Dynamic managing

principles, process, practice

Mervin Kohn, Ph.D.
Youngstown State University

Cummings Publishing Company

Menlo Park, California • Reading, Massachusetts
London • Amsterdam • Don Mills, Ontario • Sydney

ISBN 0-8465-3676-5
ABCDEFGHIJ-MA-7987

Cummings Publishing Company, Inc.
2727 Sand Hill Road
Menlo Park, California   94025

Preface

Organization presidents, football coaches, office and factory managers, or committee chair-persons, if asked to describe or explain what makes their jobs managerial, would probably find it difficult. Still, whether one is a manager in business or an administrator in a hospital, government office, or other non-business organization, the functions performed are strikingly similar. Despite differences in various organizations, managers in every organization do very much the same work and must deal with many of the same problems arising in the world around them. Regardless of the type of organization being managed, or the level within it, the process of managing is essentially the same.

College students, curious to learn the role of the manager in organizations, receive their early, and perhaps only, classroom exposure to the concept of managing when they enroll in business courses. Up to this point in their careers, having had little or no organization experience, they may have little idea of what managing actually is or of how it relates to the business enterprise. This book is intended to help students and practitioners understand the importance and dynamic nature of managing, which involves continuous action, interaction, and reaction.

A variety of disciplines have made significant contributions to the store of management knowledge. During the last two decades most of the textbooks and articles on management have been written by psychologists, sociologists, anthropologists, economists, engineers, mathematicians, professors, politicians, philosophers, and clergy. They have brought forth new perceptions of business and its mechanisms and have opened new vistas such as human relations in organizations, social influence and responsibility, and behavior-function-models concepts. Unfortunately, the vantage point of social scientists and philosophers has been that of outsiders looking in, not the perspective of those who have served in a managerial capacity and experienced many of the situations they are describing. Without discussing various schools of thought individually, this book integrates the contributions of the classical, behavioral, quantitative, contingency, and systems approaches. It is thus eclectic and synergistic, drawing important elements from these sources and combining them into a more meaningful whole from a manager's perspective.

These pages seek to develop an understanding of the principles, process, and practice of managing that apply to all organizations, large or small, and to all functional areas within them. Whether personnel management, production management, financial management, sales management, marketing management, organizational management, resources management, or management of information systems, the common denominator is management.

Incentives such as stock option plans, corporate objectives such as increasing return on investment, and controls designed to prevent shoplifting are but a few examples of activities and concepts that are identified solely with the business world. Thus, merely to deal with management in a very general way, as it applies to organizations of all kinds, is to deprive students of a degree of understanding that can only be gained by focusing primarily on business organizations and then applying the observations to other types of organizational life.

Merely possessing knowledge about managing is not sufficient for a real understanding of managing. In any discipline, knowing how each piece of information relates to, compares with, and dovetails with others helps us understand that discipline. This is equally true of managing. Thus it is the aim of this book to establish relationships between the various business and managing activities and thereby help the readers develop an understanding of managing as a process. The subject is presented in a direct, orderly, and logical fashion, challenging the readers' minds with ideas they will find stimulating even if they occasionally disagree with some. Pros and cons of different concepts are evaluated, and tenable positions to adopt are suggested.

Throughout the book, management principles are related to current practice. Realistic, practical examples are provided so students can quickly grasp the concept being discussed. Thus this text should be a tool for more effective teaching as well as learning. Its basic aim is to explain a fascinating and incredibly complex subject in a simple, understandable, and meaningful fashion. The students or practitioners will then understand the meaning of managing well enough to describe it in their own words, give examples of it, clearly see the connection between managing and other areas of the organization, and put it to practical use.

Contents

Part I

Some Basic Concepts

To understand dynamic managing as it applies to any type of organization, it is appropriate at the outset to develop fundamental, sound concepts about business, to recognize its importance in the American way of life, and to dispel some distortions and misconceptions. In establishing the role of a manager in any organization, one must base one's premises largely on the way in which business has been managed, since modern management theory has its origin in the management of business enterprises.

In many ways, the business firm is one of the most important institutions in our society. Yet, the public in general and college students in particular are not well informed about the free enterprise system and how it operates. One executive describes it in the following terms:

> I genuinely believe that free enterprise is one of the most magnificent ideas ever conceived by man. The quality of life in our industrial, capitalistic society is so overwhelmingly superior to that of other societies that the time has come to put to rest the notion that it is not.
>
> In referring to the quality of life, I am speaking of the possibility of human dignity and personal development rather than the material realizations of our society. I would advise that we avoid the temptation to justify economic freedom on the basis of its material superiority to other systems.[1]

WHAT IS A BUSINESS ENTERPRISE?

The city-owned bus line, local hospital, university, and public library all provide goods or services, employ people, and require management, yet are not considered business organizations. What is there about a business that makes it different from other institutions? To qualify as a "business," an organization must possess *all* of the following characteristics: (1) it must be profit oriented; (2) it must assume risk; (3) it must be governed by a business philosophy; (4) it must take an accounting point of view; (5) it must be recognized as a business by other organizations and by the appropriate

---

[1]Z. D. Bonner, "How Industry Can Regain Public Trust," *New York Times,* Sunday, September 1, 1974.

government agencies; and (6) it must be privately owned, controlled, and managed. Let us examine these attributes.

Profit oriented.   Although the end purpose of business is the production of goods or services, its immediate, motivating purpose is profit, or financial return in excess of cost. Thus profit orientation excludes such organizations as the Boy Scouts, churches, state highway patrols, public schools, city-owned power plants, NASA, and labor unions. The Supreme Court has ruled that labor unions are not businesses and not subject to the same laws and regulations as "profit-oriented" firms. In the eyes of the law, business involves commercial activity in search of a profit.

Risk of operations.   Anyone who owns a business risks his own time, money, and effort. This risk is recognized and accepted as an ever-present ingredient in operating a business. It includes the ultimate risk of complete failure in which owners may lose their entire investment.

Business philosophy.[2]   Business managers make decisions that deal with markets, costs, prices, competition, government regulations, economic conditions, and the community.

Business subscribes to the philosophy that it is better able than any other type of organization to produce most of the goods and services society needs. To make good this claim, businesses must not only prove their economic vitality, but also accept their responsibilities to consumers, employees, and the society as a whole. Organizations such as chambers of commerce and better business bureaus reflect business's concern for safeguarding the business philosophy.

Accounting point of view.   Given the importance of price, markets, costs, and competition in the business philosophy, an accounting point of view is essential. In business, revenues and costs must be recorded, summarized, and analyzed. Balance sheets and operating statement concepts are employed: decisions are made in terms of current and fixed assets, long-term and short-term liabilities. Business managers think and act in terms of cash on hand, inventories, accounts receivable, accounts payable, bank loans, equity, net worth, working capital, good will, and other accounting concepts.

Costs in a business or accounting sense are measured exclusively as "money outlay." If the use of a resource does not involve an actual expenditure of money it is not considered a measurable business cost. Social costs and opportunity costs, for example, are important to economists, political scientists, sociologists, and biologists, but they are not accounting costs

---

[2]The subject of business philosophy is examined in Chapter 1.

since money outlay is not involved. In recent years, however, various authorities have suggested that all organizations ought to recognize social costs. They view human resources as an asset, and human costs as part of the concept of "real" costs.

Recognition as a business.   To call itself a business, an establishment must be recognized as such by similar establishments as well as by government agencies. A motel is a motel in part because it is recognized as such by other motel operators. On the other hand, the Girl Scouts, raising funds through the sale of cookies at a profit, would not be considered a business since regular cookie vendors do not recognize it as such.

Recognition by government agencies depends on conformance to government classifications of businesses. For example, the government defines "Manufacturing" as:

> . . . establishments engaged in the mechanical or chemical transformations of inorganic or organic substances into new products, and usually described as plants, factories or mills . . . establishments engaged in assembling components of manufacturing products are considered manufacturing if the new product isn't a structure nor fixed improvement.[3]

By this definition, a company making a product of wood and metal to be sold as a bookshelf would be considered a manufacturer, whereas a company using wood and metal for building construction would not be.

Private ownership and control.   Most businesses in this country are owned by individuals who have invested personal funds in ventures of their own choosing. A person who starts a manufacturing plant not only owns it but controls its use. He can decide what to make or not to make and whether to buy machinery or lease it. In short, he determines how and when to use the factory he owns. He can also delegate to others, managers and workers, the right to use his property for a given lawful purpose. This owner-manager relationship is prevalent in small organizations typified by the proprietorship and the partnership forms.

In modern corporations, however, ownership and control have become separated into two distinct groups: stockholders and professional, or career, managers. Corporate ownership has become so widely dispersed among many stockholders that effective control has passed to non-owner managers. The principle of private ownership and control still prevails, however, in modified form. Professional managers act as trustees of the investors, representing their interests directly while remaining responsive to the interests of employees, consumers, suppliers, and society.

---

[3] "Standard Industrial Classification," Executive Office of the President, Bureau of the Budget, 1967, p. 37.

THE UNIVERSAL GOAL OF MANAGERS

The goal of every manager or administrator in every organization—business, government, philanthropic, or church—is to ensure that the members will further group objectives with the least costs in money, time, effort, resources, and unsought consequences. Thus the goal of managers is fundamentally the same in business and non-profit enterprises. Corporation presidents, college deans, heads of government agencies, and coaches in athletics all have the same basic goal. We shall be able to demonstrate this in the chapters that follow.

Like a good athlete, a manager must possess both strength and agility—that is, both a solid understanding of managing principles and a quick grasp of changing realities. He must be able to analyze new problems and mobilize diverse talents to meet them. And he must do it better than his competitors. The dynamic nature of American business requires dynamic managing.

Chapter 1

Theory and Philosophy of Managing

Despite the stories about successful managers who never studied management, most modern managers look to management theory for an understanding of organizational structures and functions, which have become more and more complex. There is no one, integrated theory of managing that is universally accepted; but there are general managing principles that have become widely established.

Managing principles are derived for the most part from actual business practice. Most of what we know about managing comes from studies of the way businesses have been, and are being, managed. The basic assumption has been that their success depends on certain things that managers do. Of course, to say that a manager has achieved successful results presupposes an understanding of what constitutes success. Some indicators of success include longevity, or the length of time the organization has been in continuous operation; the consistency with which it produces a satisfactory return on investment; its prominence within its own industry; and the degree to which it is accepted by the community it serves. Obviously, objective criteria for success must be established before principles can be proposed to account for the achievement of that success.

A solid understanding of managing requires a systematized framework to build on. The framework employed in this book consists of managing *principles, process,* and *practice.* Process refers to the functions, or ongoing activities, of managing. Principles, process, and practice all interlock, continually reinforcing and reacting to each other so that managing is always a *dynamic* function. Thus theory is not something separate from practice; it is the basis for practice.

MANAGING PRINCIPLES

Principles are the building blocks with which a sound theory of management is constructed. For our purposes the term **managing principle** means a *generalization about managing that has widespread application based on the* *causal relationship between a managerial act and its perceived conse- quences.* A managing principle, therefore, is a working hypothesis. It is not a theory or a law, nor is it universally accepted. It simply reflects the fact that managers do or fail to do things that produce certain results and that this can be widely observed. Its soundness has been established for practical purposes.

If the statements are made that "increased incentives lead to increased productivity," and that "eliminating unnecessary motions increases effi- ciency and reduces work fatigue," can these be considered principles? Since both state cause and effect, if it can be demonstrated that these rela- tionships hold for many types of work in various types of organizations then both statements qualify as managing principles. That does not mean there are no exceptions to these generalizations. It simply means that there is ade- quate indication that a given act or series of acts generally leads to observ- able results.

HOW MANAGING PRINCIPLES ARE DERIVED

There are two basic approaches to formulating managing principles: (1) the **empirical** approach, based on observation, and (2) the **rational** approach, based on deduction from other principles.

The Empirical Approach

The empirical approach involves assembling and analyzing data from actual observations, based on practical experience without reference to scientific investigation. It asks the question, "What methods have managers utilized that have worked successfully?" Through **inductive reasoning** it is possible to draw conclusions about cause and effect from accumulated observations. Such conclusions become principles of managing, statements which have widespread application and from which a store of knowledge can evolve. As an illustration, one might observe in a number of successful companies that the managers spent a considerable portion of their time planning. The hypothesis could then be made that all managers of successful businesses probably spend considerable portions of their time in planning. Should such a generalization become widely accepted, a principle is established.

Many of the early principles of managing were derived in this manner. Writers such as Frederick Taylor, Henri Fayol, and Elton Mayo—sometimes referred to as the classical theorists—described and generalized about their observations in the steel, mining, and electrical industries. Many basic principles of management resulted from observations of manufacturing and other "primary" production industries.

The criticism is often made that principles derived in this fashion are not valid since they have not been proved. On the other hand, they have not been disproved either! Proved or not, they provide useful models of cause and effect.

The Rational Approach

The rational approach to deriving managing principles involves reasoning. It asks the question, "What is the logical way of treating this problem?" Take, for example, the question, "At which level of management should certain problems be handled?" Reasoning **deductively** from principles of economy, one might reach the conclusion that the more limited the problems are in scope, the lower the level of management to which they should be referred. If this conclusion proves effective in practice and gains wide acceptance, it becomes a managing principle.

The rational approach is also used by managers in problem solving. In applying the rational approach to a problem, a manager (1) objectively defines the problem, (2) searches for a solution, and (3) tests the selected solution to see if it is reliable and valid. Let us examine the meaning of the terms we are using to describe the rational approach.

To define a problem *objectively* means to state the facts without personal bias or interpretation. To be objective is to be impersonal.

The **reliability** of a solution indicates its *internal consistency*. A reliable solution is dependable and not erratic. It is **efficient.** It will, therefore, produce consistent performance. A watch that does not vary by more than one second a month is certainly a reliable timepiece.

The **validity** of an action indicates how close the action comes to achieving the goal for which it was designed. Validity is a measure of feasibility, or **effectiveness.** It indicates the degree of successful achievement or the chances of success. If a technique or solution is valid, its effects in a similar situation can be predicted. It is thus said to have interpretive or predictive value.

Although a procedure or device may be internally consistent and very efficient, it may not be valid or effective at all for a particular purpose. For example, a shotgun fired repeatedly without a misfire can be said to be reliable. However, if only an occasional pellet strikes the target the shotgun is not a valid device for hitting a target at a distance. On the other hand, if a rifle is fired repeatedly at the same distant target and regularly strikes the center, it is both a reliable and valid instrument for that purpose. Should it misfire frequently or fire erratically, it would not be reliable and could not be a valid instrument for striking bull's-eyes. Thus a means may be reliable but not valid, but it cannot be valid unless it is reliable. Any managing procedure, technique, or device, therefore, will succeed in reaching a goal only if it possesses these dual characteristics of reliability *and* validity. This statement is another example of a managing principle. The concepts of reliability and validity are portrayed in Figure 1-1. In Figure 1-1,A, five shots

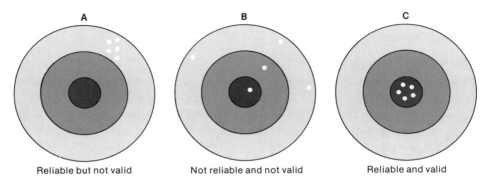

A   B   C

Reliable but not valid   Not reliable and not valid   Reliable and valid

Figure 1-1.   Targets illustrating reliability and validity.

are closely grouped together, yet none of them strikes the bull's-eye. The instrument that produced this result is said to be reliable but not valid. In Figure 1-1,*B,* the five shots are widely scattered, indicating that the instrument is neither reliable nor valid. The one shot that struck the bull's-eye may have been due to chance. In Figure 1-1,*C,* all five shots are grouped together and all have hit the bull's-eye. This drawing depicts valid results from a reliable mechanism—the ideal situation.

Organizations too may be efficient and yet not be effective. However, an effective organization is also an efficient one. In the latter case, it may be possible to further improve its effectiveness by improving its efficiency. It is advisable to bear in mind the meaning of these two terms and their relationship to each other, since they will be used frequently throughout this book. The importance of a manager's effectiveness is stressed by Peter Drucker when he states, "The executive's job is to be effective; and effectiveness can be learned."[1]

The search for a body of sound principles of management on which to base a sound theory of management must combine the empirical and rational approaches. Walter Gast called this "rational empiricism."[2]

Because managing principles indicate a cause and effect relationship, they have *interpretive* and *predictive* value. When a principle has stood the test of time and has not been disproved, it eventually evolves into a theory, or possibly a law, and becomes universally accepted, just as in the physical and social sciences. A **theory** has been defined as *a coherent system of propositions advanced to explain a phenomenon.* While the propositions on which a theory is based can be tested so that the theory can be shown to be a predictor of a phenomenon, the theory itself can never be *proved* correct.

---

[1]Peter Drucker, *The Effective Executive* (New York: Harper & Row, 1967), p. 166.

[2]Walter F. Gast, *Principles of Business Management* (St. Louis: St. Louis University Press, 1953), p. 5.

Every theory is a simplified representation of reality—an abstraction of a complex phenomenon.[3]

IS MANAGING A SCIENCE OR AN ART?

The debate about whether or not managing is a science continues. Since a **science** is by definition *a body of knowledge obtained through the use of the method of science,* the answer to this question depends largely on the degree to which the scientific method is used to determine managing principles and solve managing problems.

Briefly, the **method of science** consists of the following steps:[4]

1. Facts or data are collected in an objective manner.

2. These facts are classified in some way, usually on the basis of similarities or dissimilarities, in an attempt to make the data more meaningful.

3. From the classifications, hypotheses are formulated.

4. The hypotheses are then tested to determine their reliability and validity.

5. After the hypotheses are verified and if they stand the test of time, they then have interpretive or predictive value when applied to similar phenomena.

Consequently, replication is possible; two researchers undertaking the same investigation, working independently, and treating the same data under the same conditions, should obtain identical results.

So far relatively few managing principles have been derived by the method of science. Recent additions to the store of management knowledge have been gained largely by means of techniques other than scientific. Only in a limited way, in specialized areas such as research, testing, and new product development, has management made use of the scientific method. Whether a science of management will ever evolve is highly improbable. In referring to the hope or dream that a true science of management may someday be achieved, Professor Mee states, "This hope probably will be realized in another chapter in another book in another century."[5] Perhaps the best that can be said is that a science of management is just beginning to emerge.

---

[3]Henry Mintzberg, "Policy as a Field of Management Theory," *Institut D'Administration Des Entreprises,* April 1975, p. 12.

[4]Observe how closely the method of science parallels the rational approach which we have already described.

[5]John F. Mee, *Management Thought in a Dynamic Economy* (New York: New York University Press, 1963), p. 11.

It has often been stated that even when management attempts to use the method of science (from which managing principles are also derived), management is neither as precise nor as comprehensive as the natural and social sciences. There are several reasons why this is true:

1. The rational approach and the application of the method of science are relatively new in business and industry. As a result, managing has not developed the comprehensiveness found in other disciplines that have used the scientific approach for a much longer time. In fact, one of the more significant developments in the last seventy-five years in the field of management has been the tendency toward using the rational approach in solving management problems.

Viewed as a panorama in historical perspective, management as a distinct discipline is relatively young and still growing. Before 1900 there were only five recognized schools of business in the United States. Textbooks in management for use in business curricula appeared between 1910 and 1915, and it was not until 1924 that the first management meeting was held at the Amos Tuck School at Dartmouth College.

2. Relatively few managers are trained or experienced in using the method of science. Those who are trained may find it too time-consuming and, because of this as well as other limiting factors, seek other ways to reach decisions and to solve problems.

3. Precision measuring instruments and tools are not always available in management. A manager is forced to use relative measurement where absolute measurement is not possible or feasible. To evaluate the performance of a group of supervisors, for example, he may have to use a relative measuring device such as a carefully prepared rating scale. For his purposes, however, the relative measuring technique is just as useful and effective.

4. In the physical sciences, the researcher works with a single variable, holding all other factors constant. Managers can seldom do this. They almost always deal with people, the human element with all its frailties. The human element can never be treated as a constant; hence precision is less than in the physical sciences, though equal to that of the social sciences. Businessmen are always dealing with the unpredictable: people, governments and nature.

5. Most important, managerial decision making, unlike problem solving in the sciences, *stresses action rather than truth*. A manager's decisions must have practical application. Managers strive for *reasonable* results under uncertain conditions rather than for perfection. A method, technique, or device only has to be "good enough" to get the job done.

An **art** is a skill in doing something that one learns by experience, study, and observation: it implies proficiency. It is the practical nature of managing that makes it much more an art than a science. Although managing makes use of scientific findings and methods, it is primarily concerned with results. Even its theory stresses usefulness rather than perfection.

As an art, managing too is distinguished by proficiency developed through study and experience. It is one thing to know managing principles, but it is quite another to apply them skillfully and effectively. Knowing every managing principle does not make a manager, any more than knowing every part of the body makes a doctor. Like a skillful physician, a manager must be able to apply his knowledge to complicated, often novel problems. This requires a certain intuition. A manager must develop know-how—a practical sense—to get a job done and to understand, communicate, and get along with people, particularly those on whom he must rely to accomplish a mission.

An essential ingredient in the art of managing is found in the manager himself. An able manager must develop conceptual skills, an ability to see and understand the "big picture," to separate the forest from the trees; learn to recognize a problem and be prepared to do something about it; understand relationships; and anticipate future effects of present actions. All of these abilities can be learned, and the person who acquires them can become a highly qualified manager in a complex organization.

A PHILOSOPHY OF MANAGING

A business is a **telic** venture; that is, it exists to serve a definite purpose in society. Its operation, therefore, must meet society's expectations with respect to both goals and the means of attaining those goals.

Thus, the operation of any organization cannot be separated from the totality of human life. Business, too, can only be understood as it relates to society, of which it is a part and which is an integral part of it. To develop such an understanding requires a philosophy of business.

A philosophy of business is a system of thought based on business concepts and principles and how they relate to society. Such a philosophy helps us to understand business problems within the community and provides a logical basis for comprehending the steps a business firm takes to resolve these problems. The effectiveness and economy with which business functions are performed thus have a profound influence on the entire community and on the ability of society to realize its expectations.

A **philosophy of managing** is predicated on a philosophy of business. Just as a business has a purpose in society, so too does managing have a purpose in business. Business as a totality is a means to serve the ends of society. Managing as a totality is a means to serve the ends of business or any other institution.

Within the framework of the American enterprise system there develops a managerial philosophy which includes a sense of responsibility to owners, employees, consumers, vendors, and the community at large. Our society depends on business managers to regulate its productive capacity and to promote its economic and social well-being. To accomplish this effectively, managers must coordinate the work of many specialists. This requires them to understand human relations, to direct individual and group effort, and to know the various facets of business operations. Managing, as we will note, cannot be separated from other business activities which it affects and which have an effect on it.

Essentially, a philosophy of managing is a *value system consisting of beliefs, concepts, and attitudes adhered to by managers in their relationships with each other and with society.* It is this definition that will be meant whenever the term "philosophy" is used in this book. It is important to note from this broad definition that (1) various experience is synthesized into an organized body of thought (value system), and (2) phenomena or events are always related to human life; these are two essential characteristics of philosophy.

The concepts, beliefs, and attitudes to which managers subscribe influence the manner in which they carry out their managerial role. An understanding of their philosophy helps us to understand managerial problems and provides insight into various activities in which managers engage to resolve those problems.

Given the telic nature of managing, a philosophy of managing will always provide the following: (1) a statement of the purpose of managing in an organization (ends), and (2) a basis for identifying the functions of managing through which this purpose will be attained (means). Thus, a philosophy of managing embodies a means-ends relationship. It announces the objectives of managing and reveals the functions it will perform to achieve them, always with society in mind.

A viable philosophy of managing is *dynamic*, never static. It reflects the time and culture in which it is found. Thus it can be vastly different from one era to another, from one country to another. It changes as changes occur in the political, religious, social, and economic philosophies of our society. According to one authority, "Management philosophy for the future will evolve to accommodate the decisions and actions of managers to a changing economic, political, and technological environment.[6]

The importance of a philosophy of managing, based on sound management principles, cannot be over-emphasized. A survey of the membership of

---

[6]Ibid, p. 76.

the American Assembly of Collegiate Schools of Business (AACSB) indicates that instilling a philosophy of management, creating an "awareness of the field," and teaching principles are more important objectives than teaching special skills.[7]

THE NATURAL OBJECTIVES OF BUSINESS ENTERPRISE

Since a philosophy of managing serves the ends of business, it is appropriate to point out some of these ends as seen through the eyes of society. We shall refer to these as the **natural**[8] **objectives of business.**

In accordance with principles of social and distributive justice ("to each his due"), there are several natural objectives that can be fulfilled by business enterprise. Collectively, they are what society perceives to be the role of business. The following are some of the more important objectives.

1. **To provide want-satisfying goods and services.** Every society has basic needs which can be satisfied more efficiently through organizations than through individual effort. The business firm, an economic organization, is the most efficient producer of material goods and services that society requires and is willing to pay for. As long as the business enterprise system is capable of performing the broad production function effectively—that is, as long as business firms can satisfy society's demands for food, clothing, housing, banking, insurance, or books better than other forms of organization—this system will be preferred.

2. **To provide for the productive employment of all of the factors of production.** Whenever a product or service is produced, certain resources must first be assembled. These are the inputs from which the output, or product, is derived. In our economy, these resources—consisting principally of land, labor, and capital—are called the *factors of production*. The business organization is in general best able to allocate these scarce or limited resources advantageously, in the proper amounts and in the proper sequence, as it produces the desired goods and services. The proper amounts of input factors to produce a given output are called **coefficients of production** by the economist.

The manager, executive, or administrator is the one who decides on the kinds and amounts of input resources to use in order to produce certain outputs, or benefits. When a resource is employed there is a cost for its use. Similarly, an output usually has a value. Effective managing tries to minimize the costs associated with an expected benefit, or to optimize the

---

[7]John C. Athanassiades, "The Basic Management Course: Its Objectives, Content, and Instruction," *Academy of Management Journal*, Vol. 17, No. 4, December 1974, p. 776.

[8]As defined in *Webster's Third New International Dictionary*, "Based upon the innate moral feeling or inherent sense of right and wrong held to characterize mankind."

benefit associated with given resource costs. Since resources can generally be put to alternative uses, managers must often utilize **cost-benefit analysis** as the basis for determining the productive employment of input factors.

3. **To increase the wealth of society through the economic use of the resource factors.** In the course of producing useful material things and essential services, the business enterprise system is a mechanism that can add to the total wealth of society more effectively than any other type of organization, and society expects it to do so. Every time a new factory opens, employing only 100 persons, the local economy receives substantial benefits. In addition to the newly created industrial jobs, 65 non-industrial jobs are created to provide necessary support services. The community gains 4 new retail establishments causing retail sales to rise about $330,000 annually, bank deposits go up $230,000, passenger car registrations increase 97 units, and the community tax base is broadened. This makes possible better schools, recreational facilities, hospitals, and other civic benefits.[9]

In its operation, the business firm employs people, utilizes capital, and makes use of natural resources. It must do so in a manner that is not wasteful or destructive of society's assets. Effective use of these resources should result in increased material wealth for the community—something added for all to enjoy. Responsible business leaders are well aware of this obligation. The chairman of a leading chemical company had this to say:

> Chemistry and related sciences permit us to replace whole families of products with materials from alternate sources. For all practical purposes there is no limit to the number of molecular structures that can be constructed or modified on a laboratory basis. Products such as plastics and man-made fibers and synthetic rubber all have resulted from that kind of molecular manipulation; and here too there is a net gain in land availability, for without the synthetics tens of millions of additional acres would be committed to fiber crops or timber farming. . . . Thousands of new compounds are added to the record books each year.
>
> From society's point of view as much as industry's, the efficiency or conservation technologies pay off handsomely. You get two birds with one stone. Improving the yield in a manufacturing plant saves on raw materials and brings an environmental gain at the same time. The laws of science say that everything has to go somewhere, and the more that is turned into usable product the less waste the pollution control people have to contend with.[10]

4. **To provide a just return to the input factors.** Society expects business to award fair compensation for the contribution each factor makes in the productive effort. It expects the firm to pay a just wage to labor for its services;

---

[9]Mario A. DiFederico, "Some Reflections on the Reputation of Business," *Akron Business and Economic Review*, Vol. 3, Fall 1972, p. 7.

[10]Charles B. McCoy, "Can We Avoid a Crisis in Resources?" an address before the Economic Club of Detroit, December 4, 1972, pp. 9-10.

a fair return to capital in the form of interest; and a just return in the form of rent to the landowners. What constitutes a just return is determined partly by society's value judgments (such as its determination of minimum wages), and partly by the market mechanism which balances supply and demand forces to arrive at a price for the factor.

5. **To provide a climate in which people can satisfy a major portion of normal human desires.** Individuals become members of an organization because it enables them to realize certain material and social benefits more readily than they could by themselves. If an individual is going to spend a substantial portion of his daily life working for a business organization, he expects to find conditions there that enable him to fulfill himself as an individual.

As social beings, all individuals need something more than monetary compensation for the time and services they contribute when productively employed. They expect to derive certain basic satisfactions from the nature of their work or from the work situation. Many have strong needs for recognition, belonging, pride in their work, security, opportunity for creativity, participation, respect, and other non-material values.

The individual not only does not wish to be thwarted in fulfilling these personal objectives while working but expects the firm to provide the opportunities and the climate that will make the realization of these social and psychological needs possible. Part of a manager's responsibility is to create work situations in which every employee can satisfy a portion of his personal needs.

Modern managers acknowledge these natual objectives, these "reasons for being," of a business enterprise. Thus when the firm establishes its own corporate hierarchy of objectives, tailored to its individual requirements, it must do so within a frame of reference of the broad natural objectives that society has established for it. The acceptance of these natural objectives becomes an intregral part of a manager's philosophy.

What about profit?

Where does **profit** fit into the picture? Profit is provided for in society's concept of the purpose of business.

Society declares that the prices it would be willing to pay for the goods or services being produced should generate revenues sufficient to cover **all costs** of production. These include not only pay to the factors for their use, but also provision for replacing worn-out equipment, conducting experimental and developmental projects, insuring physical assets, providing favorable working conditions, and establishing other conditions necessary for the healthy perpetuation of the firm. Thus, broadly viewed, profits are revenues sufficient to cover all costs of present and future operations—in other words, the costs of pursuing the natural objectives of business in society. The subject of profits will be analyzed more completely in the section on corporate objectives in Chapter 3.

SUMMARY

The development of a sound theory of management depends on the continuing development of sound principles of managing. Such principles are derived scientifically, empirically or rationally, and all principles have predictive and interpretive value.

Since most principles of managing are not obtained through the use of the method of science, at the present stage of its development managing can not be considered a science. It is, however, an art in which scientific discoveries are applied in pursuing organizational goals.

A dynamic philosophy of management, based on managing principles, provides a basis for understanding the role of managing in organizations and the role of organizations in society. From society's point of view, there is a continuing need for business establishments to fulfill many essential purposes. It is the responsibility of the manager to accomplish these purposes in an efficient and effective way. He must accept them as an essential part of his managerial philosophy.

KEY CONCEPTS

Managing Principle	Effectiveness
Empirical Approach	Science
Rational Approach	Method of Science
Inductive Reasoning	Art
Deductive Reasoning	Philosophy of Managing
Rational Empiricism	Natural Objectives of Business
Reliability	Coefficients of Production
Validity	Cost-Benefit Analysis
Efficiency	Profit

GLOSSARY

art   Proficiency or skill in doing something that comes from experience, study, and observation.

deductive reasoning   Logical process that draws conclusions from general premises.

empirical   Based on experience or observation without reference to scientific investigation.

inductive reasoning   Logical process that draws generalizations from specific observations.

managing principle   Generalization having widespread application based on the causal relationship between a managerial act and its perceived consequences.

philosophy   Beliefs, concepts, and attitudes held by individuals or groups in their relationships to each other and to society.

rational   Involving reasoning, especially the objective definition of a problem and search for a valid solution.

reliability   Internal consistency or efficiency of any means, device, or technique that makes it dependable.

science   Body of knowledge that results from the use of the method of science.

telic   Purposive, leading toward an end or goal.

theory   Coherent system of propositions advanced to explain a phenomenon.

validity   Criterion of effectiveness, predictability, or successful achievement.

REVIEW QUESTIONS

1. Why is it necessary to develop managing principles?
2. How are managing principles derived?
3. Give an example of a managing principle.
4. Why is it essential to determine both the reliability and validity of any technique or device? Can you give some examples not mentioned in the chapter?
5. Explain in your own words the difference between efficiency and effectiveness.
6. Do you consider managing a science? Why? An art? Why?
7. How do you explain the fact that management is less precise and comprehensive than the physical and social sciences?
8. Do you feel a philosophy of management is useful? Defend your position.
9. Give some examples of how a business organization adds to the wealth of society.

Chapter 2

Role of Management in Organizations

Whenever two or more individuals pool their efforts and interact to achieve some mutual goal that neither could accomplish as effectively alone, a simple organization exists. As an organization matures and grows, its activities become more varied, until eventually they require management to coordinate them. No matter how rich an organization may be in human and material resources, it will not achieve its objectives unless those resources are mobilized effectively. The manager must determine how resources should be utilized for given purposes, what kinds of activities should be carried out, where, and by whom.

Though most people associate the practice of management with the industrial or commercial world, it is found in any organization which (1) carries on its work by dividing the tasks among its members, (2) integrates the members' roles into a unified working structure, and (3) requires decisions on marshalling and deploying human and material resources. Someone in every organization must assume responsibility for relating its various activities to its central purpose. This is the manager's role.

PURPOSE OF MANAGING

Managing strives to achieve coordination of all activities so they operate in a balanced way, and continue to relate to the overall objectives of the enterprise. Managing ensures that all enterprise functions perform in an integrated fashion and harmonize with each other so that institutional goals will be fulfilled. Without managing, without someone to make decisions, no organization can endure. Anarchy would cause its demise.

THE MAJOR ENTERPRISE FUNCTIONS

An **enterprise function** is *any activity designed to achieve an enterprise objective.* In a business enterprise, for example, we find such familiar activities as purchasing raw materials, buying merchandise to sell, marketing, advertising, warehousing, inventory maintenance, manufacturing, inspecting, quality control, interviewing applicants for jobs, hiring, training, planning, payroll, clerical work, security, and similar necessary functions. Functions are always *purposive* in nature, by definition.

To deal in a workable fashion with the myriad activities going on and to understand their relationships to each other, it is necessary to consolidate them into a few meaningful categories. For example, in classifying the activities listed above one could decide that purchasing raw materials and buying merchandise for resale are both "buying" activities; that marketing, advertising, and warehousing are components of "selling"; that manufacturing, inspecting, and quality control are aspects of "operating"; and that interviewing, hiring, training, planning, and payroll are "managing" functions. Establishing classifications in this manner is arbitrary, of course, and some activities could conceivably be placed in a different category. Moreover, the classifications overlap and are interdependent and interrelated. Nevertheless, for simplicity, and for discussion purposes, it is helpful to establish a few clusters of activities that are common to most enterprises.

There are three *basic* functions which are indispensable to the conduct of a business, regardless of its size or the nature of its product or service. Frequently referred to as the *primary business functions*, these essential activities are **buying, selling,** and **operating.** They occur even in a one-man business. A cobbler operating a shoe repair shop must buy leather and materials; cut, fashion, and sew them (operate); and sell the result of his productivity. These same basic activities are performed by every proprietor, although the relative importance of these activities may vary. For a newsstand operator, for example, selling might be a more important component of his business than buying.

As organizations increase in size and complexity, additional functions become necessary to make their operation economically productive. Facilitating functions, designed to assist the performance of the primary functions, are added. All four of these major activities have to be coordinated and related to each other so that organizational objectives can be met. This is the task of the manager.

Thus, all purposive organizational activities can be classified into one of five categories which we shall designate the **major enterprise functions:** (1) *buying;* (2) *selling;* (3) *operating;* (4) *facilitating;* and (5) *managing.* Let us consider the general nature of each of these clusters of activities which can be found in most organizations.

Buying.   The activities included under buying are all those associated with "procurement" or purchasing—of raw materials, supplies, equipment, machinery, parts, components, and so forth. The buying process may also involve inspecting merchandise as it arrives, or testing it for quality or conformance to purchase order specifications.

Selling.   All the numerous functions associated with the movement of goods or services from the time they have been produced to the time they are put to use are included in the selling, or marketing, function. Advertising, sales promotion, public relations, point-of-sale display, direct selling, warehousing, transportation, and packaging are a few of the components of the selling function.

Operating.   The actual production of goods or performance of services is referred to as the operating function. In a factory, the operating function is manufacturing and includes sub-functions like cutting, bending, welding, machining, assembling, riveting, testing, quality control, and other operations required to produce a product. In an airline, the operating function is chiefly moving passengers and freight. In a bank, it is providing full-service banking including savings accounts, checking accounts, safe deposit boxes, commercial and consumer loans, and similar services. In a hospital, the operating function is providing inpatient and outpatient health care. Every organization has some main activities that chiefly characterize it. These are its operating functions.

Facilitating.   The auxiliary activities that serve to support and assist the managing function and the primary functions (buying, selling, and operating) comprise the facilitating functions. Typical facilitating functions are maintenance activities such as oiling machinery, sweeping the floors, washing the windows, painting the building, and repairing electrical systems; switchboard, stenographic, typing, filing, and receptionist services; operating a computer; and security facilities. All activities which do not readily fit into any of the other four major categories are considered facilitating functions. A secretary to the purchasing agent, therefore, is performing a facilitating and not a buying function. By the same token, a secretary to the president also performs a facilitating function and not a managing function.

Managing.   The managing function includes whatever actions are necessary to insure that each enterprise function operates effectively and in harmony with all others so that the total organization is effective.

Throughout this book, whenever reference is made to major enterprise functions or to functional areas of enterprise, the reader need only recall that for our purposes there are only five to consider—buying, selling, operating, facilitating, and managing. A distinction should be maintained between the organizational functions (marketing, manufacturing, purchasing, finance, and so on) and the managing functions, which make up the managing process. It is the managing process with which we are primarily concerned throughout this entire book and to which we now turn our attention.

THE MANAGING PROCESS

Management thought has been evolving over a long period of time toward an understanding of the role of managing in all organizational systems. Particularly since Harold Koontz described management theory as a jungle in an article in 1961,[1] a number of approaches have been developed or refined in an attempt to produce a clearer understanding of management. In general, these approaches include the human behavior approach; the systems approach; the quantitative, or mathematical, approach; and the process, or functional, approach. Each perspective has advantages and limitations, but the functional approach, despite some severe critics, has become the most firmly established. William Greenwood believes that management process theory will remain the standard against which all other theories will be compared, and that it will be refined by the integration of theories from other disciplines.[2] It is the process approach, also known as the functional or operational approach, that is emphasized throughout this book. Basically, this approach explains managing as a continuing flow of activities aimed at defining and achieving organizational goals through the effective use of human and physical resources. It visualizes managing in terms of what managers do.

The current meaning of management bears a striking similarity to the definition offered in 1911 by Frederick W. Taylor. According to Taylor, managing is "knowing exactly what you want men to do, and then seeing that they do it in the best and cheapest way."[3] This dynamic concept of managing contains the elements of all later definitions. Let us examine the concept of managing as described by some of the leading management authorities:

> Management is the function of executive leadership. Managerial functions involve the work of planning, organizing, and controlling the activities of others in accomplishing the organization's objectives.[4]

---

[1]Harold Koontz, "The Management Theory Jungle," *Journal of the Academy of Management*, Vol. 4, No. 3, December 1961, pp. 174–188.

[2]William T. Greenwood, "Future Management Theory: A 'Comparative' Evolution to a General Theory," *Academy of Management Journal*, Vol. 17, No. 3, September 1974, p. 510.

[3]Frederick W. Taylor, *Principles of Scientific Management* (New York: Harper & Brothers, 1911), p. 5.

[4]Ralph Currier Davis, *The Fundamentals of Top Management* (New York: Harper & Brothers, 1951), p. 14.

Management involves the coordination of human and material resources toward objective accomplishment.[5]

Management is the process by which individual and group effort is coordinated toward group goals.[6]

Management is a distinct process consisting of planning, organizing, actuating, and controlling, performed to determine and accomplish stated objectives by the use of human beings and other resources.[7]

As a method of analyzing systems management in some detail, the four functional areas of the management process, planning, organizing, motivating, and controlling, should be examined as they would appear under systems management.[8]

Management, then, is a force that, through decision making based on knowledge and understanding, interrelates and integrates, via appropriate linking processes, all the elements of the organizational system in a manner designed to achieve the organizational objectives.[9]

A comparison of these typical definitions of management indicates a stated or implied recognition of the process concept. For our purposes, it is informative to include in a definition the kinds of activities that are essential to the act of managing. In a very general way, one could say "managing is what managers do." One could define nursing, teaching, or football quarterbacking in a similar way. Merely describing the activities in which managers engage does not indicate either their purpose or their relationship to other organizational activities, and these points are crucial to the view of managing as an integrating process. Hence we need a more precise definition. We shall use the following one throughout this text.

Managing is *a process that consists of planning, organizing, activating, and controlling the resources (personnel and capital) of an organization so they are used to best advantage in achieving the objectives of the organization.* This definition views managing as a dynamic, purposive process, a series of related and continuing activities. These same activities are performed in managing every type of organization, whether the organization is

---

[5]Fremont E. Kast and James Rosenzweig, *Organization and Management: a Systems Approach* (New York: McGraw-Hill Book Co., 1970), p. 6.

[6]James H. Donnelly, James Gibson, and John Ivancevich, *Fundamentals of Management: Functions, Behavior, Models* (Austin, Texas: Business Publications, Inc., 1971), p. 4.

[7]George R. Terry, *Principles of Management*, 6th ed. (Homewood, Ill.: Richard D. Irwin, Inc., 1972), p. 4.

[8]Michael H. Mescon, William Hammond, Lloyd Byars, and Joseph Foerst, *The Management of Enterprise* (New York: The Macmillan Co., 1973), p. 37.

[9]Earl F. Lundgren, *Organizational Management: Systems and Process* (San Francisco: Canfield Press, 1974), p. 5.

business or non-business, large or small, manufacturing or service, commercial or industrial, partnership or corporation.

THE MAJOR MANAGING FUNCTIONS (POAC)

To understand its role and how it relates to other enterprise functions, we are viewing managing as a process consisting of numerous managerial activities. Any activity necessary to accomplish a managing objective is a **managing function** and is, therefore, part of the managing process. Management functions are management means to management ends.

Of the vast array of managerial activities, those listed most frequently in books about management are planning, organizing, staffing, directing, controlling, communicating, innovating, activating, motivating, leading, supervising, decision making, budgeting, reporting, and representing. Such a lengthy list is unwieldy. To understand what part each activity plays in the managing process and how the activities interact, it is imperative that we classify them into a few major functions. But which functions are major and which are secondary or sub-functions in the managing process? This is not an easy question to answer.

Managing functions have been grouped in many ways in the past, the numbers of categories ranging from as few as two to as many as eight or ten. As a vehicle for this book, however, four broad categories, or groups of functions, will be used. Referred to throughout the book as the *major* managing functions, these are **planning, organizing, activating,** and **controlling.** Although they are not the only possible categories for analyzing managing functions, they are convenient for our purposes. Inasmuch as they correspond to stages in the managing process, they permit a dynamic analysis of managing. All other managing activities will be treated as sub-functions of the major managing functions. This provides a simple framework for our exploration into how organizations are managed. Just as it is easier to remember that there are five major clusters of enterprise functions, so too is it easy to remember that there are four major clusters of managing functions. We can use the acronym "POAC" to remember what they are.

In establishing classifications, it may seem somewhat arbitrary to place a particular managerial activity into one category rather than another. Since managerial activities frequently overlap, it might be possible to place an activity in more than one category. The problem is analogous to deciding whether a firm should be classified as a retailer, wholesaler, or manufacturer when it makes a product, distributes it to dealers, and also sells some of its output in its own retail stores. Yet if a single determination must be made, the company may logically and conveniently be classified on the basis of that segment from which it derives the largest portion of its total reve-

PLANNING	**O**RGANIZING	**A**CTIVATING	**C**ONTROLLING
Budgeting	Staffing	Actuating	Auditing
Decision	Recruiting	Motivating	Reporting
making	Hiring	Leading	Measuring
Innovating	Indoctrinating	Supervising	Comparing
Forecasting	Training	Developing	Evaluating
Policy	Assigning	incentives	Corrective
making	capital	Communicating	action
Analyzing		Directing	

Figure 2-1.   The major managing functions (POAC).

nues. Similarly, a managerial activity may logically be classified on the basis of the major function to which it makes the greatest contribution.

The four categories that we are henceforth calling major managing functions and the sub-functions within each are listed in Figure 2–1. Let us review the rationale for placing sub-functions under their particular major headings.

Planning.   *Planning consists of formulating objectives and determining ways to reach them.* That the average company president devotes most of his attention to planning has been demonstrated by an extensive survey covering 492 presidents among the 700 largest industrial, merchandising, transportation, life insurance, and utility firms in the United States.[10]

A budget is actually a type of plan, and so budgeting will be treated as a part of the planning function, even though budgets are used primarily as instruments of control.

Innovation is generally regarded as the product or end result of creativity. One tends to associate creativity with new products or other tangible discoveries, but creativity can also produce new ideas and ways of doing things, which may have critical importance for dynamic managing. Therefore innovation will be treated as a sub-function of the planning process. It should be noted, however, that innovation is not the exclusive province of the manager; rank-and-file workers can also be creative.

Decision making and planning are closely related. In the course of planning, decisions have to be made. Determining what to do and how to do it requires decision making.

Organizing.   *Organizing consists of selecting and combining resources (personnel and capital) and integrating them into a structure of relationships capable of effective action.*

Staffing is usually considered a separate, distinct function. However, since it means placing the right people in the right jobs—selecting, assigning, training, and indoctrinating them—it can be treated as a facet of

---

[10]*The Wall Street Journal,* September 29, 1967, p. 13.

organizing. Besides, few modern-day managers, personnel managers excepted, spend very much of their daily routine in activities related to staffing. Additional organizing activities include job analysis, writing clear job descriptions, and establishing job classifications that frequently are used for wage determinations.

In one research study, 452 executives at all levels of management in 13 companies reported on the percentage of their workday that was spent performing various managerial functions. Representation—portraying the organization to the internal or external community—took 1.8 percent of their time and staffing, 4.1 percent. Compared with planning, which took 19.5 percent of their time, and supervision, which occupied 28.4 percent, representation and staffing were found to be of lesser importance.[11] The administrator who engages in formal representation probably does so as a consequence of his executive position rather than because it is his role as a manager to do so.

Activating. *Activating consists of setting in motion and directing the activities necessary to the realization of managerial plans.*

Actuating means getting things started, particularly mechanical processes. Getting things done through the efforts of others is associated with a manager's leadership ability. In this book actuating and leading will be classified as components of activating.

As the term is used in this book, directing means interpreting plans for others and giving instructions for their execution. In these days of specialization, employees normally enter the work situation already possessing the necessary experience and know-how. They frequently know more about the job than the person hiring them. Much less time is required to give them direction than in the past. Moreover, when direction is required it is provided to a large extent by fellow workers rather than by the supervisor or executive in charge. The directing that is still done by managers can be considered a sub-function of the activating process.

Communicating is the interchange of thoughts and information. When managers communicate with subordinates, the exchange is very much a part of other activities that are taking place—planning, organizing, activating, and controlling. Communicating cuts across all managerial areas and in this textbook is not presented as a separate, major function. In no way does this minimize the importance of communicating. No managerial activity can occur without communicating. To explain to subordinates how they ought to do something; to address a group of department foremen; to write a memorandum to a superior; to interview an applicant for a job—all involve communicating. It is difficult, therefore, and unrealistic to treat communicating as an independent managerial activity. Because it is so closely re-

---

[11]John B. Miner, *Management Theory* (New York: The Macmillan Co., 1971), p. 76.

lated to direction and supervision, and because these latter activities are vitally dependent upon communicating, all three will be treated as components of activating.

Controlling. *Controlling consists of measuring and evaluating the effectiveness of the organization and taking corrective action if necessary.*

Reporting on the progress of activities—an example of communicating—finds its greatest use in the area of control. Measuring, comparing, and evaluating are other important components of controlling. Measurement provides managers with information about the quantity and quality of performance. With this feedback, managers can compare actual results with anticipated results. If a significant variation is observed, managers will then initiate remedial action to bring the organization back on course.

The Performance of Managing Functions

Managers do not engage in the various management functions to the same extent. An executive at the highest level of management will probably devote more time to decision making than to reporting or supervising—and make a greater contribution to his organization by so doing. A department head, on the other hand, will probably do more directing and supervising than he does staffing. The personnel manager will obviously devote greater effort to staffing and related areas, and relatively little time to corporate planning.

The degree and frequency of deployment of functions depend on at least four factors: (1) the competence of the manager; (2) the organizational level at which he is managing; (3) the type of activity being managed; and (4) the competence of the persons being managed.

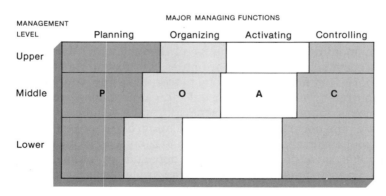

Figure 2-2. Mix of major managing functions at different levels of management.

The extent to which planning, organizing, activating, and controlling tend to vary within the management structure is indicated in Figure 2-2, which illustrates the "mix" of these major functions at different organizational levels. An executive at the upper level normally spends more time on planning overall objectives and strategies than on procurement of workers or managers for the various departments (organizing) and perhaps spends some time on corporate controls. A middle-level manager, on the other hand, may spend a somewhat smaller amount of time on planning, and a somewhat larger portion on organizing and controlling his area of jurisdiction. A lower-level manager will probably spend the least portion of his managerial time on planning the work assignments of his subordinates, and proportionally more time on supervising, appraising, assessing, and taking corrective measures (activating and controlling). The functional "mix" in the managing process, therefore, tends to vary with the level of management and with the type of activity being managed. This is a managing principle.

Interaction of Management and Non-management Functions

The managing process is highly complex, with varying degrees of interaction continually occurring among its component functions. This interaction is another reason why managing is a dynamic process. Interaction also occurs continually between managing functions and other enterprise functions (buying, selling, operating, and facilitating). Buying must be managed in the sense that it must be planned, organized, activated, and controlled. In the same sense, selling, operating, and facilitating functions have to be managed. Sales management, for example, consists of the following:

Sales planning	sales goals, quotas, sales territories, market research, sales policies, sales strategies
Sales organizing	hiring salesmen, training them, assigning them to territories
Sales activating	motivating salesmen, establishing incentive programs
Sales controlling	measuring sales results, comparing actual results with sales goals, making adjustments if necessary

The amount of management attention devoted to each of the non-management enterprise functions varies from organization to organization. In a service-oriented firm like an insurance company the buying function may be less important and require less managing emphasis than in a department store.

Managing itself requires managing! All of the different activities that constitute managing must themselves be managed. Planning must be managed; organizing must be managed; activating must be managed; controlling must be managed. Thus all five major enterprise functions must be managed. This means that all personnel and capital necessary to perform the activities associated with buying, selling, operating, facilitating, and managing must be planned, organized, activated and controlled. There are no exceptions to this principle.

Most managers, at every organizational level, do some technical or non-managerial work in addition to managing. It should be clearly understood that a person is managing only when he or she is performing a managerial function. When a supervisor shows a subordinate how to do something, he is performing a managerial function; when he does it himself, as he often must, he is performing a non-managerial act. A person may head the drafting department, supervising the work of other draftsmen; but when he is not supervising their work, he may do drafting work himself. Part of his time is spent being a draftsman; part of his time is spent being a manager of draftsmen. The president of a church sisterhood or sodality is not managing when she helps in the kitchen preparing the food for a Sunday night supper; a dean is not managing when teaching a graduate course at a university.

Distinguishing between managerial and non-managerial acts involves recognizing their characteristic functions. Although executives may and do perform non-managerial activities, those who are not managers do not perform managing activities. Thus a factory worker who is perceived by his peers as their unofficial leader is not performing a managing function since his leadership is not intentionally directed toward achieving management objectives.

The extent to which an executive spends more time with managerial duties and less time with non-managerial duties depends partly on the level at which he is managing, and partly on his ability as a manager. At higher levels of the management hierarchy, executives tend to spend a relatively greater proportion of their time in managerial rather than non-managerial acts. At lower levels, the opposite is true. The principle is graphically illustrated in Figure 2–3. The president of a corporation, for example, may seldom make a sales call on a potential customer. The sales manager, on the other hand, may do some selling in addition to directing the sales organization. In any case, he is more apt to do some selling than is the president.

MANAGEMENT versus ADMINISTRATION

A great deal of confusion surrounds the use of these two terms. At times *administration* is intended to mean the same thing as *management*; at other times its use is meant to convey a different meaning. Some clarification is needed.

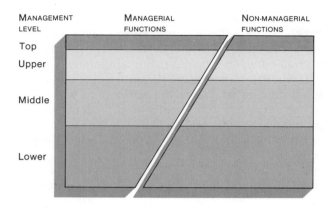

Figure 2-3.   Performance of managerial and non-managerial functions at different levels of management.

In public, quasi-public, non-profit, and government organizations, the term "administration" is used instead of management, and the title "administrator" is substituted for that of manager. Hospitals refer to their authority centers as the hospital administration; universities refer to their presidents, vice-presidents, and deans as members of the university administration; in government, the chief of the Veterans' Administration and the head of the Small Business Administration are given the rank or title of "administrator." The designation "manager" is seldom used outside of business; administrator is used in its stead.

It is when both terms are used in business that the real confusion takes place. When they are not being used interchangeably, the distinction is usually made on the basis of either (1) the level of management, (2) the kinds of decisions involved, or (3) the kinds of subordinates involved.

Administration is a collective term applied to managers at the upper or highest levels of the management hierarchy. This elite group includes the company president; vice-presidents; board of directors if the company is a corporation; and similar high-level executives.

Closely related to the position a manager holds are the kinds of decisions he makes. If they are major decisions, or "corporate" decisions such as company policies, the executive involved may be considered part of the administration. If they are less important, or relatively minor, such as "operative" decisions, the person making them would be regarded as a manager rather than an administrator. The distinction between administration and management often hinges on whether the manager is managing other managers or simply rank-and-file workers. To illustrate, a vice-president in charge of sales who has several sales managers under him may be considered part of the administration. On the other hand, the individual sales manager who directs the activities of salesmen (non-managers) is not considered part of the administration. He is simply part of management.

The distinction between administration and management in industry is very artificial. It would be a service to the entire discipline of management if it were completely eliminated. Hence the distinctions will not be made in this book. It serves the same purpose to refer to presidents and executive committees as "top management" and to indicate that corporate policy is usually formed at this level and that operative decisions are made at lower levels of management.

Regardless of which term is used, there is no essential difference between what an administrator does and what a manager does. The process in each case is identical: Managers in industry and administrators outside of industry plan, organize, activate, and control the resources of their respective organizations to achieve their respective goals.

SUMMARY

Managing is intimately involved with the other activities of an organization. It affects them and is affected by them. It is a necessary element in all organizational systems where decisions have to be made concerning the kinds and amounts of resources that must be deployed to accomplish effectively the purposes of the organization.

In every enterprise the many necessary activities that take place can be classified for purposes of discussion and analysis into five major clusters that we have designated as buying, selling, operating, facilitating, and managing. The purpose of managing is to coordinate all enterprise activities so they operate effectively and harmoniously in accomplishing organizational goals.

Managing can be viewed as a process made up of many sub-functions. Those listed most frequently by management theorists include planning, organizing, controlling, staffing, budgeting, reporting, coordinating, motivating, leading, supervising, negotiating, evaluating, directing, communicating, and decision making.

Some activities which make up the managing function are also engaged in from time to time by non-managers. It becomes necessary, therefore, to differentiate between managing activities and other enterprise activities that are non-managerial in nature. The essential difference is in their purpose. Whenever an activity is intended to accomplish a management goal, it is a managing function; otherwise it is not.

Before any of the functions of management can be understood, it is essential to identify them, define each of them, and relate them to each other and to other enterprise activities. To simplify this process, all managing functions have been grouped into four major clusters that we are calling *planning, organizing, activating* and *controlling* (POAC). All other managerial activities are considered to be sub-functions of these four.

The major management functions are closely related and interdependent; changes in one will influence the others. Although each will be dealt with as a separate entity, it must always be borne in mind that the functions are not actually separable but are intermeshed and highly dependent upon each other. They also have to be managed. Planning must be planned, organized, activated, and controlled; so must organizing, activating, and controlling be planned, organized, activated, and controlled. This is a continuing process. Another reason, therefore, why the process of managing is so dynamic is because it is also **iterative.**

There is no set order in which these four major activities take place, since they occur continuously and simultaneously. They are logically presented in the sequence in which they appear in Parts II, III, IV, and V.

To avoid confusion, the terms *administration* and *management* will be used interchangeably throughout this text since they refer to essentially the same process.

KEY CONCEPTS

Organization	Mix of Managing Functions
Purpose of Managing	Management versus Non-
Major Enterprise Functions	management Activities
Managing Process	Management versus Administration
Major Managing Functions (POAC)	

GLOSSARY

actuating   Process of getting things started.

communicating   Interchange of thoughts and information between two or more persons.

directing   Interpreting plans for others and giving instructions on how they are to be carried out.

enterprise function   Any activity designed to achieve an enterprise objective.

innovation   Product or end result of creativity.

iterative   Characterized by being repeated.

managing   Process consisting of planning, organizing, activating, and controlling the resources of an organization so that they are used to best advantage in achieving the objectives of the organization.

managing function   Any managerial activity essential to achieving management objectives.

organization   Social structure in which two or more persons interact to achieve a mutual goal that neither could accomplish as effectively alone.

representing   Portraying the organization to the internal or external community.

staffing   Organizing activity that includes placing the right persons in the right jobs by carefully selecting, assigning, training, and indoctrinating them.

REVIEW QUESTIONS

1. What is an organization?
2. In your own words, state the purpose of managing in any organization.
3. How many categories of enterprise functions have we established? Name them.
4. What are the advantages of classifying the functions of managers? How many categories have we established?
5. Why should coordinating not be considered a management function?
6. Since the process of managing is universal, does this mean that a lieutenant in the Army quartermaster corps could manage a discount department store?
7. Give an example of a situation in which a manager is performing a business activity which cannot be considered managing. Do situations like this occur often?
8. Is there any difference between the terms administration and management? Be explicit.

Part II

Planning

Basic to managing any organization is planning, which may be defined as the *process of formulating objectives and deciding what actions should be taken to achieve them.* Planning is always future oriented. To provide effective blueprints for action, planning must both project the organization's own objectives and anticipate changes in the economic, social, or physical environment that might affect them.

Planning begins with the formulation of clear objectives. Most organizations have multiple objectives related to their productive, service, and social dimensions. Some objectives are short-range; others extend further into the future. Once a group of objectives has been established, ways must be designed to pursue them successfully.

Determining what has to be done, and how, requires decision making in which a selection is made from various possible options. It may be necessary to select one plan from among several in order to resolve a problem, prevent one from occurring, or achieve new goals. To make sound decisions, managers need tools or devices to give them the necessary information and to help them evaluate various options. Management information systems can provide the input with which to do this; mathematical or quantitative aids such as equations, models, and computers help in the analysis. For an administrator, planning and making decisions are a never-ending process—a process central to the managerial role.

In Part II, therefore, our attention focuses on that portion of the managing process which is called planning. Chapter 3 describes the steps in the planning process, explains the importance of a system of objectives, analyzes the characteristics of valid objectives, and establishes the uses of planning. Chapter 4 explores the decision-making process, problem solving, and how problems are handled. Managerial aids and tools that can be used in decision making are discussed in Chapters 5 and 6. The major types of plans that are developed and employed to achieve hierarchical goals are described and discussed in Chapter 7, and some of the limitations of the planning process are pointed out.

Chapter 3

The Planning Process

Leaders in every organization must clearly perceive the group's aims and then determine how to make them a reality. The business organization is no exception. Its managers must determine what the firm seeks to accomplish and decide how it should proceed. The starting place is always *planning*.

Planning seeks answers to a multitude of questions including the following:

- What should be done?
- Why is action necessary?
- Where shall it be done?
- When shall it take place?
- How shall it be done?
- Who will do it?
- What physical resources will be required?

Planning charts a course of action for the enterprise to follow. Thus it is a process whose result (the plan) must answer all questions that have been raised. Planning *must precede* performance if the most desirable end product is to be achieved consistently at minimum cost. This is a principle of planning. Koontz and O'Donnell emphasize, "since managerial operations in organizing, staffing, directing, and controlling are designed to support the accomplishment of enterprise objectives, planning logically precedes the execution of all other managerial functions."[1] They refer to this as the "primacy of planning" since planning establishes the objectives necessary for all group efforts.

Planning *is a major cluster of activities in the managing process and consists of formulating objectives and deciding the actions to be taken to achieve them.* It is a process concerned with what has to be done and how to do it—ends and means.

---

[1]Harold Koontz and Cyril O'Donnell, *Management: A Systems and Contingency Analysis of Managerial Functions*, 6th ed. (New York: McGraw-Hill, Inc. 1976), p. 131.

Thus there are two essential aspects to planning. Merely selecting goals or targets to reach is not planning. That is only one phase of the process. The other necessary phase involves selecting or designing appropriate techniques and procedures that will be instrumental in arriving at those goals. One without the other does not provide a plan. As an example, simply illustrated, planning an advertising program consists of determining both phases:

The objective: to promote the sales of Product X
The means: selling direct to the consumer through house to house sales personnel

Since the first portion of the definition of planning involves formulating organizational objectives, a working definition of an enterprise **objective** is necessary. *It is an end (purpose, mission, result, or goal) the enterprise is expected to achieve, acquire, create, preserve, or distribute, and toward which managers direct their efforts.*

STEPS IN THE PLANNING PROCESS

To design and select specific goals and alternative courses of action to achieve them, the planner must carry out a series of activities. He must assemble, analyze, and relate all pertinent facts and assumptions about the situation, always taking into account the influence of the external environment on what he wishes to achieve. Both the aims and the course to take to achieve them must be perceived in the context of the economic, social, political, religious, psychological, ethical, and physical forces in the environment. Plans cannot be conceived and implemented in a closed, internal system. All managers, particularly in performing the planning function, must recognize and pay heed to the complex environment in which their organization operates and of which it is a part.[2] Planning, therefore, utilizes an **open-system approach.**

Essentially, the planning process consists of the following steps:

1. Formulate the task or select the goals. (What should be done? This calls for decisions.)
2. Collect and assemble essential information. (Develop inputs.)
3. Recognize the existence of uncontrollable variables (states of nature).
4. Evaluate alternative courses of action (ways to resolve the problem).

---

[2]The significance of the interaction between executive decision making and the environment is analyzed in detail in Part VI.

5. Make decisions. (Develop outputs that answer all key questions raised at the outset.)

6. Evaluate the adequacy or feasibility of the result. (Control the plan.)

It is important to observe that a plan must first determine *what* actions are required (formulate the task) and then determine *how* these actions are to be accomplished (develop outputs).

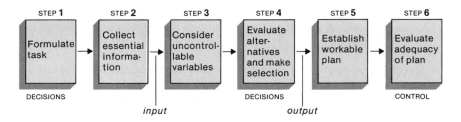

Figure 3-1.   The planning process model.

A model illustrating the planning process is shown in Figure 3–1. The first step indicated is deciding on the task or objective. Usually, there are several options. Once the objective has been established, relevant data are assembled. Recognition of the existence of uncontrollable factors is an essential part of the planning process. Workers get sick unexpectedly, machines break down, suppliers fail to deliver on time, competitors take actions that cannot be prevented, or it may snow for several days despite favorable weather forecasts. These "states of nature" constitute the variables in the model. Each alternative course of action should take into account all important uncontrollable variables and the probability of their occurring. After the alternatives have been weighed, a decision is made that results in a course of action to follow. Finally, a method of checking is provided to determine whether the plan is accomplishing its mission.

The steps in the planning process are very similar to those in the method of science, with one significant addition. The planning process should always include a method of control—some way of determining how successful the plan is. The consequences produced by any plan must be compared with those intended by the plan. If negative results outweigh positive ones, the plan may have to be modified, or a new one designed to take its place. In the control phase of planning, ways must be provided to enable the planner to determine in a quantitative or qualitative fashion that the results produced are as intended. To make such an evaluation possible, techniques to measure actual performance, to compare it with planned performance, and to permit accommodations if necessary, are included in the planning process.

Designing the Planning Process

When a manager attempts to prevent a problem from arising, or tries to solve it by careful planning, the very act of planning itself presents problems: How to plan? What to plan? Who should develop the plan? The solution for these problems requires another plan—a blueprint for planning. In addition, a person or group must do the planning. Often equipment is needed to aid them. This means that an organization for planning is necessary. In small firms, the planning "organization" is often an individual, the owner perhaps. In a very large company, the planning organization may be a staff of people, some of whom may engage in highly technical aspects of planning like economic forecasting. They will need direction and supervision. Finally, the organization doing the planning must be controlled, to ensure that it is planning as it should. Thus the need to plan, organize, activate, and to control planning is evident. As is true of all functions, *planning has to be managed.*

An organization has expectations that it sets for itself. It is constantly adding some and deleting others. Many are broad, overall targets; others are limited and pertain to specific areas or departments. Executives who develop the former are not usually the same persons who design the latter. Within each enterprise there exists a multitude of related aims. Understanding them and their relationships can be facilitated if they are arranged in an orderly and systematic fashion. Such an ordering of goals is called a hierarchy of objectives.

ESTABLISHING A HIERARCHY OF OBJECTIVES (GOAL SYSTEM)

Every institution in society has goals toward which it strives. The goals of a government, for example, include meeting social needs, such as welfare and security; of a university, teaching and research; of a hospital, diagnosing, treating, and preventing illness; of the Boy Scouts of America, developing character; and so on. For these general purposes to be achieved, they must be supported by the particular objectives of various sub-units of the institution, by its divisions, departments, and sections. Thus, if developing personal character is an aim of the scouting movement, it can only be achieved as other scouting objectives are established and met as well. Conserving natural resources, performing service, developing a respect and appreciation for nature, and other worthy achievements may be subordinate aims that must be accomplished before character development becomes a reality. There is a telescoping and cascading effect present in goal achievement. Goal setting is **synergistic;** that is, goals reinforce each other in such a way that the total result is greater than the sum of the effects taken individually. The objectives of every organization can be viewed as a structure of goals, a hierarchy or goal system.

While there are numerous ways that a structural order of objectives can be devised, a convenient way of structuring objectives is first to view the organization as a total entity with "corporate" or "strategic" objectives, and then to visualize successively smaller segments of the whole and the "operating" objectives of each. This holistic view enables us to emphasize functional relationships between the objectives of the whole and those of its subdivisions. Regardless of how an organization's objectives are classified, they are always closely linked and interdependent. Listing the "big picture" objectives of the institution and then establishing goals for each of its major subdivisions permits us to develop a complete hierarchy of purposes that can be presented and studied in a logical, orderly manner. The actual setting of objectives often involves difficult decisions, since a manager may have a choice between two or more possible goals. This problem will be discussed in Chapter 4.

Objectives of the Total Enterprise (Corporate Aims)

A clue to a business's basic purpose can often be found in the company name under which it operates. Monarch Tile Company, Anderson Electrical Supply, First National Bank, and Sam's TV Repair all indicate the general purposes of the businesses in question. Other company names, such as Roger Kent Company, Interco, and ATO, Inc., provide no clue at all. If a firm is a corporation, its purpose is stated in its articles of incorporation. However, in recent years attorneys have spelled out corporate purposes in such general terms that corporations often appear to be in business to pursue any ends they choose as long as they are legal.

While specific objectives of one company may differ from those of another, there are some objectives that are basic to all business organizations. At first glance, the goals of a small electronics company may appear to be different from those of a major chemical company, yet there are certain goals which both hold in common. One major firm states several of its corporate objectives, within a three-year time frame, as follows:

> . . . supplement subsidiaries' product lines not only with internal developments but by selected product acquisitions as well.
> . . . endeavor to maximize at all times the avenues available to the Company to sustain the optimum growth rate consistent with financial stability.
> . . . improve the existing debt/equity ratio at the parent company level.[3]

These objectives could also be corporate goals for many other firms throughout the nation. Most businesses probably include one or more of the following among their overall corporate aims: (1) survival, (2) to produce or distribute a product or service, (3) growth, (4) favorable public image, (5) innovation, and (6) improved return on invested capital.

---

[3]James J. Ling, Chairman and Chief Executive Officer of Omega-Alpha, Inc., Statement at the Annual Meeting of Stockholders in Dallas, Texas, December 29, 1972.

Survival. Businesses strive to remain afloat, in spite of shifting economic currents and other conditions of the external environment which may be hostile to their success. When a firm gets into difficulty and its continued existence is threatened, survival becomes all-important. Many huge firms including American Motors, General Motors, Penn Central, and Lockheed Aircraft have faced this situation at some point in their history. In such circumstances, all other objectives become relatively less important. Attention must be focused mainly on doing whatever is necessary to survive. Often drastic and harsh means are employed, including consolidations, shutting down departments, laying off employees, reducing, trimming, and cutting. If its existence is not threatened, the firm will direct its energies toward other company objectives.

Produce or distribute a product or service. Inherent in every business enterprise is the purpose of producing or distributing some product or service. The firm works on the assumption that the item or service is needed by society and that it has the capability to satisfy this need to some extent. As it grows, the firm may increase the number and variety of goods and services it offers. Many of these may be quite unrelated. A large corporation, for example, may have one division that manufactures shoes in multiplants throughout the country, and another that operates a chain of retail hardware stores. Despite increasing size and complexity, it continues to maintain as one of its basic corporate objectives the desire to produce and distribute needed commodities and services. The corporation carefully selects the items to offer and continues to produce them as long as a need for them exists, and as long as there is a reward to the company for providing them.

Growth. Very closely related to survival as a corporate target is growth. In an expanding general economy, failure of the firm to keep pace, or at least to expand as rapidly as the industry of which it is a part, means decline. Standing still while others grow, or developing at a slower rate, means to decline in relative importance. A continuing decline may eventually threaten survival. A firm may have to grow just to maintain its relative position!

In this total context, growth becomes another objective pursued by a majority of astute managers in today's dynamic free enterprise system. Maintaining relative position, or increasing it, can be accomplished in several ways:

■ **Through increased size.** Increased size may manifest itself in increased dollar volume or sales, additional paid employees, greater number of shareholders, increased investment in plant and equipment, broader product lines, and similar criteria.

■ **Through a larger share of the market.** Capturing a larger percentage of the market, ordinarily thought of as an indicator of growth, is not always a valid one since the size of the market itself may change rapidly. At one time, Aluminum Corporation of America enjoyed virtually 100 percent of the market. As other firms entered the industry, particularly after World War II, Alcoa's share declined, yet the firm continued to grow dramatically. To enjoy 80 percent of a $10 million market is less desirable from a growth standpoint than to hold 50 percent of a market that itself has grown to $20 million. With a declining share of the market, a firm in the second instance has grown considerably larger than when it was king of a relatively small mountain. Yet in an expanding market, large firms develop strategies to maintain or increase their proportions of it. Often this is a very difficult goal to attain.

■ **Through diversification.** To add new products, to improve existing product mix, to reduce reliance on a single item and thereby to minimize the overall risk and uncertainty associated with it, to mitigate cyclical or seasonal influences—these are some of the reasons for growth through diversification. Often this can be accomplished by merger or acquisition as well as internally.

Diversification may also be achieved by vertical integration forward or backward, or by horizontal integration. A manufacturer, for example, may integrate backward by acquiring producers of raw materials that it uses, may integrate forward by opening its own retail outlets, and may integrate horizontally by acquiring other manufacturing plants whose products complement its own. Some steel mills, auto manufacturers, oil companies, and chemical firms are highly integrated operations.

Favorable public image.   Many organizations, particularly the larger and more mature ones, desire to create a favorable image in the eyes of the community they serve. All institutions strive to establish some visual identity.

> Every corporation dealing with a product, a service, or an idea; every government; every philanthropic organization; each religion and its factions; hospitals; schools; foundations; associations; labor unions—each has a visual identity. The question is whether it has a good one.[4]

To make it a good one, some institutions maintain public relations departments and spend millions of dollars enhancing their images in the public's mind. Generally, they attempt to accomplish this in one or more of the following ways:

■ **Through establishing a reputation for quality.** If prestige is the aim, a company may spend considerable sums of money to identify itself with this concept. It may strive to become the Tiffany or the Cadillac of the industry. "You can be sure if it's Westinghouse" is a classic illustration of a desire to establish a reputation for high quality and dependability.

It is also conceivable that a firm will go to great lengths to build a reputation for cheaper quality for which it can be equally proud. Dollar Stores have established this sort of image.

- **Through establishing a reputation for service.** Firms pride themselves on their reputation for establishing and maintaining service. Sears Roebuck and Co., for example, not only installs and services major appliances for its customers, but offers to reinstall these should the customer move to another residence, even in another city.

- **Through achieving an outstanding position in the industry.** The desire to be identified as the leader, or to be considered a member of the industry leadership, is for many a desirable way of enhancing corporate personality. General Motors is proud of its position not only in the industry, but as a recognized leader in the American industrial system. Avis Inc. made advertising history with its slogan "We're only number two, so we try harder." For many years Metropolitan Life Insurance Company and Prudential Insurance Company vied with each other for the number one spot as the largest insurance firm in terms of total assets. Prudential achieved this position for the first time in 1966 and has not relinquished it.

- **Through becoming known as a "good citizen" in the community.** As part of their ethical responsibility, business executives in recent years have increasingly assumed the role of making the community a better place in which to live and to work. Their firms make generous contributions to community activities and encourage them to serve on local, state, and national committees. They have become active in drives to raise funds for the Community Chest, local symphony, art museums, slum clearance, university expansion programs, and similar social projects.

Innovation.   To become known as a pioneer in creativity, as a developer of new products or better ways to do things, is an aim of some of the bigger firms, especially those that are highly technology-oriented. General Electric's slogan "Progress is our most important product," and Du Pont's "Better things for better living . . . through chemistry" are examples.

Improved return on invested capital.   More and more institutions are establishing increased return on invested capital as an organization-wide objective as well as an indicator of efficiency. The concept is not new. It was first used in 1915 by Donaldson Brown of the Du Pont Company, which then introduced it to General Motors two years later when it rescued GM from the verge of bankruptcy.[5] It continues to be an objective for both giants.

---

[5]Alfred P. Sloan, Jr., *My Years with General Motors*, (New York: McFadden-Bartell Corporation, 1965), p. 140.

Known as the **Du Pont Formula** (expressed as an equation for computing return on investment), it is widely used by managers in other industries to evaluate performance and to indicate relationships between various phases of their operations. In each case, primary emphasis is placed on return on capital investment as a goal.

Priority of objectives.   Whatever their size or complexity, most organizations have multiple corporate objectives. Some of these have higher priority than others. However, their order of importance is not constant; priorities shift. At one stage in a firm's development, growth may be a more prominent corporate goal than improving the corporate image. At another stage, survival may take top priority. It is difficult to assess whether a particular objective in a multiple-objective organization is more important than another because there is no simple method of measuring objectives. It is more meaningful to view them collectively as a system of goals or corporate aims.

Profit.   The question may be asked, "What about profit? Why hasn't it been included among the corporate objectives? Isn't profit *the* objective of a business?"

To understand the answer to this question, one must understand the meaning of profit. Profit has both a broad and a narrow meaning. As was pointed out in Chapter 1, in the discussion of society's view of the purpose of business, profit in its broad sense means sufficient revenue to cover payment to all of the input factors. The price that a company charges for its goods and services must satisfy the consumer and at the same time make it possible for the enterprise to recover all costs of production. This means a price sufficient to pay for the use of land, labor, and capital; replacement of worn-out and obsolete equipment (depreciation); depletion of resources; research and development; insurance of physical assets; favorable working conditions; and similar considerations. Viewed in this light, profits are simply "costs of doing business." These include **opportunity costs** or "alternative use costs," a consideration of cost to the company for not employing its resources in some other way. When a firm is successful in achieving its overall objectives, it will recover these costs of doing business (profits, in the broad sense). It would not be able to pursue indefinitely its overall objectives unless it was able to generate revenues sufficient to cover all of its input costs. If it could not, it would eventually discontinue operations.

In its narrow or restricted sense, the term profit refers to "pure profit." Pure profits can be conceived as a residual, something left over after all input costs have been recovered. Is the pursuit of pure profits, then, the main goal of business? Several observations can be made:

If perfectly competitive conditions existed in our economy (obviously they do not), pure profits could only be present in the short run. If the residue was large, additional suppliers would enter the market to get their shares of the windfall. Market forces would intervene. Supply would increase and prices would fall. Eventually, supply and demand conditions would be brought into equilibrium. Pure profits would gradually disappear, and firms would have nothing left over after recovering their input costs. Since perfectly competitive conditions do not exist, and imperfect conditions do, the pure profits that do appear are the result of these imperfect conditions. If a firm has a patent on a product, or the best location in town, or some other type of "monopoly" position, it may enjoy pure profits during the period it holds this competitive advantage. Other firms, less favorably situated, would not be able to generate pure profits.

There is a limit to the amount of pure profits that even a favorably situated firm can realize. It cannot accumulate all the pure profits it wants to. Society will step in, demanding lower prices under threat of boycotting the product or finding a substitute for it; labor will ask for a share of the residue in the form of increased wages or increased fringe benefits; the government may intervene and force a rollback of the existing high price; or other industries may develop a substitute for, or a product competitive with, the existing one. In any case, forces will come into play that tend to reduce pure profits over the long run.

Even without pure profits, a firm will continue to strive toward its corporate objectives. It will do so as long as it can meet all of its factor costs and continue to grow and develop.

Profits are to our private enterprise system what breathing is to life, but they are not the purpose of its existence any more than breathing is the purpose of life. There is more to business than profits, just as there is ultimately more to life than breathing.[6]

Properly understood, profit in its broad sense acts as a motivating force as the firm strives to fulfill its overall objectives. It is similar to a catalytic agent in chemistry; it is the actuator and not the goal or end result. Pure profit is not the goal. It is transitory when it does exist, results from disequilibrium in our economy, and is residual in nature rather than purposive.

Objectives of Each Enterprise Function (Operative Aims)

When a business enterprise is viewed in terms of its major functions, objectives can be established for each. As a result, there are buying, selling, operating, facilitating, and managing objectives. Whatever the respective goals of the different enterprise functions, they cannot negate established corporate goals; rather, they must reinforce them. The goals of the enterprise are also goals of its sub-units.

---

[6]Fletcher L. Byrom (Chairman of the Board of Koppers Company, Inc.), "Guest Editorial," *Planning Review*, Vol. 2, No. 6, October/November 1974, p. 7.

Objectives for each major function, however, are somewhat narrower, more numerous, and more particularized than company-wide objectives. The pursuit of major-function objectives becomes the means through which overall company objectives are achieved. Listed below are a few illustrations of objectives that may be established within major functional areas.

- **Buying objectives:** to be fully aware of sources of raw materials, supplies, parts, and other input factors; to purchase only what is necessary, yet buy in economical quantities; to maintain minimum yet adequate supplies of materials at machine or workbench; to purchase the best quality at the best price; to cut purchasing costs.

- **Selling objectives:** to obtain a larger share of the existing market; to develop new markets or new uses for the product; to expand the product line in order to increase size of orders; to increase revenues; to improve dealer relations.

- **Operating objectives:** in a factory, to manufacture the product with minimum rejects; to produce a high-quality product for the price; to increase output; to operate with a minimum of machine "down time"; to cut scrap loss; to reduce labor cost; to improve equipment utilization; in a service enterprise, to offer full service; to insure safety; to expedite handling.

- **Facilitating objectives:** to maintain machines in good working order; to keep the physical plant in excellent condition; to assist other functional areas in achieving their respective objectives.

- **Managing objectives:** to build a capable management organization in depth; to cut administrative overhead; to encourage employee participation; to keep abreast of changes taking place in the business environment; to coordinate all business functions.

Department Objectives

In every major functional area of the business there are numerous departments and sub-units. Departments have specific goals they set for themselves. The pursuit of departmental objectives becomes the means for achieving the objectives of the functional area within which the department operates.

In a company producing steel chairs, the operating function is called manufacturing. Manufacturing includes departments such as cutting, bending, welding, assembling, quality control, paint, shipping, and others. Each department establishes and tries to attain its particular objectives. Several departments may have very similar aims. To hold rejects to a minimum may be an objective that every manufacturing department sets for itself. On the other hand, "minimizing damage to the finished chair while in transit from factory to customer" may be an objective suited specifically to the shipping department. Nevertheless, each department, in attempting to achieve its objective of holding rejects to a minimum, contributes toward fulfilling one of the indicated objectives of the overall manufacturing function, namely "to manufacture the product with minimum rejects." Thus the department objectives are mutually reinforcing.

In a service-oriented firm like an airline, one of the operating objectives is to guarantee the safety of its passengers. The flight inspection department may have among its various departmental objectives "to insure the mechanical capability of the plane before takeoff." In this instance, the department objective dovetails with the operating objective and reinforces it. A lower level of objectives always reinforces a higher level of objectives.

Job or Position Objectives

Within every department a great variety of jobs or positions are necessary to carry on the activities of the department. Objectives are established for each job in each department. The job of a Class A welder, for example, may have as an objective turning out a cleanly welded seam joining two edges of heavy steel. This job goal closely meshes with one of the welding department objectives, "holding rejected parts to a minimum."

Task Objectives

In turn, every job can be subdivided into various tasks which make up that job. It is possible to establish objectives for each of the tasks comprising the particular job. The Class A welding job could be analyzed into such tasks as selecting the correct welding tip, checking the gauges on the tanks of oxygen and acetylene, opening the mix valve before igniting the combustible mixture, and manually operating the striker. Each task has a purpose. The purpose of operating the striker, for example, is to produce a spark to ignite the gases in the combustible mixture.

Thus task objectives denote the purpose of each task in a particular job. A given task may be designed either to produce a consistent performance by the individual operator or to assure that every operator meets some general standard of performance.

Motion Objectives

The task itself can be further subdivided into elements which the industrial engineer calls "units of motion." Each unit of motion has a specific objective. Time and motion studies are performed to establish motion objectives for various tasks. Basically, the goal is to eliminate unnecessary movements.

Using "micromotion" studies, the efficiency experts Frank and Lillian Gilbreth established two important concepts: (1) the existence of basic elements common to all human work operations; and (2) the feasibility of formulating principles of efficient motion. Basic elements of motion are called

therbligs (Gilbreth spelled backwards, with the letters *t* and *h* transposed). Well-known among the fourteen basic elements are *search, select, grasp, pre-position,* and *transport.* One of the principles of efficient motion states that the sequence of motions should be arranged to encourage rhythm in the operation. (Rhythm tends to increase speed and reduce fatigue simultaneously.)

Instant videotape replay studies of highly complex activities, such as a televised event, make it possible to determine objectives of a particular motion at the precise instant it occurred. These are helpful in establishing standards of performance and discovering weaknesses in past performance.

CHARACTERISTICS OF VALID OBJECTIVES

If objectives are to serve as effective guides to action, they must possess the following characteristics:

Must be understood;
Must be concrete, specific, particular;
Must be desirable;
Must be flexible and subject to modification;
Must be balanced;
Must be attainable.

Must Be Understood

Everyone must understand precisely what the objective is. Every worker and every manager must have a clear mental picture of the aim or purpose toward which he will be working. The objective must be understood not only by all persons expected to work toward accomplishing it, but by all who will be affected in any way by it.

Must Be Concrete, Specific, Particular

An individual cannot direct his efforts constructively if the purpose he seeks to achieve is nebulous, abstract, or vague. A manager cannot be effective unless he knows precisely what his target is, nor can a subordinate perform effectively unless he knows specifically what is expected of him. Hence every objective must be clearly and concisely spelled out. The parameters or dimensions of the purpose must be so delineated that there can be no doubt about the specific, particular ends being sought. The language describing an objective ought to possess qualitative and quantitative dimensions for a definite time period. To state ''The company strives for a profit'' is a general or loose objective. To state ''The company strives for a profit before taxes of $500,000 on sales of $2,500,000 during the fiscal period ending December 31'' is a more definitive objective. It is concrete, specific, and particular.

Must Be Desirable

An objective must always be worthy—that is, beneficial, fair, or equitable both to the company and to the surrounding community. Is this department goal a reasonable one to pursue? Is this production goal desirable? The answer to questions like these must be affirmative. Where groups will be affected, one must consider whether the end is socially desirable. Its desirability must also be considered from the point of view of the individuals who are expected to direct their efforts toward its fulfillment. A manager cannot expect high motivation if a goal established for the organization is not compatible with personal goals of individuals expected to implement it. If it is not, the objective must be discarded and another one selected which meets the "desirable" criterion. An individual's personal goals and company objectives should preferably be mutually reinforcing, or at least compatible.

Must Be Flexible

Goals established in the light of existing knowledge may be inadequate to meet changing realities. As conditions alter, goals may have to be tailored to accommodate change. Sometimes an objective formulated from existing and perhaps limited information turns out to be unrealistic when additional data are produced. Under those circumstances, the original goal should be modified. Business objectives should be so designed that they allow for such modification. All objectives should be flexible enough to be converted as the situation dictates. One way to build flexibility into goals is to establish a range rather than a finite limit. Increasing the share of the market between 10 and 15 percent is a more flexible objective than setting it at 12½ percent.

Must Be Balanced

Once a hierarchy of objectives has been established, there may be a tendency for certain objectives to claim undue emphasis. Part of a manager's role is to regulate the balance among the multiple objectives within his sphere of influence. The executive vice-president, for example, must make sure that well-intentioned selling objectives proposed by his director of sales do not place too great a burden on the company's productive capacity. There is no point in selling more than can be produced, or conversely, in producing more than can be sold. Functional objectives must be balanced.

Departmental objectives must also be kept in harmony. One group of desirable goals should not be emphasized at the expense of others, unless there is a good reason for doing so at a particular time. In the long run, imbalance at any point in the hierarchy of objectives can damage the pursuit of corporate aims and ultimately threaten the successful operation of the firm. This means that the traditional goal of "maximizing" may now be obsolete. Maximizing in one area leads to dislocations in another. To maximize could mean to disrupt. To maintain a balance among objectives and smooth coordination of the various activities of the enterprise, a manager may find it beneficial to fix levels of operation below those demanded for maximizing. In today's dynamic enterprise milieu, the goal of *optimizing* is much more realistic.

Optimizing.   Unlike the classical maximizing, which seeks to achieve the greatest result, or to perform in the best possible way, **optimizing** seeks to do what is most favorable or desirable for the enterprise as a whole under the existing conditions.[7] Thus to operate a plant at 100 percent of capacity strives toward maximizing output, whereas to operate at 90 percent of capacity seeks to optimize output, to produce at a highly favorable rate under limiting conditions. In the long run, optimizing would be more desirable since the plant and equipment would not be run constantly to the point of breakdown, or the workers to the point of exhaustion. Driving an automobile at 120 miles per hour may be maximizing speed, yet driving at 70 miles per hour is optimizing its speed when other considerations, such as burning out a bearing or overtaxing the driver, are taken into account.

Where several interests are concerned, optimum means no feasible alternative exists that is preferred by some interested party and which is not detrimental to the interests of any other party.

To describe the relative nature of optimum performance, Herbert A. Simon introduced the concept of **satisficing.** Building on Abraham Maslow's psychological theory that lower-order personal needs do not have to be satisfied 100 percent before higher levels of needs emerge,[8] Simon maintained that for businesses, too, a sufficient although not necessarily a maximum level of achievement is acceptable. He states:

> In most psychological theories the motive to act stems from drives, and action terminates when the drive is satisfied. Moreover, the conditions for satisfying a drive are not necessarily fixed, but may be specified by an aspiration level that itself adjusts upward or downward on the basis of experience.
>
> If we seek to explain business behavior in terms of this theory, we must expect the firm's goals to be not maximizing profit, but attaining a certain level or rate of profit, holding a certain share of the market or a certain level of sales. Firms would try to "satisfice" rather than to maximize.[9]

This suggests that many business executives strive for what is "good enough."

---

[7] Any other alternative would be less favorable or of lesser value or utility.

[8] Abraham Maslow, "A Theory of Human Motivation," *Psychological Review*, Vol. 50, 1943, p. 388.

[9] Herbert A. Simon, "Theories of Decision-Making in Economics and Behavioral Science," *American Economic Review*, Vol. 49, No. 3, June 1959, pp. 262–63.

Typically, when the quality of work is too low, a manager will take necessary action to bring it up to par. But what about work quality that is too high? Should it be reduced? Under the satisficing concept, the answer would be yes. Why, for example, must a production order or a warehouse requisition be a perfectly typed, flawless communication? Is that degree of perfection necessary or even desirable? If the purpose is simply to communicate information that can be easily understood and acted upon, a plainly worded, handwritten note can serve the identical purpose and eliminate time spent on dictation, typing, revisions, and retyping. If "gold plated" is just as serviceable as "gold filled," there is no need for the latter. There is nothing unethical or improper in having a worker make products good enough to pass inspection and no better. In fact, it is a waste of time and money to do things in a way that is more exacting than necessary. A factory can ill afford to permit its workers to put a high polish on the necks of lightbulbs it manufactures when to do so could be costly and would serve no useful purpose. In short, if an item or service meets established, acceptable standards, it is "good enough."

Sub-optimizing. Most economists, engineers, and management theorists view sub-optimization as the result of a situation in which relatively autonomous units, in a conscientious effort to optimize their own effectiveness, decrease the net effectiveness of the organization. A manager tends to think primarily of the welfare of his own department or sector; he strives to optimize inputs and outputs in his division, often without regard to the ultimate effect on the firm. The result is **sub-optimization,** an imbalance in the total effort. A typical definition, given by Miller and Starr, states, *"when objectives are dependent,* the optimization of one can result in a lower degree of attainment for at least some of the others. This condition is known as *sub-optimization."*[10] They go on to elaborate, "If the performance of one part of a system (a subsystem) is improved and this results in an impairment of the total system's performance, we have clear evidence of sub-optimization."[11] This traditional view equates sub-optimization with mismanagement on the part of an executive who permits the situation to continue.

Deliberate sub-optimizing, however, is not mismanaging. On the contrary, it is a positive, intended act. Sub-optimizing should be viewed as an effective *means* of achieving a desirable end, not the result of undesirable actions. There are many occasions when a capable manager will intentionally sub-optimize in certain areas to achieve overall balance and to integrate functions for the corporate good. Let us examine a situation that illustrates this positive, beneficial nature of deliberate sub-optimizing.

---

[10]David W. Miller and Martin K. Starr, *Executive Decisions and Operations Research,* 2nd ed. (Englewood Cliffs, N.J.: Prentice-Hall, Inc., 1969) p. 48.

[11]Ibid., p. 55.

Assume the canning department in a brewery, operating optimally, can fill cans, place them in cartons, stack the cartons on wooden pallets, and load sixty pallets in a hour. The shipping department employs two men to operate forklift trucks. Each forklift operator transports a loaded pallet to a railroad car at the siding, stacks the pallet in the car, and returns for another load. Working at optimum, each man can handle twenty loaded pallets per hour. If the canning line continues at its optimum level of production, it will not take long before loaded pallets pile up faster than two forklift operators can remove them, despite the fact that they, too, are working at optimum level. Under the assumption that the shipping department is already working at optimum, it is not possible to add another forklift operator; the drivers would line up waiting to load and would be getting in each other's way. To require the two forklift operators to work beyond established optimums, to speed up their work above what has already been determined as "optimum" in the long run, is to invite accidents, damage to the merchandise, and excessive fatigue for the drivers. The plant manager, therefore, would instruct the manager of the canning department to "sub-optimize" his operations, slowing down the canning line to forty loaded pallets per hour in order to bring the total operation into balance. Perhaps at some future date the technology within the shipping department will have changed, permitting the handling of sixty loaded pallets per hour as an optimum performance. When that occurs, the canning department can be restored to its optimum level of output.

If optimization is a long-range goal, deliberate sub-optimization can be a necessary and desirable short-run or interim expedient to keep the total hierarchy of objectives in balance. As long as sub-optimization contributes to optimization of overall objectives, it should be considered a positive measure.

Must Be Attainable

Perhaps the most important criterion for an organizational objective is that it be attainable. All goals must be realistic and therefore capable of accomplishment.

Some theorists have suggested that organizational objectives can be classified in terms of their time reference. Within this classification objectives may be (1) **visionary** (goals in the distant future), (2) **attainable** (goals in the not too distant future), and (3) **immediate** (goals in the near future). There are some who say visionary objectives are at the top of the hierarchy—that they are the most desirable accomplishments for the organization.[12]

---

[12]Herbert G. Hicks, *The Management of Organizations: a Systems and Human Resources Approach,* 2nd ed. (New York: McGraw-Hill Book Co., 1972) p. 68.

According to our definition of a business objective, and the characteristics of a valid objective, only attainable and immediate objectives qualify. A business organization cannot achieve, acquire, create, preserve, or distribute anything visionary. If there is a possibility that someday ore can be mined on the moon, the typical mining company cannot plan now to open a mine and build a processing plant there. It cannot include such a prospect in its hierarchy of goals.

This does not mean that some part of a business organization cannot devote a portion of its thinking to visionary goals. In fact, there are corporations designed to deal with "futurology." Their purpose is to investigate the future by all technical and scientific means available to them. One of these famous "think tanks" is the Rand Corporation in Santa Monica, California, established in 1945 by the U.S. Air Force. As early as 1946 its scientists were evaluating the military usefulness of a spaceship! Government and big business need these thinkers who deal with the future. But few organizations can afford to maintain staffs of hundreds of scientists simply to explore the unknown and to deal with phenomena that have no known dimensions. As technology advances and conditions become ripe for new concepts to be accepted, what was a visionary goal often becomes an attainable one. When a goal becomes attainable, an organization can begin to marshal its resources and plan for its achievement. The goal can now take its place in the hierarchy of objectives.

RELATIONSHIP OF OBJECTIVES IN A HIERARCHY

A hierarchical structure of objectives implies certain relationships between these objectives:

1. At any level of the structure, objectives within that level are related to each other. At the corporate level, for example, obtaining a reputation for quality may enhance growth as well as achieve a larger share of the market.

2. Objectives within a given level of the hierarchy are related to objectives at any other level of the hierarchy. There is a cascading effect. Once goals have been developed, they must be clearly communicated to the next lower level.

3. The various hierarchical levels are linked together by a *means-ends relationship.* That is, the attained objectives at one level become the means for attaining objectives at the next higher level.

4. Micro-objectives reinforce macro-objectives in the family of objectives. The pursuit of sub-unit goals should always reinforce overall goals and never run counter to them. Someone in the organization should be given the authority to enforce this principle. As an illustration, consider the corporate

goal of "overall cost reduction." The inventory manager may set out to reduce storage costs. If production set-up costs are high, greater reductions may be achieved by producing in large lots to reduce unit costs—which could only be accomplished by increasing storage costs! In this instance, the sub-unit goal of reducing inventory storage costs would have to be deliberately sub-optimized by executive mandate in order to achieve the corporate objective of overall cost reduction.

5. Together, all the objectives in the hierarchy form a single network of mutually reinforcing aims.

THE USES OF PLANNING

Planning is a basic function in the managing process. Unless it is performed in an effective manner, organizing, activating, and controlling cannot be performed effectively either. An organization, as we shall discover shortly, is a controllable means for implementing plans. Without plans, there is no reason for organizing; nothing to activate; no basis for controlling. A very intimate relationship exists among these functions. One cannot occur without the others.

Planning, therefore, has two basic uses:

1. To make it possible for other managing activities to occur. We must have something for which to organize and to activate, and something with which to control.

2. To solve problems in all areas of the business. Deciding what has to be done and how to do it requires a plan of action. One has to decide among possible, desirable objectives and possible, desirable ways to accomplish them. Planning, decision making, and problem solving are intimately related.

SUMMARY

An essential component in the managing process is the planning process, a cluster of activities directed toward establishing goals for an organization and designing ways in which they can be achieved.

Most organizations have multiple goals, which comprise a network, or enterprise goal system. This system includes numerous sub-systems of objectives developed in the various divisions, departments, and sections of the organization. The relationships between objectives becomes clear when the objectives are arranged in a hierarchy.

Basic corporate objectives include survival, production of a product or service, growth, favorable public image, innovation, and increased return on capital investment. During various stages of an organization's development and maturation these objectives may shift in order of importance.

For objectives to be included in a hierarchy of objectives, they must possess *all* of the following attributes: they must be understood, concrete and specific, desirable, flexible, balanced, and attainable.

The planning process is essential because it makes it possible for all other managing activities to occur, and enables managers to solve problems or to prevent them from arising.

KEY CONCEPTS

Open-System Approach
Planning Process
Hierarchy of Objectives
Du Pont Formula
Profit
Therbligs

Opportunity Costs
Optimizing
Optimum
Primacy of Planning
Satisficing
Deliberate Sub-optimizing

GLOSSARY

deliberate sub-optimizing   Purposely setting performance in a sub-unit at less than optimum in order to achieve balanced overall organizational performance.

hierarchy of objectives   Structure of objectives arranged in descending order from corporate objectives to motion objectives.

objective   End (purpose, goal, aim) that an organization is expected to achieve, acquire, create, preserve, or distribute, and toward which managers direct their efforts.

opportunity costs   Consideration of the cost to an organization for not employing its resources in some other manner.

optimizing   Attempting to obtain what is most desirable for the enterprise as a whole.

optimum   The most favorable state under existing conditions.

planning   A major function of managing that consists of formulating objectives and establishing the means to achieve them.

primacy of planning   Planning must precede performance.

satisficing   Working toward a sufficient, although not necessarily optimum, level of satisfaction.

synergistic   Producing a total effect greater than the sum of the component effects.

therblig   A basic unit or element of motion.

REVIEW QUESTIONS

1. Comment on the statement, "Planning utilizes an open-system approach in dealing with management decisions."
2. Draw up a list of goals that you would like to achieve for yourself in the next five years. Can all of them be optimized?
3. Select one of these goals and, using the steps in the planning process, plan how to achieve this goal.
4. What is the role of profit among organizational objectives?
5, Must an organization have a balanced system of objectives? When is deliberate sub-optimizing useful?
6. What are some of the relationships between organizational objectives which are established by a hierarchy of objectives?
7. What are the dual uses of planning?

Chapter 4

Decision Making

The subject of decision making has been investigated by engineers, economists, sociologists, psychologists, management theorists, and others. Their theories differ widely, as might be expected from their different orientations. Nevertheless, most agree that decision making is a skill which can be developed.

Effective decision making is a distinguishing feature of effective performance in all organizations. Unfortunately, skilled decision makers are scarce. Managers are in great demand who can make wise decisions in a dynamic environment. These are the dynamic managers.

Decision making cannot be completely quantified; nor is it based solely on reason or intuition. Many decisions are based on emotions or instincts. Any realistic approach to an understanding of decision making must recognize the existence of these extremes. It is decision making as a *rational process* that is the subject of our interest.

THE DECISION-MAKING PROCESS

Decision making can be viewed as a process made up of four continuous, interrelated phases: *search, analysis, evaluation,* and *commitment.* Asking "What should be done?" and "What are the challenges?" represents **searching.** Asking "How can I utilize my available resources?" and "How can I take advantage of these challenging opportunities?" indicates **analyzing.** Asking "What are the costs?" and "What are the potential rewards?" indicates **evaluating.** Finally, asking "Which option shall I select?" indicates preparation for **commitment.** One writer calls these stages in the process explorative, speculative, evaluative, and selective.[1]

Decision making is a dynamic process concerned with identifying worthwhile things to do, and with selecting a course of action from among less effective courses of action. The result of this process is always a

---

[1]Philip Marvin, *Developing Decisions for Action* (Homewood, Ill.: Dow Jones-Irwin, Inc., 1971), p. 3.

decision—*a commitment to a choice from among two or more alternatives.* Marvin points out that decision making operates on a binary basis. Failure to act in any decision-making situation has the full effect of a commitment to a course of *inaction.*[2] The person who doesn't decide to do something decides not to do something.

As noted in the previous chapter, decision making is essential to the planning process, both for determining objectives and for selecting courses of action.[3] In considering objectives, it is important to decide not only what you want to do, but also what you do *not* want to do—what markets you do not want to enter, what services you do not want to offer, and at what point you want to stop doing whatever it is that your organization is doing. The objectives decided on guide further decision making by channeling the search for alternative actions and providing criteria for evaluating them. A decision is made to select one or a combination of several alternatives to which resources are then committed. This commitment to action is usually expressed in the form of some type of plan.

WHAT IS A DECISION PROBLEM?

A *change* of some kind, either in the enterprise itself or in the external environment, is usually the causal factor behind a decision problem situation. An adjustment may be necessary because something occurs that alters the existing state of affairs and requires attention, or managers may take systematic steps to bring about planned changes in existing operations to avoid stagnation. Blake and Mouton call this "change by design, not by default."[4] Planned obsolescence by automobile manufacturers is an example of this type of decision making. On the other hand, the change requiring a decision may be some undesirable deviation from a standard norm of performance. The control process may indicate that a particular situation needs to be corrected. The question is "how?"

From a behavioral point of view, a problem may be an unsatisfied need to change a perceived present situation to a perceived desired one. A solution is realized when present and desired situations are perceived to be the same.[5] Since decision making fundamentally is a commitment to some goal or to some course of action, a problem arises only when an alternative goal or alternative course exists, and a decision maker is uncertain about which goal or means to select. A **decision problem** can be defined, therefore, as an *uncertainty in a manager's mind about the best way to achieve some end or*

[2]Ibid., p. 5.

[3]The reader is referred to the model of the planning process in Figure 3–1.

[4]Robert R. Blake and Jane S. Mouton, "Change by Design, Not by Default," *Advanced Management Journal,* Society for Advancement of Management, April 1970, pp. 29–34.

[5]Edwin M. Bartee, "A Holistic View of Problem Solving," *Management Science,* Vol. 20, No. 4, December 1973, p. 439.

purpose. It is this meaning of the term *problem* to which we turn our attention.

The "best" way to do something implies that there is more than one way that it can be done—that alternatives exist. Uncertainty is present since the decision maker is not sure which of the choices to select in order to achieve his goal. **Uncertainty** is *the presence of doubt because of a lack of definite or complete knowledge about an outcome.* What is best in one situation may not be in another. Horton suggests that as a practical matter, priorities must be assigned to alternatives if only because the total amount of available resources is nearly always limited.[6] Organizations cannot do everything at the same time. Sooner or later decisions on priorities are necessary and managers will need some method of weighing the many intangible, diverse, and partial objectives. Thus, for a problem to exist, there must always be present these dual conditions: *uncertainty* and *choices.* If there are several options but no doubt about which to select, there is no problem; if there is but one choice about how to proceed, again no problem exists. If a supervisor in a factory has a choice between two locations in which to set up a new piece of machinery in his department but has no doubt that one location is superior to the other, he does not have a problem. On the other hand, if he has a choice between two sites but is uncertain which of them is superior, then he does have a decision problem to solve.

While it is true that all problems raise questions, not all questions raise problems. Fact finding is often confused with decision making. Simple information seeking, even if posed as a question, is not a problem. The answer to the question "What time does the next plane leave for New York?" poses no problem. There is only one next plane for New York. How to go about discovering when the next plane leaves could be a problem, since there may be several ways to seek this information and you may not know the best way to find out. In addition, it should be kept in mind that while all problem solving requires decisions, not all decisions are concerned with solving problems. If, in answer to a worker's question "What time shall I report for work in the morning?" the supervisor answers, "Come in at 9:00," the supervisor is making a decision but no problem is involved and no planning is required.

In the decision-making process a manager, confronted with a problem, selects a "solution" from among several alternatives. He wants to choose a course that will be most effective in reaching the goal or in solving the problem confronting him. Since there is usually some uncertainty about the future, he cannot be sure of the consequences of his decision. To estimate the consequences of various decisions he might make, a manager must have some measurable criterion of effectiveness. Typical criteria may include a validity coefficient, or an acceptable degree of perfection or compatibility.

---

[6]Forest W. Horton, Jr., "Optimization," *Reference Guide to Advanced Management Methods,* American Management Association, Inc., 1972, p. 195.

Measurements may reflect such concerns as "How much will it cost compared to another alternative?" "How much satisfaction will it produce compared to other ways?"

Because alternative courses are many, and numerous premises and variables are involved in most problem-solving situations, evaluation can be very complex. It is at this point in the decision-making process that quantitative aids to decision making can make a contribution. Newer methodologies, including computer techniques and mathematical aids that can be helpful, are described in Chapters 5 and 6.

Through quantitative evaluations, a manager may determine which outcomes are most likely to occur, and what their economic and social consequences are likely to be. Having considered the probabilities, he may act on the basis of this information, or he may choose to ignore the probabilities and take a calculated risk. In any case, he must decide!

KINDS OF DECISION PROBLEMS

Problems crop up constantly in all functional areas and at all levels of management in an organization. One is no sooner solved than another presents itself. Frequently the solution to one problem creates a new, or potential, problem. Managers, therefore, are continually involved in making decisions and solving problems. This is a never-ending process. Some problems are pressing, requiring immediate attention; others can be handled at a later date. Some are complex and broad in scope; others are simpler and more limited. Some have to do with selling; others are associated with manufacturing or with other functional areas. Since a multitude of problems of all types confront managers, it is helpful to understand and deal with them if they are grouped in some meaningful ways. For discussion purposes, all problems can be classified according to (1) time significance, (2) scope, and (3) major enterprise functions to which they relate. Special kinds of plans are then developed to handle these different kinds of problems.

Classification by Time Significance

One way in which decision problems can be viewed is in terms of their temporal demands. Since a manager can attend to only one thing at a time, it is important for him to have a sense of temporal priorities.

Urgent versus less urgent. By their very nature, some problems are urgent. They require immediate attention. An injection molding machine may be spewing out incompletely formed or misshaped pieces. For the machine to continue operating in this manner would result in costly production of non-usable parts. The problem should be rectified quickly. From the standpoint of time, it is urgent.

On the other hand, many problems are less urgent and do not require immediate attention. A mimeograph machine may print legible copies that are not uniform with respect to light and dark areas on each page. The problem needs correcting but is not urgent. Perhaps its solution is to permit the machine to continue to run until the ink presses evenly through the stencil and uniform copies appear. If that course of action does not remedy the original problem, the stencil may have to be re-inked. At any rate, this type of problem is not urgent.

Immediate versus remote. Immediate problems are the actual, present problems, whereas remote problems are the potential which may arise at some time in the future.

All urgent problems are immediate, though not all immediate problems are urgent. If a customer in a department store becomes ill and faints, the problem is immediate and urgent. A customer complaint to the adjustor in a department store may be immediate, yet may not be urgent.

A remote problem may be illustrated by a small but growing firm whose sales may eventually outrun its delivery capabilities. Presently it makes deliveries to customers via its own company-owned truck. If sales continue to accelerate, will the present truck be large enough to handle all deliveries? The problem is only a potential one. It may become immediate if sales continue to increase at a rapid rate. In time, a remote problem can become an immediate one, even an urgent one.

Recurring versus non-recurring. Many problems appear and reappear, requiring repeated attention. Others do not. In a restaurant, the same peak periods occur daily. If there are problems attendant to those peaks, they are recurring. In a factory, rising costs may be a recurring problem.

A decision to lease a piece of equipment or to purchase it exemplifies a non-recurring problem. It is a one-time decision. Whether a given mailing brochure should be printed in black or white or in color is also a non-recurring problem.

Classification by Scope

Another manner in which problems can be grouped is according to their scope. Some problems are very broad in their implications, involving many functional areas or large numbers of persons. Other problems are much more limited.

Designing the size and kind of organization that will be required to handle an anticipated increased volume of business ten years from now is a problem that has far-reaching implications, may involve many functional areas of the company, its physical plants, sales offices, suppliers, employees, and customers. This kind of determination is broad in scope. Problems which are broad in scope are generally handled by higher echelons of management.

In contrast, determining where to place the desks of two new employees in the office of an insurance company is a relatively simple problem. Limited in its scope, it is not likely to have any significant impact on other areas of the company, its customers, suppliers, or branches, and could be handled by a lower level of management, perhaps the office manager in this situation.

The more limited in scope a problem is, the greater is the likelihood that it can be referred to a lower level of management to resolve. All problems should be referred to the lowest level of management capable of dealing effectively with them. This principle is valid even for problems that are broad in scope. Although they may be handled by higher managerial levels than limited problems, they should be delegated to managers at a level no higher than is necessary to deal with them. Only in exceptional cases should a manager at a given level call a problem to the attention of someone at a higher level in the hierarchy. A competent manager normally should not ask his superior how to deal with a problem. Instead, he should report the manner in which he actually dealt with it! Only if the problem is beyond his capability and authority should he refer it to a higher level. In that instance, the higher-level executive will deal with it because it is unusual—an exception. This is known as *management by exception*. The concept is an extension of the **exception principle** first expressed by Taylor.[7] This principle, often cited in management literature, states that a manager should plan his work in such a manner that subordinates handle routine, predictable assignments while he devotes most of his time to exceptional circumstances and problems. In a control situation, a manager is not concerned with all deviations from the norm, but only with *significant* deviations, good or bad, wherever they occur. The more a manager concentrates on exceptions, the more effective his control efforts will be.

Problems broad in scope, the weighty matters which require top-level decisions, are sometimes referred to as *corporate* problems. These may have to do with product development, markets, channels of distribution, mergers, consolidations, and similar areas. They require *corporate plans* designed to meet these objectives. Those which are more restricted in scope and relatively less important, requiring the decisions of lower- rather than top-level managers, are frequently called *operational* problems. Generally, they deal with current rather than future activities. They require *operational plans* to meet current or short-range objectives. Immediate problems and urgent problems tend to be limited in scope.

The relationship between the scope of problems and the level of management dealing with them is illustrated in Figure 4-1. As indicated, top-level managers deal with corporate problems, which are broadest in scope, middle-level managers wrestle with problems somewhat narrower in scope, and lower-level managers handle problems of an operational nature, which are much more frequent and much more limited in their implications.

---

[7]Frederick W. Taylor, *Shop Management* (New York: Harper & Brothers, 1911), pp. 126–127.

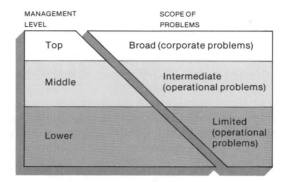

Figure 4-1. Scope of problems dealt with at different levels of management.

Classification by Major Enterprise Function

A third way in which the myriad decision problems can be classified is on the basis of the functions to which they relate. Different problems arise in marketing, production, finance, personnel, accounting, and other areas of activity. These can be consolidated into two broad groups: those related to *non-management* functions, and those which are *managerial* in nature.

Problems related to non-management functions would be of four kinds: **buying, selling, operating,** and **facilitating.** There are several advantages to grouping problems in this manner. (1) It makes problems easier to identify. Despite the possibility of overlap, it is relatively easy to recognize the problem area involved. (2) It establishes the locus of authority, enabling an executive to determine who shall have the authority to handle each problem. If it is a buying problem, for example, an executive in the buying area will deal with it. (3) It makes it possible to divide authority. Should a problem have ramifications that involve several functional areas, more than one manager may have to be called in to deal with it effectively. To paint a product black or gold may be a decision that requires consultation with the marketing manager (gold may sell better than black); the production manager (black may be easier to apply to the product than gold); and perhaps the purchasing agent (black may cost less or be easier to obtain from suppliers than gold). In this situation, the problem is multi-dimensional. Its solution is the resultant of the managerial contributions from all of the functional areas involved, a group decision reached in a participative manner.

Managerial problems also fall into four categories: planning problems, organizing problems, activating problems, and controlling problems. The advantages of grouping problems in this fashion are similar to the advantages of the non-management classification: (1) easy identification, (2) location of authority, and (3) division of authority where necessary. Thus, if the problem has to do with forecasting, an executive from the planning area will deal with it. In a large firm such as a steel mill, a bank, or an insurance company, this individual may be an economist who has the technical competence to make economic forecasts. If the problem has to do with excessive labor turnover, it is an organizing problem and will normally be handled by an officer from that area of managing, probably the personnel manager.

Complex management problems, such as the problem of labor turnover, may require the attention of more than one manager. In seeking to reduce excessive labor turnover, the personnel manager may consult with the factory superintendent. Perhaps the problem stems in part from poor personnel selection, and in part from poor working conditions or inept supervision by the line foremen. In this situation we have an example of a problem overlap between a non-management area (operating) and a management area (organizing). Representatives from both functional areas become involved in the decision problem and its solution.

It should be kept in mind when classifying problems according to time, scope, or major enterprise function that most problems are related to other problem areas. Classifications are by no means mutually exclusive; rather, they are interrelated, interdependent, and interacting. Various combinations are possible. A sales problem, for example, could be broad in scope, non-recurring, and immediate. Nevertheless, this system of classification provides a useful means of identifying problems for analysis and discussion. Particular types of plans are devised to solve them, as we shall discover in our discussion of major types of plans in Chapter 7.

HOW PROBLEMS ARE HANDLED

Recognizing and solving problems is a never-ending process for managers at all levels, in all types of organizations. There are numerous ways that managers can deal with problems that come to their attention. Among them are delay (1) in handling, (2) imitation, (3) seeking expert advice, (4) trial and error, and (5) reflective thinking. Let us examine each of these ways of handling problems.

Delay in Handling

Intentionally delaying action on a problem should not be confused with procrastination. The latter involves putting off until a later date something that ought to be done now, because a person is lazy or by habit a postponer who dislikes facing present reality. On the other hand, a decision to delay action on a problem that is not pressing can sometimes be an effective managerial strategy. There are at least four potential benefits: (1) the problem may disappear in time; (2) "sleeping on it" may give the decision maker a better perspective; (3) the accumulation of problems may permit an order of priorities to be established; and (4) several problems may often be solved with one solution. Let us examine each of these advantages.

As frequently happens during the delay interval, factors or conditions that caused the problem may change, and at a later date the original problem may no longer exist. Take as an example the office manager in an engineering department who is faced with the problem of how to redesign the filing system to accommodate increasing numbers of engineering drawings and specifications that must be maintained for long periods of time. The problem is immediate but not urgent. Thus the office manager does not seek an immediate solution but delays while he handles more pressing matters. In the intervening weeks, he is advised by his superior that all technical data in the company, including engineering, are to be microfilmed. The original problem of how to redesign his department's filing system no longer exists. In fact, had he tackled the problem at once and proceeded to restructure the filing system, it would have been a wasted and costly effort in light of the higher-level decision to change over to microfilm.

Sleeping on a problem rather than acting at once can also be advantageous. Often it permits the decision maker to see the problem more objectively, in the cold light of reality, rather than emotionally. Waiting a few days and then taking a fresh look at the problem may give the manager a new perspective, which may lead to a better solution. It may also put him in a better frame of mind, psychologically, to cope with the problem.

Delay in dealing with problems permits several problems to accumulate. One can then begin to see the forest, rather than each individual tree, and can establish an order of priorities so as to deal with the more important problems first. Sometimes it makes more sense to handle problems in a planned, sequential order than to deal with them indiscriminately on a first-come, first-served basis.

Finally, by accumulating problems one may arrive at a solution that will eliminate or mitigate more than one of them. Needless steps may be saved. To wait and then dictate one memorandum to several department heads is less time-consuming than to dictate individual memos to each, if the communication deals with a problem that concerns them all. It is not at all uncommon for one decision to cure or eliminate more than one problem when the individual problems do not have to be dealt with right away. In the example of the company-wide microfilming of all technical data, with the same solution several intra-company problems were solved, including the one faced by the office manager in the engineering department.

Imitation

In solving problems by imitation, a manager repeats what he has done successfully in the past with a similar problem, or what he knows someone else has done that has proved effective. In the former case, the manager recalls a similar set of circumstances and the techniques or measures he employed then to resolve that problem. The decision which he made then, and which worked, is now repeated in the present situation. The costs in arriving at the original decision, and all the steps that had to be taken at that time, can be saved now. The workable solution is simply imitated.

If a manager has not faced a similar problem in the past, he may know other managers in or out of the organization who have done so. He may thus be able to duplicate what they have done successfully when confronted with a similar set of circumstances.

Seeking Expert Advice

In today's highly complex organization, a manager who is a competent generalist does not always possess the technical expertise which some problems demand. He may deal with such a problem by seeking the expert counsel of a specialist, who can point out possible alternatives for him to consider in his deliberations. In industry today this is a very familiar situation. An executive may have to address himself to a problem that has legal implications with which he is not conversant. He is uncertain, therefore, how to proceed. He calls upon the company's lawyer for expert opinion and advice. With the legal pros and cons before him, he may limit his choice to the legally correct one, or to one least likely to cause legal complications. However, he may choose not to follow the course recommended by the technical expert and take a calculated risk instead. It is his prerogative not to heed expert advice, although he usually does if he seeks it.

To call upon an expert in a specialized field is part of the methodology of the competent executive whether the institution is large or small. Often the sources of such counsel in larger firms are the company's own staff departments—engineering, legal, personnel, quality control, and others.

Trial and Error

Frequently, a problem is solved by the trial-and-error method. This may work quite well in situations where the decision maker knows in advance that one of the trials contains the solution to the problem, but does not know which one.

Illustrative of trial and error is a situation in which a person knows that one of the keys on a ring will open the door to an office. He does not know which one, however. He is unable to call in someone who may be able to identify the correct key. There is an urgent need to enter the office. He decides to solve the problem through trial and error. The worst that can happen is that he may not find the solution until the last key has been placed in the lock. The most favorable result would be to discover that the first key he tries opens the door. However, the probability is that a trial somewhere between the first one and the final one available will open the door. Once the correct key is found, it can be identified and used again without delay in a similar situation.

Determining whether an early trial or a later one will produce a successful result is not merely a matter of luck. It is a matter of statistical probability. Sheer luck seldom solves a problem.

The process of trial and error also plays an important role in the learning of new operations. A superior should understand this when working with a subordinate who is new at a given assignment and is unfamiliar with the sequence of tasks involved or with the motions that make up the task. The worker will learn partly through trial and error. His errors help him to learn. The incorrect trials will become fewer. Eventually only correct motions will be made, and a rhythm will be established. The novice will become a skilled operator.

Thus, in situations where the solution to a problem is to be found among the trials attempted, dealing with problems by trial and error may be an expedient and prudent approach.

Reflective Thinking

Reflective thinking involves integrating past experience with present experience to solve a problem. For the manager, this is a process of "thinking through" a problem until he comes up with a solution.

The concept of reflective thinking is illustrated by the model in Figure 4-2.

THE PROCESS OF REFLECTIVE THINKING

How does a manager solve a decision problem by using the process of reflective thinking? An examination of the process itself will provide the answer. As indicated by Figure 4-2, it includes the following steps:

1. Clearly Define the Problem

The philosopher John Dewey said that a question well put is half answered. Whether the mathematics of this statement is true or not, it is certain that unless a problem is carefully defined it cannot be solved. Many writers echo the view that problem definition is the key to effective problem solving.[8] A manager has to know what he is trying to do, or where he is trying to go, before he can begin to accomplish his objective. The problem must be put in a precise fashion. Very often, what appears to be the problem is not the actual problem at all. A problem resembles an iceberg in that what is visible or apparent actually represents only a small portion of the problem and its true depth. It is important to get to the root of the problem and to deal with

---

[8]Thad B. Green, "Problem Definition—Key to Effective Problem Solving," *Management Advisor,* November–December 1973.

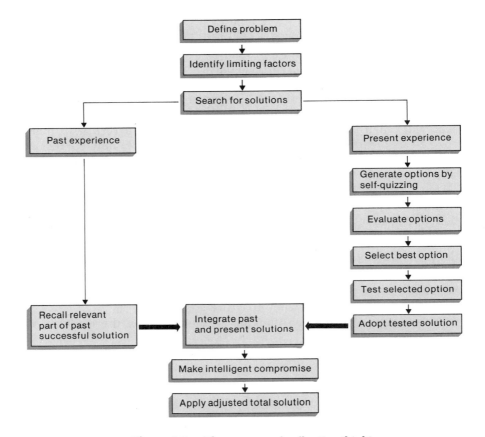

Figure 4-2.   The process of reflective thinking.

the malady itself and not just its symptoms. Treating symptoms doesn't solve problems. Symptoms, however, may furnish clues to problems.

A mother states that she has a problem. "How can I get my child to eat eggs for breakfast?" When asked why she wants the child to eat eggs, her reply is, "for the body-building protein." How to get a child to eat eggs for breakfast is not the problem; how to get the child to eat more body-building protein is. The solution then becomes a matter of finding a substitute for eggs—other protein foods. If the child enjoys some of these, the problem is solved.

Let us examine the situation in which an organization learns that the lease on the building it occupies is about to expire, and that the owner of the building is not favorably disposed toward renewing it. The organization has a problem. However, the immediate problem is not "what action to take if the lease is not renewed," but rather, what steps to take to overcome the landlord's reluctance. Knowing this, the institution can address itself toward a solution.

2. Identify Limiting Factors (Contingencies)

Generally the decision maker finds that he does not have a completely free hand in attacking the problem before him. He may be hampered either by restrictions that are part of the problem itself, or by limitations in the available means or methods for solving it. Although these limiting factors are not found in every situation, they must be taken into account in most.

In the illustration of the building lease, the problem has been stated as "what to do in order to get the owner favorably disposed toward renewing the lease." A limiting factor may be the negative personality of the landlord, which is part of the problem itself. On the other hand, how much additional rent the firm can afford to pay, the minimum or maximum length of time it can entertain on a new lease, and the concessions it would be willing to make to satisfy the landlord, such as paying the property tax or paying for maintenance and repair of the building, are examples of limiting factors related to the *means* being considered toward solving the problem. They place limits on how far the organization can go in preparing its negotiating position.

Whether limiting factors are part of the problem, or are associated with the means employed in seeking a solution, they usually take the following forms:

Manpower limitations.   In general, only a given number of employees are available to work on a project. A supervisor assigned to a mission is told that the company can spare two men to help him. These two men become the manpower limitation. He might proceed in a far different manner if he were not limited to two. Another example is that of a manager who is asked to establish a training program. The way he would set up a training program for fifty subordinates would be different from the manner in which he would proceed if only ten were involved. The kind of program designed would reflect the limitations imposed by the number of persons involved.

Space limitations.   Often the decision maker must consider the physical limitations of space. The area available, the square feet of floor space, or cubic foot of storage, or even the height of the ceilings, may be limiting factors. Charged with the task of storing incoming materials ordered in amounts larger than usual, the receiving manager might well ask: "How much floor space do I have to use? How much wall space?" Given the physical dimensions, he would work out his storage accordingly.

Financial Limitations.   Financial restrictions are very often a critical constraint on decision making. The kind of program selected to promote the sale of a new product is limited in part by the amount of money available for promotional expenditures. The kinds of tools purchased, the persons hired, buildings constructed, systems designed, all may be dependent upon financial considerations that act as limiting factors on what is eventually decided. An ever-present consideration is "What will it cost?" and "How much do I have to spend?"

Equipment limitations.   It is quite possible for a pending decision to be limited by considerations of the equipment that will be employed. Built-in limitations may exist in capacity, speed of operation, manual feed or automatic feed, maintenance requirements, or other essential characteristics. When machines are to be employed as part of the means for solving a problem or attaining an objective, the characteristics of these capital items may act as constraints. The manager will have to take them into account as he proceeds toward the solution of the problem.

Personality limitations.   Personality traits, attitudes, and value judgments of persons working on a problem, or those affected by its solution, may all influence a manager's handling of the problem. A manager will do things quite differently if his subordinates are highly motivated "self-starters" than if they require heavy supervision. Furthermore, if the people who will be affected by the decision are receptive, cooperative, and positive in their attitudes, this opens up a range of alternatives that would not be available to the decision maker if these people were not receptive, uncooperative, and negative in their attitudes. The psychology of the situation at a given moment could well determine the managerial style that is employed.

Time limitations.   "How much time do I have to get the job done?" A deadline is obviously a potential limiting factor. "How long is the project going to last?" "Will this be a one-year or five-year contract with the employees?" Such questions indicate time considerations that may well be limiting factors for the decision maker. Quite often the end result of a project that is not restricted by time limits differs from one that is. If an employee has to give his superior a report based on facts assembled in minutes, it is likely to be less accurate than the one he would provide if given much more time to gather his data. Yet, realistically, in organizational situations one seldom seems to have enough time. Many problems have to be solved now. "Now" may be an imposing limiting factor.

While other limiting factors may also be present, in general one or more of those discussed (manpower, space, finances, equipment, personalities, and time) will have to be carefully noted by the decision maker before he attempts a solution of the problem he has objectively and painstakingly defined.

3. Search for Possible Solutions

Knowing what the problem is and what limiting factors must be considered, the next step in the process of reflective thinking is to search for possible solutions. This may be done by recalling elements of previous successful experiences or by asking questions which may suggest answers.

Recalling elements of previous successful experiences. The starting point in the search for a workable solution to a problem is to refer to past experiences with similar problems.

Is there something about the present situation that appears familiar because it resembles a previous situation in some way? If so, the question may be asked, "What did I do at that time that worked successfully?" If it worked under similar conditions then, it should work now—or, at least, some elements from the previous situation should be applicable to this one. Without spending a great deal of additional effort, time, or money, one may recall part of the total solution which can be used again in the present situation.

Sometimes problems are partially solved in this manner. Part of the answer comes from the past. The remainder comes from the present. The object of reflective thinking is to integrate past and present experience into a single workable solution.

Self-quizzing. The present elements of the solution are reached by asking a variety of questions about the problem. The type of question that may be relevant will depend on the nature of the problem—specifically, whether it involves people, things, or concepts, and whether it can be solved by *extension* of an existing idea or device or whether it will require *substitution* or even a *synthesis* of ideas or talents from several sources. Self-quizzing is to an individual what **brainstorming**[9] is to a group.

The decision maker pursuing reflective thinking may ask himself the following kinds of questions:

1. Are there *other uses* for the product in addition to the original use? Kleenex, for example, can be used for purposes other than as a substitute for a cloth handkerchief. Onion soup can be used for a cocktail dip, barbecue sauce, and gravies in addition to its primary use.

2. Can another design be *borrowed or adapted*? Some of the principles involved in the construction of a butane cigarette lighter may have been borrowed from the acetylene torch.

3. Can the problem be solved by giving the item a *new shape or design*? The tapered roller bearing, modified in shape from the standard roller bearing, works in situations where the latter would not.

4. Should the item be made *more* of anything—stronger, longer, wider, taller, heavier? Would it work then? If we added overtime, would we solve the problem of bringing production into line with sales at a feasible cost?

---

[9]The group brainstorming technique was suggested by Alex F. Osborn, *Applied Imagination,* 3rd ed. (New York: Charles Scribner's Sons, 1963) p. 151.

5. Should the item be made *less* of anything—weaker, shorter, lighter? Can anything be reduced or eliminated? Removing the inner tube from the rubber tire provided a superior tire—the tubeless. Will reducing the work week to four days from five days reduce Monday absenteeism? Improve productivity? Increase employee morale? The answer may be in the affirmative.

6. Can parts be *rearranged*? Can the layout of the factory or the office be rearranged? Shifting the offices from the first to the second floor and moving the inspection department down from the second to the first floor may dramatically improve production efficiency. Rearrangement may suggest a solution. In a chemistry problem, rearranging the molecular structure could give rise to a new product or result, which might achieve what the original arrangement failed to accomplish.

7. Can a process be *reversed*? If we cannot pull the load, perhaps we can push it. In perfecting the sewing machine, Elias Howe designed the needle with the eye in the bottom instead of the top. Driving a truck in forward gear may not work in snow, but putting it in reverse may.

8. Can a *substitute* be found? If copper is in scarce supply, is there a substitute that can be used in its place? Perhaps aluminum will do the job. If printing is too expensive, can less expensive mimeographing be used as a substitute? In the 1950s, horsehides were disappearing as tractors replaced horses on farms. Wolverine Worldwide, Inc., longtime manufacturers of horsehide work shoes, experimented with pigskin as a substitute. The company found that pigskin was highly resistant to rot and provided good ventilation. The result was the famous "Hush Puppies"—tough, lightweight, water-repellent, casual shoes with the suede look. They replaced work shoes as the mainstay of Wolverine's production. Substitutes are often the answer. Can a synthetic be used in place of the genuine? Sometimes synthetics are substituted for the original material. Synthetic rubber was substituted for natural rubber during World War II and has largely replaced natural rubber since that time.

9. Can several purposes *be combined* or consolidated? The individual efforts of several people can often be combined productively into a team approach. Bifocals combine reading and distant-vision lenses in a single eyeglass. A four-in-one tool combines the utility of a screwdriver, bottle opener, can opener, and knife in a single instrument. Consolidating the advertising department and the public relations department into a single advertising and public relations department may simplify structure, improve communications control, and reduce the number of staff.

The type of creativity represented by the first seven questions is **extension,** the most widely used of all forms of creativity. The next question illustrates **substitution,** and the final one is an example of **synthesis.** These three types of creativity lead to most innovation. There is still another type of creativity which is unplanned. Called **bisociation,** it is the putting together of two unconnected and unrelated concepts or ideas to form a single new one.[10] The story is told of Gutenberg pondering how to reproduce the written word while watching grapes being pressed. In a flash of insight, he saw the printing press as the solution to his quandary. Bisociation had occurred.

Creating a new product can be viewed as a process that follows a path from initial idea to product concept, and from concept through design and development. This process is shown in the model in Figure 4-3.

Figure 4-3.   Product development process model.

The further a new product moves along this path, the more routine problem solving becomes and the less opportunity there is to shape or change the evolving product. Consequently, as product deficiencies are carried into the production stage, the more difficult it becomes to correct them.

4. Evaluate and Select Best Alternative

The answers to self-quizzing may provide several alternatives. They may suggest more than one way to resolve the dilemma. Each option must be carefully evaluated relative to the others—the advantages it possesses, the disadvantages it might create, its potential returns compared with its possible risks. How much can be won? How much can be lost? What are the chances of success? A cost-reward choice must be made. The alternative most likely to succeed is selected.

5. Test the Selected Alternative

To the extent that it is possible, the alternative selected should be tested for reliability and validity.[11] If it has these dual characteristics, it is a workable solution to the problem.

6. Integrate Past Solution with Present Solution

Any part of the solution derived from the past is now joined with the portion derived from self-quizzing. Combined, they should provide an effective solution to the total problem.

---

[10]This term was introduced by Arthur Koestler in his book *The Act of Creation* (London: Hutchinson and Co., Ltd., 1964).

[11]The reader is referred to the discussion on reliability and validity in Chapter 1.

Should the decision maker, in reviewing the past, be unable to discover any experience relevant to his present problem, he would rely on self-quizzing for the solution. In that event, the integration step would be omitted.

7. Make Intelligent Compromise

As a practical expedient, intelligent compromise is often necessary before a solution can be put into operation. The immediate superior to whom the recommendation is presented may oppose implementation of the program as it stands. He may insist on some modifications, even of a minor nature, before he gives his approval. He may want partial credit for the result. In order to gain his acceptance, it may be necessary to make him feel that the recommendation is the result of his own suggestion or creativity.

Others in the organization affected in any way by the solution may offer strenuous objection and opposition. Again, the solution may have to be modified to make it palatable to the individuals or groups affected.

8. Apply the Adjusted Solution

After the adjusted solution has gone through the process of intelligent compromise, when necessary, it is implemented, or applied to the problem area for which it was designed.

GROUP DECISION MAKING

Mention should be made of group decision making, since not all decisions are made by an individual. It was stated earlier that there are times when a number of people from different functional areas and with different perspectives need to furnish inputs and be involved in the problem-solving process. This is especially important when there is problem overlap. Let us examine three alternative methods for group decision making: *interacting, nominal,* and *delphi processes.*

The most widely used technique for group decision making is the **interacting process** represented by the traditional discussion group. Such group meetings typically begin with a statement of the problem by the group leader. This is followed by an unstructured group discussion in which information and judgments are pooled. The session ends with a majority vote or some other consensus decision.

The **nominal group technique**[12] includes a meeting with a structured format which proceeds as follows: (1) In writing, individuals silently and in-

---

[12]Andrew L. Delbecq and Andrew H. Van de Ven, "Nominal Group Techniques for Involving Clients and Resource Experts in Program Planning," *Academy of Management Proceedings,* 1970, pp. 208–227.

dependently generate ideas on a problem. (2) Each member, in turn, presents one of his ideas to the group without discussion. The ideas are summarized and recorded on a blackboard. (3) There is then a discussion, clarification, and evaluation of the recorded ideas. (4) The session ends with a silent, independent vote on priorities by a rank-ordering or rating procedure. The group decision is the pooled outcome of the individual votes.

In the **delphi technique**[13] participants are physically separated and do not meet face to face. There is a systematic collection of judgments on a particular topic through the use of a set of carefully designed sequential questionnaires based on summarized information and feedback from earlier responses. This technique is useful when respondents are geographically separated, as in a multi-plant organization, and it would be costly to bring them together on repeated occasions.

Current research seems to indicate that for solutions of fact-finding problems requiring the pooled judgment of a group of people, both the nominal group technique and the delphi method are more effective than the conventional discussion group.[14]

STYLES OF DECISION MAKING

In their daily handling of problems, managers incline toward different approaches or styles of decision making. These styles describe *how* managers decide what should be done to accomplish some mission.

While there are many styles of decision making, four are encountered most frequently in practice: (1) rule of thumb, (2) progressive, (3) follow the leader, and (4) method of science. Each represents a particular kind of managerial philosophy.

Rule of Thumb Method

The rule of thumb method, sometimes described as traditional, consists largely of using procedures and techniques that have worked in the past. The president of a successful conveyor equipment manufacturing company, when asked why women at the end of the production line painted metal frames by hand, replied, "We've been doing it that way for thirty-five years." This is management by rule of thumb. It is "doing business as usual," in the conventional way.

Frequently this method makes use of intuition. A manager may have a strong feeling that somewhere in the past a problem similar to the present

---

[13]Norman C. Dalkey, *The Delphi Method: An Experimental Study of Group Opinion* (Santa Monica, Ca.: Rand Corp.), 1969.

[14]Andrew H. Van de Ven and Andrew L. Delbecq, "The Effectiveness of Nominal, Delphi, and Interacting Group Decision Making Process," *Academy of Management Journal*, Vol. 17, No. 4, December 1974, pp. 605–621.

one was handled successfully in a given manner. Without being consciously aware of it, he may proceed in the same way now. Through intuition, he may thus gain a quick insight into the problem without employing deliberate, rational processes. When a manager indicates that he has a "hunch" about doing something in a given way, he is usually being guided by intuition. This is quite different from making a decision based solely on guesswork or chance. The two should not be confused. Intuition is not guesswork. It is the manager's perception of the current situation in light of his experience that decides which rule of thumb will be applied.

Managers who use the rule of thumb method often handle problems as they arise, "playing it by ear," rather than anticipating problems and planning in advance for potential contingencies. Their method is typified by the expression "We'll cross that bridge when we get to it." Critics describe it as "fighting fires." Still, it is commonly used with great success.

There are several advantages to making decisions by rule of thumb. It is economical and less wasteful than other methods. The manager who does things in the same proved way is cautious and accepts change only when it is necessary. He will purchase a new piece of machinery only when the old machine is no longer usable. Besides, there is little risk involved in repeating the tried and proved, and he does so confidently.

Despite the usefulness and popularity of the rule of thumb method, there are also disadvantages to doing things in a traditional way. In the first place, it tends to discourage innovation. Instead, decisions are largely influenced by habit. As with all habitual patterns, there is a tendency to include some that are not desirable or are no longer in tune with present conditions. Situations change suddenly; habits slowly. Moreover, decisions based on tradition are strongly subjective and unlikely to be free of bias.

Progressive Method

Many alert managers who wish to apply the newest techniques or procedures in their areas of responsibility adopt a progressive style of decision making. As part of their philosophy of managing, they urge their fellow managers and their subordinates to consider new ideas and to challenge old ones.

A manager using the progressive style keeps abreast of current developments and tries to be modern. It is also part of his philosophy that a good manager tries to make obsolete that which he is already doing successfully. Thus he may be anxious to pioneer and innovate. In industries dealing with drug, chemical, and food products, being progressive may be essential to keep ahead of competition and to retain one's share of the market.

The progressive method is very receptive to change and the latest innovations. Carried to its extreme of "Let's try anything new," or "Because this is new, we should adopt it," the method becomes almost an "eager beaver" approach, whose results are sometimes disastrous. A midwest brewery, for example, in an attempt to become more progressive, installed new stainless-steel, high-speed bottling equipment in a plant that was otherwise old-fashioned and obsolete. The new equipment had the capacity to bottle in one day all the beer the plant could produce in a week!

Modern managers will find it advantageous to be well aware of the total picture, to be progressive in moderation, to temper enthusiasm with sound judgment. The best conceived profit-sharing plan, incentive program, management information system, sales promotion campaign, and other worthy projects too often have been adopted by progressive managers with disappointing results. Often this can be traced to hasty decisions which were based on enthusiasm and desire to keep abreast with progress but which were not thoroughly researched and tested for feasibility before they were implemented.

The progressive method of decision making thus has its limitations too. Haste in selection of what is new may lead to errors in application. There is a tendency to fail to relate new technology to one's own particular circumstances. The computer, an important advancement in technology, may be an efficient means of maintaining inventory control in one firm, yet totally impractical for this purpose in another.

In and of itself, being progressive and receptive to new developments is not necessarily being objective nor free from bias. It may be just as subjective as the rule of thumb method. Besides, one has to be able to afford the newest developments, equipment, and procedures to replace existing ones that may still be serviceable.

Follow the Leader Method

Often managers decide on a course of action based on imitating or duplicating what leaders in their industry have done. A company will raise or lower a price, or add a new product or service to the line, because the industry leader has done so. In basic commodities such as steel or copper, prices frequently are established by an industry leader. Other members, particularly the smaller firms, follow suit. Among producers of consumer fashions, like shoes or dresses, there is again the tendency for smaller firms to follow the leaders in introducing new styles, utilizing newly developed fabrics, and employing innovative production techniques. They copy or adapt to suit their particular circumstances.

In many instances, this can be a very successful method to employ. Most smaller firms cannot afford to maintain elaborate research and development programs, or to search for newer and better ways to produce or distribute their products. They cannot afford to be innovators or pioneers at the risk of failure. Their strategy is to sit back and wait until others have done the pioneering and have worked out some of the "bugs" in the process or technique. If the new concept or product proves itself in the marketplace, then they follow in the wake of the leaders. Their research and development costs, as well as design costs, are held to a minimum.

The follow the leader technique is also employed within an organization, in response to internal stimuli. A manager in one department may emulate the performance of a manager in another department. Policies developed in one area may be duplicated in another. For many organizational leaders, innovation is confined to imitating the success of colleagues.

Following the leader has its limitations. There is the disadvantage of arriving late on the scene, particularly if the product is one of high style and short life. The leader may have become firmly established in markets that are difficult to enter at a later date, and may have already garnered the best accounts. The follower may have to settle for the gleanings. On the other hand, what may be the leavings to a large organization may be a harvest to a small organization that could not handle large orders from large users.

What is good for the leader may be disastrous for the follower. Imitating a decision without knowing the factors that entered into it could prove extremely costly to the unsuspecting follower. The leader may be able to absorb the cost of a pioneering mistake; the follower may not.

If following the leader produces rewards often enough, a tendency may develop to utilize this method exclusively and to ignore the potential of other methods. A manager may become an habitual follower and adopt a managerial philosophy that overlooks or rejects pioneering and creativity as useful strategies. Change for that person's organization becomes largely dependent upon someone else's decision.

Finally, not everyone can follow the leader. It takes a certain ability and acumen to be able to recognize a good thing when you see one. Not every manager has this unique capability.

Method of Science

The same technique used to solve problems in the sciences is used to solve management problems. A manager may also find it advantageous to apply existing principles or discoveries of the physical, biological, and social sciences to current problem areas.

This is a very desirable method to use when a firm is trying to pioneer and wants to invent or develop a line of products, as may be true of cosmetics or detergents. Research and development projects frequently utilize the scientific method, as does most laboratory testing of a new product. The method of science is the most objective style of decision making. Besides, it is the most precise and capable of exact reproduction.

As is true of any style of decision making, the method of science also has its limitations, not the least of which is that it requires a type of person who is capable of being totally objective and who is trained to employ scientific methodology in approaching business problems. Such a person must also be orderly, meticulous, logical, patient, and honest. Most people, including managers, are not so endowed. Furthermore, this method takes a great deal of time. It is not always practical in a situation where a decision has to be made quickly. If the procedures are properly carried out, the method may also be expensive. This cost may not be economically justified.

The scientific method is not applicable in all areas of operation and cannot be employed for every problem situation that may arise. Where a great many of the facts are not readily available, or when the data is limited, it would not be possible to use the method of science.

Having briefly reviewed these four methods of decision making, each with its respective advantages and limitations, one may ask, Which is best? Which should a manager use? The answer is there is no best method. A capable manager should employ the most desirable aspects of each, or a combination of the best in each, depending on prevailing conditions. This is known as the *contingency approach*. Perhaps rule of thumb is adequate and desirable in a given situation, whereas the method of science may be preferable at another time and place. The decision maker must determine what is best at the given moment, taking into account limitations of time, personnel, cost, and similar considerations. The realistic criterion in making a decision must be, "Will it get the job done?" Any method or combination of methods that satisfies this criterion is acceptable.

SUMMARY

Present in every decision-making situation are the following ingredients: decision makers, goals to be achieved, alternative ways to achieve them, uncontrollable variables, and a choice of one or more of several alternatives.

Not all decision making is problem solving. Some decisions are made under conditions of complete certainty. These, however, are the exceptions rather than the rule. It is when decisions have to made under conditions of uncertainty—when their outcomes are affected by uncontrollable variables like acts of God, actions of competitors, or sudden illness of employees—that problems exist.

Decision making is a **synoptic** process that provides a broad view of the entire problem area. Whether performed by an individual or a group, it involves the continuous, integrated phases of search, analysis, evaluation, and choice.

The decision problems that arise in organizations are numerous and often complex, and can be handled in several ways: by delay; imitating past successes; seeking expert advice; trial and error; and reflective thinking. Methods commonly used by managers in decision-making situations include rule of thumb, progressive, follow the leader, and method of science. Constantly confronted with various kinds of problem situations, a manager will deal with them in one or a combination of these ways. At all times, his criterion should be to do whatever is necessary to get the job done.

Several observations can be made concerning planning and decision making: Although planning always requires decision making, making a decision does not always require planning. Planning and problem solving are interwoven, since the decision-making process is part of the planning process and planning is part of the problem-solving process. The process of planning and the process of reflective thinking both closely resemble the method of science.

KEY CONCEPTS

Decision-Making Process
Decision Problem
Classification of Problems
Exception Principle
Process of Reflective Thinking
Limiting Factors
Self-Quizzing

Innovation
Bisociation
Group Decision Making
Decision Making by Rule of Thumb
Progressive Method of Decision
  Making
Follow the Leader Method

GLOSSARY

bisociation Chance or unplanned joining of two unconnected and unrelated concepts or ideas to form a single new one.

brainstorming Type of group creativity in which spontaneous ideas are suggested in quantity in an attempt to find solutions to problems.

decision Commitment to a choice from among two or more alternatives.

extension Type of creativity based on refinement, development, or adaptation of an existing idea.

innovation Result of types of creativity known as extension, substitution, synthesis, and bisociation.

intuition Insight based on knowledge and experience without the conscious use of reasoning.

problem Uncertainty about the best way to establish or achieve some objective.

reflective thinking Problem-solving process that integrates past and present experience in "thinking through" a problem.

synoptic Providing a broad view of the whole.

synthesis Type of creativity that results from combinations or consolidations.

uncertainty Existence of doubt because of a lack of definite or complete knowledge about an outcome.

REVIEW QUESTIONS

1. Decision making is said to be a never-ending task for an executive. Comment.
2. What is meant by the statement, "Decision making operates on a binary basis?"
3. Refer to the model of the planning process in Figure 3-1. Where does decision making play a role?
4. Is there any relationship between "change" and a decision problem? Explain.
5. Give some examples of "extension," "substitution," and "synthesis."
6. Do you believe that all organizations should be innovative and pioneering? Defend your position.
7. Give some examples of situations that may require group decision making techniques. Which group technique would you use in each situation?

Chapter 5

Quantitative Aids in Decision Making

In the course of operating a business or managing an organization, an owner or a manager constantly encounters situations that call for some kind of decision. Some problems are relatively simple, others are complex. The growing complexity of decision making, particularly in larger establishments with multiple operations, requires the use of more sophisticated problem-solving techniques. In making decisions, the executive is always conscious of the existence of constraints that are imposed on him. Some of these include limited time, money, manpower, space, knowledge of competitor's actions, and many uncertainties about which he has no knowledge and no control. Since there is usually some uncertainty about the future, a manager cannot be sure that the decision he makes will be a correct one.

Categories frequently used to describe conditions under which decisions are made are *certainty, risk,* and *uncertainty.* Certainty and uncertainty may be viewed as opposite ends of a continuum; risk represents all points between. Under a condition of certainty, perfect knowledge of the problem and the outcome is required—an infrequent circumstance. Under a condition of uncertainty, one has imperfect knowledge of the problem and no experience or knowledge of the outcome; it would be unreasonable to attempt decisions under these circumstances. Therefore, most decisions are made within the area of risk, and the amount of risk is determined by the quantity and quality of the information about the outcomes of the various alternatives. Evaluation of the alternatives is facilitated by assigning a quantitative value to each alternative considered. Under risk conditions, more than one state of nature can exist, but the probability of occurrence is known. If one wanted to wager on his ability to draw the king of diamonds from a standard deck of playing cards, the probability that it will be selected on a single draw is one out of fifty-two. Though risk is present, the amount of risk is known.

The decision maker wants to choose a course of action that probably will be effective in attaining the goals of his enterprise, or in solving the particular problem before him. If the problem has numerous variables, and these variables can be quantified in some way, the decision maker may utilize one or more of the quantitative techniques which have been developed in recent years to help managers deal with complex or uncertain situations. The techniques most frequently employed will be described briefly, on an introductory level, in this and the succeeding chapter. The purpose of this survey is to make students, and others interested in dynamic managing, aware of the existence of these quantitative tools. Such an awareness may then motivate readers to investigate quantitative techniques in greater detail in courses in mathematics and applied business, and in textbooks devoted exclusively to this subject.

For the most part, quantitative tools are used by decision makers to deal with non-people problems—problems dealing with "things." The quantitative concepts in managing that will be discussed and evaluated in this chapter are limited to the following:

1. Break-even analysis
2. Linear programming
3. Operations research
4. Probability theory

It should be kept in mind that results obtained from the use of quantitative methods as aids to managerial decision making can be no better than the assumptions and estimates on which the methods are predicated. If estimates are unrealistic, results are undependable. Every quantitative concept must reflect existing conditions accurately, otherwise misleading conclusions will result. Each quantitative concept will be examined to develop an understanding of its value to dynamic managing, as well as to discover its strengths and its limitations.

BREAK-EVEN ANALYSIS

One of the major problems a manager faces is establishing a desirable rate of output, usually in production or sales, which are the basic line activities in every business. This involves a relationship between the cost of input factors and the value of output units (revenue).

When initiating any operation from scratch, start-up costs and expenditures may exceed initial income and the enterprise operates at a loss. When total revenues exceed total costs, it makes a profit.

The break-even point should not be confused with the **equilibrium** concept described in economics in connection with marginal analysis and the "theory of the firm." In economics, a firm operating under conditions of pure competition reaches equilibrium position when its *marginal cost* and *marginal revenue* are equal. Before this point, *one* additional unit of production increases total revenue more than total costs; after this point, it increases total cost more than total revenue. Thus equilibrium is an **optimum** position and not a break-even one. Consequently, when marginal revenue equals marginal cost, the positive difference between total revenue and total cost is greatest. Therefore, profit is *greatest* when the economic firm is in equilibrium. At the break-even point, however, profit is *nonexistent.*

Bankers and credit men say they are constantly amazed by the ignorance of business fundamentals displayed by many entrepreneurs. "It's surprising how many people don't even know what they're talking about when we ask them what their break-even point will be in a new venture."[1]

The **break-even point** can be defined as *that level of operations where total costs and total revenues are equal so that there is neither a net profit nor a net loss.*

Included in the concept of **total costs** are both **fixed** and **variable** costs. Rent and insurance are examples of fixed costs, since they are present regardless of the level of operations. Sometimes these are referred to as "indirect" costs, or **overhead.** Wages and cost of materials are examples of variable costs, since they tend to vary directly upward or downward with the level of operation. Often these are called "direct" or "prime" costs. Together, fixed and variable costs make up total costs. Total costs tend to rise as output rises up to a certain point, and then decrease; total revenues rise steadily with output. Beyond the first break-even point, total revenues increase more rapidly than total costs, so that added output increases profits. At some later point, as the plant or operation approaches capacity, certain costs accelerate more rapidly than revenues until, eventually, total costs may again equal total revenues and a new break-even point is established. When total costs exceed total revenues at this higher level of operations, losses again will occur. Such a condition could prevail when an existing plant is used intensively. When this happens, it becomes necessary to work people overtime, run extra shifts, run machines without maintenance longer than is good for the machines, and hire less-skilled workers. Fatigue factors set in and other evidence of decreased efficiency becomes apparent. It is possible, therefore, for an organization to have more than one break-even point.

Graphic Determination of Break-Even Points

If the assumption is made that the price of a product is determined by the competitive market, and that a company cannot raise prices without losing some of the market, the manager will strive for an optimum level of operations, which is the point where total costs are lowest in relation to output. Such a situation is illustrated in Figure 5-1. Total costs and total revenues in dollars are shown on the vertical axis; output in units is shown on the horizontal axis.

---

[1]"Failures on the Rise," *The Wall Street Journal,* January 23, 1961.

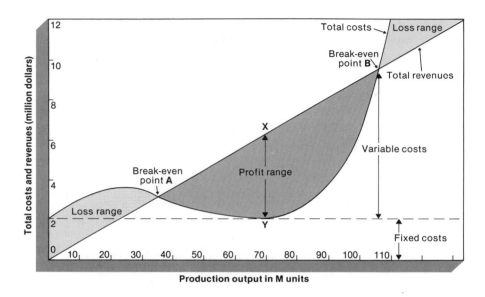

Figure 5-1.   Break-even chart.

In this illustration, total costs exceed total revenues until an output of 30M units is achieved, indicated by point A. At this point, total revenues are slightly less than $3 million, and total costs are also slightly less than $3 million. At break-even point A, total costs and total revenues are equal. Thereafter, total revenues exceed total costs until an output of 105M units is reached, indicated by point B. Here, total costs and total revenues are equal at slightly less than $9 million, and a new break-even point is reached. Beyond break-even point B, costs advance beyond revenue, and the firm suffers a loss. Maximum profit is between points X and Y, where the difference between total revenues and total costs is the greatest. Thus the firm would optimize its profit at an output of 70M units. At this point, total revenues are about $5.5 million while total costs are slightly more than $2 million.

Total profits or total losses at various levels of output can also be determined from examining the break-even chart. In addition, this chart can be used to plot the effects on profits of a change in either variable or fixed expenses.

Computation of Break-Even Points

Break-even points can be determined algebraically as well as graphically. Suppose a firm plans to sell an article for $1.50. Its variable costs total $1.00 for each item. Fixed expenses amount to $250.00. How many items must it sell to break even? How many dollars of revenue does it take to break even?

The mathematical model used to express the relationship between total revenue (units sold × selling price per unit) and total costs includes the following components:

N = the number of units produced
P = the selling price per unit
C = the fixed costs of production
V = the variable cost per unit produced

Expressed as a break-even equation, the relationship becomes:

$$P(N) = V(N) + C$$

Substituting the data in our illustration into the equation provides the following:

$$1.50\,N = 1.00\,N + 250.00$$
$$1.50N - 1.00\,N = 250.00$$
$$0.50\,N = 250.00$$
$$N = \frac{250.00}{0.50}$$
$$N = 500\ \text{units}$$

The break-even point is 500 units of production. At a selling price of $1.50 each, the break-even point in dollars is $750.00.

A practical approach to figuring a break-even point is to use previous profit and loss statement data. Ordinarily this approach is precise enough for planning purposes in most organizations. One advantage is that it will spotlight danger points so that corrective action can be initiated promptly. In addition, a break-even point based on these data is useful in setting pricing and production policies, and guiding plans for future plant expansion. The acquisition of new equipment will add to fixed expenses (amortization and maintenance costs) but will also tend to reduce operating costs. Should the purchase of new equipment not produce savings in variable costs substantially greater than the increase in fixed charges, the break-even point will be higher rather than lower.

Break-even point analysis is a relatively simple yet effective aid to managerial decision making. A manager knows that sales levels above the break-even point are profitable; sales levels below that point are unprofitable.

LINEAR PROGRAMMING

Another useful quantitative aid to decision making which can take either graphical or computational form is linear programming. This technique is used primarily in analyzing situations that can be expressed mathematically

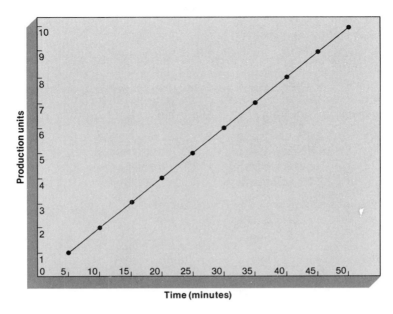

Figure 5-2.   Linear relationship of two production variables.

as linear, or straight-line, relationships. A **linear relationship** exists if *one value varies directly with any change in another value.* Most econometric models are linear. A change in factor X influences a change in factor Y. Thus, if it takes 5 minutes to produce one unit of output, it will take 50 minutes to produce 10 units. In such a situation, a linear relationship exists between time and output. The graph in Figure 5-2 depicts this straight-line relationship.

Linear programming can be applied to a number of organizational problem areas, some of which include the following:

- Allocating the use of the firm's resources to best advantage
- Establishing price-volume relationships
- Determining optimal product mix
- Minimizing warehousing and distribution costs

A few simple examples will demonstrate situations in which linear programming can be helpful.

Graphic Method of Linear Programming

Problems involving up to three linearly related variables can be solved graphically. With just two dimensions to a problem, the solution involves straight lines; with three dimensions, the solution involves plane surfaces.

Generally, it is not feasible to solve linear programming problems graphically when more than three variables are involved.

Linear programming can be applied to relatively simple situations to determine optimum allocation of company resources.[2] Consider a company manufacturing two models of a product, Model X and Model Y. Assume three main production activities are involved: metalworking, subassembly, and final assembly. Maximum hours available for each activity are:

Metalworking	1200 hours
Subassembly	1400 hours
Final assembly	500 hours

Pertinent revenue and production time data for each model are:

Model	Revenue	Production time in hours per unit		
		Metalworking	Subassembly	Final assembly
X	$20	1.0	0.7	0.5
Y	$30	1.2	2.0	0.5

The company wants to determine how many of Model X and Model Y to manufacture to derive the greatest total revenue.

The constraints within which the models must be produced can be shown graphically. In Figure 5-3, units of Model X are shown on the vertical axis and units of Model Y on the horizontal axis. Consider metalworking time. For Model X, metalworking takes 1.0 hours per unit. If the entire metalworking facilities were devoted solely to producing Model X, 1200 units could be manufactured during the 1200 hours available. Metalworking on Model Y takes 1.2 hours per unit. If the entire metalworking facilities were used for Model Y only, then 1000 units could be produced in 1200 hours. This relationship between Model X and Model Y in terms of metalworking is shown by line M–M' in Figure 5-3. It is a straight line since the relationship is linear. It intersects the vertical axis at 1200 units and the horizontal axis at 1000 units.

In similar fashion, the line indicating subassembly work can also be established. Since 1400 hours are available for all subassembly work, if only Model X is produced, which takes 0.7 hours per unit, 2000 units can be produced. For Model Y only, which requires 2.0 hours per unit for subassembly work, a total of 700 units can be manufactured. The relationship between the two models in terms of subassembly is indicated by line S–S' on the graph.

---

[2]The reader will recall from Chapter 1 that *optimum* means that which is desirable for the enterprise as a whole. Any other alternative would be less desirable, or of lesser value or utility.

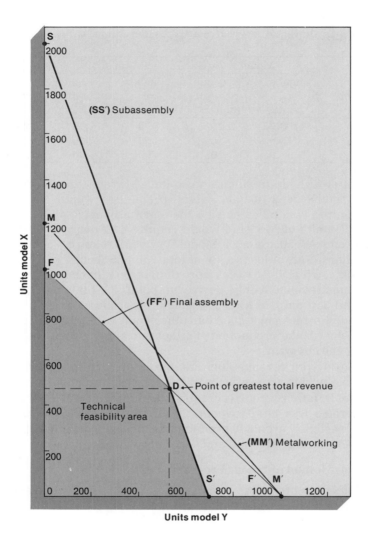

Figure 5-3.   Technical feasibility limits for combined
production of two models.

Line *F–F'* indicates final assembly. Since it takes 0.5 hours per unit for
either Model *X* or Model *Y* to go through final assembly, with 500 hours
of available time the firm could produce 1000 units of either Model *X* or
Model *Y*.

The graphic solution to the problem lies at some point within the area of
technical feasibility, represented by the polygon *FDS'O*. At any point within

Table 5-1. Revenue derived from production options between model *X* and model *Y*

Feasible point	Model X		Model Y		Total revenue (dollars)
	Number of units	Revenue per unit (dollars)	Number of units	Revenue per unit (dollars)	
F	1000	20	0	0	20,000
D	450	20	550	30	25,500
S'	0	0	700	30	21,000

that area it is feasible to manufacture both Model *X* and Model *Y*. At any point outside the area of constraints, production would not be feasible. Observe point *P*, which lies outside the feasibility polygon. At this point, to produce 950 units of Model *X* would require 475 hours of final assembly time; to produce 150 units of Model *Y* would require 75 hours of final assembly time. This adds up to a total of 550 hours of required final assembly time, which is 50 hours more than the company has available.

Maximum revenue will be derived at point *D*. At this point, 450 units of Model *X* and 550 units of Model *Y* should be produced to provide greatest total revenue for the company. At no other point will combinations of Model *X* and Model *Y*, or the production of either one alone, produce as much total revenue for the company.

Calculating the revenues for the production indicated by points *F*, *D*, and *S'*, each of which is feasible, provides the results shown in Table 5-1.

At point *D*, total revenue is greatest, amounting to $25,500. Points *F* and *S'* both produce less total revenue than point *D*. Any point other than *D* within the feasibility area will produce less income for the firm than the production of 450 units of Model *X* and 550 units of Model *Y*.

Computation Method of Linear Programming

The problem of determining optimal product mix is really one aspect of the larger problem of allocating limited resources. A relatively simple problem involving product mix illustrates how resource allocations can be determined by computation.

Consider a company which packages mixed dried fruits for sale to grocery stores. Mixed fruits are put up in 1-pound packs. Two different mixes are available. One mix contains 50 percent prunes and 50 percent apricots; the second mix contains 70 percent prunes and 30 percent apricots. On the first mix, the company realizes a profit of 10 cents per pack; on the second, 15 cents per pack. The available daily supply of prunes is 2000 pounds and of apricots 1000 pounds. The company must supply some of each mix to its customers. How many packs of each type of mix should it package daily?

A matrix containing the pertinent data is laid out in Table 5-2.

Table 5-2.   Matrix for prune and apricot mix

Dried Fruit	Mix A	Mix B	Available supply
Prunes	50%	70%	2000 lb
Apricots	50%	30%	1000 lb
Profit (cents per package)	10¢	15¢	

Examination of the data for the prunes reveals that 0.5 pound for Mix A plus 0.7 pound for Mix B must utilize, but cannot exceed, the 2000 pounds available. Similarly, for the apricots 0.5 pound for Mix A plus 0.3 pound for Mix B must use, but cannot exceed, the 1000 pounds available. This relationship can be expressed algebraically:

$$0.5A + 0.7B = 2000$$
$$0.5A + 0.3B = 1000$$

Solving the simultaneous equations, we subtract one from the other to eliminate one of the unknowns and then establish the value of the second unknown as follows:

$$0.5A + 0.7B = 2000$$
$$\text{minus } 0.5A + 0.3B = 1000$$
$$0.4B = 1000$$
$$B = 2500 \text{ packs}$$

Substituting this value for B in either of the original equations provides the value for A:

$$0.5A + 0.7(2500) = 2000$$
$$0.5A + 1750 = 2000$$
$$0.5A = 250$$
$$A = 500 \text{ packs}$$

Thus the company should package 2500 packs of Mix B and 500 packs of Mix A. These 3000 packs would use up the entire daily supply of both dried fruits. The profit for this total output would be 500 @ 0.10 plus 2500 @ 0.15, or a total combined profit of $425 per day.

Another type of problem which may be solved by linear programming is that of minimizing warehousing and distribution costs. Because it involves several product sources and several destinations for the products, this type of problem is frequently referred to in textbooks as the *transportation problem.* For example, a company has three factories and three warehouses, all separated geographically. The problem is to determine the best use of production facilities and warehousing facilities so as to minimize freight costs in shipping all of the finished products from the three factories to the three scattered warehouses. Linear programming can be used to find the solution.

OPERATIONS RESEARCH (OR)

Operations research is a loosely used, much confused, and greatly misunderstood term. In its broadest sense, it has become a catchall or umbrella for such concepts as management science, mathematical models, probability theory, game theory, factor analysis, linear programming, queuing theory, multiple regression analysis, symbolic logic, and a host of others. Although these tools are often used in OR methodology, independently, in and of themselves, they do not constitute operations research. When an individual manager employs linear programming to solve a problem, he is not engaging in operations research. He is simply using a technique that operations researchers may also use from time to time when it suits their needs. The same can be said of factor analysis, or multiple regression analysis, or any other quantitative technique. One can use these techniques without being involved in any way with operations research. What then is operations research?

The current practice of operations research derives from World War II strategic planning methods. With long-range aircraft and destroyers in short supply, England was faced with the difficult problem of how to protect convoys of ships from submarine attack. A special group of scientists from various disciplines, including the physical and social sciences, were brought together to tackle the problem of getting the most effective use from scarce and limited resources. Their work was designated "operational research." When American forces became part of the Allied effort, the work of their scientific group was known as "operations research." Scientists from various disciplines, working as a team, used scientific methods to solve military problems, particularly those involving logistics. Their work demonstrated that many complex problems, previously referred to the individual judgment of military leaders, could be handled more effectively through formal scientific analysis.

Following the war, the practice of operations research extended into the area of industrial problem solving. Formal analysis and the use of highly advanced mathematical techniques could be applied to many knotty, complex, and perplexing industrial problems.

The essential characteristics of operations research are:

1. A macro-view of a decision problem—that is, a broad view giving a perspective of the organization as a whole, or some major functional area within it.

2. A task force approach, which brings together people with backgrounds and unique specialties from different departments and functional areas of the institution, to provide the necessary expert knowledge.

3. Use of the method of science plus established findings of both the physical and social sciences.

4. An emphasis upon statistical, mathematical, and other techniques including model building.

All four parameters must be present for operations research. The
absence of any one of these distinguishing characteristics negates what is
meant by OR.

As a starting point, practitioners of OR identify and define, as precisely
and as objectively as possible, the nature of the problem and the ultimate
goal that is sought. They take into consideration all factors that could influence the result (the contingencies). They then determine the probability
that these influences will occur, and estimate the consequences under
various conditions. All feasible courses of action are investigated in the
same manner, and an overall picture of potential, simulated conditions is obtained. One of these alternative courses of action is then recommended to
solve the problem, or to achieve the desired objective.

Mathematical Model

In accounting for all contingencies and their probability of occurring, operations research quantifies the problem variables and expresses them in the
form of a mathematical model made up of symbolic equations. An example of
a very simple model is the equation for Gross National Product[3] used in national income analysis. This is expressed as:

$$GNP = Goods \text{ \& } Services \times Market \text{ } price \text{ } (P)$$

or

$$GNP = (G \times P) + (S \times P)$$

A model always serves a given purpose. Assume the problem is to decide whether it is advisable to expand production facilities to meet an
expected increase in the present demand for the company's product. Expanding the production capabilities may not be the answer. Although sales
may be increasing, there is always the possibility that the cost of sales will
increase more rapidly, and net profits will decline. If a decision is made to
increase productive capacity, it must next be decided how much to expand.

Before this question can be answered, estimates must be made of the
size of the market growth, the company's probable share of this larger
market, the likelihood that this share will continue, and other related factors. As each factor is introduced, the model grows more complex. It must be
pointed out that the accuracy of the answers produced by the model can be
no better than the validity of the estimates on which the model itself is
based. Estimates are made, therefore, on the basis of the probability of the

---

[3]*Gross national product* is the total value of all goods and services produced in the United States
during a given time period.

events occurring. The size of the expected market should be estimated in the following manner. What is the probability the market will expand between 10 and 15 percent? Between 16 and 20 percent? A *range* of estimates of feasible outcomes, rather than fixed estimates, improves the analytical procedure and increases the validity of the result.

The model must then be verified. This can be done by feeding data into the model and comparing the model's results with actual results already known to have occurred. If they match up, the model is valid. If they do not, the model is not doing what was intended and must be reevaluated and reexamined, equation by equation, until all discrepancies have been uncovered.

In government and industry, OR task forces never try to build a model that resembles reality in every detail. Not only would this require a great deal of time and expense to construct, but it would be beyond the comprehension of the normal human being. Perfection is not the object. What is sought is the simplest model that predicts outcomes reasonably well, and provides answers "to get the job done." A useful model, therefore, contains many of the characteristics of the reality it represents, but excludes those which are not critical to the outcome of the decision. Moreover, it must be remembered that a manager is not necessarily looking for a specific solution, or the theoretically "best" solution. A decision maker hopes that OR will produce a workable solution from among several possible choices, one that is best under the given circumstances—an optimum solution.

When problems are well-structured, they are solved by techniques called algorithms. An **algorithm** is *any well-defined systematic procedure*. A mathematical model is a type of algorithm used for this purpose. It may be compared to a closed-end, or closed-loop, system since it does not take into account items not built into the model. When problems are ill-structured, **heuristic** processes are usually required. The heuristic method sometimes solves problems by searching for reasonable results rather than trying to calculate the mathematically precise answer. In order to reduce the size of the problem, the heuristic process may also deliberately ignore some of the possible alternatives.

Heuristic methods, although they are unproved, or even unprovable, are useful in empirical research. Often they are based on observation or experience and employ decision making by intuition and rule of thumb, as well as trial and error. Let us assume that a hunter making his own shotgun shells produces six and then realizes that one of them has insufficient powder. He has to find the defective one, and the only equipment available to him is a balance scale. He selects three shells at random and places them on one side of the balance, and the remaining three are placed on the other side. As the scale tips, he knows that the defective shell is among the three that rose. He then selects two of these three at random and places one on each side of the balance. If the scales do not balance, the cartridge that rises is the defective one. Should they balance, then the cartridge not on the scale must be the defective one.

Most problems do not require sophisticated techniques. Plant layout, production scheduling, and most inventory control problems can be solved through heuristic processes.

Sometimes the amount of input data required to establish alternatives for solving problems is so vast, and the number of variables so large, that computations can only be achieved rapidly through the use of high-speed computer techniques. Most operations research projects today depend on the use of the computer to make OR techniques feasible.

Operations research has practical application in manpower assignments, scheduling of production runs in oil refineries, determination of optimum inventory levels, financial analysis, investment analysis, and in any major planning activity that involves an evaluation of the consequences of alternative courses of action. There will still be executives inclined to play the long shot, but operations research, if one chooses to use it, can tell a decision maker in advance what the odds are for success. Operations research is an aid to business judgment, never a substitute for it.

PROBABILITY THEORY

The same mathematical models and probability techniques used by task forces engaged in operations research can also be effective devices for an individual manager faced with problems to solve. Statistical, mathematical, and other quantitative techniques are not the exclusive province of operations researchers. In fact, they are often useful in decision-making situations which do not require operations research.

In general, a manager makes a decision under one of two conditions: (1) He has all of the necessary facts and makes his decision under conditions that approach certainty. Such a situation is said to be **deterministic.** (2) He does not have all of the facts and makes his decision under conditions of uncertainty. This situation—the more prevalent one—is said to be **stochastic.**

Deterministic Conditions

In a situation in which a manager, faced with a problem, has a significant portion of the facts before him and can make his decision under conditions that approximate certainty, the law of chance plays no part. All of the factors taken into consideration are assumed to be exact or determinate quantities. The solution is determined by precise relationships. Such was the case where break-even points and linear programming were shown to be useful. Both are examples of decision making under deterministic conditions.

Stochastic Conditions

Usually decision makers know that more than one outcome is possible for any course of action selected, but do not know how likely the outcomes are. Problems of this kind are often called *decision problems under conditions of uncertainty* since the probabilities of the outcomes of alternative courses of action cannot be known in advance.

Decision problems under conditions of uncertainty require that a choice be made between alternative courses which may be affected by one or more "states of nature." The term **states of nature** designates *events beyond a manager's control which could actually occur.* He does not know and cannot predict which state of nature will prevail at the precise time he makes his decision. If he is not sure what the weather conditions will be, or whether drilling for oil will actually locate oil, or what his competitors will do as a reaction to what he does, he is working under conditions of uncertainty. Some natural and uncontrollable factors that can occur include storms, fires, floods, earthquakes, drought, and other "acts of God."

Besides states of nature, there are other events that occur *purely by chance,* adding to the uncertainty of decisions. Machines break down, employees get sick, suppliers fail to deliver on time. These occur in the best managed organizations. Thus a number of *random variables* interact and affect outcomes. Though the individual events are unpredictable, the probability of their occurring can be estimated. Such variables are also termed stochastic variables.

The stochastic process, then, is one in which decisions are made under conditions of uncertainty by assigning probabilities to the various states of nature and to the random variables.

The **Markov process** is a special type of mathematical model in which various states of nature are described.[4] The basic assumption of the Markov process is that the probability of change from one state to another depends only on the existing state and not on how the existing state was reached. A machine may be in adjustment (state 1) or out of adjustment (state 2). If it is in adjustment, the probability that it will still be in adjustment a day later can be estimated and conversely the probability that it will be out of adjustment a day later can also be estimated. If it is out of adjustment, the probability that it will be in adjustment a day later can be estimated and conversely the probability that it will be out of adjustment a day later can also be estimated. If the machine is in state 1, the probability of its changing to state 2 a day later can be estimated regardless of the condition of the machine on day one.

---

[4]For an excellent account of this process the reader is referred to Harold Bierman, Charles Bonini, and Warren Hausman, *Quantitative Analysis for Business Decisions* (Homewood, Ill.: Richard D. Irwin, Inc., 1969) pp. 409–422.

Uncertainty is the usual situation facing decision makers, who must act nevertheless. They decide on a degree of risk taking and resolve problems within the framework of incomplete information. To fail to make a decision can be more costly than to make a decision in the face of great uncertainty. When the true states of nature are not known, the manager must act with imperfect information. In doing so, several courses are open to him. Among the aids he can consider under these circumstances are: (1) the Bayes decision process; (2) decision criteria; (3) decision trees; and (4) game theory.

The Bayes Decision Process

Many mathematicians take the position that only objective probabilities for recurring events are meaningful. In the world of business, however, objective probabilities are not always obtainable, yet decisions must be made. The Bayes decision process[5] is a logical procedure which permits the use of *subjective* evaluations of probability. Despite its subjective basis, this technique can be extremely useful. Briefly, the process consists of the following steps:

1. List the possible values for each state of nature.

2. Assign a probability factor to each state of nature.

3. Multiply the possible value for each state of nature by the probability of each state of nature to arrive at the expected value of each alternative.

The alternative with the highest expected value is the Bayes solution; this is the decision that would be taken. Let us observe, in an illustration, how this can be done.

Assume that the problem is to decide what quantity of an item to order for inventory. Here the states of nature are the possible demands for the item. These may be either 10, 50, or 100. One of these is the actual state that will occur. The decision maker can construct a probability distribution for these possible occurrences. Probabilities can be based on objective evidence from the past if the decision maker believes that the same forces that prevailed then will continue into the future. In the absence of objective evidence, he can assign probabilities that he, subjectively or intuitively, feels are appropriate. Table 5-3 shows the probabilities assigned to each of the possible states of nature, or market demands. When each possible demand is multiplied by its probability of occurrence, it becomes obvious that the decision maker should order 100 items for his inventory. The probability of the actual demand being 100, rather than 10 or 50, although not the highest order of probability, still provides the highest "expected value."

---

[5]Ibid, p. 7.

Table 5-3. Bayes decision process

Possible occurrences (market demands)	Probabilities	Expected values of occurrences
10	0.05	0.5
50	0.50	25.0
100	0.45	45.0
	1.00	

Decision Criteria

In making a decision, a manager may be guided by one or more decision criteria. The one he selects reflects his own personality to some degree. If he is a gambler by nature, or an eternal optimist, he will be guided by one standard; if he tends to be conservative, he will be guided by another; and if he is a perpetual pessimist, he will be guided by still another. Some of these decision criteria include:

■ The **maximax criterion**—maximizing the greatest possible payoff or gain.

■ The **maximin criterion**—maximizing the minimum possible gain.

■ The **minimax criterion**—minimizing the maximum possible loss.

■ The **insufficient reason criterion**—assuming events have equal probability of occurrence.

When a manager must reach a decision under conditions of uncertainty, there is no one "best" criterion to select. The choice is an individual matter, reflecting to a large extent the personality makeup of the decision maker and his philosophy of management. By nature, some managers have a high aversion to risk, whereas others do not. The degree of risk taking varies not only with the persons involved but also with the size of the risk, the level in the management hierarchy at which the decision is made, the relative importance of the event being decided, the availability of capital funds, and other pertinent factors. Let us examine these variables.

One manager may hesitate to risk the investment of $50,000 of company funds on the 70 percent chance that it may return $150,000, whereas the same individual may not hesitate to risk $50 on the 70 percent chance it will return $150. The size of the risk is a determining factor.

Managers at higher levels in an organization are probably more accustomed to taking greater risks than managers at lower levels, in large measure because the scope of decisions usually is broader at higher levels. A company president may have to consider the sizable risk involved in decisions to market a new product, to double the advertising expenditure, or to close down an entire operation. A first-line supervisor, on the other hand, has a more restricted range of risk, limited perhaps to hiring another worker, approving a rearrangement of the layout of his department, or accepting the human relations consequences of disciplining a subordinate.

Table 5-4. Maximax matrix

Strategy	Investment (dollars)	Payoff (dollars)	Probability of success
1	50,000	150,000	0.70
2	25,000	75,000	0.80

Even top managers who would go ahead with one project involving a 75 percent chance for success might not proceed with another whose chance of success was identical. One might, for example, favor investing in a sales promotion program which had a 75 percent chance for success, but would reject an equal investment in new plant and equipment unless the chance for its success was considerably higher.

Attitudes toward risk, therefore, vary with people, position, size of risk, funds available, and the nature of the event itself.

The maximax criterion. Guided by the maximax criterion, a decision maker would select the alternative that offers the greatest possible return, without regard to risk or potential loss. This can be a very dangerous philosophy under which to operate. Although it holds out great rewards and the chance for rapid success, it can also lead to disastrous errors. Such a guideline underlies the actions of a manager who "goes for broke." If he is correct in his decisions, the payoff for his company is large; if he is wrong, the firm may not survive long enough to try again.

Table 5-4 illustrates a hypothetical matrix for a maximax criterion. To keep the example simple, only two strategies are proposed. Under the maximax concept, the manager would list the most favorable payoffs for each strategy. In this example, he would select strategy number 1, which offers a payoff of $150,000 despite the fact that its probability of success is less than that of strategy number 2. Although the investment required is greater, and the risk is greater, the manager would opt for the maximum possible gain.

The maximin criterion. The maximin criterion is more likely to be adopted by a conservative manager. He would select the alternative that promises at least a minimum payoff. He would, therefore, make a decision that maximizes the minimum possible gain regardless of which state of nature occurs.

With a conservative state of mind, or a pessimistic outlook, a manager would review the matrix in Table 5-4 and select the strategy that offers the better chance for a payoff, although a smaller one. Under these circumstances, he would select strategy number 2 and would be satisfied with a payoff of $75,000 on an investment of $25,000 since there was an 80 percent chance of obtaining it. He would pass up the chance to gain $150,000 since its likelihood is only 70 percent. This decision is exactly opposite to the one in which the maximax criterion was employed.

Table 5-5. Minimax matrix

Strategy	Investment (dollars)	Maximum possible loss (dollars)	Probability of occurrence
1	10,000	3000	0.30
2	12,000	2000	0.30
3	15,000	1000	0.40

The minimax criterion. The minimax concept involves minimizing the possibility of any maximum loss. A simplified illustration will help to explain the fundamental ideas behind it. Suppose a manager has three alternative strategies open to him. He knows that each will require a different investment and that each investment could result in a loss for his company. He also has some basis for estimating the probability of each outcome. He wants to select the alternative which will hold his potential loss to a minimum. By constructing a payoff matrix from the data he has, he can analyze the several strategies. Such a matrix is indicated in Table 5-5.

Using the minimax criterion, he would select strategy number 3 even though it represents an investment larger than the other strategies. He knows that 4 times out of 10 this strategy will result in a loss, but that the loss cannot exceed $1000. If he selected strategy number 1, although he would only have to commit $10,000, and the chances are only 3 in 10 that a loss would result, the loss could amount to $3000. For strategy number 2, the chances are also 3 in 10 that a loss would result. If it did, it would be a smaller one, only $2000. Despite the fact that he would have to commit $12,000, it would be a better strategy than number 1. Thus, although his chances for a loss under strategy number 3 are greater than for either of the other strategies, his maximum loss, if it did occur, would only be $1000. To minimize his maximum loss, he selects alternative number 3 and commits $15,000.

Strategy of least regret. A variation of the minimax concept is the strategy of least regret.[6] This strategy permits the manager to select the alternative that minimizes the greatest regret he would have as a result of having made the wrong choice. It is based on the assumption that when a manager makes a decision that does not lead to the most favorable payoff, he experiences regret. By constructing a regret matrix, he can minimize his maximum regret.

Table 5-6 is a regret matrix. Maximum regret for failing to select strategy 1 is $100,000; for failing to select strategy 2, it is $50,000. There-

---

[6]L. J. Savage introduced this strategy in his paper "The Theory of Statistical Decision," *Journal of the American Statistical Association,* Vol. 46, March 1951, pp. 55–67.

Table 5-6. Regret matrix

Strategy	Investment (dollars)	Payoff (dollars)	Maximum regret (dollars)
1	50,000	150,000	100,000
2	25,000	75,000	50,000

fore, to minimize his maximum regret, the manager would adopt strategy 2. He would have less regret from failing to adopt strategy 2 than from failing to adopt strategy 1. (If he knew in advance which state of nature would occur, obviously he would select the strategy that caused him no regret.) Note that the decision of least regret is the same as that reached under the *maximin* criterion in Table 5-4. The strategy of least regret is also implicit in game theory, discussed later in this chapter.

Minimax is the most conservative of the decision criteria. It implies that a manager should do little or nothing that is risky. Using minimax as the sole determinant in decision making would be undesirable in the long run. Its consistent use would mean that a firm would eventually lose out to a competitor who was more aggressive, more willing to innovate, and more willing to take reasonable chances of suffering losses in exchange for the greater rewards.

Insufficient reason criterion. The insufficient reason yardstick will be employed when a manager does not know the probability of various states of nature occurring, or of various possible competitive actions, and does not know whether any eventuality is likely to occur more often than any other. Since he has **insufficient reason** for deciding otherwise, he assumes that *each is equally likely to occur.* He therefore assigns equal probability to each and makes his decision on that basis. Once again, a simple illustration will aid in explaining this concept.

Suppose a manager has only two alternatives open to him. He knows that four states of nature can occur. Although he knows the values for each state of nature that can occur within each strategy, he does not know the probabilities of their occurrence. Furthermore, he believes that one has just as much chance of occurring as any other. Under these conditions, he assigns equal weights to all states. Table 5-7 illustrates a matrix in which the estimated value of four states of nature, A, B, C, and D, are given for each of the two strategies. The total value for each strategy is represented

Table 5-7. Insufficient reason matrix

Strategy	Dollar values of possible occurrences				Payoff value
	A	B	C	D	
1	$15	$25	$35	$45	$30
2	25	20	15	40	25

by the average for all states of nature that could occur while that strategy is employed. It is arrived at by adding the values for each state of nature and dividing by the number of states of nature. (In this illustration there are four states of nature.)

$$\text{Value of Strategy No. 1: } \frac{15 + 25 + 35 + 45}{4} = 30$$

$$\text{Value of Strategy No. 2: } \frac{25 + 20 + 15 + 40}{4} = 25$$

Under these conditions, the manager will select strategy number 1 since it offers the best potential payoff.

It is worthwhile noting that although equal, rather than different, subjective probabilities of occurrence are assigned to the states of nature, the criterion of insufficient reason is an extension of the Bayes decision process discussed earlier in this chapter. The highest expected value decides the issue.

Decision Trees

When a decision maker has to make a sequence of decisions, and each decision has several alternatives, the use of a decision tree may be helpful. A decision tree is a graphic device for visualizing the sequence of decisions to be made and the possible outcome of different choices along the way.

Assume Company A must decide whether or not to introduce a new product on the market. The cost to market the product is estimated at $35,000. The profit that can be realized depends on two variables: (1) whether a competitive product will appear, and (2) the price that Company A can charge for its product. If no competitive product appears, Company A will set a price that will optimize its profits. Should a competitive product appear, the price Company A sets will depend upon the price of the competitive product.

A decision tree is constructed as diagrammed in Figure 5-4. It shows potential profits for different pricing decisions, as well as the probabilities of competitive reactions.

At the first decision point on the tree, Company A must decide whether or not to market the product. If it decides to market the product, it will have to decide at a later point what price to establish.

Should Company A market the product, there is a 70 percent probability that some other company will introduce a competitive product, and only a 30 percent probability that a competitive product will not appear.

If a competitive product does not appear, and Company A sets its price high, medium, or low, the potential profit is $100,000, $75,000, or $50,000, respectively. It would, therefore, set its price high and derive the $100,000 profit.

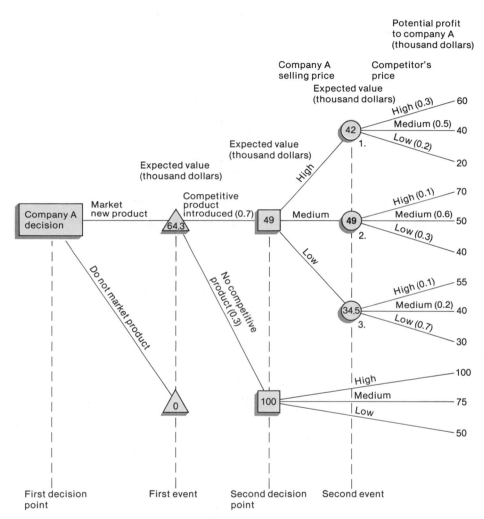

Figure 5-4.   A decision tree.

If a competitive product does appear, as is likely, Company A knows that if it sets its own price high, there is a 30 percent chance the competitor will also set a high price, a 50 percent chance it will set a medium price, and a 20 percent chance it will establish a low price to counter Company A's pricing strategy. The potential profits to Company A under these conditions are $60,000, $40,000, and $20,000, respectively. Similarly, if Company A sets medium or low prices, the probable competitive reactions are indicated, as well as the potential profits for Company A under those conditions.

To complete the decision tree analysis, one starts at the branches of the tree and works backward to the trunk. An expected value is computed for each possible set of decisions and events. Thus the expected value for the second event, under conditions of high, medium, and low competitive price reaction to the setting of a **high** price by Company A is:

$$(\$60,000 \times 0.3) + (\$40,000 \times 0.5) + (\$20,000 \times 0.2) = \$42,000,$$

which is shown in the top circle.

The expected value if Company A establishes a **medium** price is:

$$(\$70,000 \times 0.1) + (\$50,000 \times 0.6) + (\$40,000 \times 0.3) = \$49,000,$$

which is entered in the middle circle.

The expected value if Company A sets a **low** price is:

$$(\$55,000 \times 0.1) + (\$40,000 \times 0.2) + (\$30,000 \times 0.7) = \$34,500,$$

which is entered in the bottom circle.

If we retrace our steps to the second decision point, there are two decision situations. The first is based on the appearance of a competitive product and offers the options of setting a high, medium, or low price for Company A's product. As has been computed, the optimal choice, or the choice which offers the highest expected profit, is that of setting a medium price for the product. The expected profit of $49,000 is shown in the upper box at the second decision point. If no competitive product is introduced, Company A would set a high price, which would provide a potential profit of $100,000. This value is placed in the lower box at the second decision point.

Going back to the first event point, an expected value is computed by multiplying the potential profit of $49,000 by its probability of 0.7, and adding to it the profit of $100,000 (under conditions of no competition) multiplied by its probability of 0.3. The result is:

$$(\$49,000 \times 0.7) + (\$100,000 \times 0.3) = \$64,300.$$

If we subtract the $35,000 cost to market the product, the net profit becomes $29,300 ($64,300 minus $35,000). The decision would be made to market the product since a $29,300 profit is greater than the zero profit from a decision not to market the product at all. Note again the use of the Bayes decision process in assigning probabilities and calculating expected values.

Game Theory

A manager's decision strategies may be influenced significantly by competitors' actions. Factors such as the sales that are realized from the promotion of a product, the availability of skilled workers in a labor market, the number and effectiveness of dealers in a sales organization, and a host of others all depend to some extent on what competitors do. Their actions and counteractions, in response to a given strategy, are difficult to predict in advance. They are therefore considered to be uncontrollable variables. However, the variables created by competitors behave quite differently from the vagaries of Mother Nature. The technique of game theory was devised specially for analyzing competitive situations.

Game theory is similar to playing a game of chess, in which two adversaries are pitted against each other. A player makes a move, keeping in mind the move his opponent is likely to make to counter it. The opponent's countermove is made under the assumption it will produce a further reaction from the first player. The actions of one opponent influence the actions of the other.

Game theory relies primarily on a *combination of maximin and minimax decision criteria.* It assumes that a manager wants to maximize his gains and minimize his losses, and that his opponent—whether a business competitor, union official, or other opponent—is similarly motivated. Game theory provides the optimum solution, the best gains with the smallest losses, whatever the opponent does.

Certain fundamental assumptions must be made in viewing game theory as it applies to business. It is assumed that a firm:

1. has certain objectives that conflict with those of one or more firms;
2. has two or more alternative courses of action;
3. does not have complete control over the outcome of any course of action;
4. is influenced by the actions of the firm or firms whose interests are in conflict with its own.

Game theory is thus said to be concerned with "conflict-of-interest" situations. Two types of games are possible under these conditions: "zero-sum" and "nonzero-sum."

Zero-sum game.   If the gains of one firm exactly represent the losses of another, the game is described as a zero-sum game. This situation might exist when a gain in share of the market by one firm is offset by an equivalent loss in market share by the other. If two firms shared the market on a 50–50 basis, an increase by Firm A to 60 percent would mean a decrease to 40 percent by Firm B. Firm A's gain is also Firm B's loss. The sum of their gains and losses equals zero for every outcome.

A zero-sum game is rather simple to analyze, but in the realities of the business world it is seldom encountered. In most business situations, the gains of one firm are not exactly equal to the losses of another as a result of a given strategy. One firm's losses are not necessarily another firm's gains. Therefore the strategy that might be employed in a zero-sum game situation would not be useful in a nonzero-sum game.

Table 5-8. Two-person zero-sum game payoff matrix under equilibrium conditions

Firm 1 \ Firm 2	Increase dealer organization	Offer easier financing	Introduce 90-day warranty	Row minimums
Hire salesmen	600	500	400	400
Increase advertising	700	800	850	700*
Improve customer service	650	600	500	500
Column maximums	700*	800	850	

*Saddle point.

Nonzero-sum game. When the competition or conflict is nonzero-sum, analysis becomes much more complex. This is particularly true when there are many opponents or competitors. It is very difficult to anticipate the effect of a specific decision made by one firm on any one of several of its competitors. It is equally difficult to anticipate how the decision made by any of them will affect one's own firm.

To conceptualize game theory, our analysis will be confined to two-person zero-sum games.

Two-person zero-sum games. Characteristic of two-person zero-sum games is a maximin—minimax solution. The use of the minimax strategy, far from being the conservative and sometimes detrimental option that it is in decisions involving uncertain states of nature, is highly advantageous in a game against one rational opponent—especially if the opponent also adopts this strategy.

Let us assume a simple situation. Suppose Firm 1 and Firm 2 are competitors. Firm 1 is larger and better known than Firm 2. Together they share the entire market for their product. Firm 1 is considering three programs it could develop to increase its share of the market. Firm 2 also has three programs it could introduce to take some of the market away from Firm 1. Their possible courses of action are as follows:

Firm 1
1. Hire salesmen
2. Increase advertising
3. Improve customer service

Firm 2
1. Increase dealer organization
2. Offer easier financing
3. Introduce 90-day warranty

The management of Firm 1 has prepared a payoff matrix showing anticipated effects on its sales of various combinations of actions taken by it and by Firm 2. The matrix is shown in Table 5-8. The strategies of Firm 1 are listed on the left side of the matrix, and the expected payoffs indicated. The strategies of Firm 2 are listed across the top of the matrix. Its expected payoffs are also shown, since they are the negative values of the payoffs already listed. Remember, Firm 1's gains are equal to Firm 2's losses.

Table 5-9. Two-person zero-sum game payoff matrix under non-equilibrium conditions

Firm 1 ＼ Firm 2	Increase dealer organization	Offer easier financing	Introduce 90-day warranty	Row minimums
Hire salesmen	600	500	400	400
Increase advertising	800	700	625	**625**
Improve customer service	650	600	675	600
Column maximums	800	700	**675**	

Since the maximin–minimax criteria attempt to maximize the minimum gain or to minimize the maximum possible loss, in the margins of the payoff matrix are shown the "row minimums" and the "column maximums." For each strategy of Firm 1, the minimum gain it can make, if faced by the best strategy of Firm 2, is found in the row minimums. The maximum loss for Firm 2, when faced with each strategy of Firm 1, is found in the column maximums. Firm 1 will select the largest of the row minimums, and Firm 2 will select the smallest of the column maximums. In the example given, Firm 1 would increase advertising, while Firm 2 would increase its dealer organization. With these strategies, Firm 1 would gain 700 units and Firm 2 would lose 700 units. Since the maximin for Firm 1 equals the minimax for Firm 2, we have an equilibrium situation. This equilibrium point is called a **saddle point** by game theorists. If one of the competitors tried to move from this equilibrium while the other maintained his position, the mover would not improve his situation.

In business situations, the existence of saddle points is relatively rare. Usually, a payoff matrix does not have a saddle point. Let us adjust the payoff matrix, as indicated in Table 5-9. Now the minimum gain that Firm 1 can achieve is 625 units, as found in the row minimums. For Firm 2, the smallest figure in the column maximums is 675 units. If Firm 1 chooses the strategy of increased advertising and Firm 2 selects the 90-day warranty, an equilibrium situation does not exist. The precise result cannot easily be predicted, but for each firm these tend to be the best strategies to employ.

SUMMARY

In government, public, and private enterprise, problems arise that require individual or group decisions. Among the decision-making tools available are quantitative techniques ranging from simple devices to highly sophisticated and complex ones. Sometimes the solution of an algebraic equation, or a simple graphic portrayal of the data on a chart, provides the answer the decision maker is seeking. At other times, the magnitude of the problem and its many ramifications require a team of problem solvers, using sophisticated techniques and high-speed computers.

In this chapter, four quantitative techniques were reviewed and evaluated: break-even analysis, linear programming, operations research, and probability theory. Whenever decision makers do not have all the facts, yet must resolve the situation despite uncertainties about the outcome, the situation is a stochastic one. Under such conditions, where states of nature cannot be controlled and random variables occur unexpectedly and unpredictably, the decision maker uses the laws of probability to predict the outcomes. When *subjective* estimates of probability are necessary, the Bayes decision process is helpful in determining expected values of each alternative being considered. The decision maker is directed toward the alternative with the highest expected value. The Bayes process can be applied in many situations, including those in which the criterion of insufficient reason and decision trees are used.

KEY CONCEPTS

Break-Even Analysis	Decision Criteria
Linear Programming	Maximax Criterion
Operations Research	Maximin Criterion
Mathematical Models	Minimax Criterion
Heuristic Processes	Strategy of Least Regret
Probability Theory	Insufficient Reason Criterion
Markov Process	Decision Trees
Bayes Decision Process	Game Theory

GLOSSARY

algorithm A well-defined systematic procedure used to deal with a well-structured problem. A mathematical model is a type of algorithm.

break-even point That level of operations where total costs and total revenues are equal so there is neither a net profit nor a net loss.

decision tree A graphic, tree-like presentation of a sequence of decisions to be made and the possible outcomes of each.

deterministic problem A situation in which a decision maker has all the necessary facts and can decide under conditions that approach certainty.

equilibrium point A situation in which marginal costs and marginal revenues are equal and profits are greatest.

heuristic A process used when problems are ill-structured. The search is for reasonable rather than mathematically precise results and is based on intuition, rule of thumb, and trial and error.

insufficient reason criterion Decision criterion that assumes equally likely probabilities of any event occurring.

linear relationship   A relationship that exists when one value varies directly with any change in another value.

maximax criterion   Maximizing the greatest possible payoff or gain.

maximin criterion   Maximizing the minimum possible gain.

minimax criterion   Minimizing the maximum possible loss.

overhead   Fixed or indirect costs of an operation.

random variables   Events that occur purely by chance in an unexpected and unpredictable manner.

states of nature   Events beyond a manager's control which could actually occur (uncontrollable variables), but not by chance.

stochastic problem   Situation in which a decision maker does not have all the facts and must decide under conditions of uncertainty, neither the state of nature nor the random variables being known.

total costs   Fixed costs plus variable costs.

variable costs   Direct or prime costs that fluctuate upward or downward with the level of operation.

REVIEW QUESTIONS

1. What is the difference between an equilibrium point and a break-even point?

2. Assume a company wants to sell an item for $2.00. If its indirect costs total $500, and its variable costs are $1.50 per item, how many units must it sell to break even? How many dollars worth? If the company wanted to make a net profit of $200, how many units would it have to produce?

3. Refer to Figure 5-3. Suppose no final assembly is required to complete Model Y. How many of Model X and Y should the company produce to derive the greatest revenue under these changed conditions? Show, graphically, how you obtained your answer.

4. What is the advantage in preparing a range of probability estimates rather than a single fixed estimate when using a mathematical model in operations research?

5. What is a stochastic problem situation? Name some techniques available to a manager for tackling problems under conditions of uncertainty.

6. Explain the Bayes decision process. Can intuition play a role in this technique of decision making? Explain.

7. Assume a factory has fixed costs of $50,000. In a pending labor contract, its variable costs to produce a product may be either $1.00, $1.50,

or $1.75 per unit. The probabilities of each of these labor costs are 0.3, 0.6, and 0.1 respectively. Compute the expected total cost to produce 25,000 units.

Chapter 6

Additional Quantitative Aids for the Decision Maker

Besides the techniques discussed in the previous chapter, decision makers have other quantitative tools available to them. In this chapter our attention is focused on a discussion and evaluation of the following additional aids:

1. Queuing theory
2. Monte Carlo method
3. Simulation techniques
4. Economic order quantity (EOQ)
5. PERT
6. Hedging

Each concept will be examined to develop an understanding of its contribution to dynamic managing, and to point out its strengths and limitations in the decision-making process.

QUEUING THEORY

Visualize the following situations—customers lined up at grocery store check-out counters, cars lined up at a tollgate on an expressway, customers in line at a teller's window in a bank, aircraft circling the field to land, trucks waiting to get into the loading docks of a warehouse, material piling up waiting to be moved to the next station on the assembly line in a factory, a line of people waiting to register for voting, and another line waiting to purchase tickets for a baseball game. Everyone, at some time, has to wait in line for something. Your desire for service and the precise time it is available do not coincide. Since some types of waiting lines are unavoidable, people take them as a matter of course. At other times, if the line is too long and the expected wait too great, the customer may leave the queue and go elsewhere to be served. When that happens, the enterprise loses a sale and perhaps a customer.

In business, queuing problems arise when (1) men, machines, or materials must wait because facilities are insufficient to handle them immediately, or (2) utilization of facilities is less than optimum because the arrival sequence of resources using them is not regular or rhythmical, but random in occurrence. Queuing theory, therefore, is concerned with situations in which arrivals for services appear at random time intervals and servicing also takes place on a random or "first come, first served" basis. It is used where an imbalance exists between demand for service and availability of service, when a "stack-up" or "pile-up" occurs. This happens not only in production operations, but also in communications, paper work, and many of the facilitating processes in an organization.

Queuing theory, sometimes called *waiting line theory,* was developed in the early 1900s by A. K. Erlang, an engineer with Copenhagen Telephone Company. Queuing theory employs statistical probability to estimate the likelihood of waiting lines, and then weighs the cost of these lines to the institution against the cost of preventing them by increasing facilities. Costs of lost business, reduced customer satisfaction, and imbalances in the overall operation must be weighed against the expense of providing additional facilities to eliminate the queue. Factors like customer satisfaction are difficult to measure in dollars and cents, yet a manager must decide whether the expense involved in reducing a waiting line is economically justified. There exists a cost–service trade-off. Sometimes it is more expensive to eliminate all delay than to live with some degree of it. The cost of adding extra service lines like check-out counters in a supermarket, with additional expensive cash registers and less than optimally employed help, may not be justified by the added customer satisfaction.

In many situations, reasonable queuing decisions can be based on empirical data from previous experience, or can be made in a rational way based on current facts. By reviewing the experience of comparable stores, the manager of a supermarket occupying a given number of feet of selling space knows approximately how many check-out counters are required in his store. By noting the length of waiting lines at any time of the day, he can add personnel and open closed check-out stations if lines are long, or can close some registers and assign personnel to other chores if lines are short. In a factory, back records showing machine downtime may make mathematical computations unnecessary.

There are numerous queuing problems, however, which are too complex to be solved simply by reference to experience, or for which no previous experience exists, or which demand more precise answers. In such situations, waiting lines can be minimized through the use of mathematical models of queuing. Such models provide a method to determine the optimum capabilities of any service system by considering all input tasks, the cost of delaying action on these tasks, the cost of expanded facilities, potential benefits to be gained, and similar factors. One technique, called the Monte Carlo method, which will be discussed shortly, is often used to predict random events and can thus aid in predicting arrival rates at service facilities.

This is one way to reveal expected delays, particularly if the queue is not constant.

Mathematical Models of Queuing

Generally, one of two prevailing conditions produces waiting lines or queues:

1. Random arrivals from an **infinite** population to a situation in which (a) there is one service facility, or (b) there are multiple service facilities.
2. Random arrivals from a **finite** population to a situation in which (a) there is one service facility, or (b) there are multiple service facilities.

Let us examine both conditions. To keep the analysis simple, only the situation in which one service facility is available will be considered.

Arrivals from an infinite population. The following conditions are assumed: (1) there is only one service facility; (2) arrivals are from an infinite universe; (3) arrivals are independent of each other—that is, they are random; (4) service is on a "first come, first served" basis; and (5) arrivals and services occur in accordance with a **Poisson process.**[1]

Based on these assumptions, a Poisson mathematical model can be constructed to estimate various counts, such as the average number of customers arriving within a given time period, the average number of customers the facility can service within the given time period, the number of units currently being serviced (already in the facility system), the number in the queue (this does not include those being serviced), and the length of time an arrival must wait in the queue.[2]

Arrivals from a finite population. The following conditions prevail: (1) there is only one service facility; (2) arrivals are from a finite source; (3) arrivals are not independent of each other; and (4) service is on a "first come, first served" basis.

The Poisson probability technique cannot be used since the population is finite, and arrivals are not independent. An illustration of a queuing situation under these conditions is one in which machines keep breaking down and have to be repaired. Formulas can be devised to reveal the probability of all machines waiting or in process of being repaired; the probability of non-operating machines waiting or being repaired; the expected number of

---

[1] In a Poisson process, the population is infinite, the probability of an event occurring is constant, and the occurrence is independent of what has happened immediately prior to the present observation. Examples of Poisson processes are injection molding rejects per 1000, manufacturing irregulars per 100 yards of textiles, and defects per 1000 feet of rolled steel.

[2] Harold Bierman, Charles P. Bonini, and Walter H. Hausman, *Quantitative Analysis for Business Decisions*, 3rd ed. (Homewood, Ill.: Richard D. Irwin, Inc., 1969), pp. 368–370.

machines in the waiting line, and the average time spent by a machine in the waiting line.[3]

THE MONTE CARLO METHOD

It has already been noted that an essential ingredient in determining the optimum size and capability of any servicing facility is the "time of arrival" factor, which occurs in random fashion. When possible, actual observations may be made and records kept of the time and number of units that arrive for service. For example, a count could be made in a bank of the precise number of customers that wait in line in front of the tellers' windows each hour of every working day, throughout the entire year. In other situations, however, detailed observations cannot be made to indicate patterns of service loads.

Where actual observation and tallykeeping is impractical or impossible, the Monte Carlo[4] method is a simple and useful way to develop a *random sampling* of arrivals. The technique enables one to make projections in situations where work loads, machine breakdowns, illnesses, and similar conditions occur in random fashion. While the *sequence* of occurrence is unpredictable, the *frequency* of occurrence is predictable.

Both queuing theory and game theory[5] can employ the Monte Carlo method since both waiting lines and games involve random elements. In any analysis of automobiles arriving at a thruway tollgate, Monte Carlo can simulate real arrival conditions and quickly provide information equivalent to that which could be derived by actual counting and timing at the tollbooth.

In game theory, where several alternative strategies are open to a decision maker, selecting them in a consistent, patterned fashion could soon tip off the opponent. He would recognize the patterns and would take countermeasures in anticipation of them. Thus **mixed strategies** are called for, and these should be selected in a random fashion. The Monte Carlo method is one way to make random selections in a mixed-strategy game situation. An opponent would then have no way of anticipating which strategy will be employed.

Basically, the Monte Carlo method uses random numbers from which a selection can be made. A highly simplified example will indicate how it works. Assume that a company purchases automobiles for its ten salesmen. It knows that these cars will wear out at different times because of unequal travel by the salesmen. It would like to know how many additional cars it

---

[3]*Ibid.*, p. 374.

[4]John von Neumann revived this technique for the secret neutron diffusion work conducted during World War II at Los Alamos, New Mexico, and gave it the code name "Monte Carlo."

[5]The reader is referred to the analysis of game theory in Chapter 5.

Table 6-1.   Life expectancy of salesmen's cars

Expected car life (months)	Percentage of cars wearing out
12	5
15	10
18	20
21	25
24	35
27	5
	100

will have to purchase over a 5-year span in order to keep the ten salesmen on the road at all times. Listed in Table 6-1 are the probable car lives and the percentage of cars that will wear out during each life expectancy period.

For each 5 percent, a tab is made. On one tab, we write the number "12" (indicating that 5 percent will wear out in 12 months); on two tabs we write the number "15" (10 percent will wear out in 15 months); on four tabs, the number "18"; on five tabs, the number "21"; on seven tabs, the number "24"; and on one tab, the number "27." We now have 20 tabs (100 percent) which are placed in a box and thoroughly tossed to separate them.

Next, a list of the ten cars is made as indicated in Table 6-2. A tab is then drawn at random from the box. This automatically represents the life in months of car number 1, and is entered opposite Car 1 in column 1. The tab is returned to the box and thoroughly mixed with the other tabs. Another random selection is made, representing the life of Car 2. The process is repeated until the life of all 10 cars has been established and listed in column 1. Next, since none of the cars will last 5 years, we simulate the

Table 6-2.   Monte Carlo method prediction of car replacements

Car	Number of months before original and replacement cars wear out			
	1	2	3	4
1	15	39	60	
2	24	45	69	
3	24	48	72	
4	24	48	72	
5	21	45	69	
6	24	51	72	
7	21	42	57	81
8	12	36	54	78
9	27	39	63	
10	24	48	72	

replacement of every car with a new one whose life is also determined by the Monte Carlo technique. A tab is drawn from the box to establish how long each replacement car will last. Assume a tab with "24" written on it is drawn for Car 1's replacement. This means that Car 1 and its replacement will last a total of 39 months, which is listed in column 2. The tab is placed in the box and another random drawing made for Car 2's replacement. Assume this tab reads "21." This indicates that Car 2 and its replacement will last 45 months. The process is continued for all 10 cars, and the cumulative life expectancy shown in column 2.

It can be observed from the listings in column 2 that in no case would a replacement car and its original last through the 5 years. A third simulated purchase is made, therefore. After the third car is purchased, drawings are repeated on a random basis. The cumulative lives of all but Car 7 and Car 8 will reach or exceed 60 months, as indicated in column 3. A replacement will have to be made for these two automobiles to bring their extended lives to 5 years. This is shown in column 4. Thus every salesman's car will have to be replaced twice, and Cars 7 and 8 will have to be replaced three times.

The company now knows how many cars it has to purchase during a 5-year span in order to keep ten cars operating at all times. It has to buy the original ten vehicles, replace each one twice, and purchase two additional autos. Thus it has to purchase a total of thirty-two cars for its sales force during the 5-year period, the ten original ones plus twenty-two replacements.

If the life expectancy of the cars is accurately stated, the Monte Carlo procedure is reliable. To increase its reliability, a manager may want to repeat the entire Monte Carlo process several times. If there is a slight variation, the repeated procedure may produce a range of results that tells him the number of replacement cars may vary from, say, twenty-one to twenty-three.

In brief, the Monte Carlo method attempts to simulate real situations in which the frequency of occurrence of variables is reasonably predictable but for which mathematical calculations are too complex, too costly, or unnecessary to employ.

SIMULATION TECHNIQUES

Simulation is a type of "business game." It is quite different in concept, however, from game theory which has already been discussed. The basic idea behind simulation is to construct a situation which closely represents the actual one. It provides an opportunity to conduct trials or test runs under conditions that are as close to reality as is feasible.

Based on empirical data, a model is constructed and then subjected to the same influences and forces that would occur in actual practice. While these simulation models are not mathematical in the same sense as operations research models, they are quantitative representations of the entity or situation being studied. They include physical similarities, behaviorial characteristics, and interactions that would normally be present under actual conditions.

Gamesmanship is being used effectively to test ability of managers and potential managers to make decisions under conditions that closely resemble actual situations. Role playing and case study analysis are types of executive game simulation. Assessing talent in this way dates back to World War II, when criticism was voiced about the effectiveness of the paper-and-pencil test selection process for officer candidates. British War Office selection boards began observing and testing officer candidates in live situations where leaderless group problems had to be solved. This role playing methodology was adopted in 1943 by the American Office of Strategic Services when it established its legendary Area S outside Washington, D.C., and began weeding out and selecting agents for its vital missions.[6] Although the successes of the O.S.S. procedure were published shortly after the war, it was not until more than ten years later that assessment programs were considered by industry.

In May of 1957 twenty corporation presidents met in New York City to demonstrate the first practical "war games" for business executives.[7] Since then, business games have been used to simulate problems of running an industry, a company, or a particular department in a company. Its players come from production, sales, executive suites, and almost every area in the business.

Fundamentally, there are two types of business games—computer and manual. Computer games have received more publicity, although the manual simulations are probably more widely used. Both types may be designed for play by individuals or teams. The more complicated games are likely to be team or group exercises. Whether designed for computer or manual operation, business games are of several kinds. Two of the more common are general management games and functional games.

General Management Games

The focus of general management games is on allocation of resources to achieve optimum profitability, return on investment, share of the market, or some other corporate objective. The players adopt a corporate point of view. All major functional areas of the business are considered, and decisions are made at the top management level. In the American Management Associa-

[6]Leonard Sloane, "Assessing Talent," New York Times, November 28, 1971.

[7]John G. Burch, Jr., "Business Games and Simulation Techniques," Management Accounting, December 1969, pp. 49–52.

tion "General Management Game," all players work for the same company. The teams are large and the decisions to be made, in a short time, are many. Participants, therefore, are forced to delegate authority, assign accountability, measure performance, and practice a variety of management skills similar to those which would be employed under natural conditions.

Several times each year, groups of employees at Proctor & Gamble Company are organized into teams of four and spend six hours playing "Venture," a company game involving running a firm that manufactures cake mix or detergents. It gives them the opportunity to experience the total decision-making process involved in running a business. At Boeing Company, top managers play "Operation Interlock," a game that closely reflects their business and highlights their particular kinds of problems. The United Auto Workers Union uses several games for training its leaders. Sun Oil Company's annual game moves participants into unfamiliar roles—for example, assigning production experts to sales jobs, or taking executives out of the petroleum industry to compete as waffle iron manufacturers.

Functional Games

Many business and executive games are aimed at middle or lower levels of management, and stress a particular business function such as production, marketing, purchasing, or some aspect of managing, such as planning, organizing, or controlling. Du Pont uses "Realia," a computerized marketing game which simulates conditions a paint salesman encounters in his territory.[8] It is designed to improve a retailer's business. The salesman has to make the same decisions a merchant makes concerning advertising, pricing, inventory, and space allocation. He is forced to examine in-store problems from the retailer's viewpoint.

General Electric Company uses "job shop simulation" to discover the most efficient arrangement of plant equipment, and the smoothest production scheduling methods. Any number of arrangements can be simulated and tested by computer, whereas actually shifting equipment to try out changes could cause prohibitive disruptions in operations, and would be excessively expensive. In other simulation situations, toy models are used in factory and warehouse design and layout. These are arranged in countless ways. To discover which arrangement is likely to work best if put to the test of actual use, each is translated into a mathematical equation. When all equations have been run through a computer, months or years of plant and warehouse operation are simulated in seconds, and the optimum design or layout is uncovered.

Simulation has been criticized for ignoring qualitative factors and overlooking the importance of the human element. Many variables are not

---

[8]Thayer C. Taylor, "Stimulating Salesmen by Simulating Sales," *Sales Management,* May 1, 1972, p. 63.

considered. Missed deadlines, absenteeism, strikes, material shortages, plant breakdowns, data processing errors, and other factors are not shown to have a material effect on basic functions of sales and production. Even customers are assumed to be completely rational in their behavior. In reply, designers of simulation techniques argue that no simulation situation can possibly include every aspect of reality. If it did, it would no longer be a simulation of reality, but reality itself.

ECONOMIC ORDER QUANTITY (EOQ)

A manager is often faced with the problem of deciding how many of an item to purchase, or how many pieces to manufacture in a single production run to obtain the benefit of lowest unit cost, or how much raw material to have on hand to assure an uninterrupted production flow. Basically, these are problems of either procuring or producing in economic lots. What constitutes an economic lot? To determine this, the decision maker must first identify the cost factors that influence his alternatives.

In a department store, for example, this means knowing when to order, and how much to order, of styles, colors, and sizes to have sufficient depth of merchandise to service customers. The merchandising manager is concerned not only with the cost to the store of potential lost sales from inadequate inventories, commonly referred to as "stockouts," but also with the cost and risk involved in procuring and maintaining these inventories. Cost factors must be evaluated to determine the trade-off between cost and service. The inventory decision can be facilitated by using the economic order quantity model as a basic technique.

In a factory, it costs money to set up machines and make ready to manufacture a single item or a production run. **Set-up costs** are about the same for large runs as for short runs. It takes the same amount of time and money to clean a printing press for a color change whether the job to be run is for 1000 handbills or for 1,000,000. In a grocery store, it costs money to place an order, regardless of its size. There are clerical costs, administrative costs, costs of receiving and checking the incoming merchandise, and physically placing it in the warehouse or on the shelves. In the area of physical distribution, such costs are usually called acquisition costs, or **ordering costs.** Ordering costs in marketing are equivalent to set-up costs in manufacturing. As quantities (produced or ordered) increase, their cost per unit tends to decrease.

Then there are **carrying costs** to consider. The larger the lot produced or purchased, the higher are inventory carrying costs. These include interest on the investment in inventory (cost of capital) since the money could be put to an alternative productive use; record keeping such as perpetual inventory; loss or shrinkage from shelf wear; storage space or bin costs; rent; insurance against fire, pilferage, water damage; depreciation, deteriora-

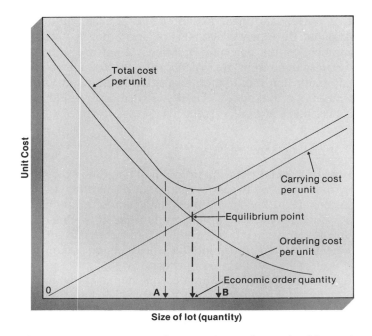

Figure 6-1.   Economic order quantity as determined by cost curves.

tion, and obsolescence; security, heat, light, refrigeration, humidity control; and similar costs of carrying an inventory. For accounting purposes, the carrying cost is usually carried on the company books as an annual dollar figure, and as a percentage of the average total inventory value.

Determining Economic Order Quantity

At some point in the cost analysis, ordering costs per unit and carrying costs per unit will balance. This equilibrium point indicates the economic order quantity, or economic lot size.

Graphic method.   The relationship between ordering costs and carrying costs is shown graphically in Figure 6-1.

The total cost curve in the figure is made up of two components: ordering costs and carrying costs. The low point on the total cost curve indicates the economic order quantity to buy or carry in stock. In principle, the EOQ is also identified by locating the point at which the ordering cost per unit equals the carrying cost per unit (equilibrium point). This point coincides with the low point on the total cost curve.

To minimize inventory costs, management will try to minimize ordering and carrying costs. Total costs are minimized at the point of intersection of the carrying cost and ordering cost curves *only* when the carrying cost function is a linear one. Realistically, conditions arise which tend to produce a non-linear carrying cost function. An example would be the case of capital cost; it is questionable that each dollar generated from the sale of inventory could instantly and automatically be reinvested elsewhere. To take another example, acquiring warehouse space is dependent on *peak* rather than average inventory values. Since this is the case, EOQ is more likely to be a range than a fixed quantity. In Figure 6-1, the EOQ range might include quantities between points A and B.

It is also possible to calculate economic order quantity by trial and error computation, or by algebraic equation. Let us examine these methods.

Trial and error computation.   Assume that a firm has an annual need for 1000 motors to use with equipment it manufactures. It estimates that its cost of placing an order at any time is $40. The value of each motor is $20. Carrying costs in inventory are estimated to be 10 percent of average total inventory value. How many motors should be bought on each purchase order? How many orders should be placed?

The number of orders placed for a given time period is equal to demand (D) for the period divided by the quantity on each order (Q). Total ordering cost per period (week, month, year, or longer) is equal to the ordering cost for each order (O) multiplied by the number of orders per period. Total ordering cost $= (D/Q)(O)$. As the size of the order increases, it takes fewer orders to satisfy the demand for that period, and total ordering cost will decrease. This is indicated by the downward-sloping ordering cost per unit curve in Figure 6-1.

The cost of carrying an item in inventory is calculated by multiplying the value of each item (V) by the percentage figure (P) estimated by management to cover taxes, insurance, interest, depreciation, and other carrying costs as a percentage of total inventory value. Total carrying costs equal the cost of carrying one item (VP) multiplied by the average inventory $Q/2$, or $(Q/2)(VP)$.

Thus, in our illustration,

$$D = 1000 \text{ motors}$$
$$O = \$40$$
$$V = \$20$$
$$P = 10 \text{ percent}$$

With this information at hand, the manager can draw up a table indicating the size of an order and the cost relationships involved for each quantity that he may consider purchasing. This data is shown in Table 6-3.

Table 6-3. Economic order quantity as determined by trial and error computation

Number of motor orders	Size of order (Q)	Ordering cost (dollars) $\dfrac{D}{Q}(O)$	Carrying cost (dollars) $\dfrac{Q}{2}(VP)$	Total cost (dollars)
1	1000	40	1000	1040
2	500	80	500	580
4	250	160	250	410
5	**200**	200	200	**400**
10	100	400	100	500
20	50	800	50	850

NOTE: Q represents quantity; D, demand; O, ordering cost per order; V, value of each item; and P, percentage figure estimated by management to cover overhead costs.

An analysis of the total cost data reveals that during the year placing 5 orders for 200 motors yields the lowest total cost. The manager would, therefore, order 200 motors 5 times a year.

Algebraic equation.   The EOQ formula represents the relationship between total, ordering, and carrying costs. The *optimum point* (EOQ), as we have noted, and which can be observed in Figure 6-1 and Table 6-3, is where *the ordering cost and carrying cost are equal* to each other.

Thus, expressed algebraically,

$$\frac{Q}{2}(VP) = \frac{D}{Q}(O)$$

Solving for Q:

$$Q(VP) = \frac{2D(O)}{Q}$$

$$Q^2(VP) = 2DO$$

$$Q^2 = \frac{2DO}{VP}$$

$$Q = \sqrt{\frac{2DO}{VP}}$$

Verbalizing the final formula, we get:

$$EOQ = \sqrt{\frac{2 \times \text{number of items per period} \times \text{ordering costs}}{\text{value per item} \times \text{carrying cost rate}}}$$

Substituting the demand, ordering cost, value of the motors, and the carrying cost rate in this formula, where $D = 1000$, $O = \$40$, $V = \$20$, and $P = 10$ percent, we get:

$$EOQ = \sqrt{\frac{2(1000)(\$40)}{(\$20)(.10)}}$$

$$EOQ = \sqrt{\frac{\$80,000}{\$2.00}}$$

$$EOQ = \sqrt{40,000}$$

$$EOQ = 200 \text{ motors}$$

Therefore, by using the formula we arrive at an economic order quantity of 200 motors which would have to be placed five times during the year to provide the demand for 1000 motors. This information enables the manager to maintain the least costly inventory program. It is the same answer arrived at by trial and error computation. Using the EOQ formula is the simplest technique for the manager to use. However, not every computation will work out exactly, as in our illustration. The manager may have to use judgment in a final determination between two alternatives, one of which may give him slightly more, and the other slightly less, than the precise number of units he needs. Since either will be less costly than any other possible choice, he will select one of them.

PERT (PROGRAM EVALUATION AND REVIEW TECHNIQUE)

The Program Evaluation and Review Technique is a type of plan which takes the form of a *network schedule*. It has been defined as a "management information and control system used in planning, scheduling, controlling, and evaluating progress on a program."[9] Its primary application has been as a control device, generally in some aspect of production or construction. PERT is a relatively recent development and, although it does not enjoy the popularity it initially did, it is often referred to in management textbooks, particularly in areas dealing with production management or production control.

To understand PERT, one must first understand the development of a scheduling procedure known as the Critical Path Method (CPM), which preceded PERT and which is an essential ingredient in it. Early in 1957, a group of operations research specialists at Du Pont, together with experts from Remington Rand, designed a procedure for scheduling chemical plant construction. Much of the credit for developing CPM belongs to James E. Kelley, Jr., at that time with Remington Rand, who introduced the "critical path" concept.

During the early stages of the development of the Navy's Polaris submarine missile, it was apparent that conventional managerial methods were

---

[9]"Army Programs—Program Evaluation and Review Technique (PERT)," U.S. Army Materiel Command, Washington, D.C. AMC Regulation 11–29, June 15, 1966, p. 3.

hopelessly inadequate to keep track of the schedule. The participation of 11,000 subcontractors introduced a high degree of uncertainty as to when crucial research and development stages would be completed. Building on the CPM technique, Willard Fazar of the Navy Special Projects Office devised PERT as a network flow chart, but, instead of assigning a single time estimate to each task as Kelley had done with CPM, he introduced three time estimates: optimistic, realistic, and pessimistic.[10] After PERT was put into operation in 1958, it was credited with reducing by two years the time required to complete the Polaris program.

For a project to avail itself of CPM analysis, it must possess the following essential characteristics:

1. It must consist of a well-defined sequence of jobs (activities) which, when completed, terminate the project.

2. Jobs must be capable of being started or stopped independently of each other within each sequence.

3. Jobs must be performed in technological sequence. (For example, the concrete foundation of a building must be poured before the walls can be erected.)

PERT, using CPM, involves two basic concepts: (1) activities and (2) events. An **activity** is the work performed by a single operator, a department, or an entire organization. Jobs or activities must have definite starting and stopping points. A starting or stopping point is called a milestone, or an **event.** An event represents a specific, identifiable goal of achievement. A PERT event does not consume time or resources; activities do.

The PERT network shows the interrelationship of activities and events required to reach an objective. Graphically, events are represented in the network by geometric symbols such as squares, rectangles, triangles, or circles. The sequence of activities is represented by arrows which connect each event with the next event in the project as it moves from start to finish.

In building a PERT network, the *first step* is to prepare a list of activities and the sequence of activities essential to complete a project.

A chart showing a simple project made up of 6 events, the sequence in which they occur, and the estimated time for the activities involved is shown in Table 6-4. The events are given letter designations, and the time for each is shown numerically. In our example, event B cannot begin until event A has occurred; event C also cannot begin until event A has occurred; events B and C must occur before event D begins; and event E must occur before event F.

Based on the data in the chart, with circles indicating events, and the estimated time shown in each circle, a network diagram can be drawn as illustrated in Figure 6-2. The arrows in the network represent the sequence of activities. The arrow from circle A to circle B indicates that event A, which

[10]Willard Fazar, "Origins of PERT," The Controller, Vol. 30, December 1962, pp. 34–36.

Table 6-4.   Network events and activities in a simple project

Event	Estimated time to complete activity (days)	Immediately preceding event
A	2	
B	3	A
C	5	A
D	6	B, C
E	2	
F	8	E

takes two days to complete, must be completed before event B can start; the arrow from circle A to circle C indicates that event C also cannot begin until event A has been completed. Similarly, events B and C must be completed before D can begin, and so on.

The Critical Path

A **path** is *any sequence of connected events in a project.* In our network diagram, there are three paths which are necessary to complete the project; path *ABD,* which is estimated to take 11 days; path *ACD,* which has an

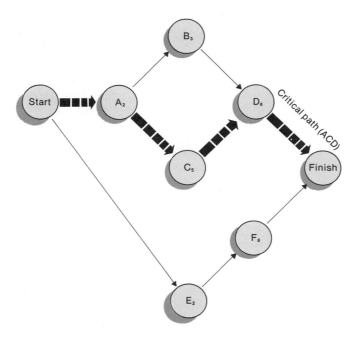

Figure 6-2.   PERT network diagram.

estimate of 13 days; and path *EF*, which is estimated to take 10 days. The **critical path** is *the one which takes the longest time to complete.* In our illustration, the critical path is *ACD.* Since this essential sequence of connected events will take 13 days to complete, the entire project cannot be completed in less time than that. In essence, the critical path is the bottleneck route. Delays in events on the critical path *will* delay the completion of the project, whereas delays in non-critical events *may not* hold up the overall completion date. However, speeding up the completion time of non-critical events such as *B*, *E*, or *F* will not reduce the overall project time since they are not on the critical path. The only way the total project can be finished in less than anticipated time is if one or more events on the critical path can be completed in less than the estimated time. Thus, if we can reduce the time it takes to complete *A*, *C*, or *D*, we can reduce the time to complete the total project, assuming all other events occur as scheduled.

Estimating Time for Activities

The *second step* in building a PERT network is estimating how long an activity will take. The important variable in a PERT system is time—the duration of each individual activity and the time required to complete the entire project. Estimating these times can be difficult.

There are two methods for estimating the time required to complete any activity in a network. The degree of uncertainty will determine which of these methods the manager decides to use. The first is a *single time estimate.* In the estimator's judgment, this is the time necessary to complete an activity under normal working constraints. The second method requires *three time estimates* for each activity: optimistic time *(a)*; most likely time *(m)*; and pessimistic time *(b)*. The three-time-estimate is used where uncertainty is involved, in situations where a manager has no previous experience to guide him.

- **Optimistic time (a).** If everything goes exceptionally well, and no unforeseen problems arise, this is the most favorable time, the shortest time, in which an activity can be completed.

- **Most likely time (m).** This is the most realistic estimate of the time an activity will take under normal conditions.

- **Pessimistic time (b).** If things go wrong, and if unforeseen problems crop up, this is the least favorable, the longest time, that it will take to complete an activity.

A weighted average time, called **expected elapsed time** *(t_e)*, can be calculated from the three-time-estimates by using the following formula:

$$t_e = \frac{a + 4m + b}{6}$$

Table 6-5. Expected elapsed time as calculated by the three-time-estimate method

	Completion time			Three-time estimate
Event	Optimistic (a)	Most likely (m)	Pessimistic (b)	$t_e = \dfrac{a + 4m + b}{6}$
A	1	2	3	2
B	1	3	5	3
C	2	4	12	5
D	2	6	10	6
E	1	2	3	2
F	6	8	10	8

Expected elapsed time as calculated by the three-time-estimate method is shown in Table 6-5.

Once obtained, the (t_e) values can be used in the network or "arrow" diagram, as illustrated in Figure 6-3. The three-time-estimates (optimistic, most likely, and pessimistic) and the calculated expected elapsed time

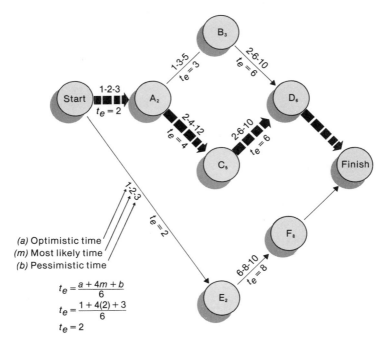

Figure 6-3. Network diagram showing expected elapsed times (t_e) calculated by the three-time-estimate method.

(weighted average time) are added to the network diagram, and the critical path is indicated.

Slack (Float)

Slack, or float, is the difference between a job's earliest start time and its latest start time (or between its earliest finish time and its latest finish time). In critical path scheduling, it is important to have this information, since slack refers to the number of days an event can be delayed without causing the total project to be delayed beyond its planned completion date.

In any project, three kinds of slack are possible: (1) slack may be **positive** (ahead of schedule), where the target date is later than the earliest finish date; (2) slack may be **zero** (on schedule), where the target date equals the earliest finish date; (3) slack may be **negative** (behind schedule), where the target date is earlier than the earliest finish date. Negative slack, when it occurs, alerts management to the existence of a time problem, spotlighting activities that need immediate attention to insure the project will be completed by the target date.

The longest path in the network, *the critical path,* is the one which *has no slack available.* Slack for critical path *ACD* is zero. All other paths in the network may have slack time or excess resources available to achieve project objectives.

Crash Programs

Frequently, management can change the time required to complete an activity by assigning more physical and human resources to that activity, increasing the costs for that activity in order to "buy time." Thus, if it normally takes three carpenters 6 days to put up walls on a house, five or six carpenters can erect those walls in fewer days, or the original three carpenters might do it in less than 6 days by working overtime. On a PERT project, the manager must decide which activities should be performed on a "crash basis" if saving time is more important than increased cost. Since a project cannot be completed in fewer days than it takes to complete activities on the critical path, the manager has to direct his attention only to those activities that lie on the critical path. In our illustration, path *ACD* is the critical one. The times and hypothetical costs for regular and crash programs for events *A, C,* and *D* are shown in Table 6-6.

Table 6-6.   Cost of regular and crash programs along critical path $A + C + D$

Event	Time required (days)		Cost (dollars)		Added cost of crash program (dollars)	Added cost of crash program per day (dollars)
	Regular program	Crash program	Regular program	Crash program		
A	2	1½	200	260	60	120
C	5	4	400	500	100	100
D	6	4½	500	725	225	150

In our illustration, the event along critical path *ACD* that can be shortened least expensively is *C*. The added cost per day to speed up event *C*, thereby saving one full day, is only $100, compared to $120 and $150 to "crash" events *A* or *D*. By spending an additional $100, the decision maker can shorten the project time to 12 days instead of 13. By spending a total of $370, and putting *A* and *D* also on a crash basis, the total project can be reduced by 3 days, from 13 to 10. The network diagram would then look like Figure 6-4.

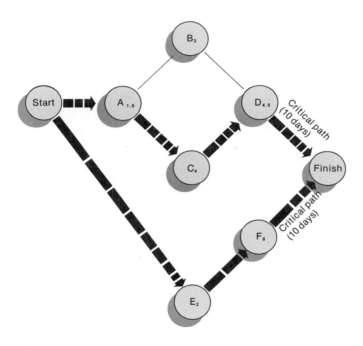

Figure 6-4. Network diagram after crash program on path *ACD*.

Path *ACD* would now take 10 days to complete and would be equal to path *EF*. We now have two equal critical paths. Any additional time savings needed on the project would have to come from shortening activities on path *EF*, or further reducing times along path *ACD*, whichever would be less costly.

A further refinement of PERT is the PERT system which keeps track of cost as well as time. Essentially, PERT/COST is an extension of the basic PERT/TIME system. Both cost and scheduling are planned and controlled within the same framework. PERT/COST adds the consideration of resource costs to the time sequence in the PERT procedures. When an activity is planned and scheduled, an estimate of its cost is also established. The PERT system then works to keep activities on schedule and costs within budget. It may sometimes be more important to know what the cost of a project will be than when it will be completed.

Although PERT provides a systematic approach to planning a series of activities, it is greatly limited in its application.

1. It does not eliminate uncertainty in the decision-making process. Using PERT, executives must still make decisions that are highly subjective.

2. It is not useful in continuous flow process activities, such as oil refining, where operations follow each other with no slack between them.

3. It is not suited for projects that are of a routine, repetitive nature such as a production run in a printing shop or textile mill. For PERT to be applicable, jobs must be "ordered"—that is, performed in a technological sequence, as in the construction of a building where the foundation must be poured before walls can be erected, or in shipbuilding where the keel must be laid before the work can begin on the superstructure.

4. When using the three-time-estimate with PERT, there is a bias toward pessimistic rather than optimistic time, so that the weighted average tends to be conservative. This permits a built-in margin for error that allows more time for an activity than is actually necessary. Such bias can become costly in terms of slowdowns within the framework of the total estimate.

5. Another objection to PERT is the expense of reviewing all time and cost figures on a periodic basis, weekly or bi-weekly, to determine where the project stands. PERT must be kept up to date, like any other type of plan. On large complex jobs this means frequent computer reviews of the changing data—a costly process.

After reaching its height in popularity during the 1960s, PERT has gradually declined in its application and is used by relatively few firms in business and industry today. Even in government, its use has decreased. At present, the Air Force no longer requires PERT to be used by suppliers in handling defense procurement contracts. There is no requirement or dollar threshold specified in the Armed Services Procurement Regulation regarding the use of PERT. According to NASA Manned Space Center, Houston, Texas, PERT, which was formerly required by NASA on contracts over $100,000, is rarely required today.

HEDGING

Most things that we do involve a degree of gambling—"taking a chance" on the eventual outcome. When a farmer plants corn, he is gambling that weather and other conditions in nature will enable him to raise a good crop, and that the price he will receive for it will be greater than his cost of producing it. When a man goes into business for himself, he "gambles" that he will be successful, and that he will do better than he would working for someone else. When a purchasing agent buys now for delivery in the future, he runs the risk that at the time of delivery the price of the item may be lower than when he placed the order. If, when he places the order, he contracts to pay the current price at the time of delivery, he runs the risk that the price then may be higher than it is at the time he places the order. He thus seeks some form of "insurance" against the risk of price uncertainty.

Hedging can be a means of reducing the gamble inherent in many decision-making situations. It is a *technique employed to protect one's self from loss by a counterbalance transaction.* Trading in the "futures market" in wheat, corn, cotton, sow bellies, copper, and other commodities is a type of hedging. Buying *and* selling commodity futures is a protection against loss due to price fluctuations that occur in the open market. Gains derived from the practice of hedging reduce the risk of loss. But for this, there is a price to be paid.

A simple illustration will indicate how hedging works in practice. Bookmakers or odds makers in horse racing or other sports events employ the concept of hedging when they "lay off" some of their bets. Let us examine how this takes place in a fictitious situation, "playing the numbers" or buying a lottery ticket.

A person buys a ticket for $1 on a 3-digit number from 000 to 999. He selects number 579. The winning number is to be determined by combining the numbers of the winners of the first, third, and eighth races at Fairmount Park. In each race, 9 horses are entered. If horse number 5 wins in the first race, number 7 in the third, and number 9 in the eighth, all holders of ticket 579 will receive $1000.

The bookie has sold 900 tickets at $1 each. The chances are very slim that many ticket holders will win. However, if only one person holds the winning ticket 579, the bookie will lose $100 since he has taken in $900 and must pay out $1000. Therefore, he will hedge his bet. He does this by getting a report on the winning numbers in the first and third races at Fairmount. Suppose they turn out to be numbers 5 and 7. Thus the only persons who can still win $1000 are those who hold tickets with 571–579. In reviewing the numbers bet with him, the bookie observes that he has a potential winner, ticket number 579. If horse number 9 wins the eighth race, the bookie must pay out $1000. To protect himself, the bookie will hedge by calling another bookie and placing a bet on horse number 9 in the eighth race at Fairmount. Assume the odds on horse number 9 are 5 to 1. He will then bet $200 on that horse. If the horse wins he collects $1000, which he uses to pay off ticket holder 579, assuring himself of keeping the original $900. If horse number 9 loses in the eighth race, the first bookie has no winning lottery ticket to pay off and makes $900 minus $200, or $700. By betting $200 of his collections he is guaranteed a gain of $700 as against a potential loss of $100 had he not hedged the original risk, and he has a chance of retaining the entire $900.

In business and industry, hedging can also be a useful technique, not only in purchasing but in other functional areas as well. Viewed in a broad context, termination agreements written into employment contracts of executives who are recruited from outside the firm are examples of hedging for both the executives and for the company. For the executive, the agreement sharply reduces the risk involved in transferring to a new company to accept a bigger job. Whether his employment contract is terminated "for cause" or "without cause," the company is obligated to continue to pay his salary for the duration of the agreed termination period. It is essentially a form of no-fault insurance in which the company does not have to show cause to terminate a contract, and the executive does not have to prove termination without cause in order to collect.

In sales, test marketing new products is a hedge against risk. It serves as a trial balloon before a firm commits itself to wide-scale development or distribution.

EMPLOYMENT OF QUANTITATIVE AIDS

There has been much discussion about the importance and relevance of quantitative aids to the corporate planning function. Frederick C. Weston conducted a study among firms listed in the "Fortune 500" and "Second 500," to determine the specific quantitative tools employed by corporate planning personnel.[11] Table 6-7 shows the results. In the table, "frequency" refers to the number of times each technique was mentioned. The percentage indicates the degree to which a particular technique is applied, relative to the others. The evidence based on ninety-three respondents indicates that simulation and linear programming are the techniques most often utilized. Other techniques are relatively less important in terms of the frequency with which they are utilized.

It is likely that some firms, particularly larger companies and high technology companies with formalized planning functions employ some quantitative tools and techniques in the planning or decision-making process. However, many do not. It is very unlikely that the bulk of the 8.5 million firms in the business population,[12] mostly small firms, rely to any major extent on operations research or other quantitative tools in arriving at either long-range or day-to-day decisions.

---

[11] Frederick C. Weston, Jr., "Operations Research Techniques Relevant to Corporate Planning Function Practices: An Investigative Look," *Academy of Management Journal,* Vol. 16, No. 3, September 1973, pp. 507–510.

[12] This figure does not include agriculture, forestry, or fishing. If these were included, the total would approximate 12 million.

Table 6-7. Quantitative tools most frequently employed by corporate planning personnel*

Technique	Frequency	Percent
Linear programming	43	21
Non-linear programming	16	8
Dynamic programming	8	4
Integer programming	7	3
Queuing theory	7	3
Inventory theory	24	12
Network analysis	28	14
Simulation studies	60	29
Other	12	6
	205	100

*From Frederick C. Weston, Jr., "Operations Research Techniques Relevant to Corporate Planning Function Practices: an Investigative Look," *Academy of Management Journal,* Vol. 16, No. 3, September 1973, pp. 507–510.

SUMMARY

A frequently observed situation on the American scene is one in which people or equipment have to wait in line for attention or service. The likelihood of waiting lines occurring can be predicted, and their cost to an organization in terms of lost customers or productivity can be compared with the cost of reducing or eliminating such queues. This cost-benefit analysis can be made by applying queuing theory and the Monte Carlo method, a useful random sampling technique for predicting the frequency of occurrence of uncontrollable variables.

Highly useful to decision makers in business and non-business organizations are simulation techniques, in which trials or test runs are conducted under conditions that closely resemble actual conditions. Among the currently popular simulation techniques are general management games and functional games.

Knowing how many of an item to purchase, or how many to manufacture in a single production run, to obtain the benefits of lowest unit costs is a problem that rears its head frequently. The answer to the question, "What is the optimum economic lot?" can be determined by an EOQ graph, trial and error computation, or algebraic equation.

PERT is a useful scheduling device for special situations in which activities are performed in a well-defined technological sequence, and each activity is capable of being started or stopped independently of the others. A network of activities can be developed, showing the critical path, or sequence which takes the longest time to complete. Total completion time can then be shortened by speeding up events along the critical path.

Hedging is a technique used to reduce risks. It is particularly useful in guarding against price fluctuations in commodities and raw materials used in production. It can also be utilized in financial planning, executive recruitment, marketing, and other functional areas. There is a cost to the practice of hedging, but it is a relatively small price the decision maker pays to reduce uncertainty and the risks attendant to it.

KEY CONCEPTS

Queuing Theory	Carrying Costs
Poisson Process	PERT
Monte Carlo Method	Critical Path Method (CPM)
Mixed Strategies	Slack (Float)
Simulation Techniques	Crash Programs
Economic Order Quantity (EOQ)	Hedging
Ordering Costs	

GLOSSARY

crash program   Speeding up the time required to perform a job or complete an activity, despite the increased costs, by assigning additional personnel and capital resources in order to "buy time."

critical path   The sequence of connected events in a project which takes the longest time to complete.

economic order quantity   Optimum quantity to order because ordering costs and carrying costs are equal.

expected elapsed time   Weighted average of three time estimates (optimistic, most likely, and pessimistic) used in determining how long an activity will take to complete.

hedging   Type of counterbalance transaction to protect one's self from loss.

Monte Carlo method   Statistical technique for predicting the frequency of occurrence of random variables.

PERT   Type of critical path scheduling used for control purposes.

Poisson process   Statistical technique utilized where the population is infinite, the probability of an event occurring is constant, and the occurrence is independent of any previous occurrence.

slack (float)   Difference between the earliest and the latest time in which a job can be completed.

stockouts   Term used in merchandising to indicate when items are "out of stock" or unavailable because of inadequate inventory.

REVIEW QUESTIONS

1. Cite two situations that lead to queuing problems.
2. What is the difference between game theory and gamesmanship?
3. What is the advantage of using a mixed strategy in marketing? Give an example.
4. List some examples of inventory carrying costs. How do they influence economic order quantities?
5. Assume a hospital needs to purchase 2000 bed sheets annually. It estimates that it costs $50 every time to place an order with a supplier. Each sheet costs $2.00. It also estimates that its inventory carrying costs for sheets is 10 percent of average total inventory value of sheets. How many sheets should it order at any one time? How many orders should be placed during the year?
6. What are some of the limitations of PERT?
7. Think of some situations in which hedging could be a useful technique to a decision maker.

Chapter 7

Major Types of Plans

The means that managers devise to achieve organizational objectives, or to solve the problems that crop up along the way, usually take the form of some type of plan.

Since many plans are actually solutions to problems, each type of problem suggests the type of plan that should be developed for it. Specific categories of problems (as they have been outlined in Chapter 4) require specific types of plans. Immediate problems demand very different plans from those projected to solve remote problems; plans designed to deal with broad problems are conceived differently from those devised to correct problems narrow in scope. Enterprise functions such as buying, selling, operating, facilitating, and managing all require special types of plans. It is important to recognize these different types of plans and to understand the nature and purpose of each.

The planning requirements of large or growth organizations cannot be met satisfactorily if managers simply deal with problems as they arise. As far as possible, problems should be anticipated. Contingency plans can help avoid "crisis management." Contingencies will still arise which have not been anticipated, and for which no standby plans exist, but if these are few they can be handled readily with improvised solutions. The need to deal with emergency situations can be reduced to the extent that sufficient contingency plans are available. In preparing for the expected, it is well to prepare for the unexpected.

Whether the organization is large or small, essential tasks of the manager are knowing how to plan, what to plan, and what types of plans to have ready. The alternative to any plan that fails to work is always another plan.

A hierarchy develops in which some plans are of greater importance than others. Together the plans form a rational structure, each fitting into the whole. In every organization, planning should proceed from the general to the particular. Knowing in a broad way what has to be done is primary. Filling in the specific details by spelling out precise steps that will be taken and the order in which they will occur follows in natural sequence. Detailed plans and standards, for example, must be developed within the framework of existing master plans and policies. The big picture has to be conceived first; the details to bring it into closer focus come second. This is an essential principle in planning.

The following major types of plans constitute a portfolio of plans developed to meet objectives at all organizational levels. It must be borne in mind that they represent *clusters* of plans which have been grouped for purposes of discussion and understanding. These major clusters include (1) master plans, (2) policies, (3) standards, (4) detailed plans, and (5) composite plans. Each category will be analyzed in some detail, and its distinguishing characteristics pointed out.

MASTER PLANS

By its very nature, all planning is future-oriented. For many organizations, it is essential to plan far ahead. A business may have to orient its thinking in terms of activities in which it may engage many years from now or which require many years to develop. Some long-range decisions are new fields to enter, major capital facilities, and developing channels of distribution. They require corporate, long-range planning regarding the development of future products, markets, sources of raw materials, labor supply, financial resources, and other equally important considerations. This is an ongoing process.

Master plans are broad in scope and usually apply to or affect more than one area of the enterprise. They are general rather than specific, and tend to deal with *non-recurring* problems. Usually, both personnel and capital considerations are involved. As an example, determining the faculty, staff, and physical plant needed to operate your university effectively twenty years from now requires master planning. Steps must be taken far in advance to insure that proper facilities are available when needed. Somebody has to be thinking ahead.

From the standpoint of time, master plans can arbitrarily be divided into two categories. (1) Those which extend a relatively short distance into the future, perhaps six months to a year or so, are called short-range or **current master plans.** (2) Those which extend further into the future, possibly five to twenty-five years, are called **long-range master plans.** In master planning, management must balance long-range and short-range goal achievement in order not to jeopardize the enterprise, and to assure that short-run expediencies do not lead to long-run disadvantages. A long-range plan to build a larger dealer organization could be disrupted by a short-range plan to curtail production and close some marginal plants. Here, too, the principle of deliberate sub-optimizing may be applied.[1]

---

[1] The reader is referred to Chapter 3 for a review of this essential concept.

Short-Range Master Plans (Current)

When an establishment makes plans in the present for something that will occur six months to a year in the future, it engages in current master planning. Since the time span is relatively short, current master plans usually contain more details and deal with more specifics than do long-range master plans.

An advertising program in which commitments have to be made a year in advance for space in publications, or for time slots on radio or television, is illustrative of a current master plan. The advertising manager has to know how much money he has to spend, decide how he will spend it, including what media he will use and how much of his budget he will allocate to each, and make other commitments such as reserving space and time in advance of the date the ads will appear. In essence, he engages in short-range master planning of an advertising program.

While lead time of six months to a year may be typical of most current master planning, in many industries normal lead time may extend several years into the future. The aircraft and automobile industries are prime examples. It has been said that an aircraft becomes obsolete before its plans leave the drafting board. In the auto industry, this year's model was conceived and implemented at least three years ago. Toolmakers require long lead times, generally as much as two years, for many of the dies and stampings that produce a car. After collecting data on auto scrappage rate, population growth, the outlook for the general economy, and other pertinent factors, auto makers draw up estimates of the total auto market for the model year in question. They then must estimate their company's share of that market, and calculate the probable demand for the various models they make. In the process, they must consider changing public taste, styling changes, and what they think their competitors plan to do. From these evaluations emerge the detailed production plans and tooling orders. Although a much longer period than a year in advance is required, for the auto industry it is still considered current master planning. In view of the necessity to predict the size and composition of an auto market three years in advance, it is not surprising that auto companies often make mistakes in judgments, such as the delay in marketing small cars after the foreign oil embargo.

Long-Range Master Plans

For an idea of what is involved in long-range master planning, consider the problem of estimating a community's need for hospital services five to twenty-five years from now. Plans for the kinds of services that will be needed, as well as the amount, are based on present information and expected trends—in health care, population, and other relevant conditions. Environmental changes are constantly occurring. Long-range planning must be sensitive to actual or potential change. When accurately recognized and planned for, environmental changes can become challenging opportunities instead of threats.

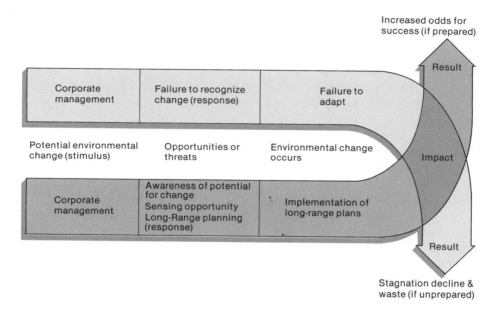

Figure 7-1.   Stimulus and response = growth (or decline).

The effects of corporate action or inaction to environmental change are depicted in Figure 7-1. Sensing opportunities to capitalize on potential change, the company initiates long-range plans to adapt. As the environmental change begins to take place, the company's long-range plan is implemented. Being prepared greatly increases the company's chances for favorable results; being totally unprepared could result in stagnation, decline, or unnecessary waste. In the case of a nuclear-powered electrical plant, for which lead time between ordering a nuclear reactor and actually producing power may be ten years, neglecting to prepare years in advance of expected plant usage would mean unnecessary hardship to both the utility and the entire community it serves.

A company can ordinarily plot its course far enough in advance to keep itself on an even keel and abreast of its competition without hectic last-minute crash programs. Long-range planning also plays a vital role in determining what acquisitions or mergers a company should undertake and the conditions under which it will attempt them.

The growing size and complexity of modern institutions, mounting costs, rapidly changing technologies, and keen competition have produced a highly specialized type of executive—the long-range planner whose job it is to come to grips with some of the unknowns about the future. What will the labor supply be ten or fifteen years from now? How fast are taxes rising? What will the political climate be? Does the physical plant have existing or potential pollution problems which might place restrictions on future activities? Will it need larger facilities and, if so, where will it get the money to finance them? These are a few of the factors the long-range planner must consider in projecting costs, size and potential of the market, changing transportation facilities and freight rates, and a host of other variables. Here is one description of the long-range planner:

> The long range planner is part of a relatively new type of corporate "radar" that's catching executives' fancies. Essentially, it scans the horizon, 5, 10 or even 20 years ahead and, assuming it works correctly, spots upcoming business opportunities and rough economic waters.[2]

While planning is not new to U.S. businessmen, the scientific, systematic, and long-range approaches are. For a few companies, long-range master planning goes back a number of years. Du Pont set up a planning department in the early 1930s, and Lockheed Aircraft did so in 1943. Since the early 1960s others have followed. Only a handful, however, including 300 of the Fortune 500 companies, have designated specific persons to develop a master plan for corporate responsibility that embraces community development efforts.[3]

In 1958 Stanford Research Institute created a Long Range Planning Service which issues approximately forty confidential industry reports a year. Each is a carefully studied look at a segment of life in the United States and the changing environment around it. These are designed to assist planners, or, if a company has no official long-range planners, to explain to its top executives why master planning is needed and what they can do to accommodate to changing conditions.

More and more companies are looking to the long-range planner for guidance, installing him as head of an entire department, or in some cases a full-scale division. The increased importance attached to the job is evidenced by the fact that planners rank considerably higher on the corporate ladder than they did just a few years ago. Economists in industry are commonplace; planning vice-presidents are no longer rare.

It should be noted that many companies are not enthusiastic about formalized long-range planning. Consolidated Foods Corporation, for one, finds it too restrictive and tends to rely more on the intuitive judgment of the men

---

[2] *The Wall Street Journal,* June 1, 1967.

[3] Stephen E. Nowlan and Dianna Shayon, "Expanding Horizons for the Corporate Planner," *Planning Review,* Vol. 2, No. 6, October/November 1974.

running its twenty-three divisions and subsidiaries. "I like our ability to move compared with a lot of ponderous formality. Flexibility is needed in any business selling fast-turning consumer goods," commented its president, William Howlett.[4]

Experience indicates that if long-range planning is to succeed, line managers running the organization should participate in the planning. Long-range planning by staff executives without extensive participation by line managers is resisted by the latter. The long-range planner and his staff design and install the planning system and teach others, from the president down, how to use it (an organizing phase of planning). A line executive will usually cooperate in implementing a plan that he has had a hand in authoring. On the other hand, corporate bonds may be sold with a 25-year maturity without having line executives participate in the decision. Most line managers do not have the technical expertise to counsel on the merits of this type of long-range planning and would comply with the recommendations of those who do.

FORECASTING

Although forecasting is not required for every kind of plan, it is essential in master planning, particularly long-range master planning, which must deal with the long-term probable effects of present causes. Future events are predicted by analyzing past information in the light of present knowledge.

Forecasting can be defined as *that aspect of planning which deals with predicting changes in the environment in which an organization operates.* Most long-range business planning begins with an evaluation of the external environment.[5] In estimating probable changes in the environment, and in planning a course of action with respect to such changes, the manager must determine: (1) whether present conditions will continue into the future; and (2) whether he should move in the same direction as the general trends; follow the trend in his own industry; buck the trends; or try to change the trends to the extent he is capable of doing so. These are difficult decisions to make correctly.

Methods of Forecasting

There are several forecasting techniques that are helpful to master planners. These include (1) trend forecasting, (2) business indicators, (3) market research, and (4) econometric models. Let us examine the essential characteristics of each.

---

[4]*The Wall Street Journal,* June 1, 1967.

[5]A comprehensive discussion of the macro-environment (social, economic, political, ethical, and physical) and its influence on managerial decision making is presented in Part VI of this book, titled Strategic Management.

Trend forecasting. One of the simplest forms of forecasting is projecting trends of past and present activities. Thus, if a firm knows its revenues have been increasing at the rate of 10 percent annually for the past several years, it may assume that revenues will continue to grow at the same rate in future years. It would then forecast revenue for the succeeding year on the basis of this year's revenue plus 10 percent. It could also project several years and extrapolate the data for any single future year from the trend line.

This technique assumes that history repeats itself, that cycles of approximately the same amplitude and duration tend to recur. It is useful only where components of the environment are slow to change or where rate of change is fairly steady (for example, life expectancy, birth rate, population increase, and GNP). Trend forecasting cannot anticipate sharp changes that may occur in the business cycle, rapid shifts in consumer tastes, unexpected movements in international affairs, or action that competition may take.

Business indicators. The term "business cycle" ordinarily describes a complete course of economic activity, embracing four well-defined phases which have been identified as *prosperity, recession, depression,* and *recovery.* This is the typical cyclical pattern.

To foretell the turns, up or down, in the economy, various indicators have been found useful: (a) certain types of activity tend to occur in advance of general business trends; (b) others tend to occur simultaneously with the trend; and (c) some tend to lag behind the trend. Frequently these are referred to as lead indicators, current indicators, and lag indicators.

Among the more reliable **lead indicators** are residential building contracts, which precede changes in the economy by about five months; paper board production, which indicates that industry will be packing and shipping either more or less of its productivity (since it has to order shipping containers months in advance); and the National Association of Purchasing Management monthly surveys. Since NAPM conducts its studies during the third or fourth week of each month and tabulates and publishes its findings by the end of that month, its data lead other advance indicators by weeks and even months.

The Federal Reserve Board's Industrial Production Index, which measures the total output of the nation's factories, mines, and power stations, is considered a key "coincident" or **current indicator** of how general business is faring. Other current indicators include quarterly changes in the Gross National Product reported by the Department of Commerce; freight car loadings published by the Association of American Railroads; and unemployment figures released by the Department of Commerce.

Among the **lag indicators,** airline traffic, which trails the ups and downs of the general business trends by four or five months, is one of the most reliable. Another is manufacturers' inventories (raw materials, semi-finished, and finished products).

Market research. As defined by one text on the subject, "Market research is the systematic gathering, recording, and analyzing of data about marketing problems to facilitate decision making."[6]

Some of the problems with which market research is concerned are customer reaction to market prices; supply and demand conditions; market potentials; stability or change in consumer tastes and buying habits; and the potential size of the market and the share the firm can expect to gain for itself. Most large businesses engage in some form of market research, and many either maintain a department for that purpose or contract for the professional services of an outside research organization to conduct marketing studies.

Trade associations gather much data that is useful in a market study. Magazines and professional marketing journals offer valuable information. Many universities maintain bureaus of business research. The federal government provides a wealth of readily available information. Often a railroad or a public utility, in an effort to bring new industry to a locality, will gather valuable statistics on local and regional markets. Frequently an industrial development corporation, sponsored by a state or municipality, will perform the same service in order to attract new industry to the area. Even data compiled by the local gas company on the number of homes heated with natural gas indicate a "potential" market for gas lights and barbecue grills, although there can be no assurance that people heating with gas will also purchase convenience items that are fueled with gas.

To determine whether a product or service will win acceptance, and to delineate the share of the market that the institution can reasonably expect to gather, three techniques of market research are frequently utilized. These are polling, motivation research, and market testing.

Polling. Users or potential users of a product or service can be questioned by telephone, mail, or personal interviews. In most types of polling or canvassing not every person or company can be approached. Often a **statistical sampling** technique is employed. The sample must be (1) large enough to give valid results, (2) truly representative of the population being studied (the group that may logically be expected to need the product or service, and be able to pay for it), and (3) randomly selected.

Sometimes those selected as the test group become a continuing panel from which organizations derive a great deal of worthwhile information. For example, each month 7000 customers selected by the Gallup organization are asked to report their soft goods purchases—what they bought and where. Using the consumer test panel information, J. C. Penney learns how people have spent their money—the items, sizes, colors they have selected,

---

[6]Edward W. Cundiff and Richard R. Still, *Basic Marketing: Concepts, Decisions, and Strategies,* 2nd ed. (Englewood Cliffs, N.J.: Prentice-Hall, Inc., 1971), p. 503.

and the pattern of their purchases. From these and other available data, the Penney Company can forecast its proportion of national sales, including its share of the market on about 500 lines of merchandise, and proceed to buy or develop the kinds of merchandise people want.

Companies develop sales and earnings forecasts as aids in making operating decisions. For institutions whose customers are other institutions, sales and earnings forecasts are frequently based on *sales force estimates* and on *customers' anticipated usage.* Sales force personnel submit to the home office forecasts of sales to present and potential accounts in their territories. These estimates, compiled nationally, by state and by region, specify not only total dollars or total number of units, but also particular categories of items, products, or brands. However, if these estimates are also to be used for establishing sales quotas, sales representatives have a tendency to minimize the forecasts.

Many institutions, especially those serving industrial customers, base forecasts on *expected purchases* by their clients. The customer and the potential customer are polled for an indication of expected use of the product or service. It should be recognized, however, that these are only estimates and do not represent firm or even potentially firm commitments.

Motivation research. Motivation research employs "in depth" interviews to detect the hidden reasons why people do, or do not do, what they say they will do. The technique is designed to probe the psychological mechanisms that determine an individual's attitudes or choices. Does a woman influence her husband to buy a sportscar because it is more convenient for her to drive to the supermarket or because it satisfies a need for status? Her answer might be that she would find it more convenient. The true reason, exposed through interviewing in depth, might be the status motive.

Obviously, motivation research requires skilled interviewers with carefully prepared questionnaires. But even skillful surveys of carefully selected samples do not guarantee accurate predictions. Paul McCracken, former chairman of the President's Council of Economic Advisors, cautions about the results of such surveys:

> Ask people this: if they expect the price level to rise more rapidly, will they step up their buying or not? A fairly high percentage will usually say they'll step up their buying. If they expect price levels to rise, obviously they'll buy now before the price level goes up. The empirical evidence is very clear and has been tested now over quite a period of time that it's the other way around. If people expect the price level to rise more rapidly, they will be inclined to spend less on big ticket items such as automobiles. . . .
>
> It turns out what they do is pretty rational. What they seem to be saying is: I think the cost of living is going to rise and of course I'd have to go into debt to buy a new car and I don't think this is a very good time to go into debt. I might

not be able to handle the payments. Consequently, uneasiness about the price level—far from stepping up consumer buying—has tended at least historically to work the other way.[7]

Market testing. A technique often used when a firm is planning to introduce a new product is market testing. As its name implies, it is a trial run of a limited market to judge dealer and consumer acceptance. Generally this technique is useful for low-priced products which have the potential for widespread acceptance. Household products like soaps, laundry detergents, dentifrices, and cake mixes lend themselves well to market testing.

The product may be tested in a single city, or in several "typical" cities or towns in a limited area, to determine customer response to package, product, price, and other pertinent market factors. Since introducing any new consumer product is a very risky endeavor, test marketing is a favored way to hedge this risk. It serves as a trial balloon to see which way the wind blows. If a brand fails in only a few cities selected as test sites, the loss may run approximately $500,000. If it is rushed into national distribution without such testing, it could be a multi-million dollar loss. Test marketing reduces the probability of a product being rejected at a later stage after a more substantial investment has been made.

A growing number of consumer products are being *pre-tested* on a small number of users before a final decision is made to test-market the items. If a product is judged to have market potential, it is first tested in a limited number of homes. If its potential seems justified on the basis of these pre-tests, it is submitted to a broader test market. A significant advance in pre-market testing is "concept testing," which entails going directly to consumers first to get their reaction to the idea of the product, frequently before the product is actually developed.[8]

Some market tests have been very successful. Others have not been. In seeking to introduce a new dentifrice, Colgate did not want to hurt its successful Dental Cream, which had already been replaced by Proctor & Gamble's Crest as the top-selling toothpaste in the late 1950s. Realizing how difficult it is to get people to try new toothpastes, to break habit patterns, it introduced Ultra Brite through a new strategy of market testing. It mailed a large tube, not just a miniature sample, to almost every household in the country. It wanted to be certain that families receiving a full-size tube would use it long enough to build a new loyalty. The strategy worked. Ultra Brite advanced from a development concept to third place in the market behind Crest and Colgate Dental Cream.

---

[7]Paul W. McCracken, "Will the New Economic Expansion Endure?" Business Outlook Forum, Honolulu, Hawaii, November 13, 1972.

[8]The reader should review the model of the product development process presented in Figure 4-3 in Chapter 4.

Many products that appeared to have done well in test markets have failed in general distribution. One baking company put a new cookie into mass markets after it did well in test cities. Nationally, it became a sales disaster. The cookie was fine when eaten fresh but its shelf-life was short. In test markets, the manufacturer was able to make frequent deliveries and watch supermarket shelves more closely than it could under conditions of national distribution.

There are individual factors that must be considered in test marketing. It is very difficult to find "typical" cities that reflect the national mix in terms of ratio of food store chains to independents, age, sex, income, family size, ethnic and religious similarities, education, and other characteristics. Some cities may be satisfactory for test marketing certain products but poor for testing others. St. Louis and Salt Lake City are poor for coffee testing. In St. Louis a regional brand, "Old Judge," dominates the market; Salt Lake City is heavily populated by Mormons, who are forbidden to drink coffee.

Econometric models.   With increased employment of economists in government and industry, the use of econometrics as a forecasting technique has also increased. It is frequently used in business-cycle analysis.

The collection of economic quantities is the task of economic statistics and economic history; the interpretation of economic quantities is the principal task of economic analysis. Synthesizing statistics, economic theory, and mathematics into a model that can be used for predicting is the task of econometrics.

Regardless of the technique that is employed, be it trend forecasting, business indicators, market research, the use of econometrics, or a combination of these, all forecasting is an "educated guess." At best, it is a "guesstimation." It is superior to making predictions purely on the basis of intuition, or on the basis of chance; but it can be, and frequently is, grossly inaccurate. In the 1930s, it was taken for granted that national population growth would terminate, to be succeeded by stability, or a declining trend. Economists then projected our 1980 population at 153 million. By 1970, it had actually surpassed 200 million. Not a very accurate forecast!

POLICIES

A second major category of plans consists of policies. In many ways these are the most misunderstood and difficult to understand of all organizational plans. Generally, they deal with recurring problems. Policies may extend over long or short time periods. They may apply to the entire institution or to specific functional areas, or to both. They may be either broad or limited in scope. Sometimes the mistake is made of referring to all types of plans as "policies." They are a distinct type by themselves and should not be confused with other types.

A **policy** is *a plan that deals with a recurring problem for which there is no routine solution by requiring the organization to recognize particular objectives and to work toward their fulfillment in some broadly defined way.* From this definition, it becomes apparent that a policy is not a fixed rule, nor is it a procedure. Both of these will be discussed later in this chapter.

A policy simply establishes *guidelines* or boundaries within which subsequent decisions are made. It takes the form of a general statement pointing out the goal toward which the organization is directed rather than a mold into which it is forced. The purpose of policies is not to achieve absolute uniformity of action but to guide people who have to develop other kinds of plans so that they will know when to make exceptions to usual practices and when not to do so.

In general, a policy has greater flexibility than other types of plans. In the progression from policies to procedures to rules, the limits become increasingly narrow and less subject to interpretation.

Kinds of Policies

Some policies focus on people and others on capital; some describe objectives and others means. In general, policies may be classified according to whether they relate to (1) personnel, (2) capital, (3) objectives, (4) means, or (5) specific organizational areas. This is an arbitrary but convenient way to classify policies. It should be pointed out that these categories are not mutually exclusive but frequently overlap. Let us examine these categories.

Focusing on personnel. Some personnel policies apply to all personnel; others concern only specific classes of employees. An organization may have a vacation policy which simply states that "all employees who have worked for twelve months shall be entitled to two weeks vacation with pay." It may have a promotion policy that announces, "It is the policy of the company to make promotions from within the company ranks whenever possible." This policy would also apply to everyone.

On the other hand, there are policies which apply only to *certain* people in the organization. An executive bonus policy is an example. It applies only to executives and not to the entire rank and file. An executive bonus policy should not be confused with an "executive bonus plan," which spells out in great detail how the policy is to be implemented. The policy does not. It merely states the *intention*. The "executive bonus plan" is designed to comply with the policy and make it effective.

A well-known pharmaceutical firm has an "Antitrust Law Compliance Policy" whose purpose is stated:

> Our Federal antitrust laws have contributed substantially to economic growth and . . . our full compliance with them is in the best interest of the company. It will continue to be our policy to comply in every respect with both the letter and the spirit of these laws, and there will be no exception or deviation from this policy.

Under the paragraph heading "responsibility," the drug firm indicates the people to whom this policy applies.

> Each individual is responsible for conducting company business within the letter and spirit of this policy. The various area heads are charged with the primary responsibility for assuring compliance within each of their areas. It is their responsibility to see that all personnel under their supervision are made fully cognizant of our company's position on this matter and that all such personnel fully comply. . . .[9]

Note that the policy does not state how they shall comply. It is much more general, simply making known its intent.

Focusing on capital. An enterprise may have a number of financial policies. It may adopt a policy of investing in new or expanding opportunities only if there is reasonable assurance of a predetermined rate of return on the capital invested. If the estimated return is less, the company will not make the investment nor proceed with the merger or acquisition.

Some firms write off as expenses of doing business all product-development costs as they are incurred. Other companies have a policy of capitalizing all or part of development costs and deferring the write-off until the product or service has been marketed.[10] Both are examples of financial policies—exactly opposite in application. For each firm the particular type of policy utilized is appropriate.

Focusing on objectives. Many institutional policies focus on objectives including service, quality, efficiency, or cooperation with others including government agencies.

The Du Pont Company adopted the following corporate policy declaration dealing with ecology:

> . . . not only to continue to comply with all laws and regulations related to environmental quality in its manufacturing, product development and transportation activities, but to continually review its products, processes and control facilities for the purpose of making improvements *beyond minimum legal requirements* that result in practical benefits to the environment.[11]

To further its corporate objective of creating a favorable public image, a firm may adopt a liberal service policy, or a liberal returned-goods policy. Sears maintains a policy of servicing major appliances purchased from its stores, even if the purchaser moves to another locality.

---

[9]Merck & Company, Policy #14, October 1, 1963.

[10]The Financial Accounting Standards Board Statement #2, "Accounting for Research and Development Costs," requires companies whose fiscal years begin on or after January 1, 1975 to recognize research and development costs in the year in which they were incurred.

[11]"The Environment: A Special Report, " *Du Pont Context*, E. I. Du Pont de Nemours & Company, Inc., Wilmington, Delaware, February 1972, p. 1.

An airline will have a preventive maintenance policy. One of its purposes is to help achieve the corporate objective of "insuring the safety of the passengers" that it transports. To implement such a policy may require larger, better trained ground crews who carry out their duties according to a routine detailed plan known as a preventive maintenance procedure. (Note the difference between policy and procedure.)

Focusing on means.   Other types of policies are stated in terms that emphasize the means to be employed in accomplishing specific goals.

One company may have a policy of obtaining business by means of catalog selling rather than direct selling; another may have a policy of selling house to house. The specifics concerning the kind of catalog, size of catalog, or frequency of publication are beyond the scope of policy. So, too, would be the details of techniques of selling house to house.

In establishing channels of distribution, one company may adhere to a policy of selling through distributors, another may sell only to retail establishments, and a third may sell only through franchised dealers. The details of complying with these respective policies will be found in additional plans that will be developed to implement them.

A brokerage firm may have a training policy which states, in a general way, that all employees must undergo a period of training as a prerequisite to permanent employment. Different categories of employees may undergo entirely different training programs in keeping with this policy. The training policy for registered sales representatives may state that each trainee must spend a month at company headquarters; become familiar with company procedures, Stock Exchange regulations, Securities and Exchange Commission regulations, bond markets, and commodities training; and then pass a comprehensive examination. Note that this policy does not spell out which company procedures must be learned, or which S.E.C. regulations must be mastered. Neither does it state the specific subject areas of questions that may be included on the comprehensive examination. It merely sets forth a general course of action as it applies to the training of registered representatives. Other aspects of its corporate training policy, as they apply to other types of personnel including clerical and office workers, will have their own specialized training programs and will emphasize methods suitable for each.

Focusing on specific organizational areas.   Many policies pertain to all or several areas of an organization; others pertain to specific functional areas or levels of management.

Special policies are required for each of the five major enterprise functions that we have identified. Thus organizations will have buying, selling, operating, facilitating, and managing policies.

Buying Policies are the guidelines laid down for any activities related to the firm's buying function. Here are some typical examples of buying policies:

- For purchases exceeding $1000, bids must be obtained from at least three suppliers.

- Preference should be given to local resources, if they are available.

- Speculative purchases of raw materials should be avoided.

- Purchases should be made only from companies that are well-rated financially and can be depended upon to make deliveries as stipulated.

For large organizations, buying policies can number in the hundreds.

Selling policies form the framework within which various selling activities take place. A pricing policy is an example. A retail store may set its selling price based on a percentage markup above the cost of the product and yet include a policy statement, "We will not be undersold." Its sales policy is to sell any item which is identical to one being sold by a competitor, at the same or lower prices. Its customers buy with assurance that the price they pay is as low as they could find elsewhere. To meet this commitment the retailer may have to buy very carefully if he is to obtain merchandise at a price low enough to permit a reasonable markup and still not exceed competitors' prices. He may have to establish buying policies that make possible the fulfillment of this selling policy. This is a good example of the interrelationship of policies across functional lines.

Another organization may have a policy of selling its product or services only to customers that are well-rated financially. Its attendant credit policy (a part of the selling function) might be to sell only to those accounts which paid their bills within thirty days, and to refuse credit to accounts which failed to pay within that time period even though they were favorably rated financially. On the other hand, a potential customer like billionaire John Paul Getty may not be rated at all, yet is likely to pay his bill within thirty days. Would you favor selling to Mr. Getty? If you would, it means a policy may be waived in special situations where it is desirable to do so.

Shown in Figure 7-2 is an advertising and sales promotion policy statement of Best Foods, a multinational food firm operating in over forty-one countries. This statement is indicative of a policy that emphasizes particular aspects of the selling function, namely advertising and sales promotion activities.

Operating policies are those policies relating to the company's main "doing" or performance function. All organizations have policies associated with their chief operating functions. If a firm engages in manufacturing, it will have production policies.

A company may establish an operating policy that is opposed to overtime work. This does not mean that it will never permit overtime; it merely states the intent of the company to avoid it. In an emergency, the company may operate on an overtime basis. Exceptions to a policy, therefore, are permissible without negating its value.

GENERAL COMMUNICATIONS

These policy statements are applicable to all Best Foods personnel. They are also binding on the personnel of its advertising agencies, and any other person or persons involved in the planning, creation, implementation, production or dissemination of advertising and promotional materials, literature, publicity, packages, labels or correspondence regarding Best Foods or any Best Foods products. These various modes of expression are referred to here, individually and collectively, as "Best Foods Communications."

Accuracy and informativeness: It is Best Foods policy that all its communications must be straightforward and accurate, and not deceptive or misleading.

Best Foods communications are intended to enable the consumer to make informed buying judgments based upon honest presentations. All communications claims require substantiation by appropriate information regarding product characteristics, advantages, use, contents and nutritional values.

Claims and comparisons in Best Foods communications will portray the product in normal use, not abnormal use, without exaggeration or cosmetic adulteration.

Good taste: Every Best Foods communication carries the responsibility to reflect favorably on the good name of the company and of each of its products. Although taste is a subjective matter, Best Foods communications will observe what we believe to be high standards of good taste and contemporary values, and will respect the values and sensitivities of minorities and special groups.

Care will be exercised to assure that phraseology used will not be misinterpreted by the consumer.

Violence will not be portrayed in Best Foods communications.

Communications addressed specifically to children will contain nothing which seeks to exploit their immaturity or which might result in harm.

Substantiation and approvals: All factual claims will be substantiated in writing with whatever supporting data are required to back up each claim.

Recipes and instructions for use will be evaluated and pretested before publication for accuracy, clarity and performance.

PRODUCT SATISFACTION

Guarantee: Backing our conviction that our products are of dependable quality and value and will perform as promised is our moneyback guarantee of consumer satisfaction.

To that end, the following statement appears on Best Foods packages: "Quality of Best Foods products is guaranteed. If not satisfied, Best Foods will refund the purchase price of the product."

In instances where this statement does not appear on a package because of size limitations the guarantee is still applicable.

Redress Mechanism: It is Best Foods policy to make refunds under the above guarantee with a minimum amount of effort and inconvenience on the part of the consumer.

OPEN CODE DATING

Although there is no legal requirement for open code dating of food products other than certain types that are highly perishable (milk, bread, etc.) Best Foods believes its customers have a right to know whether a product has reached or passed its normal shelf life expectancy.

Therefore, all Best Foods food products have plainly imprinted on the package or label a "Buy Before" date. This date gives the month, day and year after which the product should *not* be purchased.

Figure 7-2.   Excerpts from Best Foods Policy Statements on Affairs of Consumer Interest. (From Best Foods Division, CPC International Inc., Englewood Cliffs, New Jersey, September 1976.)

Facilitating policies exist for all activities that contribute to the facilitating function. An example is the policy of establishing security protection through engaging the services of an outside organization like Pinkerton or Wells Fargo, rather than hiring and training one's own security guards. In maintenance, there might be a policy regarding the care of physical equipment that would include painting the exterior of the machinery twice a year to keep the appearance of the plant attractive. The kind of paint used, or who does the painting, is not part of the policy.

Managing policies include planning, organizing, activating, and controlling policies. Here are a few illustrations.

- In planning, an organization may adopt a policy of having a standby or contingency plan available for every regular plan that is adopted.

- In organizing, a policy may be adopted of guaranteeing a qualified supply of manpower, including managerial talent. For the latter, a policy of executive development, executive recruitment, or both may be instituted.

- Activating policies may include maintaining open lines of communication, developing and instituting appropriate incentives, and encouraging leadership.

- An example of a controlling policy is a policy encouraging corrective action without delay. Establishing how often invoices and statements should be mailed to customers is another; this one related to accounts receivable policy.

Every *department* within a functional area has its own policies. A display department in a retail store may establish policies by which other departments will be guided when dealing with it. Display may announce that all items from selling departments should be submitted to it not less than sixty days prior to the date set for store window displays. This enables the display people to accommodate the window display needs of all selling departments in an orderly way.

Policy Formulation and Implementation

Policy decisions rest fundamentally on human judgment and intuition. Some policies evolve informally over a long period of time without conscious or selective formulation. They have their origin in slowly developing custom, traditions, and attitudes. Others are formulated quickly, because the situation requires rapid implementation. Both types may originate at top levels in the organization and work their way down; they may arise in a given area and remain in that area; or they may start at lower levels and permeate upward. In general, policies should be formulated by those in the organization who have the responsibility for accomplishing the particular objectives to which the policies relate.

From the top down. Some policies cut across all functional areas of the enterprise. Many are so interrelated with all areas of operations that their significance can best be understood by top-level managers. In large corporations today, for example, the chief financial officer is an important contributor to advance planning and policy formulation. Complex taxes, new accounting procedures, mergers, computerization, insurance, pensions, profit sharing, growth and expansion, and many other corporate considerations cause the chief financial officer to become involved in areas that are broader than strictly finance.

General policies or *corporate policies* affecting all areas of operations should originate with top management officials. At the highest levels, in large companies, corporate policy may be determined by the policy committee. Descending levels in the organizational structure will be guided by these policies when formulating more limited policies at their own levels.

Within functional areas or departments. Those in charge of functions or departments generally establish policies for these areas. Sales executives formulate sales policies; financial executives, financial policies; personnel executives, personnel policies; manufacturing executives, manufacturing policies; purchasing managers, purchasing policies; and so on. These *operations policies* proposed by area or department managers must be consistent with the policies established at higher levels in the management hierarchy, and especially with overall company policies. Policy established within a given functional area may influence the formulation of policy in other functional areas as well as the strategies developed to pursue those policies.

From the bottom up. At the department level, experience has demonstrated the merits of inviting supervisory and operating personnel to participate in developing and implementing policies.

Whenever possible, non-management employees should have a voice in policy matters that will directly affect them or their work. This kind of "participative management" engenders good human relations. Not only does it give managers a chance to hear workers' subjective reactions to policies, and to accommodate them, but also it gives the workers an opportunity to gratify deep-seated needs for recognition and influence on the group's functioning. Furthermore, by participating in policy making a worker develops a managerial perspective and a tendency to consider the enterprise as a whole, thereby contributing to its success.

In general, policies established at lower levels tend to function for the benefit of the sub-area itself with little or no effect on other areas. Such policies may be either temporary or permanent. It is advisable that managers review all policies periodically. Some outgrow their original purpose or usefulness. They should not be perpetuated merely because they are policies. Rather, they should be modified or replaced when circumstances call for a change.

Once a policy has been adopted or modified, it should be communicated to all affected by it, so that everyone will know about it and understand it. It is advisable to communicate policy statements at all levels in writing and to maintain a policy file that is accessible to everyone. Persons expected to conform to a policy have a right to know that such a policy exists, the purpose of that policy, and why it was promulgated.

Strategy versus Policy

Perhaps at this point it would be wise to distinguish between the term "policy" and the term "strategy," since the two concepts are often confused. They are not synonymous.

Policy suggests the directions that may be taken; strategy plots the course. Strategy is concerned with how to deploy available resources to reach a major objective in the face of obstacles. Obstacles may be competitive forces, government regulations, technical upheavals, social change, or similar forces.[12] Strategy is designed to deal with those forces in the total environment over which the organization can exercise the greatest amount of influence or control.

Policy and strategy are often interdependent and mutually reinforcing. Their relationship is analogous to that of the chicken and the egg. An existing policy may produce a given strategy; an existing strategy may lead to additional policies. Let us examine this relationship. It may be company policy to evaluate the performance of salaried employees. The implementing strategy may be to have immediate supervisors conduct quarterly appraisal interviews of salaried personnel. This strategy may lead to a policy of using the interview appraisal results as a basis for merit increases, additional training, promotions, or reassignment to another position.

The Importance of Policy

Policies are of great importance to every organized group since they tend to stabilize the institution, establish its basic identity, shape its planning, and further its acceptance by the public.

To stabilize the institution. Policies provide a conceptual framework within which other types of plans can be established to form a balanced, coordinated structure of plans. Since they serve as guides to further action, existing policies relieve managers of the necessity to ask superiors for permission to do, or not to do, certain things. As long as the managers are conforming to the organization's policies, they can safely proceed on their own initiative. Because policies tend to change infrequently or gradually, they lend stability to the organization. They provide a kind of uniformity or conformity that is desirable.

---

[12]These forces and the strategies devised to accommodate them are analyzed in Part VI.

To establish the organization's basic identity. The prominent characteristics by which a firm is known to its personnel are determined to a large extent by its general or corporate policies. Its managers and workers know the institution, its philosophy of management, and its way of conducting its business largely through an understanding of its policies. Their perception of any area of the organization is a reflection of its existing policy structure.

To shape the organization's planning. Plans developed in various areas of an institution are influenced to a great extent by existing policies. All plans are expected to accord with existing policies, and even to extend them. Since policy is the framework which shapes all decision making, everything decided or instituted is a manifestation of existing policy. The results can be no better than the framework that shaped and guided them.

To further acceptance by the public. To persons outside the firm—its suppliers, its customers, and the public in general—an organization becomes known largely as a result of its general and operating policies. The reputation that it enjoys, favorable or otherwise, is frequently the result of the way the outsider perceives the company through its policy structure. The firm is known to be liberal in its credit policy, or positive in its attitude toward employees, or "tough" in dealing with suppliers. Persons seeking employment may favor or shun a firm because of its employment policies. Investors may be attracted or dissuaded by the firm's investment or dividend policy. The consumer may buy or refuse to buy the company's products or services because of its service policy or returned-goods policy. There is little doubt that a firm's acceptance is basically a reflection of the policies by which it is known and judged.

STANDARDS

There is a third category of plans which justifies consideration as a distinct major type. What makes this group of plans different from others is the fact that their effectiveness has been demonstrated and proved before they are adopted. Usually they have their greatest application at the operating and facilitating levels of the organization, particularly in the production and clerical areas. **Standards** are developed for the solution of, or application to, a repetitive or *recurring* problem. They are distinguished from other types of plans by their relative exactness and precise definition.

For practical purposes, there are two acceptable definitions for standards. In an engineering or technical sense, a standard is *the result of a scientific search for the best way to do something.* In the broader meaning of the word, particularly where people or ideas are concerned, a standard is *a norm, a planned and accepted level of attainment or performance.* It is a prescribed way of doing something, a model or criterion of what is desirable and acceptable.

By either definition, a standard may also become a goal or objective toward which various sub-units in the organization strive. Therefore, standards tend to develop conformity of action within an organization. Depending upon their applicability, both meanings of "standard" are used in this book.

Kinds of Standards

Tangible entities, such as units produced or energy expended, are quantifiable and easily measured. Absolute measuring devices are available for weighing or counting them in an accurate, precise way. Where absolute units of measurement are available, *absolute standards* can be developed.

Intangibles, such as morale, grievances, and quality of supervision, which often reflect value judgments, cannot be quantified or determined in a precise way. This is always true when dealing with the characteristics of people rather than with things. When absolute units of measurement are not available, relative units can be devised. With these, *relative standards* can be developed.

How does an administrator determine whether some supervisors are more competent than others? Since absolute measuring devices have not been perfected for this purpose, relative techniques must be employed. Although these are less precise, they serve their purpose equally well. For example, a rating scale or value continuum indicating poor, average, and superior supervision, with perhaps gradations between these three ranges, can be established. With the same yardstick, each supervisor could be rated on characteristics related to supervision. The completed rating scales could then be compared. On the basis of these comparisons, a determination could be made that some supervisors are superior to others as measured by this device.

The technique is similar to using an intelligence test for comparing people. The test is a relative device and not an absolute one. If a person scored zero on such a test, one could not conclude that he had no intelligence. By the same token, if another person made a perfect test score, it could not be concluded that he had maximum intelligence. All that can be inferred is that, as measured by this particular test, the person with the perfect score appears to have higher intelligence than the person who scored zero.

Uses of Standards

Standards, as we have defined them, are often used in one or more of the following ways: (1) a yardstick of measurement, (2) a means of identification, (3) a means for comparison, or (4) a means for control.

Yardstick of measurement. Measurement is not possible in the absence of satisfactory units of measurement. There must be available either absolute or relative measuring units. Based on either of these, standards are developed that can be used as a measurement of quality, or as a measurement of performance or achievement.

Quite often, the intrinsic attributes of the materials from which a product is made determine its final characteristics. Thus, to produce a finished product that meets a certain standard, the specifications of the raw materials going into that product (hardness, tensile strength, ductability, conductability, and so forth) are used as the yardstick for the *measurement of its* **quality.**

In production or operations, standards provide management with specific goals, or with specific guides for attaining desired results. Two practical examples of this principle are speed in processing and the quality of the finished product. To produce quality incandescent lamps in an efficient and effective manner, it is critical that the strength of the bulb does not fall below a lower limit established and maintained through numerous tests. As a consequence, bulb suppliers are given the lower limit specification to which to adhere. To insure that weak bulbs do not enter the manufacturing process, all incoming bulbs undergo inspection based on a batch-sampling technique. Using this technique to maintain the quality of the basic material permits the factory to routinize many of its additional manufacturing decisions.

When a standard is used as a measurement of **performance,** it is often called a "job standard." A particular job will meet the standard of performance when certain specified results are obtained. Job standards, therefore, may be relative or absolute.

When there are variables present that are not subject to precise control, the performance standard developed may be a relative one. For example, what is the standard for good customer service? Good customer service is a set of conditions that prevail when service has been provided in a satisfactory fashion. Since the effort or output of employees is often difficult or impossible to quantify, a standard of acceptable behavior or performance may have to be a relative one.

On the other hand, should a typist develop the best way to insert envelopes into a typewriter for addressing, a method that produces optimum output with the fewest motions, a standard of performance also results. It becomes a job standard, in this case an absolute one. A performance standard, relative or absolute, may thus become a goal, an objective toward which to strive.

The use of standard costs as an important criterion of performance is a frequent source of dissatisfaction among managers. The inability to maintain standard costs because of variations in quality and cost of raw materials, burden or overhead automatically allocated to plants and divisions, and other factors beyond the control of the operating manager cause distrust of such standards. It is wiser, therefore, to develop multiple criteria for measuring and evaluating managerial performance.

Means of identification.   Standards are an excellent way to reduce the number of unnecessary variations in products and services and to bring conformity and understanding into practice. For the consumer, standardization means products and services which are similar, can be purchased with greater confidence, and can be used interchangeably. The standardized neck on a light bulb enables it to be used interchangeably in any lamp regardless of the manufacturer. The light socket is also standard and will accommodate the bulb whether it is made by Sylvania, General Electric, or Westinghouse.

If one purchases a 1/20, number 4 flat head, zinc-plated, wood screw he does so confidently, knowing that through this standard of identification the screw will be the same regardless of production source. In buying lumber, one may ask for "two-by-fours," which are pieces of wood whose actual dimensions are not two inches by four inches, but closer to 1¾ inches by 3¾ inches finished size. One will also discover that "9 × 12" is the identification standard for a rug whose actual dimensions are approximately 8 feet 6 inches by 11 feet 6 inches.

Means for comparison. Comparison is a process of evaluating two or more entities or attributes together to discover similarities or dissimilarities, or any relationship between them.[13] In making comparisons, it is essential that criteria be established which can be used as the basis for evaluation. Standards are a type of criteria that can be employed for this purpose. If a department store wants to evaluate how well its sales personnel are offering service to its customers, it must first have some objective criteria of what constitutes good, average, or poor customer service. In other words, criteria of standard customer service must be established. Then, the activities of sales personnel can be compared with the criteria. The standard is used as a means of comparison.

Means for control.   A great many standards are utilized as a means of exercising control in various areas of the organization. Engineering, for example, enforces standards based on the best practice that has been demonstrated for existing manufacturing technology. These standards may be modified by a permissible degree of variance or latitude to make them practicable or more workable. Such variation in a standard is called **tolerance** and is often expressed in hundredths or thousandths of an inch. Engineering standards with permissible tolerances are called **working standards.** Thus,

---

[13]More will be said about comparison as a control function in Chapter 23.

if a part is to be machined to a specific dimension, the working standard will permit a finished piece that can vary no more in either direction than the tolerance. This acts as a means of quality control.

Technical standards, inasmuch as they represent scientific determinations of the best way to accomplish some purpose, can be used as yardsticks of measurement, means of identification, and means of comparison. Other types of standards including relative norms can also be used as control devices. In general, standards tend to have greater permanency and are less subject to modification than most other types of plans. As is true of all plans, standards may be related to each other and to other types of plans. This interrelationship which we have already observed among plans will become more apparent when various types of detailed plans have been examined. We now turn out attention to these.

DETAILED PLANS

A fourth category of plans, as they have been arbitrarily established in our hierarchy, is the type which may be called detailed plans.

As its name implies, this group of plans defines objectives, means, or methods in a precise manner. These plans are more limited in scope and more numerous than other types of plans. Detailed plans cover a relatively short time span. Compared with long-range plans, they are less subject to frequent or radical modification. They deal with *both recurring and non-recurring* problems and normally apply to specific functional areas. Usually they are formulated at lower echelons of the management structure. Many are created by the first level of management—the foreman, or operative supervisor. Detailed plans can be very complex, depending on the purpose for which they are intended. A map or blueprint is a detailed plan.

Some detailed plans are designed to solve a particular problem or to be utilized for a special purpose and no other. Some may be used once and never again; others may be designed for a specific use and continue to be used for that purpose. The distinction between *single-purpose* and *routine* plans, though not a hard-and-fast one, is helpful for studying detailed plans.

Single-Purpose Detailed Plan

Single-purpose plans may be repetitive or non-repetitive. Those which are single-use as well as single-purpose in nature are non-repetitive. A trip ticket specifying that a delivery by a truck driver be made to a customer on a designated day is an example of a single-purpose, single-use plan. It will never be used again for that customer on that day.

Other detailed plans, however, are designed to be used repeatedly for a specific purpose. A blueprint of a mobile home that is manufactured in frequent, small production runs is an example of a single-purpose, repetitive plan.

The types of single-purpose detailed plans most often encountered are (1) programs, (2) projects, (3) budgets, (4) schedules, (5) agendas and business forms, and (6) blueprints and specifications.

Programs.   A program is somewhat broader than most single-purpose plans and may incorporate other detailed plans within it. It is an aggregate of several related action plans that have been designed to accomplish some common objective. One might call it a *single-purpose metaplan.*

A training program for road salesmen illustrates this concept. Such a plan may have a number of components including meetings with the sales manager to review the line of products and learn how to present them to customers; sessions with the sales promotion manager to discuss promotional strategies in selling the products; talks with the advertising manager to discuss the type of advertising assistance that will back the sales efforts; and several weeks work in the territory under the tutelage of an experienced salesman to "learn the ropes." This might be followed by a period during which the neophyte salesman takes over. He would be supervised and guided by the experienced salesman who would observe, critique, and point out aspects of performance that need improvement. Obviously this sequence is an oversimplification, but it does illustrate a single-purpose (sales training), repetitive, detailed metaplan known as a program. Other training programs may be more complex. Some are much simpler.

Programs are prevalent in all functional areas of business; management development programs, preventive maintenance programs, and others are continually being devised and implemented.

Projects.   Projects are detailed plans that are usually part of a specific program. A given project may be made up of several specialized detailed plans.

A learning project, for example, may be one component of a training program. Other projects in the program may be on-the-job training or simulator training. Collectively, such learning projects comprise a training program. The project itself may consist of several sub-plans. Many institutions have found they can reduce training time of personnel by utilizing videotape, which can be replayed to point out errors. This technique is one segment of the learning project.

Many projects are much broader and far-reaching in their effects. Marketing a new product may be a complex project that is but one of many that constitute a sales expansion program. Other related projects may focus on developing new markets for existing products, or selling existing products more intensively in present markets. Thus, in this illustration, we have three projects taking place concurrently—marketing a new product, developing new markets for existing products, and selling existing products more intensively in present markets. Related by a common purpose, they collectively constitute the sales expansion program.

Budgets. Budgets are single-purpose, single-use plans designed primarily to allocate the resources of an organization.

There are as many kinds of budgets as there are major activities in the enterprise: capital, production (units produced), cost, sales (quotas), personnel (manpower requirements), financial, and so on.

The financial budget is concerned with inputs (income or revenue) as well as outputs (expenditures or expenses). Generally, it relates to specific time periods, usually a calendar quarter, six months, or a year. Sometimes, as part of a master plan, financial budgets extend several years into the future, estimating long-term revenue and probable expenditures.

Budgets are employed most frequently as a control device. Operations are reviewed on some established time-span basis. Actual results for the period, in terms of income or expenditure, are compared with the budget (plan). If significant variations are observed, management must initiate the required action to correct the situation. The important fact to remember is that a budget is always a *plan* even when it is used for control purposes.

Budgets may cut across all areas and all managerial levels, and may parallel other organizational plans. A firm, for example, may have a total expenditure of $100 million planned as its overall budget for next year. However, that may be only part of a long-range master plan for corporate expansion involving a $700 million budget to finance diversification, new plant and equipment, increased inventories, additional personnel, and other factors.

Like other types of plans, budgets should be reviewed and adjusted to meet changing conditions and, therefore, must be flexible and open to revision when necessary.

Schedules. Detailed plans that are primarily concerned with the time sequence of operations or tasks are called schedules. They are plans with a time dimension.

Schedules have their greatest application in the operating areas. Products, including subassemblies and semi-finished work-in-process, should not be completed too far in advance of when they will be needed in a manufacturing plant. Otherwise, additional handling costs, temporary warehousing charges, and possible deterioration might occur during the waiting period. On the other hand, work completed after the time needed would be very costly and could disrupt the flow in subsequent stages of production or marketing. To maintain an even flow of operations calls for scheduling in all types of organizations. In a hospital, for example, lab tests, X-rays, and surgery are sequenced.

In scheduling, some activities take place concurrently; others have to follow one another in a predetermined sequence. Although some phases of activities are completed sooner than others, the goal is to finish the entire project on time. Schedules, therefore, are a type of plan used largely for control purposes, but also to program operations and to standardize performance. Program Evaluation and Review Technique (PERT), discussed in Chapter 6, is an example of a rather complex schedule.

Agendas and business forms. Frequently utilized by managers when conducting meetings, conferences, seminars, or conventions, agendas outline things to be done, topics to be discussed, and the order in which they will be handled. Although the format for each session may remain constant and be repeated the next time, the subjects to be discussed and included in the particular agenda vary from meeting to meeting. Each agenda, therefore, is a single-purpose, single-use type of detailed plan.

Most business forms such as order blanks, sales slips, requisition forms, or bills of lading are also single-purpose and single-use. It is true that the format is the same, but the information filled in on each varies with each use. Every purchase order, trip ticket, invoice, or returned goods authorization form, when put to use, can be viewed as a single-purpose, single-use detailed plan.

Blueprints and specifications. For the most part, blueprints and specifications are engineering or architectural plans that set forth in great detail how something is to be built or put to use. They have widespread application in operating areas, particularly in production activities.

They are also employed by drafting and design departments in preparing cost estimates, tailoring products to customer requirements, and determining the kinds and amounts of materials and manpower that will be needed. They are a type of single-purpose detailed plan, and generally are single-use.

Routine Detailed Plans

Routine detailed plans are repetitive in nature and purpose. They are intended to be used again and again. Since they are used repeatedly and are less subject to major change, writers often refer to them as *standing plans.* Some routine detailed plans are broad in scope and complex, representing a composite of subordinate detailed plans. Others are simple. Standing plans encountered most often are (1) procedures, (2) systems, (3) methods, and (4) rules.

Procedures. A procedure is a plan that provides a chronological, step-by-step sequence of tasks, prescribing a specific course of action to follow. It clearly spells out the way one is to go about doing something. As procedures are developed and refined, they become highly efficient in reaching a goal or solving a problem. They become perfected to the point where they seem to be the best way that has been devised to accomplish the purpose, to get the job done. When they reach this stage of refinement, they are frequently referred to as **standard operating procedures** (SOP).

Procedures are used in all major functional areas. Thus, within the function of comptrolling there may be an accounts receivable procedure and an accounts payable procedure. An airline, mindful of its corporate objective to guard the safety of its passengers and equipment, uses a preventive maintenance (facilitating function) procedure to implement its preventive maintenance policy. (Note the interrelationship between policy and procedure in this illustration.)

Very often procedures cut across functional lines and influence several areas within an organization. For example, the order-handling procedure usually will involve the sales department, the credit department, the accounting and billing departments, the warehouse, and the traffic or shipping department. In a hospital, the procedure for admitting patients will include the admitting office; the laboratory which performs tests and other routine work-ups on a patient being admitted; the dietician; the floor nurses; and so on. Procedures detail the precise sequence in which activities will be performed repeatedly under similar conditions. This is just as true of surgical procedures in a hospital as it is of administrative procedure in a government office or commercial enterprise.

Systems.   A system may be viewed as a *routine metaplan,* composed of several related procedures with a common objective.

Procedures can be viewed as sub-systems of the total system. Thus, the accounts receivable procedure and the accounts payable procedure, to which we previously referred, are components of an "accounting system" which may consist of several procedures in addition to these two.

Some systems are mechanical or engineering in nature. Generally these engineering or operative systems consist of smaller, self-contained sub-systems that feed into or contribute importantly to the major system. A materials-handling system in a distribution center is an example. The purpose of the system is to expedite the flow of merchandise as efficiently as possible with a minimum expenditure of time and handling. The system consists of self-contained sub-systems including motor driven belt conveyors; sections of gravity-type roller conveyors; mechanical or electrically controlled mechanisms to palletize, turn, and switch to different feeder lines; spiral chutes between floors; and timing devices to synchronize the movements. The materials-handling system just described would not be a "system" without the individual sub-systems that make it the total entity it is. It is a complete metaplan designed to achieve a specific objective. It is synergistic in that the results of the whole are greater than the sum of effects produced by its individual parts.

Methods.   Methods are plans that prescribe a way to do something. Generally methods are sub-units of a procedure; they spell out the techniques to be employed in making the procedure workable and effective. An effective procedure, in turn, contributes toward an effective system. Two illustrations will demonstrate this close interaction.

In a department store, *cycle billing* is a method often employed for charge account customers. Instead of sending out all bills on the same day of the month, one-third of the accounts may be billed on the tenth, another one-third on the twentieth, and the final one-third on the thirtieth. This distributes both the billing load and the receipt of funds more uniformly. It eliminates "bunching" or "peaking" of both billing resources and cash flow. The cycle billing method is a component of an accounts receivable procedure. The accounts receivable procedure, in turn, in a component of the store's accounting system. In a manufacturing or mill situation, product sampling may be a method utilized as one part of a quality control procedure. The latter is an integral part of the overall quality control system.

Rules.   Rules are specific statements of what should or should not be done. Some are posted in positive terms such as, "All employees will wash their hands before handling food." Others may take the negative form: "No one is permitted to enter if the red light is on." Some rules are rather complex and detailed in content; others are as simple as the "No Smoking" rule. Many rules originate internally within all functional areas; others are introduced by outside agencies. The rule governing the number of occupants permitted in a restaurant or an elevator is mandated by outside regulatory bodies such as the fire department or state safety regulations.

Rules have the greatest longevity of all routine detailed plans. They allow for no range of discretion or deviation. They must be followed precisely and observed strictly. It is important to note these essential differences between rules and policies.

When sharpened and refined through repeated use, some routine detailed plans *may eventually evolve into standards.* A highly developed and extremely effective procedure or method, which has been revised and improved until it has become the best way to accomplish a mission, begins to fit our definition of a technical standard. One way in which standards develop is through this evolutionary process of perfecting routine detailed plans.

COMPOSITE PLANS

In practice, efforts to solve problems or to achieve goals in government and industry, in business and non-business organizations, almost always result in some type of composite plan. In the normal course of planning an event, various types of plans are employed jointly or concurrently. A total plan probably includes one or more of several kinds of plans—master plans, policies, standards, and detailed plans. Whenever two or more categories of plans are employed for a specific purpose, the result is always a **composite plan.** This is the fifth group of plans as we have classified them.

While we normally do not think of it as such, planning the Christmas display windows in a department store is an illustration of the use of a composite plan. Let us briefly examine some facets of this composite.

- **Master planning** is involved, represented both by *long-range planning* of the Christmas window theme, one to two years in advance, and by the *short-range* (current) planning of the general window layouts, six to nine months in advance.

- **Policy** is involved. *Company policy* dictates that only departments, or items within departments, that fit the Christmas season will be displayed. *Department policy* (of the display department) stipulates that departments desiring to display merchandise in the windows must submit a list of suggested items not later than ninety days prior to November 15.

- **Standards** are involved. These include using fire-retardant and flame-resistant materials that meet the fire underwriters' code.

- **Detailed planning** is involved. It pinpoints the exact location of each item in the specific window. Blueprints may be drawn.

Although many more details would normally be involved in planning the Christmas window displays for department stores, this summary gives some idea of the various kinds of planning required. Since two or more major types of plans are committed to the overall objective, the "total plan" is a composite plan.

LIMITATIONS OF PLANNING

Under an orderly system of planning, more problems are solved, more missions are accomplished, fewer trials are required, fewer errors are made, less time is taken, and random activity is minimized. Yet despite the essential need for and the unquestioned value of planning, it must be recognized that the process of planning, like any other managing activity, has its limitations.

Accuracy. As can be observed from a comparison of long-range plans and routine detailed plans, the accuracy of planning varies inversely with the length of time over which the plan extends. Managers are likely to be more accurate in planning for something that will take place next week than in planning for something that will take place next year.

Difficulty.   The difficulty of planning varies directly with the size of the organization. It is usually less difficult to plan for a smaller organization than a larger one. It is less difficult to plan for a single department than for several departments or for an entire company with all of its departments. As establishments grow larger, or as departments within an organization expand, planning becomes more complex, requiring specialists to perform the function.

Cost.   A manager must always question the cost of planning in terms of time spent to formulate the plans, the manpower required to do the planning, and the resources needed to execute the plan. Inevitably, sound managerial practice requires a resolution of the question, "Is this plan economically justified?" If its cost is too high, an alternative plan that is economically feasible must be substituted. An exception to this principle is the unusual situation where a crash program is required to accomplish a particular mission. In that case, cost is no longer a primary consideration. If, for example, the objective is to "compress time," to get the job done as quickly as possible regardless of cost, then the plan devised will not be limited by short-run cost considerations. Long-run costs, however, cannot exceed anticipated long-run benefits.

Change.   Internal and external environmental changes are taking place all the time. When plans are formulated, an attempt is also made to anticipate changes that may occur and to accommodate these contingencies. Yet despite man's best attempts to predict changes within the organization, or in the macro-environment in which it operates, many unforeseen circumstances occur that make the original plan less workable or even obsolete. Plans, thus, are limited by unpredictable changes. This means that even the most carefully laid plans must be reviewed periodically and modified to accommodate shifts that have occurred since the original plan was proposed. There is a positive side to this constraint: it contributes to the *dynamic* nature of planning.

Competence of the planner.   A plan can be no better than the competence of the person who does the planning. Planning is an *art*. It takes a special type of person to plan. Not everyone is capable of planning, of solving organizational problems. A planner must possess not only skill, but intelligence and breadth of vision, and for long-range master planning must have the ability to forecast. One must be realistic and practical to be a business planner. Although not every creative person can be a good planner, every capable planner must be creative.

While planning is one of the major categories of activities in which all managers engage, non-managerial personnel should also plan. *Everyone,* even at the lowest levels in the organization, *should plan,* if only the immediate task before him. It has been demonstrated that individuals succeed best who establish ideas of what they are going to do before they start doing it. In personal planning, a person should ask, "Are my goals precisely defined so that I know what I am trying to do and how I should go about it?" If one wants to pursue *personal* goals, planning becomes a valuable ingredient in the art of "self-management." The processes of self-management and organizational management are identical. The only difference between them is in their goal orientation.

SUMMARY

The end result of both the planning process and the decision-making process is a plan of some kind. Since myriads of plans exist, it is helpful to classify them into major clusters, or types of plans, based upon similarities in their general application or the existence of some indigenous characteristics they possess. These categories include master plans, policies, standards, detailed plans, and composite plans. Although forecasting may provide data for planning at all managerial levels, it is essential to master planning. Forecasting techniques include trend forecasting, business indicators, market research, and econometric models.

Master plans can be divided into those which extend a short time span into the future (current master plans) and those which survey years ahead (long-range master plans). Policies, which are general guidelines, provide the framework for all other planning activities. Standards may be the very precise measurement criteria established by technical and engineering tests, or simply the norms of acceptable performance. Detailed plans are intended to be either single-purpose or routine. From a practical standpoint most planning probably embraces two or more of these major types of plans. In that case, the overall plan is a composite.

In all types of organizations plans are utilized, for the most part, for control purposes, to prevent problems from occurring, to correct undesirable situations, and to keep problems from getting out of hand.

Like any other managerial activity, planning has its limitations in terms of accuracy, difficulty, cost-effectiveness, competence of the planner, and the continuing need to adapt it to change.

KEY CONCEPTS

Master Plans	Econometric Models
Forecasting	Policies
Trend Forecasting	Standards
Business Indicators	Tolerance
Market Research	Detailed Plans
Statistical Sampling	Composite Plans

GLOSSARY

budget   Type of single-purpose detailed plan designed primarily to allocate resources for the purpose of control.

composite plan   Combination of two or more major types of plans employed concurrently for a specific purpose.

current master plan   Short-range master plan that prepares six months to a year ahead.

forecasting   Aspect of planning that deals with predicting changes in the environment in which an organization operates.

long-range master plan   Master plan that prepares five to twenty-five years ahead.

method   Routine plan that is a component of a procedure.

policy   Plan that deals with a recurring problem for which there is no routine solution by requiring the organization to recognize particular objectives and to work toward their fulfillment in some broadly defined way.

procedure   Routine detailed plan that provides a step-by-step sequence of tasks in a specific order.

program   Single-purpose metaplan that is an aggregate of several related projects with a common objective.

project   Single-purpose detailed plan that is usually part of a broader plan called a program.

rules   Routine plans, usually in the form of specific statements from which there can be no deviation.

schedule   Detailed plan that is concerned primarily with the time sequence of operations or tasks.

standard   Either the result of a scientific search for the best way to do something *(technical standard)* or a norm or accepted level of attainment or performance *(general standard)*.

system   Routine metaplan composed of several related procedures with a common objective.

tolerance   Permissible variation in an engineering or technical standard.

working standards   Engineering standards with built-in tolerances.

REVIEW QUESTIONS

1. List the major types of plans. What is the advantage of classifying all plans into one of these categories?

2. Name four techniques that are used in forecasting. What is your evaluation of the value of forecasting?

3. Three pre-conditions must always exist before a manager can use statistical sampling techniques. What are they? Apply this principle to testing the strength of the slotted end in wood screws that have just been produced.

4. Why can sales force estimates be an unreliable way to develop sales and earnings forecasts?

5. Is there a relationship between strategy and policy? Of what value to an organization is the existence of policies?

6. What is the purpose of strategy?

7. What does the term "standard" mean to you? Give an example from your personal experience of observation.

8. Give some examples of single-purpose plans.

9. Indicate some ways that schedules can be used.

10. Give some examples of routine detailed plans.

11. Can you think of any situation that utilizes a composite plan? Describe it.

12. How can planning be a "participative process?" Do you believe it should be? Be specific.

Part III

Organizing

The United States, like every other developed country, has become a society of organizations, each requiring many administrators and a high degree of managerial effectiveness.

Whenever an enterprise evolves beyond what an individual entrepreneur can accomplish, organization becomes necessary. Expansion leads to new activities, specialized personnel to perform them, and new departments and divisions to house them. Each of these components must be carefully fitted together in a manner that provides flexibility and adaptability in the balanced pursuit of company goals.

A manager must perceive organization as a physical and social arrangement in which capital and people are *both* essential. Neither can achieve significant results without the other. He must also recognize that the introduction of machinery or other equipment must take into account the fact that the people who will operate it are intelligent, self-seeking individuals with a broad spectrum of strengths and weaknesses, a variety of motives, and changing attitudes.

In organizing, managers seek appropriate ways to accomplish necessary goals. This means accommodating people and capital resources to each other by means of a carefully planned organizational structure within which activities are grouped in logical arrangements, and roles are designed and assigned to produce coordinated efforts.

Chapter 8 introduces some basic organizing concepts including the organizing process. In Chapters 9 through 13, the major components of the process are explored and the concepts of formal and informal organization are presented. Chapter 14 describes the main forms of organizational structure with particular emphasis on the characteristics of basic line and staff organization including their strengths and weaknesses. Adjuncts to basic line and staff organization and the newer organizational forms such as task force and matrix organization are covered in Chapter 15. The issue of centralization versus decentralization, as it applies to both authority and physical facilities, is explored in Chapter 16. Collectively, these nine chapters provide the basis for understanding the second major cluster of activities in the managing process—**organizing.**

Chapter 8

Organizing Concepts

However carefully conceived, well designed plans are meaningless by themselves and will never produce results. To make them useful and effective, they must be translated into action. Making it possible to put plans into action is one of the concerns of organizing. Organizing can be regarded, therefore, as an *implementing* function in the managing process. It, too, is a very dynamic process as we will soon observe. The interrelationship between planning and its implementation through an appropriate organization that leads to goal achievement must always be kept in mind.

WHEN DOES ORGANIZING OCCUR?

When a new enterprise is started, organizing activities become readily evident. If it is a manufacturing operation, the owners or their agents must decide where to locate; the types of machinery and equipment that will be required; the kinds of materials that must be purchased; the types of operations and services that will be performed; the personnel that will be needed to perform these operations and services; the physical plant or building that will house the business; and many other considerations. Similar activities take place in every kind of organization at its inception. It is necessary not only to make these decisions, but also to carry them out.

More common, although usually taken for granted, are the organizing activities that continue to occur during the life cycle of any existing business. They go on constantly, and must, if the firm is to remain dynamic and capable of adapting to changes that confront it. Adjustments are repeatedly called for. Typical conditions that require organizing activity are normal growth and decline; addition or discontinuance of departments or product lines; vertical and horizontal integration, mergers, or consolidations; deaths or separation of personnel; promotions or transfers; depreciation or obsolescence of plant and equipment; shifts in markets for finished products; and changes in types of raw materials used. In some industries, like automobile manufacturing, annual model changeover requires multiple organizing activities.

When too many division heads report directly to one executive, he finds himself unable to do an effective job. Consolidating or combining some divisions into groups each headed by a group executive who reports to the chief executive may solve the problem of organizational weakness at the top level. In this situation, there is a need to reduce the *span of management* to a workable number. Such *realignment* changes the structure. It too is an organizing activity.

When plans change, it is not always possible to utilize the existing organization to implement the change. There are times when partial or total *reorganization* is necessary because radical changes are involved. Dropping an unsuccessful product from the line can produce substantial reorganizing activities which are an adjustment from an undesirable to a more favorable state of affairs. This occurred in 1959 when Ford discontinued production of the Edsel at an estimated loss of $250 million, and in 1971 when, after ten years of manufacture, Du Pont ceased the production of Corfam, a leather substitute, and absorbed a loss estimated at $100 million. These are examples of radical rather than typical reorganizations. Behind the scenes, even for these giants in industry, some financial reorganization was required to accommodate the huge physical and personnel adjustments connected with these product discontinuances.

Some organizations, faced with a threat to survival, undergo drastic corporate and *financial reorganization or recapitalization* that includes closing plants, selling unprofitable divisions, discontinuing services, substituting long-term for short-term debts, converting debt to equity financing, and selling assets to improve liquidity. American Motors and Penn Central are classic examples.

THE COMPONENTS OF AN ORGANIZATION

When two or more elements interact for a common purpose, a basic **system** exists. If we substitute the word "people" for "elements," the statement becomes a definition of a simplified organization. Thus, every organization can also be viewed as a system.

The modern organization is a highly complex system designed by its managers to serve as the vehicle for the pursuit of corporate objectives. In such an organization, the following components are *always* present:

1. **Activities and tasks.** Ideas and things are being created, built, stored, distributed, and converted for specific purposes.
2. **People.** Those who do the creating and producing, and those who manage them.
3. **Capital.** The money and machinery that make it possible for people to carry out the various activities by performing designated tasks.

4. **Structure.** The arrangement and relationships of activities, tasks, people, and capital that permit them to interact in a meaningful way.

Since the components are never static, but change continually, and since the relationships also change continually, the modern organization can be viewed as a dynamic as well as a complex system.

ORGANIZATIONAL DESIGN

The manner in which the components of an organization interrelate and interact influences the design of an organization. Therefore there is no one best way to design an organization and its sub-units. Every organizational unit is custom-made. What is appropriate in one set of circumstances may be highly inappropriate in another (contingency situations).

The classical organizational design, associated with such proponents as Henry Fayol, Frederick Taylor, Luther Gulick, Max Weber, James Mooney, and others, is depicted as a pyramid with the few executive positions at the apex and the many subordinate positions at the base. Each enterprise function calls for specialized competence and appropriate authority. Where operations are routine, calling for only a moderate level of skill and ability, they require a more highly structured type of organization. Activities are regulated by policies, procedures, and rules. Human endeavors are controlled mechanistically by acceptance of responsibility that accompanies acceptance of a position in the hierarchy. People are expected to comply with directives, regulations, and standard operating methods which prescribe precisely how duties are to be performed. Authority is centralized, and authority and accountability relationships are well-defined. Such an organization has been described as **mechanistic.** This type of organization is appropriate for mass production industries such as automobile production.

Where operations are more varied and utilize a higher degree of technical knowledge and skill, they require a less highly structured type of organization. The behavioral organization design, associated with advocates of industrial humanism such as Elton Mayo, Chester Barnard, Rensis Likert, Chris Argyris, and others, deemphasizes formal authority. Participation in decision making at lower levels is encouraged. Jobs are designed to fit individuals, rather than being defined by the classical division of labor. Informality is encouraged; role and rank are minimized. Skill and professional training are the basis for differentiation. Greater delegation is possible, and the individual has a major voice in what he does and how he does it. This type of organization is described as **organic.** It is appropriate for research and development activities and the performance of staff functions.[1]

---

[1] For a description of staff functions, the reader is referred to Chapter 14.

Organization models can be viewed as two extremes on a continuum with the formal, or mechanistic, at one end and the organic at the other. Most modern organizations probably lie between these extremes in their organizational design.

Additional Determinants of Design

The size of an organization, in terms of the number of people employed, units produced, share of the market, revenues, assets, or number of stockholders, influences the kinds of coordination, management information systems, and other interacting relationships—hence the organization design. While size is relative, most of the concepts covered in this book apply to larger rather than smaller organizations. This is so not because smaller organizations do not have to be managed. Indeed, they do. In a smaller organization, however, relationships between managers and employees are more personal and less formal, with face-to-face contacts more frequent than in large groups. Since most business organizations are small, averaging fewer than seven employees, many organizing concepts such as collective bargaining, worker alienation, line and staff relationships, decentralization, training, and indoctrination will not concern them. A personnel department is unnecessary in an organization of ten, fifteen, or twenty people.

In referring to administrative organizations, particularly non-profit organizations, C. Northcote Parkinson satirically notes that the number of persons tends to multiply at a pre-determinable annual rate, even if the workload is decreasing. As long as time or space is available, if a vacuum exists, administrators will fill it by hiring more employees, specialists, and assistants. These will have to be serviced by other persons and activities. The organization increases in size and complexity. This helps the administrator to justify his importance and to fulfill his status needs. Parkinson's study of the British Admiralty led to these conclusions, which have become known as **Parkinson's Law.**[2] Frequently these situations are termed empire building. The inference can be drawn that personal considerations may also influence the design of organizations.

The nature of the task is another important influence on organizational design. In her Tavistock studies conducted in England, Joan Woodward found that successful industrial firms with different production technologies were characterized by different types of organizational structure.[3] Job-shop, mass production, and continuous process type firms all have different formal structures because the "technology" is different in each. Her investigations indicate that unit production and continuous process production are

---

[2]C. Northcote Parkinson, Parkinson's Law and Other Studies in Administration (Boston, Mass: Houghton Mifflin Company, 1957).

[3]Joan Woodward, Industrial Organization: Theory and Practice, (Fairlawn, N.J.: Oxford University Press, 1965).

more likely to resemble organic organizations, whereas mass production is mechanistic. Charles Perrow also considers technology to be a major influence on organizational design.[4]

Jay Galbraith has observed that as technology changes, a complex organization adjusts its structure in order to survive and remain effective.[5] There is general agreement that different structures and leadership techniques are needed for different situations (contingencies). Even in the production of a single product, different structures may be called for at different stages of production. Furthermore, a product or idea in the initial development stage may require a non-bureaucratic structure; when it advances to the production or distribution stage, the structure and style of leadership may change to a more bureaucratic one.

As a firm grows in size and complexity, and as it adapts to changing internal and external environmental conditions and pressures, its formal structure changes. Perrow describes a "mixed model" in which bureaucratic and adaptive structures may be found in the same organization.[6] Mixed structures probably characterize most large organizations today. Structural types emerge, develop, and become modified. They are discernible in all stages during the life of a firm.

THE METHOD OF ORGANIZING

In general, a manager performing the function of organizing will do the following things in the following order:

1. Consult the original plan for answers to such basic questions as: What has to be done? How? What resources are required? (understanding the overall plan)

2. Define enterprise activities that will be essential and the tasks required to implement them.

3. Obtain the appropriate people and equipment to do the job. (includes staffing)

4. Assign and condition these resources to their respective tasks. (includes staffing)

5. Integrate the personnel and tasks into some sort of structural order to make coordination and control possible. (This gives rise to formal organization.)

---

[4]Charles Perrow, "A Framework for the Comparative Analysis of Organizations," *American Sociological Review*, April 1967, pp. 194–208.

[5]Jay Galbraith, *Designing Complex Organizations* (Reading, Mass.: Addison-Wesley, 1973).

[6]Charles Perrow, *Complex Organizations: A Critical Essay*, (Glenview, Ill.: Scott, Foresman & Co., 1972).

Despite the fact that these are the typical steps in the process of organizing, there is far from universal agreement that this method should prevail. A number of positions have been advanced in opposition to it. Let us examine some of them.

Newman, Summer, and Warren[7] take the position that planning cannot take place without an organization to do the planning; therefore, organizing activities must precede planning activities. Actually, this is not the case since one individual can plan—it does not require the prior existence of an organization. Where complex planning does require an organization, someone still has to plan or create the "organization" to do further planning.

Others who advocate organizing first and planning later take the position that potentially valuable employees should be hired whether there are existing jobs for them or not, on the grounds that their services will eventually be needed.

This point of view can be justified only under unusual circumstances. If there is a shortage of professional or technically trained personnel, like highly specialized research chemists or computer technologists, an organization may decide to hire them whenever they are available regardless of the immediate need for their services. The institution knows it will need them eventually, as it expands. It decides to procure them now and find specific uses for their services later. Recruiting outstanding graduates from universities to become part of an executive development pool, for assignment to needed areas at a later date, is another illustration of organizing first and planning for specific use later. Many large firms do this. The executive development recruits are given a general introduction to the firm's operations, its policies, its long-range objectives, and its way of doing things. They may be given temporary assignments, perhaps rotated among various departments or divisions until a specific opening occurs. At that point, one of the trainees is given a definite assignment.

Obviously, this would not be the typical way one would go about staffing his entire organization—selecting people and machines first and finding a use for them eventually. Under certain conditions, however, it does make sense to do so.

THE ORGANIZING PROCESS

Like planning, organizing activities are an ongoing, never-ending process from the inception of an organization throughout its continued existence. Organizing, therefore, possesses the characteristics of being ephemeral because it is so dynamic.

---

[7]William H. Newman, Charles E. Summer, and E. Kirby Warren, *The Process of Management*, 3rd ed. (Englewood Cliffs, N. J.: Prentice-Hall, Inc., 1972).

Organizing is that *cluster of activities in the managing process which consists of selecting and combining suitable resources (personnel and capital) and integrating them into a structure of relationships that enables them to carry out the planned activity in a coordinated and controlled way.*

The success of any enterprise is in larger measure a reflection of its organization, but an organization does not come into being by chance or accidental happenstance. While it is a goal seeking and goal attaining vehicle, it is always the product of a continuing and refining process that sustains it and keeps it vital.

Figure 8-1.   The organizing process model.

Basically, organizing as a dynamic process consists of the following four major sub-processes:

1. Designing enterprise functions and their relationships.
2. Designing jobs and their relationships.
3. Procuring of personnel and capital to do the jobs.
4. Assigning and conditioning personnel and capital to their respective roles.

These essential steps in the process are depicted by the model in Figure 8-1. They will be discussed later in detail, each in a separate chapter.

The end product of organizing is a viable organization which acts as the vehicle for accomplishing the missions its managers set for it. Utilizing the process, managers create the organization; the organization, in turn, creates and develops the managers it needs at all levels to perpetuate the organization. It is an iterative relationship.

THE IMPORTANCE OF ORGANIZING

Some theorists question the desirability of formal organization. They believe it restricts individuals to particular pigeonholes in the structure, limiting their opportunities and usefulness. Yet as long as relationships exist and interaction occurs, formal structure will also exist. Relationships are the key to structure. This is a basic organizing principle.

Despite weaknesses inherent in any organization, many of which can be mitigated, the strengths and advantages of organization far outweigh its disadvantages. Comprehensive plans cannot be implemented without organization, nor can controlling be exercised without it. In fact, universities, hospitals, government agencies, churches, and business firms could not exist in our society without organizing activities and the presence of some type of structural order.

If the method of organizing has limitations, as it undoubtedly does, it poses a challenge to managers to do something to correct its undesirable aspects. Perhaps expanding the meaning of jobs, encouraging participative activities among employees, utilizing management by objectives where it is possible to do so, and properly matching people with their respective jobs so that talents are neither under-nor over-employed, are some means that can be used to improve the process.[8]

SUMMARY

The best laid plans have no value unless they are put into effect. Implementing any intended action to solve a problem or achieve some desired end requires resources. Acquiring or developing these resources, and blending them into a workable arrangement is the province of organizing.

Every organization consists of basic elements or components. Always present are activities and tasks, people, capital, and structure. Since these elements are fluid, changing constantly in either an evolutionary or planned manner, the organization also changes.

Organizing, therefore, is a never-ending essential process. It is a part of the total process of managing. This is true in all enterprises, both profit and non-profit. The organizational design is influenced by the environment, technology in which the enterprise operates, organizational size, personal ambitions of administrators, and other forces. Some organizations have been described as mechanistic and others as organic. Both are probably extreme points of view.

Regardless of the ultimate design that it produces, organizing is a never-ending, essential process; a dynamic sub-function of the total managing process. Basic ingredients in the process of organizing are the four steps: designing enterprise functions and their relationships, designing jobs and their relationships, procuring of personnel and capital, and assigning and conditioning personnel and capital to their respective roles.

Despite their weaknesses, formal organizations are essential. Institutions could not prevail without the presence of organizing activities and some sort of structural order.

---

[8]Ways to reduce structural rigidity are discussed at length in Chapter 11.

KEY CONCEPTS

Components of an Organization	Parkinson's Law
Mechanistic Organization	Method of Organizing
Organic Organization	The Organizing Process

GLOSSARY

organization   The end result of the organizing process.

organizing   A major component of managing which consists of selecting and combining appropriate resources (personnel and capital) and integrating them into a structure of relationships that enables them to carry out plans in a coordinated and controlled way.

system   Any situation in which two or more elements interact for a common purpose.

REVIEW QUESTIONS

1. Based on your own experience or observations, give some examples of organizational change.
2. In your own words, describe *(a)* a mechanistic organization; *(b)* an organic organization. Give an example of each.
3. Do you believe there is validity in Parkinson's Law? Defend your position.
4. Do you agree with the theory that organizing should precede planning?
5. What are the steps in the organizing process?
6. Do you believe the process of organizing is important? Why?

Chapter 9

Designing Enterprise Functions and Their Relationships

Before he can design a building an architect must know the kinds of activities that will take place in it, the reasons why they will occur, and whether some are associated in any way with others. So, too, must a manager know the kinds of activities that will be necessary to implement some plan or to solve some problem. He must also know their intended purpose and how they will be performed before he can design the appropriate organizational structure to accommodate them. The answer to a portion of his query may be found in the *master plan*, if one exists, which covers his area of jurisdiction, and within the framework of existing *policies*.

Obviously, activities to be considered will either be of a non-management or of a management nature. If they are the former, the manager will be concerned with buying, selling, operating, and facilitating activities; if the latter, his focus will be on planning, organizing, activating, and controlling functions. Some activities may be accommodated in the same organizational structure; others will require separate structures, depending on the contingencies that exist at the time.

ESTABLISHING NON-MANAGEMENT FUNCTIONS

The multiple activities that are necessary in a specific enterprise or in a given department must be clearly and concisely understood. Furthermore, decisions to conduct specialized activities effectively must be particularized. The *specific* needs and objectives of each institution or department must always be the focus of attention. This is essential, since the requirements of no two organizations are identical. The same organizing decision may be justified for one and completely unjustified for another. Let us look at some examples of this organizing principle.

In Company A, producing school chairs made of metal tubing with seats and backs of molded plastic, the operating functions (manufacturing) might include cutting, bending, grinding, drilling, polishing, and inspecting the metal parts; forming and inspecting the molded parts; and assembling the finished product. In Company B, producing a similar school chair, the manufacturing activities might include only cutting, bending, welding, polishing, and inspecting the metal parts; inspecting molded parts purchased from an outside vendor; and assembling the finished product. Although the two companies make the same product, the organizational structure in Company B differs from that in Company A. Company B has fewer departments, fewer manufacturing processes, and some that are totally different from those in Company A. Each company has operating activities especially designed for it, although the goal of each firm is identical.

The decision to assign an activity to one department rather than another depends on the logic of each enterprise's particular operations. Let us compare the selling and the buying functions in a department store. "Selling" includes such diverse activities as newspaper advertising, mailing circulars along with customer statements, waiting on customers, self-service, and similar sales efforts. "Buying" encompasses purchasing merchandise to be sold, pricing, displaying merchandise within the department for effective selling, markdowns when merchandise does not sell readily, determining which items will be advertised in the newspapers, how much advertising space to use, and similar decisions. Note that though the buyer makes decisions regarding "pricing," "displaying merchandise," "markdowns," "how much advertising space to use," and "what items to advertise," by their nature these are selling or merchandising activities. Yet in a department store, the buyer engages in many activities that are of a selling rather than a strictly buying nature since they are so closely interrelated in that type of business. The buyer generally will not be concerned with buying fixtures, mannequins, pin tickets, or even the advertising space to be used. Those activities will be performed elsewhere in the organization, by the purchasing department and the advertising department, where they can be handled more efficiently by experts in those areas of the store's operation. Thus in a department store not all buying activities are performed by its buyers, whereas many activities of a sales and merchandising nature are.

A railroad offers another example of how activities are placed in certain departments to suit its purposes and yet might be housed in entirely different departments in some other type of enterprise. In a railroad, the buying function is called purchasing. It includes purchasing materials and equipment. These have to be inspected when they arrive to insure they meet specifications. Inspection is performed by a section housed within the purchasing department. The inspected material must be stored somewhere. This requires a "stores keeping" section within the purchasing function. Stores keeping, or inventory maintenance, is usually part of the operating function in other types of business. At some point, a railroad accumulates a lot of scrap from worn-out equipment, flat car wheels, and items that have become obsolete. The sale of such material is handled by the "scrap disposal" section, a unit within the purchasing function. By its nature, scrap disposal is a selling activity, yet in a railroad it is perfectly logical for it to be located in the purchasing department. Who in the railroad is better qualified to determine to whom scrap items should be sold and at what price than the persons who bought the items originally? One could hardly expect the traffic department, responsible for selling passenger and freight service, to sell scrap also merely because scrap disposal is nominally a selling activity.

Where an enterprise function is housed in an organization is very often a matter of expediency. The function itself may be a temporary one. During World War II, for example, a manufacturer of materials handling equipment found it necessary to comply with the regulations of the War Production Board on end-use priority allocations of scarce resources like steel, ball bearings, motors, and similar items that were also sorely needed in the war effort. It became necessary to appoint someone in the company to the position of "priorities administrator." The assignment was given to its director of advertising and sales promotion, whose normal activities were curtailed because of the war. Thus priorities administration with its complement of assistants, clerical staff, and secretaries became housed in the advertising department of that company. Probably in no other company in the country was its priorities manager also its advertising manager. For that company, at that time, it made sense. With the termination of the war, the need for priorities administration terminated also.

Fixing the boundaries for particular activities and placing them where they should be in the organizational design are matters for each manager to decide. He must do what is best for his enterprise, or his area of jurisdiction in that enterprise, regardless of how it is done elsewhere, including other departments within his own institution. What may be a buying function in another company may be perceived to be part of the selling function in his.

ESTABLISHING MANAGEMENT FUNCTIONS

Managing activities must also be defined in terms of their specific purposes within a specific management area. In some enterprises, it may be necessary to designate certain individuals, or to establish separate organizational units, to engage in *planning*. A bank may require the special skills of an economist to develop forecasts as part of its corporate planning activities. A large industrial firm may require the services of an entire planning department including several economists, researchers, analysts, technicians, and other long-range planning specialists. The executive in charge may be a vice-president of corporate planning.

The performance of various *organizing* activities may require specialists also. To do a thorough job of staffing may necessitate establishing a personnel department. Some personnel departments may need skilled interviewers; an interviewing section would be established. Psychological testing may be a component of the personnel activity; this may require a testing section staffed by psychologists and trained technicians to administer and evaluate tests.

In the area of *controlling,* some enterprises require a systems department. Others need a comptroller's office, a payroll department, an accounts payable department, accounts receivable department, and so on. When the need is apparent, an organization is created to satisfy it.

Each enterprise, large and small, must examine and define its managing activities and requirements to achieve specific objectives or to tackle specific problems. Since no two firms or their problems are exactly alike, neither will their managing activities be exactly alike, and neither will the structure that houses these activities be exactly alike. Each firm's management organization must be custom tailored to its specific needs.

CAPITAL FUNCTIONS

In most firms, capital functions involve the management of funds designated for capital expenditures. In this sense, they are part of the total managing function and are usually administered by top-level managers. Usually these funds are part of a revolving or rotating fund in which monies are budgeted for the various capital needs of the company. Funds may be included in the overall capital budget for expansion, capital improvement, and similar needs, or earmarked for specific purposes such as procuring machinery and office equipment, paying advertising and promotional expenses, financing inventory, carrying accounts receivable, and other pre-planned uses. Capital considerations must always be included in the organizational design because of their ability to influence the structure. The work that people do and the relationships between jobs frequently depend on the kinds of equipment and capital facilities that are available.

DESIGN PATTERNS (CONFIGURATIONS)

Largely because of changing technologies and other environmental factors, complex organizations continue to modify their organizational design. How do executives choose appropriate designs for their organizations? Most have found it desirable, particularly for expanding organizations, to consolidate functions into practical, workable units in which similar or homogeneous activities can be performed. This grouping of similar activities tends to improve efficiency, increase organizational specialization, and minimize the costs of overall coordination. The ways in which these units relate to each other, and to the corporate whole of which they are a part, determines the overall organizational design.

When activities are grouped because they have similar characteristics, certain patterns or configurations emerge. Typically, activities are grouped according to (1) major enterprise functions (marketing, engineering, research, manufacturing, and so forth); (2) product lines or services; (3) territory or geographic area; (4) customers served; or (5) process or equipment (forging, heat sealing, cutting, and so on). Each of these has costs and rewards associated with it. The nature of these organizational design patterns, as they are observed in actual practice, and their relative merits are described in the sections that follow. The overall structure of most enterprises represents a combination of several or all of these patterns.

Functional Divisions

This structural pattern reflects the separation of all operations into the major ongoing activities such as buying, selling, operating, managing, and facilitating. The formal structure resulting from such a separation of functions in a business enterprise is shown in Figure 9-1. This pattern of organization could prevail in a small business, or one in which the line of products or services being produced and distributed remains relatively limited.

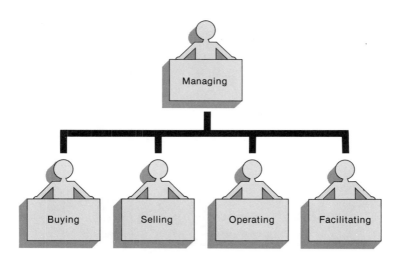

Figure 9-1.   Organizational structure by major business functions.

Functional divisions within an enterprise (for example, production, marketing, and research in industry; emergency room, intensive care, and X-ray in hospitals) have integral, specialized orientations which must be structured specially in order to advance the productivity and effectiveness of each, and the total effectiveness of the organization as a whole. Functional grouping encourages the acquisition and continued development of a high degree of specialization of both personnel and equipment and optimum utilization of these specialized inputs. It tends to minimize duplication of

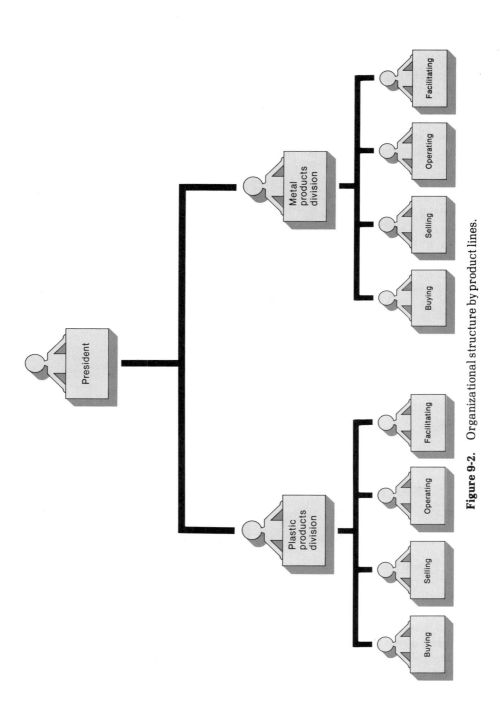

Figure 9-2.   Organizational structure by product lines.

resources by pooling and sharing them across product or service lines. On the other hand, if it becomes important to complete all tasks on all products at the same time without sacrificing quality, this is not possible under the functional arrangement. It would require long lead times, expert scheduling, and tight controls to expedite the delivery of raw materials and sub-assemblies where and when needed. In a sense, that function becomes overloaded.

Product or Service Divisions

An institution which offers diverse products or services may find it expedient to develop separate organizational units to house them. If products are predominant, each product division should be large enough to justify and sustain its own major functional areas. For example, General Motors has Chevrolet, Pontiac, Buick, and Cadillac divisions. Each has an independent sales organization, production facilities, service and management personnel. Fundamentally, GM is differentiated and structured along product lines. In department stores and discount stores, operations are often departmentalized by groups of related products, each with its own merchandise buyer. In a modern bank, organizational units to perform the varied lending services include the commercial, industrial, installment, and personal loan departments, each with its separate, specialized personnel. Hospitals offer inpatient and outpatient services, each with separate facilities and staff.

Organizational structures based on product lines and major services are portrayed by the charts in Figures 9-2 and 9-3 respectively. Figure 9-2 is

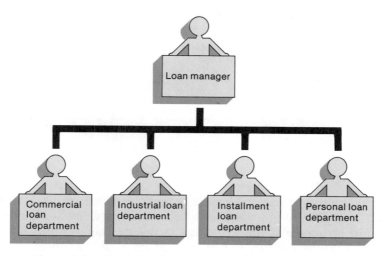

Figure 9-3.   Organizational structure by services offered.

a combination of a primary pattern based on independent product divisions, and a secondary pattern of supporting functional activities for each product offering. This arrangement is economically feasible only when the importance or magnitude of each product division can sustain separate and independent functional organizations.

Territorial or Geographic Divisions

Differentiation by territory or geographic areas is employed when the evolving enterprise has some of its important activities dispersed geographically. By grouping activities or services into territorial units, the enterprise may be able to capitalize on local conditions. Physical plants or warehouses may be grouped into "Western Division," "Southern Division," "Overseas Division," and similar designations. Territorial differentiation is particularly useful in the selling function where the special nature of geographic markets often calls for specialized sales activities. Thus the United States may be divided into territories or regions. Each would have a sales organization whose manager would report directly to the national sales manager. This type of differentiation is illustrated in Figure 9-4.

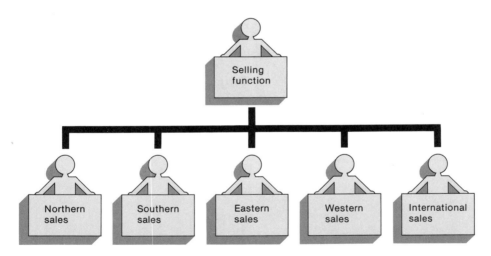

Figure 9-4.   Organizational structure by territory.

Customer Divisions

When an expanding company determines that increased emphasis should be placed on its ability to provide special customer services, it may design a portion of its structure for that purpose. In this manner, additional specialized services can be offered. In a large modern bank, the commercial loan department often is organized according to the kinds of customers served.

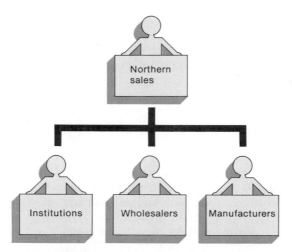

Figure 9-5.   Organizational structure by type of customer served.

The bank may assign certain loan officers to handle firms engaged in food processing; others to serve firms in textiles, apparel, and related businesses; and still others to service companies in chemical, petroleum, and paper products. In other words, the commercial loan officers service particular customer categories of business loans and no others. They become specialists in those areas, talk the language of the firms in those areas, and understand the problems peculiar to those areas. In terms of marketing channels, companies that are large enough to do so often restructure their sales efforts to cater to specific types of customers in order to serve them more effectively. Thus they may have separate sales forces to solicit more intensively and in a more specialized fashion each class of customer—institutions, wholesalers, manufacturers, and so forth.

Figure 9-5 shows "Northern Sales" subdivided according to customers served. Similar customer concentration could be developed in other territorial divisions if the situation warrants it.

An organization structured in terms of customers served enables its sales and technical personnel to become very familiar with problems and conditions that prevail in the channel of distribution they service and in which they become specialists. The representative who calls on institutional users, including hospitals, schools, hotels, and similar accounts, does not call on wholesalers or manufacturers. Similarly, the representative who sells wholesalers and manufacturers does not sell to institutions. Each becomes expert in his respective area. Normally, this benefits the salesman, the customer, and the parent company.

Process or Equipment Divisions

Differentiation by process or equipment becomes a logical form of organization where the operations require specialized skills, or their technological nature requires some degree of special concentration. Such differentiation is generally more applicable in the operating and facilitating areas of the organization than in other areas. An oil company may have separate organizations for different processes. As an example, it may have an oil exploration division, a refining division, and a petrochemical division. Each structure, with special equipment and personnel, is organized around a distinctive process. It makes good sense to concentrate resources where they are needed and where the nature of the process logically requires them to be separately housed. A chemical company or a pharmaceutical company may establish an organization with specialized equipment and technicians to perform operations of a "batch production" type, and a completely different organization for operations of a "continuous production" type. Different technologies call for different structural design. A printing plant may maintain a "job shop" to handle short printing runs, using small and relatively slow equipment. It may also have a "production shop" to produce continuous, large-quantity runs, utilizing larger, high-speed presses. From a practical standpoint, it could not afford to run a small job through its production shop, nor could it afford to produce a large-quantity order in its job shop. The printing company, in this case, maintains two distinct organizational structures to take care of two dissimilar process or equipment situations even though both involve printing.

Revision of Organizational Designs

For strategic reasons, an organization may sometimes recast its entire organizational design through a process of reorganization or realignment of previously consolidated activities. New patterns emerge. General Foods, often referred to as a case study of marketing enterprise and effective management, reorganized in 1973 in order to reverse a three-year decline in profit margins. Four of the five products divisions, including Post cereals and Birdseye frozen foods, were abolished. They were replaced by basic units (beverage, breakfast, main meal, desserts, and pet foods) to reflect categories of consumer demand and to provide what its chairman called "a better strategic focus against a given market segment."[1]

Mixed Patterns of Organization

Most large industrial and commercial firms, through growth and diversification, eventually develop such varied interests—unrelated products, ser-

---

[1]James L. Ferguson, Chairman, General Foods Corporation, as quoted by Marylin Bender, *New York Times*, June 30, 1974.

vices, customers, strategies, and techniques—that it is not feasible for all of them to be served within a single type of organization structure. As a result, combinations of all five patterns of organization are employed to accomodate the diversity. To illustrate, let us examine the structure of an existing diversified company. Interco, Inc., with sales exceeding $1 billion annually, operates in three major areas: apparel factories; general retail merchandise group; shoe factories, shoe stores, and shoe departments. Its general retail merchandise group consists of 569 retail stores separated into 4 major divisions: Central Hardware Company, Eagle Discount Stores, P. N. Hirsch & Company (256 junior department stores in small to medium-size communities in 16 states), and Sam Shainberg Company (family-type specialty stores in the South). The central Hardware Company division operates 21 giant hardware, lumber, and building materials supermarket stores in Missouri, Indiana, and California. It also has a wholesale division that distributes to independent hardware dealers. Interco's shoe factories include Florsheim Shoe Company with twelve factories; International Shoe Company (the largest in the world) with nineteen modern or updated facilities including a huge, electronically operated, conveyorized warehouse; and Interco Savage Ltd., with six plants in Canada. Each factory produces only certain types of shoes for men, women, and children, depending on the manufacturing process employed, special equipment required, and other production considerations. Thus a cursory glance at the operations of this multi-faceted firm reveals corporate pursuits requiring differentiated organization structures, and combinations of them, based upon major business activities, product lines, territory and geographic considerations, customers served, and process or equipment needed. Similar observations can be made of most large firms in every industry.

Despite their uniqueness, it is obvious that all enterprise functions are interrelated. Non-management functions are related; so too are managing functions related. Non-management and management functions are also closely related. It is also a fact that specific jobs performed within each functional area are related to each other, and to jobs in other functional areas. The relationships may be between one managerial job and another managerial job; between a managerial job and a non-managerial job; and between two or more non-managerial jobs. These multi-relationships will become more apparent as the next step in the process of organizing, that of designing jobs and their relationships, is analyzed in the chapter that follows.

SUMMARY

The first step in the organizing process is to identify and define the activities that are essential to comply with the intent of a planned course of action or to realize some desired goal. These activities will either be managerial or non-managerial. In either case, they must be designed to fit the needs of the particular decision maker and the specific organizational unit to which they relate. Activities that may be justified in one organization may not be suitable for another. No two enterprises, even with similar purposes, are organized precisely alike to accomplish their missions.

In order to promote specialization, improve efficiency, reduce costs, and accommodate to technological and other environmental influences, managers often will combine or consolidate various activities that have some commonality. As a result, design patterns emerge based on major enterprise functions; products or services; territory or geography; customers; and processes and equipment. Most large organizations require combinations of these patterns.

The relationships between the activities within each pattern, and the interactions between the various design patterns, produce the overall structural design. Since relationships are never static but continually change, so too does the overall structure.

KEY CONCEPTS

Designing Non-Management   Designing Management Functions
    Functions   Design Patterns (Configurations)

REVIEW QUESTIONS

1. Why does an organization have to be "tailor-made"?
2. List five bases that underlie the organizational design patterns in most enterprises.
3. What organizational patterns are present in the university you are attending? In your place of work?
4. Do different technologies influence organizational design? Explain.
5. Under what conditions would you recommend organization by products rather than organization by major enterprise functions?
6. Could all of the design patterns discussed in this chapter ever appear simultaneously in an organization? Defend your answer.

Chapter 10

Designing Jobs
and
Their Relationships

Not only must each function be carefully defined, but jobs within each functional area also must be carefully described. Kinds of work must be expressed in terms of amounts of work to be done, and each task must be placed into proper relationship with every other task.

If we know, for example, that necessary operations in the manufacture of metal school chairs include cutting, grinding, welding, drilling, polishing, and inspecting of components, we must also know what kinds and amounts of work constitute "cutting," "grinding," "welding," and so on. Cutting may involve several workers. One person may bring lengths of tubing to the person who operates the actual cutting machine, and a third person may stack the cut pieces on a truck for transport to the next point. In this illustration, operations in the cutting department comprise three different types of work. Furthermore, the relationship between the cutting operation and any that follow must be established. Is the next step welding or drilling? What kinds of work take place in those areas and how do they relate to subsequent stages in the production process? What does a welder do? A driller? What tools do they use? What responsibilities does the inspector have? A manager must have this information as he designs specific jobs and their relationships.

The definition of jobs and their relationships is no simple task. A number of extremely important organizing activities take place before jobs and their relationships are finally established. The major components in this process are (1) job analysis, (2) job definition, and (3) job classification. We shall examine all three to see how they contribute to an understanding of job design and job relationships.

JOB ANALYSIS

A **job** is *the kind and amount of work to be performed by a person or a piece of equipment within a given time period.* To determine this in a precise fashion requires job analysis. *Job analysis means breaking down a job into its components to determine its content.* It involves observation, as well as collection, identification, and classification of information about all phases of the job under study, whether an existing job or one that is to be created. The job is dissected to establish what is to be done, work units, frequency of performance, the tools and equipment used, the skills required, and any major problems connected with it. All the detailed tasks that go into each job are noted, with their respective purposes.

Data can be accumulated in several ways. For an existing job, a skilled job analyst may arrange meetings with an employee holding the job, observe

FACTORY JOB DESCRIPTION   CODE NO.: D-69

FINAL REVISION   GRADE: 1
                                                             DATE:
        JOB CLASSIFICATION—Inspector-Subassembly   ANALYST:

Element	Job specification
Duties	Inspect subassemblies at progressive stages and completed major assemblies such as forward fuselage, center fuselage, aft fuselage, inner and outer wing, empennage, nose, and in spacecraft such items as radar and rendezvous section, reaction control system section, crew compartment, adapter section, and preliminary fit of heat shield before two major modules or major assemblies are joined together. Inspect jig and template locations, the spline of subassemblies, installation of all non-electrical subassembly components, weld assemblies, compartment sealing, tank installation, location in ream fixtures and hole sizes. Inspect ground support equipment, landing gears, canopies, and all pressurization to determine structural soundness. Inspect final shakedown and mechanical operations of subassemblies and completed major assemblies. Use a variety of inspection aids and precision measuring instruments. Prepare documents incidental to the accomplishment of inspection function.
Educational and/or training requirements*	Must have a knowledge of shop mathematics, a working knowledge of specifications, assembly and fabrication procedures, and shop practice. Work from information such as drawings, templates, master layouts, inspection, and assembly fixtures.
Experience required*	1 to 3 years aircraft or spacecraft experience
Occupation or operation requirement*	Perform unusual and difficult work where standard or recognized methods may not be available. Considerable judgment required. Responsible for the proper performance of assignments and the prudent handling of product, tools and equipment. May work with the assistance of and/or instruct 3 or less lower graded employees.

*Elements marked with an asterisk are elements usually required but are not necessarily a requisite to the peformance of the duties described above.

Figure 10-1.   Factory job description. (From McDonnell Aircraft, September 1960.)

what is being done, and ask questions about the job and what the worker does. The observations and answers are then recorded. This technique is particularly satisfactory for jobs of a higher skill level, or those requiring special ability, including a high degree of mental aptitude. Research or creative work would be examples. Where jobs are scattered geographically, as in a multi-plant operation, carefully prepared questionnaires may be sent out to the appropriate employees and the replies collated, analyzed, and then integrated by the job analyst. For a new job, the analysis would be made by the manager of the jurisdiction in which the newly created position fits, or by a trained staff specialist. In either case, the purpose of the job, why it is needed, the tasks involved, the conditions under which it will be performed, and other pertinent questions will be answered before the new position becomes a reality.

JOB DEFINITION

After the job analysis has been completed, the information can be consolidated in written form as part of the formal **job definition.** Every well-conceived job definition should always consist of two parts: (1) the **job description,** which enumerates the duties to be performed, and the authority, responsibility, and accountability inherent in performing the job; and (2) the **job specification,** which states the qualifications an individual must possess to perform the job. Job analysis provides the data for both segments of the job definition.

Most job definitions are poorly planned and poorly written. There is little uniformity with respect to format or kinds of information that are included. Often the terminology used is also confusing. Some definitions cover only job descriptions, ignoring job specifications (personal qualifications). Others confuse the terms *duties* and *responsibilities,* or use them interchangeably. Most definitions are prepared by someone in the personnel department. In smaller companies, the worker writes his own preliminary draft, often slanted or not completely objective, which may then be rewritten at face value by someone more adept with the English language. In any case, there is vast room for improvement in this vital area of organizing. Trained job analysts should make the analysis; trained writters should write the definition. Expert job definition can significantly reduce misunderstandings and job dissatisfaction, and greatly increase the chances of placing the "right person" in the "right position."

Job Description

A job description is a detailed statement of the content of the job in terms of major tasks, the sequence of those tasks, and the conditions under which they will be performed.

The job content should also include three essential facets: (1) the *authority* that goes with the job; (2) the *responsibility* that the jobholder agrees to accept; and (3) the person to whom the jobholder is *accountable*. A job is fully described only when authority, responsibility, and accountability have been fully specified also. Unfortunately, most job descriptions do not clearly spell out all three of these most important components of the total job. The result is a great deal of confusion and misunderstanding. Admittedly, it is more difficult to fix the boundaries of authority than it is to enumerate duties and responsibility. Nevertheless, it is imperative, if assignments are to be carried out effectively, that authority be clearly recognized as an essential part of every job description. It is not enough merely to describe responsibilities and duties! Figure 10-1 is a job description for a subassembly inspector's job in a large aircraft-aerospace company. Despite the fact that it is an example of one of the better-written descriptions, having been revised several times, it still has weaknesses. Authority, for example, is not fully stated. What can this inspector do if he spots sub-standard subassemblies? The job description does not say. The description and specifications are combined instead of being separated, and the components of each are not clearly differentiated. Note that duties are listed under "Specifications." To whom is this man accountable? He is not told in this job description, and he should be.

Figure 10-2 represents a suggested revision. In it, the term "job definition" is introduced. It is divided into two segments, the job description and the job specification. The description clearly indicates duties, job requirements, authority, responsibility, and accountability. The specification states the qualifications required of the person who will fill the job. To anyone interested—a person applying for the job, a person trying to hire someone to fill the job, or a person trying to compare this job with another job that may be closely related to it—the improved document makes it easier to comprehend the designated position, "Inspector-Sub-Assembly."

Authority

Since every job description must include the authority that is an integral part of the specific job, it is necessary to understand the concept of authority.

Authority is the *right to discharge one's duties, to perform a function or task to which one has been assigned and which one has accepted.* It is a right vested in *positions* and not in people. Authority includes the right to make decisions and to discharge one's responsibilities. It enables a manager to use discretion in setting and achieving objectives within his assigned sphere of jurisdiction. It is an announcement that a person's job involves certain duties that he has the right to perform. This announcement should be communicated not only to the individual assigned the job, but also to other persons who may be affected in any way by the performance of the job. This will

FACTORY JOB DEFINITION

CODE NO.: D-69
GRADE: 1
DATE:

JOB CLASSIFICATION—Inspector-Subassembly

ANALYST:

Element	Job description
Duties	Inspect subassemblies at progressive stages and completed major assemblies such as forward fuselage, center fuselage, aft fuselage, inner and outer wing, empennage, nose, and in spacecraft such items as radar and rendezvous section, reaction control system section, crew compartment, adapter section, and preliminary fit of heat shield before two major modules or major assemblies are joined together. Inspect jig and template locations, the spline of subassemblies, installation of all non-electrical subassembly components, weld assemblies, compartment sealing, tank installation, location in ream fixtures and hole sizes. Inspect ground support equipment, landing gears, canopies, and all pressurization to determine structural soundness. Inspect final shakedown and mechanical operations of subassemblies and completed major assemblies. Use a variety of inspection aids and precision measuring instruments. Prepare documents incidental to the accomplishment of inspection function.
Occupation or operation requirement*	Perform unusual and difficult work where standard or recognized methods may not be available.
Responsibility	Responsible for the proper performance of assignments and the prudent handling of product, tools, and equipment.
Authority	May work with the assistance of and/or instruct 3 or fewer lower-graded employees. May refuse to pass any work or subassembly that does not meet established standards.
Accountability	Accountable to Senior Inspector-Subassembly. Submit to Senior Inspector-Subassembly all documents incidental to the accomplishment of inspection function.
	Job specification
Experience required*	1 to 3 years aircraft or spacecraft experience.
Educational and/or training requirements*	Must have knowledge of shop mathematics, a working knowledge of specifications, assembly, and fabrication procedures, and shop practice. Work from information such as drawings, templates, master layouts, inspection and assembly fixtures. Considerable judgment required.

*These elements are usually required but are not necessarily a requisite to the performance of the duties described.

Figure 10-2. Factory job definition.

help avert misunderstandings. It is particularly important if the position is one that confers authority over others.

Very often, when a position is created, even though a job description has been written for it, authority relationships are not too clear. The new position may exert an influence across several functional areas, and people in those areas may question the authority of the occupant of the new position. Suppose a position is created with the title of "administrative assistant to the president." Approached by the administrative assistant to cooperate in certain assignments or to follow directives suggested by him, people may question his authority and ask themselves why such requests have not been made through their direct superior whom they recognize as their "boss." Doubts concerning the newly created authority should be forestalled, perhaps through a letter or bulletin from the president announcing the new post and requesting all personnel to provide their full cooperation. Such action would tend to prevent friction, uncertainty, jealousies, and other potential dysfunctions.

Managerial authority.   When a job entails supervision of other employees, *managerial authority* is specified as part of that job description. It includes the right to make decisions, to give orders to subordinates, to assign or delegate tasks to them, to require satisfactory performance of them, and to request an accounting from them for the manner in which the tasks are performed.

Authority is not distributed evenly among the various organizational levels. It clusters around the top levels and decreases as one descends the hierarchy. This is by no means accidental. Problems broad in scope and affecting many areas of the total organization can be handled only by those in upper-echelon positions who have broad enough authority to make the kinds of decisions required to resolve these dysfunctions. More limited problems usually do not require the same breadth of authority for resolution and can be handled by persons at lower levels in the formal structure. Executives at lower levels tend to have less authority than those at upper levels. This is as it should be.

Power.   Often associated with managerial authority is the concept of power. The two, however, should not be confused. **Power** is the *ability to enforce managerial authority*. It is influence, or clout, that causes subordinates to do what the manager requests. This influence may take various forms including force and persuasion. It may be based in part on superior knowledge as perceived by subordinates. Ametai Etzioni makes a distinction between *position power* and *personal power*.[1] He believes power is derived from an organizational office, personal influence, or both.

---

[1]Ametai Etzioni, *A Comparative Analysis of Complex Organizations* (Glenco, N.Y.: The Free Press, 1961).

A manager may have the right to recommend pay increases, promotions, and other rewards; withhold these rewards; recommend transfers, demotions, firing, and other penalties; and take disciplinary action when necessary. Not every manager has these special rights, but the manager who does possesses a powerful means of enforcing compliance with his requests.

A competent manager should never substitute improper use of power for leadership. To advise a subordinate holding a temporary position that the job will become permanent if he performs satisfactorily illustrates correct use of power and managerial authority. To threaten or imply that the job will not become permanent unless the superior decides to make it so illustrates improper use of power. Such misuse is tantamount to flaunting managerial authority.

Antony Jay introduces a somewhat different view of the concept of power. He portrays power as a simple equation:[2]

$$\text{Authority} + \text{Responsibility} = \text{Power}$$

Given the right to perform and possessing the willingness to accept the obligation, a person has power.

One could modify Jay's equation to indicate loss of power or absence of power:

$$\text{Authority} - \text{Responsibility} = \text{Lack of power}$$

or

$$\text{Responsibility} - \text{Authority} = \text{Lack of power}$$

Given the authority to perform but lacking the willingness to accept the obligation, a person has no meaningful power; lacking the right to make decisions despite a willingness to perform, a person would also have no meaningful power. There is no escape from the conclusion that authority must match responsibility.

Sources of managerial authority.   What is the origin of authority, this right that managers have to direct others, to make decisions that must be carried out by subordinates? It stems basically from four sources: (1) edict or mandate, (2) social contract, (3) private property, and (4) subordinate acceptance.

Edict or mandate. In some institutions and non-business organizations including the Church, the Army, and governments, authority stems from edict or legal decree.

In the Catholic Church, for example, the Pope occupies the highest position of authority. Papal edicts that are issued are accepted, implemented, and enforced by successive levels in the hierarchy. Power is present also

---

[2]Antony Jay, *Management and Machiavelli* (New York: Holt, Rinehart and Winston, 1967), p. 140.

and may involve sanctions or penalties, the ultimate penalty being excommunication.

Authority in the United States Army also stems from legal decree. Officers of lower rank accept orders from those of higher rank almost without question. This rank-authority order is institutionalized and understood by everyone in the military. It is spelled out in the official military manuals.

The office of President of the United States is the highest position in our government. His authority is legally prescribed also. Certain presidential orders, therefore, are mandates to be followed. Cabinet members, heads of government agencies and departments derive their authority from legislation which confers certain rights upon the office holder, making it possible for him to fulfill the obligations of his office.

In the family situation, parental authority is a familiar type of authority coupled with power. When a child questions a parent's request to do something by asking "why?" the parental answer is often "Because I said so!"

Over a long period of time, therefore, members of society have become accustomed to this type of authority. When it is derived from legal decree and takes the form of an edict or mandate, authority tends to be autocratic in nature.

Social contract. To a large extent, our present attitude toward authority is culturally based. In the course of his evolution, man accepted the personal need for government and has consented to be governed. He entered into a social contract. Carried into modern-day organizations, this contractual arrangement exists in the minds of the manager and the managed. One might say that a psychological contract exists. The executive or administrator has the right to make assignments and issue instructions; the managed have an obligation to comply. Psychologically, both parties agree to this arrangement.

By custom and tradition, rank and status are associated with authority. The higher the rank or status, the greater is the amount of authority expected. This attitude toward authority is brought into the organization by both managers and workers as part of their social and cultural experience.

Right to private property. The Constitution of the United States guarantees every citizen the right to private property. In our modern free enterprise system, a man may start a business and own its assets. They are his private property. He may hire others to run his business, permitting them to utilize the assets in his behalf. In this sense, he delegates his right to private property. If they do a creditable job, the owner may reward them by paying higher salaries or bonuses, or perhaps giving them an interest in the business. In that event, they become part-owners of the firm.

In corporations, the owners are the stockholders. Obviously, if there are 1000 stockholders not all of them can manage the company. Therefore, stockholders elect a board of directors to represent them in running the business. In effect, they delegate their private property rights to the board, who has a fiduciary obligation to protect those rights for the owners. In addition, the board is accountable to the stockholders.

The directors elect a president and other officers and delegate certain authority to them, thus making it possible for them to perform their duties. Frequently, the authority associated with top corporate positions is described in a general way in the by-laws of the corporation since explicit job definitions usually do not exist for these high level posts.

Each administrative officer may have executives under his jurisdiction. Managerial authority should be an integral part of the job description of each of these lower ranking positions. Authority that originates with the rights of owners and is delegated downward throughout the organizational structure is often referred to as **top/down authority,** indicating the direction of authority flow.

Subordinate acceptance. Realistically, effective authority is unchallenged authority. Its existence is dependent upon the extent to which subordinates willingly recognize the superior's right to assign tasks, give directions, and require satisfactory performance from them. When subordinates openly or clandestinely question and are unwilling to accept the authority of their superior, they effectively undermine his authority.

The psychological concept of subordinate acceptance was advanced by Chester Barnard, who held that authority is "the character of a communication by virtue of which it is accepted by the subordinate as controlling his behavior."[3] When he receives an order, the subordinate believes his compliance will further the goals of the organization and promote his own personal goals. The emphasis is on the subordinate's willing contribution; on what he or she does rather than on what the superior says should be done.

Managers should be aware of the importance of subordinate acceptance. Fortunately, most employees are psychologically prepared to accept the authority of immediate superiors as well as executives at higher levels. They do so because their attitude toward authority in general, as we have noted, is culturally based; they are accustomed to authority that stems from legal decree; they accept the right to private property doctrine; and they recognize the rank-authority link which calls for appropriate degrees of authority at successive levels of rank and status.

Managerial authority that receives subordinate acceptance through successive levels of organization structure is called **bottom/up authority,** indicating the direction of flow. Genuine subordinate acceptance rests ultimately on recognition of the superior's competence, his human relations skill, and his influence with his superiors. Professor Berman puts it well

---

[3]Chester Barnard, *The Functions of the Executive* (Cambridge: Harvard University Press, 1951), p. 163.

when he states, "Authority is not tyranny, but the natural relation of knowledge to ignorance."[4]

Acceptance theory, while shedding some light on the source of authority in superior-subordinate relationships, does not explain the authority that a manager has to enter into a labor contract, a purchasing agreement, or a service commitment to customers. Obviously, they have nothing to do with subordinate acceptance.

Delegation of authority. It is often observed that the mark of a capable manager is his ability to delegate authority. It is impossible for a manager to do everything himself. If he is to make optimum use of his most valuable resource—the people in his organization—he must recognize others' abilities and allow them to contribute as fully as possible to the company's total effort. Delegating authority is one means he can employ to accomplish this.

It is undoubtedly true that opportunities to delegate a portion of a portfolio are more numerous at higher levels of management where the scope of the position is broader. When a manager has a limited area of responsibility and few subordinates, the opportunities decrease. Nevertheless, the extent to which a manager does delegate is an indicator of his ability. Delegation enables him to accomplish more than he could just by himself. To illustrate, a vice-president of industrial relations usually oversees most of the personnel activities that comprise "industrial relations." Many of the broad, far-reaching decisions associated with industrial relations will be made by him. Other decisions will be made by competent personnel people under him. The vice-president may personally handle delicate labor contract negotiations with unions representing skilled and unskilled workers in the organization. On the other hand, he may assign the recruiting and hiring of employees to a subordinate, perhaps the personnel manager. The latter may not do the actual recruiting and hiring; he may assign those functions to members of his department. For recruiting, he may utilize a trained professional. Since hiring involves many related activities including interviewing applicants, professional interviewers are assigned this task by the personnel manager. Thus within the industrial relations area various activities are "farmed out" to capable, trained subordinates. Each delegated function includes the requisite authority to perform the assignment in a competent manner. Thus *when duties are delegated, authority is delegated also.* There is no question that within the scope of his area of jurisdiction, any manager can delegate assignments and tasks to others. What must be understood, however, is that each assignment must also carry commensurate authority.

Delegation of authority is an expression of **participative management.** When he delegates, the manager does so on the assumption that the person

---

[4]Ronald Berman, "An Unquiet Quiet on Campus," *The New York Times Magazine*, February 10, 1974, p. 26.

to whom he has assigned an activity is capable of carrying out the assignment. He has confidence in the subordinate. The latter now takes charge and, within the limits of company policies, existing procedures, and any restraints imposed by his superior, is expected to fulfill the mission. His own jurisdiction has been enlarged. He now becomes the decision maker participating in a wider area of company activity than heretofore. He feels that he is expected to justify the confidence placed in him by performing in a creditable manner. It can be a challenging and potentially rewarding experience.

The risks of delegating authority.   Any time a person depends upon another to represent him or take his place in a situation, he runs the risk that the other fellow may perform poorly. Inherent within the delegation of managerial authority is the risk that subordinate performance will be less than expected. Should this occur, the manager may be able to offer constructive suggestions and guidance for improving performance. As a last resort, he can reclaim the assigned task and reestablish it as part of his portfolio, or he can re-delegate the task to another subordinate. From time to time, adjustments of this sort are necessary.

There is also the possibility that the subordinate will do an exceptional job. His performance may attract the attention and approval of persons higher in the organization than the manager who originally delegated the task. The assignment could develop into such an important activity, making valuable contributions to the organization's hierarchy of objectives, that a new department or division may develop and be separated from the original jurisdiction from which it sprung. However, if this serves the best interests of the organization, it should also serve the long-run interest of the manager who delegated it in the first place. It is a feather in his cap that should not go unnoticed by his superiors.

To delegate widely, as a good manager should, tends to increase his overall responsibility. He has many people to look after instead of a few. Thus, while the range of fulfillment of his own duties is greatly increased through delegation to others, the amount or degree of his responsibility is increased also.

When delegation is broad, the problem of effective control tends to increase also. There is always the possibility that more elaborate control techniques and control systems will become necessary. This is evident in larger companies where multi-plants or multi-branches are involved. Therefore it should be recognized that despite the many advantages of delegating authority certain limitations exist. These explain why many executives are reluctant to delegate.

Perhaps it should be reemphasized that *one cannot delegate what is not his to delegate.* It is not an act of delegation when a manager asks a subordinate to do something that the latter is normally expected to do. It is not delegating, either, if an executive asks someone to do something, like conducting a survey, and reserves the final decision making for himself. Delegating occurs when an executive farms out a portion of his portfolio to another, explains what has to be done and why, and leaves it to the delegatee to handle in his own manner. A competent manager would be demonstrating the correct concept of delegating if he said, "Here is a problem that exists in my area of jurisdiction. I am assigning it to you to handle and to resolve." A bonus effect is its contribution toward a sense of personal worth and importance for the person accepting the assignment.

Responsibility

Just as every job description must delineate the authority that the job confers, so must it state the responsibilities that it imposes. (Note how this is done in the job description in Figure 10-2.) It is imperative, therefore, that the concept of responsibility be clearly understood.

Responsibility is an *obligation to perform*. It is a commitment that a person takes upon himself to handle the job to the best of his ability. The source of this responsibility, therefore, lies within the individual. It is a personal bond that he creates when he agrees to accept the job. If a subordinate does not agree with the objectives of the assignment, or finds them distasteful or imcompatible with his personal objectives, he should decline to accept it, or at least make his position known to his superior. Acceptance carries the obligation to pursue the goals of the assignment to the full extent of one's capability. Though the terms are often used interchangeably, responsibility is *not* the same thing as a duty. The latter means a task, or work assignment. The two should not be confused. They are separate and distinct concepts as we are using them.

Delegation of responsibility.   A great deal of misunderstanding exists in management literature concerning delegation of responsibility. Some of the confusion is a matter of semantics since responsibility is often loosely defined as a duty of some kind, and duties can be delegated. As we have defined it, *responsibility cannot be divided or delegated.* You cannot delegate an obligation. Only functions or assignments, with their attendant authority, can be delegated.

A manager, although delegating authority, retains overall responsibility for the way in which the particular assignment is carried out. Thus when the vice-president of industrial relations assigns the tasks of recruiting and hiring to his personnel manager, he still retains the responsibility for the way hiring and recruiting are performed. In accepting these functions, the personnel manager automatically takes upon himself the obligation to perform to the best of his ability. Although he delegates the recruiting function to the professional, he cannot delegate the responsibility which became his when he accepted the assignment from his superior, the vice-president, to whom he is accountable. The professional recruiter, in accepting his assignment and the authority that goes with it, likewise automatically accepts the obligation to recruit to the best of his ability. The delegator who assigns a part of his total job portfolio to someone else does not relinquish the responsibility over it, but is always fully responsible for the entire job including the part that he delegates. Thus overall responsibility is seeing to it that all delegated tasks are performed effectively by subordinates who accept them.

If he who delegates tasks (accompanied by authority) always retains overall responsibility for what he has delegated, "buck passing" and placing blame on others for poor performance will be eliminated. This is an organizing principle.

Accountability

In our illustration, the recruiter is accountable to the personnel manager for the way recruiting is handled; the personnel manager, in turn, is accountable to the vice-president of industrial relations for this function; and the latter ultimately is responsible to the president of the organization. What does the term "accountability" mean? How does it differ from responsibility?

Accountability *is an appraisal or evaluation of the extent to which performance was discharged satisfactorily.* It is a continuing, dynamic process. The manager is accountable to his superiors for the effective performance of all functions covered by his job description and any additional ones delegated to him. After accepting an assignment, a subordinate is expected to give his superior an accounting of how well he is doing. His superior has the right to request such an accounting as part of his managerial authority. Moreover, since the superior is ultimately responsible for the subordinate's performance he must have some way to evaluate and determine how well things are going.

Most managers expect subordinates to keep records from which oral or written reports can be made. These may be progress reports on a scheduled basis, perhaps every week or every month. **Reporting** is often the means by which subordinates' performance is reviewed, appraised, and evaluated. It is a mechanism for establishing control.[5]

A review of a subordinate's performance makes further control actions possible. Should things be going less than satisfactorily, the manager can counsel, direct, motivate, and assist the worker to improve the level of performance. The subordinate obligated himself to perform to the best of his capabilities; if it turns out that his best is not sufficient to get the job done, he cannot be faulted. His superior, using tact and human relations skills,

---

[5]Reporting is discussed more thoroughly in Chapter 23.

must explain this to him and arrange for a replacement. Thus, *accountability is an effective controlling device* in the organizing process.

The Value of Job Descriptions

Job descriptions are **essential** in planning or designing the organization. Clearly spelled out, authority, responsibility, and accountability relate jobs into a structural order. It must be remembered that without structure there can be no formal organization. Collectively, job descriptions make structure possible.

Despite the need for clear-cut job descriptions to communicate specifically the essential activities associated with any position, job descriptions do have serious limitations which must be recognized. At all levels, position titles are often misleading and subject to misinterpretation. Is a stationary engineer an elevator operator or vice versa? Furthermore, managerial positions are not standardized, particularly at higher levels. The president in one organization may devote a major portion of his efforts to improving the financial capability of his institution; the president in a similar institution may direct his energies toward developing marketing plans and strategies to implement them. Moreover, establishing a priority of objectives, which is an essential component in all managerial roles, is a dynamic function and very difficult to specify precisely in a job description. The description itself must be reviewed and revised periodically to assure that it does not become outdated.

Job Specification (Qualifications)

You will recall that a properly developed job definition consists of two segments: the job description and the job specification.

A **job specification** is *a statement of the qualifications a prospective employee should have to fill a particular job*. The *description* deals with the *job* and its requirements; the *specification* deals with the *person* and his qualifications. It lists the physical and mental characteristics, skills, attitudes, aptitudes, interests, personality traits, education, experience, including supervisory experience, and any other attributes a person must possess to fit the position.

Most mis-matching of people with jobs stems from excess demands in the job specification. There is a tendency for personnel departments to require more qualifications than are actually necessary to do a job. One man told the author that he had applied for a position as a janitor, the duties of which including shoveling snow from the walks during the winter. He did not get the job because he did not qualify. The job "required" a high school diploma! It is hard to understand how a diploma is a prerequisite to do janitorial work or to shovel snow.

Peter Drucker has commented on the subject of requiring more of an applicant than the job actually entails or has to offer.

> Don't believe anybody who tells you that jobs have become more complex. It just ain't true. Sure, the salaries have changed, and the titles, and the diploma one has to have. But the jobs have not been restructured. The trouble is that these young people—and many of my students among them—are hired with great expectations of challenging jobs, then dropped into training programs. They are given fancy titles and salaries and then given a file clerk's work. It serves no earthly purpose. It's work that doesn't have to be done. . . .Nothing creates dissatisfaction faster than a big title, a lot of money and only donkey work to do.[6]

The argument frequently advanced to explain why the job specification calls for qualifications greater than the job actually demands is that the person can later be promoted to another job that will require the additional attributes. Under such circumstances an employee must under-employ his talents in the present job in the hope that someday he will be promoted or transferred to a position where he will fully employ his capabilities. There is little justification for this practice. It makes for discontent and job dissatisfaction, lowers morale, and tends to increase labor turnover. An employee may simply find employment elsewhere rather than continue to be unhappy at his present work while awaiting the development of a job opportunity more suited to his talents and abilities. Job specifications should fit the job descriptions they go with. That is what a good job definition is—a well-written job description coupled with a job specification tailored to fit it.

Unlike job descriptions, job specifications are *not* required to plan or design the structure of an organization. They are, however, extremely useful for efficient performance within the structure. Job descriptions contribute to formal structure; job specifications lead to effective utilization of that structure.

JOB CLASSIFICATION

After job definitions have been written, it is often useful to establish classifications based on similarities in duties being performed, or similar degrees of competence. **Job classification** means grading jobs based on similarities in job descriptions and/or job specifications.

A comparison and evaluation is made among various jobs to establish that despite dissimilarity in job titles they do have something in common. How much different does one job have to be from another to justify a higher rate of pay? How does a manager determine the relative compensation for factory, office, supervisory, research, and engineering work? Is it purely a

---

[6]Interview of Peter Drucker by Thomas J. Murray, *Dun's*, April 1971, pp. 40–41.

matter of supply and demand? Should supervisors in the United States Weather Service attend the same management training program together with supervisors from the records section of the United States Department of Defense? Job classifications help to answer these questions.

Methods for Comparing and Evaluating Jobs

There are three basic methods that can be used for comparing and evaluating jobs: (1) ranking, (2) factor comparison, and (3) point rating.

Ranking is the simplest and most limited type of evaluation. Each job is ranked with every other job and assigned a number. A list is compiled arraying jobs in order of relative worth to the company. The list may then be consolidated into small groupings of assorted jobs having approximately the same value. This method is appropriate for small companies, with relatively few employees, which cannot justify a more elaborate system. It is also practical for evaluating supervisory positions or classes of work requiring uncommon abilities.

Factor comparison is somewhat better known than the preceding method. This method, which originated in the 1930s in studies for the Philadelphia Rapid Transit Company, compares the factor components of each job and then ranks jobs on the basis of additive factors. The factors usually are *mental requirements, physical requirements, skill, responsibility,* and *working conditions.* Each is analyzed separately. Thus a job could rank high in mental requirement and skill factors, and relatively low in the physical requirement factor if machines do most of the work. This would be true for a toolmaker. A money value is assigned to each factor, and the job pay rate is determined by adding the five monetary values. Certain "key" jobs with assigned monetary values become the standards against which other jobs are compared.

To illustrate, when a toolmaker is paid $5.78 an hour, a lathe operator $4.80 per hour, and a drill press operator $3.50 per hour, some portion of their hourly wage is attributable to each of the five factors. Table 10-1 com-

Table 10-1.   Factor comparison for three jobs

Factors	Hourly rate of payment (dollar value)		
	Toolmaker	Lathe operator	Drill press operator
Mental requirements	1.70	0.90	0.84
Physical requirements	0.48	0.88	0.56
Skill	2.35	1.56	0.98
Responsibility	0.90	0.72	0.68
Working conditions	0.35	0.74	0.44
Total hourly pay	5.78	4.80	3.50

pares these jobs by factors and indicates the monetary worth of each factor. Generally, the mental and skill components account for major differences in pay. All other jobs in the shop are compared with these three key jobs, and a wage scale is established relative to their rates of pay. Note that factor comparisons are instrumental in relating jobs to each other. These *relationships* contribute to structural order.

Point rating is the best known and most frequently used method of comparing and evaluating jobs. It covers about 85 percent of all job classification systems.

In point rating, numerical values are assigned to each factor. In most systems, four basic factors are considered: *skill, effort, responsibility,* and *job conditions.* These, in turn, are subdivided and each sub-factor is assigned points that permit it to be weighted in importance as a job ingredient. This is illustrated in Table 10-2.

Observe in the example given that skill is weighted 50 percent, effort 15 percent, responsibility 20 percent, and job conditions 15 percent of the total value of the combined factors. This means that for every job evaluated for

Table 10-2.   Points assigned to factor degrees and range for grades*

Factor	1st Degree	2nd Degree	3rd Degree	4th Degree	5th Degree
Skill					
1. Education	14	28	42	56	70
2. Experience	22	44	66	88	110
3. Initiative and ingenuity	14	28	42	56	70
Effort					
4. Physical demand	10	20	30	40	50
5. Mental or visual demand	5	10	15	20	25
Responsibility					
6. Equipment or process	5	10	15	20	25
7. Material or product	5	10	15	20	25
8. Safety of others	5	10	15	20	25
9. Work of others	5	10	15	20	25
Job conditions					
10. Working conditions	10	20	30	40	50
11. Hazards	5	10	15	20	25

Score Range	Grades	Score Range	Grades
139	12	250–271	6
140–161	11	272–293	5
162–183	10	294–315	4
184–205	9	316–337	3
206–227	8	338–359	2
228–249	7	360–381	1

*From American Association of Industrial Management, September 1976.

classification by means of the point ratings in Table 10-2, a heavy premium will always be placed on skill and its components.

The way in which one of these sub-factors is described and its degree definitions explained, is illustrated in Figure 10-3.

PHYSICAL DEMAND

This factor measures the kind, amount and frequency of the physical effort required to perform all the job duties; and the work position in which the effort is applied in handling material, parts, tools, equipment, and in operating equipment, machines, processes and apparatus. Periods of physical inactivity must be taken into consideration.

1st Degree

Little physical effort consisting of (a) continuously lifting or moving material of negligible weight . . . (g) rarely lifting or moving light weight material in difficult work positions.

2nd Degree

Light physical effort consisting of (a) continuously lifting or moving very light weight material . . . (h) rarely lifting or moving average weight material in difficult work positions.

3rd Degree

Moderate physical effort consisting of (a) continuously lifting or moving light weight material . . . (g) rarely lifting or moving heavy weight material in difficult work positions.

4th Degree

Considerably physical effort consisting of (a) continuously lifting or moving average weight material . . . (e) occasioually lifting or moving heavy weight material in difficult work positions.

5th Degree

Heavy physical exertion consisting of (a) continuously lifting or moving heavy weight material . . . (c) frequently lifting or moving heavy weight material in difficult work positions.

Figure 10-3. Description and degree definitions for "physical demand" factor. (From "Current Job Rating Plan," American Association of Industrial Management, September 1976.)

When the degree of each factor has been determined from the description, points are assigned by referring to Table 10-2, recorded on a job classification form similar to the one in Figure 10-4, and then added together. Jobs with equivalent total points, or perhaps ranges of total points, are placed in the same classification.

JOB CLASSIFICATION

Plant Title_____Watertender_____Standard Title_____Watertender_____

Factor Reason for Classification	Code	Class-ification
1. Pre-Employment Training. This Job requires the mentality to learn to: Service, control and operate Steam Boilers and auxiliaries.	B	.3
2. Employment Training and Experience. This job requires experience on this and related work of 25 to 30 months to become proficient	F	2.0
3. Mental Skill Use considerable judgement in operating moderately complex equipment.	D	2.2
4. Manual Skill Operate Steam Boiler controls and levers in making adjustments for maintaining steam pressure.	C	1.0
5. Responsibility for Material Estimated Cost Ordinary care for part of turn to prevent $50.00 waste of water, water treatment, fuel, etc. or under to maintain efficient boiler operation.	B	.3
6. Responsibility for Tools and Equipment Close attention & care required to prevent damage to Boiler tubes caused by low water. Safety devices limit probability.	D	Hi 2.0
7. Responsibility for Operations Responsible for the continuity of operations of Boilers producing steam for mill production.	D	2.0
8. Responsibility for Safety of Others Responsible for the flow of steam.	D	1.2
9. Mental Effort Moderate mental and visual application required to tend boilers, maintain proper operation. Inspect, make minor repairs and adjustment.	C	1.0
10. Physical Effort Light physical exertion required to walk, observe, inspect, lubricate, make minor repairs, and adjust valves.	B	.3
11. Surroundings Modern type gas fired boiler house.	A	Base
12. Hazard Moderate exposure to bruises, cuts, or burns.	B	.4

Reviewed and Approved by:	Job Class 13	Total	12.7
Chairman, Union Job Classification Committee	Described By: E.F.B.	Date:	
Chairman, Management Job Classification Committee	Classified By: J.L.R.-W.H.-J.L.M.		
Union Copy☐ Management Copy☐	Approved By:		

Figure 10-4. Job classification: Watertender. (From Niles Rolling Mill Company.)

In the example in Figure 10-4, total component points are 12.7, and the job of watertender is given a classification of 13. It is quite possible that other jobs, dissimilar in title or description, will also earn the same numerical classification.

Job classifications are extremely useful in preparing equitable wage scales, planning training programs, upgrading personnel within classifications, and promoting to higher grades. Through their use, job assignments of comparable nature can be grouped within the same grade. Levels of duties, skills, experience, and responsibility can be viewed as a composite, indicating the relative contribution of each factor to the total job picture. Salary ranges can be established based on a comparison of such composites. Grade classifications for salary purposes are used by the U.S. Civil Service Commission. Dissimilar positions such as those of microbiologist, accountant, actuary, and industrial hygienist all have the same classification and comparable salaries. Job classifications are invaluable in another way. They relate jobs to each other. In so doing, they contribute to overall organizational structure.

To avoid obsolescence, job classifications should be reviewed and updated periodically. In every organization new jobs are added, others are discontinued, and existing ones change. Occasionally, points assigned to the factors may be challenged by labor unions or by individual workers and may have to be reevaluated. When jobs are reviewed and reassessed, reclassifications may become necessary and a new structural equilibrium established. Such review and reassessment assures the dynamic nature of this aspect of the organizing process.

JOB RELATIONSHIPS

As we have developed it to this point, the process of organizing includes designing enterprise functions and their relationships and designing jobs and their relationships. *Relationships are the key to structure.* Management functions are related to the non-management functions. Non-management functions are related to each other. Management functions are interrelated too. With their emphasis on authority and accountability, job descriptions make it possible to relate jobs to each other. Job classifications place comparable jobs into a structural order, thereby contributing to formal organization. The structuring of job relationships will be discussed in detail in the following chapter.

Any change in relationship causes change in structure. The original organization ceases to be. As Alvin Toffler puts it,

> . . . An organization, after all, is nothing more than a collection of human objectives, expectations, and obligations. It is, in other words, a structure of roles

filled by humans. And when a reorganization sharply alters this structure by redefining or redistributing these roles, we can say that the old organization has died and a new one has sprung up to take its place. This is true even if it retains the old name and has the same members as before. The rearrangement of roles creates a new structure exactly as the rearrangement of mobile walls in a building converts it into a new structure.[7]

SUMMARY

The second step in the organizing process is to design specific jobs for each functional area and to relate them to each other and to jobs in other functional areas. This requires a thorough knowledge of the nature of each job; its purpose; its composition, including work units and frequency of operations; tools required; working conditions; and the kinds of skills that it will require for effective performance. To obtain this information, the job designer must make a thorough analysis of an existing job which may have to be modified, or of a new job which will have to be created as he perceives it.

The information derived from the analysis is written up as a formal job definition consisting of a job description and a job specification. Included in the description is a careful clarification of authority that goes with the position, statements concerning responsibility or what the individual obligates himself to do, and designation of the person or persons to whom the jobholder is accountable and from whom he will take his orders and directions. The specification portion of the definition enumerates the characteristics or attributes that the jobholder should possess to assure the job will be handled effectively and efficiently. The authority and accountability relationships that are spelled out in the job description relate jobs to each other and contribute toward structural order.

In many organizations including government, job definitions are compiled and analyzed and, after careful comparison and evaluation, are grouped into classifications based on similarity of duties (job descriptions) or similar degrees of competence (job specifications). Job classifications are useful for establishing wage scales, training programs, promotions in grade or to a higher classification, and for similar purposes. In grouping seemingly unrelated jobs on the basis of some common denominators, job classifications contribute to overall structural design.

Designing and redesigning organizational roles, and shifting and rearranging them periodically, not only influences organizational structure but also reveals the dynamic nature of the organizing process. The managing process itself is dynamic because its major components and their sub-units are dynamic processes.

---

[7]Alvin Toffler, *Future Shock* (New York: Random House, 1970), pp. 114–115.

KEY CONCEPTS

Job Analysis	Subordinate Acceptance
Job Definition	Delegation of Authority
Job Description	Responsibility
Authority	Accountability
Power	Job Specification
Sources of Authority	Job Classification

GLOSSARY

accountability   An appraisal or evaluation of the extent to which performance was discharged satisfactorily.

authority   The right to discharge one's duties, to perform a task to which one has been assigned and which one has accepted.

job   The kind and amount of work to be performed by a person or piece of equipment within a given time period.

job analysis   Breaking a job into its components to determine its content.

job classification   Grading of jobs based on similarities in job descriptions and/or job specifications.

job definition   A statement consisting of a job description and a job specification.

job description   That portion of the job definition that consists of a statement of the content of the job in terms of major tasks, sequence of tasks, conditions under which they will be performed, and the job's authority, responsibility, and accountability.

job specification   That portion of a job definition which states the qualifications a person should have to fill the job that has been described.

power   The ability to enforce managerial authority.

responsibility   An obligation to perform to the best of one's ability the duties one has accepted.

REVIEW QUESTIONS

1. Of what help is job analysis in designing jobs? Make a job analysis for the position of a college professor.

2. Should all job definitions consist of a job description and a job specification? Why?

3. Where do managers get the authority to tell subordinates what to do or not to do? Be specific.

4. What is the source of responsibility? Explain.
5. From your own experience, give an example of an abuse of managerial power. Do all managers have power? Explain.
6. Why can a manager delegate authority but not delegate responsibility?
7. Reporting is often viewed as a control mechanism. How do you view it?
8. Do you agree with the position that it is all right to hire persons for jobs that may under-employ their talents, as long as later on they will be promoted to jobs that will require their full capabilities?
9. What is point rating? How does it contribute to job design?

Chapter 11

Formal and Informal Organizations

How well jobs will serve their intended purposes in an organization depends to a great extent on the relationships that are set up between them. Thus, in designing particular jobs a manager considers how they will mesh—how they will interact and influence each other. Certain relationships become apparent when job descriptions are written, others when job classifications are made. Additional relationships exist simply because people at work are brought into proximity with other people. Relationships of various types are the core of all structural arrangements and any change in these relationships produces an automatic change in organizational structure.

We turn our attention now to a more detailed examination of the relationships that exist in an organization and the ways in which they contribute to its overall structure. Generally speaking, job relationships are of two major types: **work relationships** and **personal relationships.** The former give rise to formal organization, the latter to informal organization.

FORMAL ORGANIZATION (WORK RELATIONSHIPS)

Work relationships are depicted graphically by an organization chart showing the structure of the formal organization, the chain of command, lines of authority, and flow of accountability. Contrary to the position of some writers, an organization chart is never an aid to designing structure. With the exception of a fixed table of organization such as the "TO" one finds in the armed services, the chart is not intended to be a blueprint of how the organization *should look.* It is a diagram of how the organization actually *does look.* The organization chart does not establish relationships. On the contrary, existing relationships are the basis for constructing the chart.

Most relationships that occur between jobs in a factory or an office result either from the flow of work, or from the authority that exists between a superior and his subordinates. The former is called a **procedural** relationship; the latter, an **authority** relationship. Their existence produces *formal* organization. Herbert A. Simon and his associates define formal organization as "a planned system of cooperative effort in which each participant has a recognized role to play and duties or tasks to perform."[1]

Procedural Relationships

Procedural relationships result from the continuity of the work. By its very nature, work flow relates jobs to one another. Generally, flow of work occurs in *serial* or *parallel* fashion, or a combination of the two.

Serial flow.   When work proceeds in a serial fashion, it moves in successive stages, each group of tasks being part of a set sequence. Tasks or operations at a given stage cannot be performed unless operations and tasks at the previous stage have already been carried out. In a restaurant, the cook must prepare the food before the waiter can serve. In an office, the customer's order goes first to the order taker and then to the order filler. On an assembly line, a man places nuts and bolts, which are tightened by a man at the next station. In a hospital, a routine work-up is done on a patient before treatment begins. At a university, registration takes place before classes are taught. Countless jobs are related because the natural serial continuity of the work forges these relationships.

Parallel flow.   Other types of work proceed concurrently, relating jobs in a parallel fashion. In the restaurant situation, the jobs of two waiters are related in this way. Both are also connected to the cook's job in serial fashion. Neither could serve unless the cook prepared the food first.

When two order fillers in a warehouse work together to fill the same order, or fill two orders separately but concurrently, their jobs are related in a parallel way. They work alongside each other. The same can be said of nurses in a hospital, or clerical workers in an office, or soldiers in a platoon.

On the assembly line, the job of the man who places nuts and bolts on the wheels on the left side of the vehicle is associated with the job of the man who places them on the right side. Their work takes place simultaneously in parallel fashion. The same is true of the men at the next station; while one man tightens the left front wheel, another man across from him tightens the right front wheel. These jobs parallel each other. At the same time, they are also related in serial fashion to the job at the previous station. This is an illustration of work flow that combines both serial and parallel relationships.

Authority Relationships

It is not only procedure that relates one job to another. In a situation where someone is in charge, directing others in the performance of their duties, the relationship is an authority relationship.

---

[1]Herbert A. Simon, Donald W. Smithburg, and Victor Thompson, *Public Administration* (New York: Alfred Knopf, 1962), p.5.

Authority relationships are often referred to as "hierarchical," indicating a structuring of authority according to rank—a chain of command. It is these authority relationships that give rise to structural types known as line organization, staff organization, and modifications of the two. These major structural types are highly complex and require careful explanation and analysis to be understood. They will be treated, therefore, in detail in a separate chapter (Chapter 14).

OVERCOMING STRUCTURAL RIGIDITY

There are those who oppose all clearly defined organizational structure on the grounds that it limits a person's usefulness. One of these is Warren Bennis, who believes that classical structure is too rigid to be effective under conditions of rapid technological change and will eventually disappear.[2] Critics of formal organization say that it ties an individual to a specific set of duties, denying him the opportunity to show what else he can do. Writing about industrial democracy, Derek Norcross observes that "ordinary workers complain openly about excessive authoritarianism, rigid work hierarchies, and the terrible negation of spirit in performing the same dull job day after day."[3]

Disenchantment is not limited to factory workers or those whose work is machine paced. A person hired as a bookkeeper may never be anything but a bookkeeper. He feels "locked in." There is ample evidence that the jobs of the bus driver, policeman, farm worker, airline stewardess, garbage collector, cashier, security guard, foreman, and thousands of others are not always glamorous, challenging, ego satisfying, or totally rewarding. Even for the self-employed, most work can at times be lonely, routine, filled with tension, or boring. Many accountants, lawyers, dentists, and shop owners would agree.

A major problem of our present-day society is how to preserve the creative power of the individual within the context of organizational life, how to reaffirm the role of the individual in a world irrevocably committed to organizational procedure. Writers frequently place the blame for the individual's slide toward anonymity on the business organization, charging that business structure is bureaucratic, stifles initiative and produces "organization men." A fundamental tenet of American political and social philosophy is freedom; yet at work the individual often feels anything but free. He is expected to do what he is told; he finds authority and rigid hierarchy, with

---

[2]Warren Bennis, "Organizational Developments and the Fate of Bureaucracy," *Industrial Management Review*, Spring 1966, p. 52.

[3]Derek Norcross, "Sweden's Newest Export: Industrial Democracy," *Parade*, December 15, 1974, p. 15.

little chance for him to make it to the top. Charles Reich makes the point "when the shape of the hierarchy is a pyramid, only a few can enjoy the satisfaction of being in superior positions."[4]

It is not the work situation itself that produces conformity. By habit, by custom, and by choice people conform to society's behavioral norms. In the work situation, they conform to the norms of both the informal group as well as the formal organization to which they have been assigned. Much of the conformity in both groups is not "conformity to" but rather "conformity within" that results because behavior patterns are carried into organizations by their members. "Man has the capacity to internalize the values of his society and subgroup, to make them 'his own', so that he conforms not only because he must, but also (and often primarily) because his inner disposition favors such behavior."[5] Obviously some degree of conformity is necessary for an organization to function.

Only when *conformity in thinking* occurs does it become a danger. When that happens, the organization itself loses its vitality, and its very survival becomes threatened. *Non-conformity in thinking* is the basis for constructive criticism, for challenging and questioning the status quo, and leads eventually to change. Sometimes called creative imagination, non-conformity in thinking often leads to innovation.

Within the confines of organization, administrators can do something to encourage initiative, to reduce the monotony associated with many kinds of work, to decrease bureaucracy, and to enhance workers' self-esteem. Here, the managers can put their human relations skills to use and can apply some of the discoveries and contributions of behavioral scientists. People are the most important asset an organization possesses. They must feel they play an integral and important role in the scheme of things, that they are needed and appreciated. Further, they must derive personal satisfactions from their work. It is part of a manager's role to provide the climate or conditions within which satisfactions can be fulfilled.[6]

What are some strategies managers can employ to accomplish these ends? In overcoming dysfunctions associated with a formal organization, such as worker alienation, the most effective methods are considered to be: (1) expanding the meaning of a job (job enlargement, job enrichment, and job rotation); (2) participative activities (use of a suggestion box, policy formulation, delegation of authority, service on committees, and mutual goal setting); (3) management by objectives; and (4) properly matching people to jobs. These strategies are complementary and tend to be mutually reinforcing.

---

[4]Charles Reich, *The Greening of America* (New York: Random House, 1970), p. 211.

[5]Rose Laub Coser, "Insulation from Observability and Types of Social Conformity," *American Sociological Review*, Vol. 26, No. 1, 1961, p. 29.

[6]This is one of the natural objectives of business as described in Chapter 1.

When employed in various combinations, they tend to produce their optimum effect. A brief review of each will contribute to an understanding of their potential in reducing rigidities traditionally associated with "mechanistic" organization structure.

Expanding the Meaning of the Job

A routine job may be less boring to an employee if he is helped to understand the meaning and importance of the work he does; the relationship of his work to work being done by others; its contribution toward fulfilling corporate objectives; his personal importance and the value of his contribution; and the opportunities present on the job that enable him to satisfy many of his personal desires in the course of pursuing organizational goals.

International Business Machines Corporation explains to its recruits from poor and depressed areas why their contribution is essential to the company's success, and how they can develop their skills to assume positions of greater responsibility with more pay.

Jobs can be expanded in meaning through: **job enlargement, job enrichment,** and **job rotation.** Many labor relations experts now believe that the time-honored method for increasing productivity through specialization, dividing work into small tasks that can be handled by relatively unskilled workers, may have been carried too far—to the point that it has sapped workers' desire to accomplish more than the bare minimum. By designing certain types of new jobs and redesigning old ones to include greater variety and increased responsibility in producing the total product, managers can improve worker morale and performance in some instances. This can lead to increased productivity, with fewer "bugs" in the product or service that eventually reaches the consumer. The dual goal is to increase production while increasing worker satisfaction.

Job enlargement (job restructuring).   One approach to job enlargement lies in centering work in small groups of men and women who are given optimum responsibility and freedom in handling it. This means rewriting job descriptions and rearranging job classifications, and may require union cooperation and approval. The president of Volvo, one of Sweden's largest manufacturers of automobiles, farm machinery, and engines says, "We are trying to create small groups of workers who develop into skilled and proud craftsmen."[7]

Maytag Company has adopted enlargement projects for some of its blue-collar workers. The company had used a group of five or six operators to assemble a 26-part water pump for automatic washing machines. The operation was redesigned so that a single worker could assemble the complete pump and be responsible for testing it. As a result, assembly operation

---

[7]Derek Norcross, *op. cit.*

costs have been cut 16 percent since the worker can arrange the parts more efficiently within his work area than was possible along an assembly line. Furthermore, quality has increased (the reject rate has dropped from 5 percent to 0.5 percent) since the operator is no longer under pressure to keep up with a moving belt conveyor. Formerly he would either let a troublesome part continue along the line or run the risk of falling behind and holding up the other workers.[8]

International Business Machines Corporation has also introduced enlargement programs. In one of its typewriter plants, when one person put together a complete tab mechanism, better results were produced than previously when six people performed this operation.[9]

Job enrichment.   Professionals in industrial relations point out that it is not necessarily repetition in a job that creates dissatisfaction. Many repetitive jobs are highly complicated and sophisticated. It is when a worker feels he is being denied the opportunity to use his skills, or when he feels his skills are not appreciated, that he becomes dissatisfied and resentful.

Work enrichment strives to replace boredom and humiliation with variety and respect. Job enrichment is a way of designing work to make it more meaningful, interesting, and emotionally rewarding. The key appears to be to give people a voice in their own destiny, and a challenge. A great many work enrichment programs are being initiated in Sweden. Among the best known are those at the huge Volvo plant where computer-directed trolleys are each manned by a group of workers who collectively assemble an entire auto rather than repeat just a single operation as the car moves along a production line.

Motorola's communication division turns out a miniature paging receiver without using the conventional assembly line. Each worker puts together the complete receiver from a combination of 80 components and is fully responsible for testing the entire unit. Enclosed with each complete unit is a note to the consumer that states: "I built this receiver in its entirety and am proud of it. I hope it serves you well. Please tell me if it doesn't." The note is personally signed by the assembler. The system provides personal involvement and a sense of accomplishment for the worker. Indications are that the technique improves quality, increases productivity, and reduces employee turnover and absenteeism at a "slightly higher per-unit cost."[10]

In other instances, assembly lines are being modified so that workers can operate as teams and thereby play a larger role in the manufacturing process. Narco Scientific Industries switched from an assembly line opera-

---

[8]Roger B. May, "Jobs of Many Blue-Collar Workers Become More Varied as Firms Try to Raise Morale," *Wall Street Journal*, April 15, 1968.
[9]*Ibid.*
[10]Joe Cappo, *Chicago Daily News*, as reported in the Youngstown *Vindicator*, September 19, 1971.

tion of ten women putting together a medical humidifier to teams of five. The results were startling: time for assembling each humidifier was reduced 25 percent. Pride was the chief reason for the improvement. The assemblers considered themselves more important as members of a small team than as members of a larger, impersonal assembly line.

One theory of motivation that explains how job enrichment increases personal involvement and commitment is "expectancy theory."[11] Basically this theory states that an enriched task is *perceived* by an individual as leading to an intrinsic reward or satisfaction.[12] While there is no universal agreement why job enrichment works when it does, programs being advanced include the following elements: (1) individuals are given wide freedom to control their work and develop their skills; (2) the worth or value of the job is explained to the worker; and (3) status differentials between a superior and a subordinate in a group, or between one group and another, are replaced by an emphasis on shared organizational goals.

Leidecker and Hall view job enrichment as a *continuous* process that includes three stages: preparation, enriching, and implementing.[13] The first stage involves evaluating organizational climate, diagnosing enrichment needs, and obtaining personnel and managerial commitment. The second stage re-evaluates existing job content and job classifications to determine how they should be changed. The third stage introduces the actual changes into the work situation, including the strategies to implement them.

Not every effort to enrich workers' jobs proves successful, however. One electronics concern abandoned the idea when it found that women employees tended to become anxious and unhappy when given the added responsibility of checking the quality of their own work. Apparently, they were their own worst critics. Maurice D. Kilbridge of the Graduate School of Business at Harvard University asserts that "trying to reverse the process of division of labor is not technologically sound."[14] In a study in which workers were given more of a job to do, he found "no overwhelming evidence that people wanted variety in their work and a lot of contrary evidence that they didn't." Some, he says, actually prefer the sense of security of a small job within small surroundings.

Whether job enrichment contributes to increased satisfactions depends to a large extent on the type of work involved, the personality of the person doing the work, and the type of supervision employed. Many tough jobs, like digging for coal, eviscerating cattle, assembling autos, and welding a ship's hull, are basically dirty no matter how much we "enrich" them.

---

[11] Victor H. Vroom, *Work and Motivation* (New York: John Wiley and Sons, 1964).

[12] For details of this theory the reader is referred to Chapter 17.

[13] Joel K. Leidecker and James L. Hall, "A New Look at the Job Enrichment Concept," *Santa Clara Business Review*, Vol. 5, Number 1, Spring 1974, pp. 41–42.

[14] Roger B. May, *op. cit.*

Some researchers have been suggesting that in addition to redesigning jobs and restructuring production techniques to reduce worker alienation, some attention should also be given to *influencing behavior* in the work environment.

Alcoholism and drug use are prevalent in industry. Referring to drug use in an auto assembly plant, the president of a local union observes

> Drugs are used here. Not so much hard stuff—they use grass, some pills. Young people are on drugs, especially marijuana, like their parents are on alcohol. There's something else to drugs. It has to do with monotony, it has to do with society. Until you show the kids a better way of life, they're gonna stick on the grass.[15]

Alcoholism costs U. S. industry about $10 billion annually in sickness or accident benefits, low productivity, lost man-hours and absenteeism.[16] General Motors and the United Auto Workers have more than 100 joint alcoholism committees functioning in plants in the United States. A study of 101 Oldsmobile workers participating in G.M.'s Recovery and Rehabilitation Program disclosed after one year: 50 percent decrease in lost man-hours; 30 percent decline in sickness and accident claims; 63 percent reduction in disciplinary action; and 82 percent decrease in job-related accidents.[17]

More recent techniques that have been suggested are the use of hypnosis, professionally administered by qualified psychologists and psychoanalysts, to reduce tensions, build confidence, and overcome alcoholism and drug use.

Another suggestion has been to provide medical care including tranquilizers and other drugs, under carefully controlled medical and psychiatric supervision, to those employees who request help in adjusting to the work situation.[18] This novel and controversial approach has not as yet gained acceptance.

Job rotation.   Another way in which the meaning of the job can be expanded is through job rotation. This technique adds flexibility to job assignments. In job enlargement, jobs have to be redesigned. In job rotation, a person is moved at an opportune time from one existing job to another existing job. In some situations, to do this will require the approval and cooperation of

---

[15]Gary Bryner, president Lordstown Local 1112, UAW, quoted in Studs Terkel's *Working* (New York: Pantheon Books, 1974), p. 193.

[16]R. C. Gerstenberg, Chairman, General Motors, "Some Facts about the GM Employee Alcoholism Recovery Program," June 14, 1972, p. 5.

[17]George B. Morris, Jr. (Vice-President Industrial Relations, General Motors Corporation), Remarks before the Association of Labor-Management Administrators and Consultants on Alcoholism, at Denver, Colorado, April 27, 1974, pp. 15–16.

[18]Stephen P. Robbins, "Organizational Psychopharmacology: Drugs, Behaviour and the Work Environment," paper delivered at the Seventeenth Annual Conference, Midwest Division, Academy of Management, April 26, 1974.

unions, and union officials may resist since job classifications may have to be modified to accommodate the shift from job to job.

If two laborers are working, one with a pick and the other with a shovel, the task of each becomes routine and probably very monotonous. If the foreman permitted one man to use the pick for a few hours and then rotate and use the shovel, while the first man who had been shoveling switched to using the pick, the work would be more varied and the men would become skilled at two operations. The work might still be boring, but less so by virtue of rotating jobs.

In many areas job rotation can be an effective technique for making tasks more enjoyable and less routine. A salesman could be permitted to call on different types of customers or to travel in different geographic territories from time to time; a typist in an inner office could switch positions with the receptionist in the outer office for a few hours during the day. Each relieving the other would reduce the monotony for both. In many assembly lines there is a relief man who spells the others who may want to leave the line from time to time for compelling reasons. The relief man is sort of a utility infielder who can fill in at several positions. His job is less monotonous than the regular jobs on the line.

Job rotation could help to make executive training more meaningful also. It might be especially useful in training managers at the lower and middle levels of the hierarchy. Moving a trainee laterally into various positions helps that person to obtain a better overall perspective of the various operations than would be possible by remaining in one position, or even moving up and down within a given functional area. Lateral rotation can broaden one's scope and open up future avenues of communication that might otherwise be closed.

Not all job rotation is helpful. For example, in a hospital a nurse's encouragement to a patient is often a prime factor in speeding recovery. This relationship requires stable daily contact between patient and nurse. Ward transfers, shift rotations, and switches in days off tend to negate this. Thus the principle of rotation may be incompatible with hospital treatment goals.

In large companies, such as multi-plant and multi-national "super firms," position rotation of higher-level executives could be self-defeating. A manager shifted frequently around the country, or the world, to take executive positions in various plants or offices, cannot build permanent attachments to the places where he temporarily resides. Instead, he tends to identify strongly with his company and the more permanent attachments that it represents to him. The company receives greater loyalty from him than does a given country or community. He becomes very dependent upon the super firm. In his case, position rotation may make of him the very "organization man" that job rotation at lower levels is intended to discourage. Position rotation must be exercised with care, lest it foster the very corporate conformity it was intended to forestall.

Participative Activities

Subordinates are more inclined to accept decisions made by their superiors if they have been asked for their views, contributed to making the decisions, or been consulted in some way.

There are at least five types of participative action which are both feasible for the organization and conducive to a supportive climate whereby individuals can derive some of the personal satisfactions they seek from their work situation. These include: (1) use of a suggestion box; (2) policy formulation; (3) delegation of authority; (4) committees; and (5) mutual goal setting.

Use of a suggestion box. Employees may be encouraged to be creative, to contribute ideas for improving a product or a service, or to voice any other constructive ideas on their minds, through a carefully implemented suggestion box system.

Forms may be provided on which the contributor can state or illustrate the suggestion. It is forwarded to a suggestion box committee, which acknowledges receipt, thanks the employee for the suggestion, and advises that it is being evaluated. The suggestion is then forwarded to the proper department head for consideration and comment. If the suggestion can be used or implemented in some way, the original contributor should be advised and should receive an adequate reward, commensurate with the value to the organization of the suggestion being adopted. If, for good reason, the suggestion is unfeasible, the contributor should be advised, with reasons, and encouraged to submit other ideas. It is preferable that all suggestion box communications be in writing. Carefully administered and properly encouraged, the suggestion box can be a valuable device to enable anyone to contribute creativity to the organization knowing that it will receive impartial consideration. It also gives that person a splendid opportunity to participate. Sometimes, this type of participation brings recognition, a sense of accomplishment, and new job opportunities.

Policy formulation. As has already been pointed out, there is great merit in encouraging supervisory and operative personnel in all departments to participate in developing policies for their specific areas of activity.[19] Whether contributions come from the whole group or from delegates who represent the group, employee representation in policy-making decisions enhances the acceptance of those policies by all concerned. Moreover, subjective reactions are quickly noted and accommodated, making implementation more viable.

Delegation of authority. Assigning to another person a portion of one's portfolio of activities, coupled with the appropriate authority to enable him to perform effectively, is in itself a type of participative action. The subor-

---

[19]This subject was covered in Chapter 7.

dinate, in accepting a portion of the manager's total role becomes a participant in the management process to the extent of his assignment. It is a compliment to an employee to be asked to take on an assignment which is part of his superior's total area of authority. It lets him know that he is considered capable of handling a particular job, which perhaps not everyone would be offered. In the act of delegating, the manager enables the subordinate to participate through performing duties that are part of a higher or broader level of activity.

Committees. While there are disadvantages as well as advantages to committees,[20] their judicious use can be another effective means to encourage employee participation.

At higher organizational levels, committees may take the form of task forces, or special study and investigative teams. Middle- and upper-level executives, both line and staff, may be invited to serve on one of these special committees to assist top management with a unique problem and to make recommendations to alleviate it. There are situations where a committee at this level may serve on a continuing basis as a type of "collateral organization" to the basic organization. Members of this type of committee not only participate but bring their personal expertise to the committee. This unique circumstance gives them the climate for personal achievement, recognition, and perhaps self-fulfillment.

At lower levels, operating employees can also serve on various types of committees. In some cases, the entire group may serve as a committee of the whole. More often, members of the group will be invited by management to serve on a committee, or they may be elected by their fellow workers to represent them. In either case, the group is represented directly or indirectly and its contributions, ideas, and points of view are considered. The entire group of employees feel they are participating, that their position is being considered in management councils, and that the group is more than a mere cog in a huge machine. One area where committees can be used effectively as a participative technique is in formulating policy. Encouraging employee input in formulating policy, you will recall, is a participative act. Utilizing a committee for the purpose adds a participative medium in which the participative act can be fulfilled.

To the extent that people in an organization are given an opportunity to serve on any type of committee—for promoting safety, developing better ways to do things, or setting policy—they can break the tedium of their work routine and assume a different role. In that new role, certain personal satisfactions may be realized.

---

[20]These are discussed in our study of committees as adjuncts to basic line and staff structure in Chapter 15.

Mutual goal setting. According to some companies, allowing workers to participate in decisions affecting their jobs has a tonic effect on production results. Texas Instruments, Inc. initiated a pilot project in which 3000 blue-collar workers were grouped into teams and permitted to participate in determining how various jobs were to be set up to accomplish agreed-upon goals, and what tasks each team member would perform. The results were so successful that it was decided to expand this participative device to include 8000 workers and their supervisors. Mutual goal setting resembles and is closely related to "management by objectives," which also has a participative aspect to it.

Management by Objectives (MBO)

Management by objectives, often referred to as "management by results" or "supervision by results," focuses attention on *what* must be accomplished (goals) rather than *how* it is to be accomplished (methods). It allows the subordinate plenty of room to make creative decisions on his own. The supervisor is available for advice, counsel, and direction should the subordinate seek this assistance.

MBO has several unique advantages: (1) the superior and subordinate jointly arrive at a consensus of what should be accomplished (the participative aspect); (2) the subordinate is encouraged to make his own decisions, within the limits of the assignment and existing company policies and regulations, about the most effective way to achieve the agreed-upon results; (3) the supervisor measures and evaluates performance in terms of accomplishment rather than ability to carry out orders.

Management by results gives an individual or group some leeway to use imagination or creativity to accomplish the mission; fosters a feeling of independence; provides an incentive to achieve the goal; and permits a feeling of true participation in the task from its inception. When it comes to evaluating satisfactory performance, the results speak for themselves. The mission was either accomplished or it was not!

Frequently it is possible to establish time spans in terms of objectives. A salesman may concur with his sales manager that six months is a reasonable time to pioneer and develop a sales territory. Mutually, they establish a criterion of successful accomplishment, perhaps a given number of new customers to be added to the company books within the time limit. The salesman is then left more or less on his own to get the job done. He is responsible for the results at the termination of the agreed-upon time span.

A sales manager and his superior, the vice-president in charge of sales, could agree that company sales should be increased by 10 percent at the end of a 12-month period. After mutual concurrence on the time span, the sales manager assumes the responsibility for implementing the overall sales goal.

He, in turn, may establish objectives and time spans with each of his subordinates, the individual salesmen.

Management by objectives is not without its critics. Harry Levinson believes the ordinary MBO appraisal process, far from being a constructive technique, raises great psychological issues.[21] He believes that since it is based on a reward-punishment psychology, the process, in combination with performance appraisal, is self-defeating and serves to increase pressure on the individual while giving him a very limited choice of objectives. It is probably true that MBO tends to emphasize the quantitative rather than the qualitative aspects of performance in terms of goal achievement, and also deemphasizes the qualitative aspects of the way in which goals are pursued.

Properly Matching People to Jobs

The concept of management by results assumes that the employee has been properly selected and trained for the job, and is capable of deciding what procedures to initiate, or how to adapt existing ones, to accomplish the assignment. But this is not always the case. A great deal of worker dissatisfaction can be attributed to a misfit, a poor assignment, or misuse of the worker's talents. It may be the result of improper selection, inadequate training, or both.

Not all routine leads to worker alienation. There are instances in which workers find mass production work, or highly routine work, very satisfactory and welcome it as an opportunity to daydream, talk to fellow workers, and avoid direct supervision. In a plant that manufactured materials handling equipment, women at the end of the assembly line painted the completed steel sections by hand. All day long they hand-brushed paint on steel, but they enjoyed their work. It required only surface attention. They had ample time to daydream or socialize, and were seldom bothered by their foremen.

It has been suggested that where work has been highly simplified and routinized, mentally retarded persons can perform it satisfactorily and actually outproduce persons with normal intelligence by wide margins and with high levels of safety. A mentally retarded employee told an anxious social worker, "Don't worry about me getting hurt on the job. I've learned in business its only them that can think that gets hurt."[22]

Just as the blind have demonstrated their ability to perform in exemplary fashion complex jobs requiring high degrees of skill, and just as the deaf naturally do jobs under conditions of high noise levels that tax normal hearing, the educable mentally retarded (EMR) may very well find repetitive

---

[21]Harry Levinson, "Management by Whose Objectives?" *Harvard Business Review*, July–August 1970, pp. 125–134.

[22]Chris Argyris, "We Must Make Work Worthwhile," *Life*, May 5, 1967, p. 56.

detailed work that is monotonous and stultifying for some to be agreeable and even challenging.

Proper use of job definitions in which the job is clearly described and the qualifications of the prospective employee are carefully spelled out will reduce mismatches. Hiring the right person for a given job will go a long way toward reducing worker dissatisfaction. The concept of job definition, a prerequisite for properly selecting and matching people with jobs, was discussed at length in the previous chapter.

INFORMAL ORGANIZATION (PERSONAL RELATIONSHIPS)

Every formal organization maintains established work procedures and has its unique chain of command. Within these highly structured formal organizations personal relationships develop because jobs are performed by persons who are brought together initially by the nature of their work. As people, they interact. Slowly, there evolves a loosely knit, simply structured, informal organization, which includes managers as well as workers and which may extend beyond the work situation. It is the *non-work role* that leads to autonomous group behavior, sometimes called "informal organization."

Origin and Nature of Informal Organization

Man is naturally gregarious, a social being whose need for social interaction is one of his strongest and most urgent drives. People constantly seek new ways to establish a sense of belonging. These are provided, in part, by work associations. Social relationships are established which tend to serve the personal goals of the individual, his needs and his aspirations. Becoming a member of a group that shares similar goals and aspirations establishes a common bond. It fosters a sense of identity with a peer group, whose influence over him may become stronger than that exercised by management.

Formal organizations are job-oriented in terms of functions and authority; informal organizations are people-oriented in terms of personal and group goals. The informal organization never appears on an organizational chart, and it is seldom included in the overall planning of a company's operation. It is not established by authority or decree but develops as people associate with one another. A manager can create a formal organization and abolish it. He cannot create an informal organization or abolish it. It evolves within the formal, structured organization. As long as people need social intercourse, informal groups will exist.

Normally individuals develop social contacts with co-workers they see most often or with whom they work in close proximity. Waiters in a restaurant, order fillers in a warehouse, workers on the assembly line, and sewing machine operators seated near each other strike up conversations, share experiences, help each other out when in difficulty. They may eat lunch together, play cards during the lunch hour, bowl on the same team, invite each other to their homes, and gather families together for a picnic in the park. The social ties tend to become stronger over time, and often enduring friendships develop.

Most individuals become members of more than one informal organization. Informal groups develop quite spontaneously. A man may eat lunch with certain associates. After eating, he may play cards with another group, comprised of some of his luncheon companions plus others who now join the card-playing group. In this situation, he is a member of two informal groups—his lunch companions and his fellow card players. Should his work as an assembler in the shop also bring him into contact with the packers in the shipping department, he may strike up a social relationship with these workers. In that case, he becomes part of yet another informal group. These social contacts may also extend beyond the work situation.

Advantages of Informal Organization

The existence of informal organization has many advantages for its members and for the formal organization as well.

It provides social satisfaction.   The informal situation offers a person some of the social contact and recognition he seeks. As we have previously observed, many jobs in industry require only a small portion of a person's total capabilities; he frequently finds himself under-employed. In his role as worker, particularly in a large organization, a person may feel unimportant, just another social security number on the payroll. To his fellow workers, however, he has a personal identity. He can be himself, share his experiences, even "let his hair down." He may have found a sympathetic ear, someone to whom he can unburden himself, someone to whom he can talk. He can also enjoy the satisfaction of having others share their experiences with him, as they express themselves and perhaps confide in him. He is no longer just a number on the time card. With his peers he is important. He is somebody.

It helps to indoctrinate new workers.   The informal group can serve as an excellent medium to overcome the strangeness or unfamiliarity of a new job. Rather than risk the embarrassment that he may feel in repeatedly going to his supervisor for information, the new employee turns to his fellow workers for answers to such questions as, "Where do I get supplies? How long do we take for coffee breaks? What sort of person is the supervisor?" The peer group guides the neophyte and sets the example of acceptable behavior. Members of an informal group often turn to each other for advice and direction on how to do something, rather than seek help from the foreman or supervisor.

It provides a communication medium. Through the various informal groups to which an individual belongs, he learns what goes on in the organization and hears the latest news. In addition, the informal network enables a person to transmit information to others. A communication interchange is available that otherwise would not be.

It provides stability. The informal group becomes more than a collection of people on the job. It develops its own ways of doing things. It has its own code of honor, its own standards of conformity. Some are for the purpose of making things easier for its members. In a bank, tellers who have completed their daily tallies will help other tellers who are not finished and will receive the same assistance when they need it; waitresses in a restaurant may "pool" their tips and divide them equally; retail sales clerks may "spell" one another, giving each an opportunity to take an unscheduled break in the routine. The informal work group becomes a loosely knit but highly effective organization within the structured formal organization.

It develops solidarity. Strength exists in numbers. A group can exercise effective influence on individuals or groups outside itself. The position of the group can be made known to managers, unions, and to other informal groups. A total sense of group allegiance develops.

Disadvantages of Informal Organization

While there are distinct advantages to informal organization, there are also disadvantages.

It may create dissatisfactions. If a group does not accept a worker, he may find his work more distasteful than he would otherwise. His dissatisfaction may cause excessive absenteeism, or he may request a transfer, or perhaps quit the job completely.

It may determine output. The informal group may set its own work pace, and agree on a level of output which does not permit one member to outperform another. A new worker is often cautioned, "Slow down, buddy. Don't make waves." The group may establish goals that are at variance with those announced by management. Astute managers should recognize that this can occur and develop ways to accommodate both points of view.

It may enforce severe self-regulation. The informal organization tends to discipline its members through social pressures, social ostracism, or in extreme cases through physical threat or harm. Failure to comply with group standards of acceptable work output could lead to attempts by the group to bring the dissident member into line. The group can make life miserable for the non-conformist. Subtle attempts may be made to upset his work routine or to prevent his functioning effectively. Social ostracism or exclusion from the group privileges is a severe penalty for a person who must have group acceptance and approval to satisfy his strong need for social interaction.

It develops additional conformity. Wholehearted association with an informal organization demands that a person accept another kind of conformity in addition to that of the formal organization. In an attempt to avoid conformity and routine, he gravitates toward an informal group but finds this acceptance has its price. He is expected to conform to the codes and standards of the informal group and to identify with its interests and goals. Under these conditions, a person exchanges one type of conformity for another!

Leadership in Informal Organizations

Most informal groups tend to be small. Each has its leader, who was not elected or appointed but earned this status because of age, seniority on the job, dominant personality, special capability, physical strength, or some other characteristics.

In larger informal organizations there may be more than one leader whom the group will follow under given circumstances. An individual with more formal education than the others may be looked up to in matters that require formal communication. He may be asked to speak for the group in dealings with management, the union, or other informal groups. Another member, possessing more job experience and "know-how" may be consulted when direction or guidance is needed in handling a work assignment or solving some problems connected with it.

Often the leader of the informal organization must gain and maintain the recognition of its members, either by working with management or by working against management. Managers should recognize that this condition prevails. Knowing and understanding the leadership of the groups with whom he deals can be extremely useful to a manager.

A manager can build favorable relationships with informal leaders in several ways. He can consult with the leaders and seek their advice on technical matters or human relations problems. He can request their assistance and cooperation in indoctrinating new members and training them to become competent workers in their formal job assignments. Open, two-way communications can be encouraged on a continuing basis for mutual benefit. A manager must be careful not to reduce the status of the leader in the eyes of his constituents, and especially careful not to show favoritism or partiality.

Unions and Informal Organizations

Where present, the union is itself a formal organization that parallels the business organization. It has its own hierarchy of authority, its own organizational structure. A unionized employee finds himself a member of two formal organizations. Where the goals or purposes of the two are in opposition or at variance, the employee may face a conflict of divided allegiance.

The union additionally provides a climate in which new and different informal groups develop, built around union relationships, union activities, and union interests. Thus many of the advantages and disadvantages of informal organizations that are present in the job situation also exist in informal organizations within the union.

The presence of unions adds formal and informal structures to those found in the work situation, thereby making the total condition more complex and increasing its ramifications.

Management and Informal Organizations

Informal groups have it within their power to make a manager appear to be competent or inept. An astute manager recognizes the implications of this and can do several things:

1. Recognize the existence of informal organizations and let his employees know that he accepts and understands the need for them.
2. Before initiating action of any kind, consider the effect it might have on informal organizations. Changes requiring members to deviate from accepted norms of informal group behavior will be resisted.
3. Attempt to integrate the objectives of informal groups with those of the formal organization.
4. Maintain an equilibrium between both groups. This is essential if corporate objectives are to be achieved and maintained.

Work relationships and personal relationships tend to become bound together until they are inseparable. The latter have tremendous impact on work situations. Every business, except the one-man firm, is a society. People in that society relate to each other in many ways. The manner in which people mesh while working influences their satisfaction and ultimately determines the efficiency of their performance and the teamwork that develops. Formal and informal organizations can become a highly effective cooperating system.

SUMMARY

Relationships are always present in every organizational setting. Some relationships exist because the nature of the work associates one job with another as a matter of work flow. In addition to these procedural arrangements, there are also authority relationships, such as that established when someone is placed in charge of a group of workers. Together, procedural relationships and authority relationships produce the type of structure known as formal organization.

Many people criticize formal organizations as being too mechanistic and too rigid, limiting a person's usefulness. There is no way to eliminate the formal organization, but there are ways to reduce its limitations. Some of the strategies a manager can employ to reduce worker dissatisfaction and alienation are to expand the meaning of jobs to the workers, encourage participative activities, institute MBO programs when feasible, and properly match people to jobs in the course of filling job openings.

On the job, workers have contact with each other and many strong personal ties develop. Personal relationships produce another type of structure known as informal organization, with its own leaders, code of ethics, standards of behavior, advantages, and disadvantages.

Formal organizations and informal organizations tend to become inextricably woven together. The latter have a profound influence on the operation of the formal organization. A modern manager cannot afford to overlook the importance of informal organizations and should recognize the opportunities they present to help the formal organization achieve its planned goals.

KEY CONCEPTS

Procedural Relationships	Job Rotation
Serial Flow	Participative Activities
Parallel Flow	Mutual Goal Setting
Expanding the Meaning of Jobs	Management by Objectives
Job Enlargement	Personal Relationships
Job Enrichment	

REVIEW QUESTIONS

1. What kinds of relationships are present in work situations?
2. What is a formal organization? How does it originate?
3. Is conformity necessary in formal organizations? In informal organizations? Explain.
4. Give some examples of job enlargement, job enrichment, and job rotation. How do they differ?
5. What do you think of trying to influence change in worker behavior in addition to changing the work environment? How can it be accomplished?
6. Make a list of some participative activities that can reduce worker alienation.
7. What do you think of MBO?

8. How does MBO differ from mutual goal setting?

9. What are some advantages of belonging to an informal organization? Are there any disadvantages? Explain.

10. If you were a manager, how would you work with informal organizations within your formal organization?

Chapter 12

Procuring Personnel and Capital (Staffing)

The reader will recall that the process of organizing involves four major steps: designing enterprise functions and their relationships; designing jobs and their relationships; procuring personnel and capital; and assigning and conditioning personnel and capital to their respective duties.

Thus far, we have dealt with the first two steps in the process. Designing functions and their relationships and designing jobs and their relationships constitute the *planning functions* of organizing. They tell us what the organization ought to be. Without appropriate personnel and capital, however, we still do not have an organization. The organizing plan must be implemented.

Procuring personnel and capital, and then assigning and conditioning them to their respective jobs are the remaining steps in the organizing process. They are the *organizing functions* of organizing. Personnel procurement is one segment of the concept of *staffing*. Staffing is usually handled by trained specialists rather than by individual managers. Many firms have a staff department, the personnel department, that handles hiring, training, and most of the essential employee services. An industrial relations division is commonplace among the larger firms.

PERSONNEL PROCUREMENT

Getting the right people into the right jobs is essential if the organization is to be effective. At the outset, one must be realistic and accept the fact that jobs cannot be designed to fit people in a precise way, and people cannot be found who fit jobs in a precise way.

Selecting people improperly results in mal-assignments or misuse, which may create two negative conditions: over-employment or under-employment of their talents. In the former situation, when an individual finds himself in a job that is a little over his head he feels tense, insecure, and frightened. To relieve his anxieties he may turn to tranquilizers, liquor, or other forms of relief. His usefulness becomes limited. After a fair trial period he may have to be transferred to a position more suited to his abilities.

Errors in selection lend some support to the facetious **Peter Principle,** which states that managers tend to be promoted to the level of their incompetence.[1] According to Peter, a successful manager in one position is promoted to a higher one until he is finally "promoted over his head." On the other hand, this "principle" ignores the possibility that the area which a person oversees may grow in size and complexity until it outgrows the capability of the administrator holding the position. In such a situation, he also finds himself "in over his head" and probably should be transferred or replaced.

Under-employing the talents of employees is probably the more prevalent condition. The major effect of under-utilization is labor turnover. Managers are to blame for insisting on more competence than the current job requires. Companies insist on college graduates for positions which do not require this level of education. Frequently, a high school graduate or a graduate of a vocational school would do a better job. The college graduate is hired, finds the work boring, and quickly loses interest if his college degree does not seem to move him up the ladder quickly enough. He quits. Unfortunately, young people who quit because they are under-utilized are often persons with high potential, who have confidence in their capabilities and who would be willing to work hard to accomplish their personal goals if the job assignments were challenging. A study by General Learning Corporation indicates that between 1967 and 1975 industry will require 31.5 million new employees with less than four years of college.[2] There is an increasing demand for public vocational education to meet the needs of students and employers.

Even a high school educational requirement may not be related in any way to job performance ability. It may even be considered discriminatory against minority groups because of their presumed lack of educational opportunity. In 1971, in Griggs v. Duke Power Company, a suit was brought by a group of black laborers who wanted to apply for the higher-paying job of coal miner with the same company. The firm's employment policy specified a high school diploma as a prerequisite. None of the laborers had one. The United States Supreme Court ruled that the company's employment policy violated the Civil Rights Act of 1964. The key point was that the educational requirement was not actually necessary for job performance.

It is necessary to exercise judgment in fitting people to jobs, and jobs to people. There must be some flexibility. The job definition is our starting point. It contains the job description indicating the content of the job and the conditions under which it is performed, and the job specification outlining the qualifications an individual should have to do the job. Selective use of

---

[1]Laurence J. Peter and Raymond Hull, *The Peter Principle* (New York: Bantam Books, 1969).

[2]*Trends,* Whaley–Eaton Service, May 1, 1972.

these elements provides the manager with the tools for matching people and jobs appropriately.

Let us examine a hypothetical example, the job definition of riveter in the tail assembly of an aircraft. Highly simplified, a portion of the *job description* might be written as follows:

■ **Duties:** Rivet panels in aft fuselage sections. Work to exacting standards. Use automatic riveting tools.

■ **Conditions of work:** Difficult because of very close, confined quarters. Must perform under cramped conditions for extended periods. May have to work in kneeling or prone position.

The *job specification* might include:

■ **Skills:** Complete familiarity with the use of automatic riveting tools.

■ **Experience:** Five years experience as a riveter, with at least two years experience in aircraft fuselage riveting, preferably aft fuselage sections.

■ **Physical characteristics:** Should not be more than 5'4" in height. Maximum weight 125 lbs. In good physical health.

■ **Mental characteristics:** Should have no previous history of claustrophobia (fear of being closed in). Enjoys working alone.

In this hypothetical example, we are told about the work and the conditions under which it will be performed as well as the personal qualifications necessary to fill this job. There would be no point in hiring a skilled aircraft riveter 6 feet tall, weighing 195 pounds even if he enjoys working alone and does not have claustrophobia. Nor would there be justification to hire a 5'4" very experienced aircraft riveter weighing 120 pounds if he does not like to work alone or has a strong dislike for closed-in places. Both would obviously be misfits for this particular job.

Sources of Personnel

Knowing the types of jobs to be staffed, and the qualifications required to fill them, staffers must locate the appropriate manpower resources. They can either select from among persons presently employed by the organization, or turn to outside sources.

Within the organization. Capable talent is frequently available among existing employees. A person may be *transferred* from a present position to a new one at the same job classification level. This is known as a "cross-promotion" or **lateral promotion.** Or, a person may be promoted and receive an increase in pay, responsibility, and status.

If the position is a managerial one, the candidate may be available because he has been a member of the company executive training program.

To insure the availability of promotable people, one large firm maintains that "a strong executive *development* program is the only real insurance against the undesirable alternative of an executive *recruitment* program."[3] Over the years, many firms have filled key executive positions with men who matured in their own organizations. This is analogous to organized baseball where players can either be developed internally through the "farm system" or acquired outside through the "bonus system."

Having several people in training for each managerial position and each executive trained to handle several assignments is commonly referred to as having **management in depth.** Failure to develop management in depth can often lead to discontinuance of the firm. In a comprehensive study of transition in the wholesale drygoods industry, one of the reasons attributed to the demise of the two largest firms in the country was lack of depth in management.[4]

Where non-managerial positions are involved, firms use in-plant training to develop the necessary personnel. During the latter half of the 1960s, when skilled workers were scarce, small employers utilized on-the-job-training to provide their needs. Shop schools were improvised to produce the talent required for job openings. Under normal conditions, on-the-job-training is one of the most effective methods of internal development.

The policy of **promoting from within** has several advantages. (1) It increases motivation and employee morale. Workers know that job opportunities are filled by upgrading and promoting present employees. (2) Labor turnover tends to be reduced. (3) Management already knows the people being moved into position openings and can reduce the time and money spent in indoctrination.[5]

Promoting from within also has a number of disadvantages which should be recognized:

1. It can lead to "in-breeding," the development and perpetuation of habitual company practices. A man developed in the corporate mold tends to acquire ingrained characteristics that are difficult to alter. A great deal of what he knows and does is the result of years of learning the company's way of doing things. Fresh points of view are much less likely to be introduced when promotions are made from within, and the traditional way tends to continue. Proponents of promoting from within say that in-breeding can be reduced when executives attend management development programs at universities to gain fresh perspectives and knowledge of the latest developments in management and behavioral science; attend professional associa-

---

[3]Rockwell Report, *The Wall Street Journal*, May 18, 1964, p. 5.

[4]Mervin Kohn, *The St. Louis Merchant Drygoods Wholesaler in Transition*, Ph.D. dissertation, St. Louis University, 1957.

[5]Indoctrination is discussed in Chapter 13.

tion meetings to participate in informal discussions, read journals, hear lectures, and attend workshops and seminars which bring them up to date in their field of specialization; and participate in community activities where they can occupy key positions of leadership in civic, fraternal, and other groups and thereby derive valuable experience which is carried back to the work situation.

2. The most capable persons available are not always selected when the firm limits itself to searching internally to find people to fill vacancies. Better qualified men and women might be found if the organization permitted itself to look beyond its own portals.

3. Rivalries and jealousies may develop. When a managerial vacancy occurs in a department, there is a natural tendency for the remaining members to think of themselves as eligible for the succession. One person may feel that having been there the longest, he should be selected; another may sincerely believe that she is the most competent; a third may think that his close personal relationship with superiors who will make the selection will give him the nod over his fellow workers. In any event, should one of them be selected, the others may nurture a strong dislike for the successful one, festering a rivalry and jealousy that could impair the operation. However, if a person is brought in from outside, or from another branch or division, the unselected insiders tend to close ranks in opposition to the outsider. Should this person prove to be capable, the initial collective resentment would soon vanish.

Outside the organization.   For many organizations, it is imperative to go outside to obtain people to fill vacancies. Even for firms that do have a policy of promoting from within, upgrading people to higher-level positions creates openings at lower levels. Filling these necessitates hiring from outside. External sources may be required also when rapid expansion occurs, or when specific skills are not to be found internally.

Most organizations utilize one or more of the following resources in seeking new employees: recommendations from present employees; classified advertising; employment agencies; professional recruiters; and union arrangements.

Recommendations from present employees. Hearing of a vacancy in his department, a worker may suggest to some friend or relative that he apply for the position. During periods of economic prosperity and tight labor conditions, such as occurred during the 1960s, firms often ask employees to suggest people for job openings. They also ask suppliers, customers, and stockholders to direct technically trained people to the firm for employment consideration.

Classified advertising. For office personnel, semi-skilled or unskilled help, and for some types of white-collar and lower-management jobs, classified advertising is the device used to procure personnel. The effectiveness of this technique could be improved by discontinuing the use of blind-box-number ads and listing the name of the firm seeking applicants. While there are numerous reasons why box numbers are used, there is something very unfair about expecting applicants to apply for a position with a company whose identity is unknown to them. Many potential employees will not reply to box numbers.

Employment agencies. Many employers utilize the services of employ-ment agencies in recruiting personnel. Capable agencies can be instrumen-tal in pre-selecting applicants based on the hiring firm's specifications, and can then refer for final selection those who seem to fit the job definition. Most of the larger firms pay the fee to the employment agency for this service.

Professional recruiters. For middle- and upper-level managerial posi-tions, professional recruiters may be used. Some institutions contract with a recruiting firm, which is a type of employment agency specializing in placing management-caliber personnel. These firms may call themselves "career advancement" or "executive assessment" companies. Many personnel de-partments have their own internal recruiters who travel the country seeking employees for various departments of the company. Frequently company recruiters visit college campuses primarily to interview graduating seniors in chemistry, physics, engineering, and business.

What do personnel people look for when they interview a prospective college graduate? One study indicates that among differentiating, qualitative factors, five are considered more important than the others. Off-campus interviewers ranked these in order, as follows: (1) general ap-pearance, (2) applicant's future potential to the company, (3) personality, (4) conversational or communication ability, and (5) scholastic record.[6] The relative ranking of all fourteen factors is shown in Table 12-1

Limited evidence seems to indicate that success in business and scholastic record are related. American Telephone and Telegraph Company compared academic records with salaries of 17,000 of its executives and found that of the men who had been in the top third of their classes scholas-tically, 45 percent were also in the top third of the company in salary; of the bottom third scholastically, only 26 percent were in the top pay bracket.[7] On the other hand, a team of Harvard researchers led by sociologist Christopher Jencks reported that I.Q., amount and kind of schooling, home background, and heredity seem to bear little relationship to earning power

---

[6]Mervin Kohn, "Hiring College Graduates through Off-Campus Selection Interviewing," *Public Personnel Management,* Vol. 4, No. 1, January–February 1975, pp. 23–31.

[7]Frederick R. Kappel, "From the World of College to the World of Work," speech delivered at Westminster College, Fulton, Missouri, April 5, 1962.

Table 12-1. Criteria used in evaluating job applicants*

Rank	Criteria	Number of times ranked from 1 to 5 rank					Weighted total mentions	Percentage weighted total mentions
		1	2	3	4	5		
1	General appearance†	9	6	2	1	6	83	15.7
2	Applicant's future potential to company	8	3	4	1	5	71	13.4
3	Personality‡	7	4	4	1	5	70	13.2
4	Conversational or communication ability	2	6	7	4	3	66	12.5
5	Scholastic record	3	4	6	6	–	61	11.5
6½	Overall interview impression	4	5	–	6	4	56	10.6
6½	Past work experience	2	3	6	7	2	56	10.6
8	Applicant's future ambitions	–	2	3	2	5	26	4.9
9	Extracurricular activities	–	–	1	3	4	13	2.5
10	Pre-employment personnel tests	–	–	1	1	3	8	1.5
11	Faculty evaluation	–	1	–	1	–	6	1.1
12½	Personal references	–	–	–	2	1	5	0.9
12½	Military service or veteran	–	1	–	–	1	5	0.9
14	School attended	–	–	1	–	–	3	0.6
	Total	35	35	35	35	39		99.9

*From Mervin Kohn, "Hiring College Graduates through Off-Campus Selection Interviewing," *Public Personnel Management*, Vol. 4, No. 1, January–February 1975, pp. 23–31. Reprinted by permission of the international Personnel Management Association, 1313 East 60th Street, Chicago, Illinois 60637.

†In the questionnaire, traits of general appearance were provided and included: neatness, grooming, dress, and personal cleanliness.

‡Examples of personality traits included the following: sincere, agreeable, well-mannered, social awareness, and attitudes.

in later years. What matters most, Jencks suggests, are luck and the right personality.[8] In the Kohn study, scholastic record ranked fifth and personality third in importance in decisions to hire college graduates.[9]

Union arrangements. Where unions are associated with the business firm, recruiting for some jobs may have to be accomplished through the union, or with union approval. As in the case of the construction industry, the union hiring hall may be the source for obtaining new employees to fill job openings.

USE OF IMPROVED PROCUREMENT TECHNIQUES

Knowing the type of person needed to fill a position, and having sources of personnel available both within and outside the firm, enhances the process of acquiring the right person for the job. Business organizations can further improve their chances of selecting the most suitable person by improving their procurement techniques.

Evaluating a prospective employee's previous work history, checking the opinion of others, conducting a well-conceived personal interview, and administering personnel tests are ways to determine a person's fitness for a job. Each is a valuable tool in hiring. The proper use of several or all of them generally provides more information than any one by itself. Their improper use, however, will result in a lower return on "investment in personnel" than is necessary.

Well-Constructed Application Forms

A carefully prepared application blank is an effective tool for raising the quality of personnel procurement. It is probably true that what a man has done in the past is one of the best indicators of what he is likely to do in the future. The application blank is a device that should provide a great deal of information about what a person has done in the past. Most information offered without the guidelines provided by an application form is subject to errors of memory, fabrication, and exaggeration, some degree of falsification and embellishment, and a psychological tendency to repress unpleasant information or unsuccessful experience. Thus it is advisable to use a comprehensive, carefully constructed application blank. Information contained within it can provide valuable clues to the interviewer as he uses it in conjunction with the interview guide.

Most application forms are poorly designed, too lengthy, and ask many questions that are ambiguous and subject to misunderstanding or misinterpretation. For example, the question, "Where were you born?" is ambigu-

---

[8]Christopher Jencks, *Inequality*, (New York: Basic Books, 1972).
[9]Mervin Kohn, *Op. cit.*

ous. A person might answer "at home," "in a hospital," "in the city," and in many other ways. If the question is intended to seek information as to city, state, or country of birth, it should do so in very specific terms, leaving no room for doubt or confusion. Moreover, many forms contain questions of a personal nature unrelated to the person's fitness for the job. Others are designed to make psychological evaluations of the candidate based on the way he handles certain items. For example, an applicant could indicate his answer by encircling an item, underlining, placing a check mark, or crossing out certain unwanted selections. If he uses one of these options consistently, he may be evaluated as "consistent," or "determined," or "well organized." Should he use several of these methods in responding, he may be considered "inconsistent," "flighty," "poorly organized," and so on. Since the validity of such approaches is difficult to demonstrate, subjective evaluations of this type are unwarranted.

The well-designed application blank should seek only that information necessary and pertinent to a factual appraisal of a person's capability to fill the job under consideration. The format should be as concise and brief as possible, consistent with its purpose. It would be helpful if choices were limited to placing a check mark in an appropriate square. For example, marital status could be handled in the following manner:

single ____ married ____ separated ____ divorced ____ widowed ____.

The candidate simply checks the appropriate one.

It is strongly recommended that the use of *personal* references be dropped from application forms. The time-honored procedure of checking personal references too frequently is a waste of time. No applicant will ever knowingly supply the name of a person he believes will say something negative about him. The applicant may even advise his friends that they may be contacted for references and ask them to "put in a good word for him." Personal references tend to be stacked. Realizing this, many firms have discontinued their use. A.T. & T. is one of them.

Checking with previous employers is far more effective than checking personal references. Former supervisors who have observed the applicant at work are able to provide information pinpointed to specific job behavior. A telephone call to these work references will frequently reveal much more than a form letter. One can detect from the reference's voice and way of saying things much that never would be revealed in writing.

In developing an application form that will assist in doing an intelligent hiring job, a manager must bear in mind that the Civil Rights Act of 1964 prohibits discrimination in employment practices because of race, color, sex, religion, age, or national origin. In addition, the Fair Credit Reporting Act of 1971 requires employers to tell applicants when a retail credit check is being made and if it is the cause of an applicant's rejection.

Interviewing Procedures

A personal interview is a two-way street that should permit a frank, honest exchange of information between two parties. Any interview that accomplishes less than that is self-defeating. On the one hand, it allows the company to discover valuable information about an applicant which will not be revealed from psychological testing, reference checking, or previous work information. On the other hand, it provides an opportunity for the job seeker to learn many things about his prospective employer that he cannot discover through any other medium. Skillfully conducted, the personal selection interview supplements information that can be derived from using other techniques. Additionally, it provides essential information that helps an applicant decide whether the position with that organization is really for him.

While many factors contribute to an effective interview, it is imperative that the following three be carefully considered: (1) the interview setting; (2) capability of the interviewer; and (3) proper interviewing tools.

The interview setting.   The physical environment in which an interview is conducted will have a bearing on the results. Unfortunately, most firms do not pay sufficient attention to the necessity of providing a setting that enhances the meeting of two strangers.

Interviews have been conducted through a hole cut in a glass partition that separated the interviewer, seated at a desk on one side, and the interviewee, standing on the other—hardly a setting conducive to obtaining the best available talent! The interviewing locale should be quiet, private, and tastefully furnished, and should provide a chair no less comfortable for the applicant than for the interviewer.

Capability of the interviewer.   It takes a great deal of skill to interview. It is an art that requires considerable human relations ability. Interviewers must like meeting people and helping them. An applicant enters an interview at a psychological disadvantage, and interviewers should understand this. The interviewer must quickly establish rapport, set the applicant at ease, meet him as an equal. Having done this, a skilled interviewer asks pertinent questions, none of which should embarrass the applicant or make him uneasy. The results of any interview will never be better than the capability of the person assigned to conduct it.

Proper interviewing tools.   To facilitate the interview, and to reduce subjective judgments, there are various tools available. Two of these are the interview guide and the interview report.

The **interview guide** is a planned format designed to *standardize* selection interviews and to make them more objective. It is a printed form that lists a number of information areas, including work history, health, education, and personal, social, and financial data. It may ask for a simple statement or answers to brief specific questions: "Please describe the kind of work you did in your last job"; "How will your schooling help you to be successful in the job for which you are being considered?"; "What do you do in your spare time?"; "Why do you want this job?". The answers are recorded on the form.

The **interview report** is used by the interviewer to *summarize* the information recorded in the interview guide, and to prepare a rating scale based on his interview impressions. The report rates from "unsatisfactory" to "outstanding" the following factors: appearance, friendliness, poise, conversational ability, alertness, personality, drive, and information about the general work field. Such information does not appear in the interview guide. The interview report also contains recommendations with reasons to hire or not to hire, and the type of work for which the applicant appears best qualified. The report should be completed soon after the applicant has left the meeting, while the information is fresh in the interviewer's mind. It can be referred to on subsequent occasions when a person may be interviewed again for a higher-level position.

Personnel Tests

While a great deal of knowledge is obtained from evaluating the application blank, and from a face-to-face objective interview with the job applicant, there may be additional information the employer would like to have about the prospect which can only be obtained from personnel tests. Carefully selected and skillfully employed, personnel tests can be a useful tool in the personnel selection procedure.

There are many varieties of personnel tests, but the three types most frequently employed are (1) psychological tests, (2) performance tests, and (3) trade knowledge tests.

Psychological tests.   Of all procurement techniques, the most frequently misused, and least understood, are psychological tests. Insufficient attention has been paid to their limitations, to the qualifications of persons who administer them and those who interpret their results, to standardized test conditions, and to the anxiety and psychological condition of the person taking the test. Most psychological tests are of the "paper and pencil" type, designed to measure intelligence, aptitudes, interests, personality traits, emotional stability, and additional factors. Others are of a "motor" type, designed to measure reaction time, manual dexterity, finger dexterity, eye–hand coordination, and other traits involving acuity or movement.

Psychological tests have been classified on the basis of the following criteria:

1. *Speed versus power.* Speed tests have a time element built into them so that few people can complete the test in the allotted time. The assumption is that the more capable person will produce more correct answers within the

time limit than will the less capable person. Thus speed of performance has an appreciable effect on test results. When there is sufficient time for every person to consider every item on a test and to indicate his answers, it is called a power test.

2. *Verbal versus non-verbal.* Response to verbal tests requires comprehension and use of words and language, whereas the non-verbal test does not require these attributes in order to respond. Manipulation is substituted for verbal response, and may take the form of matching blocks, fitting pegs into a board, or placing irregular objects into matching cutouts on a plane surface.

3. *Individual versus group.* Individual tests are administered to one person at a time, whereas group tests are given to groups of people simultaneously. The ACT Assessment for college entrance is a group test; the driver reaction time test to determine eligibility for an automobile driver's license is an individual test.

4. *Objective versus subjective.* Objective tests are of various types, the more familiar being true-false, multiple choice, completions, and matching. The objective test derives its name from the objectivity of the scoring method. Essay-type tests, on the other hand, are largely subjective. The results are based on the scorer's interpretation of what has been written. Even with trained scorers, there is a built-in scorer unreliability. Give the same essay answer to different capable scorers to review, and their evaluations will vary. The same limitation prevails with projective tests such as writing a story about what you see in a picture or illustration. The Rorschach Test and Thematic Apperception Tests are projective tests that take unusual skill in administering and interpreting.

The use of psychological tests as a procurement device has two basic purposes. The first purpose is to predict the likelihood of a person succeeding in the job for which he is being considered. If it later develops that predictions based on test results are not much better than could have been made without their use, then the tests failed to achieve this purpose. The second purpose is diagnostic. It may uncover relative strengths essential for effective performance, or weaknesses that would limit a person's effectiveness in the job. Such diagnoses might spot areas where additional training and instruction would contribute to successful job performance; determine the degree of creativity that a person possesses; or discover considerable deviation from normal behavior which might disqualify the person for the job. Of the two uses, their use as a predictive device has more relevance in business hiring. However, even for this purpose, psychological tests must be used with extreme caution and discretion.

In business and industry, the psychological tests most widely used in personnel procedures are those designed to measure intelligence and aptitude. In general, these have their greatest value in group testing, particularly where massive screening is necessary and where little other basis exists for selecting a few from the many. Their validity is based on group results and group data. In other words, intelligence tests and aptitude tests, while useful for predicting group results, are not valid for predicting what an individual person within the group will or will not do based on his test score.

Inadequacies and unfairness in the use of intelligence tests in industrial hiring were vividly brought into the open in the famous Motorola case of 1964. The Illinois Fair Employment Practices Commission ordered the company to stop using a general ability test in its hiring practice because it discriminated against "the hitherto culturally deprived and the disadvantaged groups." This issue had been troubling social scientists and educators for a long time.

In Griggs v. Duke Power Company, the Supreme Court also ruled that testing for employment or promotion must be "job-related" rather than general, and that the burden of proof is on the employer. Thus, if a specific level of intelligence is required by the company for a particular assembly line job, the employer must be prepared to provide by validation studies that the requirement is necessary for the proper performance of the job. As a result of this decision, personnel managers will have to place greater reliance on techniques other than intelligence tests in hiring and promoting. In Youngstown, Ohio, the Civil Service Commission wisely decided not to require the city's garbage truck drivers and loaders to take a civil service test for these positions in its sanitation department. Many of the older long-time employees who were doing their work in excellent fashion were afraid they would lose their jobs because they were illiterate and could not pass the tests.

Where personnel departments find psychological tests of aptitude, personality, interests, attitudes, or emotional stability helpful in selection or promotion, the use of a group of tests rather than a single test is usually more meaningful in measuring a trait. A series of tests covering many traits produces a "profile" which is a more valid overall appraisal. Although a battery is generally more valid than a single test, there are exceptions. A major producer of objective tests had this to say:

> . . . I'll never forget our experience with an Army test to identify potential radio repairmen. We developed an elaborate battery; then we cross-validated it with some of the kids who went to radio repairmen's school. We came up with the awkward answer that the entire battery was not as good as one question: "Would you like to be a radio repairman?"[10]

---

[10]Lyle W. Spencer (President, Science Research Associates), *University of Chicago Magazine,* May–June 1963.

Performance tests.   Performance tests are those in which the applicant actually demonstrates his ability to do the job.

If a man applies for a job as a tractor-trailer driver, for example, giving him an opportunity to "spot" a trailer by backing it into a loading bay would be a quick way of observing whether he can do what he says he can. A woman who applies for a position as a stenotypist can quickly demonstrate her ability by taking dictation on her machine at the prescribed number of words per minute, and then transcribing them. Similarly, a performance test can be given to a stenographer or a typist. Not only will the actual performance indicate the operator's speed, but accuracy can easily be determined as well. Performance tests are not always feasible, but where they can be used they are one of the best procurement tools.

Closely related to performance tests are *simulation tests*. Since the actual conditions may not be available, simulated conditions and situations are provided. An example would be a road test in which the driver, sitting behind a mock-up dashboard and steering wheel, views a screen depicting highway driving conditions, road signs, oncoming traffic, and the behavior of drivers of other vehicles. He is observed or his movements recorded as he reacts to changing situations. Another example is a training simulator of a cockpit of an airplane, where the conditions are almost realistic, and the prospective pilot is asked to put the ship through its paces.

Trade knowledge tests.   While trade knowledge tests do not indicate how well an applicant can perform, they do indicate his familiarity with the content of the job. Thus, if a man indicates that he is a practitioner of a given skill, the relevant trade knowledge test will enable a personnel technician to determine whether the applicant is familiar with the job functions, terminology, equipment used, and other pertinent information. It indicates whether he is knowledgeable about the job or not.

A man claiming to be an automotive mechanic, for example, should be able to explain what engines, carburetors, axles, differentials, transmission, and ignition systems are and how they are related to each other. He should "speak the language." A radio mechanic, welder, electronics or electrical man, if he is what he says he is, should be familiar with the theory, symbols, and equipment involved in the work. This does not necessarily mean that he is competent or can even do the work. But it does indicate that he is familiar with the trade or craft, and perhaps if given some training and on-the-job experience could quickly fill the job in question. A person having absolutely no familiarity with the trade would find it extremely difficult to fake his way through a trade knowledge test.

Thus we have observed that the function of staffing can be expedited when adequate job definitions, sources from which prospects can be obtained, and improved procurement techniques exist.

REQUIREMENTS FOR AN EXECUTIVE

Most of what has been said so far about staffing refers to rank and file employees in an organization and to lower- and middle-level managers. Does a firm look for something different in hiring or promoting an upper-level or top-level manager? Should he possess skills or characteristics different from those of lower-level managers? The answer to these questions is yes.

Characteristics of an Executive

Robert Frost once observed that if a man works faithfully eight hours a day he may eventually get to be a boss and work twelve hours a day. While it is difficult to describe a "typical" executive, men who arrive at the top managerial posts in organizations usually possess a favorable combination of the following characteristics or attributes: personal endowments, favorable personality, and managerial skills.

Personal endowments.   Five traits that are sought in high-level executives are intelligence, open-mindedness, desire for responsibility, high movitation, and adaptability.

Intelligence. Most top-level managers possess a high level of intelligence including great analytical ability. Most have college degrees. In a study of 200 executives promoted to president or vice-president of their companies, 77 percent were college graduates; only four percent had only a high school education or less.[11] In another survey covering 492 presidents in 700 of the largest companies in industrial, merchandising, transportation, life insurance, and utility fields, 35.7 percent had graduate degrees. More than 83 percent had at least a bachelor's degree; only 16.7 percent did not have a degree.[12] A sheepskin, which implies sufficient intelligence to complete college-level studies, is almost a "must" to reach the top rungs of the corporate ladder today.

Open-mindedness. Top-level managers tend to be rational and logical in their approach to situations. They are usually more objective and less prone to personal bias in evaluating problem areas and making realistic recommendations than others lower in the organizational hierarchy.

Desire for responsibility. Executive-caliber managers welcome responsibility and have a deep sense of obligation to their company, its employees, its customers, its suppliers, and to the community. Leaders in business and industry, in their role as top managers, are concerned individuals.

High motivation. Corporate executives have an intense desire to succeed. A top manager is ambitious and continually seeks new opportunities. He welcomes challenges, wants more than his present job offers. He pos-

---

[11]*The Wall Street Journal,* December 7, 1966, p. 9c.
[12]*The Wall Street Journal,* September 29, 1967, p. 13.

sesses an unusual amount of drive. Often he will prepare himself for promotion by mastering the essentials of the job above him.

Adaptability. A top executive is flexible and adaptable. He is capable of changing his attitude when necessary and is not fixed or rigid in his position.

Favorable personality.   Personality is largely the result of a person's experience and development as a member of society rather than of native endowment. **Personality** represents *that part of one's self that is exhibited to others.* As such, it includes such outward manifestations as integrity, fairness in dealing with others, friendliness, honesty, cheerfulness, and likableness. It includes charisma and charm. It is the totality of an individual's behavior and emotional characteristics as others perceive them.

A manager's personality, which is manifested in face-to-face relationships, is important to a subordinate. Irritability, lack of understanding, aloofness, partiality, insincerity, and other negative characteristics detract from a subordinate's expectation of his superior. A worker's role-perception of a manager includes the expectation that he will be a person the worker will like, trust, respect, find fair, and who is approachable.

It is particularly important for a manager to be approachable. A man on the job likes to know that his boss is a person to whom he can talk, not only about job-related problems but about personal problems as well. An astute manager must recognize and appreciate the importance of this expectation. As busy as he is, he must arrange his time in order to be reasonably available to his people should they want to discuss things with him. A manager who is respected, trusted, and sought out by subordinates when they need his advice and counsel increases the probability of being successful when he enlists their cooperation in directing their efforts toward organizational objectives.

From the manager's point of view, while there is no one best style of leadership for every situation in which he finds himself, his chances to perform well are increased if he occupies a position that is compatible with his personality.

Managerial skills.   In the early pages of this book, it was pointed out that managing is an art; the manager is a practitioner, utilizing his talents and skills. At this point, we shall examine what some of those skills are. They include conceptual, human relations, and specialization skills.

Conceptual skill. Conceptual skill encompasses the ability to "see the big picture," to recognize and understand broad relationships, to work with abstractions, to develop models. It enables a manager to recognize problems and to solve them. Probably the outstanding trait of a top executive is the ability to get right to the heart of a matter, to separate the essential from the non-essential, and thus make decisions. Most people are not blessed with this capability. An executive's decision-response to changing events in his internal and external environment is conditioned by his interpretation of those events. Conceptualization is important because it strongly influences overt behavior. Inability to conceptualize is evidenced by inappropriate managerial action in which effort is focused on solving a non-existent problem while the actual problem is not perceived, or in applying inappropriate action to a real but ill-defined problem, or in treating symptoms rather than causes.

Problem-solving ability is one of the characteristics sought by top executives when considering managers for promotion. The person who can cut through a maze of data, varied information, and red tape to get to the core of the matter is the one with the best chance of making it to the top. Instead of contacting his boss with "We've got a problem. What shall we do about it?" he will work out a solution on his own initiative and will report: "This was the problem. These were the options open to me. This is what I did. Here are the results."

The renowned industrialist and oil tycoon, J. Paul Getty, makes this statement about hiring or promoting an individual to an executive post.

> How do I judge whether or not a man is—or would be—a good executive? I hold that the first acid test of an executive is his ability to think and act for himself. He should have the intelligence and ability to originate ideas, develop plans, implement programs, solve problems, and meet situations without running constantly to his superiors for advice. In my opinion, a man who cannot do these things is not an executive.[13]

It is characteristic of the top executive, the "generalist" in industry, that he possesses conceptual skill that enables him to coordinate and integrate all activities of his organization toward a common objective. It has been said that the attitudes of a top executive color the character of the organization's response, and determine the "corporate personality" that distinguishes one company's way of doing business from another's. These attitudes are a reflection of the administrator's conceptual skill. Conceptual skill tends to deal with *ideas*.

Human relations skill. This skill involves dealing with *people*, principally those within the organization. Directing human activities requires the ability to work with people, to develop team effort toward corporate goals. In general, meeting people well and working well with them is the key to human relations skill. However, there is some evidence this is less necessary at the corporate level of management than at operating levels where more frequent face-to-face relationships with subordinates occur.

One of the important ingredients in human relations skill is leadership ability. Few men are natural leaders. Most intelligent, willing men can

---

[13]J. Paul Getty, "What Makes an Executive," *Playboy*, Vol. 9, No. 5, May 1962, p. 95ff.

develop qualities of leadership adequate to meet most situations they will encounter during their careers as managers.

Specialization skill. Expertise, technical competence, and knowledge and proficiency in a particular specialty are included in this concept. This kind of skill is more relevant at the operating and middle-management levels of the business than at top levels. Specialization skill is essential for the accountant, engineer, purchasing agent, or quality control manager. At the corporate level more generalized than specialized experience is required. Specialization skill tends to deal with *things.*

The relative importance of these management skills (conceptual, human relations, and specialization) at different levels of management is shown in Figure 12-1. Considerable conceptual skill, some human relations skill, and relatively little specialization skill are utilized by the top-level manager. The job of the corporate "generalist" primarily requires that he see the forest rather than the trees, quickly visualize relationships, spot problems and make decisions from a broad perspective to coordinate the multi-activities of the organization. The nature of his job at the apex demands less utilization of technical skill. At the lower levels of management, particularly where a face-to-face relationship exists between superior and subordinate, there is need for the manager to demonstrate a considerable amount of technical skill and a lesser degree of conceptual skill. Superior technical competence may be a primary requirement of the manager at this level, and a basis for justifying his leadership role in the eyes of his subordinates. To do his job effectively, he will also rely to a larger extent on his human relations skill than does the top-level manager. Between the corporate manager and the operative manager are the middle-level managers, serving as heads of functional

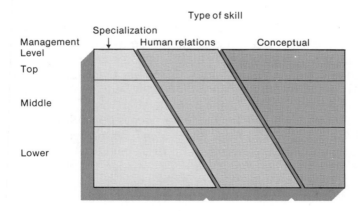

Figure 12-1.   Relative importance of major managing skills at different levels of management.

areas like sales, production, and purchasing. They discover that their positions utilize a more balanced mix of managerial skills than is required for performance at other management levels.

In time of stress, such as a sharp or prolonged profit decline, a serious curtailment of market share, or similar dire contingencies, a board of directors may have to consider replacing the organization's chief executive officer in order to turn the company around. Should the new chief executive be drafted from a top-level job within the company or should the position be filled by an executive who has had no prior connection with the firm?

It is very likely that the existing unsatisfactory state of affairs stems from a failure of incumbent management to accommodate to changing conditions, and it is unlikely that corrective action taken by incumbents will be extensive enough to improve the situation. First, in all probability an executive from within participated in and agreed with decisions that led to the present state of affairs. He would be reluctant, therefore, to make important changes that might be required in policies, goals, and relationships and would be constrained by previous precedents, commitments, and loyalties. Second, organizations tend to be colored by the personality of the president or chief executive. Studies have shown that executives tend to promote subordinates who tend to think and act as *they* do. While this may be desirable for stability and continuity, it tends to restrain significant change.

These restraints will not hamper a new chief executive selected from the outside. He will view the organization's problems with greater objectivity and feel free to formulate new plans, new views or resource allocations, and new ways to implement them. Usually he will also enjoy the support of executives in the organization who are looking for new leadership to deal with the problems that have been plaguing them.

Limited evidence seems to indicate that under conditions requiring sweeping adjustments, organizations should bring in a top executive from outside. In one study of ten major publicly held firms that changed their top executives in order to improve profitability, five companies promoted an insider and five brought in an outsider. Of the six firms that significantly improved their profit trend, five were those that had brought in an outsider.[14] All five outsiders had succeeded in turning their companies around, whereas only one of the five insiders was successful. While it is possible to theorize that the successful firms might also have turned around if headed by an insider, and that the unsuccessful firms might not have done any better if the assignment had been given to an outsider, it appears that a board of directors faced with a decision of replacing a chief executive in order to improve a poor profit picture would do better to select an outsider.

---

[14]Arie Y. Lewin and Carl Wolf, "When the CEO Must Go," *Advanced Management Journal*, Vol. 39, No. 3, 1974, p. 59.

Transferable management skills. The question is frequently raised concerning "transferability of managerial skills." Can an executive in one type of industry be hired successfully to fill an executive role in an entirely different industry? Are all managerial skills transferable? Can they be put to use at comparable managerial levels in any organization? Let us observe.

The skills required at upper management levels are transferable! The president of a department store could probably assume the presidency of a bank; the president of a railroad could direct the overall activities of a soft drink bottling company. There are countless examples of presidents and vice-presidents of firms leaving to accept an equivalent or higher-level post with a firm in an entirely different industry, and doing so successfully. A vice-president of a major oil company becomes president of a large integrated wood and paper products company; an owner of a small but promising advertising agency sells out to become president of Good Humor, leaves to become an executive vice-president of Colgate Palmolive, and winds up as chief executive of Norton Simon, Inc. The conceptual and human relations skills that an executive possesses are transferable. Specialized skills, even if he possesses them, are only minimally required to function effectively at this high level. Furthermore, in addition to possessing transferable skills, executives of this caliber are exceptionally talented individuals and have the capacity to be top executives almost anywhere.

In the *middle* to upper-level range of management, skills are also transferable. A sales manager for a shoe manufacturer may well be able to perform as a sales manager for a ladies sportswear factory, or in other consumer-oriented product areas, especially if the channels of distribution are similar. Sales managers are able to direct sales activities in many product areas, including those which are unrelated, since their work chiefly requires a high degree of conceptual and human relations skills, both of which are transferable, and a lesser degree of specialized or technical competence.

It is unlikely that specialized expertise employed at *lower* management levels can be transferred. The very nature of specialization is self-limiting. A man is skilled for a "particular" job. The foreman supervising "lasting operations" in a shoe factory probably could not step into the role of foreman supervising an equal number of subordinates in the grey iron casting department of a foundry. Each position requires a specialized, unique understanding and mastery of technical know-how which takes years to acquire and which does not have transferable dimensions. "Lasting" operations are not "casting" operations. Each of these managerial positions requires less use of conceptual and human relations skill relative to technical competence for satisfactory performance. It should be noted, however, that mere possession of specialization or technical skill does not qualify a man to be a manager, even at the lowest level of management. An excellent sales-

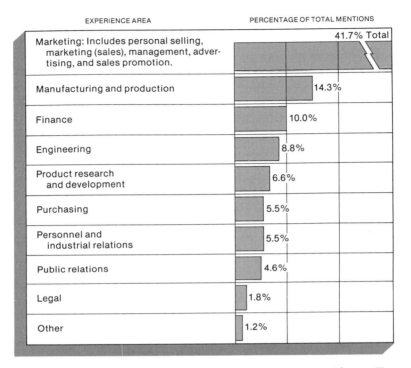

Figure 12-2.   Primary experience areas of company presidents. (Reprinted by permission from Sales & Marketing Management. Copyright 1966.)

man may not make a good sales manager; a technically trained and competent factory worker may not make a good factory superintendent or even a good foreman. Qualities in addition to technical skill are required to become a manager even at the lower levels of the hierarchy. Personal endowments, favorable personality traits, and human relations skill are among them.

A number of studies have been made to determine the primary experience of top executives. One of these, covering presidents of industrial firms, indicates that backgrounds in marketing and manufacturing are the most direct route to the top. In another survey of presidents, 960 corporations with net worth of over $1 million were selected at random from Dun & Bradstreet's Million Dollar Directory. Heads of 389 companies who replied indicated their primary areas of experience were sales or marketing, followed by manufacturing and finance. The results of this study are summarized in Figure 12-2.

Indications are that in companies producing industrial and consumer goods, the primary routes to the presidency are marketing and manufacturing. This is not surprising since selling and operating are the basic line functions in all business operations, whereas finance, engineering, personnel, and law are staff activities.

PROCUREMENT OF CAPITAL

Procurement of personnel, though a very necessary component of organizing, is not in itself sufficient to produce an effective organization. The tendency when dealing with the concept of "procurement" is to overlook completely the role of capital or to minimize its influence on job design and ultimately on overall structural design. Without the necessary tools, equipment, and machinery, people will not be very productive. Resources required to implement the plan, to reach a goal, or to solve particular problems include both people and capital.

Every job requires a full complement of facilities to make performance meaningful and productive. In fact, without capital equipment and a structure to house it, there would be no jobs. Jobs require raw materials, inventories, replacement parts, and cash on hand. It is only as managers convert dollars from capital funds into profitable job-making facilities that continuing jobs come into being.

There are two primary sources for obtaining capital funds for business: investors and lenders. **Investors** provide the *equity capital,* whereas **lenders** provide the *debt capital.* After operations have been established at a profitable level, a portion of the firm's revenues, called *retained earnings,* are reinvested or "plowed back" into the business for further growth or improvement. They are an extremely important source of capital and have been estimated to constitute between one-half and two-thirds of all investment. Depreciation allowances, when earned in the course of successful operation, also provide a source of "cash flow" to be re-used in the business.

Depreciation, or capital recovery, should allow for replacement of worn-out or obsolete plant and equipment, but because it is based on *historic* costs, it does not allow for inflation. Allowable depreciation of facilities is falling short of replacement costs by $16 billion a year and the gap will widen as costs escalate. Tax reformers have suggested that one means to alleviate the situation would be legislation permitting accelerated depreciation. Organizations would accrue depreciation allowances as rapidly as possible and this would become an important determinant in capital planning.

With accelerated innovation, improved technology and increased specialization, the number of dollars required to create and maintain a job has grown very rapidly. The Chamber of Commerce of the United States made this observation in one of its studies:

> The great rise of our living standard over that of our forebears is largely traceable to invention, discovery, science, engineering, managerial know-how,

and the great increase in the average investment per job. The worker today is essentially the same organism that he was at the time of Aristotle. He still has only two hands, his back is no stronger, and his I.Q. no higher. He is better educated and generally more skillful; but, basically the difference between the output per worker today and the output of decades and centuries ago is due to this technological revolution bringing more and better tools. . . . [15]

In the early days of the automobile, it took a skilled worker over 8 hours to shape the top half of a gas tank, using hand tools. Today, it is accomplished in 20 seconds by a forging machine.

One of the greatest challenges facing American industry is finding the necessary capital to finance expansion. Edgar Speer, Chairman of U.S. Steel Corporation says:

> The main question now is how does a business accumulate enough cash to expand. For the past decade and a half, there has not been enough of the gross national product going back into business to renew plants and build new capacity. [16]

It has been estimated that during the next decade at least $250 billion will have to come from new ownership, or equity capital. Yet since 1958 the investment group primarily composed of small, individual investors has been a net *seller* rather than purchaser of stocks.

Some business leaders, economists, political scientists, and investment analysts indicate that incentives which encourage individual investors to provide the needed equity capital have been largely eliminated by the anti-investment bias of our tax laws. These include double taxation of dividends, stringent capital gains taxes, and unrealistic depreciation allowances.

Some idea of how much investment is necessary for each industrial job, and how the amount has been increasing, can be obtained from comparing figures published by the First National Bank of New York in 1960 with those compiled in 1975 by the author. The Bank figures covering the 100 largest corporations in the country showed they employed 6.5 million workers and utilized total assets of $136 billion—an average capital investment of approximately $21,000 per employee. [17] The examination by this author of the 100 largest corporations in the *Fortune* list of 500 industrial companies in 1975 indicated they employed 8.3 million workers and used total assets of 428.0 billion—an average capital investment per employee of $51,784, an increase of more than 148 percent in just 15 years. Moreover, during the same period, the number of employees increased by 28 percent, whereas the total

---

[15]*Brevits*, Vol. Q, No. 4, February 15, 1960.

[16]Edgar Speer, from an address before the local chapters of the Steel Service Center Institute and the Purchasing Management Association in St. Louis, Missouri, September 28, 1974.

[17]*Brevits, Op. cit.*

amount of assets increased by 215 percent! To increase productivity in our highly industrialized economy apparently requires that industry must become increasingly "capital intensive." Simply hiring capable people to fill necessary positions is not enough. The concept of "procurement" as a stage in the organizing process, therefore, includes personnel *and* capital. Both are components of job design.

Productivity of Capital

One of the fastest ways to improve the profitability of a business is to improve the productivity of capital. If capital turnover can be increased from one time a year to 1.2 times a year, total return on capital can be increased 20 percent.

Fixed capital and **working** capital require different approaches in managing their productivity. Unlike fixed assets, working capital is not "directly" producing capital but rather is "supportive" capital. In a typical business it strongly supports inventory and accounts receivable (inventory management and credit management).

Like any other segment of a business, capital productivity must be managed. This position echoes that of Peter Drucker who states:

> It is high time that American business managers, in the great majority, learn and accept that managements are paid for managing productivity, especially the productivity of capital, on which, in the last analysis, all other productivities depend; that the productivity of capital can be managed, and that the productivity of capital *must* be managed.[18]

One way to improve capital productivity is to use capital more intensively, to turn it over more frequently. One firm, Palm Beach Company (men's clothing), estimates that for each day it decreases the length of time its accounts receivable are outstanding (average collection period), it increases its cash flow by $322,000.[19]

SUMMARY

Designing functions and their relationships and designing jobs to fit those functions provide a plan for an organization, but without people and capital there is no organization.

Getting the appropriate personnel to fill the jobs is part of the staffing process. Basically, people can be obtained from within the existing organization or they can be recruited from outside. There are advantages and disad-

---

[18]Peter Drucker, "Managing Capital Productivity," *The Wall Street Journal,* July 24, 1975, p. 14.
[19]Palm Beach Company, Annual Report to Stockholders, January 30, 1976, p. 4.

vantages to utilizing either source. Whichever source is tapped, the chances of placing the most suitable person in each position opening is greatly improved when procurement techniques are carefully developed and utilized. Properly employed, application blanks, selection interviews, and personnel tests can be valuable tools in the staffing process.

In selecting executives, some of the basic attributes sought include personal endowments, favorable personality traits, and managerial skills. At certain levels of management, particularly top and upper levels, management skills are transferable.

Often overlooked but extremely important in the organizing process is the procurement of capital. Few jobs have much productive meaning without the necessary tools and equipment (capital). Realistically, jobs are the end product of continuing infusion of capital into our productive systems. This is true whether the organizational design is for hospitals, universities, libraries, steel mills, or other public and private institutions. One essential although frequently overlooked way to "procure" capital is through capital management or improved capital productivity.

KEY CONCEPTS

Matching People and Jobs	Performance Tests
Peter Principle	Trade Knowledge Tests
Management in Depth	Characteristics of Executives
Promoting from Within	Transferability of Managerial Skills
Procurement Techniques	Procurement of Capital
Psychological Tests	Productivity of Capital

GLOSSARY

conceptual skill   The ability to recognize and understand broad relationships, to work with abstractions.

depreciation   An allowance in the form of a charge against earnings for replacement of worn-out or obsolete facilities.

interview guide   A planned format designed to standardize personnel selection interviews.

interview report   A form that summarizes the results of a selection interview and rates the job applicant on points that do not appear in the interview guide.

lateral promotion   A transfer to a new position at the same classification level.

personality   That part of one's self that is exhibited to others.

Thematic Apperception Test   A projective type of psychological test.

REVIEW QUESTIONS

1. Why is it so important to select people carefully for job assignments?
2. What is the difference between executive development and executive recruitment? Give an example of each.
3. What is the meaning of management in depth?
4. What are some advantages to a policy of promoting from within? Some disadvantages?
5. Name several procurement techniques that can be improved in the staffing process. Suggest one way to improve each technique you have mentioned.
6. List several characteristics of top executives you know. How do they compare with the attributes of executives listed in this chapter?
7. Are there differences in the "mix" of management skills at various levels of management? How do you explain this?
8. If you had to replace the chief executive in an organization because of a crisis situation, would you promote an insider or hire an outsider to take over? Why?
9. Can managerial skills be transferred? Be explicit.
10. How important is procurement of capital in the organizing process? What are the main sources of capital in industry? In government?
11. Suggest one way to improve productivity of capital. Give a realistic example to illustrate your position.

Chapter 13

Assigning and Conditioning Personnel and Capital (Staffing)

Staffing is not complete with the procurement of personnel. Once people have been hired for particular jobs, they must be introduced to the work situation, with its network of procedural and authority relationships, and trained in any special skills they may need. Capital resources, too, require a "breaking-in period." Thus the final stage of the organizing process is assigning and conditioning personnel and capital. For personnel, this stage has two parts: (1) orientation, or indoctrination, and (2) conditioning, or training.

ORIENTATION OF PERSONNEL (INDOCTRINATION)

Every employee, whether manager or worker, requires a period of orientation when placed in a new job situation. This is an adjustment period in which one has to learn to feel at home in a new and strange situation. For a person who accepts a job in a new city, the transition is doubly difficult. In the beginning, everything is unfamiliar. New relationships have to be established, not only work relationships but personal relationships also.

Every employee should know how his job relates to other jobs, and where he stands in the chain of command. An employee should never be placed in the position of having to take orders from two or more people who give the impression they have the right to tell him what to do. Often one or more of these persons does not actually have the right but simply assumes it without challenge. If an employee is uncertain whether people asking him to do something have the actual authority to do so, he becomes confused and resentful. Ambiguity in authority relationships is not conducive to effective control. The orientation process should prevent this.

A new employee should be introduced to his associates by the department head and made to feel welcome. Procedural and authority relationships between the newcomer and his colleagues should be explained to him. Either the department head or someone designated by him should familiarize the newcomer with the location of his desk or work station, the location of the lunchroom, restroom facilities, his locker, where to obtain supplies, and so forth. Everything possible should be done to make him feel at ease.

The orientation or indoctrination period should also be used to acquaint the new employee with company policies, fringe benefits, departmental policies, and pertinent rules and regulations that will affect him and his performance on the job. The early impressions he gains will have a lasting effect, and it is important that these impressions be favorable and conducive to a rapid adjustment to the job. Helping him to develop proper work attitudes is part of the orientation process. Getting to work on time, coming in every day and remaining for the entire day, accepting supervision, and learning that constructive criticism does not mean personal rejection, are some of the attitudes and habits that have to be developed.

The need for orientation is vividly reflected in one of the demands made by registered nurses of the Ohio Nurses Association, who went on strike against the Youngstown Hospital Association in December 1974. In their contract, nurses insisted on the "implementation of a sophisticated orientation program for new nurse employees."[1] A fourteen-week program was written into the contract when the strike was settled and an agreement ratified in February 1975.

Testifying before a Senate subcommittee, the president of the United Auto Workers local at Lordstown, Ohio, where conveyors transport 103 Vega cars out the factory door every hour, charged lack of corporate concern for the orientation of new assembly line employees:

> He is brought into the plant and his orientation session ends and starts with his papers on insurance and his assignment to a foreman who immediately puts his warm body on the line.[2]

Too many firms pay too little attention to the importance of a well-planned program of induction and indoctrination. It is time to recognize this as a significant phase of the staffing process.

Sociometry

There is some research evidence that when workers are allowed to choose the people with whom they would like to work, output is greater than that of similar groups not permitted to make this choice. The study and measurement of feelings of group members toward one another is called **sociometry.** Sociometric rankings have been used to establish work groups which have proved to be more effective teams than groups randomly selected. One study

---

[1]*Youngstown Vindicator,* (Ohio), December 12, 1974.
[2]Gary Bryner, President UAW Local 1112, Lordstown, Ohio, testifying before Senate Subcommittee on Employment, Manpower and Poverty, July 25, 1972.

indicated that carpenters and bricklayers permitted to choose their own teammates outproduced other teams. Results were reduced labor and material costs, an overall saving of 5 percent in total production costs, and reportedly more satisfied workers.[3] In a Swiss appliance factory, sixty workers who had arbitrarily been divided into three groups of twenty were permitted to regroup themselves on the basis of personal likes and dislikes; within three weeks they increased production by 24 percent.

Teamwork

Assembling an organization of small, closely knit units whose members have similar interests, likes, social and economic backgrounds, education, and other uniform characteristics leads to cohesiveness and fosters teamwork. A cohesive work group will exhibit a smaller degree of variability of output than a less cohesive group. It is important to remember, however, that its level of output may be higher or *lower* than that of a less cohesive group. In general, cohesiveness results in higher productivity only if the group recognizes, and willingly accepts as legitimate, management's request for increased productivity targets. Should the cohesive group reject management's position, lower productivity will result.

Teamwork, a situation in which members subordinate personal achievement to the effectiveness of the whole, requires *cooperation* and *coordination*. The willingness of people to work together toward desired objectives is not sufficient alone. Their efforts must be synchronized and a sequence established for performing their respective tasks. Three or four men driving a stake with sledgehammers may be perfectly willing to cooperate, but unless their blows are timed and coordinated they will interfere with each other and produce chaos instead of constructive results. Actually, there are three types of teamwork present in organizations: the crew, the task force, and the interchangers.

The crew.   The members of a crew tend to suppress personal hardships and discomforts to carry out rote assignments directed toward a goal they consider highly desirable. Everyone acts in concerted fashion, willingly subordinating himself to the authority of the leader who is likely to employ an autocratic or authoritarian managerial style. Strict as it is, this style is probably best for this type of teamwork, which requires strong concerted efforts. A group of oarsmen in a shell, competing in a regatta, obey the authoritative commands of the coxswain to "stroke" a given number of beats per minute. The result is precision rowing, even when the beat is increased. Another example of a crew at work is a group of men shovelling sand into a truck under the watchful eye of the section chief.

[3]Raymond A. Van Zelst, "Sociometrically Selected Work Teams Increase Production," *Personnel Psychology*, Vol. 5, Autumn 1952, pp. 175–185.

The task force.[4]   In a task force, each member contributes his special skills and ideas to a project that requires inputs from several different areas. The work of a product development group comprising a designer, an engineer, a cost expert, a marketing specialist, and a production man, all of whom contribute to the overall mission, would constitute a task force or project assignment. The managerial style used in overseeing this type of team is generally supportive. The relationship among task force members tends to be collegial.

The interchangers.   In certain types of precision teamwork, members are prepared to interchange tasks or roles readily, to fill in where needed. They are trained to perform more than one job well. The surgical team, working on a heart transplant in a hospital operating room, is an example of this sort of team effort. One nurse can perform the duties of several of the others if requested to do so; surgeons can step in and take over for each other whenever necessary. In this situation, the managerial style is generally collegial.

Although one does not usually think of it as such, the relationship between the job of a heavy equipment operator and that of an ironworker is also a type of teamwork. One operator puts it this way:

> There's a bit more skill to building work. This is a boom crane. It goes anywhere from 80 feet to 240 feet. You're setting iron. Maybe you're picking fifty, sixty ton and maybe you have ironworkers up there 100, 110 feet. You have to be real careful you don't bump one of these persons, where they would be apt to fall off.
>
> At the same time, they're putting bolts in holes. If they wanted a half-inch, you have to be able to give them a half-inch. I mean, not an inch, not two inches. Those holes must line up exactly or they won't make their iron. And when you swing, you have to swing real smooth. You can't have your iron swinging back and forth, oscillating. If you do this, they'll refuse to work with you, because their life is at stake.
>
> They're working on beams, anywhere from maybe a foot wide to maybe five or six inches. These fellas walk across these.
>
> They have to trust you. If there's no trust there, they will not work with you. It has to be precision.[5]

Are there any actions which a manager can take to develop teamwork? The answer is yes. Among them are the following:

1. Assemble people who like each other. This will reduce the possibility of friction, personal misunderstandings, and jealousies.
2. Instill in members the importance of their contributions to the team effort, of their need to act and think as part of a team and not as

---

[4]The task force is discussed in greater detail in Chapter 15. Managerial styles are described in Chapter 18.

[5]Studs Terkel, *Working* (New York: Pantheon Books, 1974), p. 23.

individual performers. Help them to think "group" rather than "individual."

3. Provide special help and encouragement to workers who have difficulty in making friends, who are not outgoing, or who are reticent.

4. Keep the group together by resisting excessive requests for transfers. At the same time, a manager must not thwart opportunities for promotions by denying legitimate requests.

5. Provide group incentives in which members share in the rewards of successful team efforts.

6. Utilize a managerial style that fits the type of teamwork required—that is, autocratic for the crew, supportive for the task force, and collegial for interchangers.

THE CONDITIONING PROCESS

Conditioning, sometimes called **occupational socialization** or **organizational socialization**, is the process by which an individual learns the objectives, norms, and preferred ways of doing things within an organization or one of its functional areas. It occurs most dramatically when a person enters his first job. It reoccurs when he moves from one department to another, or from one rank level to a higher level. It takes place again when he leaves the organization to enter another. The speed and effectiveness of conditioning influence employee loyalty, productivity, and effectiveness. To a large extent, organizational effectiveness is a reflection of its ability to socialize new members.

Generally, conditioning personnel is a more elaborate and time-consuming process than orientation or indoctrination. Conditioning may be **formal** and include some type of training program; or it may be **informal** and left largely to the supervisor, or to fellow employees who are more experienced and will help "break in" the new member. Conditioning is primarily concerned with helping the new worker to learn the duties of his job and to perform them in the most effective manner.

The conditioning process, particularly the formal type that includes specialized training, can be a very expensive one. It costs, as a national average, approximately $8,800 to train a salesman before he is proficient enough to carry his own weight and pay his own way.[6] For salesmen of industrial products, the average cost is over $11,000. For a registered representative (account executive) with a major brokerage firm, the training program includes a period of seven months in investment schooling covering

---

[6]This cost estimate does not include the new man's salary, but does include aptitude testing, travel, hotel and meals, field supervisor's time, car allowance, insurance, and fringe benefits.

corporation finance, bond markets, commodities, and Securities and Exchange Commission regulations. Three months are spent in the branch office, three months in a company-conducted formal school in New York City, and one month back at the branch office. Total cost to the parent company has been estimated at $15,000 for each trainee.

When it comes to training groups, there is some evidence of a relationship between trainer styles and group development. Ivancevich studied two groups of managers involved in a cognitive-oriented training program. The structured, or directive, style was found to be more effective in producing group cohesiveness, minimizing participant conflict, increasing communication, improving group productivity, and encouraging favorable attitudes toward the trainer than was a less structured trainer style.[7]

Training Programs

Various types of formal training are practiced in industry. The more familiar ones include on-the-job training; vestibule school; committees and conferences; study programs; and executive training programs.

On-the-job training. On-the-job training is frequently employed in the operating and facilitating areas of the business—on the production line where machines are operated or products assembled, or in the office where bookkeeping or accounting machines are used. The operator should either be given explicit directions or he should be shown what must be done to perform the operation properly. He should be told why it must be done this way. The operator then tries it himself under guidance, until he is sufficiently proficient to take over without direct supervision. In time, he makes fewer mistakes and achieves the performance standard expected of him by his supervisor or by the informal group of which he becomes a member. When a person has worked on a similar machine before but now has to learn the differences in the new one, the re-training is called **discrimination training.**

Vestibule school. As its name implies, the vestibule school is conducted outside the regular work area. Perhaps a machine is set up in a room where the newly inducted employee can practice, get the feel of the machine, and make mistakes or damage raw materials in the learning process. When he has mastered the intricacies of the machine and the operations, he is assigned a similar machine on the line in the shop area. He did his practicing in the "vestibule." The use of aircraft simulators, in which pilots are trained before taking the controls of the actual aircraft, is a type of vestibule school in which learning takes place and new skills are acquired without fear of

[7]John M. Ivancevich, "A Study of a Cognitive Training Program: Trainer Styles and Group Development," Academy of Management Journal, Vol. 17, No. 3, September 1974, p. 428.

serious injury or permanent damage to personnel or equipment during the training lessons.

The key elements in the operative training process, either on-the-job or vestibule variety, are (1) explanation, (2) demonstration, (3) performance under direct supervision, (4) performance under intermittent supervision, and (5) independent performance. Since this sequence of steps in the training process produces a trained worker, we can say that this hypothesis also is a managing principle.

Committees and conferences. Although committees and conferences will be discussed primarily as adjuncts to basic line and staff structure in Chapter 15, it should be pointed out here that they also serve as training grounds, particularly for junior executives and executive development trainees. Associating with senior executives, the executive trainee has a unique opportunity to understand the company through exposure to various points of view expressed by committee members, to visualize operations from a broader perspective, and to observe successful executives in action. As "low man on the totem pole," the trainee may be asked to do some of the legwork for the committee, to research necessary data or information, and to report his findings. He may be questioned and find it necessary to defend his position or his recommendations. This is not only excellent experience for him and an opportunity to become acquainted with the way executives function and the way decisions are made, but it also enables senior executives to observe how he handles himself and to evaluate his development and readiness to take on more difficult and perhaps more important assignments.

Conferences provide a medium for discussing special problems and exchanging ideas. Conference training generally consists of a small group and a leader who jointly discuss a subject. Each member develops new ideas and begins to recognize and understand new relationships through mutual exchange with the others. The conference is especially effective in training key personnel, supervisors, and executives. To obtain superior results from training of this type, there should be active participation by all conference members within a climate that encourages inputs.

Study, lecture, and laboratory courses. Employees may be assigned special study, such as reading assignments and home study courses, to develop their knowledge and understanding of particular areas. They may be required to attend lectures conducted by company specialists on a broad range of topics including leadership, labor laws, safety, human relations, company organization, grievance procedure, and management regulations. Laboratories may be held also where trainees are required to engage in role-playing, speed reading, interviewing, and other activities that lend themselves to laboratory techniques. Formal training of this type is very helpful in developing foremen and supervisors. Most major consumer goods companies use videotape techniques for training their sales representatives before sending them on the road.

Executive training programs.   An individual being trained for a managerial assignment may first be introduced to all the operations in the organization so that he will understand the relationships among them and be able to visualize how his particular position relates to the whole. Department stores, such as Macy's in New York, have utilized the "flying squadron," in which a man or woman spends a short time working and observing in each area, from the shipping dock to the executive offices, and thereby gains an impression of the total operation before settling down to a specific assignment.

Internship training is frequently employed to advantage. Joint programs between business firms and universities are being developed which provide for general education as well as specialized job-related instruction. Such programs may include courses in general management, human behavior in organizations, executive development, or more specialized instruction in accounting, labor legislation, finance, and other relevant areas. The United States Civil Service Commission has successfully developed a "Management Intern Program,"which includes university courses in management developed exclusively for its selected supervisory candidates.

Many major organizations that have management development departments now offer courses which include such training methods as videotaping and television recording of participants as aids to their personal development.

Theory Z

What determines individual commitment to organizational goals? Lyndall Urwick suggests that the agreement between the individual worker's interests and the organization's interests hinges on the worker's dual economic identity.[8] As Urwick views it, the economic process consists in relating the behavior of the individual as a *consumer* to the behavior of *the same individual* as a *producer or distributor*. He believes the closer the work situation is to the worker's perceived role as a consumer or producer-distributor, the greater is the likelihood that he or she will identify with organizational goals. This relationship is called "Theory Z."

In a manufacturing unit, decisions of an individual in his role as a producer seem very remote from his decisions as a consumer. The manufacturing organization tends to place a higher priority on commitment to the work itself than to the more remote identification with customer service objec-

[8]Lyndall F. Urwick, "Theory Z," *S.A.M. Advanced Management Journal,* Vol. 35, No. 1, January 1970, pp. 14–21.

tives. On the other hand, in a service-oriented unit, like a retail outlet, commitment to the firm's customer service objectives and identification with customers may be very important corporate objectives. The sales person in a retail organization is an active party in customer interaction, can more readily perceive himself in the role of consumer, and can identify with goals intended to serve the customer.

A subsequent study of a Dayton, Ohio department store tends to support Theory Z.[9] It revealed that sales personnel, identifying with their role as consumers, may be willing to compromise the organization's interest in situations they perceive to be in conflict with the customer's interest. An example is that of revealing ahead of time a forthcoming storewide sale at reduced prices.

The Dayton study also indicates that of various factors that explain an employee's lack of identification with organizational objectives, customers, and the work itself, the one that stands out is **anomie**. Anomie has been defined as a condition of rootlessness or lack of personal attachment, so that normative standards of conduct are weak. It denotes a directionless orientation toward societal values. The high-anomie individual does not participate in organizational values and remains relatively uncommitted despite attempts at training and orientation. The typical technical and customer-relations types of training do not fulfill their development needs since these approaches are not designed to reduce anomie. This situation should be recognized by managers charged with instituting and supplementing a training program. Perhaps attention should be directed toward reducing anomie if successful conditioning is to be achieved.

As has been indicated, not all conditioning is formal. Moreover, it is probably true that for most firms conditioning of employees to their new jobs is informal in nature, left largely to the immediate supervisor or to fellow employees. This is substantiated in a study conducted at a United States Government installation, where workers were asked to designate the source from which they *primarily* received help in learning the duties of their present job. The largest single source, indicated by 29.2 percent of the respondents, was "an experienced fellow employee"; 23.4 percent indicated "catching on as best I could"; while 22.2 percent listed "my supervisor." Only 4.5 percent received help primarily from "attending formal training sessions."[10]

The reader will recall from our discussion of personal relationships in Chapter 11 that one advantage of the informal organization is its capacity to aid in indoctrinating new workers, in assisting them to make the adjustment, and in offering guidance and direction on how to do the work.

---

[9]Thomas J. Von Der Embse, "Critical Factors in Organizational Commitment and Performance," *Bulletin of Business Research, Ohio State University,* Vol. 47, No. 6, June 1972, p. 4.

[10]U.S. Army Transportation Material Command Survey, 1961, p. 12.

ASSIGNING AND CONDITIONING CAPITAL

Whether obtained from lenders or investors, or generated internally, capital funds must be assigned or earmarked for special use. That is part of the organizing process.

Most capital is available as part of "capital budget," a single-use type of plan designed to guide capital expenditures for a given time period. It is a rotating fund, portions of which are designated for a particular function or purpose. The sales function might require funds for advertising and sales promotion, training salesmen, purchasing automobiles for salesmen, and similar needs; the manufacturing function might require funds for raw materials, new machinery and tools, a new plant or an addition to the existing one; financing could well require funds to carry increased inventory build-up, or to carry increased accounts receivable resulting from the increased sales developed from the advertising and sales promotion expenditures. The receivables become cash, and the cash is again assigned to meet some requirement. This is a circular flow process.

When dollars from capital funds take the form of machinery and equipment, a period of conditioning may be required—in other words, a "breaking-in period" to "get the bugs out." Even a new automobile has a breaking-in period before its moving parts mesh properly. In large plants, where technology requires huge capital expenditures for equipment, the conditioning period can be lengthy and costly. As part of a modernization program, a large, profitable midwestern steel plant installed a block-long, $30 million computerized strip mill and then showed a financial loss for six consecutive quarters until the major bugs were eliminated from the new system. Situations like this are not uncommon. Costs associated with breaking in a new system or process are commonly called "start-up costs."

Defining business functions and their relationships; defining jobs and their relationships; procuring personnel and capital to perform the jobs; and assigning and conditioning personnel and capital—these sub-functions collectively constitute the process of organizing. They make it possible for plans to be implemented, and provide the structure through which coordination and control can be achieved.

SUMMARY

Two very important ingredients in the staffing process, itself a component of the total organizing process, are orientation or indoctrination of personnel, and conditioning them to their new work situations. The importance of properly assigning and conditioning people resources is frequently overlooked or given only minimal attention even by the largest organizations. Making an adjustment to a new situation is a difficult transition for most people. They need help, encouragement, and guidance until they "settle in" to the new job and its unfamiliar surroundings. Aiding the uninitiated to develop favorable impressions and proper work attitudes is a significant aspect of the orientation process.

Grouping persons with similar backgrounds, interests, capabilities, and motivation, particularly if they have a voice in their peer group selection, leads to cohesiveness and creates a climate that is conducive to teamwork. Sociometric grouping should be part of the induction process.

Conditioning may be formal or informal. Usually formal conditioning includes on-the-job training, the vestibule school, service on committees, and for managers an executive training or development program to nurture the skills and the dedications required to achieve corporate goals. Lyndall Urwick suggests that a person's commitment to organizational goals in economic undertakings depends on his perception of his role as a consumer or a producer–distributor and how close the work situation approximates the interest of the consumer compared to that of the producer–distributor. Urwick calls this human behavior in economic situations Theory Z. Informal conditioning is that which occurs because the immediate supervisor is supportive of an individual's efforts, or because fellow workers are helpful, cooperative, and encouraging.

Capital also must undergo a conditioning process. New equipment or machinery must be broken in and the bugs discovered and eliminated before it works at its optimal capability. Start-up costs for a new process or technology can seriously hamper short-term goal achievement and must be considered as part of the total organizing process.

KEY CONCEPTS

Induction	Occupational or Organizational
Orientation	Socialization
Sociometry	On-the-Job Training
Teamwork	Vestibule School
	Theory Z

GLOSSARY

anomie   A condition characterized by lack of personal attachment or involvement and reluctance to comply with normative standards of conduct.

discrimination training   Training an already trained worker to adapt to a new piece of machinery or equipment.

sociometry   The study and measurement of feelings of group members toward each other.

teamwork   A situation in which members of a group subordinate personal achievement to the effectiveness of the group.

REVIEW QUESTIONS

1. What are some advantages to providing an adequate program of induction or orientation for new employees? Suggest some things that you believe should be included in such a program.

2. What is sociometry? What is its value?

3. Describe three types of teamwork. What actions can a manager take to develop and encourage teamwork?

4. What is the value of the conditioning process as it relates to personnel?

5. List several types of formal training that are used in industry. Which of these could be used in any kind of organization?

6. What are the key elements in the operative training process? What role does the instructor or supervisor play?

7. Explain Theory Z.

8. Does anomie help to explain why current types of formal training may not succeed in getting individuals to identify with organizational goals? What would you recommend to overcome this obstacle?

9. How can you justify including "assigning and conditioning capital" in the organizing process?

Chapter 14

Organizational Structure (Line and Staff)

Organizing has been portrayed as a process in which major areas of work, or enterprise functions, are subdivided into various kinds of jobs that need to be performed, and staffed with people specially selected for those jobs. Viewed in this way, organizing is achieved by division of work, and delegation of duties and attendant authority.

Authority relationships are the bonds that unite the subdivisions of work into an effective organization. Just as an organization has a hierarchy of objectives, so too it has a hierarchy of managerial authority to see that those objectives are met. Operating decisions must serve corporate objectives. Specialized tasks must be coordinated. Authority provides direction, through managerial decisions and their implementation. Thus the locations of decision making in an organization largely determine its *authority structure*.

AUTHORITY HIERARCHIES

As we have already noted, structure is the result of multiple relationships (group activities, job definitions, job classifications, procedures, systems, interpersonal relations) within an organization. Although patterns of differentiated relationships[1] produce structure on the basis of organizational needs, activities, technology, and requirements at a given time, structure is also created because a hierarchy of authority relationships exists.

Authority is greatest at the top levels of management, where it originates, and decreases in a scalar fashion as it is transmitted down to the lower levels. James Mooney called this the **scalar chain.**[2] Such a downward flow of authority typifies the chain of command found in the traditional formal organization in which an authority hierarchy is always present.

Flow of authority as it might exist in the sales area of a firm is indicated in Figure 14-1. The chain of command, through successive vertical levels, is from national sales manager to assistant national sales manager, to divi-

---

[1]This topic was discussed in Chapter 9.
[2]James D. Mooney and A. C. Reilly, *Onward Industry* (New York: Harper & Brothers, 1931), p. 31.

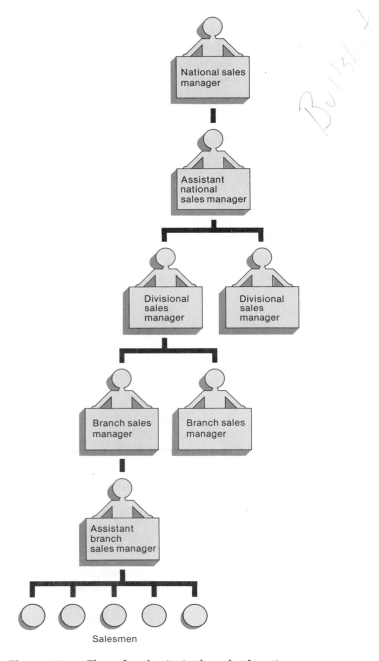

Figure 14-1.   Flow of authority in the sales function.

sional sales manager, to branch sales manager, to assistant branch sales manager, to salesmen (non-managers).

Thus, in any given functional area, different levels of managerial duties carry appropriate levels or degrees of authority. In this context, the relationship between the national sales manager and the branch sales manager is vertical. On the other hand, if the position of the national sales manager is compared with that of the national production manager, the relationship is not scalar. They are executives in different functional areas but at the same level in the corporate structure. There is no authority relationship between them. Any relationship is a functional one. Rather than vertical, it is horizontal or lateral; communication between them is lateral also. In Figure 14-1, a lateral relationship exists between the divisional sales managers. Theirs is a horizontal relationship to each other, and a vertical relationship to their mutual superior and their respective subordinates.

In management literature reference is frequently made to **levels of management.** While it is impossible to establish clear-cut demarcations, levels have often been identified as top, upper, middle, and lower. These levels in the corporate hierarchy are shown graphically in Figure 14-2.

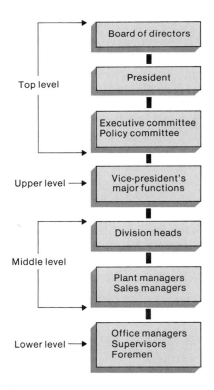

Figure 14-2. Levels of management.

From an overall corporate perspective, *top-level* management comprises the board of directors, president, executive committee, and corporate policy committee. *Upper level* indicates the vice-presidents in charge of major business functions (perhaps our national sales manager and national production manager would be among them). *Middle level* embraces division heads, plant managers, sales managers, personnel managers, purchasing agents, engineers, and similar executives, both line and staff. *Lower-level* management generally refers to office managers, supervisors, and foremen. They are the "first line" managers. Their subordinates are not managers but workers, the "operative" personnel.

Structural Types

Hierarchical or authority relationships produce two major structural types. They are: (1) basic line organization and (2) modifications of basic line organization. Both are often pictured by means of an organization chart or diagram.

It is extremely important to remember that every organization chart based on authority relationships is merely a graphic representation of the existing flow of authority. The purpose of the diagram is to show which positions in the organization have authority over others, and to indicate to which superior each subordinate is accountable. All that it is intended to show is the direction of authority and accountability flow and nothing more.

If two persons are shown at the same level in the organization chart, it does not imply they are equal in rank, authority, or status. It simply means that each is subject to the authority of the same superior at the next higher level and is accountable to him. Most students of management have gained the erroneous impression that when an organization chart shows the purchasing agent and the sales manager, for example, on the same level (middle management) both have equal rank, prestige, and influence. Such is not the case. A sales manager may have several hundred men working for him and may earn a salary and a bonus several times larger than the purchasing agent, who may have only a dozen subordinates in his department. Moreover, the value of the sales manager to the successful operation of the company may far exceed that of the purchasing agent. There is no basis to assume from the diagram that both men are equal. One must constantly keep this in mind in order to comprehend structural types of organizations that are based solely on authority relationships. The organization chart is not intended to indicate what ought to be; it represents what is. It is not normative; it is actual in its representation of formal structure.

BASIC LINE ORGANIZATION

Authority relationships give rise to the basic form of organization known as **line organization.** In the superior-subordinate relationship, authority flows

in a straight line through successive management levels. Hence, the deriva-
tion of the terms *line authority* and *line organization.*

Every organization begins as a line organization. Only those functions
that are *basic* to the performance of major operations, or that contribute
directly to accomplishing major corporate objectives, are considered line
activities. In most firms, from the simplest to the most complex, **sales** and
production are the basic activities. All others should be viewed as aiding or
facilitating the successful operation of these two essential line functions. In
this light, many very important business activities associated with buying,
finance, personnel, warehousing, traffic, accounting, maintenance, legal
work, and advertising are not basic or directly responsible for achieving
major corporate objectives. However, there is no disputing the fact that they
are necessary since they serve the line activities and make it possible for
them to function more effectively. In fact, line executives at times engage in
many of these indirect or staff activities. When these non-basic activities
grow in importance and begin to take up a great deal of time, specialists are
often hired to handle them. Collectively, all purposive activities other than
basic line activities are usually considered *staff functions.*

The organization illustrated in Figure 14-3 shows the two major line
activities—sales and production—and the vertical flow of authority within
each.

While "pure line" does not exist except in the very early stages of
organizational development, there are certain characteristics that describe
all basic line structure. Four of the more important are the following:

1. Each superior has the authority to make decisions and to implement
   them.

2. At any level, each subordinate is subject to the authority of only one
   person at the next higher level, and is accountable only to that person.

3. All lines of authority lead in a straight line from the top level (ownership) to successively lower levels (operating and facilitating).

4. Great specialization takes place at the operating and facilitating levels.
   Here, through division of labor, work is divided into small units and
   workers become expert at handling them.

As a simple, one-man business matures many changes take place. The
original entrepreneur, who may have produced the product and also sold it,
soon finds that both activities require full time and attention. He may,
therefore, decide to handle the manufacturing duties himself and hire someone to do the selling. As business prospers, he will hire more production
workers and spend more time supervising their activities. He will add more
equipment, perhaps move to larger physical quarters, divide the manufacturing function into specialized operations so that each worker becomes
very proficient at his job. Several more salesmen may be added and eventually a sales manager appointed. Before long, the originator of the business

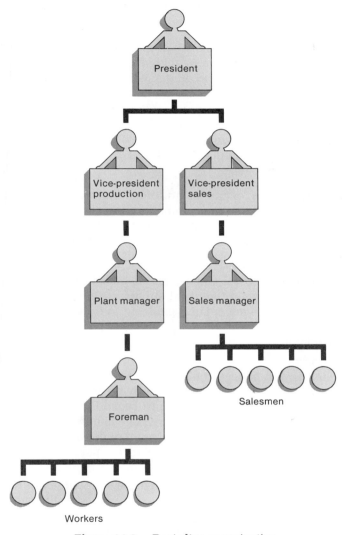

Figure 14-3.   Basic line organization.

may hire someone to act as factory manager, freeing himself to oversee the entire expanding operation. A basic line organization develops in terms of functional patterns. However, as more people are hired and the operation continues to become more complex, it can no longer effectively accommodate growth and expansion simply by vertical development. Its size and shape change. Major weaknesses become apparent:

1. Top line executives become excessively burdened with all management activities. There is simply too much for each person to do unless provision is

made for delegation of some aspects of the management functions to subordinates.

2. Specialization in the performance of management functions is not possible. Because of the lack of time or technical competence, managers in a basic line organization cannot become specialists in planning (long-range planning, policy formulation, setting standards, scheduling, establishing budgets, reviewing and revising plans, and so forth); nor can they become specialists in organizing (job analysis, writing job definitions, interviewing, hiring, and performing other organizing activities); nor experts in controlling (accounting, record keeping, assessing results, and performing additional controlling activities).

3. As line organization expands, additional levels of management are added which stretch the span of communication between the top and lower echelons. (For an illustration of this in the area of sales, the reader is referred to Figure 14-1.) Communication between levels of the structure becomes more difficult and more time-consuming.

4. The span of management can become too broad, making it very difficult for managers to direct the activities of subordinates. Span of management has become an important concept in organizing. We shall examine this next.

Span of Management

"How many subordinates can a manager supervise effectively?" This is the question implicit in the concept of span of management. Span of management has been referred to in various ways by writers on management subjects. Although Fisch, in an article in the *Harvard Business Review* in 1963[3] claims to have coined the term *span of management*, Koontz and O'Donnell used the term in 1955.[4] Frequently called span of control, span of authority, or span of supervision, the concept is based on the psychological limits to an individual's "span of attention."

Obviously as a firm grows in numbers of personnel the interactions and interrelationships increase also. In addition, many more informal groups or cliques develop and exert an influence on the formal organization. A manager cannot be assigned more subordinates indefinitely without reaching a point where it becomes very difficult for him to give adequate time and attention to each of them. Managing capabilities become spread too thin. Unless a manager is alerted to do something about it, the law of diminishing returns, in the form of diminishing management effectiveness, sets in.

---

[3]Gerald G. Fisch, "Stretching the Span of Management," *Harvard Business Review*, Vol. 41, No. 5, 1963, p. 74.

[4]Harold Koontz and Cyril O'Donnell, *Principles of Management: An Analysis of Managerial Functions*, 5th ed. (New York: McGraw-Hill, 1972), p. 248.

Table 14-1.   Potential superior–subordinate contacts as number of subordinates increases

Number of subordinates	Total number of potential contacts
1	1
2	6
3	18
4	44
5	100
6	222
7	490
8	1080
9	2376
10	5210

A French industrial consultant interested in this problem analyzed communications between superiors and subordinates, and worked out a mathematical formula for determining the number of possible contacts that could theoretically occur.[5] Here is **Graicunas' formula:**

$$C = n\left(\frac{2^n}{2} + n - 1\right)$$

where C = total number of contacts and n = number of subordinates. Applying this formula to an organization of only ten subordinates gives the results shown in Table 14-1.[6]

The key observation is that within an expanding organization, *the number of superior-subordinate relationships increases at a much faster rate than the rate of increase in the number of subordinates.* For example, if the number of subordinates is increased from 2 to 3 (50 percent), the number of potential relationships increases from 6 to 18 (200 percent); an increase from 2 to 5 subordinates (150 percent) produces an increase in potential relationships from 6 to 100 (1,515 percent). The progression is greater than geometric: it is exponential!

The Graicunas approach has a number of weaknesses. First, it did not consider relationships that can exist between members of the organization and persons outside the organization. To have done so would have vastly increased the number of potential contacts. Second, the formula provides the number of potential or possible contacts, not the number that actually occur. Third, since not all contacts take place at the same time, or within the same time span, a manager may never be subject to all of the possible contacts and certainly not simultaneously. Fourth, Graicunas assumed that all relationships occur with equal frequency. Fifth, he also assumed that every con-

[5]V. A. Graicunas, "Relationship in Organization," *Bulletin of International Management Institute,* March 1933, pp. 183–187.
[6]An alternate formula, $C = n(2^{n-1} + n - 1)$ will provide the same results.

tact is equal in intensity. In actual practice, relationships between a manager and his subordinates vary considerably from organization to organization, and are not predicated simply on the assumptions which Graicunas made. In spite of these limitations, there is little doubt that with expanding business organizations, the difficulty of the executive's job increases as the complexity of his organization increases.

Again the question crops up: How many subordinates can a superior manage effectively? To arrive at an answer is far from simple. The number of persons a manager can handle depends on several factors:

- **Whether he is engaged in executive or operative supervision.** The level of management has a bearing on management span. In general, the span of management is broader at the operating level than at the executive level.

- **The nature of work being supervised.** If the work is routine and repetitive, more workers can be supervised than if the work is intermittent, complicated, one-of-a-kind in nature, or very creative. Practical realities like the complexity of the product line are also a factor.

- **Geographic dispersion of subordinates.** A study by Udell of span of control as it applies to chief executives in marketing and sales indicated a positive rather than a negative relationship between span of control and geographic dispersion of subordinates.[7] Apparently, limited dispersion does not affect the size of span, whereas substantial dispersion *increases* the span of control.

- **Capabilities of the subordinates.** In general, well-trained, self-reliant, competent subordinates require less individual supervision. Therefore a manager can deal with more subordinates of this type. The greater the capacities and skills of the subordinates, the broader the span of management that is feasible.[8]

- **Capabilities of the superior.** Some managers are simply more competent than others. They are less easily distracted, less susceptible to the negative effects of pressure, and capable of dealing with more people. Some have a greater capacity for work, possess greater human relations skill and leadership ability. Some are more knowledgeable; some have greater energy; some are more highly motivated or ambitious.

- **Management style.** The organization's philosophy of management determines its management style and affects the span of management. If management welcomes and encourages participation, has a supportive attitude toward its employees, provides a climate that encourages and

---

[7]John G. Udell, "An Empirical Test of Hypotheses Relating to Span of Control," *Administrative Science Quarterly*, Vol. 12, 1967, pp. 420–439.

[8]See Marshall W. Meyer, "Expertness and the Span of Control," *American Psychological Review*, December 1968, pp. 944–951.

enables subordinates to fulfill a substantial portion of their individual goals and desires in the course of pursuing the objectives of the organization, then a broader span of management is possible. When goals of the firm and goals of its members are compatible, broader spans of management occur.

- **Incentives.** If a favorable incentive system exists that motivates workers and managers to increased performance, broader spans of management are possible. A base pay rate coupled with a bonus may inspire workers to act as self-starters who require less supervision. A bonus, stock option plan, or chances for advancement may induce a manager to produce better results. Proper incentives may enable him to broaden his span of management.

Although it is difficult to set definite spans of management, since the number of subordinates that a manager can handle depends to some extent on the situation, ranges have been suggested. Stieglitz indicates that spans for middle managers range from 4 to 11; those for first-line supervisors from 8 to 22.[9] In a later survey covering 274 company heads he reported spans ranging from 1 to more than 20. In about 80 percent of the cases, however, spans varied from 4 to 10.[10] Dale offered the suggestion, later echoed by Keith Davis, that the number of people having *access* to an executive may be considerably larger than the number requiring close, immediate, or direct supervision.[11] In such a situation, Davis suggests that spans range from 5 to 15.[12]

How many subordinates, then, can a manager direct effectively? The optimum range of *operative* supervision is probably between 10 and 30 subordinates (for clerical workers, possibly 12 to 15). The optimum range of *executive* supervision is probably between 3 and 10 subordinates.

A number of additional studies tend to confirm these optimum ranges. An American Management Association survey of 38 chief executives in companies with sales of $1 billion or more revealed a span of management (SOM) that ranged from 3 to 12, except in four companies in which more than 12 officers reported to the chief executive.[13]

An interesting aspect of the AMA study is the increase in span of management as company size (measured both by sales and number of employees)

---

[9]Harold Stieglitz, "Optimizing Span of Control," *Management Record,* Vol. 24, No. 9, September 1962, pp. 25–29.

[10]Harold Stieglitz, *The Chief Executive and His Job* (New York: National Industrial Conference Board, Inc., 1969), pp. 15–17.

[11]Ernest Dale, "Planning and Developing the Company Organization Structure," Research Report No. 20 (New York: American Management Association, 1952), p. 57.

[12]Keith Davis, *Human Relations at Work: The Dynamics of Organizational Behavior,* 3rd ed. (New York: McGraw-Hill, 1967), p. 190.

[13]K. K. White, "Understanding the Company Organization Chart," American Management Association Research Study 56, 1963, p. 61.

Table 14-2. Span of managment of chief executive in 38 companies with annual sales of $1 billion*

Size of span	Number of companies
3	1
4	1
5	3
6	2
7	4
8	8
9	2
10	4
11	3
12	6
Over 12	4
	38

*Adapted from K.K. White, UNDERSTANDING THE COMPANY ORGANIZATION CHART, AMA Research Study 56, American Management Association, 1963, p. 61.

increases. According to Fisch, the positive relationship between company size and span of management is easily explained. He says, ''The larger the company, the greater is the likelihood of diversification; and the greater the degree of diversification, the larger the size of the SOM.''[14]

Variations in spans of management are also observed when different types of businesses are considered. A highly integrated production factory, for example, in which each production unit tends to be dependent upon other production units, may require close supervision of all activities to maintain coordination and control. In this situation, the factory superintendent may be able to direct the work of only a few supervisors.

Joan Woodward's study of industrial organizations suggests there may be optimum spans of control associated with successful organizations, and that spans are influenced by the type of technology or process used in production. In unit production firms the number of people directly accountable to the chief executive ranged from 2 to 9; in mass production firms, the range was from 13 to 14; in process production firms, the range was from 5 to 19.[15]

In a department store each buyer possesses considerable expertise in his or her specialty area. Moreover, the operation of each department is relatively independent of activities in other departments. The sporting goods department, the shoe department, and the furniture department are all

---

[14]Gerald G. Fisch, *op. cit.*, p. 81.

[15]Joan Woodward, *Industrial Organization: Theory and Practice* (London: Oxford University Press, 1965), p. 52.

more or less autonomous units, although they may share certain storewide services like security, maintenance, warehousing, and personnel. Since individual departments do not have to be closely controlled, the merchandising executive can exercise a broader span of authority, overseeing the activities of many buyers and department managers rather than few. Retailing, in other words, tends to have a broader span of management than manufacturing. This is borne out in a survey dealing with the proportion of executives to non-executives in 82 retailing and manufacturing firms employing a total of more than 500,000 people. Retailing executives constituted 11.4 percent, whereas manufacturing executives comprised 13.6 percent of the work force, indicating that retailing had the broader span of management.[16]

Tall versus Flat Organizations

Whether organizational structure is tall or flat is not accidental. It is a reflection of management policy to optimize the span of management. Implementing this policy creates various levels or layers of management. The broader the span of management, the fewer the levels and the flatter the organization; the narrower the span of management, the more numerous the levels and the taller the organization.

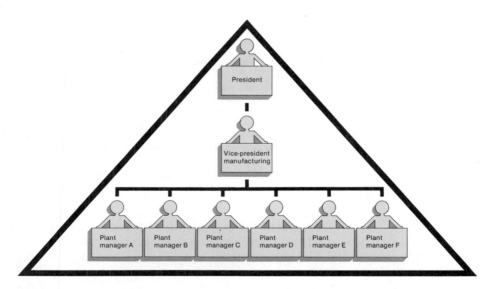

Figure 14-4. Flat organization: Three levels of management. Maximum span of managment is six; total number of managers is eight.

---

[16]Robert D. Loken and Winfield C. J. Thake, "How Many Managers Are There?," *Current Economic Comment*, University of Illinois, November 1952, pp. 18–27.

As shown in Figure 14-4, a flat organization results from a broad span of management. In this illustration, there are three levels of management. At the second level, the vice-president of manufacturing has six plant managers reporting to him. Lines of communication are short. A total of eight managers are involved.

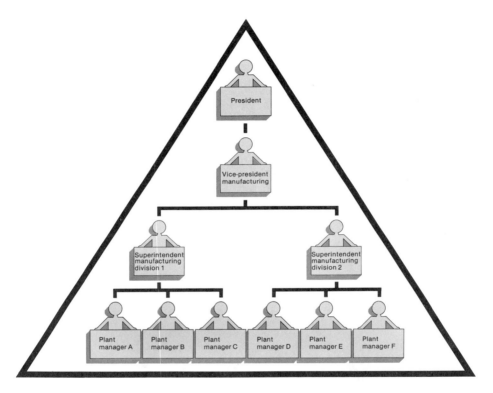

Figure 14-5. Tall organization: Four levels of management. Maximum span of management is three; total number of managers is ten.

Figure 14-5 illustrates some modifications in the structure. The span of management has been reduced. To accomplish this, one more level of management has been added. The organization has become "taller," now having four levels. At the second level, the vice-president of manufacturing now has only two subordinates, division superintendents, reporting to him. At the third level, the superintendent of division 1 has plant managers *A*, *B*, and *C* reporting to him, while plant managers *D*, *E*, and *F* report to the superintendent of division 2. Maximum span of management for any executive has been reduced to three, but two new managers have been added so that we now have ten managers on the payroll instead of eight. Lines of communication are longer, increasing the chances of potential misinterpretation or abstraction of directives, and lengthening the time it takes for information to be transmitted up or down.

In very large corporations, particularly multi-plant and trans-national firms, it is not uncommon to have 10 or 12 levels intervening between operating employees and top-level management. In such a tall organization, however, communication effectiveness is limited, and more elaborate and more costly control systems become necessary. Distorted or abstracted communications and delays in decision making are smoke signals that too many levels of supervision are present.

It is obvious that reducing the span of management at each level also means increasing the chain of command. As intervening managers are added, the cost of managing increases. One has to weigh the advantages of reduced span of management against the disadvantages of increased levels and accelerated cost. Each layer increases organizational costs, which include salaries, fringe benefits, office space, and facilitating costs including communication expenses. The goal is to strike a balance between the economies of a broad management span and the cost of the necessary support activities as SOM expands.

If a large corporation is supporting one extra layer of middle management or supervision, the cost can run into millions of dollars annually. Fisch indicates huge dollar savings are attainable in the middle management and supervisory levels.[17] One way to increase the span of first-line supervisors is to eliminate as many of their non-managerial duties as possible. A substantial portion of non-managerial work (clerical details, for example) can be provided by the facilitating units in the organization.

No organization can be fitted into a particular mold. Each firm must decide what is best for its type of operation, its management style, and its competitive and marketing strategies. It must then structure its organization accordingly. In Sears, Roebuck, for example, levels of supervision are held to a minimum. In some of its stores, as many as thirty-two department managers report directly to the store manager; in others, department managers report to five or six division managers who in turn report to the store manager. Sears thus has a flat organization structure; at the top level, as many as forty executives may report directly to the president.

Despite continued investigation by behavioral scientists, there is no universal agreement on desirable spans of management, or the effectiveness of flat versus tall organizations. In one study, for example, the time required to make decisions was found to be faster in flatter organizational structures.[18] Another experimental study indicated that groups operating within

[17]Gerald G. Fisch, *Op. cit.*, p. 79.

[18]H. R. Jones, Jr., "A Study of Organizational Performance for Experimental Structures of Two, Three, and Four Levels," *Academy of Management Journal*, Vol. 12, No. 3, September 1969.

a relatively tall organization structure exhibited significantly better profits and rate of return on revenues than groups operating under a flat structure.[19] Apparently there are advantages to both flat and tall organizations, depending on the objectives or circumstances. There seems to be little doubt that there is a practical limit to the number of people an individual can manage effectively and efficiently, but the number will vary from one organizational situation to another. This is a basic principle of span of management.

The tendency today is for the organization chart of most businesses to flatten out. Technologically oriented, innovative, highly motivated young people who now enter industry are not content with the apprenticeship system of management development that has characterized most large companies. They want more face-to-face interchange with top management and less rigidity, red tape, and delay in communications. This kind of direct contact tends to reduce the layers between top management and competent subordinates being groomed as replacements. As has already been observed, the more capable, competent, motivated, and self-reliant the subordinate, the broader can be the management span, with a flatter structure the resultant. Research findings suggest that managerial satisfaction is higher in smaller organizations with a flat structure. In one study, 1,900 managers were categorized as belonging to tall, intermediate, or flat organizations and were surveyed by questionnaire. In organizations of 5,000 or fewer persons managerial satisfaction was greater in the flat structure; in larger organizations satisfaction was greater in the tall structure.[20] A similar study of 2,976 managers in thirteen nations produced equivalent results.[21] House and Miner believe that such results suggest that at some point in the growth of an organization it may be desirable to formalize hierarchical relationships and establish limited management spans.[22]

MODIFICATIONS OF BASIC LINE ORGANIZATION

Organizational growth and environmental pressures inevitably require modifications of the basic line organization. While many modifications can and do occur, the more important ones are functional organization, staff organization, and various combinations of these.

---

[19]Rocco Carzo, Jr. and John N. Yanouzas, "Effects of Flat and Tall Organization Structure," *Administrative Science Quarterly*, Vol. 14, No. 2, June 1969, pp. 178–191.

[20]Lyman W. Porter and Edward E. Lawler, III, "The Effects of 'Tall' versus 'Flat' Organization Structures on Managerial Job Satisfaction," *Personnel Psychology*, Vol. 17, No. 2, 1964, pp. 135–148.

[21]Lyman W. Porter and J. Siegel, "Relationships of Tall and Flat Organization Structures to the Satisfactions of Foreign Managers," *Personnel Psychology*, Vol. 17, 1965, pp. 379–392.

[22]Robert J. House and John B. Miner, "Merging Management and Behavioral Theory: The Interaction between Span of Control and Group Size," *Administrative Science Quarterly*, Vol. 14, 1969, pp. 451–464.

Functional Organization (Multiple Authority)

Functional organization is a type of structure that exists when authority is exercised *across* organizational lines. It requires an agreement or willingness to subordinate one area of an organization to another under given circumstances, particularly those calling for special expertise. Such functional or "multiple" authority results either in multiple line or multiple staff structure. A highly simplified model of functional organization appears in Figure 14-6. The dotted lines—unfortunately not yet a standard device in organization charts—indicate that *functional authority* exists between positions linked in that manner.

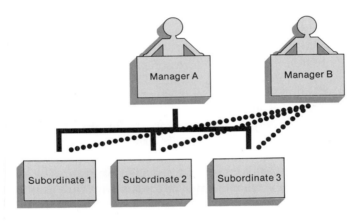

Figure 14-6.   A simple functional organization.

Certain characteristics are evident in multiple line or multiple staff structure based on functional authority.

1. Each superior has the right to make decisions and to enforce them.
2. At any level, a subordinate may be subject to the authority of more than one person at higher levels, and may also be accountable to more than one person at those higher levels.
3. Two or more superiors at any level may have authority over the same person at lower levels.

It must be kept in mind that functional authority conferred upon an individual is based on that individual's possession of special expertise, which is required for specific situations or contingencies.

Functional organization may be understood by observing situations in which it operates. First let us illustrate some **multiple line** situations.

On a freight or passenger train, the locomotive engineer normally is subject to the authority of the dispatcher, who advises when to leave the originating point and when to arrive at various destinations. On its run from St. Louis to Kansas City the train stops in Columbia, Missouri, where the master mechanic, upon inspecting the drive shaft and finding it defective, orders the train not to proceed until the defect is corrected. The engineer now finds himself taking orders from the master mechanic.

The comptroller of a company is interested in analyzing and controlling selling costs. With the knowledge and approval of the sales manager, he sends a message to all salesmen requesting them to mail directly to his attention each evening a special report indicating the number of prospects called on, number of sales made, miles travelled, expenditures for gas, oil, meals, and other pertinent information. Normally, salesmen send their orders, sales correspondence, and other sales-related communications directly through the sales chain of command. In this special situation, however, they send the comptroller's report directly to the latter's office and not through the sales hierarchy.

A saleslady in a department store sells several hundred dollars worth of merchandise to a customer who wishes to have it charged to her account. The saleslady has to check with the store's credit department to verify that the account is in good standing. If not, the sale is disallowed until the customer reestablishes credit with the store. In this instance, the sales clerk is subject to the decision authority of the credit department rather than to the authority of a superior in the sales department.

Multiple staff situations are also prevalent in business. A firm's purchasing department may wish to enter into a contract with a supplier of raw materials or semi-finished products. Before concluding negotiations, the purchasing agent receives from the firm's legal department an opinion that indicates the contemplated agreement would violate existing federal anti-trust laws. A staff officer (legal department) in this case makes a decision that is binding upon another staff officer (purchasing agent). The purchasing contract has to be revised.

In a large multi-plant organization, at each factory an accountant keeps records in a form that is helpful to his boss, the plant manager. There is also a central accounting office at the parent company headquarters. Central accounting requires each factory accountant to maintain standard accounting procedures to enable the parent company to consolidate essential accounting information from each plant. In this situation, the accountant at the plant is not only subject to the authority of his line superior (the plant manager) but also to that of a staff executive at central headquarters. Moreover, the standard accounting procedure requirement demanded by central accounting is binding upon the accountant at the plant. He is expected to comply.

Advantages of functional organization.   There are a number of advantages to functional authority.

1. *It relieves the line officer of some of the burdens of his position.* In specific situations that arise, someone else is given the authority to act under clearly specified conditions. These are well understood by all persons involved including managers and subordinates. The dispatcher knows that under conditions affecting the safety of the train and its passengers the master mechanic may make a decision and give orders to the engineer. The locomotive engineer knows this also and finds no conflict between following the original orders of the dispatcher and the present order of the master mechanic.

2. *It saves a great deal of time.* It is much faster to send reports directly to the comptroller each evening than to send them through regular sales channels and then on to the comptroller. Days and weeks of sales analysis time can be saved, and the statistical information can be kept current, useful, and readily available. The sales manager knows the circumstances under which his salesmen send reports directly to the comptroller, and not to him through the normal chain of command. The salesmen understand the special conditions under which they deal directly with the comptroller and not with their usual line superiors.

3. *It shortens the communication gap.* Going directly to the person who can make the specialized decision shortens the span of communication, reduces the possibility of misinterpretation, abstraction, editing, and delay in response. Under functional authority any employee who wants expert advice concerning or affecting an aspect of his job is encouraged to contact directly the most knowledgeable person in the organization. As a result, lower-level employees can sometimes bypass their immediate supervisors, and managers can bypass their direct superiors. The credit department in the department store, by approving or negating a sales transaction directly, shortens the communication span.

4. *It expedites implementation of a decision or policy.* The purchasing contract is reviewed and ruled upon by the legal department before any harmful results can occur. The train is halted and the possibility of damage to it is prevented; repairs can commence without delay. To go through chain of command channels would take longer, and the decision might come too late to be effective.

The bridging of the communications flow, instead of going through normal channels, is an extension of Fayol's **gangplank principle**,[23] which pointed out that rigid adherence to formal lines of authority could prove needlessly time-consuming when speedy decisions and actions are imperative. In Figure 14-7, if D required information that E could provide, instead of going through channels of command from D to B to A and down through C,

---

[23]Henri Fayol, *General and Industrial Management* (London: Sir Isaac Pitman and Sons, Ltd., 1949). The original work in French appeared in 1916.

he would proceed directly to *E*, and the interchange would take place. The superiors of *D* and *E* should be informed that contact is being made and should be advised if a significant agreement or determination between *D* and *E* has been reached.

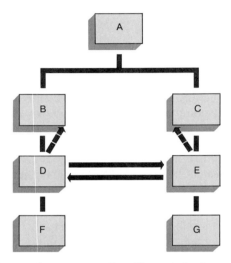

Figure 14-7.   Fayol's gangplank.

5. *It may reduce the cost of operation.* For salesmen to send the comptroller's report through regular sales channels would be far more expensive in terms of mailing costs and re-handling than to mail them directly to the comptroller's office each night.

Disadvantages of functional organization.   While there are many advantages to the use of functional authority, there are at least two potential disadvantages that should be pointed out.

A tendency may develop to circumvent the normal chain of command in situations other than those special ones for which functional authority is intended. If continued, this could eventually erode or weaken normal line authority. This is a potential danger.

If the special circumstances under which functional authority operates are not clearly spelled out and understood by everyone affected by its practice, confusion could result and normal functions be disrupted. A subordinate must never find himself in the position of asking, "Who is my boss?" Such a situation would be contrary to Fayol's classical principle of **unity of command,** which states that a person should normally receive orders from only one superior.[24]

---

[24]*Ibid.*

The best way to avoid some of the problems, friction, and confusion caused by functional authority is to make certain that the precise functional authority assigned to a manager is clearly specified. There are two ways that this can be done: (1) by a clear statement of authority in the job description[25] and (2) by a directive from the line superior who has granted the authority announcing the specific arrangement to all persons who will be affected. Either technique should clearly spell out the line, staff, and functional authority relationships that exist. A staff manager, for example, may have functional authority over operating departments if this is specifically granted to him by the line superior to whom he is directly accountable and who has jurisdiction over those operating departments. If it is a permanent rather than a temporary grant, it will eventually become a part of that staff manager's job description.

In modern business, especially in large corporations, daily activities cannot be conducted effectively solely on the basis of line structure. Modifications are necessary. Some form of functional organization properly employed, when added to basic line, permits flexibility, adaptability, and effectiveness. Functional authority is a necessary technique in dynamic managing.

Staff Organization

The responsible line executive usually has neither sufficient time nor technical competence to study all phases of the functions under his jurisdiction. In small businesses the owners or their appointees may be able to perform all of the managing functions adequately. But in large-scale organizations, which may have grown through mergers, acquisitions, and vertical or horizontal integration, and possibly developed into multi-plant and even multi-national organizations, this is clearly impossible. The increasing complexity of markets and technologies requires staff specialists.

Staff brings to the organization the advanced, specialized training and experience that the line manager lacks. The line manager cannot keep up with developments in every area of business, yet needs the best information to act on. In today's fast-changing technology, even a staff expert, including the engineer, chemist, physicist, or researcher, soon learns that his own store of knowledge and techniques becomes insufficient or obsolete within a few years. He must keep abreast of his field or lose ground to younger, more recently trained graduates of universities and research centers.

There are several characteristics that identify the basic staff organization.

1. A staff position is always related to a line position whose occupant has authority over the holder of the staff position.

---

[25]For a discussion of job description, the reader is referred to Chapter 10.

2. Staff has the authority to make decisions within its assigned area of specialization but does not have authority to impose these decisions on the line organization unless provisions have been made for functional authority.

3. Great specialization in management activities occurs in staff areas.

Staff organization complements the work of the line officer. It does so by relieving him of some of the specialized management functions for which he may not be technically qualified or for which he no longer has the time even though he may have the competence. The purpose of staff is to make it possible for line to do a better job, to accomplish its goals more effectively. The modified organization becomes a line-staff structure. The intimate relationship between line and staff can readily be observed in the military, where the general has his staff officers (operations, ordnance, intelligence, supply, and so on) on the one hand and his corps commanders, field officers (infantry, artillery, armor, and so on) on the other.

A simplified chart showing staff organization in a business setting is illustrated in Figure 14-8. (It would be extremely helpful if literature dealing with management theory indicated all staff relationships on an organization chart by means of *broken lines*. Such standardization would make it much easier to identify line and staff positions.)

In Figure 14-8 all of the executives shown are subject to the authority of the president and are accountable to him. Nothing in the chart is intended to indicate that the other positions are equal in rank or importance. Moreover, the fact that the position "assistant to the president" is shown at a higher point on the chart than other executive positions does not mean that it is

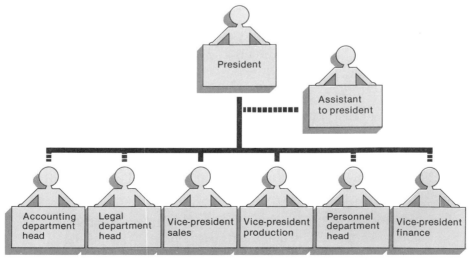

Figure 14-8.   Organization chart showing staff organization (*broken lines*).

more important than the others, nor that the man occupying the position is their superior. Not at all. Solid lines leading to a position indicate that a line relationship exists between the subordinates and the superior; broken lines indicate that a staff relationship exists. In Figure 14-8 both the vice-president in charge of sales and the vice-president for production are line executives who report directly to the president. The assistant to the president and the heads of the accounting, legal, personnel, and finance departments are staff executives (broken lines) who also report directly to the president. The relative importance of any one position compared with another cannot be determined by examining the organization chart. All the chart shows is the direction of authority and accountability flow, and whether a given position is line or staff.

Most modern firms, particularly the large multi-market and transnational ones, utilize a management structure that *combines* line and staff organization. Kinds and numbers of line and staff positions are continually reviewed and modified. The objective is to find the organizational structure that will be most effective in achieving corporate goals. At Chrysler Corporation, for example, at one time fourteen executives reported to its president, Lynn A. Townsend. After eighteen months of study, the management structure was revised and the span of management reduced so that only nine executives reported directly to him. The revised structure consisted of six "staff" vice-presidents (administration, finance, legal affairs, engineering, product planning, and staff operations) and three "line" group vice-presidents (U.S. auto manufacturing and sales; international operations; and defense, space, and diversified products).

Staff Functions

Staff activities supplement the basic line functions, increasing their ability to accomplish their missions. A manufacturing plant exists primarily to *make* and *market* products. These are its line functions; all others are staff. Similarly, a department store is in business primarily to buy and sell merchandise. These activities contribute directly toward the store's overall objectives; any other activities contribute indirectly by making the basic functions more effective.

To serve the line organization, staff engages in three main kinds of activities:

1. **Advisory.** To guide, make suggestions, recommend, produce ideas;
2. **Service.** To perform essential services, or assist various segments of the organization;
3. **Control.** To coordinate, regulate, and relate various activities to each other.

These three types of staff activities are not mutually exclusive. They are closely related, interdependent, and reinforcing. Considerable overlapping occurs. Some staff personnel may engage in all three types of activities, although not necessarily simultaneously. In addition, these activities may be performed for other staff groups as well as for line units. The personnel department (a staff unit) may hire employees for production and sales (line units) and also hire people for the purchasing, accounting, legal, and other non-line departments. Purchasing buys for other staff departments as well as for line departments.

Advisory activities. Persons engaged in advisory work offer specialized counsel in their area of expertise to anyone who requests it. An executive desiring to improve the public image of his division may ask the firm's public relations department for ideas on how this goal may be achieved. The public relations department will make recommendations, which the division manager may or may not follow. Perhaps the company has a chance to gain a new customer if it offers a special price advantage. Is it legal to do so? The sales manager may ask the legal department for counsel. The purchasing agent wants to enter into a contract with a supplier of raw materials over an extended period. He asks the legal department to look over the contemplated agreement and advise him if it is legally in order. Thus the legal department was consulted and offered specialized advisory service to a line manager in the first instance and to a staff manager in the second.

Advisory staff specialists find themselves in a difficult position since they can neither force others to seek their advice, nor force them to heed it. They may therefore have trouble, on occasion, justifying their value to the company. The results of their contribution to the organization are difficult to demonstrate or to measure. Advisory staff people are sensitive about this.

Service activities. Many staff functions are designed primarily to perform essential services for various segments of the organization. The medical department gives physical examinations to all employees in all departments. The company cafeteria is operated for the benefit of all employees. If there is a company store, it offers merchandise at a savings to all workers who wish to make purchases. The personnel department may interview, test, and do preliminary screening of prospective employees for all departments. These types of service activities are performed for all line and staff departments without being initiated by line or staff managers.

Other service activities may be initiated only at the request of a manager. For example, a manager may request that the purchasing department order special equipment that he wants for his department. He may ask the maintenance department to repair his desk, or fix the leaking radiator. The maintenance department performs the service when it can fit the request into its schedule and its procedures. Data processing is another type of service that may be requested by a manager. But he may have to wait his turn before the data he wants processed will be handled; there may be numerous projects and requests ahead of his. Such situations have a tendency to restrict the line manager's activities and encourage behind-the-scenes influence or "pulling rank" to obtain more favored treatment. Politicking puts undue pressures on the service staff and may lead to human relations problems that require someone with authority to resolve inter-group frictions.

Control activities. Frequently staff groups are given authority to coordinate and regulate activities outside their own areas of specialization. They have "functional authority" to act in a control capacity, to make decisions that are binding upon executives and workers in other areas. When an employee reports for a routine physical checkup to the medical department, the physician may discover a physical disability potentially dangerous to the health of the worker or the safety of his fellow workers. The doctor's "recommendation" that the man not continue to work until the disability is treated and corrected has the force of a directive. It is really a control decision that is binding upon the employee's supervisor. A safety inspector, discovering a defective machine or a hazardous situation, may order the machine shut down immediately until the problem is corrected. He does this without first obtaining formal approval from the worker's line superior. If quality control determines that a product is not up to standard, it has the right to reject it or order it returned to the production area for reworking or correcting. When the legal department advises the purchasing department that its contemplated purchasing agreement with a supplier would be in violation of existing antitrust laws, the purchasing department cannot proceed. The legal opinion, in this instance, would be binding upon the purchasing department.

Types of staff positions. Sometimes staff positions are classified as "general" or "specialized." General staff usually serves a single manager. Specialized staff, however, possesses some expertise within a relatively narrow area of activity that is available to all managers and all departments. The legal, purchasing, personnel, quality control, production scheduling, and auditing departments are examples of specialized staff units.

The four types of staff positions most frequently encountered in organizations are: staff assistant, staff executive, staff department, and staff consultant. Of these, the staff assistant is a general staff position and the others are specialized.

Staff assistant. Not only does the staff assistant serve one particular manager exclusively, but he is more often a *generalist* rather than a specialist in some specific management area. The position is that of an administrative assistant and frequently bears the title of "assistant-to." Thus he may be referred to as assistant-to-the-president, or assistant-to-the-director of sales promotion, depending on the title of the line or staff officer to whom he is assigned.

The staff assistant should not be confused with a line assistant, who may bear a very similar sounding title like assistant sales manager, assistant plant manager, or assistant office manager. A line assistant is a line manager, one level below the superior in the chain of command. Line assistants have the right to make decisions and to enforce them just as any line manager does. An "assistant-to," like any other staff person, generally does not have the right to enforce decisions.

Furthermore, the staff assistant should not be confused with personal staff, like a secretary or stenographer, who may be specialists working for one manager exclusively but who are not managers themselves. The nature of their duties is not managerial but facilitating.

The idea of having staff assistants to top managers in organizations is not new. The origin of the "assistant-to" position in business has been traced to the railroad industry at the turn of the century when most railroad executives had a clerk as an aide.

The position of staff assistant is becoming increasingly popular and provides an opportunity to learn the business at the top. In addition, rubbing shoulders with people who are important in the company offers an "assistant-to" experience, privileged information, and the visible exposure needed for advancement. To be a right-hand man to an important executive can be a stepping stone, a unique opportunity. Some assistants-to are paid as much as $75,000 a year. Former chief executives like Ralph Cordiner of General Electric, Mark Cresap of Westinghouse, and K. S. Adams of Phillips Petroleum were once assistants-to. Frequently, the heir-apparent to a top executive post is designated assistant-to by the man whose post he will eventually fill. Such action may stamp out rivalry for the position among senior executives and make it clear to all that the assistant-to will succeed to the post when the current chief executive steps aside. There are situations in which an executive may occupy an important line position in addition to being an assistant to another executive. The president and chairman of the board of General American Life Insurance Company came to the organization as administrative vice-president *and* assistant to the president, was later named executive vice-president, and subsequently was promoted to president and chief administrative officer.

The duties of the staff assistant are usually varied. He assumes many of the tasks that his line superior normally would be expected to perform. He may also handle special assignments and do the leg-work in certain broad areas of corporate planning, acquisitions, and public relations. He may act as trouble-shooter when special problems arise, travel to plants and branches as the special representative of his superior, and brief his mentor on things to look for or questions to raise in the process of controlling various areas within his chain of command.

Staff executive. The staff executive is a highly trained *specialist* accountable to a line executive at a high level of managerial authority. He usually is an expert, highly skilled in one or more areas of management.

To aid in *planning*, a firm may need staff executives highly competent in research, forecasting, or formulating special types of corporate plans. Economists and research statisticians are examples of staff executives who have special competence in areas associated with the planning function.

To assist in *organizing*, the firm may utilize specialists in job analysis, in writing job definitions, or in some other rather narrow personnel area. It may also require an authority on wage negotiation, a psychologist trained to administer and evaluate employment tests, or several specialists in corporate organization and reorganization including mergers and acquisitions.

Activating may require a highly trained executive proficient in installing and administering incentive systems including incentive wage programs, bonus plans, and stock option programs.

In *controlling*, staff executives specially trained in matters dealing with control may be essential. One may be a specialist in developing control systems to safeguard company assets; another an expert in accounts receivable procedures.

Staff executives may also be employed in non-management areas. In finance, for example, the staff executive may be well versed in money markets, methods of raising capital, ways to invest surplus funds, conserving cash, and related matters. In law, one may be a specialist in a particular branch of law such as antitrust, leases, or labor legislation. The purchasing agent is the staff executive with specialized knowledge about suppliers, products, prices, delivery dates, and other matters related to the buying function.

Staff department. Usually, because of the growth and development of a staff executive's activities, it becomes necessary for him to have some assistance. He may require secretarial, stenographic, and clerical help. He may also need an assistant to share some of his responsibilities. As personnel are added, a department evolves. The organizational structure within a staff department, like all organizational structure, originates basically as line. A chain of command develops with levels between the top staff executive and his subordinates. Authority relationships are established. The staff executive, within his domain has the right to make and enforce decisions. Within his staff department he is the "line" executive. Sometimes staff specialists including staff executives are added to the expanding staff department to enable it to function more effectively. In a large personnel department, for example, it may become necessary to hire a medical doctor and a nurse to give first-aid and periodic physical examinations to all company employees. The doctor and the nurse are staff specialists within a staff department. It is not uncommon for a staff executive to have an "assistant-to."

An organization chart of a staff department (personnel department) appears in Figure 14-9. Note the similarity between its structural organization and that of a line department. One observes the existence of levels of

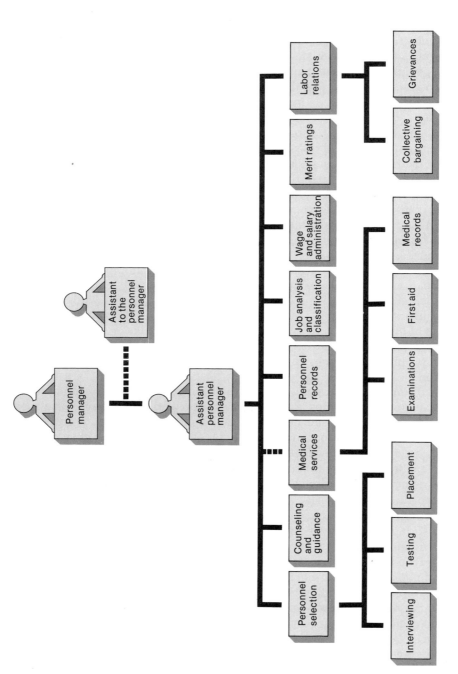

Figure 14-9.   Organization chart of a personnel department.

management, a chain of command, span of management, and basic line and staff relationships.

Staff consultant. There are two types of staff consultants in business and industry:

1. *Within the firm,* particularly if it is a multi-plant or global company, there may be an executive who functions as an overall corporate generalist and whose job it is to see the big picture of total operations in an objective way. He makes recommendations to top management on how to run a tauter ship, make more effective use of the company's total resources, and balance its various operations for greater efficiency. Consolidations, avoidance of duplication, and discontinuance of certain activities may be some of his recommendations. Top management decides whether or not to implement such recommendations.

2. *Outside the firm,* there are individuals and companies that are paid a fee for performing a specialized service which the firm cannot perform for itself because it lacks the capability or manpower, or because it wants an outside point of view. Such an outside consultant may be engaged to make a marketing study, recommend an advertising program, improve employee relations, conduct a management evaluation, recruit a top executive, uncover potential acquisition or merger candidates, conduct an accounting audit, or render similar specialized services. In some instances, the outside consultant will merely make a report and offer recommendations. Whether they are implemented rests with the top management that engaged its services. In other situations, such as conducting an accounting or financial audit, or engaging outside legal specialists to act for the company, the services or findings of the consultant are more than advisory or recommendatory: they are binding on the company. Under these conditions, a "functional authority" relationship exists, having been conferred on the outside staff consultant by the line executive when he contracted for its services. It should be emphasized that the value of the outside consultant rests not merely on his specialized skills but on his detached perspective. As an outsider, he can view the situation in a more impersonal and objective manner. In addition, he brings to the organization his knowledge of similar problems in other firms in the same industry, or solutions that have worked elsewhere, often in entirely different industries.

ORGANIZATIONAL CONFLICT

In many organizations, line and staff work together as a harmonious team. This is the ideal situation. Line managers are supported in their efforts by a group of highly trained staff experts who, when called upon, investigate and offer effective solutions to some of the complex problems that arise in the operation of modern business.

Very often, however, working relations between line and staff departments are less than harmonious. Line managers feel that staff people are crowding them, encroaching on their territory. Staff people are uncertain what role they are expected to play, and what authority they actually have. Friction, distrust, and inefficiency result. If continual hassles persist between the two, decisions are impeded, constant jockeying for recognition and assertion takes place, and coordination suffers.

From the line manager's perspective, the staff organization (1) tends to exceed its advisory role and to assume line authority, (2) fails to see the entire picture and all of the relationships and ramifications that exist beyond its own restricted area of specialization, (3) does not always give sound and realistic advice, and (4) constantly strives to justify its existence, and increase its prestige.

The staff point of view, on the other hand, is that line managers (1) resist new ideas, (2) fail to recognize the contributions of staff, and (3) do not delegate sufficient "functional authority" to staff to implement its recommendations.

One of the reasons for the lack of agreement between line and staff is a fundamental difference in philosophy between them. Staff is creative, innovation-minded, and strongly motivated to introduce change or to question existing ways of doing things. Line tends to prefer things routinized, following prescribed patterns. Like most individuals, line managers dislike sudden change and disruption of the usual, regardless of the reasons for it. Thus, when staff recommends change, particularly abrupt change, line is psychologically geared to resist. When things go wrong, however, line managers welcome suggestions to correct or improve the situation and may eagerly seek the advice and recommendation of staff specialists.

Despite the fact that differences or conflicts often occur between line and staff personnel, there is no question about the need for staff in modern industry and no doubt that its contributions far outweigh its disadvantages. In a sense, the presence of conflict between these organizational units is a positive force in organizational dynamics.

Conflicts also arise in other organizational situations—between managers and workers, managers and other managers, between departments or divisions, and between companies belonging to the same parent company. The psychological conflict between an assembly line worker and an inspector is tersely expressed in the following statement:

Inspectors are like parasites—they don't produce, they don't add something. They only find error.[26]

---

[26]The view of a young union leader in an automobile assembly plant, as quoted by Studs Terkel in *Working* (New York: Pantheon Books, 1974), p. 192.

Humanizing the work place can be undertaken as a joint, cooperative, non-adversary effort by management and the union. Irving Bluestone, vice-president of the United Auto Workers, says:

> The initial key to achieving this goal may well be the open, frank, and enlightened discussion between the parties, recognizing that democratizing the work place and humanizing the job need not be a matter of confrontation but of mutual concern for the worker, the enterprise, and the welfare of society.[27]

Hard-driving, ambitious men who strive for the upper management positions generally step on a few toes along the way. This is also true of ambitious men elsewhere—in politics, the military, and other fields. Conflicts are inevitable—and not always bad for the organization. Of 600 high-level executives interviewed in a survey conducted by Opinion Research Institute, 62 percent said it was impossible to avoid conflicts with other people; only 37 percent thought it was "very important to avoid such conflicts."[28]

There is some evidence that the climate for conflict varies with the number of members in the group. Obviously, the optimum number depends on the group's function. However, as group size increases there tends to be a loss of group cohesion; cliques and factions form whose objectives may be incompatible with the objectives of the organization. Furthermore, even-numbered groups have been found to display greater disagreement than odd-numbered groups. Frank and Anderson measured the conflict level in groups of two, three, five, and eight working on solutions to a human relations problem. They found higher levels of conflict in even-sized than in odd-sized groups.[29] They also found greater perceived unpleasantness and alienation by members of the even-sized groups. A similar finding has been reported by Maier. In studying three- and four-member discussion groups, he found that four-member groups were less inclined to cooperate and compromise than were three-member groups.[30] On the other hand, research evidence on two- and three-person groups seems to indicate that the two-person group is more stable than the three-person group. This seems to reinforce the old adage "two is company and three is a crowd."

Types of Conflict

There are four basic types of conflict and combinations of these that can arise in an organization. The first is *issue* conflict, which is usually a

---

[27]Irving Bluestone, as quoted by Derek Norcross in "Sweden's Newest Export—Industrial Democracy," *Parade Magazine*, December 15, 1974, p. 15.

[28]*The Wall Street Journal*, November 21, 1961.

[29]F. Frank and L. Anderson, "Effects of Task and Group Size upon Group Productivity and Member Satisfaction," *Sociometry*, Vol. 34, 1971, pp. 135–149.

[30]N. Maier, "Decision Making in 3 vs. 4 Person Groups," *Personnel Psychology*, Vol. 25, 1972, pp. 531–534.

disagreement between two or more groups arising from differences in organizational viewpoint. For example, an academic department in a university may want to tighten grade standards in order to improve the quality of its graduates. The admissions office, however, feels it necessary to keep enrollments high. Interdepartmental conflict will result.

The second type of conflict is *interpersonal*. This is conflict between two individuals and is based on personal differences. It may originate as an issue conflict and develop into a personality clash.

A third type of conflict is *role* conflict. This occurs when an individual faces pressure from several sources. If a plant manager is asked by a manufacturing vice-president to increase the output of Product A, for example, and the sales vice-president calls for more of Product B, the plant manager faces a role conflict caused by the incompatible demands made upon him.

The fourth type of conflict is *intrapersonal*. In this situation, an individual's values and beliefs are incompatible with his actions. A chemist may believe it is wrong for a country to use napalm as an instrument of destruction. His company may ask him to develop cheaper ways to make napalm. His required behavior will be in direct conflict with his belief.

The Effects of Conflict

In the past, all conflict has been viewed as dysfunctional or destructive. Conflict can be constructive, however, and can play a creative role in producing organizational objectives.

Traditional management theorists saw organizational conflict as destructive, and the elimination of all dissent as management's role. However, the issue conflicts generated by friendly competition may be highly desirable, although the interpersonal conflicts characteristic of cutthroat competition are usually destructive and should be eliminated. The **behavioralist** philosophy has been that conflicts exist and should be resolved amicably. The **interactionist** approach differs from the behavioralist in that it recognizes the absolute necessity of organizational conflict, encourages it, and considers the management of conflict a major responsibility of all administrators at all organizational levels.[31] Interactionists believe that organizations which do not stimulate conflict increase the probability of status quo existence, inadequate decisions and stagnation. While there is general agreement that change brings about conflict, the belief that conflict is both a source and result of change is not yet universally accepted.

---

[31]Stephen P. Robbins, *Managing Organizational Conflict* (Englewood Cliffs, N.J.: Prentice-Hall, 1974) pp. 12–14.

SUMMARY

Authority relationships, created when certain people in an organization are put in charge of the work of others, the latter being accountable to the former, tie together the various jobs into a coherent organization.

Authority flows through successive layers or levels of subordinates in a vertical or straight line fashion and produces a type of structure known as *basic line organization*. All structure based on authority relationships originates as line organization. With growth and development of institutions this basic structure becomes modified. Two important modifications that develop are functional organization and staff organization. Both evolve to offset the excessive burdening of line executives, to enable greater specialization in the managing functions, to improve the span of communication, and to optimize management effectiveness in dealing with subordinates.

Functional organization exists when authority crosses normal organizational lines, bypassing the usual chain of command. The conditions under which this happens should be carefully spelled out to avoid any confusion, misunderstanding, or conflict. Functional authority permits increased flexibility, adaptability to special situations, and improved effectiveness.

Staff organization supplies the necessary support activities to line organization, including advisory, service, and control assistance that increases both efficiency and effectiveness of organizational pursuits. Support activities typically are provided by staff assistants, staff executives, staff departments, and staff consultants, both internal and external. Combinations of line, multiple line, staff, and multiple staff structure types are present in almost all organizations today.

Because of fundamental differences in managerial philosophy, there is often conflict between line and staff executives. Conflict also occurs in relationships other than managerial. It is present also between managers and non-managers, workers, departments, divisions and even subsidiaries of the parent organization. Four basic types of conflict are issue, interpersonal, role, and intrapersonal. The emerging concept of organizational conflict is that conflict, particularly issue-oriented conflict, should be encouraged and managed as a means of promoting beneficial change.

KEY CONCEPTS

Scalar Chain

Levels of Management

Line Organization

Span of Management

Graicunas' Principle

Tall versus Flat Organizations

Functional Organization

Gangplank Principle

Unity of Command

Staff Organization

Organizational Conflict

GLOSSARY

functional authority   Authority that is exercised across organizational lines rather than through the normal chain of command.

scalar principle   Managerial authority scales downward by degrees from top levels through successively lower levels in an organization.

span of management   The number of subordinates a manager can supervise effectively.

unity of command   A situation in which each subordinate is subject to the authority of only one superior.

REVIEW QUESTIONS

1. How would you categorize various levels of management? What kinds of positions would you include in each of your categories?

2. What are the essential characteristics of a basic line organization? Of a staff organization? What are the main differences?

3. What is the important concept to remember about the work of Graicunas?

4. What are some of the factors that influence the number of subordinates a manager can supervise?

5. The statement has been made by some writers that "the real cause of formal organization is the limitations of the span of management." Do you agree?

6. It has also been said that functional authority violates the chain of command and disrupts the organization's effectiveness. What is your view?

7. What are the chief staff functions? Give examples of each.

8. What causes conflict between line and staff? How can it be reduced?

9. List and discuss four types of organizational conflict.

10. Compare the traditional, behavioral, and interactionist points of view concerning organizational conflict. To which do you subscribe? Why?

Chapter 15

Adjuncts to Basic Line and Staff Structure

To increase organizational flexibility, and thus the organization's ability to respond to changing conditions, modern management has added a number of important adjuncts to the basic line and staff structure. They support and reinforce activities at various levels, making it possible to achieve line and staff objectives in a more orderly way. Adjuncts to line and staff are of five major types: (1) committees, (2) task forces, (3) matrix organizations, (4) conferences, and (5) conventions.

COMMITTEES

A committee is a group of persons, either elected or appointed, who meet by intent to consider matters assigned to it.

Not all committees are adjuncts to line and staff organization. The board of directors and the executive committee of a corporation are committees, to be sure. They are line committees with extensive authority. They are not adjuncts to the basic line and staff structure; they are part of the line structure.

Committees which are adjuncts to regular line and staff organization draw their members from them. Often membership will include both line and staff people, *workers* and *managers*. Generally members are appointed by an executive who has the authority to ask colleagues or subordinates to serve on committees for some special purpose within his jurisdiction. Forming a committee represents a type of delegation of authority, in that the manager assigns duties and confers specific authority upon a group, empowering them to act.

Usually the committee consists of people who devote only a part of their time to their committee roles, since they normally have other duties to perform. Under certain conditions, however, committee work may be a full-time assignment temporarily replacing the committee members' usual activities. Whether a committee becomes a permanent part of the total organization structure depends on the specific purpose for which it was formed as well as the regularity of its performance. In some firms, committees are an important part of management structure; in others they are incidental and temporary. Committees that function on a continuing basis may be considered a type of **collateral organization.**

Committees are brought together for many reasons. A frequent purpose is to evaluate existing activities. The committee may review certain activities and make recommendations for improving their effectiveness. It investigates the areas assigned to it, reports its findings, and proposes modifications or revisions. A university faculty peer evaluation committee charged with assessing teaching, scholarship, and service of its colleagues fulfills this purpose. In this sense, the committee performs a control function.

A committee may also be empowered to make decisions and enforce them. After studying a problem area and producing recommendations, it may proceed to implement them. Its decisions are then binding on the enterprise as a whole or on some part of it, perhaps those functional areas represented within the committee. When a *staff* committee is given the authority to enforce its decisions, to implement its findings and recommendations, it is called a **plural executive.** Although adequate research on the subject is lacking, it appears that the plural executive is most effective in policy formulation, settling jurisdictional disputes, and establishing organizational objectives.

Some committees develop plans. At the highest levels, corporate policy committees engage in corporate planning on a broad scale. At lower levels, committees may be charged with operative planning, as illustrated by the work of a research and development committee or a new product development committee.

Committees often facilitate communication, both laterally and vertically in the organization. *Lateral* communication may be established between members who would not come into contact otherwise, thereby enabling them to exchange ideas and information. A *vertical* channel of communication may also be established, with the direction of flow either from the committee chairman to the members or from the members to the committee chairman. If the head of the committee is a manager who appointed it, such vertical flow upward provides him with important"feedback" that he might otherwise not receive.

Because several points of view are represented in a committee, problems can be seen from a broader perspective. The committee also permits differences of opinion to be expressed, invites suggestions for solutions, and welcomes constructive ideas.

Employee participation can be strongly encouraged through committees, as we noted in our review of various participative activities in Chapter 11. For example, at the department level, committee interaction induces employees to contribute to the formulation of departmental policies or to the establishment of specific programs. Indirect benefits accrue also. Committee members can break the tedium of their normal work routine and assume a new and different role that is rewarding and enables them to achieve personal satisfactions. It can be an instrument to reduce worker alienation.

Committees operate at all levels of the management hierarchy. There are top-level committees, divisional committees, and department committees. Top-level, or corporate committees, that are adjuncts to line and staff include the corporate policy committee, finance committees, and audit committee. Divisional committees within particular functional areas may include a bonus and budget committee, or a product development committee whose membership probably represents several functional areas including product design, engineering, production, sales, and budgets. Note that in this example the committee is a mix of *both* line and staff people. Committees also exist at the department level and include the safety committee, grievance committee, and suggestion committee, among others.

Types of Committees

Since there are so many kinds of committees, attempts have been made to classify them in various ways. Let us examine a few ways in which they can be grouped for study.

Line committees versus staff committees.   Basically, if a committee has the authority to make and enforce decisions, it is a line committee. A committee made up entirely of line managers and their line assistants, such as a collective bargaining team, would be of this type. If the relationship of a committee to its superior is advisory in nature, then the committee is a staff committee regardless of the source from which its members have been drawn. A committee appointed by a manager to recommend ways to improve human relations is an example of a staff committee.

Formal versus informal.   A formal committee is one that has a definite and usually permanent place in the organization. Its duties and charge are clearly spelled out. Examples are the budget and grievance committees. The informal committee is not provided for in the organization structure. It may be created to explore a situation in an unofficial way. A committee appointed to evaluate employee morale and report its findings to the manager is an example of an informal committee.

Standing versus temporary.   Another way to distinguish between committees is to consider them as standing (permanent) or temporary (ad hoc). In most cases, a formal committee is also a standing one. Not all formal committees are permanent, however. A committee given a specific charge may be organized in a formal way. When it has fulfilled its mission it is disbanded. It was formal, yet temporary. Others may be informal and rather permanent. Again we refer to the manager who establishes a committee to advise him on how to improve human relations in the organization. This committee may continue to function indefinitely.

Advantages of Committees

There are a number of advantages to be gained by an organization through the intelligent use of committees. Let us observe some of these.

1. The committee assembles a wider range of backgrounds, experience, abilities, and points of view than can be found in any one person. Many problems are so complex that the most capable manager could not possess all the knowledge and experience required to arrive at wise solutions to all of them.

2. Interests of various segments of the organization can be seen from a more balanced perspective. Before arriving on the committee, individuals may have seen and understood problems only from their own particular vantage points. Sales, for example, may have been concerned only with its own problems without regard to those existing in other areas. When limited resources are to be allocated, one tends to see only his own need for them and to be unaware that others have equally strong needs for the same resources. Exchanging viewpoints helps committee members to look beyond the confines of narrow self-interest toward a broader perspective, and to clarify misunderstood or misinterpreted points of view. Special committees facilitate the exchange of information between groups whose interests and attitudes would otherwise not be understood because normally there is little or no direct contact between them.

3. The committee creates a favorable climate for implementing decisions. An idea or plan agreed upon by committee members who represent various segments of the organization has a better chance for acceptance and implementation. No area affected by the committee decision is taken by surprise; all had some voice in determining the outcome. At least they had an opportunity to listen and to be heard. They are motivated and obligated to carry out the committee decisions. The implementation process thus has built-in support. Persons outside the committee who are affected by its decisions are more likely to cooperate since their interests were represented in the committee. Resistance to change is reduced.

4. The committee can be an excellent training ground for executive development. A trainee or younger executive receives visible exposure, has a chance to watch his superiors in action and to listen, observe, and learn. He may be given "leg-work" assignments and opportunities to demonstrate his ability. He may witness the decision-making process in action and perhaps participate in the deliberations. His chances for recognition and possible promotion are increased.

Disadvantages of Committees

Committee format cannot be fully understood without also recognizing some of its potential disadvantages.

1. A committee may be influenced too greatly by its chairman. It is said that the deliberations of a committee often reflect the influence or personality of its chairman. Should this person be the executive who appointed the committee, and be a domineering person, free discussion and flow of ideas may be stifled. When a top officer who chairs a committee gives the impression that he favors subordinates who approve his ideas and suggestions, "yes-men" appear. Under these conditions, the advantages of a committee effort are lost.

2. Committees can be costly. A great deal of time can be consumed in committee meetings in discussions and free exchange of ideas. Much additional time is spent outside the meeting in fact-finding, research, and preparation for the meeting. Individuals are taken away from their regular duties, which may suffer. The total cost of meetings should be weighed against the advantages to be gained. Direct and indirect costs of committees can be sizable. The hourly cost of a committee meeting based solely on salaries of its members can be staggering.

3. There is danger of compromise. To arrive at decisions, committees must frequently make compromises to satisfy various members. There is a tendency to seek the lowest common denominator. The desire for unanimity or simply an agreement may produce a watered-down version of the original proposal. Instead of black or white, the result may be gray. Besides, politics may influence the decision. One member may support the position of another with the understanding the support will be reciprocated. "You scratch my back and I'll scratch yours" may be the basis for reaching an agreement.

4. Undue conformity may result. If members see eye to eye on everything, if there are no disagreements, no differences of opinion, or divergent points of view expressed, the value of the committee is greatly reduced.

5. It may be difficult to establish meeting times. It is not always convenient for each committee member to be available when and where needed. The larger the committee, the more difficult it is to establish a time and place for meetings.

6. Deliberations may be influenced by status or rank. Committee personnel tend to give considerable weight to the formal rank its members hold outside the committee. It is likely that in committees which include representation from several levels in a chain of command, members from the lower levels will not participate effectively. Discussions will continue to be influenced by their superiors.

7. Committee members may be excessively burdened. In many organizations—universities for example—individuals may serve on several committees in addition to their regular duties. This makes heavy demands upon their time. They may feel "committeed to death." Concerted managerial effort to capitalize on the advantages and to minimize the disadvantages can make committees more effective.

TASK FORCE (PROJECT TEAM)

There is a growing impetus for modern management to deal with specific problems through a special kind of committee called a "task force" or "project team." Task force or project management has several underlying characteristics that differ from the usual kinds of committees. It is (1) temporary, (2) organized around specific problems to be solved, (3) composed of a team with diverse professional skills including line and staff, and (4) composed of members differentiated not by their formal status or rank in the company but by the special talents and expertise they bring to the particular problem.

Project management is widespread in the aerospace industries, where large numbers of persons are assigned to the design, development, and production of entire specific projects. They are placed on detached service from their regular duties and are assigned to the project from its inception to its completion. Other industries are also using task forces.

In general, the project form of organization promotes the coordination of various specialties to achieve project completion on time and to meet established budgets or quotas. It possesses the flexibility to tackle quickly problems that develop within one specialized area, without serious disruption of the performance of other areas. There are some offsetting disadvantages, however. If a project requires only a portion of a specialist's time and talents, he is actually under-employed while he is assigned to that project. Should two projects be going on simultaneously, each requiring part-time use of two specialists, say a design engineer and a systems analyst, it may not be possible for these specialists to allocate their time and efforts proportionately to both projects. In this case the parent organization may have to hire or assign four specialists (a design engineer and a systems analyst for each project), thereby under-employing the talents of all four and incurring increased costs because of the duplication. In addition, the long-run technical development of the respective specialties suffers because the original supervisor of these specialists is no longer responsible for them while they are on detached service to the project.

To illustrate the negative effects of rapid change and the temporary nature of many jobs in modern industry, Alvin Toffler cites task forces and project management.

The high rate of turnover is dramatically symbolized by the rapid rise of what executives call "project" or "task force" management. Here teams are assembled to solve specific short-term problems. Then exactly like the mobile playgrounds, they are disassembled and their human components reassigned.

. . . Unlike the functional departments or divisions of a traditional bureaucratic organization, which are presumed to be permanent, the project or task force team is temporary by design.[1]

Toffler has predicted the breakdown of bureaucracy and calls the rise of project-oriented management **ad-hocracy.** As projects are completed or discontinued, the project team is deleted from the organization and disappears from the existing structural design. For some members of a task force this lack of permanence may be disruptive, particularly if they lose touch with developments at their home base and have to readjust and catch up when they return. In many situations, the use of project teams may not require drastic readjustment on the part of its members, particularly if they serve on the project team while retaining their regular positions in the organization. They may be able to devote the necessary time to both areas.

Two actual situations are illustrative of project management. Boise Cascade Corporation's executive committee, concerned with several problems related to the company's ability to adjust its organization to meet changing conditions, including management obsolescence, called upon its Human Resources Committee to organize a project called "The Organization Renewal Project."[2] Four operating and staff executives, with the assistance of two outside consultants, formed the project team. Observe that in this instance the task force included members from outside the organization.

At Sun Oil Company, an industrial products team composed of engineers, researchers, and sales people cooperate on a project called Hydrocarbon Management, a program of services designed to manage the flow of oil from development through marketing, as well as in-plant use, recycling, and disposal.[3] Its purpose is to conserve oil—anybody's oil. Each member of the project team is involved in the sale of lubricants and oil; the sale of engineering services, in-plant management services, and recycling equipment; and the sale of programs for waste oil disposal.

MATRIX ORGANIZATION

Matrix organization is closely related to and an extension of project organization. According to Luthans, "the matrix organization is a project

---

[1]Alvin Toffler, *Future Shock* (New York: Random House, 1970), p. 119.

[2]"Organization Renewal Project," paper prepared by the Organization Renewal Project Team, Boise Cascade Corporation, July 1971.

[3]Camille J. Dawson, "New Life for Used Oil," *Our Sun,* Sun Oil Company, Vol. 39, No. 2, Summer 1974, pp. 12–13.

organization plus a functional organization rather than a variation of project organization."[4]

As we have viewed an organization, it is a dynamic instrumentality designed to meet specific needs. As needs change, managers seek new ways to meet them. Brought about by rapidly changing technology and the necessity for rapid and highly specialized accommodation, matrix organization is one of the newer ways developed by managers to modify organizational design to fit changing conditions.

Galbraith suggests that "the matrix organization grows out of the organizational choice between project and functional forms, although it is not limited to those bases of the authority structure."[5] A matrix organization may be viewed as a hybrid containing elements of both project organization and functional organization. It attempts to derive the benefits of both. In a general way, project managers define what has to be done and functional managers determine how to do it.[6] Matrix organization is especially useful when several projects are operating simultaneously and each requires the use of the same functional resources of the overall organization.[7]

There are various kinds of matrix designs. One schematic description of a matrix structure appears in Figure 15-1.

The major difference between project and matrix organization is that in matrix organization personnel and facilities of different functional areas are loaned or made available to the project while normal functional activities continue. In Figure 15-1, for example, the product design department continues to design other projects in addition to handling design for Projects A, B, and C. The engineering department continues to offer engineering services to the entire organization while serving Projects A, B, and C. The same applies to the production and quality control departments in our illustration. In other words, a given project probably could not support or afford its own product design, engineering, production, and quality control activities and therefore uses existing functional facilities. In most organizations the cost, including overtime if necessary, of using these specialized facilities is charged to the project requesting the assistance. Who decides whether overtime is warranted? Obviously, there is need for close cooperation between a project manager and the managers of the respective functional departments.

Matrix organization has a number of serious limitations. If several projects are going on simultaneously, they compete with each other for functional services. Moreover, someone other than the individual project

---

[4]Fred Luthans, *Organizational Behavior* (New York: McGraw-Hill, 1973), p. 174.

[5]Jay R. Galbraith, "Matrix Organization Designs: How to Combine Functional and Project Forms," *Business Horizons*, February 1971, pp. 29–40.

[6]D. R. Kingdon, *Matrix Organization* (New York: Harper & Row, 1973), p. 20.

[7]Joel E. Ross and Robert G. Murdick, "People, Productivity, and Organizational Structure," *Personnel*, American Management Association, September–October 1973, pp. 9–18.

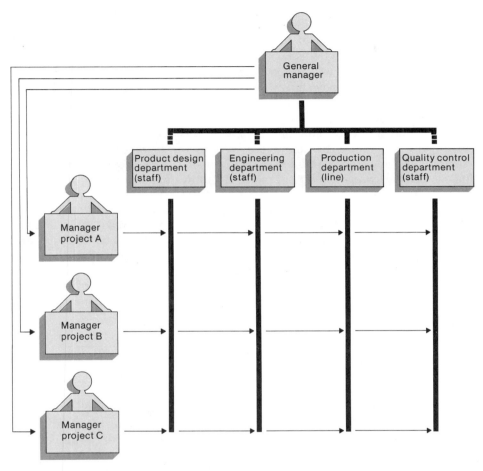

Figure 15-1. Matrix organization.

manager has to decide whether Project A should be given higher priority than Project B or C. Otherwise, managers of the functional areas have no way of determining which project should receive their attention first. Their primary responsibility is to insure an even flow of work. What is beneficial to the successful operation of their functional areas may not be suitable for the successful completion of a specific project. A manager of a functional area is not in a position to make the decision to sub-optimize the normal activity of his function in deference to the project goals, nor to sub-optimize a specific project deliberately for the benefit of the overall enterprise.[8] If deci-

---

[8]The reader is urged to review the concept of deliberate sub-optimizing, discussed in Chapter 3.

sions of this type are to be made by the general manager, as depicted in Figure 15-1, the latter has increased his span of management beyond that of overseeing the activities of his functional subordinates. He now has the added responsibility of being coordinator of all ongoing projects.

Is matrix the answer to the organizational planner's prayer for effective structure? Some say that if "who does what, when, and for whom" is clearly delineated—if every detail is spelled out in writing—matrix structure will work. Others stress that the difference between success and failure of the matrix concept lies in an equilibrium of power between project managers and functional managers. Where the *technical* aspect is a key variable (as in defense and aerospace industries), matrix organization can be effective. However, many agree that "things are very different when it has to turn in a profit."[9]

John Mee says, "the concept of a matrix organization entails an organizational system designed as a 'web of relationships' rather than a line and staff relationship of work performance."[10] This implies that line and staff functions are placed in a position of supporting the project; that the prime emphasis is on horizontal and diagonal communications; that the project manager often lacks sufficient authority to support his responsibility; and that the relationship of project to function has a limited existence.

CONFERENCES

Conferences are frequently utilized in various organizations to assist managers, both line and staff, in fulfilling the objectives of their functional areas.

In some companies, particularly those with far-flung branches and personnel widely scattered geographically, the daily "conference call" is a most valuable adjunct. This takes place over the telephone. Participants in the conference call are briefed about the previous day's events and plans for the current day. Usually the flow of communication is from the manager to his subordinates, who spend most of the time as listeners, although some time is allotted for questions and comments. This type of conference technique is far less costly than trying to bring all the parties together physically in the same room at the same time from all parts of the country.

More common is the conference in which department heads or key personnel meet with their superior periodically, in an informal way, to talk things over, exchange views, and reach agreement on how they may synchronize their efforts to accomplish mutual objectives. It also permits the superior to brief several subordinates at one time rather than having to

---

[9]John Perrham, "Matrix Management: A Tough Game to Play," *Dun's Review*, August 1970, pp. 31–34.

[10]John F. Mee, "Matrix Organization," *Business Horizons*, Summer 1964, p. 70.

brief everyone individually. It saves valuable time for both the superior and subordinate when the conference technique is used.

At Occidental Petroleum Corporation, quarterly management review meetings are held. Fifty top management executives, including key officials of divisions and worldwide subsidiaries, meet in person to report on current affairs in their respective jurisdictions, discuss problems, and formulate plans for the future. Concerning the value of these conferences, Occidental's board chairman had this to say:

> Of major benefit are the opportunities these meetings offer for the cross-fertilization of ideas—methods which will work well in one division may also work well in an unrelated division.
>
> More efficient utilization of corporate facilities and new ideas for ways of dealing with division and corporate matters are examined. Significantly, all members of the board of directors attend these two-day meetings, giving your directors and corporate management the opportunity to discuss matters first hand with the executives throughout the company's organizations who are directly involved in the creation of sales and profits.[11]

Conferences have most of the advantages of committees and fewer of the disadvantages. Like the committee, the conference can be an excellent training ground for up-and-coming executives who have a chance to see and be seen, to hear and be heard. Often some of the details or simple administrative tasks are assigned to the junior member. This can be an opportunity for him to demonstrate his dependability and capabilities.

CONVENTIONS

Another adjunct to line and staff structure is the convention, which may be regional or national in scope.

Regional conventions may be convened a few times during the year for the purpose of bringing like personnel together to discuss matters of mutual concern. Thus the national sales manager could meet with sales personnel from several states in a geographic region to deal with matters of regional significance. At a later date, another convention could be held with branch managers and salesmen from a different geographic area to discuss matters of particular importance to that region.

National conventions usually take place on an annual basis. The familiar type is the national sales convention, although national conventions of other functional areas of business are held also. For example, a company may hold an annual convention of its supervisory personnel. Such a meeting may provide speakers on topics such as costs, equipment, personnel, estimating, leadership, safety, company policies, and corporate plans for the

---

[11]Armand Hammer, Annual Report for 1972, Occidental Petroleum Corporation, March 20, 1973, p. 25.

future. The national sales convention is typical of a popular and successfully employed technique in American industry. Personnel widely dispersed geographically are brought together in one place, making it possible to achieve certain objectives that could not be achieved otherwise. A number of advantages accrue from national conventions:

1. The convention is a means for bringing together on a face-to-face, get-acquainted basis people of similar backgrounds, interests, and experience. This may be the only direct way for them to meet in person and get to know each other.

2. A convention provides a favorable medium for mass communication. It is an opportunity to introduce management plans and announce and demonstrate new products, marketing techniques, advertising and promotional aids, production techniques, and related matters.

3. An opportunity exists to exchange experiences and share expertise. An outstanding salesman, for example, can share with his fellow salesman some of the selling techniques he employs. Workshops or simulated role situations can be used to demonstrate effective selling methods.

4. Organization ties are strengthened. Whether at formal convention sessions or at its informal social gatherings, people of like interests meet each other and company executives whom they otherwise might never know except by name. Solid ties are established. A community of interests and an esprit de corps develops.

5. The convention offers an opportunity to reward and motivate personnel. Through the national convention, a particular functional group such as the selling organization may be openly recognized for its contribution to the corporate success, and encouraged to continue its efforts.

As an adjunct to line and staff organization, the convention makes it possible for objectives of the company to be met more readily. It reinforces the classical and widely held principle of **unity of direction,** introduced by Fayol, which affirms, ''one head and one plan for a group of activities having the same objective.''[12]

SUMMARY

In most organizations traditional line and staff structures are not sufficiently refined to accomplish all of the organization's needs, particularly those which call for intricate working relationships and more intimate links among people and groups. As result, a number of adjuncts to line and staff

[12]Henry Fayol, *Industrial and General Administration,* (International Management Institute, 1930.) p. 221.

have evolved to bridge the gap. These include committees, task forces, matrix organizations, conferences, and conventions.

These adjuncts may be interrelated and tend to complement each other. Through their use managers and non-managers, line and staff personnel, become more closely associated.

Committees, conferences, and conventions are probably the more familiar adjuncts. Committees may be temporary or permanent, formal or informal, line or staff in nature. Staff committees that are given line authority are called "plural executives." Conferences tend to be informal and excellent media for lateral communication and cross-fertilization of ideas. Conventions, both regional and national, are held less frequently than committee or conference meetings but tend to embrace larger numbers of people. The convention can also be a superior medium for lateral or horizontal communication. In practice, it reinforces the unity of direction concept.

The newer adjuncts to organizational structure are task force or project teams and matrix organization. Task force groups are assembled primarily because of the need to deal with specific problems or goals; are temporary; are comprised of specialists recruited for their individual expertise; and provide a collegial relationship among members, in which normal hierarchical rank is laid aside. An extension of the project team is the matrix organization in which projects dovetail with functional areas to accomplish the project objectives. In matrix organization, it is necessary to utilize existing enterprise functions, which continue to pursue their own objectives while cooperating simultaneously with project objectives. Close coordination is essential, and that may require the services of a general manager or coordinator of projects who establishes priorities. He may even deliberately sub-optimize functional operations or those of particular projects in order to achieve total organizational balance in terms of resource allocations or goal pursuits.

All five adjuncts contribute added flexibility and dynamism to existing formal organization.

KEY CONCEPTS

Committees	Matrix Organization
Collateral Organization	Conferences
Task Force or Project	Conventions
Management	Unity of Direction
Ad-hocracy	

GLOSSARY

ad-hocracy   A term used to describe the rise of project-oriented organization.

collateral organization   Committees that function on a continuing basis.

committee   A group of persons, elected or appointed, who meet by intent to consider matters assigned to it.

matrix organization   An intricately linked cooperative relationship between project organization and functional organization.

plural executive   A staff committee that has been given authority to implement its decisions.

unity of direction   A principle that states there should be one head and one plan for all activities that have a common objective.

REVIEW QUESTIONS

1. What is meant by the term "collateral organization"?
2. Make a list of some essential purposes that can be achieved through the use of committees.
3. What are some advantages of the use of committees? What are some of its potential pitfalls?
4. What are the essential distinguishing characteristics of a task force? Does it differ from a project team?
5. Under what circumstances would you recommend the use of a matrix organization? Give some examples.
6. Do you believe that matrix management will replace traditional structure? Defend your position.
7. If you were in charge of an organization, under what circumstances would you make use of conferences?
8. Why are regional and national conventions valuable adjuncts to normal organization structure?

Chapter 16

Centralization and Decentralization

Closely related to authority relationships and delegation of authority are the concepts of centralization and decentralization. In the vocabulary of management, centralization and decentralization are somewhat ambiguous terms. Theoretically, they represent extreme positions on either end of a continuous scale. Actually, they are relative terms since no organization can be completely centralized or decentralized. Complete centralization, taken literally, would mean that subordinates would have nothing to do. Complete decentralization would mean the existence of sub-units totally unrelated to each other or to the parent from which they originated. They would be strangers, with no means for coordinating their efforts toward a mutual or joint goal. There would be no unity of direction.

To understand centralization and decentralization, it is necessary to recognize that each consists of two facets: (1) plant, personnel, and equipment (the locus of activities), and (2) authority (the locus of decision making). Authority includes decision making in the exercise of the major management functions, namely planning, organizing, activating, and controlling.

One must carefully distinguish between these two essential components. Describing a firm as "decentralized" could mean that it has factories or offices scattered throughout the world. It could also mean that its chief executive has delegated a substantial part of his portfolio and powers to lower levels of management. Still another meaning could be that only certain, but not all, functions are performed by detached groups instead of by a unified division or service entity. Does centralization or decentralization refer to plant, personnel, and equipment or does it refer to authority? It is important to recognize that *both* components are involved, and various combinations or degrees of mix are possible and actually do occur.

REASONS FOR DECENTRALIZATION

In the normal course of development from a small to a large company, a firm expands its activities and its spheres of interest. It may branch out. A manufacturing enterprise may open factories and sales offices in various parts of the country; a retail chain opens stores regionally or throughout the nation; brokerage firms open offices in many cities; airlines open ticket offices in hotel lobbies in major traffic areas. The *normal pattern of growth* leads to a dispersion of physical facilities of plant, personnel, and activities from its original home base.

The *nature of the product or of the industry* itself has a bearing on the need to decentralize. Industries such as railroads, steamship lines, telephone companies, and airlines could not grow without decentralizing. Dispersion of facilities is essential in broadening their services to include more recipients. In other industries, where a product rather than a service is the core concern, the nature of the product bears on the decision to decentralize. If the basic raw material ingredient in the finished product is relatively abundant and its acquisition cost inexpensive relative to the cost of transporting it, the tendency is to locate the manufacturing facility either near its ultimate market or near the source of its raw material. Under these conditions, the ideal situation prevails when raw material and end users of the product are not too distant from each other. Beer is an example of such a product. Its major ingredient by weight or volume is water, a relatively abundant, inexpensive, and accessible resource. It is more expensive to ship the finished product to markets than it is to build breweries close to population centers. Growth in this industry thus takes place mainly through decentralization. The manufacture of cement, in which the basic ingredients are the relatively abundant limestone and sand, is also dispersed over many locations. The manufacture of women's clothing, on the other hand, tends to be concentrated in one location. In this case, the costs of the components, namely cloth, styling, and labor, are high relative to the cost of shipping the finished product over distances to end users.

In addition, many *external factors* have contributed to and encouraged growth through dispersion. Improved *transportation* has been a dominant influence. Modern, concrete all-weather highways, the growth of the trucking industry and its improved equipment, development of the airlines, and the construction of huge tankers and pipelines are all indicative of how it is possible to move merchandise in large quantities or to offer services rapidly over long distances. This development encourages firms to reach out farther from home base for markets and for raw materials. If distances between plants, warehouses, depots, branches, or sales offices have been a restraining factor in the growth and expansion of commerce and industry, improved transportation has greatly reduced the limitation.

Improved *communication* has been another force encouraging growth through dispersion. The telephone with private WATS lines (wide area telephone service), two-way radio, television, computerized management information systems, and other communication advances have made it possible for scattered divisions of a firm to keep in touch almost constantly without regard to distance.

Wars, too, have stimulated decentralization. During World War II, for example, the broadening of the war effort required firms to expand their operations and to build new plants to serve the government in building ships, planes, tanks, and guns. For national security reasons, one of which was potential enemy bombing, plants producing war materiel were scattered to many geographic areas, and in many cases were hidden or camouflaged from view. A team of nuclear scientists under the direction of the renowned Enrico Fermi did their secret nuclear fission work under the spectator stands of Stagg Field at the University of Chicago. For these and other external reasons, decentralization was encouraged.

When an organization increases in size or scale it also increases in *complexity*. This is particularly true when the size increase takes the form of proliferation into a multi-plant or multi-market structure. The number, frequency, and difficulty of decisions demanded of top management are greatly increased. If these decisions concern a wide variety of products or services, different markets, or discontinuous operations requiring frequent modification and dissimilar technology, the need for quick, informed decisions will reinforce the tendency to decentralize into self-contained, manageable subunits. Decentralization is intended to provide the benefits of both large-scale and small-scale operations. The effectiveness of decentralizing the decision-making process is directly related to the amount of freedom for decisions that is allowed at that point which most directly feels the impact of those decisions.

Often *environmental factors* cause organizations to change their mode of operations through diversification. In response to rising anti-smoking agitation, the tobacco industry, as an example, diversified into such fields as shipping, oil refining, foods, health products, land development, pet foods, liquors, and breweries.[1] This defensive strategy of diversification was actually a form of decentralization. Vertical and horizontal integration might also be viewed as types of decentralization.[2]

COMBINATIONS OF CENTRALIZATION AND DECENTRALIZATION

Centralization can be regarded as **concentration** (of physical facilities or decision making); decentralization can be regarded as **dispersion** (of physical facilities or decision making). The typical organization exhibits characteristics of both. This can be observed from examining Figure 16-1, which depicts a matrix of combinations of these components, namely *plant, personnel, and equipment; and authority.*

---

[1]Joseph Rosenberg, "Heard on the Street," *The Wall Street Journal*, October 4, 1974, p. 23.

[2]Vertical and horizontal integration are discussed in connection with growth as a corporate objective in Chapter 3.

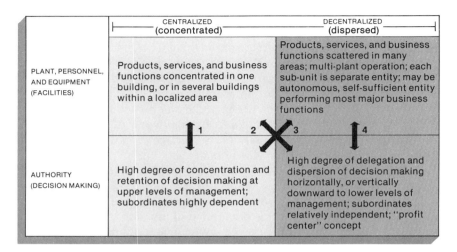

Figure 16-1. Centralization–decentralization matrix.

Four possible combinations are indicated by the four arrows. The mix of centralization and decentralization varies with each firm and with each industry.

1. **Centralized** plant, personnel, and equipment with **centralized** authority. Under these conditions, physical plant and its personnel are concentrated in a local geographic area. All products, services, and functions are handled in one or a limited number of buildings. Management retains tight control over its authority. It performs all management functions, makes decisions, gives orders. Very little delegation takes place. Authority is centralized. A situation involving this combination of the components might prevail in a closely held, perhaps individually or family owned, relatively small company with a modest offering of products or services.

2. **Centralized** plant, personnel, and equipment with **decentralized** authority. Under these circumstances, the firm has its physical facilities and personnel centered in one place. Products and services therefore are centralized. Within the central plant, however, management does delegate assignments along with substantial authority to subordinates. This means the right to make decisions is transferred in some degree horizontally from line to staff, or vertically downward from higher to lower echelons. In the latter situation, it constitutes a downward shift of authority that also includes the right to enforce decisions at that lower level. It places ultimate authority to decide and ultimate accountability for results as far down the line as effectiveness permits. A relatively small firm whose owners or managers have faith in the ability and competence of their subordinates and willingly assign

specific areas to them to take care of, simultaneously granting them the right to implement the assignments, typifies centralized plant, personnel, and equipment and decentralized authority.

3. **Decentralized** plant, personnel, and equipment with **centralized** authority. In this situation, the business has its physical facilities dispersed geographically. If it is a manufacturing plant, its factories and assembly plants are located in various parts of the country and perhaps throughout the world. Some of its products may be produced in one plant while other products may be produced and warehoused elsewhere. Most large chain store operations are decentralized in terms of scattered stores and personnel. Food chains like A & P, or variety stores like Woolworth's, are examples. Illustrative also are discount stores, department stores, franchised operations, and branch banking. The store manager may make limited decisions, perhaps in local hiring, firing, scheduling of work hours, vacations, and other areas of restricted scope. Yet major decisions involving brand policy, pricing, store layout, retirement programs, purchasing, inventory, credit and collection procedures, and so on are centralized at the home office of the parent organization. Thus authority to perform a limited number of management functions is delegated to the extent necessary to enable the decentralized plant to operate effectively. Major decisions, particularly those of broad character and company-wide significance, are made at the central facility or home office.

4. **Decentralized** plant, personnel, and equipment with **decentralized** authority. With this combination of the two components, the physical properties, products, services, and functions are wide-ranging. They are scattered into many geographic areas and, in some cases, internationally. Individual plants or divisions are created, each with its own functional areas—buying, sales, operating, facilitating, and managing. Each may possess its own line and staff structure. Management within each sub-unit has a great deal of decision-making authority. The divisions are relatively independent of the parent organization.

A rather recent decentralization technique is the **profit center** concept. A sub-unit performs the major activities involved in a product or product line. Its chief executive functions very much like the head of any small company but is held accountable by the parent company for the profit generated by his unit. Under these conditions, each sub-unit may be created as a relatively autonomous, self-sufficient profit center. It is fully responsible for results and possesses sufficient authority to fulfill that responsibility. General Motors, with its Chevrolet, Pontiac, Oldsmobile, and Cadillac divisions, is a classic example. Each automotive division is not only autonomous but competes with others for the consumer auto market. Authority is not completely decentralized, however, since corporate policy and executive committee decisions continue to be made at corporate headquarters.

Whether to follow a policy of centralization or decentralization depends very much upon the particular company, the type of business it is in, its overall strategy in the marketplace, its long-range plans, and its corporate objectives. It also depends on external environmental factors including general business conditions, governmental activities, union activities, shifts in consumer buying habits, international conditions, and many others. What is good for one company may not be good for another. A few years ago, Macmillan Company, the publishing house, centralized its warehousing activities by closing six warehouses scattered around the country and concentrating its inventory of 10 million books in one facility at an estimated savings of $200,000 a year. On the other hand, Firestone Tire & Rubber Company decentralized its warehousing, bringing its inventories closer to its customers. It opened nine new warehouses and estimated that it had saved $750,000 a year. Although taking opposite courses, both firms had similar goals: reducing the cost of getting merchandise from the factory to the consumer. If centralization worked for Macmillan, why was it not the answer for Firestone? A major factor is the widely different nature of their businesses. Many orders for books are small, for few books, and can easily and inexpensively be shipped by mail from almost any point. Firestone's orders are for more bulky items like tires and major appliances. With shipping costs an important consideration, it would be impractical for Firestone to attempt to serve its nationwide dealer network from a central warehouse.

There are advantages as well as disadvantages to both centralization and decentralization which should be recognized. Let us examine some of the more important of these.

ADVANTAGES OF CENTRALIZATION

Certain advantages are associated with centralization:

1. *Executives gain prestige and power.* Highly concentrated authority gives a manager in any functional area a great deal of power. He has a firm grip on the activities under his jurisdiction and is a "key man" in the structure. This may be essential during a crisis or when rapid decisions are necessary. Authority concentration also creates a climate that is consistent with the needs of executives who seek status, prestige, and power in an organization.

2. *Uniformity is fostered.* In a centralized organization it is easier to develop uniformity in practices, in policies that apply to all functional areas, and in the implementation of decisions. Management can run a "taut ship." Centralization is a superior means to achieve conformity and coordination.

3. *Full utilization of plant, personnel, and equipment is promoted.* Over the years the meatpacking industry has built slaughtering capacity high enough to handle seasonal demands in livestock marketing. Much of this capacity, concentrated in relatively few railroad terminal areas, was under-employed much of the year. In an attempt to make its overall operations more profitable, Armour & Company closed nine slaughterhouses, reducing facilities by 20 percent. As result, it operated its remaining plants at 90 percent of capacity, up from 65 percent before the consolidation. When machinery and equipment are more intensively utilized there is less need for overtime work. Full utilization of main office specialists is more likely to occur under conditions of centralization.

4. *Full utilization develops top-quality experts.* The scope and volume of work are sufficient to require intensive use of managers' specialized talents. Greater opportunities to use one's talents are conducive to developing expertise. Top managers given these opportunities can make better decisions than less experienced managers.

5. *Duplication of functions is reduced or eliminated.* One person handles a portfolio, or one group performs a complete function. Only one advertising manager is needed, or one public relations department to serve the other major activities. One sales organization sells all products rather than each product line maintaining its own sales force.

6. *Elaborate control systems and procedures are not required.* A centralized group of activities is simpler to control. Control techniques and procedures are less complex and less costly. Integration of the activities of sub-units is facilitated.

7. *A strong top management team develops because of the proximity of top executives.* Even if the centralized organization is a large one, the opportunities for managers to see and be seen by each other, to meet in the elevator or the company dining room, makes relationships less impersonal. Personal ties gradually develop and are reinforced. Strength and solidarity are fostered more readily.

8. *A "corporate personality" can more easily develop.* Centralized conditions tend to promote the development of a corporate image. Many of our large business enterprises still bear the names of their founders and many more bear their imprint. The attitudes of its top executives, reflected in their managerial philosophy, influence the organization's responses. These responses determine the corporate personality, which distinguishes the way the particular company does business. Centralization synthesizes corporate attitudes and value systems as they are reflected in its leaders, making possible the development of an identifiable and recognizable corporate image.

DISADVANTAGES OF CENTRALIZATION

There are also a number of disadvantages associated with the concept of centralization.

1. *There is danger of "putting all your eggs in one basket."* A company takes big risks when it depends on just one executive in each functional area. Should that person die, or leave the organization for any reason, the firm would suffer a great loss. With operations centralized in one plant or in one localized complex of buildings, a fire, explosion, or strike could cripple all activities, bringing operations to a standstill.

2. *It is necessary to develop standby personnel.* To reduce the dependency upon key executives in case of emergencies, and to develop greater depth in management for purposes of growth or expansion, it becomes necessary to hire and train replacements. This is a form of insurance which can be very costly. To carry excess personnel, particularly in the middle-level ranks, where salaries are higher than at lower levels, is an expensive luxury when plans to utilize these people are indefinite. Yet not to have them available if the situation requires them is equally or perhaps more expensive. Weighing the cost of keeping them against the potential cost of not having them when they are needed leads to the conclusion that some provision for standby personnel is essential in organizations that are highly centralized.

3. *Diversification or expansion is restricted.* The lack of management in depth, characteristic of centralized enterprises, makes diversification or growth difficult. If a company wants to open another facility, it does not have specialized line and staff executives available to man the expanded operation. The firm simply does not have the manpower to spare from existing activities to staff additional facilities. In addition, it could not consider opportunities to acquire other firms if the acquisition required the injection of fresh managerial talent, engineering know-how, or specialized expertise. Such additional manpower resources are not readily available within a highly centralized firm.

4. *There is decreased opportunity to delegate authority.* Under highly centralized conditions the opportunities to delegate decision making are greatly restricted. Even if the management's philosophy leaned toward participation in the decision-making process, persons to whom authority could be delegated are limited in number.

5. *Local needs are not clearly seen.* In situations where plant, personnel, and equipment are decentralized, while authority and major decision making are centralized, there is a built-in inability for managers at the home office to see clearly the needs that exist in localities where its decentralized

units operate. If buying is centralized for a chain of stores, merchandise that might sell in a particular locality is often overlooked. Requirements in one geographic area may be quite different from those in another. Working at a distance, centralized management cannot perceive as readily nor accommodate as quickly to local needs.

ADVANTAGES OF DECENTRALIZATION

There are some advantages that accrue from a policy of decentralizing. Some of these tend to offset the corresponding limitations of centralization.

1. *Risks are spread out.* The effect on the firm from a loss of personnel or physical plant is greatly minimized. The company is not dependent upon one plant or one person. Fire, bad weather, labor strife, loss of life, and other contingencies do not disrupt the entire operation. They do not cause as severe an impact on total company sales and earnings. The importance of this "hedge" is underscored by the experience of leading companies. Several years ago, the California facilities of three of the nation's leading breweries were shut down for a seven-week period because of strikes. Yet each of these companies recorded higher annual sales and earnings as the stepped-up performance in plants in other geographic areas more than took up the slack.

2. *Innovation is encouraged.* Plans, creative ideas, or new techniques can be tried on an experimental basis in one plant or in one market before widespread adoption. A new idea or a new piece of equipment can be tried in one facility or one department. If it fails, it does not affect in any substantial manner the remaining operations throughout the company. A particular facility or market can be used as a testing ground without impairing or disrupting the overall operations of an entire organization.

3. *Generalists can be developed more readily.* In firms operating many plants, stores, or offices scattered throughout the country, and in many cases throughout the world, management personnel with decision-making authority have opportunities to develop into general managers rather than remain narrow specialists. They acquire the necessary training and experience that enables them to succeed to corporate management positions. An alert, progressive firm makes a concerted effort to develop executive talent in anticipation of need. The president of such a company had this to say:

> The diverse nature of our business permits such a program to be carried out quite effectively. In baseball parlance, it might be said that, within our organization, we have a number of wholly-owned farm teams. We employ able management candidates in these units, develop them under our guidance and with

our methods, keep track of their progress. Then, when an opening occurs in the top management group, it is probable that a capable executive already exists with one of these "farm" units.[3]

4. *Expansion or diversification is easier to achieve.* As a company adds products to its line, it can set up separate organizational units to produce and distribute them. It has the personnel ready. If mergers or acquisitions are contemplated, the firm has a broader pool of managerial talent developed and available if needed.

5. *Delegation of authority is stressed.* Whenever decentralization of plant, personnel, and equipment occurs, a certain amount of decentralization of authority must take place also. Delegation of authority can be implemented more readily under decentralization. Top managers can willingly share part of their executive burdens with capable managerial subordinates, permitting decision making to occur at lower levels, and freeing themselves for more important matters.

6. *Full advantage can be taken of local conditions.* Decentralized units operating in a given locality are more sensitive to the needs and demands of that area. They are right on the spot, able to recognize and interpret local needs. They understand more keenly local consumer tastes and buying habits. In addition, they are in a position to utilize local resources. They have access to local suppliers, information on local labor markets, sources for raw materials or semi-finished and finished components. In short, they have their fingers on the local pulse and can make on-the-spot decisions. This is one of the reasons why Sears, Roebuck has established regional buying offices in Los Angeles, Dallas, Minneapolis, Atlanta, and Kansas City. It is interested in locating sources of supply within regions in which it sells. Thus it becomes both a buyer and a seller in given localities, particularly those with rapid growth. This points up a basic change that is taking place in manufacturing and merchandising in most lines of goods: the advent of regional buying coupled with patterns of regional distribution. This innovation is designed to shorten in-transit time and the number of times an item is handled physically from manufacturer to consumer, making possible cost-cutting along the way.

DISADVANTAGES OF DECENTRALIZATION

There are also a number of disadvantages connected with decentralization, some of which tend to be offset by the advantages of centralization.

---

[3]W. F. Rockwell, Jr. (President, Rockwell Manufacturing Company), "Rockwell Report," *Wall Street Journal*, 1963.

1. *Communication becomes more difficult.* As the various segments of an organization continue to proliferate, communication both laterally and vertically is impeded. Among managers working on products in detached, autonomous subdivisions, interplay of ideas is greatly reduced. A communication gap develops that separates the research labs, the marketing specialists, the quality control people. Lines of communication are lengthened. The time it takes for information to travel up and down through various organizational layers from corporate to operative levels is increased. Under such conditions, the advantages of rapid, timely communication are often lost.

2. *Costs may rise sharply.* Additional managerial personnel are needed as decentralization proceeds. The firm needs several plant managers instead of one, several sales managers, engineering heads, and other line and staff personnel. This adds rapidly to fixed costs and overhead. Moreover, additional capital requirements are placed on the firm to finance the building of new plants and facilities, the purchase of additional machinery and equipment, and the cost of re-staffing. Ampex, a major electronics corporation, estimated that its decentralization move added several million dollars to overhead in one year.[4]

3. *Duplication of services and facilities occurs.* Unless carefully controlled, additional plant and facilities tend to duplicate others already in existence. If the newer facilities are not fully utilized, or if the existing ones are utilized less as a result of the addition of newer ones, the entire operation becomes less effective and more costly. Under-utilization that results from duplication of services and plant can be a major drag on overall profitability. In an attempt to reduce its overhead and increase its profitability, Ampex began by eliminating duplicate division staffs. Central corporate offices were established to supervise accounting, legal work, industrial relations, marketing, research, and advanced development. Nearly 200 jobs were eliminated. A single advertising agency replaced five agencies serving one of its divisions. Four sales offices in Los Angeles were combined into one. The video and instrumentation divisions, whose products were similar, were combined. Each salesman began to represent the company's full product line instead of the products of just one division, thereby eliminating duplicate customer calls.[5] This firm had to swing back toward centralization to bring its operations into balance. When General Electric began to decentralize between 1951 and 1955, it split its operations into 113 departments, each with a large degree of autonomy. There was a tendency toward "excessive

---

[4]"Rx for Ampex," *The Wall Street Journal,* Vol. XLII, No. 234, September 1961, p. 1.
[5]*Ibid.*

fragmentation." For example, the company created three separate G.E. turbine departments—small, medium, and large. As a result, an electric utility company got to know G.E.'s small turbine experts, but when it needed a medium or large turbine it had to get acquainted with other G.E. personnel. With such fragmentation, carefully built customer contacts are wasted. Because of duplication and overlapping in services and facilities, G.E. has retreated from decentralization in many areas of its operations. For example, in its Aircraft Gas Turbine Division there were two departments concerned with jet engines. One handled engineering and development; the other produced engines. Each had its own marketing, finance, and engineering staffs. The division manager consolidated the two departments. Consequently, he was able to pare his staff of non-production people by more than 800, with annual savings of 5 to 6 million dollars. The consolidation also made it easier for customers, who now had one marketing manager and one engineering manager to deal with instead of two.[6]

4. *Less expert personnel may be employed.* Decentralization requires able managers who can accept authority and responsibility. Unless the company is already deep in managerial talent or potential, it finds itself reaching deeper into the barrel to come up with capable people to staff its decentralized operations. If a company believes it already has the "best" factory superintendent available in one of its operations, then it must seek someone less than best to staff its second unit. By the time it seeks a twentieth or thirtieth manager for a similar position, it may be reaching toward the bottom of the talent barrel.

5. *Personal ties with top management are difficult to form.* When managers are separated geographically from home office executives, it is much more difficult for close personal ties to develop. The old adage, "out of sight, out of mind," tends to operate. The familiarity and congeniality that develop from close proximity are less likely under decentralization than under centralization. As a result, the development of a strong, solid management image is greatly impeded. Whatever advantages accrue from working at corporate headquarters, from having an office in the headquarters building, from seeing and being seen by top management, are lost under decentralized conditions.

6. *A narrow or self-interest point of view may develop.* When each decentralized division tends to concentrate primarily on its own self-sufficiency and to work toward its own particular goals rather than those of the total organization, cooperation and coordination become difficult. One division may hoard its scarce talents and be reluctant to share them with other divi-

---

[6]*The Wall Street Journal,* March 22, 1961, p. 1.

sions in the company. This often happens in the area of research. Focusing on its individual aims, research may fail to see the needs of production or sales. Exploratory research, five to ten years and more away from concrete reality, has become a luxury that few companies can afford. At American Standard Corporation, central research has been reorganized to concentrate on discoveries that can be exploited quickly in the marketplace. Its vice-president stated, "What I tried to do when I came was to bring the technical people closer to our present products."[7]

When conditions dictate various types of cutbacks in an organization, it is difficult to get independent units to take the initiative unless the decision is imposed from above. Under decentralization, separate units tend to lose their willingness to understand and share corporate objectives. Their perspective narrows and their vision becomes more limited, colored by self-interest and limited objectives.

7. *More complex controls are required.* It is obvious that it takes more elaborate and extensive control to coordinate the activities of a sprawling organization than a tightly knit one. Thus more complex controls, a larger staff of control-oriented managers, and more expensive control devices are required. Rather complicated control systems must be developed if unity of direction is to prevail. It is generally more difficult to exert effective control in a decentralized structure than in a centralized one.

Today, with the advent of the computer, electronic data processing, and rapidly advancing technologies, there is a propensity in modern industry and commerce to *decentralize* plant, personnel, and equipment and some degree of line authority, but to *centralize* other types of authority, particularly those related to staff activities and managerial control activities. It is easier to decentralize line functions, especially the operating functions, and more difficult and less effective to decentralize staff or "corporate" level functions including finance, legal, basic research, and similar corporate staff activities. As a result, these functions and others including accounting, inventory, payroll, and billing tend to be centralized.

Even under decentralization, a certain amount of centralization is imperative to insure that the advantages of decentralization will be achieved. The goals of a business organization should emanate from the core or center. Decisions required to implement these goals should be shifted, to the fullest extent possible, to those in the periphery, who will also be held accountable for results. There would then exist centralization of objectives at the corporate level and decentralization of decision making at the implementing or operative levels. This is the way giants like J.C. Penney and General Motors operate.

---

[7]Dan Cordtz, "Bringing the Laboratory Down to Earth," *Fortune*, January 1971, p. 119.

At Penney's, the management philosophy embraces centralization of policy and decentralization of responsibility and implementation. However, decentralization works only when it is tied to *accountability*. There is an annual setting of goals by the president and those concerned with each profit segment. At these sessions, responsibilities for performance are accepted. A commitment is made before the whole group to strive for agreed-upon objectives. Every six months there is a checkup, a hard look taken at how close the company is coming to reaching its goals.

The heart of General Motors' decentralized management system is cost control, pricing, and budgets. GM operates under a philosophy developed in 1920 by its chief executive, Alfred P. Sloan, Jr., who called it "decentralization with coordinated control."[8] Each of General Motors' twenty-nine divisions is headed by a general manager who functions independently in running his operation. He has authority over how to market his products; whether to add products to his line; and where to buy his supplies including going outside the company's own supply divisions if he can get a superior item or a better price. Each division manager reports directly to a group vice-president. The group vice-presidents answer either to the president or to the vice-chairman of the board. All corporate-level decisions are made by GM's two top policy-making bodies: the finance committee and the executive committee. At General Motors, it is the finance committee that wields the most power.[9]

A system of accountability, from lower to higher management levels, remains a vital necessity if decentralization is to achieve the goals it sets for itself.

If the multiple activities of an organization require precise integration, it is advantageous to do this from a central point. Production control is an example. Activities which tend to be more independent, such as merchandising or marketing, and which extend over a broad geographic area, lend themselves to greater decentralization. As an organization relates to outside groups, it is often desirable to centralize the points of contact. Dealings with major suppliers, major customers, labor unions, and government agencies are examples of this concept. Decentralization lends itself best to decisions relating to internal rather than external operations.

SUMMARY

A great deal of misunderstanding exists concerning the meaning of centralization and decentralization. Decentralization is not synonymous with authority delegation, nor does centralization mean a failure to delegate

---

[8]Alfred P. Sloan Jr., *My Years With General Motors*, MacFadden-Bartell Corporation, 1965, p. 119.

[9]"The Ten Best Managed Businesses," *Dun's*, Vol. 96, No. 6, December 1970, pp. 31–32.

authority. The concept of centralization and decentralization refers not only to authority, but also to resources including physical plant, personnel, and equipment. Both components, **authority** and **resources,** must be considered.

Various combinations of centralization and decentralization of authority and resources are possible. At some point in their development, organizations may have centralized authority and centralized facilities; centralized authority and decentralized facilities; decentralized authority and centralized facilities; or decentralized authority and decentralized facilities. The latter situation is often represented by the profit center concept in which a separate sub-unit is relatively autonomous and self-sufficient but is accountable to the parent company for profit generation.

There are advantages and disadvantages to centralization. There are also advantages and disadvantages to decentralization. Whether or not an organization decentralizes depends on its own normal growth patterns, which may or may not lead to geographic dispersion of physical facilities; the nature of the product or the service; the influence of external factors; the long-range aims of the organization; scale or size and complexity of operations; changing technologies including information systems; and many other variables. The interrelationship of these variables and their influence on a given situation (contingencies) determine the degree of centralization or decentralization required.

Centralization may be appropriate for some organizations and inappropriate for others. In general, the introduction of electronic data processing equipment and other advances have led to a reversal, or at least a slowing down, of the trend toward decentralization. There is a tendency today, even where physical facilities are dispersed, to centralize many of the staff activities and controlling activities within the parent organization. Corporate policy formulation, finance, accounting, basic research and development, data gathering and storage, legal services, industrial relations, market research, and advertising are examples of activities that tend to be centralized. Line activities tend to be decentralized, whereas staff activities tend to be concentrated.

KEY CONCEPTS

Centralization	Dispersion
Decentralization	Profit Center
Concentration	

GLOSSARY

centralization   Concentration of resources (plant, personnel, and equipment) or decision-making authority.

decentralization   Dispersion of resources (plant, personnel, and equipment) or decision-making authority.

1. Explain how the nature of a product has a bearing on the decision to decentralize. Give examples.
2. What are some of the factors that contribute to a decision to decentralize? To centralize?
3. What two components must be taken into account in any discussion of centralization or decentralization?
4. Distinguish between delegation and decentralization.
5. What are the advantages of centralization? The disadvantages?
6. What are the advantages of decentralization? The disadvantages?
7. What activities do you believe lend themselves to decentralization? Give examples.
8. What activities are probably more effectively handled if centralized? Give examples.

Part IV

Activating

The best-conceived plan and the finest organization are of little value until someone with the authority to do so presses the starter that sparks them into action.

It is part of the role of an executive to make certain that ideas that have been *spelled out* are also *carried out* by employees at all organizational levels. Activating is thus a function of managing. It implies making a plan operational, getting people to understand what is expected of them, and encouraging and supervising them in the pursuit of organizational objectives. It is one of the most important facets of the role of a manager.

Activating may be defined as *that cluster of activities in the managing process which, through the exercise of leadership and the proper use of incentives, causes the organization to carry out its planned activities.* As its name implies, it too is a dynamic process—as we shall observe.

Causing the organization to carry out its plans stresses the implementing and actuating functions, which are essential ingredients in the activating process. Managers are responsible for setting activities in motion and keeping them moving in the right direction. This means working with and guiding people who have been assigned important roles designed to attain pre-established objectives. To work with personnel in all functional areas, at all organizational levels, requires of a manager an understanding of what motivates people and a profound respect for the kinds of personal needs that people must satisfy. In addition, causing an organization to respond calls for leadership *and* the proper use of incentives to motivate individuals to perform to the best of their capabilities. In today's modern organizational setting, one without the other will not achieve optimum results.

To lead and to motivate, managers must communicate effectively with subordinates so that the latter understand what is expected and have some basis for knowing how well they are succeeding in carrying out their assigned roles.

The major components of the activating process are the subjects of Chapters 17 through 21. An analysis of motivation, including a summary of generally accepted motivation theories, is presented in Chapter 17. The role of leadership, theories of leadership, and managerial styles are explored in Chapter 18. First-line management, direction, the role of the supervisor, and patterns of supervision become the subject of Chapter 19. Various types of incentives are introduced and evaluated in detail in Chapter 20. Chapter 21 deals with the process of effective communication as an essential function linking all organizational activities.

These five chapters, comprising Part IV, collectively provide the basis for comprehending the third major cluster of activities in the managing process, which we are designating as **Activating.**

Chapter 17

Motivation

As a prelude to analyzing and discussing various managerial actions that constitute the process of activating, it is advisable that we turn our attention to the subject of motivation. To appreciate fully the roles of leadership and incentives, for example, it is necessary to recognize that both require an understanding of human motivation.

To understand the performance of individuals in a work setting and to attempt to solve people problems that arise one must recognize the complexities of human motivation and the dynamic interactions that occur when people enter and pursue a career in an organization. The relationship between the individual and the organization develops through mutual influence, confidence, and bargaining to establish a workable psychological contract.[1] Schein suggests that concepts must be developed to deal with the process by which the psychological contract is initially *negotiated*, and the process by which it is *re-negotiated* during an employee's career with the organization.[2] The dynamics become apparent when one examines individual motivations *and* organizational climate and practices.

THEORIES OF MOTIVATION

It is a fundamental assumption that man is a goal-seeking creature who strives to satisfy a great many needs in order to fulfill himself. If careful investigation can determine what these goals are and why man seeks to achieve them, managers will be better equipped to understand themselves and their fellow workers. They can then plan ways that enable employees to fulfill personal needs and reach personal goals. At the same time, enterprises will also benefit. Personal aspirations of workers and corporate goals of organizations can be dealt with in ways that make them mutually reinforcing. Individuals could then derive personal satisfactions by pursuing the purposes for which the organization exists.

---

[1]The reader is referred to Chapter 10, where the psychological contract as it relates to authority is discussed.

[2]Edgar H. Schein, "Occupational Socialization in the Professions: The Case of Role Innovation," *Technology Review*, October–November 1970, pp. 32–38.

Motives are *inner drives or urges based on unfulfilled desires or fears consciously or subconsciously possessed by all individuals.* People act the way they do partly because certain drives compel them. One may want social acclaim, another companionship; one may fear unemployment and its consequences, while another desires an opportunity to express himself. Motives are hidden cravings, whether for simple things like food or for complex ones like power.

There are many ways to classify such needs. A simple breakdown is to divide them into two basic categories: (1) physiological or bodily needs, and (2) psychological and social needs.

Physiological needs are those necessary to maintain life; are universal among all people everywhere. They include the need for air, food, water, bodily elimination, sleep, warmth, and sex. Physiological needs differ in intensity, are relatively independent of one another, and must be satisfied repeatedly at relatively short intervals.

Psychological and **social** needs are mental and emotional in nature, and tend to develop as one matures. Examples are the need for recognition, belonging, self-respect, confidence, affection, and self-development. They are nebulous and hence more difficult to pinpoint and recognize than physiological needs. Nevertheless, any actions that a manager takes will affect the psychological and social need fulfillment of his subordinates. He must, therefore, give careful consideration in advance to the effect any decisions he makes will have on them.

Knowing that physical and psychological needs exist in no way indicates which are important at any given time, nor whether some are more important than others to most individuals. Which unfulfilled needs can be used most effectively to motivate employees to strive for corporate objectives? Psychologists and sociologists recognize that personal needs do have a certain general priority. Bodily needs must be met and thus claim first priority. As they are satisfied and diminish in relative importance or intensity, other needs demand attention and satisfaction. Much research has been conducted on this subject.

Maslow's Hierarchy of Needs

A general theory, structuring needs into a hierarchy, was advanced by Abraham Maslow and has gained wide acceptance.[3] Maslow based his findings on the following important propositions concerning human motivation.

1. Man is a want-satisfying creature. He has continuing wants. What he wants at any given time depends to a large extent on what he already has or upon what he expects to receive. When some wants are gratified, others spring up to receive attention. It is a never-ending process.

---

[3]Abraham H. Maslow, "A Theory of Human Motivation," *Psychological Review*, Vol. 50, 1943, pp. 370–396.

2. Satisfied needs do not motivate. Once a need has been satisfied, it no longer acts as a motivating factor. Only unsatisfied needs motivate. A hungry man may take any kind of work to earn enough to satisfy his immediate hunger. Once that hunger has been satisfied, he may become more selective and will not continue to take any kind of work. The significance of this principle is profound, and managers must not fail to understand that even partially satisfied needs diminish in their ability to motivate.

3. There is an ordering of needs. Man's needs organize themselves into a hierarchical structure according to their "prepotency." The appearance of a need usually rests on the prior satisfaction of another, more prepotent, need. Needs do not exist as miscellaneous wants that are satisfied in random fashion. Instead, they are well organized into related groups, each group having a different level of importance.

Maslow arrived at a need priority structure consisting of five levels: (1) physiological, (2) safety, (3) love, (4) esteem, and (5) self-actualization. A modified model of this hierarchy of needs appears in Figure 17-1.

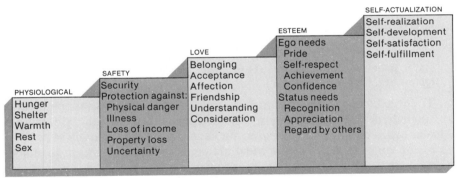

Figure 17-1. Hierarchy of human needs.

Physiological needs. At the lowest level of the structure are the physiological needs. They are basic and necessary to sustain life. We have identified them as "bodily needs" necessary for survival. When all needs in the hierarchy are unsatisfied, the physiological needs will dominate, indicating that the lower order of needs must be taken care of first. In our affluent society, we tend to overlook these needs since most people can satisfy them without too much difficulty. They tend to be taken for granted and would, therefore, be unusual rather than typical motivators of people. Man lives by bread alone only when there is little bread to be had. From a manager's point of view, the more important needs are those higher in the hierarchy. There are exceptions, of course. When very tired, an executive may yearn only for an opportunity to rest.

Safety needs.   With physiological needs reasonably met, those at the next higher level begin to influence man's behavior. Safety needs are often referred to as "security needs." They include protection from physical and bodily danger or injury; safeguards against illness; prevention of economic disaster; avoidance of the unexpected; and preference for the conventional forms of behavior. Included in this concept of safety and security is man's desire for assurance that his ability to satisfy his physiological needs will continue, that he will be able to provide the basic necessities not only today but also tomorrow. In the business environment, job security is a fundamental need of workers. For many, it is more important than rate of pay or opportunities for advancement.

With organizational relationships changing so rapidly, there is need for reassurance. Without it, organizational control becomes much more difficult. Toffler describes a shifting organizational situation:

> Today the average individual is frequently reassigned, shuffled about from one sub-structure to another. But even if he remains in the same department, he often finds that the department, itself, has been shifted on some fast-changing table of organization, so that his position in the overall maze is no longer the same.
>
> The result is that man's organizational relationships tend to change at a faster pace than ever before. The average relationship is less personal, more temporary, than ever before.[4]

To introduce stability into fast-changing structure is to reduce feelings of insecurity on the part of worker and manager alike. As John Mee puts it, "Almost every manager is engaged in a career race between his retirement and his obsolescence in his job. Most managers will be fortunate to enjoy a photo finish."[5] When sweeping reorganization occurs, as often happens after a merger between two firms, many departments are eliminated. Excess executive "fat" is trimmed. People are let go. Histories of conglomerates reveal that management personnel of acquired companies remain with the new setup an average of two years. It takes about a year for executives on both sides to recognize that an undefinable incompatibility exists, and about another year to conclude that the relationship must be severed. One is never sure that his own job is secure, that it will not be the next to be eliminated. Should the department itself continue, a succession of department heads replacing each other after short tenure generates a feeling of instability throughout the entire organization. Morale is lowered and labor turnover

---

[4]Alvin Toffler, *Future Shock,* (New York: Random House, 1970), p. 119.

[5]John F. Mee, *Management Thought in a Dynamic Economy* (New York: New York University Press, 1963), p. 76.

accelerates. It is imperative that conditions be stabilized, perhaps through re-assignments, so that employees and managers are reassured. Otherwise, effective managerial control is unlikely.

The fear of changing technology, as a threat to job security, influences a worker's behavior. He may join a union because it holds out promise for job security and offers seniority as one instrument to accomplish it. Most fringe benefits, such as workmen's compensation, are desired because they instill a greater sense of security than do pay raises, profit sharing plans, and other forms of inducement.

Workers expect paid holidays and vacations and health and accident insurance. They would like to have disability insurance and life insurance provided also. In recent years, there has been increasing emphasis on retirement benefits. Many forward-looking firms are developing retirement programs that include not only monetary provisions but also assistance in preparing employees psychologically for retirement. The steel industry has been a leader in developing "pre-retirement planning" programs.

In two of the pioneering steel companies, initial interest in pre-retirement is generated by letters sent to employees as they reach age 55. Jones and Laughlin Corporation holds sessions every year under the guidance of a staff doctor and personnel specialists. The need to plan for the future is emphasized, and questions such as where to live, health practices and preventive medicine, the biology of aging, management of finances, and other pertinent subjects are discussed. At Inland Steel, the program evolves in five chronological stages: when a person is 55, 60, 64, 60 days from retirement, and past 65. When interviewed about the program, an employee said, "Well, I know what this did for me. It encouraged me to make plans, to be ready for the later years, to stand on my own feet."[6]

Financial pressures restrict a retiree's plans to take an active part in community life. A conflict arises between his inability to pay his own way and his desire for stature, something he possessed while he worked. Born of a philosophy associated with the depths of the Great Depression, mandatory retirement at age 65 and younger may now be an obsolete concept that results in a great disservice to capable individuals and a great loss to society. It should be re-examined and reappraised. Perhaps the "step down at 60" succession policy for top management that exists at firms like Westinghouse is too costly in the long run. In Japan, for example, more than half of those over 65 continue to work. A tradition of this sort breeds respect for age and prevents discrimination against older workers in general.

It is a costly waste of an enormous resource to withdraw those over age 65 from the market by mandate, if they are physically and mentally sound and willing to continue working. The option should rest, in part at least, with

---

[6]Merrick Jackson, "Plans that Improve with Age," *Steelways*, November 1963, p. 21.

the potential retiree. When a retirement date is *established jointly*, then the pre-retirement program should be instituted. Such a program, mutually developed, strengthens individual self-reliance and assures more bountiful years ahead. The company benefits, the employees benefit, and society benefits.

Closely related to fringe benefits are good physical working conditions. Efforts should be made to minimize—and wherever possible, eliminate altogether—hazards or injuries to physical and mental health. Adequate protective and safety devices should be installed on machinery and power tools. Safety clothing, safety shoes, goggles, and helmets should be furnished where needed. Offices and plants should be well lighted, well ventilated, and air conditioned if practical. Workers expect and managers should provide first aid facilities; good lunchrooms with wholesome, well-prepared food at reasonable prices; lockers; and clean restrooms and washing facilities. These are very important to employees. Despite this fact, they are less than adequate in most of our factories and commercial establishments.

The importance of good working conditions is expressed by an auto assembly line worker at the most modern plant of its kind in the world.

> When it is 95 outside, it is 120 or so in the paint shop . . . you have no ventilation really at all. And of the noise level in the body shop which was cited a year and a half ago as higher than acceptable standards, I know I put cotton in my ears, because I cannot take it too much longer.
>
> In the 1930s our fathers or forefathers revolted. They wanted the rights for a union. In 1970, we revolted and all we want to do is improve on things. That is all we want. Why should we be criticized for something like that? All we want is improvement in working conditions . . . .[7]

The Federal Occupational Safety and Health Act, which became effective April 28, 1971, establishes new and far-reaching regulations for working environments and safety practices in all industries. So important is employee safety and health, and compliance with the law, that companies are creating top-level management positions to deal with these matters in all areas of operations. At GF Business Equipment, Inc., for example, there is now a director of corporate safety and ecology.

From a manager's point of view, providing too many fringe benefits may make employees overly dependent on the sources of this security, encourage complacency and subservience, and tend to make workers less productive as they opt for security rather than some higher level of aspiration.

Love needs (social needs).   When physiological and safety needs have been relatively well satisfied, the next higher order—social needs—becomes important. A person's desire for belonging, acceptance, love, attention, affec-

---

[7] Dan Clark, member UAW Local 1112, Lordstown, Ohio, testifying before the Senate Subcommittee on Employment, Manpower, and Poverty, July 25, 1972.

tion, and friendship must be gratified. He wants *to give as well as receive* these. Deprived of this opportunity, he will want them as intensely as a hungry person wants food. The relatively high standard of living enjoyed by members of our industrialized society encourages this emphasis on social factors. Under subsistence conditions, employees would have less inclination to concern themselves about satisfying social needs on the job.

By nature, man is a social animal. His social longings do not cease when he is on the job. For employees whose home life is unsatisfactory, associating with fellow employees on the job gratifies a portion of their total social needs. Identifying with a group and enjoying a feeling of belonging influence worker attitudes as well. Studies provide some evidence that workers who belong to small, closely knit work groups have higher morale than those who work alone or are part of a huge group with whom they cannot identify or relate personally. Not only does a worker desire to feel wanted by his co-workers, to help them and be helped by them, but he also seeks acceptance from his superior. He wants some degree of attention from his foreman or supervisor, including understanding and consideration.

When managers misunderstand the necessity for employees to gratify their social needs and attempt to discourage informal groups, they will often find themselves facing hostile, antagonistic, and uncooperative subordinates. Moreover, the inability of workers to satisfy needs at this level may contribute toward emotional and mental health problems, which are costly to the well-being of any organization.

Esteem needs. Esteem or ego needs are next in order of ascendancy. Today, workers are demanding something beyond economic satisfactions; they want greater status, greater recognition from the community. They are turning away from material things and demanding "ego things"—self-esteem *and* the regard of others. **Self-esteem** needs include personal achievement, self-respect, high regard for one's personal ability, a feeling of importance, and pride in one's work. **Esteem from others** includes the need to know that others think us worthy, believe we are important, and consider our contributions important. These are **status** needs. The janitor, file clerk, and administrative assistant all need to be reassured by others that they are important and that their work is important to the whole.

Referring to workers in an automobile assembly plant, its local union president says:

> Assembly workers are the lowest on the totem pole when it comes to job fulfill-ment. They don't think they have any skill. Some corporate guy said, 'A monkey could do the job.' They have no enthusiasm about pride in workmanship. They could care less if the screw goes in the wrong place. Sometimes it helps break the monotony if the screw strips.[8]

---

[8]Gary Bryner, president of Lordstown Local 1112, UAW, as quoted in Studs Terkel, *Working* (New York: Pantheon Books, 1974), p. 192.

Being able to satisfy self-esteem and status needs leads to feelings of self-confidence and prestige. Unlike the lower order of needs, esteem needs are seldom fully satisfied. A person can never have a feeling of too much esteem. It is almost an insatiable need, which strongly motivates people.

Self-actualization needs.   At the apex of Maslow's need hierarchy is self-actualization,[9] also called self-realization or self-fulfillment. "What a man can be, he must be."[10] This means a strong desire to make the most of one's capabilities, to realize fully the potential with which one is endowed. For a doctor, it would mean not only serving as a physician but becoming the most competent physician he is capable of being; for a mother, to be the best mother she possibly can be; for a sales manager, to be the best within the limits of his ability; to a top-flight athlete, to be a "star." It is extremely doubtful, however, that most people aspire to this top level of need fulfillment. Most doctors would be satisfied and take pride in being good doctors without aspiring to the upper limits of their potential. The same can be said for athletes and business managers. Self-actualization is a plateau that motivates the few rather than the many.

Man's lower-order needs are satisfied primarily through economic behavior. Physiological and safety needs are satisfied largely through pay, fringe benefits, and seniority. Higher-order needs are satisfied through psychological and social behavior. As long as lower-order needs remain unsatisfied, it will be difficult to motivate employees by appealing to higher-order needs. However, when lower-order needs are reasonably well taken care of, managers will have to emphasize those of a higher order if workers are to be motivated to further action.

It must be recognized that there is a great deal of overlap in this concept of hierarchy of needs and a great deal of interdependence among various levels. There is no clear-cut demarcation between one level and the next. Grey areas exist. An individual's needs tend to be partially satisfied in all areas. Safety needs do not disappear when social needs and some esteem needs emerge. They simply become less acute than they were. Nor do needs have to be gratified 100 percent before higher needs begin to emerge. The need hierarchy concept has general rather than specific application. It represents needs of people as a group rather than as individuals.

It would be very difficult, if not impossible, to determine that for a specific person the desire for acceptance was at his social need level and not at his "ego" need level. Moreover, an older person has different motivation than a younger person. For a young employee with a growing family, money as a means to satisfy physical and security needs is a strong incen-

---

[9]The term "self-actualization" was introduced in 1939 by Kurt Goldstein in *The Organism* (New York: American Book Company).

[10]Abraham Maslow, *Op. cit.*, p. 382.

tive. For an older employee, whose children have grown up and whose security needs are less intense, doing a good job and being recognized for his contribution are usually much stronger motivations.

Herzberg's Motivation-Hygiene Theory

A somewhat different view of human motivation has been offered by Frederick Herzberg. Herzberg's original research was based on interviews with 200 engineers and accountants.[11] Each was asked to think of a time when he felt especially good and a time when he felt especially bad about his job, and to describe the conditions that led to those feelings. It was discovered that different kinds of conditions caused good and bad feelings. Thus, if recognition led to a good feeling, the lack of recognition was seldom given as the cause of a bad feeling. Based on the study, Herzberg reached the following conclusions:

1. There are some job conditions which, when absent, operate primarily to dissatisfy employees; yet their presence does not motivate employees very strongly. Herzberg called these **maintenance factors,** since they are necessary to maintain a reasonable level of satisfaction. He pointed out that though many of these factors traditionally have been perceived by managers as motivators, actually they are much more powerful as "dissatisfiers" when they are absent. All **dissatisfiers** describe in some way the *environment or context of the job.* They help avoid psychological and physical discomfort at work. They are preventive factors that support and maintain mental health. Hence Herzberg also refers to them as **hygiene factors.** According to him, there are eleven hygiene or maintenance factors present in the job situation: (a) salary; (b) possibility of growth; (c) interpersonal relationships with supervisors; (d) interpersonal relationships with subordinates; (e) status; (f) interpersonal relationships with peers; (g) technical supervision; (h) company policy and administrative practices; (i) personal life; (j) working conditions; and (k) job security.

2. There are other job conditions which, when present, help build higher levels of motivation and job satisfaction. However, if they are absent, they do not cause the worker much dissatisfaction. Herzberg describes these as "motivational factors" or **satisfiers.** If managers have wondered why improved working conditions and increased fringe benefits do not increase employee motivation, the answer is that these are primarily maintenance factors that prevent job dissatisfaction when present, but which do not motivate. Motivators are the factors that meet man's need for psychological maturation. Rather than describing the job context or environment, satis-

---

[11]Frederick Herzberg, Bernard Mausner, and Barbara Snyderman, *The Motivation to Work* (New York: John Wiley and Sons, 1959).

fiers describe the *job content.* They relate to the individual's performance on the job, and the intrinsic satisfactions he derives both from his performance and from the recognition he obtains from others when he performs well. Unlike the hygiene factors, which are related to the environment in which the work is performed, *motivational factors are centered within the job itself.* The original Herzberg study listed five motivational factors or satisfiers: (a) achievement; (b) recognition; (c) the work itself; (d) responsibility; and (e) advancement. Herzberg later pointed out that recognition without achievement is simply a human relations "Attaboy."[12]

Herzberg's work has generated a great deal of criticism as well as interest. One of the criticisms has been that the conclusions were drawn from a limited study confined to a small group of professional workers. The prime commitment of professional workers may be to their profession rather than to the company for which they work. As professionals, therefore, they may have been more highly motivated. Non-professionals may be less motivated under the same conditions.

Another criticism is that the difference between reported sources of satisfaction and dissatisfaction could conceivably be an expression of the respondents' defense mechanisms. When things are going well a person is likely to give himself credit for the achievement. But when a person is dissatisfied he is likely to blame the company or his boss rather than his own inadequacies. Generally, when some misfortune happens to *us,* we tend to attribute the cause to some factor in the environment, to something produced by the organization and outside of our control; but when the same misfortune happens to *someone else,* we tend to attribute the cause to something inherent in *his* makeup or personality, to some lack or failure on his part. In his later writings, Herzberg recognized the validity of this criticism. In acknowledging that it is not possible to motivate anyone to perform well who does not have the ability to do so, Herzberg says,

> Often, employees will use motivation as a smokescreen behind which to hide their lack of know-how. It is easier and more generous to one's ego to suggest that the company is not providing sufficient reasons to work hard than to admit to a personal deficiency in ability.[13]

Furthermore, the demarcation between motivational factors and hygiene factors is not clear-cut. One factor can cause job satisfaction for one person and job dissatisfaction for another. Limited testing of less than well paid blue-collar workers indicates that pay and job security, considered maintenance factors by Herzberg, are considered motivators by the

---

[12]Frederick Herzberg, "Avoiding Pain in Organizations," *Industry Week,* December 7, 1970, p. 47.

[13]Frederick Herzberg, "Management of Motivators," *Industry Week,* February 15, 1971, p. 53.

blue-collar workers. This is probably true of clerical workers and $2.30 per hour salesclerks.

As incomes rise for all in the future, unions striving to obtain white-collar members will have to stress the motivators that satisfy social and psychological needs. Simply promising more pay, better fringe benefits, security, and the like will not attract these workers.

There is some similarity between the Maslow model and the Herzberg model, as shown by the comparison in Figure 17-2. Maslow focuses on the *totality* of human needs. Herzberg deals with persons in the *job situation only.* His findings seem to indicate that when workers have reached an ac-ceptable level of socio-economic progress, as in the case of managers, pro-fessional workers, and perhaps some white-collar workers, higher orders of needs become the more important motivating ones. It is quite probable that Maslow's three lower levels of needs have been reasonably achieved by

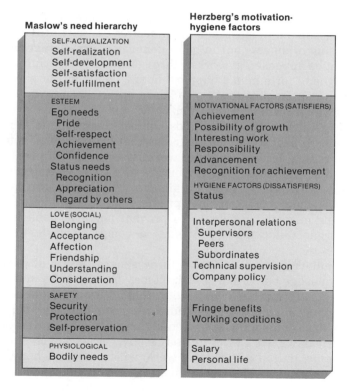

Figure 17-2. A comparison of Maslow's need hierarchy and Herzberg's motivation–hygiene factors.

these persons. In the job context, for these people satisfaction of lower-order needs is equivalent to hygiene or maintenance factors; they do not motivate but their absence would cause dissatisfactions.

As may be true of unskilled or semi-skilled workers, those who have not achieved sufficient social and economic progress will not fit too well into the motivation–hygiene model. For them, Maslow's lower orders of need satisfactions may act as motivators. Additional money may motivate a non-management employee who is at a minimum wage level, whereas achievement and possibility of growth with the company are more effective in motivating managers and professionals.

Herzberg's motivational factors seem to parallel Maslow's esteem needs. It is extremely doubtful, however, that any counterpart to Maslow's highest level, self-actualization, exists in the Herzberg model. For most workers, excluding professionals and those with a high degree of technical competence or those working at or near the top level in the managerial hierarchy, self-actualization, if it is attainable at all, cannot be accomplished on the job during working hours. Furthermore, it may be expecting too much to assume that most individual desires can be fulfilled at work. In fact advertising often sets out to build **consumer dissatisfactions,** many of which cannot be appeased at work or through work. Portraying a product or service designed "for a man's happiest hours," such as stereo components or a vacation trip, implies that these hours occur when he is not working, when he is away from the job situation.

Herzberg's two-factor model adds another dimension to the hierarchy of needs concept because it demonstrates that motivational factors during working hours are derived from the work itself. Potential progress in this area lies in intrinsic motivation of workers who have advanced beyond the economic subsistence level. What is gained by treating employees well, if according to the theory this does not produce job satisfaction or motivated behavior? The answer is obvious. To prevent negative behavior that can cause the organization many problems, a company must maintain good hygiene.

Most employees work at one of three general **levels of performance.** The first is *average performance,* which may be below the individual's capabilities but is acceptable to management. At this level, both parties enter into a psychological contract to provide an agreed amount of service for an agreed compensation under agreed conditions. This is the well-known concept of "a fair day's work for a fair day's pay." A second level is *poor performance,* below that of a fair day's work, which occurs when the hygiene factors are inadequate. The worker feels he is not being paid a wage commensurate with his abilities and reduces his performance to a level he thinks is sufficient in terms of his own standard of justice or fairness. Improving the hygiene factors does not lead to good performance, but may raise performance to the level of average performance or at least insure that it will not become poorer than it already is. The third level is *good performance*, which can only be achieved by providing opportunities to experience the motivators and not by increasing the amount or degree of maintenance factors.

Herzberg points out that all hygiene needs are very short-term. If a man receives a salary increase, he will be pleased with the increase but will become unhappy with his new salary after a surprisingly short time. Herzberg makes two additional observations: (1) that all hygiene falls back to zero (no matter how many salary increases a man has received in the past, when he wants a salary increase—he wants a salary increase); and (2) that "all hygiene has an escalating zero point."[14] (This means that if a man received a $4,000 salary increase one year and the next time is offered a $2,000 increase, psychologically he would feel that he was being asked to take a $2,000 cut. The new zero point is $4,000.)

Motivating people is seldom easy. It must be viewed as a three-faceted phenomenon. First, the subordinate must want something. He must *desire* it strongly enough to do something about it. Second, he must have a means of getting it. The individual must see the *path* or road that will carry him to achievement. Third, a person must *believe* that his efforts, if successful, will be rewarded. Many people have aspirations and see ways of achieving them but lack the faith that their efforts will be rewarded fairly.

The three-dimensional position is supported by two relatively recent motivation theories that have been advanced, namely, *path–goal* motivation theory and *instrumentality–expectancy* theory. Let us examine each of these.

Path–Goal Motivation Theory

A link between satisfaction, motivation, and the organizational goal of productivity was suggested by Brayfield and Crockett, who stated:

> It makes sense to us to assume that individuals are motivated to achieve certain environmental goals and that the achievement of these goals results in satisfaction. Productivity is seldom a goal in itself but is more commonly a means to goal attainment. Therefore . . . we might expect high satisfaction and high productivity to occur together when productivity is perceived as a path to certain important goals and when these goals are achieved.[15]

Georgopoulas and his associates provide empirical support for this concept in their test of the "path–goal hypothesis."[16] They suggest that an individual's motivation to produce at a given level depends on his needs as

---

[14]Frederick Herzberg, "Avoiding Pain in Organizations," *Op. cit.*, p. 48.

[15]A. H. Brayfield and W. H. Crockett, "Employee Attitudes and Employee Performance," *Psychological Bulletin*, Vol. 52, 1955, p. 416.

[16]B. S. Georgopoulas, G. M. Mahoney, and N. W. Jones, "A Path–Goal Approach to Productivity," *Journal of Applied Psychology*, Vol. 41, 1951, pp. 345–353.

reflected in the goals toward which he is moving *and* his perception of the usefulness of productive behavior as a path to the attainment of those goals. They found that workers who expect productivity to result in long-run financial benefit are more inclined to be high producers than those who believe that productivity is unrelated to, or inhibits, the attainment of monetary reward. They also found that workers who expect increased productivity to lead to greater acceptance by co-workers are more likely to be high producers than those who believe productivity to be unrelated to, or an inhibiting factor in, gaining co-worker acceptance. Some workers ranked opportunities for economic gain high in importance; others viewed social consequences as being more important.

The core concept of path–goal theory is the degree to which an individual *perceives* that a given path will lead to a particular goal.

Instrumentality–Expectancy Theory

The instrumentality–expectancy theory states that motivation results from an assessment by an individual of the following: (1) the anticipated **value** of the perceived outcome of his behavior, and (2) the strength of his **expectancy** that his behavior will actually result in the realization of the outcome.

Vroom has developed a model which suggests that a motivational force equals the value of the perceived outcome *multiplied* by the strength of the expectancy that the outcome will materialize.[17] This can be stated as a simple equation:

Motivational Force = Value of Perceived Outcome × Expectancy That
Outcome Will Materialize.[18]

Vroom introduces two concepts to explain how outcomes are determined. These are **valence** and **instrumentality.** Valence refers to the strength of an individual's desire for a particular outcome. Instrumentality indicates an individual's perception of the probability of first-level outcomes (organizational goals) leading to the achievement of second-level outcomes (worker goals). If a person desires promotion and feels that superior performance will lead to that end, his first-level outcome is performance and his second-level outcome is promotion. We would expect motivation toward superior performance because promotion is important and superior performance is perceived as instrumental in its accomplishment.

An additional concept in Vroom's theory is **expectancy.** This is the belief, expressed as a subjective probability, that a given act will result in a particular first-level outcome. Expectancy differs from instrumentality in that it relates personal efforts to first-level outcomes, whereas instrumentality relates first-level and second-level outcomes to each other.

---

[17] Victor H. Vroom, *Work and Motivation* (New York: John Wiley and Sons, 1964).

[18] This model is an application of the Bayes decision process described in Chapter 5.

This motivational model, unlike the Maslow and Herzberg models, stresses *individual differences* in motivation and explains how goals influence individual effort. Motivation will not improve performance if ability is low or perceptions of expectations are inaccurate.

Vroom investigated graduate students' preferences in selecting the organizations in which to begin their managerial careers. He found a relationship between organizational attractiveness and the extent to which it was perceived to be instrumental in individual goal attainment.[19] A more recent study tested expectancy theory concepts on business school students to measure occupational preferences as distinguished from occupational choice and occupational attainment.[20] It found valence and instrumentality concepts useful in understanding occupational preference. However, it was not able to demonstrate a precise relationship between occupational preference and valence and instrumentality. Because of this, Wanous concludes "one cannot say whether valence and instrumentality perceptions caused occupational preference (as implied by expectancy theory), whether occupational preference (due to other factors) caused perceptions of valence and instrumentality, or whether both caused each other."[21]

Achievement Motivation Theory

There are theories of motivational behavior that focus on achievement needs and place greater emphasis on individual and group behavior than on organizational situations. Achievement needs, you will recall, are at the higher level of need satisfaction and are included among the esteem and self-actualization needs in Maslow's need hierarchy. Achievement is also included among the motivators in Herzberg's motivation–hygiene theory.

One of the leading proponents of achievement need approaches to motivation is David McClelland. McClelland has demonstrated through years of research that individuals who make high scores on a "story telling from pictures" test designed to measure achievement needs subsequently perform more effectively in competitive achievement situations.[22] McClelland's "n Ach" (need for achievement) measure is based on the Thematic Apperception Test (TAT), which is a projective technique developed many years earlier by Murray to measure personality traits.[23] Murray's original TAT utilized photographs that subjects viewed. They then wrote a story describing what they saw in those pictures. McClelland has developed impressive evidence that even the growth of nations is closely related to their people's

---

[19]Victor H. Vroom, "Organizational Choice: A Study of Pre- and Post-Decision Processes," *Organizational Behavior and Human Performance,* Vol. 1, 1966, pp. 212–225.

[20]John P. Wanous, "Occupational Preferences: Perceptions of Valence and Instrumentality and Objective Data," *Journal of Applied Psychology,* Vol. 56, No. 2, 1972, pp. 152–155.

[21]*Ibid,* p. 154.

[22]David C. McClelland, *The Achieving Society* (New York: Van Nostrand Reinhold Co., 1961).

need for achievement, and that achievement motivation is an important ingredient in entrepreneurship. McClelland claims that the modern businessman's main motives are not self-interest or quest for profits per se but a
strong desire for achievement.[24] People with high "n Ach" set goals which
are difficult and challenging but which can be achieved with effort and
thereby provide the needed satisfaction.[25] They tend to calculate risk
carefully and strive for results where the probability of success is
reasonably high. Employees with a low need for achievement and a high fear
of failure tend to shy away from challenges and responsibilities. Most
people are of the latter type. However, McClelland believes that motivation
for achievement and power can be developed with training and experience.[26]

It must be borne in mind that not all employees can be motivated. Some
employees' lack of identification with organizational objectives may be
largely due to anomie. Moreover, Urwick's Theory Z[27] suggests that a
worker's *perceived role* of himself as a **consumer** or **producer** is a determining factor in his willingness to identify with organizational objectives. If he
perceives himself as a consumer and the organization is consumer oriented,
he can be motivated; if he perceives himself as a producer and the organization is production oriented, he will also be motivated. However, if his role
perception and the organization orientation are opposites, it is unlikely that
he will become highly motivated.

IDEALISM VERSUS REALISM

Satisfying higher-level personal needs in an optimum way within the work
situation probably is a goal more idealistic than realistic. All that a manager
can reasonably be expected to do is to provide a climate in which organizational needs and individual needs are made more compatible. Where organizational goals will not suffer as a result, individual needs should be
optimized. Where organizational needs are paramount, and mutual reinforcement cannot be achieved between them and individual needs, the latter
will have to give ground.

Organizational goals should be designed to harmonize as much as possible with employee goals, once managers have learned to understand what
these employee goals and aspirations are, and why it is important to
employees to achieve them. The work of the social scientist has been and

[23]Henry A. Murray, *Explorations in Personality* (New York: Oxford University Press, 1938).

[24]David C. McClelland, *Ibid*, p. 233.

[25]David C. McClelland and David G. Winter, *Motivating Economic Achievement* (New York: The
Free Press, 1969), pp. 50–54.

[26]David C. McClelland, "That Urge to Achieve," *Organizational Psychology* (Englewood Cliffs,
N.J.: Prentice-Hall, 1971), pp. 123–130.

[27]Theory Z is discussed in Chapter 13.

can continue to be very helpful in this area. As part of their training, managers should be exposed to the findings of the sociologists and the psychologists. A strong background in the application of psychological principles is a plus factor in a manager's kit of skills.

Company and employee goals are frequently assumed, both by management and workers, to be conflicting, to be poles apart. Conflicts will always exist.[28] There is no way to eliminate them completely, and the organization would probably be worse off without them. Happy workers are not necessarily productive workers. Healthy expressions of differing positions lead to constructive change. As was pointed out much earlier in this book, nonconformity in thinking often leads to innovation.[29]

If thoughtfully and properly selected, goals may often be complementary and integrated in ways that satisfy aspirations of both workers and management. Some illustrations of **mutually reinforcing** goals include training and developing employees at all levels; providing opportunities for advancement; improving education; coupling reduced labor costs with increased employee responsibility and suitable rewards; and harnessing production performance to financial incentives or other types of need satisfaction.

It is also important to recognize the likelihood that instead of motivation leading to achievement, *achievement may lead to motivation.* When a salesman makes repeated calls without producing a sale, the result is low motivation. On the other hand, when a salesman is successful and makes repeated sales, he may become highly motivated to continue. Perhaps for too long we have been placing the cart before the horse.

In the final analysis, employees know that their needs for security, recognition, advancement, growth, and job satisfaction can best be satisfied by the kind of managerial philosophy that understands these needs, empathizes with them, and, within the limits of the technological and job situation, creates a climate that is conducive to their satisfaction. The manager who genuinely attempts to integrate the interests of employees with the interests of the firm when this is feasible, who recognizes that people will do things willingly for the organization only if they derive personal satisfaction from doing them, is the type of leader who will succeed in achieving results through cooperation. This type of manager operates effectively with both employee and management groups.

SUMMARY

To cause an organization to produce results, a manager must perform many activating functions. Included among them are the exercise of leadership

---

[28]The reader is referred to Chapter 14 for a review of organizational conflict.
[29]This was discussed in Chapter 11.

and the judicious use of incentives. Both require some basic understanding of human needs and the ways in which needs are satisfied—in short, a knowledge of human motivation.

Many theories have been advanced to explain motivation. A widely held general theory is Maslow's, which groups personal needs into five priority levels in a need hierarchy. This theory treats needs in terms of man's total needs. Herzberg, focusing on man's needs only while on the job, introduced a two-factor theory, which has been called motivation–hygiene theory. This view suggests that certain job conditions, when absent, tend to dissatisfy workers although their presence does not motivate very strongly. These are the dissatisfiers, sometimes called hygiene or maintenance factors. Other conditions associated with the content of the job do tend to motivate, but when absent do not seem to cause much worker dissatisfaction. These are the satisfiers or motivators.

All motivation theories appear to approach motivation as a three-faceted phenomenon composed of an individual's desire for something, his perception of a path that will lead to attainment or satisfaction of that desire, and his belief that following that path will ultimately reward him for his efforts. The newer theories, namely path–goal theory and instrumentality-expectancy theory, tend to reinforce this three-faceted concept. Although the more recent theories are still in the process of validation, they shed some additional light and understanding on motivation.

Realistically, one cannot expect an organization to satisfy the totality of an individual's needs during working hours. Current managerial philosophy should include an obligation to provide the organizational climate within which personal goals and organizational goals can be compatible so that the pursuit of organizational goals can also lead to personal satisfactions and vice versa. This does not preclude the need for continued, healthy disagreement, which often leads to innovation and constructive change.

KEY CONCEPTS

Motives	Path–Goal Theory
Maslow's Need Hierarchy	Instrumentality–Expectancy Theory
Motivation–Hygiene Theory	Achievement Motivation Theory
Levels of Performance	

GLOSSARY

dissatisfiers Job conditions which, when absent, tend to dissatisfy employees but do not motivate very strongly when present.

expectancy The belief, expressed as a subjective probability, that a given act of an individual will lead to a particular organizational goal.

hygiene factors   Another term for maintenance factors, job conditions which support a reasonable level of satisfaction. They are associated with the job environment.

instrumentality   An individual's perception of the probability of organizational goals leading to the achievement of personal goals.

maintenance factors   Job conditions that tend to support and maintain mental health. Their absence causes dissatisfaction, although their presence does not motivate very strongly. Sometimes called hygiene factors.

motives   Inner urges or drives based on unfulfilled desires or fears consciously or subconsciously possessed by everyone.

satisfiers   Job conditions which help build higher levels of job satisfaction and motivation but which do not cause much worker dissatisfaction when absent. They are centered within the job itself. Sometimes called motivators.

valence   Strength or intensity of an individual's desire for a given outcome.

REVIEW QUESTIONS

1. Why is it important to understand motivation in order to understand the role of leadership and incentives in the activating process?
2. What are the two general categories into which all human needs can be placed? Give examples of needs that fit each category.
3. Describe briefly Maslow's hierarchy of needs. Give examples as you do so.
4. Do you believe self-actualization is an attainable level for most people? Why?
5. Explain briefly Herzberg's Motivation–Hygiene Theory. What is its usefulness?
6. In what areas do Maslow and Herzberg seem to parallel each other? Where do they differ?
7. Describe three general levels of performance. How are they related to levels of need satisfaction?
8. What does the term "escalating zero point" mean? Give an example.
9. What makes motivation a three-faceted phenomenon?
10. In your own words, describe path–goal motivation theory.
11. What is instrumentality–expectancy theory?
12. Briefly explain achievement motivation theory.
13. What is a realistic position to take concerning motivating people during work hours?

Chapter 18

Leadership

Having undertaken the first two major managing functions, we have a plan and we have an organization. People have been hired, assigned their roles, indoctrinated, and trained; they know what is expected of them, and they have the tools they need. Now they must be guided and motivated to fulfill the assignments they have taken on. This is the function of leadership.

Leadership is necessary in all organizations, including all segments of business. It is essential also in all areas of managing—planning, organizing, activating, and controlling—but has greater relevance in the activating and controlling sectors. It is in the exercise of supervision and some forms of corrective action that the leader meets the led more frequently and directly. Hence it is here that leadership is put to its firmest test.

In business, as in other organizations, the ability to lead must be learned and cultivated through experience. Leaders in industry are not born; they are developed. The art of leadership is acquired only through years of practice in applying the principles of getting along with people, understanding them, and appreciating why they think and act as they do. One should not assume that leadership is synonymous with managing. A good manager is a good leader, but a good leader may not be a manager at all. Leaders are present not only in the managerial hierarchy but also in informal work groups, as was pointed out in Chapter 11.

WHAT IS LEADERSHIP?

Although volumes have been written on the subject, there is no universal agreement on what leadership actually is or how it is defined. It has been viewed as an ability to influence subordinates to want to do what they have to do. It has been defined as the art of inducing subordinates to accomplish their assignments with zeal and confidence.[1]

Viewed from the standpoint of results, **leadership** can be defined as *getting people to do what the leader wants them to do because he has influ-*

---

[1] Harold Koontz and Cyril O'Donnell, *Management: A Systems and Contingency Analysis of Managerial Functions,* 6th ed. (New York: McGraw-Hill, 1976), p. 587.

enced or inspired them to believe it is what they want to do. Thus one individual exerts *influence* over others, bringing their perceptions of goals into line with his own. There are actually two dimensions to this definition. The first is the leader's presumed ability to motivate others to do what needs to be done. The second is the followers' tendency to follow those they perceive as instrumentalities for satisfying their own personal goals and ambitions. Leadership, therefore, is a double-edged sword. No person can be a leader unless he can get people to do what he wants done, nor will he succeed in this unless prospective followers also perceive him to be a means of satisfying their own personal aspirations. The leader must be able; the followers must be willing.

The leader provides a purpose, the task of building something, the chance to believe in something important or compelling. Leaders "have their eye on a goal, and somehow those who work for them are given to feel that they are not just earning a salary, but serving a cause."[2] J. Douglas Brown said this about leadership:

> The image of the leader is not his superficial self, but rather the personification of a system of values which he has demonstrated over time.[3]

There is no question that leadership is an essential element of the successful organization. Employees' efforts must be mobilized in every area of the organization. Be it a large functional area like sales or a relatively small clerical section in some department, the manager must exercise leadership with employees if he is to achieve the objectives that have been established for his area of jurisdiction. He hopes to gain their cooperation because of their identification with those objectives, because of their loyalty and admiration for him, or both.

The most important task of a manager is to see that his organization, represented by the personnel assigned to him, functions effectively. This can only be accomplished if subordinates produce results that are in keeping with organization objectives. The manager demonstrates his leadership when he guides and encourages them to strive toward these ends. As frequently happens, company goals and employee goals do not coincide. Typically, management is concerned with production, revenues, costs, quality, and profitability; whereas employees tend to be concerned with wages, working conditions, security, recognition, and opportunities for advancement. When personal goals and company objectives are out of phase, the leadership challenge to the manager is increased. It takes real leadership ability to integrate the interests of individuals with the interests of the firm. Managerial leadership is based on the recognition that people will do things

---

[2]Antony Jay, *Management and Machiavelli* (New York: Holt, Rinehart and Winston, 1967), p. 131.

[3]J. Douglas Brown, "The Attributes of the Effective Leader," *University: Princeton Quarterly*, No. 58, Fall, 1973, p. 20.

willingly for the organization only if they derive certain personal satisfactions from doing them. Managers must understand what these satisfactions are and must develop techniques that permit them to be achieved.

THEORIES OF LEADERSHIP

Attempts have been made to explain how a superior influences a subordinate or group of workers. These are offered by some writers as theories of leadership. Most frequently invoked to explain what makes a leader are: (1) trait theories and (2) situational theories. Let us explore these in some detail.

Trait Theories

Traits may be defined as distinguishing qualities or characteristics. For a long time personal traits have been used to explain successful leadership. Executive recruiters rely heavily on the trait approach in selecting managers. They consider it as valid as any other method of selection. Researchers, on the other hand, are divided on the subject. There is some general agreement, however, on what leadership qualities are—in other words, what characteristics a business leader ought to possess. Some attributes associated with leadership as it is perceived by managers include the following abilities:

1. **To motivate and stimulate people.** A leader has the ability to inspire his followers, often by example. It has been said that the true mark of a leader is his ability to motivate men of ordinary stature to extraordinary performance. This can often be accomplished by encouraging peer-group loyalty.

2. **To communicate.** Superior communication skills enable a leader to convey an idea effectively or get across the merits of a project. Usually this is done verbally. On the basis of his studies, Stogdill concluded that leadership is associated with intelligence, including judgment and verbal facility.[4]

3. **To possess conviction.** A leader must hold strong convictions and have confidence in the goals he espouses. His followers thus sense his strong beliefs and his feeling of assurance. They become aware that he is vitally concerned about the position he has taken and about their roles in it. Ghiselli found that leaders who have the drive to act independently and have confidence in themselves tend to be more successful in achieving organizational goals than those who do not.[5]

---

[4]Ralph M. Stogdill, "Personal Factors Associated with Leadership," *Journal of Applied Psychology*, Vol. 25, January 1948, pp. 35–71.

[5]Edwin E. Ghiselli, "Managerial Talent," *American Psychologist*, Vol. 18, October 1963, pp. 631–641.

4. **To instill confidence in others.** Followers will seek the leader's help, advice, and opinion not only on matters pertaining to the business or their job but on personal problems as well. They feel that their leader is someone to whom they can talk. They have confidence in him and in his ability to guide them in the proper direction. They believe in him. They trust him. They feel he is interested in their well-being—that even when he is firm, he is just.

5. **To delegate and have confidence in subordinates.** A good leader recognizes the strengths and weaknesses of his subordinates and the extent to which he can entrust important assignments to them. He believes in their integrity and, therefore, expects much of them. Guided by his perceptions of their ability, he lets them know he believes in them. Fiedler suggests that successful leaders may be more perceptive than unsuccessful leaders. He has found that effective supervisors are more proficient in differentiating between their best and poorest workers than are less effective supervisors.[6] Possessing this capability enhances the ability of a leader to succeed in "getting things done through other people."[7]

6. **To make decisions.** After considering the facts and various points of view, the successful executive quickly and decisively makes up his mind about the course to follow, and does it.

Relying on a trait approach exclusively, assuming that a person who is inspirational, confident, intelligent, perceptive, and decisive has a better chance of leading successfully, has numerous shortcomings. First, trait theory does not weight the relative importance of these various characteristics. Second, it ignores the influence and significance of subordinates on leadership results. Third, no distinction is made between traits valuable in *reaching* and those necessary to *maintaining* a leadership position. Finally, trait theorists overlook the fact that environmental factors influence leadership development, growth, and permanence—that the situation often makes the man. It helps to be in the right place at the right time!

Closely allied with trait theories is the **great man** approach frequently used by historians to explain major changes in the history of an organization or society as the result of innovative efforts of a few superior individuals, the giants of their time. Jennings refers to these great men as princes, heroes, and supermen.[8] Most social scientists believe that the great man theory of leadership is fiction. However, there is little doubt that the imprint of top-level managers is often clearly seen in successful organizations.

[6]Fred E. Fiedler, *A Theory of Leadership Effectiveness* (New York: McGraw-Hill, 1967).

[7]This phrase is credited to Clarence Hicks, former head of Industrial Relations for Standard Oil Company of New Jersey, who used it in a speech in 1930. He indicated that he heard it in the early 1900s but never could discover who originated it.

[8]Eugene Jennings, *An Anatomy of Leadership* (New York: McGraw-Hill, 1972).

Situational Theories (Contingency Theories)

Contingency theory, in general, may be called the "it all depends upon the given situation" theory. A contingency theory of leadership is no exception.

In recent years, theoreticians have begun to formulate approaches to leadership which stress the leader's ability to adapt to contingencies, including environmental factors over which he may have little or no control. The assumption is that the leader is one who can adjust to a particular group under varying conditions. Thus the primary ingredients in contingency theory are the **leader,** the **group,** and the **situation.** The situation variable is of major importance in determining who the leader will be and what he can accomplish.

It was in studies of leadership that contingency theory first found expression. As early as 1948 Stogdill stated, "it becomes clear that an adequate analysis of leadership involves not only a study of leaders but also of situations."[9] An interesting experiment conducted by Bavelas indicated that recognition as a leader depends to a large extent upon the strategic position he occupies in the communications network, rather than upon personality characteristics.[10] Slowly, the situational approach to leadership gained support. A landmark was Tannenbaum and Schmidt's article in 1958 which identified certain forces in the manager, in subordinates, and in the situation that called for different types of leadership.[11]

By 1960 this approach was widely accepted. Additional research was provided in 1967 by Fred Fiedler, who also contributed the term "contingency," which has tended to replace earlier situational terminology. Fiedler's research has focused on *adaptive* leadership. From a study of interacting groups, he developed a *contingency model of leadership effectiveness,* which included as situational factors (a) position power, (b) the task structure, and (c) leader–member relationship.[12] Let us examine these factors.

Position power.   Position power refers to influences inherent in the position. It includes such authority as the right to hire and fire, and to recommend or withhold promotions and pay raises. It also includes the manager's status in the organization and the support he receives from his superiors. The concept of position power was originally introduced in 1961 by Etzioni,

---

[9]Ralph M. Stogdill, *Op. cit.*

[10]Alex Bavelas, "Communication Patterns in Task-Oriented Groups," in D. Lerner and H. D. Lassell (Eds.), *The Policy Sciences* (Palo Alto, Calif.: Stanford University Press, 1951), pp. 193–202.

[11]Robert Tannenbaum and Warren H. Schmidt, "How to Choose a Leadership Pattern," *Harvard Business Review,* Vol. 36, March–April 1958.

[12]Fred E. Fiedler, *Op. cit.*

who believed power is derived partly from the office one holds in an organization and partly from personal influence.[13]

The task structure. Leadership effectiveness is a function of the degree to which a follower's job is routine or varied. By their nature some tasks are easy to define, to perform, and to measure and evaluate objectively. Others, such as creative work or staff jobs, are more difficult to define, and their results are more difficult to measure.

Leader–member relationship. A personal relationship exists between a leader and members of his group which is significant in determining leadership effectiveness. Included in such a relationship is the confidence that subordinates have in the leader and their loyalty to him, as well as his regard for them. If a favorable interpersonal relationship exists, effective leadership is enhanced; if an unfavorable relationship exists, the probability of leadership effectiveness is materially decreased.

Later, in a factor-analysis study of 88 companies, Wofford established five independent situational factors that influence the effectiveness of leadership. These were (1) degree of centralization of decision making, (2) organizational complexity, (3) size of the organization, (4) structure of the work group itself, and (5) organizational layering and communication.[14]

Combining interaction between situation variables and the behavior of the leader, the contingency model provides a useful way of analyzing and understanding leadership as it exists in business organizations. Together, trait theories and situational theories offer a better insight into leadership than either does alone.

The way a manager leads, or the kind of leadership he represents and demonstrates, is also largely a reflection of his attitude toward his position and toward his subordinates. His leadership style is directly related to, and is a manifestation of, his personal philosophy of management. This will have been influenced, in part, by the leadership style and management philosophy of his own superiors.

McGregor's Theory X and Theory Y

In his classic work Douglas McGregor suggests that there are two basic opposing philosophies of management that determine the character of the enterprise and influence successive generations of management. Each philosophy is based upon a set of assumptions about people which represent

---

[13]For a review of Etzioni's views and a discussion of position power as it relates to authority, the reader is referred to Chapter 10.

[14]J.C. Wofford, "Managerial Behavior, Situational Factors, and Productivity and Morale," *Administrative Science Quarterly*, Vol. 16, March 1971, pp. 10–17.

extreme and opposite positions on a continuum. McGregor called one set of assumptions "Theory X" and the other "Theory Y."[15]

Theory X Assumptions about People

1. The average human being has an inherent dislike of work, is lazy, and will shun work if he can.
2. Because of this dislike of work, most people must be coerced, controlled, directed, and threatened with fear of punishment or deprivation to get them to put forth the effort to achieve organizational goals.
3. The average human being prefers to be directed, wishes to avoid responsibility, has relatively little ambition, and wants security above all.

According to McGregor, the bulk of present-day management principles are based on Theory X. Whether this is actually so is highly questionable.

Theory Y Assumptions about People

1. For most people, the expenditure of physical and mental effort in work is as natural as in play or rest.
2. External control and the threat of punishment are not the only means for bringing about effort toward organizational objectives. Man will exercise self-direction and self-control in the service of objectives which he accepts and to which he is committed.
3. Commitment to objectives is a result of rewards associated with their achievement.
4. The average human being learns, under proper conditions, not only to accept responsibility but to seek it.
5. The capacity to exercise a relatively high degree of imagination, ingenuity, and creativity in solving organizational problems is widely, rather than narrowly, distributed in the population.
6. Under conditions of modern industrial life, the intellectual potentialities of the average human being are only partly utilized.

McGregor believes that Theory Y assumptions provide a better explanation of human behavior and dictate a different managerial strategy for dealing with human resources. According to Theory Y advocates, managers should plan ways to make organizational and individual goals compatible and mutually reinforcing. Managers should develop policies and techniques to support on-the-job need satisfaction and opportunities for individual development.

---

[15]Douglas McGregor, *The Human Side of Enterprise* (New York: McGraw-Hill, 1960).

Which set of assumptions is correct? Neither one. It is very unlikely that any manager is completely Theory X oriented or Theory Y oriented. In all probability, his attitude toward subordinates lies somewhere between these extreme positions. Besides, there are probably situations in which he may act in terms of Theory X values because conditions dictate that he should. An emergency or crash program may be that sort of situation. On the other hand, there are probably times when he acts in terms of Theory Y values because conditions are favorable. Thus managers may be Theory X oriented at certain times and Theory Y oriented at other. At best, it can only be said that a given manager *tends to be* Theory X oriented, or that he *tends to be* Theory Y oriented.

Theory X probably works best where output can be quantified or measured objectively, as in the case of a punchpress operator or a salesman with a quota to meet. Where output is difficult to measure, as in creative work performed by a research technician or a copywriter, Theory Y may work better. Where the worker is unskilled and needs training and direction, Theory X may be preferable; where the employee is a skilled technician, artisan, or draftsman who knows more about the particular task and how it should be performed than does his boss, Theory Y may very well be employed. The assumptions a manager makes about a subordinate rest largely on his evaluation of the subordinate's qualifications and abilities. You do not tell an expert welder how to weld. You assume he knows how, because he is an expert. You can, therefore, tend toward a Theory Y position. The competent, responsible employee is given considerable latitude in his work. In general, Theory X tends to emphasize dependence, domination, and control. Theory Y tends to emphasize independence, freedom, and participation.

Leadership: A Continuum

With multiple factors determining successful executive action, it is likely that relationships between managers and subordinates are not polarized but exist somewhere along a scale of values. As indicated in Figure 18-1, at one end of such a continuum is the type of manager who makes all the decisions and announces them to subordinates. At the other extreme is the type of manager who allows subordinates numerous decision-making and problem-solving opportunities. Most managers, in their day-to-day activities, probably fall somewhere in between. This continuum concept of leadership behavior, as it relates to *decision making,* was advanced by Tannenbaum and Schmidt. Figure 18-1 is based on their work.

According to Sayles, "We are coming to understand that decision making is an organization process. It is shaped as much by the pattern of interaction of management as it is by the solitary ruminations of the rational

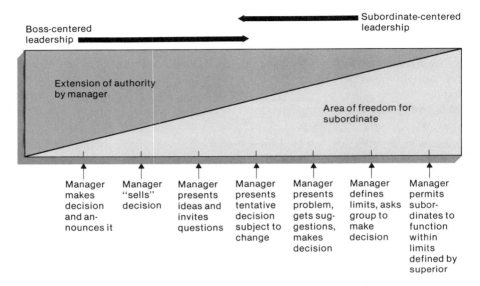

Figure 18-1.   Continuum of leadership behavior. (From Robert Tannenbaum and Warren H. Schmidt, "How to Choose a Leadership Pattern," *Harvard Business Review*, Vol. 36, March–April 1958, p. 96. Copyright © 1958 by the President and Fellows of Harvard College; all rights reserved.)

individual."[16] In fact, we have already indicated that some types of problem situations call for group decision making, particularly when there is problem overlap between two or more functional areas.[17]

MANAGERIAL STYLES

As we have observed, managerial leadership involves much more than relationships between superior and subordinate. Managerial acts affecting workers are also influenced by available resources, shifting environmental forces which may be interpreted as threats or challenges, corporate policies, managerial philosophy, and many additional factors.

A knowledge of the human need hierarchy described by Maslow,[18] the motivation–hygiene factors in the job situation proposed by Herzberg,[19] and

---

[16]Leonard Sayles, "Managing Organizations: Old Textbooks Do Die!," *Columbia Journal of World Business*, Fall 1966, p. 82.
[17]See the discussion of group decision making in Chapter 4.
[18]This is covered in Chapter 17.
[19]*Ibid.*

the Theory X–Theory Y assumptions advanced by McGregor, coupled with modern theories of leadership, enable us to understand several management styles that are present, in varying degree, in modern-day enterprise. These may be categorized as (1) autocratic, (2) paternalistic, (3) supportive, (4) collegial, and (5) laissez faire.

Autocratic

Classical or traditional management theories emphasize that a specific job should be performed in a given way as prescribed, and that the work should be closely supervised to insure that the worker does exactly what he is supposed to do. Control is established through authority. "Do as I say" is the prevailing philosophy of the autocratic manager. This managerial style is Theory X oriented and assumes that rank-and-file employees cannot be trusted to do a full day's work, and if left on their own will engage in wasteful activities. Jobs are organized, methods are spelled out, standards of performance are set, rules are established, and performance goals are determined by the manager. Compliance is sought primarily through use of economic pressures or the "stick approach," which includes threats of withholding rewards, reprimand, and outright dismissal or transfer. Decision making is centralized in the manager, who holds tightly to his authority. As a result, this managerial style frequently is described as "authoritarian" or "be strong" management. While it may have been necessary and was certainly effective during the early days of the development of the managerial enterprise system in this country, it is used to a more limited extent today. The autocratic managerial style is still evident as a vestige of the industrial revolution, when labor was untrained, unskilled, and considered a raw commodity.

There are some advantages to this autocratic managerial style. Many people, by virtue of their experience and upbringing, are used to being told what to do and how to do it. They prefer it that way. Tell them what to do, and they will follow the instructions to the letter. Leave it up to them to decide what has to be done and how, and they become lost. This type of management has the further advantage of enabling decisions to be made quickly and without challenge since authority is centered and not questioned. When the work situation is very highly structured, less competent managerial personnel can be utilized to enforce established rules and insure compliance in reaching limited objectives.

Paternalistic

Partly as a reaction to unionism following World War I, management adopted a "fatherly" or benevolent attitude toward employees and began to provide better wages, improved working conditions, and various programs designed to improve the worker's lot. Perhaps many genuinely felt that to "be good" to employees was a better way to deal with them than to "be strong," that is to say, autocratic. Employee welfare and betterment programs were introduced. In the 1930s, under the influence of New Deal thinking, fringe benefits were designed to provide security to the employee and to reduce the degrading consequences of massive unemployment. Managers, unions, and government began "taking care of" the needs of working people. This management style is paternalistic. Traditions and precedents are important elements in its philosophy. A paternalistic attitude toward employees lies somewhere between Theory X and Theory Y, and probably leans in the direction of Theory X. Routine maintenance factors are satisfied, and the employee becomes highly dependent on the business organization for his security and material satisfactions. The belief of the paternalistic manager is that a happy, contented worker is a productive one.

The great weakness of a paternalistic management style is that it builds resentment among employees who do not want "hand-outs." Besides, once they regard fringe benefits as part of the total compensation package to which they are entitled, they take them for granted. Management must find some other way to motivate workers. Properly presented, employee services and fringe benefits belong in a personnel program. They reduce tension, labor turnover, and labor unrest. But they do not motivate workers to contribute more than a minimum or average level of performance, the psychological contract already referred to as "a fair day's work for a fair day's pay." Good or exceptional performance cannot be stimulated by paternalism.

Writing in the *Harvard Business Review,* Johnson and Ouchi show how Japanese companies in this country and in Japan have outproduced American companies because Japanese managers are not paternalistic. The authors indicate what they believe are the important elements in Japanese managerial style that account for the improved results.

> In our study we observed five important aspects of this managerial approach: (1) emphasis on a flow of information and initiative from the bottom up; (2) making top management the facilitator of decision making rather than the issuer of edicts; (3) using middle management as the impetus for, and shaper of, solutions to problems; (4) stressing consensus as the way of making decisions, and (5) paying close attention to the personal well-being of employees.[20]

Concern for the whole employee, not just for his work performance, is characteristic of the Japanese manager. The results have been low rates of absenteeism, low turnover rates, increased output, and improved product quality.

---

[20]Richard Tanner Johnson and William G. Ouchi, "Made in America (under Japanese Management)," *Harvard Business Review,* Vol. 52, No. 5, September–October 1974, pp. 61–69.

Supportive

The current trend in American organizations is a shifting from authoritarianism and paternalism toward greater individual freedom and participation in decision making. While some few small companies may be managed under dictatorial or benevolent styles, the increased complexity of modern business operation makes it imperative for most managers to rely heavily on the expertise of others. Maier says, "Involving people in change thus becomes an important change method."[21]

The concept of supportive managerial style is based on the "principle of supportive relationships" proposed originally by Rensis Likert, who wrote:

> . . . The leadership and other processes of the organization must be such as to insure a maximum probability that in all interactions and all relationships with the organization each member will, in the light of his background, values, and expectations, view the experience as supportive and one which builds and maintains his sense of personal worth and importance.[22]

This implies two important conditions: (1) it is not objective reality, but how an individual perceives things that counts; and (2) to be supportive, experiences must be perceived as contributing to or maintaining a person's sense of personal worth and importance. Note the striking similarity between these two essentials, "personal worth" and "importance," and the esteem needs identified by Maslow almost twenty years earlier. They are also comparable to Herzberg's on-the-job "motivators"[23] and to McGregor's Theory Y assumptions. Note also that, at a later date, in dealing with the role of pay increases and promotions in *managerial* motivation, Lawler views *perceived expectations* of managers, not objective reality, as essential determinants in their effectiveness.[24]

Under supportive management styles, the attitude of managers toward employees lies somewhere between Theory X and Theory Y, and probably leans in the direction of Theory Y. Supportive or **participative management** lends itself best to less structured and more varied work like research, selling insurance, or craft work, than it does to repetitive work. The work of Lawrence and Lorch indicates that attempts at participative management in *routine* situations can be counterproductive.[25] The reader will recall that in

[21]Norman R. Maier, *Psychology in Industrial Organizations* (Boston: Houghton Mifflin, 1973), p. 601.

[22]Rensis Likert, *New Patterns of Management* (New York: McGraw-Hill, 1961), p. 103.

[23]These were proposed in his book, *The Motivation to Work*, published in 1959.

[24]Edward E. Lawler, *Pay and Organizational Effectiveness: A Psychological View* (New York: McGraw-Hill, 1971).

[25]Paul R. Lawrence and J. N. Lorch, *Organization and Environment: Managing Differentiation and Integration* (Homewood, Ill.: Richard E. Irwin, Inc., 1969). See also Charles Perrow, "The Short and Glorious History of Organizational Theory," *Organizational Dynamics*, American Management Association, Summer 1973.

Chapter 11 five *non-routine* opportunities (use of a suggestion box, policy formulation, delegation of authority, committees, and mutual goal setting) were suggested in which participative management is desirable.

Participative management, to be successful, depends on leadership and the application of "motivators" rather than on authority and economic sanctions. This position is supported by Sayles, who states, "Observation suggests that the manager accomplishes his objectives by moving about the organization and persuading people with special knowledge and points of view to agree with him against those who seek an alternative objective."[26] Management provides a climate that encourages employees to develop their potential. Its orientation is to support an employee's willingness to perform, to accept responsibility, and to handle delegated authority. Through delegation, managers encourage employees to participate and to become involved. More emphasis is placed on an informal environment, and more attention is devoted to managing "change" than to managing "status quo." Supportive style recognizes the need for and the value of informal organizations within the formal structure and encourages the development of independent thinking. The supportive manager welcomes the ideas of others, encourages originality, accepts the risk of his subordinate's mistakes as he would any other investment risk, limits his criticism of their failures, and rarely tells others how to do something. He takes into account the expectations of his subordinates and sees to it that they perceive his actions as being supportive.

Supportive or participative management finds broader application under conditions of decentralized plant, personnel, and equipment with decentralized authority.[27] Under these circumstances, managers of sub-units have a great deal of decision-making authority. They are responsible for results, as occurs in the "profit center" concept. **Management by results** prevails when the sub-unit manager is given considerable free rein, is "supported" in his efforts by his superiors, but is bound, nevertheless, by some adequate system of control in which accountability for his actions is a major ingredient. This situation corresponds to the area of greatest freedom for a subordinate as depicted in the continuum in Figure 18-1.

The managerial grid.   To establish the relationship between organizational demands (concern for results) and human demands (concern for people), Blake and Mouton introduced a two-dimensional grid.[28] Concern for people is shown on the vertical scale as a continuum, scaled from a low of 1 to a high

---

[26]Leonard Sayles, *Op. cit.*

[27]The reader is referred to quadrant 4 in Figure 16-1.

[28]Robert R. Blake, Jane S. Mouton, Louis B. Barnes, and Larry Greiner, "Breakthrough in Organization Development," *Harvard Business Review*, Vol. 42, No. 6, November–December 1964, p. 133.

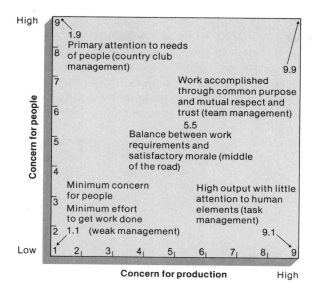

High

9

1.9
Primary attention to needs
8 of people (country club
management)   9.9

7   Work accomplished
                           through common purpose
                           and mutual respect and
6   trust (team management)
                           5.5
                    Balance between work
5   requirements and
                    satisfactory morale (middle
4   of the road)

Minimum concern   High output with little
for people   attention to human
3   elements (task
Minimum effort   management)
to get work done
2 1.1 (weak management)   9.1

Low 1   2   3   4   5   6   7   8   9

Concern for people (vertical)

Concern for production   High

Figure 18-2.   The managerial grid. (From Robert R. Blake,
Jane S. Mouton, Louis B. Barnes, and Larry Greiner,
"Breakthrough in Organization Development," *Harvard
Business Review*, Vol. 42, No. 6, November–December
1964, p. 133. Copyright © 1964 by the President and
Fellows of Harvard College; all rights reserved.)

of 9; concern for output is depicted on the horizontal axis, also as a continuum from a low of 1 to a high of 9. The resulting grid is shown in Figure
18-2.

Five combinations of managerial styles of behavior can be identified:

- **1.1** Manager shows minimum concern for either people or production
  (weak manager).

- **9.1** Manager stresses results with minimum attention to human factors
  (job oriented).

- **1.9** Manager gives primary attention to personnel and secondary attention to output (worker oriented).

- **5.5** Manager attempts to balance work results and workers' satisfaction (middle of the road).

- **9.9** Manager strives for high output and high concern for personnel
  (theoretical ideal).

According to Blake and Mouton, only the 9.9 style of managerial behavior
depicts successful integration between organizational and human values. It

is highly unlikely, however, that the management philosophy in most organizations would accept the 9.9 emphasis in its operations. It is possible, however, to devise executive development programs that are *directed toward* 9.9 orientation. Such programs may include laboratory–seminar groups, conferences to develop inter-group exchange, and mutual goal setting, which may lead to management by objectives or supervision by results.

Collegial

There is a growing tendency toward the use of a newer managerial style known as the "collegial" style, which is an extension of the supportive or participative style. This style is particularly suitable where research and professional employees are concerned. Scientists, lawyers, engineers, and other staff specialists often view themselves more in their roles as professionals than as employees of the organization. They belong to professional associations in which a collegial atmosphere prevails. This carries over to the job situation, where they prefer a high degree of autonomy and on-the-job freedom. There is a high degree of peer-group loyalty. Members of such a peer group want to have a voice and some choice about projects and assignments on which they work, and great latitude in how they approach and solve problems once they accept the assignments. They do not like to be bossed. Managers who accept this collegial style are Theory Y oriented and tend to recognize the importance to these workers of Maslow's higher level of need satisfaction. They also understand that Herzberg's motivators will be more productive with this group than increased hygiene factors.

Under task force or project management (discussed in Chapter 15), the collegial style may prove to be quite effective internally. It should be recalled that one of the underlying characteristics of the task force is that its members are not differentiated by rank. They are not authority conscious among themselves. They are brought together because their skills and expertise are needed to deal with a particular problem. As members of the task force, they view themselves as colleagues. The relationship of the executive to the task force reporting to him tends to be supportive.

In other situations, where managers view their fellow managers and highly trained subordinate specialists as "colleagues," the term "associate" is becoming increasingly popular, particularly in large business organizations. The collegial atmosphere that generally prevails within our universities and institutions of higher learning is slowly being adopted by industry. The designations "associate marketing director" and "research associate" already exist. The term "associate" implies co-equal rather than subordinate. Its spreading acceptance reflects a notable change in managerial philosophy and a shift away from vertical chains of command and hierarchical authority to lateral or horizontal patterns of relationships and communication.

Laissez faire (free rein)

Under the laissez faire style, subordinates are given complete freedom in determining their activities. The officially designated leader does not participate to any great extent. The atmosphere that prevails is very permissive, almost the opposite extreme of the autocratic situation. The philosophic orientation of laissez faire strongly reflects Theory Y assumptions about people.

In practice, there is very little active, positive leadership or decision making on the part of this type of manager. In terms of our definition of leadership he comes close to abdicating his leadership role. Unless extreme care is exercised, effective managerial control will be lost and a chaotic condition may result.

MANAGERIAL STYLE	MASLOW	HERZBERG	MCGREGOR
COLLEGIAL	Self-fulfillment	Motivators	Theory Y
SUPPORTIVE	Esteem	Motivators	
PATERNALISTIC	Love Security	Hygiene	
AUTOCRATIC	Lower-order needs	Hygiene	Theory X

Figure 18-3. Relationship between managerial styles and motivation theories.

The relationships between the four previously discussed managerial styles and several theories of motivation are diagrammed in Figure 18-3. There is a close relationship between managerial style and both the levels of need fulfillment described by Maslow, and the hygiene factors described by Herzberg. As one ascends the need hierarchy, the managerial style alters. For example, self-fulfillment, the use of motivators, and a Theory Y managerial philosophy are all identified with a managerial style that we have been describing as collegial.

Managerial styles are not mutually exclusive, however. There is considerable overlap and interaction. The style of a given manager will vary from time to time depending upon the situation. A manager is not always autocratic or always supportive. He may be autocratic at times and supportive at others. There may be times when he will act like a father or big brother. Circumstances frequently dictate the managerial style best suited to the situation.

House uses path–goal motivation theory as a basis for understanding why different leadership styles are likely to be more effective in different situations.[29] When the job is highly structured, he believes directive leader behavior may have negative effects on employees. When the job is less formalized, more ambiguous, or more open to managerial discretion, a directive style may clarify the relationship between individual activities and the objectives of the job and, thus, may be positively related to individual performance and satisfaction. House believes that the motivational functions of the leader consist of increasing personal payoffs to subordinates for work–goal attainment, and making the path to these payoffs easier to travel by clarifying it, reducing roadblocks and pitfalls, and increasing the opportunities for personal satisfaction en route.[30] Making the path easier and more satisfying to follow has significant implications for leader behavior.

Leadership styles may be arbitrarily classified in many ways, as we have already observed. It has been suggested that various situational factors (contingencies) may contribute to the type and degree of authority that is exercised in different managerial styles. Directive (autocratic), participative (democratic), and free rein (laissez faire) patterns tend to be associated with such variables as task variability, technical level of operations, technical training of employees, skill level, and availability of time for making decisions.

This suggests that under certain conditions autocratic style will be appropriate. It emphasizes tightly held authority and order giving. Enforcement depends on the power to discipline, to reward or punish. Under somewhat different conditions, democratic style is demonstrated. Instead of telling subordinates what to do, the democratic leader encourages participation by seeking advice, ideas, and suggestions. Problems are often solved through group decision making. Finally, given certain other conditions, a laissez faire style may obtain. Subordinates are permitted to set their own objectives and to develop their own techniques to achieve them. Decision making is no longer in the hands of the manager; authority is almost totally decentralized.

According to Professor Jim Windle of Purdue University, although democratic leadership is in vogue today, "it is more of a Holy Grail than a practical strategy that will enable today's typical manager to improve his leadership behavior in the day-to-day job."[31] He believes that "the manager

---

[29]This theory was discussed in the previous chapter.

[30]Robert J. House, "A Path-Goal Theory of Leader Effectiveness," *Administrative Science Quarterly*, Vol. 16, No. 3, September 1971.

[31]Jim L. Windle, speech before American Society of Personnel Administration, Minneapolis, Minnesota, June 17, 1974.

who insists on being democratic all of the time ends up with a peculiar form of pseudo-democracy. He ends up usually with a naive attempt to attain wisdom by pooling well-intentioned ignorance."[32] There are many who believe that persistent attempts always to be democratic, regardless of the contingencies, may actually indicate that a manager is evading his responsibility, that he may no longer be managing.

Realistically, supportive and collegial styles of managing are not relevant to a great many and perhaps most job situations. For example, on such routine jobs as checking gauges in an electric generating plant, watching the controls in a petroleum refinery or in a hospital intensive care unit, and similar non-varied tasks, there is no such thing as outstanding performance—only competence. What constitutes outstanding performance for the woman who packs chocolate candies into a cardboard box? Can she work more rapidly than the conveyor belt permits? Can the plant security guard walk his beat any faster or be any more mentally alert than the job calls for? Because of the dimensions of the job itself, an average or "adequate" level of performance may be all that is required, or all that can be asked, for most work being performed and will not change regardless of managerial style. Under certain job conditions, therefore, the conforming worker, who is not dissatisfied, may be the most desirable. In a Gallup Poll conducted in 1971, 81 percent of those interviewed indicated they were satisfied with their jobs. Job satisfaction was expressed by 83 percent of whites compared to 63 percent of blacks. In any case, more people appear to be satisfied with their jobs than are dissatisfied.

The president of Continental Airlines reiterated this point when he accepted the "Man of the Year" award from UCLA's Executive Program Association.

> May I suggest that there are many millions of workers who actually, honest-to-God, like their jobs and are proud of their skills? Accepted doctrine seems to insist that employees hate work, hate the boss and have to be cuddled and cajoled into punching a clock because they would much rather be down at the library improving their minds or out on the beach playing in the sand.
>
> Ladies and gentlemen, despite what you hear, most people enjoy going to work in the morning. Honest! They find their tasks interesting—even challenging—their fellow workers like-minded people with whom they can share occupational concerns. Many grow to be their best friends. The cadence of the job has a healthy rhythm. Their rewards are tangible and satisfying.[33]

SUMMARY

Leadership is an essential function in all organizational endeavor. A good manager is also a good leader.

---

[32] *Ibid.*

[33] Robert F. Six, as quoted in *The Wall Street Journal*, September 7, 1972, p. 12.

Leadership is a matter of influencing others and causing them to pursue organizational goals while achieving personal goals and satisfactions.

Trait theories, great man theories, and contingency theories have been advanced to explain leadership. While there is no universal acceptance of any theory, all of them shed some light on the question. Leaders do have outstanding attributes that attract followers. On the other hand, the work group and external conditions also contribute to making a leader. There is great validity in the concept that the situation makes the man.

Leadership has been categorized into managerial styles described as autocratic, paternalistic, supportive, collegial, and laissez faire (free rein). McGregor's Theory X–Theory Y suggests that managerial style is based on one or the other of two opposing philosophies of human behavior. In all probability, managers do not fall neatly into one or another of these categories. It is more likely that a manager may be autocratic at times and supportive at others. Under special circumstances (contingencies), he may find it more suitable to treat those for whom he is accountable as colleagues or co-workers. It is also possible for a manager to exhibit more than one managerial style in his relationships with various members of the same group, dealing in a different manner with some than with others in order to achieve overall results.

In a general way, a manager should be flexible. Ideally, he should use whatever managerial style the situation calls for. A leadership style that gets results in one situation may not achieve the same results in a different situation. Thus different styles of leadership may be appropriate within specific contexts such as specialized functional areas or different production technologies. The industrial leader has a great propensity to change and is able to alter the attitudes and behavior of others.

KEY CONCEPTS

Trait Theories	Paternalistic Management
Great Man Theory	Supportive Management
Contingency Theory	Managerial Grid
Theory X–Theory Y	Collegial Management
Autocratic Management	Laissez faire Management

GLOSSARY

autocratic management   An authoritarian leadership style, in which authority is highly centralized in the manager. Sometimes it is called "be strong" management.

collegial management   A leadership style that recognizes fellow workers as colleagues or co-equals rather than subordinates.

free rein management   A laissez faire style of management that leaves all decision making in the hands of subordinates.

leadership   Getting people to do what the leader wants done because he has influenced or inspired them to believe it is what they want to do.

paternalistic management   A leadership style that tends to be fatherly and benevolent in its philosophy toward workers. Sometimes it is called "be good" management.

supportive management   A leadership style that encourages participative activities. It is sometimes called democratic management.

traits   Distinguishing qualities or characteristics.

REVIEW QUESTIONS

1. Define leadership. Why is it important?

2. What are some attributes or personality traits that leaders are said to possess?

3. Are all outstanding leaders good managers? Defend your position.

4. Are great leaders great men? Are great men great leaders? Is there a difference?

5. What are the basic ingredients in any contingency theory of leadership?

6. In your own words, summarize McGregor's Theory X–Theory Y. With which theory do you personally identify? Why?

7. Describe five managerial styles that exist in some degree in modern-day organizations.

8. What are some factors found in Japanese managerial style that make it different from American managerial style? Do you believe they have merit?

9. Turn to Figure 18-2, the Blake and Mouton managerial grid. Where do you think you fit on this grid? Why?

10. What do you think of laissez faire management? What are its risks or limitations? When would you use it?

Chapter 19

Supervision

At all levels managers supervise a considerable portion of the activities of subordinates in their charge. To some extent executives at high levels supervise managers immediately below them. However, the term supervising usually applies to managing that occurs at the operating and facilitating levels of the organization and extends over *non-management* personnel. Regardless of the level at which it occurs, supervising is a **line** function.

For our purposes supervision refers to managing at that level where management and non-management personnel are in direct contact, as in the case of the foreman and his subordinates on the production line, the sales manager and the salesmen, or the office manager in charge of the clerks and typists in the purchasing department. The foreman, sales manager, and the office supervisor are managers dealing directly with non-management people. The point at which initial contact occurs between supervisors and workers is *where the management hierarchy begins*. In this sense the position of the supervisor is the first rung on the ladder of management; supervision is first-line management.

Supervision is another instance of "getting things done through others"; it is an essential component of the activating phase of managing. Causing the organization to carry out the planned activity through the exercise of leadership, evaluating the performance of the organization, and taking corrective action if necessary are ingredients in the supervisory function. Thus supervisors are very much involved in all facets of managing, particularly in the *activating* and *controlling* functions. A supervisor must exercise leadership to guide subordinates, as individuals and as a peer group, toward fulfilling organizational objectives. He must communicate managerial decisions from higher levels to them, motivate them, measure their response, and communicate their feelings and needs to higher management echelons. He must also institute or put into operation remedial steps when they are necessary. It takes real managerial ability to supervise effectively.

THE ROLE OF DIRECTION

In every enterprise various resources are combined in proper proportions to produce a given output of products or services. It is the **human resource** factor with which the directing function is concerned. This applies to government, universities, hospitals, churches, the military, labor unions, professional groups, as well as business organizations.

Many writers in the field of management refer to direction as an independent major management function. In their treatment of direction they include such diverse elements as giving orders or issuing directives, various types of leadership, managerial styles, morale, human relations, supervision, discipline, communication, and initiating almost any type of organized activity. To view direction in the sense of "directing *all* employee activities" is much too broad a concept to be meaningful and is very confusing for students of management. Does a member of the board of directors engage in directing? Obviously the term direction has more than one meaning. We shall use it in a much more restrictive sense and shall define it more narrowly.

The working force must know what is expected of them before they can proceed. This is essential, and direction provides the answer. **Direction** means *interpreting plans for others and giving instructions on how to carry them out.* A highly successful executive makes this observation:

> Time is money in business; misunderstandings in the interpretation of requests, reports or instructions can prove very costly. Thus the good executive is one who can explain things and tell people what needs to be done quickly and clearly.[1]

In the early days of the development of our managerial enterprise economy, shortly after this country shifted from a predominantly agricultural to an industrial society, there were very few skilled or trained factory workers who could operate power-driven machines, work with tools, or do assembly work. They had little or no experience. Managers had to spend considerable time telling workers exactly what to do, and teaching them how to do it. But we have come a long way since then. Workers today are better educated than their forebears. After years of specialization, most employees come to the job with considerable experience and know-how. Moreover, there are increasing numbers of people with training in very complex technologies, and with highly developed professional skills. It is common, and even expected, that skilled workers and specialized staff know more about a given area than does their boss. In large organizations today,

---

[1] J. Paul Getty, "What Makes an Executive," *Playboy*, Vol. 9, No. 5 (May 1962), p. 95.

problems are so complex that no one manager has all the technical information and competence required to make the right decisions solely on his own. It is usually necessary to call for expertise from subordinates in various areas of specialization. Possessors of these skills, like craftsmen, need little or no direction in how to apply them to a given situation. A welder does not have to be shown how to weld; a pattern maker does not have to be taught how to make a template; an econometrician knows how to make projections.

There is considerable evidence that when a worker does need direction it is provided more often on an informal basis by fellow workers and not by the supervisor. In a survey of civil service personnel, one of the questions asked the **primary** source from which they received help in learning the duties of their present job. The relative ranking of their responses was as follows:[2]

From an experienced fellow employee	29.2%
Catching on as best you could	23.4
Your supervisor	22.2
The employee who formerly held the job	6.5
No one—didn't need help	6.3
Attending formal training sessions	4.5
No one—would like to have help	.7
No answer	7.2

Among over 400 respondents, only 22.2 percent received direction primarily from their supervisors. More than half learned the duties of their jobs from fellow employees or on their own (self-direction).

Direction is still the province of the supervisory function. Most management decisions are probably communicated through supervisors. It is in the process of giving directions, or interpreting assignments, that most of the explanation and instruction occurs. Direction, therefore, is highly dependent upon formal communication, usually speaking, writing, or demonstration.[3] Although much ongoing direction is formalized, not all is communicated by the foreman or supervisor. At Eastman Kodak, for example, workers learn how to repair or adjust machines, while working at their own pace, by receiving instructions from a tape recorder and viewing pictures of parts as they are projected on a screen.

From our definition of direction, it becomes obvious that it is neither an independent nor a major managing function. However, it is closely associated with supervising and is an important ingredient in the activating process.

---

[2]"Survey of Civilian Personnel Management," U.S. Army Transportation Material Command, St. Louis, Missouri, December 13, 1961, p. 12.

[3]The subject of communication will occupy our attention in Chapter 21.

Supervision is *a major activating function which insures that plans are understood and are being followed.* It is concerned with seeing that direction leads to action and that action is taking place currently. There can be no supervision of a completed phase of activity, nor of a future one. The supervisor is an overseer. He constantly must ask himself, "Are things going the way they are supposed to?" There is nothing disciplinary in the concept of supervision. It is constructive, positive, and goal-oriented.

THE SUPERVISOR'S ROLE

The job of the supervisor is a most difficult one. The role is especially difficult for a new supervisor who has just been promoted to that position. Many advance by having been outstanding workers. However, the abilities that made them outstanding workers do not necessarily make them competent managers. As we have noted earlier in our discussion of the transferability of managerial skills,[4] the possession of specific technical skills tends to be relatively less important as a person ascends the management structure. This is one of the concepts with which the first-time manager has to contend in making the transition from worker and technical specialist to supervisor. He is required to develop and use new skills and talents. He must now apply human relations skills as he becomes increasingly aware of, and a stronger proponent of, company goals and objectives in his new role as a manager and decision maker. He must learn to plan, organize, activate, and control.

The supervisor's position may be tenuous. It is not uncommon for foremen to be appointed on a temporary basis. When the work force is cut, they may be bumped back with the workers. When business turns brisk, they may again be elevated to the supervisory ranks. Thus a foreman may not know where he stands. He is uncertain about his status. The situation is further complicated where unions are present. By accepting a supervisor's position, a man loses his union seniority. If he is later returned to operative work in his department, he must start at the bottom of the seniority list. This is one reason why capable people turn down the opportunity for promotion to supervisory positions.

As our industrial society changed, so did the role of the first-line supervisor. Fifty years ago a foreman had tremendous power. He did all the hiring, made work assignments, and had sole right to discharge. He had authority that could make or break a worker. With specialization, various staff groups arose. The methods department decided how men should work, production control people decided on scheduling, personnel people did the interviewing and hiring, and quality control inspectors decided if products were up to acceptable specifications. Each new staff group, in effect, took

---

[4]For a review, the reader is referred to Chapter 12.

from the foreman some of the activities for which he had been responsible. When unions made their appearance, workers were no longer completely dependent upon the foreman. His authority was further weakened. It became more difficult for him to make his orders stick. Thus staff activities and union influences have altered the role of the foreman. In addition, to strengthen its position in dealing with unions, management established company-wide uniformity in policy by centralizing personnel activities including promotion, discipline, and salary administration under one industrial relations department. As a result, the position of the first-line supervisor became very vulnerable. During World War II, therefore, thousands of supervisors formed their own union, The Foreman's Association of America. The National Labor Relations Board gave it the same recognition as other unions until the Taft-Hartley Act was amended in 1947, and the law changed to specify that supervisors are members of management—a legal position which still holds today.

Current Views of the Supervisor's Role

There currently are three widely held views of the supervisor's role in the organization: (1) marginal man, (2) man in the middle, and (3) key man.

The marginal man. More often than not, supervisory competence is assumed to exist when the title "supervisor" is bestowed upon an employee. The new supervisor finds himself in limbo—temporarily ignored by management, not yet accepted by peers, and rejected by his old buddies. He is on the periphery of the principal activities within his department, not quite outside and not quite in. In larger companies, he is bypassed by staff executives; in smaller companies, by the owner–manager. Where unions exist, they tend to work with higher levels of management. The supervisor wants to act like a manager, yet he does not participate to any significant extent in the councils of management. Staff specialists make many decisions which are communicated to him merely to re-transmit to his workers. In labor relations activities, his role is largely a passive one. The supervisor begins to have doubts that he should ever have accepted the promotion. He feels like a marginal man. This feeling of being on the fringe of everything is more marked among supervisors who work the night shift. They often continue activities which originated during the day shift and in which they played no role and made no inputs. A survey of 242 steel industry foremen indicates:

> This front-line supervisor is a man on a tightrope. Badgered by the union, harrassed by top management, he is faced daily with getting work out and maintaining harmony in the ranks above and below him.[5]

---

[5]*The Wall Street Journal,* November 26, 1968.

The survey also found that most foremen believe their working conditions are the worst in the plant, that their prestige is nil, and that their future "indicates little hope of improvement."[6]

The man in the middle.   According to a second point of view, the supervisor acts as a buffer, a human demilitarized zone between two opposing forces, management and workers. He feels pressures from above and below. Management expects him to see that their plans are followed, that company goals are reached, that loyalty and discipline are maintained, that costs in terms of tardiness, absenteeism, and waste are kept to a minimum. Being cost-conscious and goal- or production-oriented, management expects the supervisor to accept its position as his own. His subordinates also expect his loyalty. They want him to represent their point of view to his superiors, to be their spokesman, their champion. As an individual, the supervisor experiences a strong pull to be both a good member of the management group and a good member and leader of his employee group. He does not want to make a mistake. He wants to avoid criticism and conflict. He has a dilemma. Being caught between opposing forces and not knowing whether to run with the hare or hunt with the hounds produces a situation that has aptly been called "supervisory schizophrenia."[7]

The key man.   The traditional role of the supervisor is that of a key man in the organization. He is a part of the management structure and is the closest link between management as a group and workers as a group. Within the scope of his job definition, he has authority to make assignments to subordinates, interpret and implement company and departmental policies, and see that things get done. He is the key member of management in developing attitudes. Management, as a whole, is seen in the same light as the worker sees his supervisor. Workers, on the other hand, are viewed much the same as management views the supervisor. He reflects the attitudes of both groups, and is in a key position to do so. Besides, he is the chief communication link between management and workers and is, therefore, able to facilitate or to hinder the flow of ideas and information upward and downward.

REINFORCING THE SUPERVISOR'S POSITION

While the position of a supervisor, particularly the first-time supervisor, often is that of a marginal man, or of a man in the middle, it is so important to the effective functioning of the organization that it must be reinforced and supported to fulfill its rightful role as "key" man. Efforts must be made by

---

[6]*Ibid.*
[7]Graham Cole, "Supervisory Schizophrenia," *Industry Week*, December 21, 1970, p. 36.

higher management to emphasize the management role of the supervisor and to eliminate the "superclerk" image. Not only must first-line supervisors be told they are part of management, but they must be regarded and treated as management by their superiors.

The following courses of action taken by higher management will assist the supervisor to believe in his role as a key man:

1. **Elevate the supervisor's role.** This means recognizing the importance of the supervisor's role and bestowing upon him the rights, status symbols, and privileges to which all managers are entitled. Upper management must include supervisors in decision making, particularly in decisions affecting their departments; set their pay on an equitable level with other members of management, and with workers whom they supervise; and provide rewards based upon performance.

2. **Give the supervisor a greater voice in company affairs.** Permit him to help formulate policy at his managerial level. Give him greater voice in hiring, at least in making the final determination between two or three candidates selected by the personnel department for his approval; in promotions; recommending wage increases; setting work standards; scheduling; and handling grievances including matters of discipline.

3. **Provide counseling.** Supervisors should be given an opportunity to meet with their superiors, preferably at regularly scheduled intervals, to bring up problems, receive advice, offer constructive suggestions, and indicate ways that upper management can make the supervisor's performance more effective. This also permits upper levels to receive feedback on decisions affecting workers. Meetings at which counsel is freely sought and freely given builds confidence in the supervisor and makes him feel a part of the management group. In these meetings he becomes aware of the extent of his actual or expected contribution toward the work of his unit.

4. **Provide special training.** For the first-time supervisor, training programs are essential. They help him to develop an understanding of the supervisor's important role, and the attitudes and behavior subordinates expect of him. He is introduced to human relations concepts and broadens his understanding of ways to lead and to motivate. Increased supervisory knowledge and an understanding of how to deal with people help him to become the key man his new role calls for. His attendance at supervisory training sessions emphasizes to him, to his peers who also attend, and to his subordinates that he is an accepted member of the management team.

For the established supervisor, training and development can be furthered by membership in supervisory management associations and attendance at regional and national supervisors' conferences. Appointing a supervisor to committees which enable him to broaden his perspective while serving with other management people, some of whom hold higher positions in the management hierarchy, and supplying him with literature and information that keep him abreast of recent developments will enhance his self-development. Through education, experience, and training, supervisors learn how to deal with change.

A great many firms today have supervisory development programs. They are designed to influence the behavior and attitudes of first-line supervisors toward those they supervise; to increase their knowledge of the total organization, its products, and its goals; to increase their managerial skills; and in general, to improve their performance as supervisors. Some of the topics included in a supervisory development program are written and oral communications, the supervisor's role in quality and cost control, individual and group motivation, financial reports, handling complaints and grievances, developing subordinates, and counseling. The training supervisor in a large paper products company comments on the results of his company's supervisory training and development program:

> The men complete their training knowing they have a very definite responsibility to deal fairly, intelligently, directly, maturely, and honestly with those they supervise; to admit mistakes when necessary, and to seek the employees' help when it is needed.[8]

5. **Reduce non-management duties.** Richard Gerstenberg, chairman of the board of General Motors, indicates what his firm has been doing to strengthen the role of the foreman.

> In our GM Assembly Division, we are redefining the foreman's job to strengthen his role as a manager of people. In this program, an hourly employee helps the foreman perform a variety of non-management functions. This allows the foreman more time to develop a personal, more understanding relationship with the men and women under him. It is paying off. We are achieving better quality, lower costs, higher morale, as well as gains in productivity. It is only one of many new efforts we are undertaking.[9]

An additional benefit from eliminating many of the non-managerial duties of first-line supervisors is the probability of increasing their span of effective management.[10]

PATTERNS OF SUPERVISION

The task of a supervisor is to insure that his instructions to follow a prescribed course of action are proceeding on schedule. In dealing with

---

[8]"Training Gears Northwest for Change," *Potlatch Story*, Potlatch, Inc., January 1971, p. 15.

[9]Richard C. Gerstenberg, "Productivity: Its Meaning for America," address at the annual meeting of the American Newspaper Publishers Association, New York, April 26, 1972.

[10]For a review of the span of management concept, the reader is referred to Chapter 14.

subordinates, some supervisors get better results than others. Different managerial styles may account, in part, for the differences in results. In Chapter 18 it was pointed out that managers tend to be either autocratic, paternalistic, supportive, or collegial in their attitudes toward subordinates, and that any one of these styles can be very effective in the right situation. As first-line managers, supervisors also tend to practice one or more of these styles in dealing with subordinates under their jurisdiction. As a result there have evolved two rather distinct kinds of supervision. (1) The first is based on the **orientation** of the supervisor, either toward the job itself or toward the employees' needs. (2) The second is based on the **intensity**, or closeness, of his supervision.

Job-Centered versus Employee-Centered Supervision

A number of studies have been made to investigate patterns of supervision in hospitals, industry, and government agencies. The findings of Rensis Likert, one of the pioneers in this area, indicate a relationship between productivity and patterns of supervision.[11]

Among groups of clerical, sales, and manufacturing employees, Likert found that some work sections were high-producing and others were low-producing. The criteria for "high-producing" included greater output, fewer rejects, lower absenteeism, reduced labor turnover, and high morale. The criteria for "low-producing" were the opposites of these. The researchers noted that first-line supervisors of high-producing sections tended to be employee-centered, whereas those of low-producing sections tended to be job-centered. When the term **job-centered** (or task-centered or production-centered) supervisor is used it means a first-line manager who focuses primarily on the job to be done. He tends to structure the work of his subordinates; emphasizes methods, procedures, and standards of production; and often adopts an autocratic or authoritarian style in his dealings with them. The **employee-centered** (or group-centered) supervisor is primarily concerned with the well-being and motivation of his subordinates. He shows concern for their problems; focuses attention on building work groups that effectively seek high performance goals; and tends toward a democratic, participative, or supportive style in his dealings with them. The employee's welfare comes first; the job to be done is important too, but it comes second. The employee-centered supervisor, therefore, encourages "supervision by objectives" and "supervision by results" as techniques for getting the job done. In terms of his attitude toward subordinates, the job-oriented supervisor tends to be inclined toward McGregor's Theory X, whereas the employee-oriented supervisor leans in the direction of Theory Y.

Figure 19-1 indicates the relationship between supervisory orientation and productivity found in one study. Productivity in sections whose super-

---

[11]Rensis Likert, *New Patterns of Management* (New York: McGraw-Hill, 1960).

NUMBER OF FIRST-LINE SUPERVISORS WHO ARE:

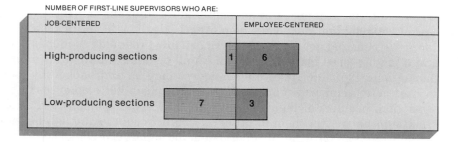

JOB-CENTERED	EMPLOYEE-CENTERED
High-producing sections	1	6
Low-producing sections	7	3

Figure 19-1. Productivity and supervisory orientation. (Based on findings of Rensis Likert, *New Patterns of Management,* New York: McGraw-Hill, 1961.)

visors showed a pattern of employee-orientation is compared with productivity in sections whose supervisors displayed a pattern of job-orientation.

The implication is that high production results from employee-oriented supervision, and low production results from job-oriented supervision—that the type of supervision is the causal variable. Is this a valid conclusion? There is considerable room for doubt. Although employee-orientation is undoubtedly important, it is not sufficient in itself to account for high production. There are many other contributing factors.

1. Productivity may influence the style of supervision. It is very possible that *because* work groups are high-producing and meeting production goals, their supervisors can adopt an employee-oriented posture. The supervisor can now focus on the needs of his subordinates as individuals. It is also possible that *because* work groups are low-producing, their supervisors must adopt a job-oriented attitude. To bring a low-producing section to a higher performance level may require a supervisor to be job-oriented, at least in the short run.

2. External behavior patterns may be a factor. The way individuals have learned to respond to situations outside the workplace carries over into their behavior as members of a work group. As employees, they have different expectations. Some prefer to be asked; others like to be told. One reason for using an autocratic or authoritarian style is that many people actually welcome it. Psychologists call these persons "authoritarian personalities." Basically, the authoritarian personality tends to be rigid in his beliefs; seems to adhere to conventional values; is intolerant of weakness in himself and others; is suspicious; and respects authority to an unusual degree.[12]

3. Employee-orientation and job-orientation are extremes on a continuum. No supervisor always acts in one way or the other. A supervisor may be

---

[12]Elliott Aronson, *The Social Animal* (San Francisco: W.H. Freeman and Co., 1972), p. 186.

employee-centered at times, and job-centered at other times. Even within a high-producing section not every employee is dealt with in an employee-centered fashion; and not every employee in a low-producing section is dealt with in a job-centered manner. It is not an all or none situation. In a high-producing unit, the majority of the employees may be approached by their supervisor in an employee-centered fashion, but the other employees in the same section, because of their dispositions, may require him to use a job-centered approach with them in order to obtain results. Although he may have displayed both patterns of supervision, the supervisor is judged overall to be an employee-centered person. Yet would high production in the section as a whole have occurred if the supervisor had not found it necessary to be job-centered, and Theory X oriented, in his dealings with some of its members?

4. The technical and specialization skills of the supervisor may be just as important in influencing output as his human relations skills. The overall competence of the first-line supervisor is judged by criteria of productivity. Productivity may reflect not only the supervisor's leadership ability, communication skills, and managerial competence, but also his technical and specialization skills, which set the standard to be followed.

Close Supervision versus General Supervision

Another aspect of the Likert studies focused on the degree or intensity of supervision to which first-line supervisors were themselves subjected. Some supervisors have superiors who oversee their work in a very close fashion; others have superiors who supervise them in a more general or "loose" way.

In a study of clerical workers, some groups were found to be more productive than others. Supervisors of the various sections had superiors who tended to work with them in either a close or a general way. Figure 19-2 presents a summary of the data.

NUMBER OF FIRST-LINE SUPERVISORS WHO ARE:

	UNDER CLOSE SUPERVISION	UNDER GENERAL SUPERVISION
High-producing sections	1	9
Low-producing sections	8	4

Figure 19-2. Productivity and degree of supervision. (Based on findings of Rensis Likert, *New Patterns of Management,* New York: McGraw-Hill, 1961.)

Here the conclusion appears to be that general supervision produces better results than close supervision—that the pattern of supervision is the causative factor. Again, there is considerable room for doubt.

1. There is no clearly established relationship of cause and effect between the two variables. If a study indicates that low-producing departments are supervised by men who themselves are closely supervised, this does not mean that close supervision caused low productivity. Neither does it mean that general supervision caused high productivity.

2. It is possible that productivity influences supervisory patterns. Because a section is a high-producing one, its supervisor can oversee its members' efforts in a more general way. It is less necessary for him to exert pressure, to nag or hound them to do the job. When productivity is low, the supervisor may find it necessary to oversee his subordinates in a close manner in order to raise the level of output.

3. Close supervision or general supervision may simply reflect a transfer of supervisory patterns. Supervisors who are recipients of general supervision are more likely to practice general supervision themselves; those who are supervised closely tend to supervise closely. In other words, a first-line supervisor tends to imitate his boss's style of supervision.

4. Degree of supervision may be related to span of authority. The size of the subordinate group is a factor influencing supervisory style. Broad span of authority is more conducive to general supervision. If the number of subordinates is small, the supervisor can oversee the work of his subordinates in a closer fashion. When there are many to oversee, he simply does not have the time to oversee everyone's work closely; general or loose supervision is more feasible and close supervision less likely.

5. The nature of the work is a factor in the degree or intensity of supervision required. The same degree of supervision indicated for clerical workers may not be indicated for other types of work. Craftsmen, for example, do not require close supervision and would resent it if it were offered. Well-trained, skilled professional workers require less supervision. They are used to accepting responsibility for an assignment and being held accountable for results. When goals or objectives are set and met, supervisors tend to interfere very little with the work of their subordinates. Supervision by results, under which each person knows what is expected of him, can be employed. The worker who watches the dials in a power plant, or operates valves in an oil refinery or processing plant, does not require close supervision. Even the mass production worker, who is confined to a fixed work station and whose output is geared to the rate of work flow, does not require close supervision. A bookkeeping department requires less supervisory attention than a mail room.

6. A supervisor may use close supervision with some workers and general supervision with others in the same section, yet his style of supervison will be characterized as either close or general. New workers generally require closer supervision than experienced ones in the same group.

7. Leadership, communication skills, and technical competence of the supervisor may play a significant role in getting subordinates to accept the goals of the organization as valid. If the group is persuaded to adopt a favorable attitude toward the organization's goals, and to work to achieve them, it will become a high-producing section whether it is closely or loosely supervised.

8. The type of incentives offered may be an influencing factor. Employees working on a piece rate or production bonus system of pay generally require less supervision than hourly workers. This is not difficult to understand. The more they produce satisfactorily, the more they take home in pay. The incentive provides the reason to maintain a high level of output.

9. The effective supervisor may have "influence" or clout with higher levels of management. When a superior is successful in obtaining favorable response to his requests of upper management, the confidence of his subordinates is reinforced; when he is repeatedly turned down by higher-ups, his men lose confidence in his ability to go to bat for them. Their effectiveness as a group is impaired. It is very possible, therefore, that close supervision *with influence* will lead to better results than general supervision *without influence.* This position tends to be supported by the research findings in a study by Evans at the University of Toronto. Evans states:

> Where upward influence is low, the most considerate supervisor may be unable to deliver the rewards that were implicitly promised; therefore, path-goal instrumentalities will be unrelated to supervisory behavior.[13]

This dovetails with the earlier work of Pelz, who found that subordinates were satisfied only if the supervisor (a) was considerate *and* (b) had high influence. If he was considerate but had low upward influence, subordinates were very dissatisfied.[14]

General supervision in business probably can be used, therefore, if the following conditions prevail:

1. the leadership qualifications and ability of the supervisor to motivate are high;

2. the nature of the work provides intrinsic satisfaction;

---

[13]Martin G. Evans, "Leadership and Motivation: A Core Concept," *Academy of Management Journal,* Vol. 13, No. 1, March 1970, p. 102.

[14]D.C. Pelz, "Influence: A Key to Effective Leadership in the First-Line Supervisor," *Personnel,* Vol. 29, 1952, pp. 209–217.

3. workers have accepted management goals as valid and compatible with their personal goal expectations;

4. consistency and coordination are relatively unimportant;

5. subordinates have the capability and desire to accept responsibility;

6. it is not imperative to get immediate, short-run results;

7. the span of authority is broad, and the supervisor has a large number of subordinates to oversee;

8. the proper incentives or motivators are present.

One might ask whether no supervision would be more effective in obtaining results from subordinates than close or loose supervision. Why not simply have a group of individuals read some instructions on what is expected of them and leave them on their own to carry out the instructions—a sort of free-rein supervisory style? Some work has been done to test this approach. In one study, twenty National Guard trainees were required to monitor a panel of lights that lit up in sequence, and were to press a button whenever an interruption occurred in the sequence. Twenty additional subjects, after identical training, were told that periodically during the test period they would be visited by a lieutenant colonel or a master sergeant. Four visits were actually made to each subject. The performance of the "supervised" subjects was then compared with that of the "unsupervised" subjects. Those who were subjected to unannounced visits by their superiors maintained a significantly higher level of performance than those who monitored the light panel unsupervised.[15] The occasional visits by a superior who merely observed but said nothing appeared to have a reinforcing effect on their performance.

There is nothing wrong with being "job-oriented." By definition, *managing is goal-oriented.* All supervisors, as first-line managers, must also be goal-oriented. Their job requires them to see that planning is carried out, that goals that have been set are being achieved, that the means selected are being utilized properly. Behavioralists must recognize that the practice of good human relations in business is not an end in itself but rather another valuable means to accomplish some corporate end, to achieve the goals for which the particular organization exists. The supervisor is there to get the job done. Therefore any pattern of supervision must reflect this essential function of a manager.

The nature of the job, the characteristics of the workers performing the job, the climate in which the work is undertaken, the personal qualities of the supervisor himself, and his influence with higher-ups, all play a role in determining the way in which the work will be done and the pattern of supervision that will be utilized.

---

[15]B. O. Bergum and D. J. Lear, "Effects of Authoritarianism on Vigilance Performance," *Journal of Applied Psychology*, Vol. 47, 1963, pp. 75–77.

In the short run, to obtain immediate results, as might be required in a "crash program" or emergency situation, job-oriented supervision and close supervision are probably more effective.

In the long run, particularly where the work is creative, flexible, and non-routine, employee-oriented supervision, close **or** general, may be contributing factors toward accomplishing these goals: improved productivity, improved morale, lower absenteeism, reduced tardiness, decreased labor turnover, increased efficiency, and reduced cost.

ATTITUDES AND BEHAVIOR

Fundamental changes are occurring in society. People are less willing to accept pressure and close supervision. The trend in home, school, and community is toward greater freedom. American youth are participating increasingly in decisions that affect them. In the political realm, the voting age has been lowered to 18. On college campuses, students are represented in deliberations of faculty and staff committees, with voting privileges on many matters including curriculum changes and required courses. At some institutions, students evaluate the faculty and publish their findings.

Since World War II, there has also been a substantial increase in the educational level of the work force. As people become better educated, their expectations rise in terms of responsibility, authority, and rewards they should receive. Added emphasis in high schools and colleges on participation, independent inquiry, democratic values, and individual initiative increases the probability that individuals will carry these accepted and expected values into the work situation.

One of the most important of the subjective factors that influence the way we perceive situations is mental **set.** A study by Kelley found that those who were previously led to expect to meet a "warm" person not only made different judgments about him but also behaved differently toward him than those who were expecting a "cold" one.[16] Strickland indicated the influence of set in determining how closely superiors feel they must supervise their subordinates. Because of prior expectation one person was trusted more than another and was believed to require less supervision, even though performance records were identical.[17]

Expectations have a profound effect on employee attitudes. **Attitudes** are *mental sets concerning some fact or state of affairs.* They result from the relationship between what a person expects and what he actually experiences. When experience (reality) falls short of expectations, **unfavorable** at-

---

[16]H. H. Kelley, "The Warm-Cold Variable in First Impressions of Persons," *Journal of Personality,* 1950, pp. 431–439.

[17]L. H. Strickland, "Surveillance and Trust," *Journal of Personality,* 1958, pp. 200–215.

titudes occur. When experience equals expectations, a **neutral** attitude, neither favorable nor unfavorable, exists. When experience exceeds expectations, **favorable** attitudes tend to result. Attitudes are considered to be one of the most important determinants of a worker's behavior. How he acts in a situation depends on satisfactions or dissatisfactions he experienced previously in a similar situation. As expectations change with fundamental societal changes, attitudes shift also. Since expectations alter, actual experience must change too at the same or more favorable rate. Otherwise, employee attitudes will be less than neutral; they will be unfavorable.

While changes in attitudes do cause changes in behavior, what has only recently begun to be understood is that changes in behavior can also cause changes in attitudes. The traditional belief is that behavior of people is greatly influenced by the attitudes they hold—that attitudes lead to behavior. Frederick Herzberg thinks this is placing the cart before the horse.

> Attitudes of employees, it is believed, are the key to their work performance and therefore employee relations efforts must be directed to ascertaining these attitudes and developing programs to modify them. Proper changes in an employee's attitudes should then lead to the desired behavior. Incredible sums of money have been spent by organizations on morale surveys and attitude change programs ranging from elaborate communication systems to group psychotherapy. This has been a scandalous waste. The whole premise is wrong.
>
> Attitudes *do not* lead to behavior. It is rather the other way around. Behavior leads to attitudes.[18]

Stereotypes that people have of others do tend to change when persons are brought together on an equal status basis working side by side. For example, the attitude that blacks are lazy, shiftless, and undependable quickly vanishes when black and white miners work together underground where they need and depend upon one another to accomplish their mission. Changes in behavior relationships produce changes in attitudes, causing some stereotypes to weaken and disintegrate.

SUMMARY

Supervision, in its traditional meaning, refers to first-line management, which occurs where foremen and supervisors come into direct contact with non-management personnel. Supervision is the first or lowest rung on the management ladder.

Supervision is a component of the total activating process and is primarily concerned with overseeing various activities to insure that plans are

---

[18]Frederick Herzberg, "Management of Motivators," *Industry Week*, February 15, 1971, pp. 53–54.

being executed properly. One important element in supervising is direction, seeing to it that all plans are understood and instructions are provided for carrying them out. There is a great deal of evidence that most direction is either informal or is not directly supplied by the supervisor even when it is formally communicated.

The role of the supervisor is a difficult one and a most important one. The position has been viewed as that of a marginal person, a person in the middle, or a key figure in the organization. There is some validity to each premise. Efforts are being made, however, to elevate and restore the supervisory position to its legitimate "key man" role.

Behavioralists have identified distinct patterns of supervision based on the orientation and managerial philosophy of the first-line manager. A supervisor tends to be either job-oriented or employee-oriented. If he is job-oriented, the supervisor focuses primarily on getting the job done, relying heavily on policies, rules, procedures, and work standards. If he is employee-oriented, he directs his efforts toward building peer group loyalty and enhancing employees' job satisfaction, in the belief that subordinates will then respond with superior results.

Behavioralists have also investigated the impact of degree of supervison on productivity. Some first-line managers supervise rather closely; others supervise more loosely.

Although the results are not conclusive since other variables influence results, including the direct connections or clout that a supervisor has with higher-ups, there may be some long-run benefits to be gained from employee-oriented, general supervision. Faster, short-run benefits may be obtained from job-oriented, close supervision. Probably mixes of supervisory styles are more effective than any single style by itself.

Attitudes or mental sets are an important influence on the behavior of both workers and supervisors in an organizational setting. Traditionally, attitudes have been thought to influence the behavior of both groups. There is ample reason to question this one-sided causal relationship. Empirical evidence suggests that behavior can also cause changes in attitudes. Both influences must be understood if supervision is to succeed in its essential mission.

KEY CONCEPTS

First-Line Management	Job-Centered Supervision
Direction	Employee-Centered Supervision
Marginal Man	Close Supervision
Man in the Middle	General Supervision
Key Man	Attitudes

GLOSSARY

attitudes Mental sets concerning some fact or state of affairs, based on the relationship between expectations and actual experience (reality).

direction Interpreting plans for others and giving instructions on how to carry them out.

employee-centered An attitude of a manager in which concern for the employee's welfare comes first; concern for output is important but secondary.

job-centered An attitude of a manager in which concern for output and the job to be done is of primary importance; employee welfare is less important.

supervision A major activating function that insures that planned events are understood and are taking place currently.

REVIEW QUESTIONS

1. Where does the management hierarchy begin?
2. Give two or three examples of first-line managers.
3. Why is direction no longer considered a major managing function in modern-day organizations?
4. Mention three widely held current views of the role of the supervisor. Do you agree with them?
5. How have staff activities and union influences altered the role of the foreman? What is the legal position of a foreman?
6. What are some ways that you would suggest to reinforce the supervisor's position as a manager?
7. What is the difference between job-oriented and employee-oriented supervision? Is one superior to the other? Defend your position.
8. Under what conditions would you recommend close supervision? Loose or general supervision?
9. Do you believe changes in attitude cause changes in behavior or that changes in behavior cause changes in attitudes? Explain clearly.

Chapter 20

Incentives

Leadership alone, whether at upper or at supervisory levels, is insufficient to make an organization accept the plans of management and put them into effect with dedication and enthusiasm. The attitude of subordinates toward such objectives as achieving sales and production quotas; reducing tardiness, absenteeism, and quality defects; offering constructive suggestions; and being a part of and identifying with the total organization is influenced by factors other than leadership. One of these is **incentive.** In addition to leadership, it takes incentives to influence people to do what management wants done.

The relationship between various kinds of incentives and employee performance is a complicated and most important one. In industry today there are few jobs in which some type of incentive system is not being applied. Many territorial salesmen work under an incentive pay arrangement; sales personnel in retail establishments often receive bonuses like "PMs" (pushing marked items); a substantial number of factory workers operate under a production bonus plan; an increasing proportion of upper-level managers are offered stock options, bonuses, and profit-sharing opportunities.

Developing and instituting various types of incentives is a *staff* function. Staff specialists and, in large companies, staff departments design and supervise the operation of incentive systems. Within the sales division, for example, there may be a bonus and budgets department that sets sales quotas and establishes bonuses for equalling or exceeding them. Working closely with the company's marketing and forecasting specialist, the bonus and budgets director can establish equitable territorial sales budgets and provide commensurate bonuses. Stock option plans to induce key personnel to enter and remain in the employ of the company, and to promote the success of the business, are generally administered by a stock option committee. In the operating area, work measurement and incentive pay may be handled by a productivity systems department, a specialized staff group within the industrial relations division.

Incentives must be carefully differentiated from motives. Motives were described earlier as "inner drives or urges" based on unfulfilled needs of individuals. They are inherent within each person. Incentives, on the other hand, are external stimuli. Hunger is a motive (internal); an appetizing steak is an incentive (external).

An **incentive** is *an inducement to perform*. It is a stimulus to action, to undertaking an assignment.

The distinction between incentives and motives is a practical as well as a theoretical one. Since incentives are stimuli that spur people to action to satisfy motives, the manager must determine which types of incentives are best suited to satisfy specific kinds of motives. Making this determination requires planning and an understanding of human nature. Developing and selecting appropriate incentives is part of the overall planning of both activating and controlling.

Basically, all incentives are either positive or negative, taking the form of rewards (carrot approach) or punishments (stick approach). A positive incentive arouses a motive to gain some satisfaction; a negative incentive arouses a motive to avoid some dissatisfaction. The use of a positive incentive is generally more effective than the use of a negative one. However, a negative incentive to induce an individual to act in a given way is more effective than no incentive at all. While the prospect of gaining satisfaction is a more powerful inducement than the prospect of avoiding dissatisfaction, a combination of the two is still more effective.

In teaching animals to perform, offering rewards like lumps of sugar encourages them to repeat the performance. On the other hand, slapping a child's hands may be an effective way to discourage his picking up an object that may be harmful to him. As early as 1903 E. L. Thorndike described this dual phenomenon as the **Law of Effect**. According to the Law of Effect, *behavior which is rewarded tends to be repeated, and behavior which is punished tends to be eliminated.*[1]

Psychologist Harry Levinson believes the carrot and stick approach may work well for animals but not for humans because it fails to take into account the deeper emotional components of human motivation. The assumption that people are motivated solely by external rewards and punishments Levinson calls the **Jackass Fallacy**.[2]

OPERANT CONDITIONING (BEHAVIOR MODIFICATION)

There are other researchers and writers who favor the use of positive incentives exclusively. One of these is B. F. Skinner, a behavioral scientist, who

---

[1] E. L. Thorndike, "The Original Nature of Man," *Educational Psychology*, Vol. 1, Teacher's College, Columbia University, Bureau of Publications, 1903.

[2] Harry Levinson, *The Great Jackass Fallacy* (Boston: Division of Research, Graduate School of Business Administration, Harvard University, 1973).

introduced the concept of "positive reinforcement" as a factor in operant conditioning.[3] Based on the Law of Effect, operant conditioning (sometimes called behavior modification) is intended to increase the probability or the frequency of occurrence of a desired response through the technique of **positive reinforcement,** that is, the presentation of rewards.

The basic distinction between classical conditioning (illustrated by Pavlov's salivation experiments with dogs) and operant conditioning concerns the *consequences* of the conditioned response. In classical conditioning, the sequence of events is independent of the subject's behavior. In operant conditioning, rewards occur as a consequence of the subject's response.

Behavior modification has been successfully applied in changing the behavior of rats, pigeons, chimpanzees, and humans under controlled laboratory conditions. Skinner says:

> Up to now it's been most effective in psychotherapy, in handling disturbed and retarded children, the design of classroom management, and in programmed instruction. It is possible that we're going to see an entirely different kind of psychology in industry. It is not something that can be taken over by the nonprofessional to use as a rule of thumb. It requires specific analysis and redesign of a situation. In the not-too-distant future, however, a new breed of industrial manager may be able to apply the principles of operant conditioning effectively.[4]

The behavior (operant) that is desired must be measurable. Hence activities involving ideas or creativity are difficult to deal with in operant terms. The technique lends itself to situations in which a worker has physical tasks to perform repetitively each day. Clerical tasks and most manual activities are of this type; easy to observe and measure, they are more amenable to conditioning.

One widely reported use of PR (positive reinforcement) in industry has been the experience at Emery Air Freight. Small shipments to the same destination fly at lower rates when packed in containers than when sent separately. By encouraging employees to increase their use of containers (from 45 percent to 95 percent of all possible consolidated shipments), Emery realized an annual savings of $650,000. Two factors were instrumental in this success: the use of recognition and rewards such as praise for compliance; and the introduction of feedback, letting employees know the results of their efforts. Of the two contrived reinforcers, continuous feedback, provided daily, has been the more influential producer of results. In

---

[3]B. F. Skinner, "Operant Behavior," *American Psychologist,* Vol. 18, No. 7, 1963, pp. 503–515. See also Skinner's *Contingencies of Reinforcement* (New York: Appleton-Century-Crofts, 1969).

[4]"Conversation with B. F. Skinner," *Organizational Dynamics,* Vol. 1, 1973, pp. 31–40.

fact, whenever Emery stopped providing continuous feedback, performance rapidly reverted to previous low levels. It should be noted that Emery does not use money as a positive reinforcer.

The reinforcement approach to control of human behavior has received sharp criticism and resistance. The major objections have been (1) operant conditioning techniques manipulate people and raise serious ethical considerations; (2) conditioning restricts an individual's freedom of choice; (3) relying exclusively on external rewards conditioning tends to ignore the fact that people can be motivated by the job itself; (4) a continuous reinforcing schedule must be maintained or desired behavior will disappear and revert to its previous state; (5) the cost of this procedure in terms of time, money, and supervision may limit its usefulness.

Positive and negative incentives often take the form of **inducive** and **coercive controls.** Inducive controls are programs or regulations that offer reward for compliance. Examples are bonuses, published recognition, promotions, and other positive forms. Coercive controls, on the other hand, are procedures or rules that require the performance of certain actions, or restraint from actions, in order to avoid penalties for non-compliance. The regulation, "Punching the time card for another employee is grounds for dismissal" is an illustration of a coercive control. Both positive and negative types should be employed if human efforts are to be directed effectively.

In order to recognize and examine the more common incentives, it is helpful to place them into categories for discussion purposes only, accepting the fact that they are interrelated, mutually reinforcing, often overlapping, and seldom employed alone. The major kinds of incentives can be classified as (1) tangible, (2) intangible, (3) group, and (4) negative.

TANGIBLE INCENTIVES

Tangible incentives are easy for people to recognize, lending themselves more readily to human awareness than any other type. They are rewards that can be seen and felt. They are material. An individual can appraise them at actual or approximate real value. Tangible incentives can be subclassified as monetary or non-monetary.

Monetary Incentives

Outranking all other incentives in the frequency of their use and the staff attention given to them are the monetary incentives. For most people in modern society, monetary rewards are the most transferable means of satisfying most of their basic needs. Satisfaction of physiological, security, and social needs can largely be achieved with money. Other incentives tend to have little motivational value if monetary incentives are perceived to be inadequate. Monetary incentives take a variety of forms including salaries, day wages, incentive wages, commissions, production bonuses, profit sharing, and stock options.

Salaries are generally paid bi-weekly or monthly to white-collar workers including office and clerical, and supervisory or higher-level managerial personnel. Employees who draw a monthly salary enjoy higher status than employees who receive a paycheck each week. In addition, the amount of wage one receives also influences his posture within his peer group and the total organization. The size of a paycheck matters a great deal to every worker in the organization, not only for what it can purchase but also for the status it signifies. While "money isn't everything," for most employees it is a very powerful inducement to perform.

Day wages are those paid on the basis of some time unit, such as $3.00 per hour or $20.00 per diem. Among industrial engineers there is a strong belief that day wage workers are not strongly motivated and exert only minimum effort in the performance of their jobs, considerably less than they are capable of producing. Being paid on an hourly basis also carries less status than does a monthly paycheck. This means that day workers, less motivated, tend to produce less than workers on salary. In addition, hourly wage workers usually require closer supervision than workers on incentive pay plans.

Incentive wages are either some type of piece rate that links earnings directly to total units produced, or a kind of production bonus that provides extra payment for output in excess of a quota or for completion in less than standard time.

In American industry, productivity is generally understood to mean the amount of output per worker per unit of time. Increased productivity is considered to be one of the more important economic goals to which our country aspires. Economists tell us that when productivity increases at a faster rate than population growth, the standard of living rises. When productivity increases at a rate faster than the rate of increase in wages, inflation can be controlled and purchasing power of the worker's dollar increases. Labor unions are concerned with advancing the worker's standard of living. Management is concerned with lower costs of production, lower prices to the domestic consumer, and keeping U.S. products competitive in the world market. Both groups, therefore, have an important stake in increased productivity. The key issue is whether productivity can be increased and how. In a 1976 study conducted by the Gallup Poll, 50 percent of the workers interviewed said they could accomplish more each day if they tried, with three out of five in this group indicating they could increase their output between 20 and 50 percent.

Among various industry groups, it is estimated that 27 percent of all production workers are paid on an incentive basis.[5] The figure is about 40 percent in manufacturing plants.

While output of the production worker was increasing 83 percent during the 1960s, productivity of the clerical worker was increasing only 4 percent. One solution, according to training consultants, is incentive pay. However, most non-production jobs cannot be programmed precisely. For individual work measurement, the following conditions must prevail: (1) rate of production is controlled by the person doing the work; (2) relatively continuous supply of work exists; (3) definite procedures for processing work exist; (4) output can be quantified. Efforts are being made to establish standards covering the "facilitating functions" including filing, typing, secretarial work, office routines, and clerical duties, but these have not been too successful thus far.

Aetna Insurance Company's productivity systems department ran a feasibility study on activities associated with issuing insurance policies. It uncovered work flow inefficiencies. Work standards were established. Incentives paid on a weekly basis were put into effect. Before the program was installed, employees had been averaging 11 new contracts each per day. In the first week under incentives, the average jumped to 23.6. Backlog work was reduced to a current basis, personnel was reduced 32 percent through normal turnovers and transfers, and the processing time for a policy was cut from 9 days to 2.[6]

There are some disadvantages to incentive pay, which should be pointed out. Workers do not always produce to their capability under an incentive wage plan. When rates are set liberally workers often restrain themselves in the belief that large bonuses, earned from all-out effort, will eventually result in a cut in the piece rate. They establish a production "bogey," pegging it to a given level so their earnings will not tempt managers to cut rates. The informal work group expects each of its members to comply with the bogey. If any one does not see it this way, the others keep him in line.

Another potential disadvantage of incentive pay is that quality of work may suffer. In order to turn out quantity, incentive pay workers may try to slip through items slightly below standard. Quality standards must be enforced through more rigid inspections. Inspection costs, therefore, are generally a little higher than when people are paid day rates.

---

[5]L. Earl Lewis, "Extent of Incentive Pay in Manufacturing," *Monthly Labor Review*, U.S. Department of Labor, Bureau of Labor Statistics, May 1960.

[6]"Getting the Office Moving with Incentives," *Industry Week*, March 29, 1971, p. 42.

One of the outstanding advantages of incentive wage plans is that employees working under such plans require less supervision. The supervisor is less likely to prod for higher output. Employees can adjust their work pace to their personal needs and requirements. Under these conditions, supervision can be general rather than close.

Despite the advantages, incentive pay has been losing ground to straight-time pay during the past twenty-five years. There are at least three reasons why this is happening. (1) First, machines have been replacing manual labor. **Mechanization,** the substitution of machine for physical effort, has been steadily increasing. Semi-automatic and automatic machines and production lines are common. Conveyors run at pre-determined speeds, pacing the work of individuals. Under these conditions, a person cannot work harder and turn out more. In addition, **automation,** the substitution of machines for physical *and mental* effort, has eliminated many jobs that formerly were piece-rate jobs. (2) Second, some unions oppose incentive pay. While textile, shoe, and steel industry unions strongly favor incentives, other unions have held down their use. The union philosophy, in general, supports hourly rate of pay for workers. (3) Incentive wage plans cause administrative problems. Some jobs are not quantifiable or measureable and therefore cannot be put on piecework. Having some day workers and some pieceworkers causes earnings disparity. Pieceworkers earn more, making day workers dissatisfied. Besides, work standards upon which incentive pay is based must be revised and brought up to date. Any attempt to change work standards is resisted by the affected workers. As the job changes but the standards do not, rates may get to be relatively "loose." Men who work under loose rates can earn a great deal of money without having to work very hard. Day workers, aware of this, become more dissatisfied.

Where feasible, incentive pay plans should be used only where the worker can increase output through his own efforts. In addition, they should pay more for effort that exceeds rather than simply meets standard. Moreover, standards should be fairly determined, and revised when job changes occur. Also, the results of effort in the form of increased pay should reach the worker promptly, preferably in each paycheck. Finally, the plan must be simple enough for workers to understand, and for supervisors to administer.

Commissions are frequently used both to compensate and to motivate. For sales personnel, a *straight commission* basis is similar to a piece rate for a production worker. When a man receives a commission for his efforts, he is paid a percentage of the net sales he produces. If his commission is 5 percent, he will receive that amount on his successful efforts with no ceiling on his ability to earn. Somes sales people receive a *base salary plus commissions.* Others may be guaranteed a *salary against commissions* and receive whichever is higher. Another form of compensation is the *draw against commissions,* which means that each pay period the salesman draws a certain stipend that is credited against his commission account as it accrues. The draw is a type of payment in advance, but is not guaranteed. It is often used as a means of financing a salesman until he can build up his territory or develop a clientele.

A commission rate system can offer one of the strongest incentives to increased effort. It is a very simple plan for employees to understand and for management to administer; earnings can be computed quickly as sales results are achieved. It does have some marked disadvantages, however. A straight commission places a heavy burden on the beginner, who may not earn enough to keep going. He may become discouraged and quit. The draw against commission alleviates this condition somewhat although the beginner may be apprehensive that he will not be able to generate enough commissions to earn his draw. Under a commission type of monetary incentive, earnings tend to be uncertain and can fluctuate widely. For many, the uncertainty about earnings causes worries and a threat to their security needs. They would prefer the certainty of a steady income. For this type of personality, a straight commission would be a disservice rather than an incentive. For a seasoned sales representative, however, a commission arrangement with no ceiling on his ability to earn is a powerful inducement to perform. Many top-flight salesmen indicate that they would not want to work under any system of financial remuneration other than a straight commission. Many of them earn considerably more than their sales managers.

Production bonuses are rewards in addition to the regular type of compensation. They are premiums paid for output or service beyond that which was contracted for. A firm which has had an unusually profitable year may pay Christmas or year-end bonuses to its employees. Except as they are directly related to production, it is doubtful that such bonuses act as incentives. When they are not production-related, they may even be looked upon as acts of paternalism by the employer and as evidence that wages and salaries were lower than they should have been all along.

Many incentive wage and bonus plans have been developed since the turn of the century to cover production workers. Most of them have enjoyed modest success and fallen by the way. Among the better known were the Halsey, Gantt, Taylor, Rowan, Emerson, and Bedaux plans. They are still studied and discussed by students of industrial or production management interested in gaining an historical perspective. Today there are very few companies that use any of these plans.

In place of individual task and bonus plans, company-wide plans have been developed to stimulate productivity, secure widespread employee participation, and achieve cost savings as well. Among the better known are the Scanlon Plan and the Rucker Plan, although both have passed the zenith of their popularity. Increased productivity means a larger wage pool and more money per worker. This implies that increased efficiency, not the number of workers, causes the increment in output. A plant-wide incentive means that earnings of each employee are dependent upon the effort of the entire plant. Increased effort by any one individual brings to him personally only negligible higher rewards.

Profit sharing is a type of incentive program in which individuals participate in the profits of the firm. It has largely taken the place of earlier bonus systems. Beyond some established minimum, a percentage of the company's profits before taxes is paid to each employee as a bonus. Under some plans, the bonus is paid in cash directly to the employee at the end of each year. Under others, called *deferred* plans, the monies are paid into a fund and are distributed as retirement or death benefits. In this way, the company may obtain the advantages of both incentive and fringe-benefit values.

Although profit-sharing plans are not new to American industry, only in recent years have they gained widespread popularity. Some of the best known profit-sharing programs are those of American Motors, Kaiser Steel (both of which are cost-savings plans), Sears, Proctor and Gamble, and Eastman Kodak. Despite their popularity, especially among smaller firms, company-wide profit-sharing plans are believed by most managers to have little incentive value. The company makes contributions only in profitable years. Profits depend on many factors beyond the workers' control or individual performance. Moreover, most employees do not understand how profits are computed and may feel they are being short-changed. When deferred plans are used, employees tend to view profit-sharing as merely another fringe benefit. There is no direct relationship between how diligently they work and how much they receive. Moreover, the time span between performance and reward is too great. From a psychological standpoint, the more closely the reward follows the desired response, and the more clearly it is related to it, the more effective the reward will be. For incentives to be effective, people must be able to see the results now, not at some distance into the future.

Stock options are a type of incentive program in which individuals earn the opportunity to obtain an ownership interest in the firm for which they work. They have become particularly important for middle- and upper-level management people. In general, stock options allow an executive to purchase a specified number of shares at some future time. His cost is based upon a price (usually market value) which existed at the time the options were issued. Thus, if the price of the stock advances during the waiting period, the executive has a built-in profit when he pays for his shares. However, should the market price fall during the option period, he is not obligated to exercise his option. He simply chooses not to buy the shares. In many instances, companies lend executives the money to pay for the shares if they decide to exercise their options. Other firms arrange for payment to be made in partial installments. One method used is a payroll deduction, a sort of interest-free time payment plan, until the shares are fully paid for. While there is an incentive advantage to an executive under a stock option plan, its greater value is to the company as an effective means of attracting and holding key employees.

To remain abreast of the times and to take advantage of changing tax laws, executive stock plans have been changing. The net result has been a move away from restricted and "qualified" stock plans toward "non-qualified" options, "phantom shares," which essentially are stock credits, and "tandem" plans, which combine qualified, non-qualified, and phantom stock plans.

Essentially, a **qualified stock option plan** prescribes an issue price at least equal to the market price of the stock at the time the option is granted; an option period limited to five years; a period of three years the stock must be held by the purchaser before he can sell it and qualify for capital gains consideration; and no deduction for federal income tax purposes by the issuing company. Because of these restrictions, companies have been substituting **non-qualified plans,** which do not require Internal Revenue Service approval, permit greater flexibility, and tax advantages to the issuing corporation. Non-qualified options may be held ten years before they are exercised instead of only five years, meaning that there is more time for the market price to rise above the option price.

Phantom stock enables executives to profit from stock they do not actually own. In its simplest form, in lieu of options, it awards "units" equal to a certain number of *imaginary shares* of company stock. The recipient of units is entitled to the dividends those shares produce annually. Dividend payments are usually accumulated in the executive's account until his retirement. Under some plans, in addition to the dividends the executive receives, on a *deferred* basis, the cash equivalent of the market appreciation over the years of the non-existent shares, or its value in actual shares. As an illustration, assume an employee is awarded 100 units in 1976, when the market price of a common share is $28. If the employee retires some years later, at which time the market price of the stock is $40, he would receive either $1200 in cash ($12 of market price appreciation × 100 units) or 30 shares of stock ($1200 ÷ $40 per share). Outstanding features of the phantom plan are that an executive does not risk a cent of his own, nor does he have to worry about financing the purchase of shares. For the company, phantom distributions are tax deductible when the money is paid out. For the recipient, as with other types of deferred compensation, no tax is due until he retires. At that point, his income is almost certain to be lower, and his tax rate lower. The disadvantage is that he does have to pay the regular income tax rate and not the capital gains rate to which a qualified stock option plan would entitle him. The advantages, however, far outweigh the disadvantages.

The number of qualified stock plans has been declining, while tandem options, non-qualified stock plans, and phantom plans have been increasing in popularity. In 1971 these three types accounted for 31 percent of all stock option plans.[7] By 1972 the number of companies relying solely on qualified stock options had dropped to 49 percent; the other types had risen to 51 percent.

Resembling stock option plans for middle- and upper-level managers are **stock purchase plans.** These programs have objectives similar to those of the stock option plans and cover employees at all levels in the organization. In addition, stock purchase plans increase an employee's sense of identification with the company. In most plans employees can purchase periodically, for cash or through payroll deductions, shares of company stock which give them a stake in ownership—the risks as well as the rewards. In their dual status, employees, as owners, receive quarterly and annual reports, learn about their company from an entirely different perspective, and appreciate more keenly the need for effectiveness and profitability to keep the managerial enterprise system a viable and continuing one.

Non-Monetary Incentives

The second type of tangible incentives consists of those which are non-monetary in character. Like all tangible incentives they are easy to recognize, they are material, and their value can be determined. They do not, however, directly involve "coin of the realm." Non-monetary incentives are exemplified by prizes, recognition pins, trophies, awards, vacation trips at company expense, and similar inducements.

These kinds of incentives have significant motivational value. Often they stimulate motives that are not readily satisfied by purely monetary inducements. In addition, they often involve public display, which helps to satisfy other types of motives that cannot be fulfilled by a paycheck. Thus, to a salesman who is already earning a good income, a set of golf clubs might be a more effective incentive to excel than a cash prize equivalent to their cost. A company-paid trip to Hawaii for an outstanding salesman and his wife might also be a stronger inducement than cash.

Often organizations award scrolls, recognition pins, or certificates of merit for outstanding performance. Youngstown Sheet & Tube Company has a "Pro Program," initiated in March 1972, that gives union employees recognition *and* tangible awards for "extra" individual effort on the job. It is designed not only to encourage productivity gains, but also to enhance the steelworkers' status and security. Recognition is provided in the form of certificates of merit, and by means of in-plant and public announcements.

---

[7]*Industry Week,* February 1, 1971, p. 24.

Coupled with these non-monetary incentives is a monetary one also. Ten shares of stock in the parent company are given out with each Pro award. To give recognition to employees nominated as Pros, but not finally selected by the plant selection committee, a commendation is entered into each nominee's employment record. If three commendations are entered in a calendar year, the employee is awarded five shares of stock.

Bethlehem Steel has PEP program (Pinch Every Penny) designed to reduce employee errors. At one of its mills, during one month steel shipments of poor quality or incorrect specifications cost over $585,000 in customer claims; at another, a cold steel slab fed into a rolling machine caused $90,000 in damage to the machinery; a boiler was operated without water; a crane was run off the end of its runway; an 11-ton steel roll was machined 2 inches too short. To fight such errors and production downtime, employees wear buttons stating "Down with Downtime" and "Watch Your Wasteline." The PEP program also features cost-cutting talks to workers by supervisors.[8]

A much older and more widespread plan to increase worker efficiency is "Zero Defects," or "ZD." At Martin Marietta's plant in Orlando, Florida, in 1962 a quality control engineer named Philip Crosby succeeded in cutting defects on Pershing missiles to half the accepted level. When his boss complained that was still too high, Crosby agreed. "If management tolerates a low standard, people work to that standard. Well, why not a no-defects job?" He persuaded workers in his department to sign a no-defects pledge. They soon surprised the Army by delivering a Pershing missile two weeks ahead of schedule with no detectable defects among its 25,000 parts.[9]

In today's complex defense industry, a simple mistake can lead to million dollar losses. A $1 million Jupiter missile, for example, exploded because of one faulty soldering connection that cost about 50 cents.[10] The central theme in Zero Defects programs is simply "Do it right the first time." Managers have found it can be done if workers are (1) informed that no errors will be condoned; (2) made to understand that every little bolt-tightening or wire-soldering job is very important; (3) given recognition for quality work. The Norden division of United Aircraft Corporation awards red vests to workers in departments that have achieved low error rates. Litton Industries issues lapel buttons with a caricature resembling the fictional character Zorro brandishing a rapier. Such a lapel button indicates to everyone that the wearer has achieved a low error rate and has earned the right to wear the insignia. It acts as an incentive to others to earn that

---

[8]*The Wall Street Journal*, March 16, 1971.
[9]*Time*, November 6, 1964, p. 94.
[10]*The Wall Street Journal*, April 6, 1965, p. 1.

privilege also. Outside the defense and aerospace industries, one encounters such slogans as "Good enough is not good enough," "Less than perfection is imperfection," and "Safety is no accident."

The cost of incentive programs like Zero Defects is relatively small. Estimates range from $1.50 to $10 per employee. Given these low costs, it is not surprising that non-monetary incentives produce greater results, dollar for dollar, than do monetary incentives.

INTANGIBLE INCENTIVES

Beyond some point, both monetary and non-monetary tangible incentives wane in appeal and effectiveness.

When a person is receiving satisfactory take-home wages, additional pay increments become proportionally less effective as an inducement to perform. This is probably truer of older than younger persons. An older person whose children have grown up and left home is less swayed by money incentives. Instead, he has a strong motivation to do a good job and be recognized for the contribution he makes to the company.

Among executives who quit a job and change to another, it has been determined that money ranks as low as fifth among the reasons. More important factors seem to be dissatisfaction with the job itself; poor chance for advancement; conflict, particularly with the boss; and altered duties or status because of corporate reorganization.

One young executive explains his reason for leaving his job as follows:

> I left one company because I felt my mind wasn't being stretched enough on the job. I was twenty-seven at the time. I went to the executive vice president of the company to resign. A few days later he called me into his office. He said: "Look, I've talked to the president about this. This isn't the kind of thing we usually say, and there can't be any promises about it. But we think you may be the president of this company someday. I'll never make it, I'm fifty-five now. But you may. So when you think about leaving, consider that." I know it sounds ridiculous for a man of twenty-seven, but here's what I said to him. "I've always assumed I could get to be president. If I didn't assume that I would have left a long time ago. But what I've decided is that this job just isn't interesting enough. Being president wouldn't satisfy me." I guess it was a pretty egotistical thing to say. I know he was startled. But that was honestly the way I felt about it, and I left.[11]

Another executive put it this way:

> I guess if I had an opportunity to be president of a small company, I might take it—but as always "for the challenge," not the money alone. You reach a point

---

[11]Walter Guzzardi, Jr., "The Young Executives," Part III, *Fortune*, September 1964, p. 162.

where financial remuneration doesn't mean as much as the chance to do things. It isn't the buck that triggers me. It's what you're doing, what you create, what you see in the future.[12]

The young executive wants more freedom to act. Large companies delegate wide fields of action to their divisional and departmental managers. Decisions push up from those levels for approval at the top.

Intelligent management is becoming increasingly aware that many motives cannot be satisfied merely through offering tangible incentives—that many can only be satisfied by intangible inducements which possess greater subjective significance for individuals. Although there may be some interrelationships and interdependence among them, intangible incentives can be classified into two more or less distinct groups: (1) those which are intrinsically significant, and (2) those which are extrinsically significant.

Intrinsically Significant

From an individual's point of view, **intrinsically significant intangible incentives** are *those of a personal nature.* They appeal to individual needs for performance felt to be rewarding in itself. Most of these needs are related to self-esteem. They include the need for self-expression; the need for personal achievement and a sense of accomplishment; the need for challenging work, with the chance to put personal capabilities to use; the desire to make a contribution, to give as well as to receive; and the need for opportunities to satisfy curiosity. Working simply for the enjoyment of work, to perform because the act of performing is itself personally gratifying, is illustrative of incentive that has intrinsic significance. It has meaning and provides satisfaction to the person himself. For capable people, the greatest incentive is often the prospect of achieving something difficult.

Plateaus of successful achievement have been established within the insurance industry. The zenith is called "The Million Dollar Round Table," an industry-wide organization independent of any particular insurance company. To be eligible, a life insurance salesman must sell $1 million of insurance annually. Not only does he receive the usual percentage of premium income for his efforts, but he also becomes a member of this elite group. To a man who makes the Million Dollar Round Table for the first time, it means a deep feeling of personal achievement, an accomplishment, a satisfaction of his ego need, proof to himself that he could do it. For that person, membership in the Million Dollar Round Table is an intrinsically significant intangible incentive.

Asking a skilled artisan or craftsman to handle a very difficult assignment, or to do a job that takes utmost skill and precision, can also be an in-

---

[12]*Ibid.,* p. 192.

tangible incentive that is intrinsically significant to the worker. He welcomes the challenge that the intricate work demands. He can derive satisfaction from his creation. The net result gives him a sense of accomplishment. He is personally proud of the result. He may even feel that only he could have accomplished it.

Extrinsically Significant

From the individual's point of view, **extrinsically significant intangible incentives** are *those of a social nature.* They fulfill social esteem needs, including a feeling of belonging (being part of the "in" group), recognition, and acceptance. These needs are satisfied by *outside* approval of an individual's performance—approval, for example, by one's peer group or by society at large. Extrinsically significant incentives can only be satisfied through social interaction, through social relationships, through the esteem of others.

To the insurance salesman who has become a member of the Million Dollar Round Table, his acceptance into this select group by its members, the recognition given him by colleagues who have not achieved this distinction, and the status recognition granted him by the public are all extrinsically significant. The desire to continue to receive this social approval becomes a powerful inducement for him to retain his position in the Round Table, and to continue to sell $1 million worth of life insurance next year, and the year after. Membership is both an intrinsically *and* extrinsically significant intangible incentive.

For a typical employee, the desire to receive the approval and respect of one's boss is a compelling incentive. In one study it was found that supervisors who gave encouragement to employees to upgrade their performance were rated highest by subordinates. Supervisors who listened to subordinate's problems were ranked a close second.[13] Workers will do certain things, and repress the desire to do others, in order to gain the superior's recognition and approval, and to maintain it for the duration of employment. Supervisors must recognize the validity of this extrinsically significant intangible incentive and provide the climate or opportunity that makes its fulfillment possible.

For most employees the desire to be accepted by both the formal and informal work groups of which they are a part is also a compelling incentive.[14] Everyone likes to feel he is accepted, and believes that no barriers should prevent his being welcomed by his associates and becoming a member of the

---

[13]Yoram Zeira and Ehud Harari, "Planned Organizational Change in Multinational Corporations," *S.A.M. Advanced Management Journal,* Vol. 40, No. 3, Summer 1975, pp. 31–39.
[14]For a more thorough discussion of informal groups, the reader is referred to Chapter 11.

"in" group. Managers can assist in the fulfillment of this social need by grouping workers into teams which are not too small or which comprise an even number rather than an odd number of persons. Often, putting three people together leads to a grouping of two against one. Placing four or six persons together reduces this possibility. All may remain together. Should a pairing-off occur, the probability is that there would be two against two, three against three or four against two. One person would probably not be left completely on the outside.

In addition to social need fulfillment, a security need is also satisfied. As a member of a group, the worker is protected from many external pressures with which he could not successfully deal as an individual. Groups can resist demands for additional output or higher-quality workmanship; an individual would find it difficult. A group unofficially sets the norm for all. Its members agree on the output each will produce so that no one appears less competent than the others, and no one outperforms anyone else. Having set the norm, the group will not tolerate goldbricking or soldiering by any one of its members. It has a strong code of ethics.

To gain group acceptance an individual will do certain things, such as complying with the group norm, and refrain from doing certain things like being "an eager beaver." A waitress may have to agree to go along with the accepted way of pooling and sharing all tips; a clerk may find himself answering the telephone for someone away from his desk. Toffler says, "A great deal of human behavior is motivated by attraction or antagonism toward the pace of life enforced on the individual by the society or group within which he is embedded."[15]

Opportunities for promotion. The opportunity for advancement to positions of greater status or increased responsibility and challenge can be an effective motivator. As we noted in Chapter 17, promotion or advancement is listed as one of Herzberg's motivators. A highly interesting sidelight is that promotion seems to be more rewarding when it is unexpected.

The doors of advancement should be open for all to enter. Moreover, opportunities for moving forward should be created. A policy of "promotion from within," especially in a growth firm, is one way that such opportunities can be developed. Perhaps the steps in the succession upward can be clearly pointed out to members of a department or functional area. This enables them to establish targets of accomplishment based on their capability, experience, ability to get along with others, leadership characteristics, and other criteria for advancement. Promotions should be encouraged by superiors and not blocked. In one large paper products company, a suc-

---

[15]Alvin Toffler, *Future Shock* (New York: Random House, 1970), p. 42.

cessful salesman in one of the branch offices was never recommended for a mangerial position in other branches when vacancies occurred because his manager did not want to lose the substantial sales volume he contributed. In time he left the company and went to work for a competitor. This frequently happens. Although many people are not promoted because they lack the ability to handle a position at a higher level, others with talent are denied the chance because they are extremely proficient where they are, and their absence would be missed by their present superior. Although it is not an easy decision for a superior to make, in justice he must not stand in the way of a capable subordinate. He must make it possible for a competent person to succeed just as he would expect his superior to make it possible for him to climb upward in the organization.

Many alert firms are encouraging employees to keep abreast of changes and new developments in their areas of specialization by joining professional associations and attending their meetings. Many companies are subsidizing the cost of sending their people back to study and improve their capabilities, assuring them that promotions will be the reward for self-improvement. The technical requirements of modern industry indicate that a great many supervisory positions can be handled only by persons who have special training. Some of this specialization can only be acquired away from the job, perhaps by attending classes at a university.

Where unions exist, the chances for a man to move ahead on the basis of his ability and competence are severely limited because of the emphasis on seniority rather than merit. It has been estimated that as high as 80 percent of contracts written between management and unions make seniority the sole factor in determining promotions or layoffs.

Peter Drucker believes that young people who enter business today want more responsibility, more challenge, more self-discipline, and a more demanding job. Rather than having a big title at age 24, a young person wants more rungs on the ladder, because the more rungs there are the more he can climb.[16]

Standard Oil Company of New Jersey maintains an executive review system that is repeated all the way down the organizational ladder to the smallest overseas affiliate. In selecting men for promotion, executives are asked to recommend persons they believe will be able to progress at least *two steps* up the organizational ladder. In theory, this prevents the promotion of a man who is not capable of moving up further. It also reduces the possibility of over-employing his talents at the existing level, or making him feel that he will be getting in above his head in a job that is too big for him. This strategy tends to outwit the Peter principle.[17]

---

[16]Peter Drucker, "Our Top Heavy Corporations," Duns, April 1971, pp. 39–40.

[17]This was discussed in Chapter 12.

Regard for status. There is no denying the value of status to most people, whether at work or away from the work situation. Writers on this subject point out the importance of status to members of every community at all socio-economic levels. **Status** is *the rank or position of prestige one enjoys relative to others.* It is an indicator of one's place in the "pecking order." Studies indicate a close relationship exists between an occupation's prestige in the community and the satisfaction people derive from working in that occupation. In the eyes of the community, doctors, college professors, and lawyers enjoy higher status than businessmen, clerical workers, or blue-collar workers. Within the business organization itself, the higher a person's position in the hierarchy, the higher his status. An executive with high status expects and receives greater deference than one who occupies a lower rung on the ladder.

In Sweden, at Asea, a manufacturer of electrical equipment, company offices have been moved onto the factory floor so that engineers, product-design people, and other white-collar workers share facilities, as well as inconveniences, with blue-collar production workers to reduce status differences between them.

Because status is so important to people, they will work hard to achieve it. Managers should recognize this and attempt to satisfy employees' need for status achievement. The extent to which managers consciously do so will have a direct bearing on their ability to motivate and to control effectively.

A brief examination of some existing status indicators will suggest their importance as incentives.

Job titles. The title "staff assistant" may be more ego-satisfying to an employee than "chief clerk." In society and in business today, we are more prone to identify people by timeclock or social security numbers than by name. It is not difficult for managers to select appropriate titles for various types of work to enhance the status of persons doing that type of work. Appropriate titles can elevate the work from a degrading or demeaning level to one of social acceptance. In one situation brought to the attention of the writer, the task of operating the dumbwaiter in a hospital kitchen was performed by a young man whose job title was "dumbwaiter operator." Before long everyone was calling him "dummy boy" or simply "dummy." After his objections were voiced through the grievance procedure, the title in the job description was changed to "Dietary Worker, Grade III." In time people stopped calling him "dummy."

Pay scale and method of payment. In business organizations, status is related to pay scales: higher pay implies higher status. When managers revise wage scales, they may unknowingly alter the rank of employees. The difference of only a few cents per hour may have a significant effect on the status of a particular job. Moreover, a job that does not require an employee to punch a timeclock has higher status than one that does. After all, executives do not punch timeclocks. There is a strong tendency today away from the use of timeclocks, particularly for salaried employees.

Workers in general consider the piecework pay system demeaning. In Sweden, workers have been clamoring for an end to the piecework system. Yet they do not want a complete changeover to fixed wages. Indications are that they prefer a combination pay package in which 70 to 90 percent is fixed, and additional compensation comes from premiums or production bonuses for meeting or exceeding standards.

Seniority. A person who has worked for a company for a long time generally enjoys higher status than a newcomer. Where seniority is officially sanctioned in terms of first to be promoted and last to be laid off, it becomes a very important status influence. Often it carries with it preference in assignments of day-shift work, overtime, and vacation dates.

Company car. Some firms provide company cars for employees to use in the performance of their duties. Often the make or model of car is a status symbol. An employee of General Motors Acceptance Corporation who had been driving a company-provided Chevrolet proudly announced to this author that he had been promoted and was now driving a Pontiac.

Parking space. In companies that provide parking lots for employees, a highly regarded symbol of status is a reserved parking space, particularly with the employee's name painted on it. In addition, the closer or more convenient its location to the front door, the higher the status implication. Such spaces are usually reserved for top-level persons in the chain of command.

Location of desk. A desk in the front section of a large general office is considered evidence of higher status than a desk in the rear. A shared desk is a mark of lower status than a private desk. A person whose desk is placed back to back with that of another person enjoys lower status than one whose desk is physically separated.

Telephone. Even a simple symbol like the telephone has status connotations. An employee who has no telephone has lower status than one who has the use of one. Moreover, it is a loftier status symbol to have a private telephone than to share a phone with someone. Even the location of the phone may be important when it is shared; to have the phone on your desk carries greater prestige than to have it located on your neighbor's desk and to have to ask him to pass it across to you.

Secretary. It is a mark of status to do work that requires a private secretary. That is higher on the status totem pole than sharing secretarial services or having one's typing done through the stenographic pool.

Private office. A man with a private office enjoys greater prestige than one who shares an office with others. Even the semblance of privacy, such as a low partition surrounding his desk, indicates higher rank in the scheme of things than a desk exposed in an open area. Among executives who have a private office, status can be determined by an examination of the trappings in each office. Desktop pen stands are illustrative: a two-pen desk indicates a young executive on the way up; a three-pen desk means he is approaching the top; and a four-pen stand indicates that he has arrived at the summit. Draperies, wall-to-wall carpets, and original art on the walls are additional top-level status symbols. A man with three armchairs in his office in addition to his own swivel chair at his desk is an important executive, but he is outranked by the VIP whose office is larger and who has a couch in addition to the chairs.

GROUP INCENTIVES

A third category of incentives consists of group incentives. These may be tangible (monetary or non-monetary) or intangible (intrinsically or extrinsically significant). When men work in groups or crews, in which it is difficult or impossible to distinguish between one man's contribution and another's toward total results, a group incentive may be used. The entire group is rewarded for outstanding performance, for exceeding a standard, or beating a quota.

A group incentive is monetary if the reward is a group piece rate or bonus. If the bonus is shared equally by members of the work group, this tends to alter their relationships dramatically. Each person becomes responsible to the others.

Other forms of reward may be tangible non-monetary, or intangible. Suppose there was a sales contest among branch offices in the sales organization. If every salesman in the successful branch was to receive an all-expenses-paid trip to Bermuda, the group incentive would be tangible but non-monetary. Should the contest be one in which published rankings of group achievement appeared in the company house organ, or in sales bulletins to all sales representatives, it would be an intangible incentive, and it could very well be intrinsically as well as extrinsically significant. Departments in factories are often ranked in terms of safety records, zero defects, and similar achievements. If workers are told that all members of the winning department will also receive an award or recognition pin, a non-monetary tangible incentive has been added. Thus a combination of group incentives is often utilized. *Inter-group competition* can be an effective way to actuate people and direct them toward a purposeful goal. It is far more effective than competition among individuals within a group. In fact it is doubtful that planned competition among individuals produces beneficial results sufficient to offset the side effects, which tend to be highly negative.

Group incentives seem to work better when groups are small. There is a comraderie, a closeness, and a willingness of one to come to the aid of another if necessary. In a factory or manufacturing plant, group incentives are less effective when groups are large. There is less cohesiveness, and an individual worker feels his personal increased effort only produces a reward for someone else, probably less capable or less inclined to give his best efforts.

NEGATIVE INCENTIVES

The last major category comprises negative incentives. All inducements are basically either positive or negative, the former involving rewards and the latter associated with punishment or threat of punishment.

A list of various negative incentives includes suspension, layoff, demotion, transfer, firing, reprimand, loss of promotion, no pay increase, undesirable work shift, isolated work station, and fines or other penalties for rule infractions.

Although one tends to think of negative incentives as being undesirable, without their presence positive incentives would be much less effective. Without penalty for failure there is less incentive for success. If there were no coercive controls to restrict certain types of action, nor any penalties for non-compliance with established procedures, overall organizational performance would sink to a level approaching mediocrity. People would do only what was necessary "to get by." A situation would develop in which the efficient and the inefficient were rewarded equally. From a human relations standpoint, there would be much less respect for authority of any kind. Effective direction of human efforts would become more difficult and, in many instances, perhaps impossible to achieve. This applies to the informal as well as the formal organization.

It is essential to understand that all negative incentives must be directed toward positive ends. Their purpose is no different from that of any positive incentive previously discussed. The aim of placing any constraint upon individual or group action is to assure effective implementation of existing plans in order to attain desired results. It must also be recognized that people cannot be expected to maintain a high level of performance if motivated *solely* by the desire to avoid the threat implied in negative incentives.

Despite improved results that are obtained when negative inducements are coupled with positive ones, a manager should be aware that negative incentives can produce undesirable side effects. To protect themselves against possible recrimination for any act that could be questioned, subordinates tend to "cover their tracks." They find ways to justify what they have or have not done and may produce witnesses to substantiate their position. If an employee is of a nervous or anxious disposition, the fear of losing his job threatens his basic security needs and can cause serious mental and emotional stress that may even require medical or psychiatric attention. He becomes a less effective worker. Fear of penalties for doing or suggesting something that could be misinterpreted tends to discourage initiative and creativity. Improperly used, therefore, negative incentives can be counter-productive. Both the individual and the institution suffer.

As a practical matter, the use of negative incentives, as part of a total incentive system, may be limited by contractual arrangements including union agreements. To demote, fire, or lay off a worker may require union approval, or may have to follow prescribed procedures. A layoff, for example, may be determined by seniority rights provided in existing contracts.

MORALE

Developing and installing a well-conceived system of incentives is a necessary function in activating. In a well-managed enterprise, in which leadership is properly exercised and carefully selected incentives are skillfully applied, the organization achieves good morale. **Morale** is the willingness of members of the group to seek their individual satisfactions by pursuing the purposes for which the group exists. The greater the willingness, the higher the morale; the lower the willingness, the lower the morale.

Some behavioralists interpret management's attitude toward employees to mean "management's responsibility for the feelings and morale of people is secondary."[18] This is a misinterpretation of managerial goals. Modern managers are deeply concerned about human interests and organizational morale. But managers cannot and should not be held responsible for the *total* well-being of employees. That would be asking for the impossible. They are responsible, however, for exercising great care *to create a work environment* that enables employees to gratify many personal aspirations while on the job and encourages them at the same time to contribute as fully as possible to enterprise objectives. It is only in this sense that enterprise objectives are primary and feelings of employees are secondary. Making employees happy is not the primary objective of the managing process in a profit-oriented enterprise.

SUMMARY

In an organizational setting, a superior manager at any level in the hierarchy is likely to be a superior leader also. Leadership alone, however, will not cause members of the organization to strive for organizational goals. It requires leadership coupled with appropriate incentives to get individuals to do what their leaders want done. Especially is this true when individuals affiliate with an organization primarily for economic reasons, to make a living, rather than for altruistic reasons.

Simply stated, incentives are either positive or negative inducements to perform. Sometimes the former has been called "offering the carrot" and the latter "applying the stick."

---

[18]Edgar A. Schein, *Organizational Psychology* (Englewood Cliffs, N. J.: Prentice-Hall, 1965), p. 49.

Positive incentives can be categorized as tangible, intangible, and group rewards. Tangible incentives are those which can easily be seen, felt, and evaluated. Usually they take some monetary form like wages, commissions, piece rates, profit sharing, stock options, and stock purchase plans. Many tangible incentives are non-monetary and stimulate motives that are not satisfied by monetary inducements. Particularly is this the case when people are already earning good salaries or wages. Awards, loving cups, trophies, zero-defects pins, certificates of merit, and so on, are examples of tangible non-monetary incentives.

Intangible incentives can be separated into two groupings, although they are often interrelated. Those which are important to an individual for personal reasons are called intrinsically significant and include the need to satisfy self-esteem, personal achievement, personal expression, individual accomplishment, and similar drives. Those which are of a social nature and can only be satisfied by outside approval are called extrinsically significant. Included are a feeling of belonging, recognition, group acceptance, esteem of others including one's boss, opportunities for promotion, and a regard for status.

Group incentives may be tangible, intangible, or combinations of both. Examples are group bonuses to be shared, published rankings of competing groups in an organization, and various forms of group recognition.

Negative incentives are always to be viewed as being directed toward positive ends. Constraints are placed on individual or group action to insure effective implementation of action that is designed to achieve desired results. They should be used with great discretion so as not to cause harmful, unintended side effects. Improperly implemented, negative incentives can be counterproductive.

Capable leadership coupled with appropriate incentives should produce good organizational morale. This means that members of the organization willingly strive for institutional goals because personal goals are also being gratified.

KEY CONCEPTS

Law of Effect	Non-Qualified Stock Options
Jackass Fallacy	Phantom Stock
Operant Conditioning	Tandem Options
Positive Reinforcement	Intrinsically Significant Incentives
Inducive Controls	Extrinsically Significant Incentives
Coercive Controls	Status
Tangible Incentives	Group Incentives
Profit Sharing	Negative Incentives
Qualified Stock Options	Morale

GLOSSARY

automation   The substitution of machines for physical and mental effort.

coercive controls   Procedures, rules, and regulations that require actions or restraint from actions to avoid penalties for non-compliance.

extrinsically significant incentives   Intangible incentives of a social nature.

incentive   An inducement to perform.

inducive controls   Programs or procedures that offer rewards for compliance.

intrinsically significant incentives   Intangible incentives of a personal nature.

Law of Effect   The phenomenon, described by E. L. Thorndike, that rewarded behavior tends to be repeated, and unrewarded or punished behavior tends to be eliminated.

mechanization   The substitution of machines for physical effort.

morale   The willingness of members of a group to seek individual satisfactions by pursuing the purposes for which the group exists.

operant conditioning   Modifying behavior by offering rewards or punishments as a consequence of the subject's response.

positive reinforcement   The use of a positive external reward as a stimulus to increase the probability or frequency of occurrence of a desired response.

status   The rank or position of prestige one enjoys relative to others in the social order.

stock option   The right usually given to an executive to purchase shares in a corporation at some future date at a price based on their market value at the time the option is issued.

tangible incentives   Inducements that are material, either monetary or non-monetary.

REVIEW QUESTIONS

1. The carrot-and-stick approach to motivating people has been called the great Jackass Fallacy. What is your view?
2. What is operant conditioning? Do you favor its use?
3. What conditions must prevail in order to standardize clerical output?
4. What are some advantages and disadvantages to incentive pay programs?

5. Explain the phantom stock plan. Would you like to share in one? Why?

6. Give an example of an intrinsically significant incentive. An extrinsically significant one.

7. List some status indicators that are important to people on the job.

8. Are negative incentives useful to a manager? Are they necessary? Why?

9. What is morale? How is it produced in an organization? How can it be improved?

Chapter 21

Communication

Communication is a very broad and pervasive activity, which cuts across all areas of the organization and connects the organization with the external community. It is so commonplace we tend to take it for granted, yet no organization could exist without it. Interaction could not occur without some type of communication, and the development of highly complex organizations would be impossible.

Normal interaction between people requires some type of communication. Workers may converse simply to pass the time of day. At other times, communication may be more purposeful. When used to achieve management objectives, communication becomes a managing function. Communication is a necessary ingredient in all managing activities.

In person-to-person relationships, a manager must convey thoughts, ideas, feelings, and decisions whenever he is planning, organizing, activating, or controlling. To explain what has to be done; to write a memorandum to a superior; to interview an applicant for a position; to address a meeting of department heads; to give a talk to the Kiwanis or Rotary Club; to discuss the renewal of a bank loan with a bank officer; to listen to the complaint or grievance of an employee—all require communication.

Keeping employees informed about company activities, policies, and intentions can make "big business" of communications programs. The International Association of Business Communicators estimates that more than 15,000 employee newspapers, magazines, and pamphlets are published in the United States.[1] Buick Motor Division of GM purchases an early morning hour on the Flint, Michigan radio station and presents a show called "The Factory Whistle" to give workers the time, weather, sports, traffic news, and information about Buick. American Telephone and Telegraph Company uses television to produce a daily fifteen-minute news show, and a continuous "bulletin board" of spot announcements, aimed primarily at corporate headquarters employees.[2]

---

[1] *Industry Week*, December 7, 1970, p. 34.
[2] *Ibid.*, p. 35.

In organizations, people provide information in a variety of ways including memoranda, policy statements, forecasts, reports, and computer printouts. In recent years a computer-based system for providing data, known as a "management information system," or MIS, has come into prominence. An organization can have more than one MIS. It is common to observe the existence of a personnel information system, financial information system, production information system, and others covering additional specialized areas. Where several exist, they can be regarded as subsystems of the overall corporate MIS.

THE PROCESS OF EFFECTIVE COMMUNICATION

Every production process has two outputs: the *product* and *information*. When information is interchanged, communication occurs. Various estimates, ranging as high as 75 to 95 percent, have been made of the amount of time the average person spends either sending or receiving information.

Communication is *an interchange of thoughts and information between two or more persons*. The critical components of this definition are the terms "interchange" and "two or more persons." Where an executive is personally involved, interchange takes place between himself and at least one other person. For *interchange* to occur, the *recipient must respond* in some manner.

Communication, therefore, is a dynamic two-way process: *transmission* and *response*. When a person simply expresses himself, he may not be communicating. Expression is a one-way release; communication implies a reciprocal participation. If the idea received by the subordinate is the one his superior intended to convey, *effective* communication has taken place. If the idea received is not the same as the one transmitted, effective communication has not occurred. In that event, the sender has not communicated; he merely has expressed himself.

The process of communicating, and the mechanics involved in it, can be very elaborate. In its simplest form it comprises three elements: (1) sender, (2) message, and (3) receiver. In responding to the message, the receiver may then become the sender, while the original sender becomes the receiver; hence the two-way process. This is indicated in Figure 21-1.

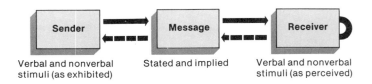

Figure 21-1.   The basic communication process.

In their respective roles in the communicating process, both the sender and the receiver should seek answers to the following questions in order to achieve effective communication:

1. What is the core thought or gist of the message?
2. What facts or data support the thrust of the message?
3. What is *implied* as well as stated?
4. What response is the message expected to produce?

In order for the receiver of the message to respond appropriately, he must rely upon his senses (taste, touch, sight, smell, hearing, kinesthesis) to gain its real meaning. The data of sensation produce a mental image, an awareness of the environment. This process of constructing meaning from sensation is called **perception** by the psychologist. The senses used most frequently in perception by a potential respondent are those of sight and hearing.

Purposes of Communication

From the perspective of a business executive who has a responsibility to employees, stockholders, community, suppliers, customers, and various government agencies, the basic objectives of communication are threefold: (1) to inquire, (2) to inform, and (3) to persuade.

A manager must seek and acquire pertinent data (inquire); provide information to others and develop understanding (inform); and initiate or reinforce attitudes and action (persuade). Whether one works in the order department, credit and collections, personnel, production, marketing, public relations, finance, or purchasing; whether the form of communication is formal or informal, verbal or non-verbal, these are the basic objectives of communication.

In dealing with subordinates, a manager who achieves both the second and third objectives of communication discovers that he has successfully developed teamwork.[3]

$$(\text{to inform}) + (\text{to persuade}) = \text{teamwork}$$

Communication Skills

Communication skills deemed important by executives include listening, non-verbal, speaking, reading, and writing.[4] The typical manager's use of these communication modes has been studied. One such study specifies the

---

[3]Various types of teamwork are discussed in Chapter 13.
[4]James A. Belohlov, Paul O. Popp, and Michael S. Porte, "Communication: A View from the Inside of Business," *The Journal of Business Communication*, Vol. 11, No. 4, Summer 1974, pp. 53–59.

percentage of time devoted to each basic skill as (1) listening—32 percent; (2) body language (non-verbal)—30 percent; (3) speaking—21 percent; (4) reading—11 percent; and (5) writing—6 percent.[5] Earlier studies indicate that as much as 45 percent of an executive's time is spent in listening.

One authority has indicated that after listening to a ten-minute talk students are only 25 percent efficient in remembering the substance of the talk.[6] Research also shows that managers, like most people, are notoriously poor listeners.

Most of us have developed common bad listening habits, some of which are: (1) assuming the subject will be boring; (2) tuning out the speaker because of his delivery; (3) becoming subjective and allowing emotion to disrupt the listening process; (4) concentrating solely on facts and excluding principles or generalizations (seeing the trees but not the forest); (5) being distracted or allowing the mind to wander; and (6) pretending to be attentive. Making a determined effort to avoid these deficiencies can improve a manager's listening efficiency above the 25 percent level. This would be a decided plus for managers since employees strongly desire to be heard, very often on matters that do not pertain to their work.

KINDS OF COMMUNICATION

While numerous classifications can be developed to describe various types of communication, for our purposes it is sufficient simply to say that communication is either formal or informal.

Formal Communication

Formal communication is *direct* communication between sender and respondent. This type of communication takes several forms. Chief among them are verbal and non-verbal.

Verbal communication.   Verbal communication may be either written or oral. *Conversation* is probably the most common type of verbal communicating. *Writing* is a second widely practiced form of verbalization. Filing cabinets in offices contain substantial evidence of correspondence, memoranda, bulletins, reports, orders, billings, catalogs, drawings, and other documents that are of a written or facsimile nature.

Is oral communication more effective or less effective than written communication? Is a combination of oral and written more effective than either one alone? One research study indicates that the oral–written combination is never inappropriate and is effective most of the time. It is especially useful in situations requiring immediate action or where follow-

---

[5]Paul Mali, *Managing by Objectives* (New York: John Wiley & Sons, 1972), p. 287.
[6]Ralph G. Nichols, "Listening, What Price Inefficiency?" *Office Executive*, April 1959, pp. 15–22.

up is desirable. The "written only" method was most effective where information required future action, or where the information was general. The "oral only" method was ranked most effective for reprimands (disciplinary action) or for settling a dispute among employees about a work problem.[7]

Non-verbal communication. Non-verbal communication takes myriad forms. Contrary to popular belief, speaking and writing are not the only ways that people communicate directly with each other. Silence, gestures, and demonstrations are also effective, direct ways to communicate.

Silence is often an effective way to convey a message. A communication may even be planned in such a manner that silence is an intended response. When a sales manager enters a meeting to address a group of salesmen who are busily talking to each other, he may ascend the stage, take a position at the lectern, and say nothing. The audience will soon heed his presence and his silence. They perceive that he is waiting for them to simmer down before he begins his address. A written invitation extended to a group of people to attend a conference may state, "Please advise if you are unable to be present," or "regrets only." If no replies are forthcoming, the respondents' silence signifies they will be present.

Gestures are frequently utilized to convey meaning. Facial expressions; a wink; nod of the head; shrug of the shoulder; look of dismay; whistle; display of emotion such as anger or tears; grimace; sneer; hand signals; and similar expressions are all types of gestures or physical actions (body language) that are intended to convey a message. Thus, when a manager asks a subordinate to do something, the latter may respond with some type of gesture that conveys directly to his boss that he is pleased or displeased.

Demonstration is another effective way to deliver a message without verbalizing. Showing a person how to operate a machine or piece of equipment is frequently more effective than telling him or writing directions for him. In other words, actual performance can itself be a way of communicating. The manager or trainer in essence is indicating, "Observe what I do and you will learn how to do it also."

Informal Communication

Informal communication is *indirect* communication and is generally referred to as the **grapevine.** The grapevine coexists with the formal communication system. It is an expression of the natural tendency of people to communicate. Contrary to the popular conception that grapevine information is inaccurate, research indicates that in normal work situations over three-fourths of grapevine information is accurate. One researcher claims grapevine ac-

---

[7]Dale A. Level, Jr., "Communication Effectiveness: Method and Situation," *The Journal of Business Communication,* Fall 1972, pp. 19–25.

curacy of 80 to 99 percent for non-controversial company information and somewhat lower for personal or highly emotional information.[8] A possible explanation for the reported accuracy of the grapevine is that the information tends to satisfy social and security needs of individuals and, therefore, does not become distorted in transmission.

There are a number of interesting positive features of the grapevine which can be noted. It is fast. It cuts across all organizational lines. It is effective. It provides managers with feedback.

The most important undesirable or negative feature of the grapevine, one which can cause friction, dissension, and misunderstanding, is **rumor.** Rumor is grapevine information of the scuttlebutt variety: hearsay information widely disseminated without an authoritative source. It contains just enough fact to make it believable, or distortion of fact presented in a logical way that makes it credible. Since rumor generally is incorrect, the best way to combat its negative influences is to uncover its cause and to present the correct facts, as early as possible, from an authoritative source in a formal communication.

Feedback

Some types of response to communication are referred to as "feedback." Feedback can occur in several ways. It can be formal such as verbal reports requested by higher levels of management of lower levels. When a manager asks subordinates to evaluate a particular proposal and then receives spoken or written comments, the totality of responses constitutes feedback. Feedback can also be formal and non-verbal, positive or negative. Drooping eyelids in response to a boring speech, fidgeting, and even silence are examples of feedback that should tell the manager something—that he is not getting through to the intended recipients, that he is really not communicating with them. Letting employees know how they are doing, perhaps through periodic reviews and appraisals, is another important form of feedback.

When feedback is informal, it is part of the indirect communication system that we have described as the grapevine. Complaints and expressions of hostility or resentment that permeate the informal communication system and eventually come to the attention of managers in an unofficial way are examples of feedback that travels the grapevine.

BARRIERS TO COMMUNICATION

Communication flow may be impeded by three types of barriers that are usually present. These can be categorized as (1) physical, (2) personal, and (3) semantic.

---

[8]Keith Davis, *Human Behavior at Work*, 4th ed. (New York: McGraw-Hill, 1972) p. 263.

Physical barriers are environmental influences such as distance, distracting noises, interference (jamming) that leads to garbled transmission, and other physical limitations.

Personal barriers are socio-psychological, based on judgments, emotions, stereotypes, bias, and similar individual values. People see and hear what they are "programmed" to see and hear by virtue of their personality and experience. Aronson identifies socio-economic status as an important cause of prejudice.[9]

Semantic obstacles arise because symbols, including words, can have a variety of meanings. They are subject to multiple inferences and meanings. These, too, are the result of differences in personality, experience, and cultural background.

Let us list and examine some of the specific barriers to effective communication.

1. **Distortion.** Sometimes distortion occurs because of mechanical failure such as defects in the optical system, or false reproduction caused by change in the wave form of a signal. When confusion exists because of a twisting of the true meaning of an idea or concept, it can sometimes be overcome by empathy—putting oneself into another's position.

2. **Filtering.** This is a sifting of information to make it appear more favorable (or unfavorable) than it really is.

3. **Overloading.** The communication system is taxed by increasing the number of communications transmitted through the organization. Increasing the number does not necessarily increase the flow.

4. **Layers.** The number of levels through which a communication must travel often affects the action that will result.

5. **Semantics.** Many words have multiple meanings that vary with the situation in which they are used. Take the word "hot," for example. A person may say, "I am hot," meaning warm. A stove may be hot, indicating a greater degree of heat than in the first usage of the word. A basketball player may pump in six consecutive field goals and be described as hot. Or, you may do something and describe the results as "not so hot," meaning less than favorable. Hot merchandise (stolen), hot sauce (spicy), and hot under the collar (irked) show additional connotations of the word hot. You can think of many others.

Some words have meaning in one language or one culture and may have no meaning or an entirely different meaning in another. In the United States, a closet is a place to store clothing; in England it means a toilet. There are words for which no counterpart exists in any other language, and still other words which lose their original meaning in translation.

---

[9] Elliott Aronson, *The Social Animal* (San Francisco: W. H. Freeman and Co., 1972) p. 186.

6. **Routing.** Generally, the more circuitous the route, the greater is the barrier to effective communication.

7. **Timing.** To obtain results, some messages should be released simultaneously to everyone; others should be released selectively according to a predetermined schedule.

8. **Interpretation.** Often the intended meaning of a communication is changed through one's perception of the intended meaning (inference). Communications are interpreted in the light of one's own subjective evaluation or experience.

9. **Readability.** When words of ten syllables are spoken, and long complicated sentences are written, it becomes very difficult for the average person to comprehend the messages. Communications should be tailored to fit the language development and comprehension levels of their intended receivers.

10. **Abstraction.** When anything is omitted in the description of an actual situation, whether intentionally or not, abstraction occurs. To know what a headache is, one must have experienced a headache. If you describe a headache, your narrative would be an abstraction of reality. The abstracting process omits details so that we communicate about reality as we conceive of it, not as it actually exists.

Abstracting can be a very useful process when employed as a basis for classifications. Examine Figure 21-2 and consider the various levels of

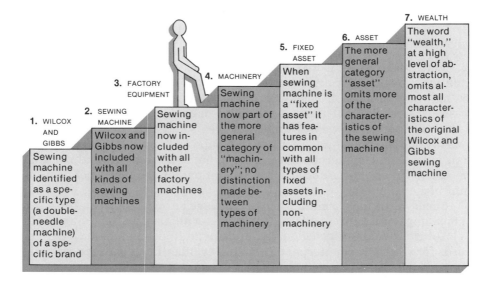

Figure 21-2. The abstraction staircase.

abstraction[10] used in classifying a sewing machine. At the base of the staircase, the first level of abstraction, the sewing machine is a very specific one, a Wilcox & Gibbs, double needle machine. At higher levels of abstraction on the staircase, the meaning of "sewing machine" gradually changes to a very general category as specific details are omitted. At the highest level, the original characteristics of the object have almost completely disappeared and the sewing machine now is simply included in the concept of "wealth."

CHANNELS OF COMMUNICATION

Channels of communication indicate the direction of communication flow. In most business organizations there are four directions of flow: (1) downward, (2) upward, (3) lateral, and (4) diagonal. These are depicted in Figure 21-3. Let us turn our attention to each of them.

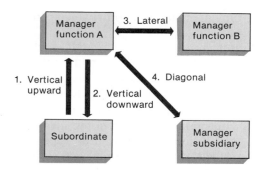

Figure 21-3. Communication as a four-directional flow.

Downward Communication

Downward communication is frequently called *top–down communication* since the flow is from upper to lower levels in the organization structure. Formal channels of communication follow the structure of authority relationships. In the typical situation of downward communication, information must go "through channels," through the formal chain of command. Someone issues a directive or request to a subordinate who, in turn, transmits the information to his subordinate, and so on down the line to the ultimate recipient who is expected to respond in some particular way.

Top–down communication, therefore, tends to be **directive,** to have the purpose of initiating activity. It is an integrating force that ties together dif-

---

[10]The level of abstraction concept was introduced as the "structural differential" by Alfred Korzybski. See his *Science and Sanity, An Introduction to Non-Aristotelian Systems and General Semantics,* (International Non-Aristotelian Library Publishing Company, 1933), Chapter 25.

Table 21-1. Information loss at successive levels
of a company hierarchy

Organizational level	Percentage of information received
Board of directors	100
Vice-presidents	63
General supervisors	56
Plant managers	40
General foremen	30
Workers	20

ferent levels of the corporate structure. By means of downward communication top-level managers disseminate corporate objectives, policies, procedures, and other pertinent unifying information that fosters stability and uniformity within levels.

Downward communication is not free of difficulties or limitations. Following are some typical obstacles to downward communication.

Abstraction. As information passes through successive levels in the hierarchy, particularly in a multi-plant or multi-national firm, changes occur in interpreting and re-transmitting. Messages may reach the ultimate recipient in greatly modified or even distorted form.

A study covering 100 representative companies indicates that a tremendous loss occurs as information flows from top levels through successively lower levels.[11] An adaptation of the results appears in Table 21-1. An average of only 20 percent of the communication sent downward through 5 successive levels below the board of directors reached the worker level in the 100 companies surveyed.

Lack of understanding by subordinates. Uncertainty can be present as to whether the communication applies to everybody or just certain people. Is it simply for information purposes and enlightenment, or should it be acted upon? Should the information stop at that level, or should it be transmitted to levels lower in the hierarchy?

Creditability of the source. As perceived by the recipient, if the originator of the message is considered to be an expert, to be trustworthy, and to have the requisite authority, the communication will be acted on quite differently than it would be if the opposite perceptions were held. Status considerations also affect credibility. A communication from a person of high-level rank carries more weight than one from a person with low-level rank. Prejudice,

---

[11]Ralph G. Nichols, "Listening Is Good Business," *Management of Personnel Quarterly*, Vol. 1, No. 2, Winter 1962, pp. 2–9.

too, is a factor. Subordinates are more readily influenced by persons they like. They resist being persuaded by someone they dislike.

Order of presentation of material. If two or more messages follow in succession, the order of presentation influences the effectiveness of downward flow. There exists a **primacy effect** in which the first communication is more effective because it tends to "inhibit" or block the learning or comprehension of the second. There is also a **recency effect** in which the most recent information is more effective because of the phenomenon of "retention." The *interval* of time between the two communications can be a *determining factor.* A short interval between two messages or instructions favors the primacy effect. If there is a long interval between the two communications, and a decision must be made immediately after receiving the second, the recency effect is favored.

Timing.   Communication released at an inappropriate time may be ineffective. Obviously, a request to employees to increase efficiency in the plant would carry little weight if the employees were about to go out on strike.

Upward Communication

Upward communication is often called *bottom-up communication* because the direction of flow is from lower levels to successively higher levels in the organization. Top management depends upon a steady stream of information from all areas in order to make intelligent corporate decisions. Effective upward communication furnishes management with quick and accurate reports on what is happening at lower levels. Accountability, in which a superior expects a subordinate to account for the way he has carried out his assignments, may be involved. The subordinate is obliged to keep the superior well informed and may use progress reports and summaries to do so. Managers should encourage free flow of upward communication. Subordinates could then express their opinions and offer suggestions for improvements. Under such circumstances, communications may take the form of summaries, proposals, and recommendations.

A banking executive contends that an employee regards being in on things as second only to obtaining a decent wage as the most desirable characteristic of a job. "Being in on things" implies upward communication as well as downward communication. Both help to establish an environment of high performance, initiative, and a feeling of importance.

> If what you're doing is OK, you'll get credit. If what you're doing is not OK, you'll get credit for not hiding it and you'll get instructions on how to correct it.[12]

[12]Sam D. Young, President of the El Paso National Bank, as quoted in "Closed Loop," *MBA Magazine,* July/August 1974, p. 8.

Bottom–up communication, then, tends to be **non-directive** and cannot, per se, initiate any activity. It is of a questioning or reporting nature. Written grievances, suggestion systems, complaints, and union publications serve as means of upward communication. They provide management with facts and data upon which to make decisions. They are the needed feedback management seeks.

Like downward communication, bottom–up communication also has limitations. These may take the following forms.

Abstraction. Subordinates have a tendency to condense or summarize material which their superior must read. They may have been instructed to submit reports in digest or summary form because the superior is pressed for time. The condensed version may omit some important details. Furthermore, subordinates tend to withhold information which they think is unpleasant and which would displease. Distortions and covering-up occur. Sometimes distortions are deliberate to avoid blame or self-incrimination; at other times, they are the result of coloring or personal bias that places data in a favorable light. The subordinate feels this is what the superior is expecting or would prefer to hear.

Status considerations. Unsure of what is expected of him, a subordinate may remain silent or communicate in a vague or general way rather than risk his reputation by reporting something which may make him appear incompetent.

Barriers. It may be difficult to obtain a face-to-face meeting with a superior who is a busy person and whose time is valuable. The subordinate may have to make an appointment. He may have difficulty getting past the secretary, who wants to know the purpose of the visit. Psychological and social barriers, including those attached to membership in the informal organization, discourage upward flow of communication. The subordinate must not lose face with his fellow workers, who may misinterpret his motives for seeing the boss. The superior himself may become a barrier to effective upward communication flow by failing to demonstrate "listening skill." He may fail to attend to what is being communicated to him. As a result, he deprives himself of valuable information and unwittingly discourages future upward flow of information from lower levels.

Lateral Communication (Horizontal Communication)

Sometimes called "cross communication," lateral communication is another direction of communication flow that is essential for efficient operations. This type cuts across departments or functional areas. It takes place among people who are at the same level in the management hierarchy. The manager of production, for example, must maintain communication liason with managers in sales, accounting, or purchasing. Without lateral communication, many important functions could not be coordinated. Control would be extremely difficult and cumbersome, if not impossible, to achieve. Mistakingly, top-level managers tend to view annual reports to stockholders as a type of lateral rather than bottom–up communication. They should revise their perceptions to reflect their actual relationship to the shareholders from whom their authority is derived.

Lateral communication can be facilitated in several ways. One of the simplest would be for a high-level manager to send copies of essential communications to all interested parties. From his point of view, he is sending information to several subordinates at the same time. From their point of view, as colleagues on the same managerial level, they receive the information simultaneously and are all equally well informed. Another means to insure horizontal communication is to use committees, conferences, and conventions in which people, particularly those from different geographic areas, can be advised what is going on in the same functional areas in other parts of the country and other parts of the world.

In large organizations, lateral communication is very difficult to achieve. As a business organization grows and becomes more stratified, often the only sharing of ideas and interaction between groups is at the very top. Very often field managers in large companies do not really know their counterparts in another division, let alone what they are doing, even though they may all work in the same city. Finding ways to overcome this is one of management's biggest communication jobs. The president of Rockwell Manufacturing Company states it this way:

> We're also continually trying to create the means by which ideas can be shared and communicated across the organization between managers at these levels.
>
> There's a very human tendency for specialists to hang together and ignore, or even actually resist, idea inputs from "outsiders." It's difficult to overcome, but we know it's worth it: We've found there's a direct correlation between a manager's horizontal communications ability and his potential for advancement.[13]

In universities, hospitals, government offices, the military, civic organizations, and almost all other organizations, lateral communication is almost non-existent. The statement that the left hand is often unaware of what the right hand is doing is almost a truism in the organizational setting.

Diagonal Communication

The fourth direction of communication flow is diagonal. While not employed as frequently as vertical and horizontal channels, diagonal communication is important, nevertheless, to people in the formal organization who can neither send nor receive messages effectively through other channels.

---

[13]"Rockwell Report," The Wall Street Journal, December 12, 1966.

In the multiple-line or functional-authority situation, diagonal communication takes place. Recall the case described in Chapter 14 in which the comptroller of the company wanted to make a study of sales costs and requested all salesmen to send special reports directly to his attention instead of going through regular channels in the sales chain of command. In this situation, the direction of communication flow from salesmen to comptroller's office was diagonal rather than vertical upward and then horizontal. In terms of saving time, effort, and cost, the advantages of diagonal communication are apparent.

The task force is another situation that readily lends itself to diagonal communication. Task force members, it will be recalled, tend to have equal status without regard to formal rank while they are members of the special project group. In their role as members of the task force, they are not subject to the authority of their department head or hierarchical superior. If input or cooperation is requested by them of top-level managers of various functional areas, the response comes as a memorandum "to all task force members."

In conglomerates, communication between parent company and subsidiaries that are not wholly owned is neither vertical nor lateral: the channel of communication is diagonal.

The importance of diagonal communication can again be noted in multinational and multi-market companies. At Eaton Corporation, with operations in twenty-two countries, plans and policies are made on the basis of major product groups without regard to geography. Communication between plants within each product group, and among product groups, is diagonal in flow.

Continuing interaction between people is necessary for a business organization to survive. Communication makes it possible for interaction to occur. To a business leader at any level in the organization communication is part of the art of dealing effectively with people. Nowhere is its importance more clearly demonstrated than in the area of supervision, as we have already observed.

Despite the importance of effective communication, it is unusual to find organizations that make periodic appraisals of their communication systems. Even the few who want to do so often lack the know-how. One researcher points out the need for a continuing program of appraisal because variables that effect changes in marketing, production, and finance also require changes in the MIS.[14] Another researcher has suggested a method by which communication systems can be examined and audited.[15]

---

[14]Lucien Spataro, "Management of Communication," *Journal of Business Communication*, Vol. 6, No. 4, 1969, pp. 6–9.

[15]Howard H. Greenbaum, "The Audit of Organizational Communication," *Academy of Management Journal*, Vol. 17, No. 4, December 1974, pp. 739–754.

Like all management functions, communication must be planned, organized, activated, and controlled. Moreover, the economic feasibility of communication systems in terms of cost versus benefits should be determined and continually reviewed. In the long run any MIS has to be worth its cost to the organization. Reviews and audits are *control phases* of the communication function.

SUMMARY

No organization can endure unless its members can communicate. People have to have some way to convey ideas and information to each other.

Typically the communication process involves transmitting a message from a sender to a receiver who must respond. In order to respond, the receiver must first perceive the transmitted signals accurately with his senses. Communication, thus, is a two-way process whose basic objectives are to inquire, to inform, and to persuade.

Skills associated with communication include listening, body language, speaking, reading, and writing. Studies indicate the time an executive spends in using these skills follows the above descending order.

Communication is either formal (direct) or informal (indirect). Not all formal communication is verbal, however. Many non-verbal forms of communication are widely used including silence, gestures, and demonstration. Informal communication is represented by the grapevine, which conveys information quickly and accurately, cuts across organizational lines, and provides needed feedback. Feedback may also be formal. Progress reports illustrate formal feedback.

Not all communication flows easily and smoothly within an organization. Barriers of physical, personal, or semantic nature exist which impede communication efficiency and effectiveness.

The directions of communication flow, often called channels of communication, are downward, upward, lateral, and diagonal. Downward communication through successive hierarchical levels tends to be directive, intended to initiate action. Upward communication from subordinates to successively higher levels in the management structure tends to be non-directive, usually reportive. Both types have serious limitations. Lateral and diagonal flows are the most neglected in all organizations. Top-level management should develop effective ways to provide information to every segment of the total organization so all are well informed and never in the dark on important issues. This means improving the quality of top–down communication, encouraging bottom–up communication, and working harder to develop horizontal and diagonal interchange. It also means that periodic reviews and audits should be made of communication systems to insure they are current, productive, and cost-effective.

KEY CONCEPTS

Process of Communication	Rumor
Communication Skills	Abstraction Staircase
Formal Communication	Channels of Communication
Informal Communication	Primacy Effect
Grapevine	Recency Effect

GLOSSARY

abstraction   Expressing a quality apart from the actual object or specific situation so that details are omitted.

communication   An interchange of thoughts or information between two or more persons, in which the recipient must respond.

feedback   A form of upward or downward flow of information, formal or informal, in an organization.

grapevine   A type of indirect, informal communication.

perception   The process of constructing meaning from sensations.

primacy effect   If two messages follow in succession, the first tends to inhibit or block comprehension of the second.

recency effect   If two messages follow in succession, the second tends to be more effective because of the retention phenomenon.

rumor   Grapevine information of the hearsay type which usually is a distortion of the true facts.

semantics   The meaning and connotation of words.

REVIEW QUESTIONS

1. Would you consider singing while in the bathtub communicating?
2. When would you consider communicating to be a managing function?
3. What is perception? What senses are utilized in perception?
4. Which objectives of communication lead to the development of teamwork?
5. List several direct ways to communicate which are non-verbal. Are they effective?
6. Is the grapevine useful to management? How accurate is it?
7. List the basic communications skills that executives believe are important.
8. How can we improve our bad listening habits? Be specific.
9. What are some of the commonly observed barriers to effective communication?

10. Explain the "abstraction staircase." What does it mean to you?
11. What are the main channels of communication?
12. List the disadvantages associated with top–down communication flow.
13. Describe the primacy effect on information effectiveness. Describe the recency effect. What conditions favor one over the other?
14. Give some illustrations of bottom–up communications.
15. What is horizontal communication? Give an illustration. Why isn't it used more?
16. Give an example of diagonal communication.
17. Give some examples that indicate the controlling phase of communication.

Part V

Controlling

Capable managers keep abreast of what transpires by observing, reviewing, and evaluating performance at all levels. Organizational performance should conform to the criteria that have been established by the planning process. Policies, standards, budgets, rules, procedures, and other types of plans generated by the planning process provide the bases for determining effective performance. Standards must be met; procedures must be followed.

When actual results are found to vary significantly from those which were intended, the administrator must discover the reason and, if necessary, take realistic steps to adjust the condition before it becomes aggravated and causes irreparable damage. In so doing, he reduces the gap between the norm and the actual until they are brought into balance.

Chapter 22 introduces some basic concepts of controlling including the controlling process and the purpose of control systems. The major components of the control process are the subjects of Chapters 23 and 24.

Methods of measuring and evaluating organization performance and comparing it with planned performance, the use of records and accounts, and the techniques for evaluating employee and capital performance are discussed in Chapter 23. The concluding chapter in this section on the controlling process deals with the means of reducing significant variations that exist between conditions as they are and conditions as they ought to be. Various types of corrective action are analyzed and discussed. All of the chapters comprising Part V provide a basis for understanding the fourth and final cluster of activities in the managing process, which have been presented as **controlling.**

Chapter 22

Controlling Concepts

Controlling is a function of managing. It implies examining an operational plan in which people are working toward designated goals, observing and measuring their progress to determine whether they are on target, and bringing them back on course should they stray too far from the charted plan of action. It is the fourth major cluster of managing activities as they have been developed and consolidated in this book and one of the most important facets of the manager's role.

Controlling is that *segment in the managing process which measures and evaluates performance, and takes corrective action when necessary.* Thus controlling is essentially a *regulatory* process. Like the other major managing processes, it is dynamic and transitive.

Because of industry's great complexity and multi-faceted activities, it is more difficult than ever before to keep various phases of operations in balance. Frequently some functional areas in the same organization work in seemingly unrelated ways, heading in different directions to accomplish their own particular goals. Production people charge full speed ahead while the sales force may find itself slowed down. The warehouse begins to bulge with cartons of unsold, and perhaps unsaleable, merchandise. Balanced operations require controls to regulate all aspects of organizational activity.

There are as many kinds of controls as there are organizational activities: financial controls, production controls, quality controls, accounting controls, inventory controls, and so on. This means that various persons in the organization are assigned the task of examining ongoing activities; they or others must determine whether what is going on is what should be going on. If actual results differ substantially from the prescribed norm, something must be done about it, and someone must have the authority to do it.

Managerial control means different things to different people depending upon their perspective. At top levels of management this concept involves appraising *overall* results. "Corporate control" is concerned with broad areas of activities, with corporate objectives and how successfully they are being realized. Is the firm maintaining its share of the market? Is it doing everything possible to maintain a reputation for quality or service?

Does it have a favorable public image? Is it realizing an adequate return on capital investment?

At low levels of management, the controlling concept has a narrower focus, as exemplified by the supervisory activities of foremen who check the work progress of employees under their jurisdiction and make adjustments where necessary. Is a project falling behind schedule? Are controllable costs higher than anticipated? Is a particular subordinate doing his work effectively? Is employee morale in the department as high as it should be? These and related questions indicate the subjects of "operative controls."

THE PURPOSE OF CONTROLLING

Whether at corporate or at operating levels, the purpose of controlling is to bring about a condition or state of affairs that can be described as being "under control." It is to insure that all activities are operating and will continue to operate as they should, resulting in a balanced and coordinated effort toward previously established goals.

To meet very high production demands at its assembly plant in Lordstown, Ohio, considered to be one of the most modern auto plants in the world, General Motors speeded the automated assembly to a point where workers stated they could not keep up with it. They are alleged to have sabotaged Vegas by deliberately leaving bolts untightened, sealing wrenches or other tools inside the car body, and generally not taking pains with craftmanship. The result was to raise the costs of assembling Vegas, rather than lowering them as the new factory was intended to do. Said one worker,

> "You couldn't ever get anybody to admit it, but there's a difference in a car that comes off the line on a Wednesday and on a Friday. By the end of the week, everybody's in a bad attitude—they've been on you all week, and you just don't give a damn anymore.[1]

A major corporation has issued this astute comment:

> If we had to pick one pivotal factor in AMF's remarkable growth record, it would probably be this: a disciplined emphasis on management controls that guide and benefit every business unit.[2]

Controlling fulfills its purpose in two ways: (1) by preventing problems from arising, and (2) by identifying and correcting problems if they do arise. It is both *preventive* and *remedial*. Thus AMF sees control as an early-warning, fast-response communications system that flags problems, triggers alternative solutions, and tracks progress continuously.[3]

---

[1] *The National Observer*, March 18, 1972, p. 7.

[2] AMF Incorporated, advertisement, *The Wall Street Journal*, March 13, 1973, p. 13.

[3] Ibid.

THE PROCESS OF CONTROLLING

Having laid the groundwork through sound planning and good organization, a manager can direct his attention to insuring that activities are operating as intended, and that goals are being achieved. Regardless of the level at which managerial control occurs, the process is essentially the same. Basically, controlling is an **implementing** and **appraising** function in which a manager does the following:

1. Observes and measures the actual performance of his organization.

2. Evaluates and appraises performance by comparing observed and measured results with predetermined, intended results (the original plan).

3. Takes remedial or corrective steps to bring actual and expected results into line with each other if a significant variance exists between them. (This may call for additional leadership, improved communication, and new or different incentives.) These three steps in the control process and their interrelationships are illustrated in Figure 22-1.

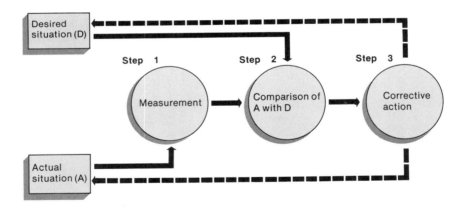

Figure 22-1. The control process model.

Observe how the control process contains a regulatory or feedback system. A manager measures actual performance, compares this against the planned situation, identifies significant deviations, then develops and implements a program for corrective action which requires a change either in the original standard, in the actual performance, or in both.

As is true of all segments in the managing process, the controlling process is an ongoing one.

THE CONTROL SYSTEM

Maintaining a controlled condition throughout the total organization, particularly the widely dispersed, large-scale operation, requires an overall *system* of controls tailored to the needs of its various sub-units or divisions.

To understand what a control system is and how it operates, it is necessary to recognize that it is always a *network* consisting of a great many sub-sytems. Some sub-systems are very simple; others are highly complex and sophisticated. Each has its particular objectives and is tailored to accomplish specific goals and to deal with specific problems that exist or that could arise. Nevertheless, sub-systems are intimately linked so that a great deal of interaction, interrelationship, and interdependence exists among them. A **control system,** then, *is the sum of all control sub-systems plus their patterns of relationships at any given time.* As sub-systems change to accommodate changing conditions in their respective areas, the total system changes also. Thus, a control system is not static or fixed but is a *dynamic,* ever-changing totality which, to paraphrase the words of Shakespeare, "alters as it alteration finds."

PURPOSES OF CONTROL SUB-SYSTEMS

There are a great many reasons why sub-systems of control exist in all areas, in all types of organizations. Among these reasons are: (1) to standardize performance, (2) to measure performance, (3) to safeguard assets, (4) to standardize quality, (5) to plan and program operations, and (6) to motivate personnel. They dovetail with each other, are interacting and mutually reinforcing, as we shall observe.

To Standardize Performance

Many sub-systems of control are designed to standardize performance in given areas of operations. The broadest forms of controls are *policies*. As has already been pointed out, policies help to standardize performance by establishing guidelines within which activities should take place. In all areas of organizational pursuits, at all managerial levels from uppermost to supervisory, policies act as guides, pointing the way. To the extent that they prescribe boundaries or general limits for further activities, policies aid in standardizing performance and developing conformity. Like many plans, they have a managerial control purpose.

Sometimes it is advisable to develop performance standards in order to increase efficiency, to increase productivity, or to reduce costs. When a typist devises a new way to insert envelopes into the typewriter so that more can be addressed in a given time period with less fatigue, a *standard* of efficient performance will result. Eventually this may become the performance standard for all typists in the organization, a form of "production" control in the facilitating area. Another example of how a standard can become a control device and lead to increased productivity is to be found in grocery distribution and warehousing. Grocery manufacturers and chain retailers use a 48 × 40 inch pallet for stacking and transporting cases of foodstuffs, whereas many wholesale warehouses use a 40 × 32 inch pallet. As a result, when a trailer load of food products moves from manufacturer to wholesale warehouse to chain retailer, pallets must be unloaded by hand, re-loaded by hand on smaller pallets, then unloaded again by hand to larger pallets—a process estimated to take 4 hours. If manufacturers, wholesalers, and retailers used the same size pallet, the process could be reduced to 30 minutes. The standard pallet would become a simple sub-system of control. It would reduce costs and increase productivity.

Additional sub-systems that standardize performance are time and motion studies; instant videotape replay; inspections; production schedules; use of standard order blanks, specification forms, and purchase orders; and written procedures. A properly signed requisition becomes an order for the parts department; a voucher signed by a department head becomes an order to the treasurer to pay out company funds; a signed payroll authorization becomes an order for the paymaster to make out checks for employees whose names are listed. These are examples of routine controls through the use of directives. **Directives** *are orders, applying to specific situations, to initiate action toward a stated goal.* Thus directives also act as control sub-systems that establish performance standards.

There are times when standardizing performance to increase efficiency or to cut costs takes a turn quite different from the expected. In an effort to reduce costs at the research and development complex at Aerospace Corporation in Los Angeles, lights burn constantly, day and night. There are no switches to snap off lights. The buildings were designed that way. After a careful engineering study the company discovered that fluorescent light tubes require less current than ordinary bulbs but wear out faster if turned off and on. So, as one of the executives put it, "We leave them on all the time. The savings are substantial."[4] In this limited instance, having lights burn constantly is a standard way to control costs.

To Measure On-the-Job Performance

Numerous controls are designed to measure performance. These become the bases for judging the work of individuals, groups, departments, and even entire functional areas.

Planning contributes substantially to this purpose. *Budgets* of standard costs, production *quotas* that set output per machine-hour, a *standard*

---

[4]*Newsweek*, November 12, 1962, p. 84.

number of rejects permissible for a given volume of output, and other performance plans are criteria for judging both an individual's effectiveness and the organization's effectiveness. *Schedules* indicate when a job should be completed and ready to ship out. Sales *quotas* direct personnel toward a sales objective and become the yardstick with which to measure sales accomplishment. In engineering, the *specification* is a control device that permits management to determine permissible performance. Amounts to be spent for organizational purposes are controlled by financial *budgets* (financial control).

How does an executive measure the performance of managers? How does he or she determine whether supervisors or foremen are performing effectively? Where value judgments are involved and attitudes or other psychological factors are being evaluated as components of satisfactory performance, quantitative tools are generally unavailable and it may be necessary to use relative measuring devices such as efficiency ratings to make qualitative evaluations. An objective rating scale can be employed. When this technique is utilized, a more valid measure of performance will be obtained if the subject is rated by his superior, his peers, and his subordinates. This provides a three-dimensional or three-tiered evaluation of managerial performance. Such a merit rating technique not only measures effective performance but may also become a standard to control all future evaluations of this sort. It is a sub-system of managerial control.

To Safeguard Assets

Some sub-systems exist primarily to safeguard the assets of the institution against theft, fraud, spoilage, shrinkage, misappropriation, or misuse. Erosion of assets may occur *from within*, as when employees cheat or steal in petty or major ways; or it may be *externally* caused, intentionally or otherwise, by customers and suppliers.

Employees often take home scraps of material, tools, even office supplies like pencils and erasers. It may never enter their minds that this is stealing. Others, in a rather professional manner, deliberately plan to take larger quantities or larger size items and are, therefore, well aware of what they are doing. Dishonest employees are said to account for about two-thirds of retail stealing, twice as much as shoplifters. It has been estimated that profits and dividends could be increased as much as 50 percent if the employee theft problem could be eliminated.

In light of these facts, what precautions can organizations take? Some systems that have been adopted are relatively simple. Breweries permit employees to drink beer at lunchtime and during "breaks" without charge; candy factories allow production workers to eat all the candy they want; bakeries sell leftover bread and cake at greatly reduced prices to workers. Knowing that these products are there for the asking reduces temptation that might otherwise be difficult to resist. Some firms supply uniforms without pockets, or ban employee parking near the back door of the building. Stationing a guard at the gate to check packages carried in or out, requiring employees to sign a register when they enter or leave the building after business hours, and using closed circuit television to monitor work areas, are additional techniques currently in use to minimize employee theft. Varying the security routine—for example, shifting guard posts—also helps to reduce in-building thefts.

Many products like meats and foods are prone to normal spoilage and shrinkage. Mechanical systems to control these conditions include adequate refrigeration, controlled temperatures and humidity, and devices to reduce physical handling.

Various sub-systems have been devised to protect assets from fraud, misappropriation, or misuse. The person who takes in cash at the register is given a receipt from the person who receives the proceeds. The work of accountants is checked by auditors. The operational systems and the accounting systems are separated from each other. Checks and balances of this sort are referred to as **internal control**. In principle, there is a division of authority in which the person doing the work does not check his own results. To implement internal control, elaborate accounting and electronic data processing equipment may become part of the sub-system. Machine-printed figures are difficult to alter, and totals can be locked in so that only an authorized person can get at them.

Customer pilferage and theft is a major problem for business and requires special control sub-systems designed to eliminate it. The use of large circular mirrors in retail stores; two-way mirrors and hidden cameras in banks; photographing checks to be cashed as well as the casher of the check; and employing guards or plainclothes employees to keep customers under surveillance are some examples of controls devised for this purpose. To prevent shoplifting losses, a revolutionary electronic device utilizes a tiny dot concealed in the price tag of a garment or product. When an item is paid for at the check-out point, the electronic dot is deactivated. Otherwise, it triggers an alarm signal at all store exits. In New York City, one small chain of cafeterias, the Exchange Buffet, operated successfully for seventy-eight years and employed a very simple, yet unique, sub-system of control—the honor system! The customer ordered what he wanted, and upon leaving simply told the cashier what he had consumed. He received no luncheon check. There was no check either on his honesty.

To guard against air hijacking, metal detectors were introduced into airports in 1972. Passengers about to board an airliner, along with their carry-on luggage and packages, are scanned electronically. Scanners are also used routinely by the post office and customs authorities to detect weapons or explosive devices.

To protect against deception or fraud by suppliers, or against unintended errors such as shortages, common techniques employed are inspections, testing for performance, verifying physical count recorded on the bill of lading with the amount shown on the purchase order, weighing, measuring, and checking the specifications to determine that what is received conforms to what was ordered. Each method is a sub-system of control.

To Standardize Quality

To assure that products or services meet the company's own specifications, or those of its customers, many sub-systems are employed to standardize quality and to insure uniformity. Representative are the use of blueprints, inspections, quality control techniques including statistical quality control, and scrap or defective items reports.

Quality control and inspection are now automated in many situations. In petroleum refining, equipment turns valves on and off automatically in response to gauges located in a central control area. In many industries **non-destructive testing** is frequently employed. NDT techniques include such sophisticated technology as ultrasonics, radiography, liquid penetrants, magnetic methods, and eddy-current testing. As cars come off production lines at American Motors a computer calculates exhaust emission readings by a predetermined formula, matches the results against applicable standards, and then reports any abnormal conditions so that remedial action can be taken. In checking nuclear power stations for safety, the Atomic Energy Commission uses ultrasonic testing of circulation loops to determine if cracks and other defects are present.

In some types of production, such as the manufacture of bolts and screws, the cost of testing each item for quality control purposes is prohibitive. In others, the test is by nature "destructive." To test the soundness of an electric fuse means to destroy it. If the fuse blows, it *was* a "good" fuse. Testing paper to establish tearing resistance, bursting strength, folding strength, resistance to color fading, and other characteristics requires the destruction of the paper. In situations like these, 100 percent inspection is not feasible. It becomes necessary to resort to some sort of sampling to determine that quality and uniformity are being maintained. All sampling techniques presuppose that a small percentage of defective units is permissible, otherwise 100 percent inspection would be required. A modern technique is **statistical quality control.** In this procedure, the sample must be selected at random, be of sufficient size, and be "representative" of the parent batch from which it was drawn. Tests are made on the sample group. From the results, based on statistics and laws of probability, conclusions are reached about the original parent population and whether or not it meets acceptable quality levels.

To Plan and Program Operations

Frequently it is necessary to develop controls for planning and programming operations. Let us examine some situations in which this occurs.

To convert raw data into finished records quickly and accurately requires a special sub-system to perform relatively simple computations, and produce an enormous volume of information. Such a sub-system is **electronic data processing.** Banks could not operate in today's check-writing age without electronic posting systems that total deposits, withdrawals, and balances on the customer's statement sheet and the bank ledger simultaneously. Magnetic ink characters identify customers' account numbers on all checks. These characters are transferred to a magnetic tape that activates a printer which produces customer statements.

J. C. Penney uses electronic data processing to control a substantial portion of its inventory and re-order activities. Sales tickets have holes punched in them which indicate item, size, color, price, the store selling the product, and other pertinent information. These are mailed daily to New York or Los Angeles where the information is read into a computer (step 1 in the control process). Every two weeks the computer compares the information from the tickets against the "program" for the relevant store (step 2 in the control process) and determines when the store will need an additional supply of any item. It issues orders for replenishing stock where it is needed (step 3 in the control process). Under this system a store is seldom out of any item and sales are not lost because of a NS (no stock) condition. Another great advantage is that the sales clerk does not have to be tied up taking a physical inventory. "Instead of being under the counter counting stock, she can be standing up taking care of customers," says a Penney official.[5]

Less sophisticated inventory controls are also used. More and more firms are using two-way radios or tape recorders as aids in inventory-taking. With a two-way radio, one employee calls out the items in stock while another, often some distance away, acts as recorder and writes down the items and quantities. With a tape recorder, a single employee can transmit inventory data on tape for transcription by a typist later on. This latter technique is often used in retail inventory control.

One control that has proved especially effective in preventing duplication and simplifying record-keeping and inventory control is the **number coding** system of listing and storing parts. Caterpillar Tractor Company found a part that had been identified and stored in several places under the following names: spacer, shim, washer, collar, and orifice. Coding it by number instead of name reduced from hours to minutes the time spent in locating it when needed. After coding, another manufacturer discovered one of its divisions was making a part at a cost of $31 that another division was buying from an outside vendor for only $2.10.

---

[5]*Investor News*, Francis I. DuPont & Co., December 1965, p. 10.

A relatively simple control sub-system can be observed in printed checkbooks. A slip of paper near the end of the book reminds us that we are running low on check blanks, and that it is time to re-order.

Color coding is another type of control that can be used effectively. This concept is by no means new. Archeological findings indicate that such a system was used in the Babylonian granaries about 500 B.C. Harvested grain was stored in huge sealed pottery jars. In each seal was implanted a colored reed, varied to indicate the age of the grain, so that the older was used first. Today, telephone companies use color-coded wires to simplify installations, maintenance, and repairs.

Computers help to automate electric generating plants, chemical plants, steel mills, paper production, and even ice cream making. Airlines, committed to meticulous scheduling of high-priced equipment, could not effectively allocate mobile resources and crews without computers. In a very real sense the computer itself has become a production machine. In many universities it is used to schedule classes and make room assignments.

Another technique for planning and programming operations is **scheduling**. Its use leads to substantial improvement in manufacturing efficiency and to significant upgrading in office efficiency. Effective scheduling requires proper sequencing and flow of work, and the logical development of work centers. It includes determining optimum batch sizes, time intervals for dispatching work, and an overall timetable for the entire project or process. A schedule thus becomes a sub-system of control enabling a manager to plan and program certain types of operations.

To Motivate Personnel

Within the context of human relations skills, which managers are expected to practice, various controls may serve the purpose of motivating employees. Setting up some machinery that recognizes and rewards achievement is one way to accomplish this. The suggestion box has previously been recommended as a way to encourage subordinates to participate in company affairs. It serves another purpose also. It is an effective way to motivate people, to enable them to express their creativeness, and to reward their participation with monetary and other types of recognition. Between 1942, when its suggestion plan was introduced, and 1972, General Motors' employees have received more than $155 million for 3 million suggestions that were adopted, covering almost the entire spectrum of GM operation. They included safety innovations, better quality, improved design, better methods, time and material savings, job improvements, and upgraded housekeeping. The success of the plan is evident when one considers that of 482,000 employees eligible in 1971, 231,000 actually submitted suggestions.[6]

---

[6] *Youngstown Vindicator*, (Ohio), February 28, 1972.

Profit sharing, stock purchase plans, promotion programs, and bonus systems are additional control devices designed to motivate employees, including executives, and to reduce their inclination to seek greener pastures elsewhere.

DISADVANTAGES OF CONTROLS

Various sub-systems, like those which have been described, make up a totality that is casually referred to as "the organization's control system." Regardless of whether viewed from a macro-perspective as a total entity or from a micro-perspective as individual sub-units, controls have a tendency to produce certain unwanted reactions. These are inherent in the system and often are interrelated. Some of the more obvious negative aspects of controls are (1) the development of a narrow viewpoint, (2) the tendency toward short-run expediencies, (3) falsification in reporting, and (4) reduced morale.

Narrow Viewpoint

Controls tend to restrict vision to those organizational segments specifically covered by the sub-systems. They act as blinders, focusing attention on limited areas and limited objectives, often without due regard for broader organizational perspective and total organizational targets. For example, a group of controls designed to increase quality, if directed narrowly toward that sole purpose, could have a disastrous effect on productive output. Rigid inspection to assure the highest quality standards, while meritorious in and of itself, could reduce effective output to a trickle. Conversely, a system of controls designed to increase output, by focusing on that limited objective, could produce many items of questionable quality. Narrow controls tend to create an imbalance in overall objectives. This may call for additional controls to forestall imbalances or to correct them when they occur.[7]

Tendency to Emphasize Short-Run Expediencies

The attempt to produce immediate, desirable, measurable results by instituting special controls often leads to long-run disadvantages. Control techniques may be designed to speed production. Do they accomplish this by neglecting proper machine maintenance? In the short run, the objective to improve output is realized. In the long run, it may be self-defeating because inadequate maintenance control will mean increased machine downtime and subsequent decrease in output. Controls that focus on getting a job done to meet a deadline, or to fulfill a contract, may insure the fulfillment of those objectives in the short run, but at what long-run cost in attitudes, morale,

---

[7]We have previously suggested "deliberate sub-optimizing" as a strategy to accomplish this. The reader is referred to Chapter 3.

and physical and psychological reactions that translate into tardiness, absenteeism, and labor turnover?

A sales promotion manager relates this experience:

> The sales department suggested a "cents-off" deal on my largest bottle size for shipment in mid-December. They reckoned that the trade would have to buy the deal, and that this would mean we would make quota. They were right, but my share of sales didn't rise a fraction of 1%. There was, instead, a tremendous consumer swing from the middlesize bottle to the largest size—the one that was promoted. Total grand sales were fractionally up in January, but reduced by the same amount in February. The point is simple: I'll try to avoid promotions that bring short-term gains and no long-term benefits.[8]

Evasion through Falsification in Reporting

Adjustments are often made in record-keeping and paper work to circumvent the purpose for which the particular controls were designed. These may take the form of **padding** figures to give the appearance of an accomplishment superior to the actual one, or of **withholding** information to portray a result that is less than the actual one. Both types of evasion are common and are used to suit the convenience of those in the organization who may be judged by the results obtained through controls, or who will be affected by the way those results are interpreted. In production, units may be rushed to completion with some disregard for normal standards so that results can be counted within that production period. This tactic of speeding output in order to meet a production quota or deadline, with little or no regard for the negative consequences that could be produced by the unusual acceleration, is frequently referred to as **bleeding the line.** Work in progress may be assigned a higher dollar value than it is really worth in order to make it look good on paper. Shipments that will leave the warehouse on Monday of next week may be invoiced on Friday of this week and be counted in this week's billings. While padding is a common practice, the strategy of holding back is just as frequent. If the sales department has already achieved a satisfactory month of billings, merchandise shipped out during the last few days of that month may not be invoiced until the first of the following month. This overflow is used to get next month off to a flying start simply by dating the invoices appropriately. When a buyer in a department store is expected to beat last year's figures for a given period by 10 percent, there is a tendency on his part to meet that projection but not to beat it. To do better than the projection means that the results achieved become the base that he will be expected to exceed for the following year. In effect, he makes it harder for himself if he raises the plateau against which his next performance will be judged. Therefore he tends to do no more than the con-

---

[8]*Advertising Age,* January 18, 1971, p. 48.

trol system asks of him. One company that uses a "Zero Defects" incentive plan discovered that some of its inspectors, eager to make their department look good, covertly turned back defective parts to be re-worked without reporting them. As a result, the company got an excessively rosy picture of its defect rate.

Possible Reduction in Morale

Those subjected to controls, and cognizant of their inherent weaknesses, are critical of them. In their minds is raised the disturbing question of the "integrity of control." Aware of the narrow perspective that controls induce, of the tendency of the control system to emphasize short-run expediencies, and of their own efforts to evade through falsification, personnel may react with lowered morale. They become less willing to pursue organizational objectives when the negative aspects of controls are at variance with their personal beliefs and value systems. Operators will often try to hide poor work or cover up in some way so that it is not discovered by inspectors and returned to be re-worked. The job of checking quality is made that much more difficult. To overcome the obstacles placed in their way, inspectors appear to be eager to spot trouble and to be particularly critical in their evaluations. In the minds of the operators and their supervisors, inspectors try to find errors merely to justify their existence as inspectors. Mutual suspicion and distrust are generated.

There is still another facet of controlling that must be considered. As was true in our consideration of planning, organizing, and activating, the question must be asked of controlling: "Is the cost of an overall control system, or of any of its particular sub-systems, economically justified?" Let us examine an actual situation.

> The investigation of the unsolved theft of $1,500,000 from a mail truck near Plymouth, Mass. in 1962 has cost more than the amount taken by the holdup men, it was reported today. William White, chief postal inspector for New England, said 60 postal inspectors are still working on the case, the biggest mail robbery in American history.[9]

Only the United States Government can afford such systems of control! Managers in commerce and industry cannot. They must always take into account the value of the objectives being sought and compare this with the cost of the control system designed to achieve it.

Suppose top managers of a chain operation are concerned about eliminating shoplifting that, company-wide, amounts to $1 million annually. A number of remedies can be suggested. Wells Fargo guards can be hired, "sensormatic" devices can be installed, plainclothes persons can be added

---

[9]*St Louis Post-Dispatch* (Missouri), January 3, 1965, p. 22A.

to keep their eyes on potential suspects, merchandise can be kept under lock and key, remote TV screens can be installed, and so on. The cost of these control sub-systems could be several million dollars annually, hardly justifiable in the face of a $1 million savings objective.

As have most major retailers, J. C. Penney Company experimented with a computerized cash register system that would give the company up-to-the-minute reports on sales, inventory, and buying trends. Its vice-president and director of finance and administration alertly raised the question of how much point-of-sale data is really needed and how often. "Do you need it instantly, or each hour, each day, each week, or what? You have to arrive at some economic optimum."[10] Managers must be alert for the point of diminishing returns beyond which the cost and complexity of a given system begin to exceed its value. Control systems should justify their cost and performance.

Despite the limitations and the undesirable reactions that control systems produce, there is no question about the need for them in every effective organization. Without controls there would be no continuing organization. Organizations could not survive.

THE MAJOR CONTROL FUNCTIONS

To achieve the purpose of controlling, namely, to insure that all enterprise activities are functioning the way they should, a manager will engage in a number of specialized activities that collectively constitute the process of controlling. The major control functions are (1) measurement, (2) comparison, and (3) corrective action. These essential activities in the process are intertwined, mutually reinforcing, and interdependent. They are discussed in the chapters that follow.

SUMMARY

As we have viewed it, the managing process comprises four major clusters of managerial activities. Activities are associated either with planning, organizing, activating, or controlling. Thus, all remaining managerial activities that have not been grouped under one of the first three major aggregates can be considered controlling activities. It must be remembered, however, that although these various activities have been classified for purposes of discussion and analysis they actually are intermeshed, complementary, interacting, and inseparable in actual practice.

A plan of action, once it has been put into operation, must be checked regularly to insure that it is accomplishing its purposes. This is the role of

---

[10]*Business Week,* June 5, 1971, p. 71.

controlling. It is concerned with keeping the organization operational, measuring and evaluating its performance, and keeping it steered on course. Controlling requires an understanding of what motivates people; a demonstration of leadership coupled with appropriate incentives; ways of measuring employees' efforts and comparing their accomplishments with intended results; and means of correcting any wide discrepancies that may exist from time to time. Success in these efforts leads to balanced and coordinated action on the part of the total organization as it pursues the aims for which it was created.

To assist a manager in performing the essential functions of controlling, control systems must be fashioned to meet the needs of every organizational subdivision. There are, therefore, as many kinds and types of controls as there are organizational activities. An overall control system is the totality of all existing sub-systems and their relationships to each other. Although each sub-system has its particular goals, collectively these systems focus on the overall goals of the total organization so that the principle of unity of direction is maintained.

There are disadvantages to be found in the use of controls. They should be acknowledged and understood. Nevertheless, they do not negate the fundamental value of control systems and their importance in the controlling process.

KEY CONCEPTS

Process of Controlling	Internal Controls
Control Systems	Non-Destructive Testing
Control Sub-Systems	Statistical Quality Control
Directives	Bleeding the Line
Three-Tiered Rating Technique	Major Control Functions

GLOSSARY

bleeding the line   The tactic of speeding output to meet a production quota by a deadline, with little regard for the negative consequences.

control system   The sum of all control sub-systems plus their patterns of relationships.

controlling   That segment in the managing process which measures and evaluates performance and takes corrective action when necessary.

directives   Orders, applying to specific situations, to initiate action toward stated goals.

internal control   A system of checks and balances to safeguard an organization's assets. It is based on a division of authority separating the performance of an act from the auditing of that performance.

REVIEW QUESTIONS

1. Do you agree that controlling is both an implementing and regulating activity? Be specific.

2. What is the fundamental purpose of controlling? How does controlling fulfill its purpose?

3. In your own words, describe the process of controlling.

4. What are control systems? How do they originate?

5. State one purpose of control sub-systems and give an actual example of a sub-system that is directed toward the purpose you have mentioned. List some additional purposes of control systems.

6. What relationship is there between specific types of plans and the purposes of various control sub-systems?

7. Are there weaknesses or limitations associated with controlling? Prove your position.

8. What are the major control functions?

9. How are the major control functions related to other managing functions? Give specific examples.

Chapter 23

Measurement and Comparison

It has been stated previously that in the course of controlling, managers engage in a continuing series of activities designed to achieve a balanced and coordinated organizational effort. By way of review, these actions include:

1. measuring the performance of the organization;
2. evaluating and appraising performance by comparing actual results with intended results;
3. taking steps to remedy any significant deviation that exists.

Measurement, the first step in this control process, is largely a *staff* activity conducted by specialists. Many of the components of measurement call for technical expertise. The results are then conveyed to line managers to assist them in an overall appraisal of the functioning of the areas in their charge.

Measurement is a *control function that provides information about the quantity, quality, and economy of group response to managerial decisions.* It is a sub-system of control.

A manager has to know what is actually taking place in his organization before he can determine whether performance is meeting, exceeding, or falling below expectations. Before a comptroller or any other manager can determine whether budgets are being followed, he must have all the necessary information on actual operations. A sales manager cannot know if sales personnel are meeting or exceeding quotas until he learns what their actual sales records are. Success cannot be evaluated until actual results are known. This requires some way of measuring activities to determine their existing levels. Without measurement, managers would have to guess about results or use other, less reliable or valid, methods.

To obtain quantity, quality, and economy information about an organization's operations, there must be a process by means of which information can be gathered and interpreted. Measurement is such a process; it is a continuing function of controlling. The process of measurement has a number of necessary components: (1) techniques of measurement; (2) records and accounts; (3) units of measurement; and (4) measurement tools.

Deciding which technique is appropriate, what kinds of records and accounts will be kept, what type of measuring unit to employ in a given situation, and which measurement tools best suit the intended purpose, all require planning. They are additional evidence of the close relationship that exists between planning and controlling and the fact that controlling must be *planned*. Procuring the needed equipment such as bookkeeping machines or calculators, and obtaining the necessary personnel to operate them, are *organizing* activities that occur within the control process. One is constantly reminded of the interrelationship of all management functions and the fact that they occur continuously and concurrently in all areas, at all management levels.

TECHNIQUES OF MEASUREMENT

From a business management perspective, organizational measurements fall into two classes: (1) those concerned with corporate control and the achievement of an overall endeavor; and (2) those concerned with operative control and the achievement of more limited objectives. In the first instance, measurement is in terms of company-wide objectives or results. What is our present share of the market? Do we have a good corporate image? What is our current return on capital invested? These are the kinds of broad questions that corporate measurement must address. In the second instance, the questions are more localized and are likely to be concerned with direct productivity. What are current factory direct-labor costs? How many calls did salesman Jones make last week? What is our present cash position? Each area being measured requires different measurement tools. These will be discussed at a later point in this chapter.

Whether managers are engaged in corporate or operative measurement, two techniques commonly employed in both areas, with great effect, are observation and reporting.

Observation

Almost daily the chairman of the board of a large department store chain walked through the St. Louis store, where corporate headquarters were housed, to observe the level of activity. He asked questions of employees, invited comments from customers, and, in a general way, noticed what was going on. He was employing a time-honored technique of measuring: personal observation.

Executives of large companies spend a considerable portion of their time visiting branches and factories, often around the globe. First-hand contact and observation tells them many things that are impossible to learn indirectly through oral or written reports. Very often these observations discover sensitive areas, latent trouble spots, or potential bottlenecks that can be forestalled if spotted soon enough.

At the operative level, there is no substitute for direct observation in checking the performance of subordinates. While personal observation may be time-consuming, it is an essential part of every supervisor's job. It gives the supervisor an advantage which managers at higher levels generally do not have. The further removed a manager is from operating activities and intimate personal contact, the more dependent he becomes on secondary sources including reports. In smaller companies it is common practice for top executives, particularly a production executive, to walk through the plant every morning and talk to the foremen and the workers about their work and their families. The level of activity, the behavior of employees, their reactions to suggestions, response to questions, and the level of accomplishment can all be directly observed and used to form a mental picture of "what is going on." In most "work measurement programs," observing how many tasks an employee normally performs during a specified time period is one of the techniques employed by the job analyst in determining whether productivity is above or below standard.

Reporting

Control can be effective only if progress toward objectives is promptly made known to the manager in charge. Part of the task of measuring performance is to plan and design a reporting system that will provide timely and accurate information.

The modern concept of managerial control includes a report system that supplies information on developments in all areas and pinpoints the reasons why they have occurred. Data then reach the executive in a form that enables him to make comparisons and to take action that may be indicated. Sales reports broken down by products and territories prove more meaningful than simple totals of units sold. Wages may appear to be high. Why? Because output was high also and required more people to produce it? Because wage rates had risen? Because labor was less efficient? Or a combination of these factors? Explanations accompanying the data make control reports meaningful and useful to a manager. In addition, this type of report helps the executive to identify trends that provide a guide to future action on his part.

In general, reports are a type of upward or lateral communication which let a manager know what is going on. Control reports are intended to reveal not only what is going on at any given time, but also the *meaning* of what is going on. A control report is to a manager what a sextant is to a ship's captain. It tells him where he is, at any point in time. A **control report** is *an oral or written message that conveys information which can be used for evaluating performance and deciding whether some change is necessary.*

Managers depend upon a continuing flow of information. Control reports indicate to an executive the extent to which delegated functions are being effectively handled by subordinates. By combining reports and summaries from various areas and establishing relationships among them, an executive builds an impression of the existing state of affairs. To formulate the total information picture he needs, today's business executive must rely on reports in addition to personal observations. He also spends a portion of his time preparing similar reports for his superiors.

Kinds of control reports.   Control reports take many forms. All, however, are oral, written, or a combination of these. Oral reports may be presented face-to-face, over the telephone, or at group meetings with department heads and division chiefs. Although written reports do not require the physical presence of the person submitting them, it is preferable that he or she be present if possible. This permits questions and answers, and discussions about the information submitted. Among the more common forms of reports are the following:

- **Narrative:** descriptive, verbal reports.
- **Statistical:** reports which rely largely on numbers and symbols.
- **Periodic:** reports issued on a regular, scheduled basis (daily, weekly, monthly, quarterly, annually).
- **Progress:** interim reports between the start and completion of a project. They are sometimes referred to as follow-up reports.
- **Special:** reports sent irregularly in response to specific, non-routine requests. Often they deal with intangibles.

The typical control report is probably a combination of several of these basic types.

Control reports, therefore, are a form of *accountability* in which a subordinate summarizes the activities under his jurisdiction and accounts to his superior for results that he has previously committed himself to achieve. It can be said that "reporting by results" is a control aspect of management by results (the MBO concept).[1]

RECORDS AND ACCOUNTS

Before a control report can be issued, it is necessary to accumulate, in some meaningful fashion, the data on which the report is based. Although personal observation is extremely valuable as a control technique, it lacks a certain amount of accuracy, objectivity, and definitiveness. Maintaining records and accounts are essential sub-functions of measurement which are

---

[1]For a review of this concept, the reader may refer to Chapter 11.

designed to convert both individually observed and measured data into permanent and meaningful form.

If a manager could be absolutely certain that actual behavior in his organization would always conform to planned behavior, from a control point of view there would be no need for records and accounts. Since he cannot be certain, he needs records that are designed to help him make judgments of actual conduct. The kinds of records that must be kept for control purposes differ, however, from those kept primarily for maintaining an historical account of the institution's development. For control purposes, records must have immediate, practical usefulness. They must be in a form that expresses organizational behavior in quantitative and qualitative terms, enabling the manager to compare it with some yardstick or standard of accomplishment. Thus, as a measurement sub-function, the chief purpose of keeping records and accounts is to provide the means for making comparisons.

Records and accounts generate masses of information for a manager. The *recording function* is concerned with receiving, accumulating, classifying, and converting information into meaningful and useful form. Bits of data must be fitted together and transformed like raw material in the production process. A deck of IBM cards contains a vast amount of raw information which is absolutely useless for measurement purposes until someone compiles tabulations and cross-tabulations, and tries to classify the results by statistical devices or reasoning. Data half-digested can be misleading or unusable. Most corporations allocate considerable resources to collecting data but spend less time and effort deriving *meaning* from the data. The final step in the processing of information is drawing conclusions from well-digested data.

Business records can readily be classified according to business functions. We speak of production records, sales records, financial records, personnel records, accounting records, and many others. Most of these are maintained by staff personnel or facilitating personnel like clerical workers.

One of the distinctive features of modern capitalistic production is that it is managed by executives who are removed from direct contact with technical details. Accounting serves as a connecting link between decision making and the industrial process which management directs and controls. The businessman must constantly keep tabs on what is going on. The owner of a department store must know which departments and which items are generating sales volume and whether they are profitable. The manager of a factory must know the value of goods in process as well as the amount of money owed to suppliers. The demand for pertinent information is ever-present in all enterprises. The aim is to have a system of records and accounts that will provide most readily the kinds and amounts of information a manager needs in order to make necessary assessments of his operations. An **accounting**

system is *a set of related procedures designed to provide management with continuing information covering business and financial transactions.* In this sense an accounting system is one segment of a total management information system (communication system).

UNITS OF MEASUREMENT

Organizational behavior must be described and recorded in quantifiable units whenever possible. Generally speaking, the units are of two basic types (1) Those which lend themselves to precise measurement are *absolute* or *direct* measuring units; (2) those which cannot be precisely quantified are *relative* or *indirect* measuring units.

Absolute Measuring Units (Direct Measurement)

Various absolute units of measurement are utilized in business. The most frequently encountered are unit of output, unit of cost, and unit of energy expended. These are expressed in numbers, pounds, gallons, feet, dollars, kilowatts, and similar universally accepted designations. Sometimes these units are related to each other and are expressed as a ratio, such as number of orders per dollar of salesman cost; output per man hour; kilowatt-hours; and other established relationships. There is always the danger that if a manager's performance is measured *solely* on the basis of output, he will be tempted to be wasteful of inputs. Thus output *relative* to profits, or output *relative* to assets employed, can be more meaningful units of measurement.

Measurements of output per unit of applied direct labor are not difficult to obtain. Work that is highly repetitive, flows at a fairly steady rate, requires little judgment or conceptual skill, and is highly objective, can be measured and quantified rather accurately and easily. Work that is creative, occurs at irregular intervals, requires conceptual skill, and varies in its makeup is more difficult to measure. In general, therefore, it is easier to measure and quantify line activities than staff activities. For example, how do you quantify the performance of the legal department, the research and development unit, the personnel department, or the advertising and public relations section? The nature of their activities makes them difficult to measure and appraise. In these instances, accurate direct measurement cannot be achieved.

Relative Measuring Units (Indirect Measurement)

The problem of measurement can also be considered in terms of tangibles versus intangibles. Cards filed, policies in force, tons of scrap, broken tools, personal calls made, and finished goods in inventory are tangible achievements. They represent a physical count of similar units which, when added together, give a picture of actual accomplishment. Such data can be manipulated statistically and can be analyzed and interpreted with a high degree of fairness.

Within the typical organization, however, there are numerous intangible results on which data cannot be gathered in a direct fashion. The development of executives, efficiency of purchasing, effectiveness of communication, level of employee morale, and effectiveness of various supervisory styles are a few intangibles that are difficult to measure and quantify directly and precisely. Improved units of measurement and tools of measurement must be developed if these activities are to be controlled more effectively. For intangible achievements, those which involve value judgments, and those which concern people rather than things, relative measuring units are substituted.

How does a manager decide that a supervisor is developing leadership characteristics in his subordinates? Or that there has been an improvement in employees' attitudes? He makes use of an instrument of relative measurement such as an efficiency rating, a scale based on some continuum of values that has no finite limits, no precise bottom or top. The more objective the rating scale, the more reliable and valid will be the measurement. Some attributes that are measured by rating scale technique are initiative, cooperation, loyalty, tactfulness, resourcefulness, ambition, and creative ability.

Many organizations use morale or attitude surveys to learn how employees feel about the work they are doing, their supervisors, policies, or the enterprise as a whole. Generally the technique used is a questionnaire carefully devised to meet the needs of the particular institution and to fit a given situation. At best, surveys of this type are approximations. Often the results are ambiguous. Frequently employees are not cooperative or, through lack of understanding, give misleading information. Many surveys are expensive and time-consuming. Despite their inadequacies, they are one means of measuring these intangibles, and superior on the whole to guesswork or chance.

MEASUREMENT TOOLS

Having determined the appropriate measurement technique to use, knowing the kinds of records and accounts that are needed to provide information in a meaningful way, and having decided on the proper unit of measurement, the manager still needs tools with which to record and measure performance.

Managers must develop and use measurement tools that are appropriate for given situations. Tools suitable in one operating area, to determine economy of tasks, may be totally unacceptable in another operating area. The situation is analogous to that of a skilled mechanic who uses a socket wrench in one situation, an open end wrench in another, and a box wrench in a third. In addition, tools of measurement suitable in operating areas may not be applicable in corporate areas.

While many measurement tools are utilized in industry for control purposes, three are widely accepted. They are (1) statistics, (2) time studies, and (3) computers. Let us examine each of these briefly.

Statistics

Statistical data are used for a wide range of measurements including work, time, effort, money, space, quality, manpower, and general progress. For business purposes, **statistics** may be defined as *a branch of mathematics dealing with the process of collection, analysis, interpretation, and presentation of numerical data.*

Some data are obtained from the internal records of the enterprise. Other necessary data may be provided by trade associations or governmental agencies. It may also be necessary to *collect* some at first hand. For example, sampling techniques and statistical quality control (discussed in Chapter 22) are statistical tools often used to measure performance as well as to standardize quality. Both require *first-hand* collection of data on a continuing basis.

The second step is *analysis*, which requires classification of data, establishing meaningful categories into which the material may fit. Four of the more important bases for classifying statistical data are (1) quantitative, (2) qualitative, (3) chronological, and (4) geographical.

In classifying data on a quantitative basis, the distinction is one of *amount*. An example is the "aging" of past due accounts receivable according to the number of days overdue. On a qualitative basis, the distinction is one of *kind*. Thus, a textile inventory would be classified as woolens, silks, cottons, polyesters, and so on. On a chronological basis, prices, sales, and output of finished products are sorted over a *time period*, by months or other intervals. A record by states, counties, sales districts, or foreign versus domestic establishes a geographical or *territorial* distribution.

The purpose of business statistics always is to provide information, predicated on unbiased facts, that can be used for decision making. In the third step of the process, the statistical investigator is best qualified to *interpret* statistical data and make recommendations to management for action. The statistician knows the meaning and degree of accuracy of the original data; is familiar with how it has been classified and manipulated; is aware of the limitations to which his conclusions are subject.

Finally, data should be *presented* in tables or charts in a way that helps the manager to visualize the situation easily, or to draw his own conclusions. The physical appearance of the table or chart is most important to the accomplishment of either of these objectives.

Time Studies

Time study is a more precise tool of measurement than statistical handling of data. Its greatest application lies in the operating areas of an enterprise and to a lesser extent in clerical or facilitating areas.

The trend is toward the use of micro-motion studies, which synchronize camera, clock, and motions. Instant replay makes it possible to review almost at once an activity just completed. The series can also be run in slow motion. Overall elapsed time can be established as well as time values between intervals of motion. Mathematical relationships and judgment are used to determine time values based on motion values. One object is to discover faster and more efficient ways to do routine tasks. Often this can be accomplished in a very simple manner, without micro-motion studies, as by moving a file cabinet closer to the clerk who uses it most often.

Not only do time studies record the situation as it exists, but they are most useful in developing standardized tools, equipment, and work flow. "Time standards" and "production standards" are reverse sides of the same coin. For example, a time standard establishes a job as a 2-minute one; a production standard establishes that a man ought to perform the job 30 times in an hour. As a training film, a micro-motion study can be used to show workers the right and wrong way to do something.

It should be noted that unions are generally opposed to time studies to measure performance. They tend to view all time studies as an attempt to speed-up work, to weed out incompetents, and to increase the output of everyone else.

Despite their limitations, time studies are a valuable tool of measurement. How long does it take the average office worker to open a letter and throw away the envelope? Only time study can provide the accurate answer. It takes 7.027 seconds, according to the analyst who uses time-and-motion study techniques.[2]

Computers

Another tool of measurement is the computer. It provides rapid assimilation, digestion, and transfer of information that portrays conditions as they are at the moment. A computer system performs four basic functions: (1) it accepts data, (2) stores it, (3) processes it, and (4) records the result.

At one large insurance company each person submits a daily employee log that separates the hours spent on productive and non-productive work. Reports, rating each employee's performance weekly, and showing average productivity for the year to date, become printouts and are sent to supervisors and vice-presidents.

---

[2]*The Wall Street Journal,* June 2, 1968.

A large, integrated paper products firm using a computer as a tool of measurement reports:

> In addition, we have designed the program so that the computer gives us thirteen different reports. One daily, seven weekly, and five monthly. Now we can keep track of every job, know its status, and record its costs.[3]

When the computer becomes the record keeper, clerical personnel are released to participate in planning and performing other kinds of work.

The real value of the computer to the manager in today's highly complex, demanding milieu is that with proper programming it can quickly select from huge amounts of stored data only that material which is relevant and important to the issues he is considering.

Measurement *provides the basis or standard for comparison.* It is a necessary prerequisite to a manager's appraisal of his own competence in terms of results. Without measurement, comparison could not take place.

COMPARISON

We turn our attention now to the second essential control function—comparison.

Comparison is a process of evaluating two or more attributes to determine ways in which they are similar or dissimilar. Comparison, evaluation, assessment, and appraisal are all interrelated, and the terms are often used interchangeably.

As a facet of controlling, **comparison** is the function of *determining the degree of relevance between actual performance and planned performance.* The *assessment* is made largely by mathematical and statistical techniques. It too is primarily a *staff* function.

In making comparisons, it is essential that criteria be established that can be utilized as a basis for evaluation. That which has been observed, reported, or measured must be compared with some criterion. In management, the criterion is an existing goal or plan of some type. Standards are one category of plans that often serve as criteria for this purpose.

Through comparison, the outcome of the use of any plan becomes observable. A manager can make a judgment on the way that others in the organization have executed it. He can relate things as they are to things as they should be; people as they perform or have performed, to people as they should have performed. In order for comparison to be meaningful to a sales manager, he should know how many units or how many dollars his sales organization should have achieved as well as how many they did achieve. For

---

[3]*The Potlatch Story,* Potlach Corporation, January 1972, p. 3.

control purposes, it is meaningless for a financial manager simply to know the amount of working capital his firm possesses, as reflected in the balance sheet, unless he also has some criterion of what constitutes a desirable amount to have on hand. Too much working capital, relative to an acceptable level, could easily mean the firm was under-employing its resources, keeping more cash and liquid assets available than the business requires at its current level of operations. On the other hand, too little working capital, relative to the same acceptable level, would be interpreted in exactly the opposite fashion. It is imperative to establish what is an acceptable level. This information is provided in the budget, quota, specifications, or some other type of plan.

In addition, it is the comparison function that enables managers to measure their own competence. Management can appraise the entire range of its effectiveness in planning, organizing, activating, and controlling. In the final analysis, the only logical purpose of comparison is to appraise or evaluate management. "How am I doing?" is the basic question a manager seeks to answer by comparing performance against plan. The ultimate responsibility is his.

Variance

As a control function, comparison seeks to discover variance. **Variance** is *any deviation of the actual from the norm.*

In business the norm often is not actual! Comparison seeks to uncover any discrepancy between what is and what should be. The important thing that a manager looks for when he examines two balance sheets, operating statements, sales records, or production periods is the difference between them, the variance.

When performance equals or closely approximates expected results, no immediate further control efforts are required. However, when variance does occur it is an immediate signal that performance is deviating from the targets that were sought. It must then be determined whether the difference is a *significant* one. Significant differences can be determined statistically, by *staff* specialists. Small deviations may be perfectly acceptable. Significant variation, however, requires additional control efforts. The primary mission of comparison, therefore, is to locate and recognize situations and conditions where *significant* deviations from planned performance are occurring. These should be reported promptly to the responsible line executive.

As a managerial function, comparison is closely related to supervision. It acts as a follow-up to supervision upon the completion of some project or phase of a planned program. As was previously pointed out, there can be no supervision of a completed or future activity. Supervision is concerned with directions being carried out currently, with observing and evaluating action informally while it is going on. Comparison, on the other hand, evaluates action formally, after it has been completed.

THE EXCEPTION PRINCIPLE (MANAGEMENT BY EXCEPTION)

Only *significant* deviations between actual performance and planned performance should be brought to the attention of the executive having overall responsibility. This principle of management by exception (previously mentioned in Chapter 4), which focuses attention on the unusual, is not a new one. There is evidence that it was practiced by Moses on the advice of his father-in-law, Jethro, in the story of Exodus.

> Moreover thou shalt provide out of all the people able men, such as fear God, men of truth, hating covetousness; and place such over them, to be rulers of thousands, and rulers of hundreds, rulers of fifties, and rulers of tens.
> And let them judge the people at all seasons: and it shall be, that every great matter they shall bring unto thee, but every small matter they shall judge: so shall it be easier for thyself, and they shall bear the burden with thee.[4]

These remarkable passages contain not only evidence of the exception principle but also of the currently accepted concept of delegation of authority to which we have frequently referred.

The actual terminology has been credited to Frederick W. Taylor, often referred to as the father of the scientific management movement. Taylor stated:

> ... the manager should receive only condensed, summarized, and invariably comparative reports, covering, however, all of the elements entering into the management, and even these summaries should all be gone over by an assistant before they reach the manager, and have all of the exceptions to the past averages or to the standards pointed out, both the especially good and especially bad exceptions, thus giving him in a few minutes a full view of the progress which is being made, or the reverse, and leaving him to consider the broader lines of policy and to study the character and fitness of the important men under him.[5]

It is interesting to note that "both the especially good and especially bad exceptions" were to be brought to the manager's attention. Realistically, it may be just as important for a manager to know when actual results are far superior to planned results as it is for him to know when actual results fall significantly short. *Positive* as well as *negative* exceptions should

---

[4]Exod. 18: 21–22.

[5]Frederick W. Taylor, *Shop Management* (New York: Harper & Bros., 1911), pp. 126–127.

be dealt with by a superior. Success, therefore, as well as failure must be analyzed. In modern-day organizations of all sorts, the tendency is to question only the shortfalls and to take the successes or overages for granted.

As supervisors and higher-level managers check reports, those activities which have been performed as intended require no further attention. Where performance varies significantly above or below expected results, a manager can concentrate his attention on those exceptional situations. A very busy executive may even request subordinates not to send any reports of activities that conform to standards, but to report only those which do not meet agreed objectives or those which far exceed them.

If a manager seriously adopts the principle of "exception reporting" as the basis for monitoring control reports, he will discover that the number of exceptions are an *index* of his own ability to plan in any area. For example, if a marketing manager plans a campaign to sell one million units of a product, and assigns quotas to twenty-five sales territories, the actual sale of a million units may give the surface appearance of a successful campaign (no variance appears after comparison). However, if exception reports indicate that as many as twenty of the twenty-five territories were 30 percent above or below assigned quotas, he didn't really have much of a plan to start with.

Management by exception should not be confused with management by results (management by objectives). The latter, discussed in Chapter 11, is a type of participation in which subordinates and their superior jointly establish goals to be achieved while the techniques for accomplishment are left to the subordinates. At periodic intervals and at the end of agreed time periods, superior and subordinate review the progress that has been made. If performance is significantly less than the established goals, management by exception comes into play. The question then becomes, what can be done about it? If a manager is to improve delegated performance, he has to do more than point out it is below par. He has to make recommendations or invite suggestions to remedy the deficiency. Without management by exception, monitoring the multiple operations of widely diversified corporations which have been developing since the 1960s would be physically impossible.

Frequently, especially in diverse, transnational, and multi-market companies, reporting and comparing take place simultaneously. Agendas at summit meetings of international firms cover a broad range of subjects. High on the list of many is a monthly performance review in which a comparison is made between reported results and original forecasts or projections. Subjects discussed range from engineering advancements, product development, and competition, to finance, banking, and consumer and business trends. Many divisions in large companies operate under both current and long-range master plans, such as one-year and five-year plans. Financial statements and operating data are reviewed by the corporate staff each month. At these meetings executives review what happened during the past month, analyze the aggregate results, and concur on future actions to realize these master plans.

The computer, which serves as a tool of measurement, is also an instrument of comparison. In addition to its capability to add, subtract, multiply, and divide, the computer has the capability to *compare*. It can, for example, perform such jobs as screening credit applications by comparing names and addresses of applicants with a master list of known and proved bad risks. At Potlatch Corporation, the computer aids in evaluating progress.

> Once a week we get a backlog report from the computer. To this we add new jobs, and make our schedule for the upcoming week. We send this schedule back to the computer, and at the end of the week it gives us a report of how we performed against the schedule.[6]

PERSONNEL EVALUATION

Another aspect of comparison relates to the **performance appraisal** of personnel, including managerial personnel. Assessing employees' performance is an integral component of the function of comparison. Performance rating of personnel, however, is a *line* function.

One of the reasons credited for the success of Standard Oil of New Jersey, and for its ranking among the ten best managed companies in American industry, is its system of executive appraisal. Every Monday afternoon five top executives, who comprise its compensation and executive development committee, meet in the board room to review and evaluate the company's top management positions. One of its executives explains:

> From the moment an individual goes on the payroll, his work is reviewed annually and his potential assessed. In each instance, this evaluation work is done by the man's immediate supervisor who, in turn, is being evaluated by his boss, and so on up. And one criteria used to evaluate a Jersey manager is how well he spots and advances management talent. That's why the system works, because each manager is held accountable for the advancement of personnel beneath him.[7]

At Rockwell Manufacturing Company, credit for spotting marginal and inefficient producers is given to its improved performance appraisal system. According to its company president, this system has provided a sound basis for salary increases and promotions. "We're putting just as much time and attention into building our 'people inventory' (compared to physical inventory). And that's the inventory on which the future of the business rests."[8]

---

[6]*The Potlatch Story*, Potlatch Corporation, San Francisco, Ca., January 1972, p. 3.

[7]"The Ten Best Managed Companies," *Dun's*, Vol. 46, No. 6, December 1970, p. 29. See also "Promotional Opportunities" in Chapter 20 of this textbook.

[8]*The Wall Street Journal*, October 23, 1967, p. 15.

Not all organizations, however, make an evaluation and inform their members how well they are performing. In a survey of civilian personnel conducted at Headquarters, U.S. Army Transportation Materiel Command, respondents were asked if their supervisor informed them how well they were performing on the job. Their responses were tabulated as follows:

frequently	13.7%
occasionally	34.1
rarely	22.2
annually	14.6
never	14.1
no answer	1.1

In this study, 85 percent were seldom, if ever, informed how well they were performing in the job assigned to them.[9]

A modern performance appraisal system in which managers appraise the performance of subordinates should originate in the *job description* of all personnel. The worker's job description should state that his performance will be reviewed by the superior to whom he is accountable; the superior's job description should specify that he is expected to appraise the performance of his subordinates and will himself be appraised by his superior.

Whether simple or complex, every appraisal system should always include the following two essential components: (1) The rated person should be given a copy of the rating to *review* and (2) should have the right to *appeal* if he believes it is inaccurate or unfair. If he is vindicated, the rating should be amended before it becomes part of the permanent personnel file.

Appraising or evaluating the performance of an organization's resources has its limitations. Included among them are personal bias, positive or negative, which can enter the evaluating process. Every subordinate is partly appraised on how well he identifies with his superior and helps the latter achieve his purposes. A heavily subjective element enters into every appraisal. Then too, some managers may not evaluate all employees honestly; marginal and unsatisfactory performance may be given an average rating, necessitating the boosting of all other ratings to compensate. Thus the organization obtains a false impression of the quality of its people resources. Also, many superiors dislike having to judge the competence of others when objective criteria are unavailable. Harry Levinson states:

> My own observation leads me to believe that managers experience their appraisal of others as a hostile, aggressive act that unconsciously is felt to be hurting or destroying the other person. The appraisal situation, therefore, gives rise

---

[9]"Survey of Civilian Personnel Management," Headquarters, U.S. Army Transportation Materiel Command, St. Louis, Missouri, December 1961, p. 5.

to powerful, paralyzing feelings of guilt that make it extremely difficult for most executives to be constructively critical of subordinates.[10]

While it may be impossible to eliminate all subjective bias from performance appraisals, a multi-dimensional approach tends to provide a composite that is more valid than a single judgment. In the case of a manager, a **three-tiered system** can be employed.[11] The manager is given three ratings: one by his subordinates, one by his peers, and one by his superior. At a university, the evaluation of faculty in a three-pronged manner could well be a fairer appraisal than a single rating as a guide for merit-related salary increases and promotions. In this situation, the faculty member could be judged, with three *different* value scales, by students, colleagues, and his department chairman and dean.

In the case of non-management personnel, a two-tiered system may have to suffice. In this instance the employee may be evaluated confidentially by his fellow employees and separately by his superior. The composite should be a better indicator of performance than either rating alone, particularly if the rating device has been standardized.

SUMMARY

How well is the entire organization performing? How well are individual sub-units performing? How effective am I as a manager? Questions like these can only be answered by collecting information that reveals the existing state of affairs and then comparing it with the intended state of affairs. The hope is that *what is* will compare favorably with *what should be*.

A determination of the existing state of affairs calls for measurement. Measuring output or stage of development requires appropriate techniques, records, measuring units, and measuring devices. Common techniques in measurement are observation and reporting. Record keeping and accounting provide the information a manager can later use for making comparisons. Measuring units may be absolute in terms of output, cost, and energy expended and are often expressed in terms of dollars, pounds, numbers, kilowatts, and similar designations. These can be used to measure "things" and the results of line activity. Other measuring units are relative and imprecise. They measure intangibles and those factors which call for value judgments. They measure attributes like morale, loyalty, attitudes, creativity, and results of staff activity that are difficult to quantify. Statistics, time studies, and computers are some of the tools that are employed.

[10]Harry Levinson, "Management by Whose Objectives", *Harvard Business Review*, July–August 1970, p. 127.

[11]This was discussed in Chapter 22 in the section on standards used to measure on-the-job performance.

Having measured the organizational performance, a manager can evaluate its effectiveness and his own by comparing the actual results with intended results. The chief purpose is to uncover any significant variation, positive or negative, and to understand why it exists. Part of the process of comparison involves an evaluation of human resources and calls for a performance appraisal of employees and managers. If the appraisal takes the form of a rating, a three-tiered rating system is more desirable than a two-tiered system, and both are preferable to a single judgment.

KEY CONCEPTS

Techniques of Measurement	Statistics
Control Reports	Comparison
Records and Accounts	Variance
Absolute Measurement	Exception Principle
Relative Measurement	Performance Appraisal
Tools of Measurement	Three-Tiered Evaluation

GLOSSARY

accounting system   Set of related procedures designed to provide management with continuing information covering business and financial transactions.

comparison   A control activity designed to determine the degree of relevance between actual performance and planned performance.

control report   An oral or written message that conveys information that can be used in evaluating performance and deciding whether some change is necessary.

measurement   A control function that provides information about the quantity, quality, and economy of group responses to managerial decisions.

reporting   Transmitting information upward or laterally to advise a manager about what is happening.

statistics   A branch of mathematics dealing with the process of collection, analysis, interpretation, and presentation of numerical data.

three-tiered rating   A rating system in which a person is evaluated by subordinates, peers, and superiors in order to provide a composite appraisal.

variance   Any deviation of the actual from the norm.

REVIEW QUESTIONS

1. Of what practical importance is measurement? What relatively simple techniques can be employed to measure performance?

2. Why are accounting and record keeping necessary components of a total management information system?

3. When would you use absolute measuring units? Relative measuring units? Why?

4. Give some illustrations of when you would use time studies. What is the difference between a time standard and a production standard?

5. What is the relationship between supervision and comparison?

6. Explain "management by exception." Do you feel it is a useful monitoring policy for a manager to adopt? Why?

7. It has been said that it is the "people inventory" on which the future of business rests. Do you agree?

8. What features would you build into an employee performance appraisal system? Justify your position.

Chapter 24

Corrective Action

The third and final major control function is corrective or remedial action. If a significant variation is discovered between performance as measured and performance as planned, a manager must decide whether action must be taken to correct the situation.

Not all significant deviation requires corrective action. Often variance can be pinpointed and the reason for its existence explained and understood without the necessity for anything to be done about it. It may be a one-time occurrence. Assume, for example, that an electronics company planned to sell and produce 30,000 diodes during a given period. It may discover that it produced 40,000 units. Investigation reveals that instead of a 5000 order from one of its regular customers, it received a 15,000 order because the principal supplier to that customer was shut down by a strike. There is a significant variance in output, but it is not likely to recur once the strike has ended and the customer resumes his normal relations with his principal supplier. Stockpiling in anticipation of an industry-wide strike could readily account for excessively high manufacturers' inventories during a given year.

Where corrective action is indicated, it is fundamentally a *line* function, performed by line managers. As an example, a foreman ultimately must translate a budget variance into direct action, whereas a divisional supervisor translates it into an impersonal directive to that foreman. Both line managers recognize that steps must be taken to bridge the gap and to eliminate it.

If significant deviations from the norm are not dealt with promptly and effectively, repercussions can occur. Serious damage and permanent losses could result from continued inability to recognize and identify the causes of variance and to act promptly to alleviate them. In extreme situations, the very safety and survival of the institution may be threatened.

Corrective action is *a major control function in which steps are taken to eliminate significant variance between actual performance and planned performance.* The purpose of remedial action is to correct deviations that have been observed and to reduce or eliminate them so that coordinated activity can continue.

SYMPTOMS VERSUS CAUSES

Correction is not always a simple matter. It may require the selection of one from among many possible managerial actions, depending upon the circumstances. In this area experience plays a very significant role. Knowing what to do promptly, without hesitation, is the hallmark of a seasoned executive. Before he can do this, however, he must be able to isolate and identify which of the many possible causes is creating the problem. There may be more than one. To be able to identify causes, and not just symptoms, is a skill that must be developed.

Relying heavily on reports and accountability, control systems provide a good method of "smoking out" problems by recognizing symptoms of variance. Wasteful practices, sloppy housekeeping, idle men and machines, under-utilized skills, unexplained delays, slowdowns, interruptions, failure to meet deadlines, customer complaints, interdepartmental frictions, unusual errors, excessive scrap rate, high overtime charges, inventory imbalances, slow collections, increased tardiness, absenteeism, and labor turnover are a few examples of symptoms. They are clues to where to begin to look for causes before applying corrective measures.

At higher levels in the management hierarchy, spotting causes and not just symptoms before suggesting remedies requires a high degree of conceptual skill. The answer to sharply declining sales volume is not necessarily to add more salesmen, nor to motivate existing sales personnel toward better performance. Falloff in sales may be the fault of product design or the inability of the firm to meet competitive marketing strategies.

An adequate system of controls will reveal where failures are taking place, who is responsible for the areas in which they are occurring, and what should be done not only to correct them but to insure that they will not recur.

Identifying who is in charge of areas where significant variance is apparent, and holding that person accountable for correcting the problem, requires human relations skill of the highest order, as well as the ability to recognize the actual problem. As an example, a manager cannot saddle a foreman with costs over which the latter has no control. If operating volume declines, causing a foreman to be confronted with under-absorbed fixed costs, it is not his fault. When a foreman runs into variances caused by factors beyond his control, yet continues to be held accountable, he may become frustrated and lose motivation. Not only will he fail to live within the budget, but he may no longer even try. In fact, he may seek ways to beat the system. He should never be held to account for factors that he cannot indeed control. The *underlying* cause must be recognized and corrected.

KINDS OF CORRECTIVE ACTION

Basically, there are only four recourses open to a manager: the reevaluation or revision of planning, organizing, activating, and controlling. He must critically examine the way in which he has performed the major functions of managing. Somewhere among these functions lies the explanation of the variance that needs adjusting. Something must be amiss in the POAC process. Weakness may exist in more than one of these areas. The manager is faced with the problem of finding answers to the question, "Where did we go wrong?" And, he must act promptly to make the necessary adjustments, before more serious and perhaps permanent damage results.

Reevaluation and Revision of Planning

Reevaluation of planned performance implies an examination of both facets of planning: the **objectives** and the **means** of accomplishing them.

It is not surprising that actual operations do not always turn out as well as anticipated. You will recall that the planning process itself is imperfect at best. In both long-range and current master planning, staff executives have to make forecasts and use them as the bases for predicting sales, competitors' actions, availability of capital, and many other factors. They are "educated guesses," which may turn out to be less accurate than managers thought they would be. The adequacy of the long-term plan can be no better than the forecast data on which it was based. Objectives reflect the planners' estimates of what the organization can probably accomplish with its particular resources in a particular environment.

It is always possible that the objectives were unrealistic, unbalanced, or otherwise inadequate. Necessary modifications may then be made. One thing a company must never do: it must never revise a target downward merely because it is difficult to achieve. If the target was originally set at an appropriate level, it probably is still appropriate. If it is not, it should be revised for that reason only.

One reason goals may no longer be appropriate is that changes may have taken place in the environment in which the business operates. Some of these changes are very difficult, or perhaps impossible, to predict in the forecasting process. A sudden change in the international situation, imposition of wage and price controls, a major strike, a regional disaster like an earthquake or flood, governmental tightening of fiscal and monetary controls, and legislative or regulatory changes are examples of environmental factors that cannot be foreseen or anticipated in a precise fashion. When they occur unexpectedly, business planning must be altered promptly to accommodate these drastic changes.[1] A complete review of the company's hierarchy of objectives is in order. Corporate objectives and operating objectives may no longer be appropriate.

It is also possible that the means selected to accomplish the objective are not sound. A company may have to revise its strategy to accomplish the same objective. Its existing strategy may be ineffective and inadequate although the target is appropriate.

A company may be trying to increase sales volume 10 percent by adding additional salesmen. Perhaps it could have achieved these results by increasing its advertising appropriation, or strengthening its dealer organization instead of adding sales personnel. The means may have been unwisely selected. Perhaps a procedure is not quite effective for the purpose; a method could be at fault. Improper routing or scheduling could be producing bottlenecks in order processing, billing, or production. Often, the means, the strategies being employed to accomplish a desirable end, are themselves inadequate or inappropriate. Revising, correcting, amending, or substituting a means may resolve the problem.

Reevaluation and Revision of Organizing

Any malfunction or maladjustment in the organizing area could be the cause of variance between desired and perceived results. Does the firm have the right personnel and the right equipment to carry out its projects? Have personnel been properly trained and assigned to their respective roles? Have jobs been properly defined? Are they related to each other in a sound structural order? What kind of place is this to work? Among the answers to these types of questions may lie the explanation for observed deviations from the expected. A manager must reexamine how well he has handled the organizing function of managing.

The fault could lie in many areas. The astute manager, therefore, must determine where the broken or weak links are in the chain. Is it possible that subordinates do not understand their duties and what is expected of them? Is there any confusion about lines of authority? Perhaps disorganized work relationships are causing work flow to be improperly planned or timed. There may be hidden problems in the personal relationships of members of the informal organization which are affecting the quantity or quality of work. Conferring with the leaders of the informal organization may shed light in this area. Their aid may also be necessary to correct any faults if they do exist.

If a firm does not have the right people in the right jobs, perhaps its process of procurement is faulty, including its techniques of procurement.

---

[1]External environmental factors and their influence on managerial decisions are the subject of Part VI, which follows this chapter.

Perhaps the job specifications are requiring greater capabilities of the individual than the job demands so that he is soon dissatisfied, and his discontent is reflected in his performance.

A middle-level manager may have more subordinates reporting to him than he can handle effectively. His span of authority may be too broad, and he may be giving only surface attention to some areas within his jurisdiction. He may be trying to manage too many areas and failing to do a good job in each. A restructuring of his responsibilities may be necessary, or he may need an administrative assistant.

From an overall point of view, certain activities may be centralized where decentralization would be more effective; other activities that are decentralized might produce better results if centralized. This may be particularly true of multi-market, multi-plant, and transnational companies.

Should the solution to the problem that produced the variance lie within the realm of the organizing function, a change of personnel, a change of equipment, a realignment of functions may be indicated—in short, a *reorganization* of modest, or even major, proportions.

Reevaluation and Revision of Activating

Inadequacies, weaknesses, or undue stresses in the activating process may reveal it to be the main source of excessive variation between actual and anticipated results.

Could there have been inadequate recognition and understanding of human motivation, failure to demonstrate leadership, lack of effective supervision including direction, misuse or failure to use appropriate incentives, or a breakdown in communications somewhere? If the answer to this question is yes, we have uncovered another locus of cause.

Foreman, supervisors, and high-level managers may be falling down in their ability to exercise leadership in getting subordinates to strive toward company goals. Where individual goals and organizational goals conflict, it takes leadership to integrate these divergent interests. This may require a manager to adopt a managerial style that is appropriate to the situation. Perhaps he is autocratic when he should be supportive; should supervise more loosely rather than so closely. Where leadership is faulty, it must be remedied. Someone at a higher vantage point should have the authority to make this determination and to suggest appropriate changes in managerial personnel if that course of action is indicated.

Normal interaction among people requires open lines of communication. Many disruptions in normal operations can be attributed to poor communications between management personnel and non-management personnel, and between various levels of management. In business, it has often been said, "the right hand doesn't know what the left hand is doing." Under these conditions, it is not difficult to understand how variance can occur. If it is true that the average person spends anywhere from 75 to 95 percent of his time sending or receiving information, the significance of adequate and proper transmission and reception becomes apparent. If communication does not inquire, inform, or persuade, it is failing in its basic purpose. The manager who succeeds in supplying information and developing understanding among his subordinates, and who initiates and reinforces attitudes among them, develops teamwork. Channels of communication should never become clogged. Interchange of thoughts and ideas should flow smoothly in all directions: downward, upward, laterally, and diagonally. If there is no flow, or even poor flow, in one of these directions, it may be the trouble area. In large organizations especially, communication becomes difficult. Not only are there eight or ten tiers through which communication must flow downward and upward, but often the only perceptible horizontal communication is that which takes place at the top level. This means that many executives in an organization are uninformed and, therefore, unaware of what is going on around them.

Direction is another activating area where variance may originate. Plans may have been incorrectly interpreted for subordinates, and instructions on how to carry them out may have been poorly conveyed. Where this occurs, one can expect significant deviations between planned performance and actual performance. If people in the organization do not know exactly what is expected of them, if things to be done and the way they are to be done are not clearly understood by them, it is very unlikely they will perform as management expects. It is possible that subordinates who resist controls do so because they do not fully understand the control system or its purpose.

It may be that a system of incentives intended to encourage workers and managers to put forth extra effort is improperly designed. Some incentives get better results than others. Under some conditions, the carrot may be better than the stick; under others, the stick may be more effective. Beyond a satisfactory level of economic security, increases in salary or fringe benefits have a lower inducement effect than do intangible incentives. Incentives which address themselves to satisfying esteem and self-fulfillment needs become more effective when security and social needs are already being met. The correct mix between positive and negative incentives is essential. Perhaps a review of this area will reveal that the inordinate use of negative incentives is causing stress in the organization, and making individuals less rather than more productive.

Reevaluation and Revision of Controlling

If no serious dislocations in planning, organizing, or activating can account for significant differences between observed results and desired results in any segment of the organization, the fourth and final area that a manager must reappraise is the control function itself. The weakness may be in controlling.

Where could malfunctions in the control system occur? The answer is that errors can occur in any of its sub-functions or sub-systems. That means there could be some weakness or inadequacy in measurement, record keeping, reporting, or comparison.

The process of measurement itself could be at fault. The measuring devices could have been unreliable. So, too, could records and accounts have been kept inaccurately. Human error can always creep into any accounting system. Moreover, relative measurements, by definition, are never precise. Where used, they offer many opportunities for divergences to occur that cannot be explained simply on the basis of chance, or random fluctuation. Measuring the value of creative work, or measuring creative output, is a tricky task at best. There is ample room for differences in judgment when subjective evaluation must be employed. Where direct and accurate measurement of any value cannot be achieved, direct and accurate results cannot be realized consistently either. Some variance, therefore, may have its roots in the imprecision of relative tools of measurement. When a manager uses observation as a basic indicator of how well things are going, he may be deceived by what he sees. As a completed product moves from factory to the shipping dock to be loaded, the people handling it may appear proud and happy while he watches them. But are they?

And what of reports? Are they accurate? Are they reliable? Do they state conditions as they really are or the way a manager would like to believe they are? How efficient is the reporting system? Does every manager and supervisor know to whom he is directly accountable? In a large organization, the answer may not be clear-cut. In reporting, as in all types of communication between superior and subordinate, a great deal of abstraction takes place. In an effort to boil down information to one page from twenty, a great deal of detail becomes lost, and the final report may be a distortion, albeit unintended, of the actual.

Finally, mistakes can occur in the process of making comparisons. Judgment errors do occur whenever one tries to compare, assess, evaluate, or appraise. Two sets of criteria must be essentially or basically similar before they can be compared. They must be related to each other in some identifiable way. To compare two dissimilar variables and arrive at a conclusion is tantamount to arriving at an incorrect one. Yet this is frequently done in business. An explanation of variance can often be attributed to a comparison that was made between two sets of data that were never really comparable to begin with.

DISCIPLINARY ACTION

In some instances, where it can be established that a significant difference is the result of an individual's failure to live up to the performance called for in his job definition, or the result of a culpable failure to conform to policies, instructions, and rules, disciplinary action may be necessary. It is a type of remedial or corrective action open to a manager. A person is disciplined not because he is bad, but because he has omitted or failed in some particular act expected of him and to which he has agreed, or has committed an impropriety.

When it becomes necessary to invoke disciplinary action, it should *always* be directed toward positive ends. Its intent is constructive and not punitive. Its purpose is to close the gap between actual results and intended results. As a managerial process, taking disciplinary action is designed to control individual and group behavior to assure proper performance on their part in the future.

It is evident that disciplinary action can be positive or negative. Positive action may take the form of encouragement, rewards, and additional training. Negative action includes the use of penalties for non-compliance.[2]

Characteristics of Disciplinary Action

Because of their importance, problems associated with the use of disciplinary action have been given much attention by many writers. For disciplinary action to be effective, it must exhibit the following characteristics: it must be (1) *expected,* (2) *impersonal,* (3) *immediate,* (4) *consistent,* and (5) *limited to the specific purpose.* A brief examination of these attributes will provide insight into their nature and importance.

1. **Expected.** Rules and regulations—that is, expectations—are established well in advance. Unexpected discipline is almost always considered unfair. Clear warning must state that a given action will lead to discipline, as well as the type or amount of discipline that will accompany the infraction. Frequently advance warnings will take the form of posted rules, as indicated in the following actual examples:

> No one is permitted to punch the timecard for another employee. Penalty is automatic layoff without pay for three days.

> Employees leaving the premises by rear exit will lose one day's work without pay for first offense; immediate dismissal for the second offense.

In these examples, negative sanctions are imposed for non-compliance in order to discourage it. Many writers do not believe in a negative form of disciplinary action even though it is directed toward positive ends. Wiard points out, "There may be cases where the use of punishment has resulted in

---

[2]These are closely related to the subject of positive and negative incentives, which are discussed in Chapter 20.

improved performance, but they are few and far between."[3] While it may not lead to "improved" performance, punishment does discourage repetition of the unwanted act!

2. **Impersonal.** Discipline should never be aimed at punishing the particular person or group guilty of an infraction, but rather at correcting the situation. It should be based on facts, not on personalities. The manager must take the position, and make it perfectly clear, that he is not finding fault with the individual personally but with the discrepancy which exists and which must be corrected.

3. **Immediate.** Corrective action should be taken as soon as possible after the deviation is discovered. The more quickly the disciplinary action follows the offense, the more likely it is that the offender will immediately associate the disciplinary action with the offense. This does not imply that final action will be taken without a full investigation of the facts in the case.

In an article relating to building and implementing an effective performance appraisal system, Zimmerer and Stroh point out that more good is accomplished by preventing mis-direction of energies than by waiting until some scheduled evaluation date to inform employees of their past "sins."

> If a manager were to tell me that for the past six month I had failed to perform a certain task in a satisfactory manner, and this was the first time I had been informed of this, my response would be simple: For one month I was wrong, but for the next five months that poor performance was his fault, because it was his responsibility to tell me the results of my work. I assumed that my performance was acceptable, because I did not hear differently. If I were told that my performance was substandard, I could have changed.[4]

Early identification and discussion of problems permit remedies to be applied before poor performance becomes habitual. The practice becomes an employee development function of managers at this point. Thus the early discussion is a positive step in helping employees toward self-improvement rather than a negative one of judgment and punishment. The manager has an opportunity to develop working relationships based on sincerity, objectivity, mutual trust, and respect.

4. **Consistent.** Rules and regulations are established for everyone, not just the violators. They must be fair and just. The concept of what is just should never disregard the worker as a human being. Otherwise, we create situations like that described by a former steelworker:

---

[3]H. Wiard, "Why Manage Behavior? A Case for Positive Reinforcement," *Human Resource Management,* Summer 1972, pp. 15–20.
[4]Thomas W. Zimmerer and Thomas F. Stroh, "Preparing Managers for Performance Appraisal," *SAM Advanced Management Journal,* Vol. 39, No. 3, July 1974, pp. 40–41.

I can recall when a friend of mine was killed in a car accident, and I took the day off to attend his funeral, and I was disciplined for two days because this was an unexcused absence.[5]

A line manager must not be guilty of favoritism or of being more lenient with one offender than with another. Consistency in disciplinary action is basic to sound human relations. Impartiality contributes stability to the organization. To tell one violator, "I'm going to let it go this time, but don't let it happen again," means the superior must say the same thing to the next violator in order to be consistent in his attitude toward disciplinary action. Regulations must be enforced uniformly.

5. **Limited to the purpose.** After disciplinary action has been taken, the superior should resume a normal attitude toward the subordinate. To treat a subordinate as though he is permanently "in the doghouse" is punitive and not positive in attitude. It encourages hostility and becomes self-defeating to the basic purpose of discipline, namely to close the gap that existed between actual performance and the norm.

There are times when the negative type of disciplinary action requires a personal **reprimand.** When this is indicated, it should be done in private. Remember, it is not punitive in intent, and it is not personal. A man would rather take a blow to his body than a blow to his self-esteem. Therefore a reprimand should not make a public spectacle or whipping boy of the subordinate. Praise can be given in public; a "bawling out" should be handled in private. Since a reprimand, or "disciplinary interview," is a procedure for correcting the employee so that he will do a better job, the time spent away from his job station must be considered as compensated time. Where such situations have gone to arbitration, it has been ruled that just as a worker is paid for training periods and orientation periods, so must he be paid for the time he spends in his boss's office for the purpose of being reprimanded.

In today's modern enterprise system most firms have an established system for handling disciplinary action. This is true of small as well as large firms, and is particularly true in firms that are unionized. Such a system is a **progressive** one which calls for increasing penalties for each successive infraction, ranging from a simple warning to the extreme penalty of dismissal. Generally the sequence of penalties under such a system of disciplinary action is: (1) oral warnings, (2) written warnings, (3) layoff, and (4) dismissal.

When a rule has been violated, the employee is first given an *oral warning.* Coupled with it, the supervisor should take all steps to aid the violator so that the infraction will not recur. For a second offense of the same nature, a *written warning* is issued. This usually becomes a part of the employee's personnel record and is tangible evidence that there has been a recurrence of the violation and that the employee has been so advised. Repeated infractions may be followed by a *disciplinary layoff* of several days or a week. The loss of income may be an effective negative incentive to get the point across to the employee that repeated violations of regulations will not be tolerated. Information that a disciplinary layoff occurred also becomes part of the personnel file. Finally, as a last resort, and only under the most extreme situations, the penalty of *dismissal* is used. Discharging a person is such a severe penalty both to the worker and to the company that it should be used with great restraint and only when no other recourse is feasible.

Another type of disciplinary action used as a remedial measure is **demotion.** Ordinarily it is used sparingly to remedy situations where an employee has been assigned a job that is "over his head," a job that is too big for him. Sometimes it is used where an employee is no longer able to perform effectively. To reduce the possibility of humiliation that can accompany a demotion, astute managers prefer to transfer a man laterally, without a reduction in pay, to some other area where he can handle the work that approximates his level of capability. Ordinarily this is a more humane course of corrective action than an outright, visible demotion.

SUMMARY

When it becomes apparent to a manager in any jurisdiction that things are not working out the way they should, that there is a significant gap between what was intended and what actually occurred, he must ask why.

If the discrepancy is one that can be laid to some unusual circumstance that is not likely to recur, or if it is one which is self-correcting, the manager need not do anything further. On the other hand, if the disparity indicates that steps must be taken to eliminate it before it gets out of hand and threatens the success of the organization, corrective action is called for.

In the final analysis, corrective action means reevaluating and reappraising the managing process itself, since lack of agreement between the norm and the actual is the result of some failure in one or more of its subfunctions. The root cause always lies somewhere in planning, organizing, activating, or controlling. Failure may have occurred in more than one of these major areas so that correcting shortcomings in one area may not be sufficient.

When disciplinary action is necessary, it should always be administered in a positive, constructive way. Its purpose is simply to eliminate the unwanted gap between actual results and intended results. If a reprimand is justified, it should be a private matter between subordinate and superior. Dismissal of an employee should be used only as a last resort when all other corrective efforts have failed.

KEY CONCEPTS

Disciplinary Action   Progressive Disciplinary System

Reprimand   Demotion

GLOSSARY

corrective action   A major control function in which steps are taken to eliminate significant variation between actual performance and planned performance.

disciplinary action   A type of remedial or corrective action in which the performance or behavior of a person or group is brought into conformity with organizationally prescribed patterns of conduct.

reprimand   A negative type of disciplinary action involving formal reproof or censure.

REVIEW QUESTIONS

1. Do all significant variations from the norm require corrective action? Explain.

2. Why is it important to distinguish between symptoms and causes in dealing with remedial action? Give an example of a symptom. A cause.

3. Where would you begin to look for underlying causes of significant variations that should be eliminated?

4. Do you believe that when disciplinary action is indicated, both rewards and sanctions should be used? Give an example of a situation in which you believe sanctions would be desirable.

5. List some characteristics of an effective system of disciplinary action.

6. What is a "progressive" system of disciplinary action?

Part VI
Strategic Management: Adjusting to the Macro-Environment

A business firm does not operate in a vacuum, isolated from other organizations or from the environmental forces which surround it. We have already observed how an organization's internal environment (micro-environment) influences its various functions. Changes that take place internally such as hiring of additional personnel, promotions, transfers, personality clashes, disagreement between supervisors and employees, introduction of incentives, and similar developments inevitably affect the operation of the firm and compel its managers to act and react. There is also another environment consisting of forces outside the firm, an external climate in which the company operates and to which it must also relate. It is this **external environment** (macro-environment) that we shall explore in the last part of this book.

There can be no meaningful analysis of environmental forces under static conditions. Static conditions do not exist in practice; consequently planning beyond the immediate future must always take into account change and uncertainty. One must bear in mind that the total environment is always in a state of transition or flux. This is one of the reasons why long-range planning is so difficult, and frequently inaccurate. Writing about the American democratic system, the eminent historian Daniel Boorstin observes:

> When we think about American democratic society, then, we must learn not to think about a condition, but about a process; not about democracy, but about the quest for democracy, which we might call "democratizing."
>
> The most distinctive feature of our system is not a system, but a quest, not a neat arrangement of men and institutions, but a flux.[1]

Those portions of the total environment that influence goal setting and goal attainment are often referred to collectively as the **task environment.** Prominent in the task environment are customers, suppliers, competitors, and regulatory groups including government agencies, unions, and business

---

[1]Daniel J. Boorstin, *Democracy and Its Discontents: Reflections on Everyday America* (New York: Random House, 1974), p. 122.

and professional associations. They represent various economic, social, political, religious, psychological, and physical forces at work in the total environmental system. A continuing interaction occurs between an organization and its task environment in a dynamic economy.

The critical test of the managing process is its effectiveness in dealing with these dynamic environmental influences which constantly demand its attention. A great many forces generated in the external milieu bombard the firm constantly, making repeated demands upon it. These shifting forces act both as deterrents and challenges to the firm as it strives to meet its desired objectives. In fact, the goals of an enterprise are achieved only to the extent that it adjusts successfully to these never-ending environmental changes. In the long run, inability on the part of business managers to cause the firm to accommodate to these shifting pressures leads ultimately to the failure of the enterprise.

Many of the top industrial firms in the United States fifty years ago are no longer on the scene today, largely as a result of their inability to adapt successfully to changing conditions. This concept of adaptation to environmental change has long been understood by the modern-day manager and is well expressed in a full-page color advertisement by Gulf Oil Company which states, "The only way a company can keep succeeding as the years go by is to keep adjusting its vision to changing needs."[2] Joseph Hall, board chairman of Kroger Company, is credited with having said, "If there's anything normal for the retail business, it is change." The president of Keystone International, Inc. had this to say:

> 1973 was a year of great change in the world and at Keystone International, Inc. A year of rising demand for products. Of uncontrolled cost inflation. Profit freezes in the United States. Material and labor shortages worldwide. A year of indecision on Wall Street and in Washington. Monetary fluctuations around the world. A year of the worldwide energy crisis. Of worldwide problems to evaluate these items. A year of many adjustments.
>
> At Keystone, many changes are taking place in an effort to manage our company under these changing conditions.[3]

Institutions that do not adapt to changing times either disappear or see their functions taken over by other institutions. Managers of modern businesses have the obligation, the essential task, to deal with change. Some changes tend to evolve slowly and develop gradually over time; others are more rapid, more dramatic and traumatic. How to deal with the problem of adapting the business organization to environmental changes is now being referred to by many management theorists as **strategic management.**

---

[2]*The Saturday Evening Post,* 1959. Coincidentally, this publication, which was founded by Benjamin Franklin around 1776 and was a weekly magazine until 1965, ran into serious cost problems and ceased publication in 1969. It resumed operations in 1971 as a quarterly, switched to six issues a year in 1973, and is currently issued nine times a year.

[3]Galen T. Brown, president, Keystone International, Inc., letter to stockholders, April 1974.

There is a strong positive relationship between strategic managing and long-range planning. After much research on the subject, Igor Ansoff concludes:

> I feel reasonably confident in advancing the conclusion that strategic planning is a preferred alternative to growth through fully decentralized adaptation without the benefit of an explicit strategy.[4]

An independent study by Robert House and Stanley Thune corroborates the effectiveness of long-range planning for company performance.[5]

In Chapter 7 it was pointed out that long-range planning must be sensitive to actual or potential environmental changes, and that these changes can be challenging opportunities as well as threats.[6] In the early 1960s, for example, Whirlpool Corporation recognized the future of permanent press fabrics and became the first company to market washers and dryers designed to accommodate these new materials. In the 1970s, on the other hand, working mothers, fewer children, and growth in the use of paper products in place of cloth could indicate a potential need for smaller washers and dryers.

Corporate long-range planning today is in the hands of the "futurists" whose work is beginning to be called "social and political forecasting," "environmental scanning," or "early warning systems development."

MAJOR SEGMENTS OF THE EXTERNAL ENVIRONMENT

The long-range planner must always take into account the interactions of the total environment of which his organization is a part, and their influence on what he wishes to accomplish. His goals must be perceived in relationship to changes that continue to occur in the world around him.

Sound strategy dictates that a manager marshal his resources to cope with and adapt to those elements in the macro-environment over which he can exert the greatest degree of influence or control. This is a principle of strategic managing.

The macro-environment is a composite of all external forces which impinge upon the operation of the firm. It is indivisible. Its components are inseparable. For purposes of analysis, however, it is helpful to delineate a few major segments of the external environment. In attempting this, we must bear several facts in mind: the segments are arbitrarily determined and are not the only subdivisions that could be established; all segments are interrelated and interdependent; changes in one produce changes in one or more

---

[4]H. Igor Ansoff, "Strategy as a Tool for Coping with Change," *Journal of Business Policy*, Vol. 1, No. 4, Summer 1971, p. 6.

[5]Robert J. House and Stanley Thune, "Where Long Range Planning Pays Off," *Business Horizons*, August 1970.

[6]The reader is referred to Figure 7-1.

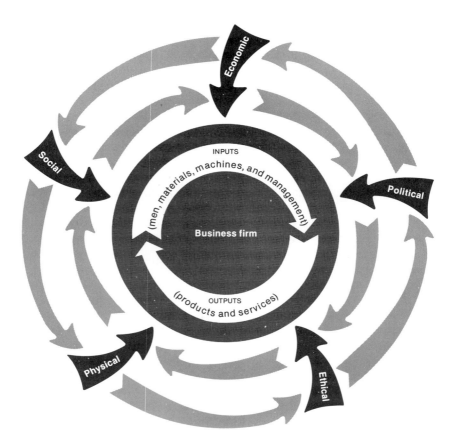

Figure VI-1.   The business firm and its external environment.
Forces influencing the business firm.

of the others; and some of the components of a given segment might with
equal justification be included within the framework of a different segment.
The movement of people to the suburbs, for example, could be treated as a
phenomenon occurring in the social segment or, with full justification, as a
change taking place in the economic sector. Placing it in one segment rather
than in another is an arbitrary determination justified by convenience and
the purpose intended.

For discussion purposes, therefore, the major subdivisions into which
the external environment will arbitrarily be divided are: (1) **social,** (2) **economic,** (3) **political,** (4) **ethical,** and (5) **physical.** Each of these will be discussed in a separate chapter. Their relationship to each other, and to the
business firm that influences them and is influenced by them, is illustrated
in Figure VI-1.

Chapter 25

Adjusting
to the Social Environment

The social environment is that portion of the external environment which deals with changes in behavior patterns of people and relationships among groups in society and the effects that these changes have upon the operation of business. While there are many sub-components of the social environment, only the following influences will receive our attention: (1) size and demographic distribution of the population; (2) rate of population increase; (3) birth rate; (4) number and size of households and family formations; (5) age distribution; and (6) social stratification. Changes in each of these areas significantly affect managerial decision making.

SIZE AND DEMOGRAPHIC DISTRIBUTION OF THE POPULATION

Some idea of the pace and impact of population change in this country can be gained from observing that of all persons living in the United States in 1975, 66.7 percent had no memories of World War II and its accompanying controls on wages and prices; approximately 50 percent were born after the Korean War ended; almost one-third had not yet been born when Alan Shepard launched into history with the first manned space shot in 1961; and approximately 13 percent were born after astronauts Edwin Aldrin and Neil Armstrong landed on the moon in 1969 and made the dramatic announcement, "That's one small step for man, one giant leap for mankind."

Bureau of Census projections indicate that the population of the United States, which was 180 million in 1960, will approach 230 million by 1980, an increment of almost 28 percent in 20 years. The tremendous population growth in this country has prompted business to make major adjustments to serve the multi-needs of an expanding society.

Not only has the population been growing and changing in many ways, but there have also been marked shifts in its geographic distribution. People have been moving from certain states to others, and from rural areas to the cities. One study indicates heavy migration during 1960–1970 *to* Florida, Nevada, Arizona, California, and Alaska, with the likelihood that it will continue to flow to these states during the 1970–1980 decade. The same study indicates heavy migration *from* North Dakota, District of Columbia, Arkansas, West Virginia, and Mississippi.[1] About two-thirds of the more than 3,000 counties in the United States actually had more people moving out than in during the past decade.

There is a continuing movement also toward metropolitan areas. Medium-sized cities having populations of 750,000 to 2 million persons are growing at the fastest rate.[2] Most of the growth in metropolitan areas is in the suburbs. In their book *The Year 2000* Kahn and Wiener estimate that three metropolitan areas will proliferate into **megalopolises** that will contain 44 percent of the 318 million people projected for the beginning of the new century. Twenty-five percent will live in "BosWash," the area between Boston and Washington; 13 percent will live in "ChiPitts," from the Great Lakes area around Chicago through Cleveland to Pittsburgh; and 6 percent in "SanSan," the area between San Diego and San Francisco.[3]

It is likely that 75 percent of the entire population will be living in as few as 25 cities by the turn of the century. The core areas of these cities will contain large numbers of minority groups, dependents, aged, and infirm persons who will place a heavy strain on schools, hospitals, recreational facilities, transportation systems, housing, and a multitude of related services.

In Figure 25-1 the bars on the left show that 136 million, or about two-thirds of the 205 million people in the U.S. in 1970, lived in metropolitan areas. The chart also indicates that more people now live in the suburbs than in the central cities. Suburbs grew about 25 percent between 1960 and 1970 (bars at right); the central cities and all non-metropolitan areas taken together also gained, but at less than half of the 13.7 percent growth rate of the nation.

The implications of these shifts, in terms of availability of labor supply, concentration of markets for consumer goods, development of new patterns of living, altered buying habits and consumer tastes, and increased social problems, must be analyzed and understood in order for business managers to make appropriate adjustments. As an example, the shift to the suburbs and the communications revolution have led to significant changes in the way customers of mail order catalog companies place their orders. For many of these companies, telephone orders and local catalog sales offices have become more important volume producers than the mail. Montgomery Ward & Company, which now derives only about 10 percent of its catalog

[1]Pietro Balestra and N. Koteswara Rao, *Basic Economic Projections, United States Population 1965–1980,* (Menlo Park, Ca.: Stanford Research Institute, 1964), p. 63.

[2]Lawrence A. Mayer, "New Questions about the U.S. Population," *Fortune.* February 1971, p. 85.

[3]Herman Kahn and Anthony J. Wiener, *The Year 2000: A Framework for Speculation on the Next Thirty-Three Years* (New York: Macmillan, 1967).

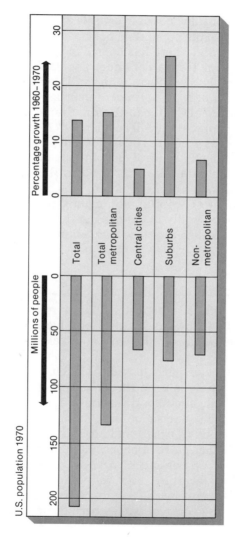

Figure 25-1. Population shifts: 1960–1970. (From Tom Cardamone for *Fortune,* February 1971, p. 83.)

volume from mail orders, has been opening more catalog stores and agencies in suburban areas.

RATE OF POPULATION INCREASE

Business managers must consider not only overall growth, but also the *rate* of population increase. While the population has been increasing, the rate of increase has not been constant. There has been a trend toward a slowing in the rate of growth. If recent trends continue, population increase in the 1970s is projected at roughly 22 million, with total population of only 227 million by 1980, a growth of only 11 percent.[4] Reports by both the National Fertility Study and the National Center for Health Statistics indicate that if present trends persist our population will reach only 270 million by the year 2000, a figure lower than that predicted by sociologists Kahn and Wiener.

Knowledge of the changing rate of population increase enables the astute manager to plan the rate at which to adjust his firm's productive capacity, channels and agencies of distribution, advertising and sales promotion budgets, and manpower, capital, and management requirements in order to accommodate successfully to changes in this segment of its social environment. Slower population increase can actually boost living standards for all.

BIRTHRATE

During the 1950s births totalled about 4 million annually and somewhat higher than that during the following decade. Total births seem destined to increase until at least 1980 although they are not likely to reach an annual level of 5 million by then.[5]

This baby boom has been parlayed into big business. An enormous amount of consumption activity is generated by each annual baby crop. A total annual birth gain of only 4 million translates during their lifetime into: 8 billion dozen eggs, 70 million quarts of milk, 48 billion pounds of meat, fish, and poultry, 53 billion pounds of bread and cereals, 134 billion pounds of fruits and vegetables, 1 billion pairs of shoes, 63 million suits and dresses, and 11 million new autos.[6] Processors of orange juice, manufacturers of baby foods, infant clothing, furniture, toys, and diaper services are only a few enterprises being challenged by shifts in numbers of births.

Although most of the huge crop of babies born during and shortly after World War II have married and reared families of their own, there is

[4]Lawrence A. Mayer, *op. cit.*, p. 81.

[5]*Ibid.*

[6]James L. Phillips, "Baby Boom: Big Business," *Brevits*, issued bi-weekly by Vance, Sanders & Co., Boston, Mass. No. 5, March 9, 1964.

evidence they have done so at somewhat older ages, and child bearing has either been delayed or spread out over a longer span of years. The paradox has been that while marriages have been on the rise, the birthrate has been declining. From 25 babies per 1,000 population in the mid-1950s, it dropped to 17.3 per 1,000 in 1971.

The pattern of child bearing today suggests an average of 2.1 infants per mother, the lowest on record. This drop in what demographers call the "total fertility rate" has prompted predictions of zero population growth in 70 years, provided immigration to the United States stops. Should the trend persist it will cause revisions in long-range economic forecasts.

Changes in the birthrate, whether a decreasing rate of increase or an actual decline, produce immediate impact. Diaper services may notice a slackening in growth of demand; retailers of infant clothing, cribs, buggies, and blankets may find it advantageous to offer a greater assortment of merchandise for older children to offset real or expected declines in the infant market. Gerber Corporation, once exclusively a baby food processor, has diversified into toys, as well as hospitalization insurance for adults. Johnson & Johnson has shifted its marketing emphasis from exclusive use of its products for infants to use by adults as well. Its advertising copy in recent years stresses that if baby talc and infants' shampoo are good for baby's sensitive skin and scalp, they must be good for mothers and athletes as well.

NUMBER AND SIZE OF HOUSEHOLDS AND FAMILY FORMATIONS

It is estimated that the number of households in the United States increased about 1 million per year during 1960–1970, and will increase by 1.3 million annually during the next decade.[7] In 1970 there were about 62 million households in the United States. A considerable portion of the increase has been in **individual households**—persons living alone, chiefly widows and divorced women, or those sharing a home with people who are not relatives. This relatively rapid increase in the number of primary individuals reflects the increasing proportion of older persons in the population, and the increasing tendency of these persons to maintain their own homes. The number of older Americans who maintain their own places of residence instead of living with relatives has more than doubled since 1950. The increase in primary households is also explained in part by the "my own apartment syndrome" of the young adults who, after completing their schooling and obtaining their first full-time employment, leave the family household to set up their own homes. This is evidenced by the large number of "singles" apartment complexes that are being built.

Increases in new household formations have great implications for businesses related in any way to housing or consumer durable goods. More

[7]Lawrence A. Mayer, *Op. cit.*, p. 84.

households translate into increased demand for housing and the products that go into housing.

Families have been getting smaller. Indications are that young parents want smaller families than did their parents. Many reasons have been advanced to explain the trend toward smaller families including the use of contraceptive pills and devices, legalized abortion, concern about air pollution, the rising cost of raising and educating children, overcrowding and environmental problems, more working women, and organized efforts like the Zero Population Movement launched in 1969 by Paul Ehrlich, the Stanford University biologist.

In 1965, average family size was 3.71 persons. By 1980, it is projected to be only 3.21 persons. This trend toward smaller family size requires additional adjustments for business firms. It means, for example, that homes in the future will be smaller, have fewer bedrooms and bathrooms, and will require smaller-capacity refrigerators in the kitchen. In the automobile industry there probably will be fewer station wagons produced. On the other hand, the market for the Pill will be potentially greater.

AGE DISTRIBUTION

Not only has the population been growing and changing in geographic makeup, but its composition has also been shifting in terms of age groups. In 1910, for example, there were 3 million persons over 65 years of age; in 1970, there were almost 20 million (9.4 percent); in the year 2000, it is estimated by some demographers that 30 percent of the population will be 65 or older. Bernice Neugarten rejects this contention, however, and believes it will range between 10 percent and 12 percent for the next two or three decades.[8] The projections in Table 25-1 seem to support her position.

In addition, while age groups have been increasing in total numbers, the rate of change has varied considerably. Table 25-1 is a population projection by age groups from 1965 through 1980. While total population is likely to increase on the order of 28 percent, substantial differences will occur in the rate of change among age segments. Some age groups will increase by as little as 1.7 percent; other by as much as 65.7 percent.

A number of additional observations can be made. Based on 10-year intervals, the largest segment of the population has been the 5–14 age group, accounting for about 20 percent of the total in each of the years shown, followed by the 15–24 year-olds. By 1980, almost two-thirds of the U.S. population will be under 35 years of age, and almost three-fourths will be under 45 years. Those 65 years and older will constitute slightly less than 10 percent, which means that only about 25 percent will be between 45 and 65.

---

[8]Bernice L. Neugarten, "The Young–Old," *University of Chicago Magazine,* Autumn 1975, p. 22.

Table 25-1. Projected population of the United States by age group: selected years 1965–1980*

Age group	1965 Population (thousands)	Percentage	1970 Population (thousands)	Percentage	1975 Population (thousands)	Percentage	1980 Population (thousands)	Percentage	1965–1980 Percentage increase
Under 5	22,141	11.4	23,895	11.3	25,630	11.2	27,375	11.0	23.6
5–14	38,983	20.0	42,431	20.1	46,253	20.2	49,794	20.0	28.0
15–24	30,125	15.5	35,702	16.9	39,285	17.1	43,218	17.3	43.5
25–34	21,906	11.2	24,534	11.6	30,675	13.3	36,296	14.6	65.7
35–44	24,344	12.6	22,901	10.8	22,098	9.7	24,758	10.0	1.7
45–54	21,976	11.3	23,329	11.1	23,677	10.3	22,357	9.0	1.7
55–64	16,941	8.7	18,597	8.8	20,071	8.7	21,406	8.6	26.4
65 and over	18,081	9.3	19,740	9.4	21,563	9.4	23,715	9.6	31.2
Total	194,497	100.0	211,129	100.0	229,252	100.0	248,919	100.0	28.0

*Derived from statistical data contained in *Basic Economic Presentations, United States Population 1965–1980*, by Pietro Balestra and N. Koteswara Rao. Menlo Park, Ca. Stanford Research Institute, 1964.

This shifting in the age distribution of our country will have far-reaching effects upon the decision makers in our businesses during the next decade. The major population explosion will occur in the family-forming age groups, which means a further expansion in housing and consumer goods and services. A leading manufacturer of mobile homes, recognizing the impact of this age stratification on its future operations, made this statement to its stockholders:

> It is estimated that one-third of today's existing housing will be demolished and replaced by 1990. Probably 30 to 35 million new units of all kinds will be required to meet the demand between 1970 and 1985, conservatively. The biggest market will be in the young marrieds. This 35-and-under segment of the population will be growing twice as fast as the population as a whole during the current decade. The mobile home industry expects to capitalize on this as 55% of the purchasers of mobile homes fit into this category. This segment will increase by 50.7% during 1970–80 while the population as a whole will increase 22.1%. The second largest buyer of mobile homes are retired families 55 and over. This category is also growing rapidly. Growth of these segments should provide an increased stream of new potential customers.[9]

The youth market possesses awesome purchasing power and to a large extent influences family buying decisions. Young adults are in the market for television, boats, bicycles, books, first homes, camping vans and do-it-yourself supplies. Advertisers are well aware of the buying power in the under-25 age group. Rather than directing their media efforts to the broad mass, advertisers are targeting their approach, trying to reach specific people in specific age groups.

A study by *Life* of 30 million persons aged 10 to 17 revealed some startling statistics. They buy more than 35 percent of all sportswear, are estimated to buy 20 percent of all cars sold, account for 44 percent of all camera sales, 55 percent of all soft drink sales, and 35 percent of the movie audience. The girls purchase 33 percent of all hair dryers and 23 percent of all cosmetics, and spend over 20 million dollars on lipstick alone.[10] It has been estimated that for every lipstick a woman of 40 buys, a woman of 20 will purchase five.

For the construction and home furnishings industries, the coming bulge in the 25 to 34 age group is particularly meaningful. According to the First National City Bank, New York, less than one-fifth of American families buy a house before the family head is 25, but about one-half do when the family head is between 25 and 35.

Beer sales have been increasing. Most of the growth can be attributed to factors not planned or controlled by the brewers themselves. The expand-

---

[9]Town and Country Mobile Homes, Inc., 1972 Annual Report, p. 6.
[10]*The Wall Street Journal*, May 24, 1967.

ing population between the ages of 21 and 39 is the primary cause of beer sales growth. This age group, which consumes nearly 70 percent of this beverage, has been growing rapidly.[11]

Management, particularly in expanding companies, can expect a ripple effect as the percentage of persons aged 35 to 44 drops by 1980. A potential shortage of "middle management," which is drawn from this age group is likely.

There is ample evidence also that adjustments are being made in anticipation of a shortage of 45–54 year-olds, an **executive age gap,** which has been projected. Statistics on business growth suggest that the demand for executives will be one-third greater in the mid-1970s. Gerald L. Phillippe, General Electric Company chairman, describes managerial leadership as "the most critical factor" confronting any concern like GE whose sales have doubled every 10 years. "Where do we get the men to manage twice what we are managing now, in a tremendously more complex environment?" he asks.[12] Speedy recognition and promotion of potential leaders, especially young people, is the principal way many corporations hope to meet these demands. By the 1980s, substantially more 40-year-old and 30-year-old people will occupy top-level management positions. The chances are favorable that there will also be additional numbers of women, as well as older men, in top executive positions during the coming decade. This means revisions will have to be made in existing programs aimed at "early retirement" and fixed date mandatory retirement of competent older executives.

Firms with in-depth executive talent will be in the best position to consider expansion programs, mergers requiring executive know-how for success, or even programs calling for decentralization of plant and personnel. To avoid the executive age gap, to have available executive talent in depth, it may also be necessary for business leaders to embark on recruitment programs, to develop or expand management training programs, or even to take defensive measures to guard against raiding or pirating. They will have to offer present managers attractive incentives to remain with the firm, including the opportunity for rapid promotion to responsible positions. Under these conditions, business leaders must be careful not to promote young men into positions they cannot handle effectively, lest the Peter Principle become operative. Short-run expediency could lead to long-run disadvantages for both the individual and the organization.

When asked what the rising average age of the U.S. population might mean for Gillette Company in the 1980s, its director of commercial research recommended that the company design and market more products aimed at the previously ignored over-55 age group.[13]

---

[11]*Industry Week*, December 14, 1970, p. 57.

[12]*The Wall Street Journal*, January 2, 1968, p. 1.

[13]Liz Roman Gallese, "The Soothsayers," *The Wall Street Journal*, March 31, 1975, p. 10.

In terms of that segment of the population aged 65 or older, the implications are also vast. The migration of older persons to warmer climates accounts for a substantial portion of the population influx to Florida, California, Arizona, Nevada, and Texas. This is likely to continue at an accelerated rate. Huge retirement centers are being developed with housing, including condominiums, designed for the retiree.

If as many as 15 percent of the population should be 65 years and older by the year 2000, it is likely that more than 30 percent will be drawing social security benefits (persons are now eligible at age 62, and life expectancy then will be 50 percent greater). Moreover, only about 40 percent of the citizens (those between the ages of 18 and 62) will be contributing toward the payments. Will this call for changes in existing social security administration? There are additional implications when one considers that in the 65 and older age group there are 50 percent more women than men.

Another configuration that is appearing as a result of people living longer and in relatively better health is a group in the 55 to 75 age range which Neugarten calls the **young-old**.[14] This is not only a relatively healthy group (not more than 1 in 4 is estimated to have any limitations on activities because of health) but also an increasingly comfortable one economically.

Challenging opportunities to develop geriatric centers, manufacture leisure time products for fishing, golfing, boating, and camping, and produce and distribute medical, nursing, and pharmaceutical products are some that will be present. Managers with vision should plan today to capitalize on opportunities that are inevitable tomorrow among our nation's senior citizens.

SOCIAL STRATIFICATION

The importance of status, or social position, is another dimension of the social environment of which business executives are keenly aware.

People are very status conscious and seek various symbols to advance their relative social position. In *The Status Seekers,* Vance Packard vividly points out the social importance to most people of church affiliation, the neighborhood in which one lives, the occupation or profession one follows, and similar status considerations. Two cars in every garage, color television, and a pleasure boat (preferably a large one) are familiar symbols in the community today.

Recognizing that people are acutely status conscious, managers take advantage of this social awareness in developing their marketing strategies. In advertising its Lincoln Continental cars, Ford Motor Company made these statements: "These are cars apart and above"; "At the top of the class"; "The Continentals: the final step up." Emphasis is placed on the car, not as a superior vehicle of transportation, but as a symbol of status. Should non-

[14] Bernice L. Neugarten, *op. cit.,* p. 23.

smoking become widespread as a status symbol, manufacturers of cigarettes will have considerable adjustments to make as the number of smokers declines.

SUMMARY

The forces that make up the social environment are dynamic, changing, and powerful. These shifting forces affect the operations of all organizations. The business organization is no exception.

Shifts in size and distribution of the population, the rate of population change, the birth rate, number and size of households and family formations, changes in age distributions, and shifts in social stratification are all taking place. Business organizations can do little to change the direction or intensity of these social phenomena. Nevertheless, management must recognize the existence and implications of these forces and make decisions that permit fruitful accommodation to them. Recognizing potential social trends provides lead time for business decision makers to benefit from them as challenging opportunities. Failure to do so may mean painful and costly readjustments that could threaten survival.

KEY CONCEPTS

Demography	Executive Age Gap
Megalopolis	Young–Old
Individual Households	Social Stratification

GLOSSARY

demography   The study of the size and density distribution of human populations.

megalopolis   A population center that includes several contiguous metropolitan areas.

social environment   That portion of the total external environment that deals with behavior patterns of people and relationships among groups in society.

REVIEW QUESTIONS

1. What is the social environment?
2. List some of the sub-units into which the social environment can be divided.

3. Why is it important to a business manager to know the distribution of the population? Give examples.

4. If you knew the birthrate was declining, what changes would you make in your plans if you owned a diaper service company?

5. Of what value is it to you today to know that 25 years from now 15 percent of the people in the U.S. will be 65 years of age or older?

6. Do you think your chances of being promoted to a managerial job are increasing or decreasing? Why?

7. What is the makeup of a college class likely to be within the next 25 years? Justify your position.

Chapter 26

Adapting
to the Economic Environment

The economic segment of the total environment deals with production and consumption activities of individuals and organizations that influence the operation of business enterprises and all other institutions.

A review of developments in a few sub-areas of the economic sector will serve to illustrate the tremendous impact economic changes have on business. The sub-areas considered here are (1) gross national product; (2) location of markets; (3) income; (4) standards of living; (5) buying habits; (6) competition; (7) technology; and (8) government spending. They are all interrelated and interacting. Changes that occur in one sub-sector will produce changes in others.

GROSS NATIONAL PRODUCT

The gross national product is a compilation by the United States Department of Commerce of the total market value of all *final* goods and services produced in the United States in any given time period. It consists of consumers' expenditures and government expenditures plus gross private investment. In general, GNP does not include *intermediate* products. Thus a suit of clothes is a final product, and is included in the gross national product; but the cloth from which the suit was made or the wool from which the cloth was made are not included in order to avoid double counting.

As Figure 26-1 reveals, gross national product has been increasing steadily since 1935 and has spurted upward dramatically since the end of World War II in 1945. Estimates are that it will reach $1.4 trillion in 1975 and $2.0 trillion by 1980.

Of particular interest to business managers is a breakdown showing how much of this increase represents inflation and how much is the result of increased productivity. If, for example, GNP increases 9 percent in a year, an inflationary growth of not more than 3 to 4 percent would be acceptable. The balance, about 5 to 6 percent, would represent an increase in real productivity per capita, a very welcome rate of national growth for a maturing economy.

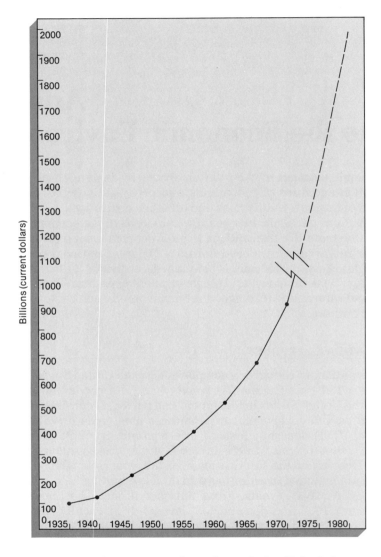

Figure 26-1. Gross national product of the United States: 1935–1980. (Based on Statistical Abstract of the United States, 1972; *United States Industrial Outlook 1972 with Projection to 1980*. United States Department of Commerce.)

The short-run effect of changes in gross national product is dramatically revealed in the machine tool industry. Historical research within the

National Machine Tool Builders' Association indicates that a 3 percent drop in GNP can trigger a 41 percent decline in machine tool orders.[1]

The critical component in the GNP is the inflation factor, and no enterprise can escape its devastating effects. Beginning in 1964, prices climbed an average of 4.4 percent a year until the mid-1970s. In 1974 they soared to an annual rate of 15 percent as measured by the Consumer Price Index. The U.S. economy faced the unique dual problem of combating both inflation and a mild depression, which saw unemployment reach the undesirably high level of 8.5 to 10.0 percent.

Traditional economics suggests that if business institutions raise their rate of capital investment, the resulting increase in productivity will hold the price level down. However, worldwide experience during the mid-1970s tends to indicate that higher levels of capital formation will not save a nation from inflation. A comparison of nations on the basis of gross fixed investment as a percentage of GNP in 1974 showed Japan at the top with 36 percent, France next with 28 percent, followed by Germany with 26 percent, and the U.S. at the bottom with a rate of 18.2 percent.[2] The Chairman of Citicorp, parent company of First National City Bank, says:

> Unfortunately, these higher investment rates do not produce lower inflation. The fact is that Japan, the country with the highest rate of investment, also has the highest rate of inflation. France, with the next highest rate of investment, produces the next highest rate of inflation. Of all these countries the United States actually had the lowest inflation rate in 1973.[3]

There has been a movement in recent years to modify the measurement of economic growth by substituting **net economic welfare** (NEW) for GNP.[4] NEW subtracts some of the non-productive costs associated with growth to give a more realistic indicator of rate of growth than is currently provided by GNP. Under NEW, growth has been at a slower rate than the GNP indicates. Whichever measurement is employed, managers will still be concerned with the proportion of economic growth that is real and the proportion that reflects inflation.

LOCATION OF MARKETS

There are at least three types of markets that hold great interest for an owner or manager of a business. He is concerned with (1) labor markets, (2)

---

[1] For a discussion of the use of the GNP as an economic indicator in forecasting, the reader is referred to Chapter 7.

[2] Walter B. Wriston, "Capital Formation—What Is the Question?" remarks before the Business Council, Hot Springs, Virginia, October 12, 1974, p. 3.

[3] *Ibid.*

[4] Paul A. Samuelson, *Economics,* 9th ed. (New York: McGraw-Hill, 1973), pp. 195–197.

markets for raw materials, and (3) markets for the sale of his products or services. He must be assured of a steady source of labor and raw materials, and ready access to the end users of his output. Changes in the availability or accessibility of any of these markets greatly influence his decision making.

As population shifts, markets tend to shift also. The trend toward concentration of people in major metropolitan areas and the development of megalopolises has already been noted.[5] If 44 percent of the people are going to reside in three of these sprawling centers, as predicted, with perhaps 75 percent living in as few as 25 cities, then markets for labor and consumer products will become concentrated also. This will call for changes in production and marketing strategies of business executives.

A manufacturer of coffee, toothpaste, or deodorant will know where the potential consumer market exists for 75 percent of its output. Production facilities will be located nearby. Breweries, for example, will produce beer close to the ultimate consumers, where population is concentrated, rather than ship the finished product long distances from point of production to point of consumption. To be competitive, manufacturers of beer cans will find it advantageous to build can-making facilities close to the beer-producing plant, reducing or eliminating shipping costs and offering superior delivery service to their customers. Advertising and sales promotion efforts will become regionalized, concentrating on a rifle rather than a shotgun approach to markets.

Shifts in population also mean a readjustment to those business firms whose former customers have been moving away. As an example, when blacks move to northern cities from rural southern areas, the migration leaves a void that is difficult to fill. It is reflected in fewer customers for southern retail establishments and a decrease in the number of service-type companies. In short, businesses so affected must make serious adjustments to this changing condition if they are to survive.

The labor market also is affected by shifts in the geographic distribution of people. Population outflow from a region can cause serious dislocations in availablity of labor. If labor supply evaporates, existing firms are hard pressed to find a replacement pool of labor resources. Firms planning on expansion will not locate in an area where the contemplated labor market is unstable or shrinking.

Markets for raw materials have been changing, requiring business firms to revise their former methods of operation. Included in the cost of raw materials is the cost of transporting them to the site where they become components in the production process. As was indicated in Chapter 16, this is a factor in the decision to decentralize. In the meat packing industry, for ex-

---

[5]The reader is referred to Chapter 25.

Table 26-1.   Total personal income:
1963–1972*

Year	Total income (billions of dollars)
1963	465
1964	497
1965	538
1966	587
1967	629
1968	688
1969	750
1970	806
1971	861
1972 (Oct.)	962

*From United States Department of Commerce.

ample, processing plants are now located where cattle are raised—primarily where corn, their chief source of feed, is grown. No longer are cattle shipped hundreds of miles from grazing grounds to stockyards and slaughterhouses. Chicago and East St. Louis, Illinois have ceased to be meat processing centers of the United States. Today about 75 percent of all cattle slaughtered in this country, about 27 million head annually, are brought to mature weight on feedlots. The feedlot is the most efficient and economical way to put weight on cattle.[6] Located adjacent to feedlots, processing plants are modern, one-story, highly efficient production units. Dressed beef, the finished product, is now shipped long distances, instead of cattle on the hoof. It costs only 2 cents per pound to ship steaks from Colorado meatpackers to Chicago markets, a distance of 915 miles.[7] Other food processors, too, are locating closer to raw material supplies. Campbell Soup has opened plants in areas where vegetables are grown, not too far from centers of population where the canned goods will be consumed.

INCOME

There is ample evidence that income has been increasing and its distribution shifting since the era of Franklin D. Roosevelt. Changes in income affect standards of living and influence markets. Increases in retail sales volume are a reflection of increases in personal income.

Changes in personal income from 1963 to 1972 are shown in Table 26-1. The increment has been more than 100 percent in less than a decade. Today, personal income exceeds $1 trillion a year. Multiple paychecks within

---

[6]Lawrence A. Mayer, "Monfort is a One-Company Industry,"*Fortune*, January 1973, p. 91.
[7]*The Wall Street Journal*, June 7, 1972, p. 9.

families tell part of the story. The number of working women has increased about 10 million (50 percent) since the late 1950s, compared with an approximate growth of 15 percent in number of working men.[8] Another factor has been a sharp decline at the poverty level during the last decade. The number of persons subsisting at the poverty level has dropped from 40 million to 24 million between 1959 and 1969.[9]

Almost half of all disposable personal income is of the "discretionary" type, that portion beyond the amount required for the necessities of life. Increased discretionary income coupled with declining poverty provides the consumer with a broad range of options: to save more; to invest in further income-producing or growth situations; to spend more for clothing, consumer durables, recreation, travel, books, magazines, and education; or to devote a portion of time to alleviating social problems or working for other worthy causes.

Consumption patterns alter with changing income patterns. Higher levels of income and lower levels of poverty translate into a changing proportion of income that is spent for food, housing, clothing, and luxuries. Increased affluence has rendered obsolete Engel's Law,[10] which states that the lower a family's income, the greater the percentage of that income that will be spent on food. Growing disposable income has boosted beer sales, for example. Because beer has become a home commodity, increased income enables consumers to stock it and consume it during periods of leisure. This trend has produced a noticeable shift in beer markets. In 1947 approximately 43 percent of all beer was consumed in bars and taverns; by 1970, the figure had dropped to 30 percent. Today, more beer is sold in supermarkets than in any other outlet. Now the eight-pack is the conventional unit of sale.

STANDARDS OF LIVING

Largely as a result of increased income, living standards in the United States have been rising too. Many items formerly considered luxuries are now regarded as necessities, including washers and dryers, air conditioners, dishwashers, and garbage disposals.

Most households possess an automobile, and many of them two or more, particularly where the wife is also employed or where there are teen-age children. Today air conditioning is standard equipment in many car models and is no longer an "optional" luxury item.

---

[8]*Ibid.*, December 11, 1972, p. 1.

[9]Lawrence A. Mayer, "New Questions about the U.S. Population," *Fortune*, February 1971, p. 85.

[10]Ernst Engel, Prussian statistician whose 1857 studies of consumption based on income led to generalizations known as Engel's Laws.

A television set is a familiar sight in the typical home and more than one is not uncommon. Affluence, coupled with the increasing teen-ager segment of the poulation, has brought a second telephone into many homes, as well as stereo sets and cameras. Magazines, newspapers, and tape collections are commonplace. A college education, once limited to the wealthy, is now nearly as routine as a high school education formerly was.

With rising **discretionary income** and education levels, Americans are likely to be more fastidious, demanding better quality, better service, and greater variety in the goods and services offered in the marketplace. Today consumers seek more convenience foods like "boil in a bag" vegetable mixes, prepared and frozen products of endless variety, pre-packaged meats, TV dinners, and the like.

More people make more frequent use of medical and dental care, nursery and pre-nursery school, baby sitter services, multi-insurance coverage, services of bankers, stockbrokers, lawyers, and other professionals. Consumer credit, including deferred payment plans, is increasing. "Fly now—pay later" is becoming a common practice. The portion of each dollar spent on these kinds of services has been rising since the 1950s; in 1954 it was 35 cents and by 1970 it reached 46 cents.

Only a part of this increased spending on services can be attributed to affluence and increased demand in a changing society. A considerable portion is also inflationary. The cost of services has been rising more rapidly than the rate of increase in discretionary income.

The significance of these changes in living standards is not lost on business managers. They are well aware that increased interest in travel, hobbies, do-it-yourself projects, and the arts, and the parallel upgrading of tastes, present both a challenge and an opportunity for them.

BUYING HABITS

Increasing income, moves to the suburbs, shorter working hours and more leisure time, improved living standards, and concerns about social and economic problems have produced changes in consumer buying habits. This becomes the concern of any company selling consumer goods and services.

People are not merely able to buy more, but are also more selective in their buying. Many executives believe that taste is improving and that it is wise corporate policy to anticipate it. "We try to design just ahead of the market so that when public taste advances, we are ready for it," states the manager of General Electric's Industrial Design Department.[11]

GE is also anticipating the possible impact of energy conservation on the 1980s. If consumers are deeply concerned about energy conservation, it

[11]*Markets of the Sixties,*(New York: Harper & Brothers 1960), p. 123.

may mean that G E and others will have to develop products that consume less energy.

Which group of people are first to set the buying patterns that others follow? The evidence is strong they are not those with the most money, but rather the "suburbanites" (a status connotation with very strong appeal). They are persons who are moving upward on the income scale, and also moving around geographically; most have acquired a good deal of formal education; and their work and leisure activities bring them into contact with a wide variety of people. Opinion Research Corporation calls them "high mobiles" and claims they were the first to buy electric blankets, low-calorie beverages, dining credit cards, food freezers, colored bed sheets, and wall-to-wall carpeting.[12] Today suburbanites start mass fashions. Business can look forward to frequent and extreme changes in style and fashion, and probably to an endless and rapid series of fads. These include fashions in clothes and grooming for men as well as women. Today "fashion goods" is a large new market category that extends beyond clothing and shoes.

In general the trend has been toward casual living. People want simpler, more comfortable clothing. As a result, the "casual look" has been accentuated. It is common to see women wearing shorts in the supermarket in suburbia. Slacks and sport jackets have taken the place of suits and offer greater flexibility in the male wardrobe. Sportswear is more suited to suburban living. Headwear, with the exception of sport caps, has almost disappeared from the scene.

In architecture, the two-story house has given way to the ranch house and the ranch house to the split-level. There are many who say that the "house" is replacing the car as the great American status symbol. Town-house apartments and condominiums are examples.

Shopping habits have been changing also. More shopping is done as a family unit, frequently at the one-stop shopping malls which have proliferated, and which offer the convenience that consumers want. Since husband and wife both often work during the day, evening shopping has been on the rise.

With projections for 1980 indicating that 60 percent of the food will be eaten outside the home, compared with only 30 percent in 1972, Green Giant Comany, producer of canned and frozen vegetables, has gone into the restaurant business. Its president stated, "We felt it important to be strong in this area if we wanted to remain strong in the food business."[13]

Outdoor barbecueing has become a way of life in the suburbs. Only since the advent of suburbia have we been able to purchase charcoal for

---

[12]*Ibid.*, p. 125.
[13]*Business Week*, August 5, 1972, p. 75.

outdoor grills from almost any filling station, grocery, or drugstore. Business firms do accommodate to society's changing living and buying habits by altering their own modes of operation.

COMPETITION

In our market enterprise system, imperfect as it is, competition is a strong regulating factor. It prods managers to keen awareness of what the "competition" is doing and what they, in turn, must do to retain their relative positions. Firms have to competitive, meaning that they must offer the buyer as much for his dollar as he can obtain from another source; or the worker as much for his services as the next firm offers; or the investor as much for the use of his equity as he could obtain by investing it elsewhere. Competition has many facets and does battle in many arenas.

Competition among Firms in the Same Industry (Intra-Industry)

The most obvious type of competition is among firms in the same kind of business. Department stores compete with each other to attract the consumer. A steel mill competes with another steel mill for markets. A bank competes with other banks by offering "full-service" banking. On a regional or national basis, chains compete with other chains. A & P competes with Kroger, Safeway Stores, Food Fair Stores, and Loblaws. Each competes with the others and with independent stores as well.

Among firms in the same industry, there is also competition for labor resources, especially for skilled or technically oriented personnel. In addition, they may vie for raw materials that may be in short supply. To generate electric power, fuel is needed to produce steam. Natural gas, being in short supply, is limited to homes for heating, air conditioning, cooking, and similar purposes, and to smaller industrial and commercial establishments. The electric companies, therefore, turn to coal as an alternative. Largely because of the pollution factor, low sulphur coal is more desirable for their purpose than high sulphur coal. Power plants, therefore, compete to obtain sources for this relatively scarce raw material which is so essential in their operation.

Competition among Different Industries (Inter-Industry)

Frequently one industry will compete with another for the same markets. The steel industry vies with the aluminum industry for the use of their respective materials in the production of cans. In announcing that it had developed a lighter, less expensive aluminum can than those currently in use, Aluminium Corporation of America indicated that the 12-ounce containers weigh about 30 percent less than existing all-aluminum cans and "appreciably less than tin-free steel cans."[14] A spokesman for American Can stated, "It will certainly help the aluminum people remain competitive with the steel industry in the production of cans."[15] However, the steel industry has come up with an alternative. Their new beer and soft drink cans made out of "skinny tinplate" are 40 percent lighter than the old tinplate cans, yet as strong and safe as the others.[16]

Copper contends with steel for end users. When copper is in short supply, its price rises. As a result, many firms which use copper in conductive cables are forced to substitute copper-coated steel instead. For construction uses, concrete competes with steel in special shapes like I-beams and H-beams. Plastic pipe competes with steel pipe for water lines and irrigation systems. Cotton competes with synthetics for finished textile products. Gas vies with coal, oil, and electricity for heating and cooking purposes.

The examples of competition among industries is almost endless. Not only do giants within industry compete with each other, but industries vie with each other for sources of labor, raw materials, and markets for their finished products or services.

In recent years shortages of raw materials have intensified the competition among industrial users. Without adequate raw materials no industry, and no firm within a particular industry, can maintain production levels. Today a large number of materials are in short supply. The effect on some companies has been severe. A Senate study of the 500 largest American industries identified 63 different material shortages, of which 39 were primary materials such as chemicals, petrochemicals, steel, and copper, and 24 were secondary materials like paper and plastics.[17]

One of the critical shortages has been energy. Business and industry account for nearly 70 percent of all the energy used in our country. To a large extent, the rapid growth of U.S. industry can be attributed to low-cost energy, much of it in the form of imported oil. When the Arab countries raised crude oil prices in 1973 and put an oil boycott into effect, the repercussions were enormous. Primarily, it signalled that the era of low-cost energy has ended and is not likely to recur.

Increased petroleum prices have changed the relative economics of new energy sources. Prices of $10–$15 per barrel increase the feasibility of turning to oil shale recovery, secondary recovery from low-yield wells, and the development of solar and nuclear energy. Gerald Decker of Dow Chemical summarizes the impact of high petroleum prices:

---

[14]*The Wall Street Journal*, February 27, 1968.

[15]*Ibid.*

[16]"Profile of an American Industry," *Steelways*, May–June 1969.

[17]Report of Permanent Subcommittee on Investigations of the Committee on Government Operations, United States Senate, August 1974.

I should probably say, in the context of the long-range picture, that it is really more of an interim period from 1980 to 2000 that we need to primarily look to coal and nuclear. Beyond that, I think we need to go to sources that have an even longer time base, such as solar, fusion, and geothermal.[18]

Several other courses are open to professional managers. They can focus on increasing efficiency in energy use; it has been estimated that a 15 percent efficiency increase can save the equivalent of 4 million barrels of oil per day. They can introduce products which require less energy to operate; re-design production facilities to conserve fuel; and develop substitutes for feedstocks that currently are used to produce synthetics and man-made fibers.

Reflected in increased prices for gasoline, higher petroleum prices have produced sudden shifts in demand on the part of the consumer. Witness the change from large to small automobiles. Higher prices for oil were probably more responsible for inflationary pressures on the U.S. economy and the unfavorable balance of trade payments during 1974–1975 than any other single factor. In today's economic environment, managers face an entirely new set of conditions imposed by the "energy gap." The need to integrate the planning function with the production–distribution system has never been greater.

Foreign Competition (Extra-Industry)

Foreign producers also provide fierce competition for American firms. This competition assumes two forms. First, not only do domestic firms compete with each other for foreign markets, but they also struggle with foreign firms for many of the same markets. To gain a foothold for air conditioners in Western Europe, a Japanese firm sold them below cost for three years.[19] Secondly, foreign firms seeking markets in the United States offer severe competition. When they export to this country they offer equal or superior quality, foreign styling and the status connotation that goes with it, lower price, or a combination of these factors which add up to "good values" for American end users and tough competition for their American counterparts. Nisson Motor Company and Toyota Motor Company established footholds in the U.S. by offering dealers higher commissions than were paid on American cars and on other imported cars, plus generous advertising support.

Although transistor radios and TVs have been imported into this country since the 1950s, in recent years shoes, textiles, and steel have been greatly affected by imports. Let us see how this has occurred.

[18]Gerald L. Decker, (Utilities Manager, Dow Chemicals Company), "Energy Conservation," *Phi Kappa Phi Journal,* Winter 1975, p. 23.

[19]Louis Kraar, "How the Japanese Mount That Short Blitz," *Fortune, September 1970, p. 127.*

Ladies' dresses and play shoes, high-fashioned and well-made, pro-duced on American lasts in Italy and Spain, have been entering the United States in increasing quantities, as have lower-priced shoes from Hong Kong and Taiwan. Men's and boys' dress shoes come from Italy, Spain, and Majorca; excellent work shoes of horsehide from the Iron Curtain countries including Roumania and Yugoslavia. Canvas shoes and thong sandals (with soles made from discarded U.S. rubber tires) from Taiwan, Japan, Korea, and Hong Kong offer the severest competition to domestic manufacturers whose labor and material costs are no match for the imports. Many American manufacturers have discontinued producing these items.

The American textile industry has fought a losing battle to maintain a two-way street in international trade. Since 1958 the United States has run a deficit in its textile trade account. As many as 50 nations actually prohibit the importation of American cotton textiles, while another 30 have tariffs and taxes high enough to shut us off effectively from those markets. In addi-tion, it is difficult for American textile mills to find an imaginative approach to meet domestic competition from foreign firms when American textile workers earn an average of $2.43 per hour compared to 45 cents in Japan, 31 cents in Hong Kong, 15 cents in India, and 11 cents in South Korea, Pakistan, and Taiwan.[20] Cheap labor is only part of the story. Productivity of Asian textile workers has been raised to a higher level than that of American workers through the building of the most modern plants, the in-stallation of the newest high-speed equipment including water jet looms that are three times faster than conventional American looms, and other ad-vanced technology.

Finished textile products, both cotton and synthetics, have also been flooding domestic markets. The impact on certain fields is massive. Men's and boys' shirts, pajamas, ladies sweaters, dresses, blouses, bed sheets, blankets, men's suits, and knit shirts are a few examples. While this has not augured well for domestic textile mills and manufacturers of textile prod-ucts, it has offered opportunities to many retail firms. They have been able to offer the American consumer less costly merchandise for the purpose, and to enjoy higher markups than they could reasonably expect on American merchandise. Many low-budget chain stores enjoy a markup of 65 percent on Asian shirts instead of 50 percent on domestic shirts, and still sell them to the consumer for less.

Until 1959 the United States was a net exporter of steel. By 1971, how-ever, we exported approximately 2 million tons and imported almost 18.3 million tons, about 17.8 percent of total U.S. steel consumption, a record to date.

Most imported steel comes from Japan and Western Europe, made in the most modern, best equipped facilities, rebuilt largely with American financial and technical assistance after World War II. Japan accounts for

[20]John M. Mecklin, "Asia's Great Leap in Textiles," *Fortune*, October 1970, p. 77.

almost 50 percent of all steel imports into the United States. While American steel mills are investing billions of dollars in research and new facilities including new basic oxygen furnaces to reduce costs, they cannot make up the vast differential in labor costs which favors the foreign steel producer. Delivered prices of foreign steel in the United States have averaged $30 to $40 per ton below the prices of steel produced in this country. The price gap in 1975 was between $50 and $100 a delivered ton depending on the product.[21]

In 1971 the United States was the world's largest steel producer, with Russia second and Japan third.[22] If present trends continue, Japan is expected to forge ahead and become the world's number 1 steel producing nation, with the United States dropping into third or fourth place.

TECHNOLOGY

In this highly imaginative, innovative, and technology-oriented world in which we live, a manager must accept the fact that there is probably a better way to produce the things that his company makes, and a better way to do almost everything that he does. He is made ever aware of this by changing technology, which is a part of the economic environment in which his organization functions.

Technological change is the process by which new methods, new machines, new techniques, and new products are discovered and developed to the market stage; introduced in production and consumption; and improved, refined, and replaced as they become obsolete.[23] The rapidity of technological change is summed up in the following statement:

> Starting with the birth of Christ, the first doubling of knowledge occurred by 1750, the next doubling by 1900, the third by 1950, and the fourth by 1960. For just a moment, look upon the last 50,000 years of man's existence in terms of life spans. Approximately 800 persons could cover the entire period. Of these
> . . . 650 would have spent their lives in caves,
> . . . only the last 70 had any effective means of communication,
> . . . only the last 6 ever saw a printed word,
> . . . only the last 4 were able to measure time with any precision,
> . . . almost everything that makes up our material world was invented during the lifespan of the 800th person,
> . . . more technological progress will be made during the first half of the life of the 801st person than during the entire lifetime of the previous 800.[24]

---

[21]*Industry Week*, December 23, 1974, p. 51.

[22]*Ibid*, May 24, 1971, p. 12.

[23]"Changes in the World Induced by Technology," General Electric *Campus Monogram*, Academic Year 1972–73, p. 4.

[24]"Road to 1970: Environment of Change," Equity Research Associates, New York, N.Y., September 20, 1966, p.3.

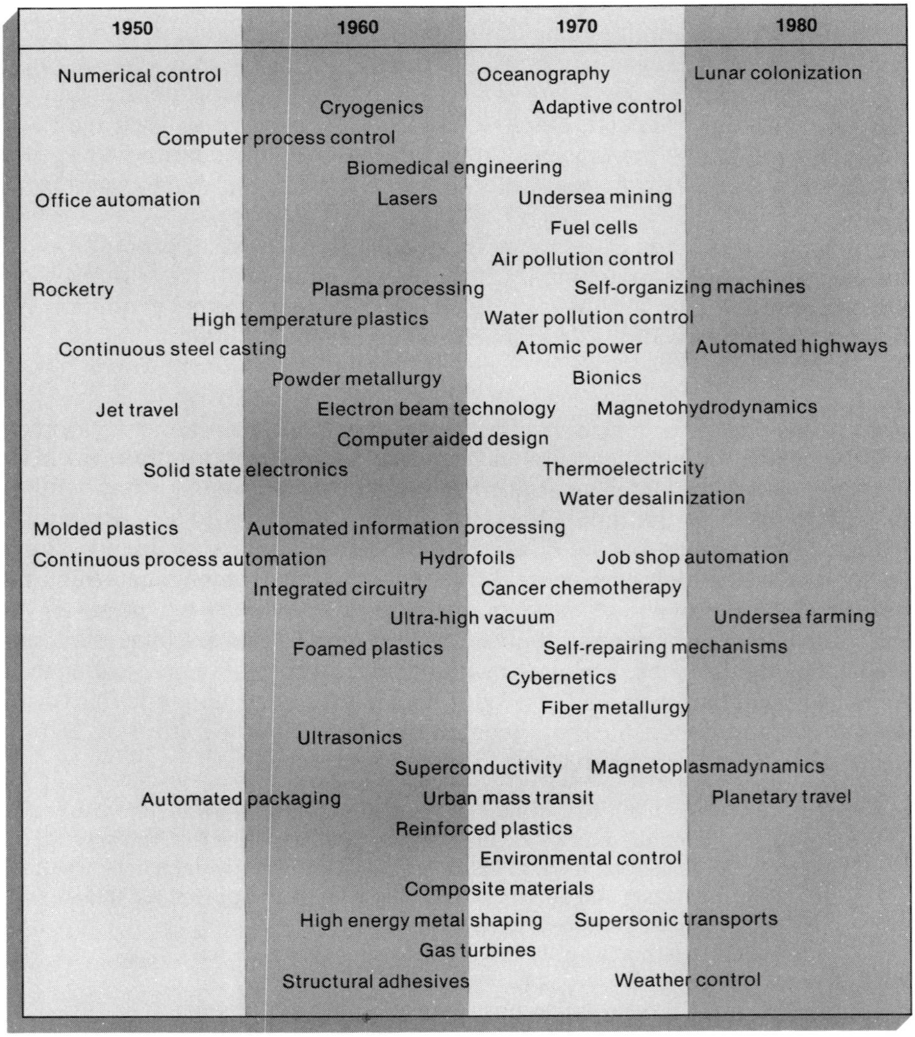

1950	1960	1970	1980
Numerical control		Oceanography	Lunar colonization
	Cryogenics	Adaptive control	
	Computer process control		
	Biomedical engineering		
Office automation	Lasers	Undersea mining	
		Fuel cells	
		Air pollution control	
Rocketry	Plasma processing	Self-organizing machines	
	High temperature plastics	Water pollution control	
	Continuous steel casting	Atomic power	Automated highways
	Powder metallurgy	Bionics	
Jet travel	Electron beam technology	Magnetohydrodynamics	
	Computer aided design		
	Solid state electronics	Thermoelectricity	
		Water desalinization	
Molded plastics	Automated information processing		
Continuous process automation	Hydrofoils	Job shop automation	
	Integrated circuitry	Cancer chemotherapy	
	Ultra-high vacuum		Undersea farming
	Foamed plastics	Self-repairing mechanisms	
		Cybernetics	
		Fiber metallurgy	
	Ultrasonics		
	Superconductivity	Magnetoplasmadynamics	
	Automated packaging	Urban mass transit	Planetary travel
	Reinforced plastics		
		Environmental control	
	Composite materials		
	High energy metal shaping	Supersonic transports	
	Gas turbines		
	Structural adhesives	Weather control	

Figure 26-2. Spectrum of emerging technologies and markets. (From Equity Research Associates and Midwest Research Institute.)

Largely stemming from the mobilization of scientists and technologists during World War II, discoveries such as antibiotics, atomic power, cryogenics, jet planes, radar, transistors, computers, lasers, x-ray astronomy, and other innovations have given a new dimension to the industrial thrust of our country.

Figure 26-2 indicates a continuum of technological advancements from 1950 through 1980. It portrays the magnitude, depth, and importance of this segment of the economic environment. Many advances have already been realized; others are in various stages of development.

One of the more exciting technological possiblilties for producing strategic raw materials now in short supply is underseas mining to recover manganese, nickel, cobalt, and copper. Ocean floor mining may be economically feasible within five to ten years and will greatly reduce our dependence on foreign sources. Underseas farming is another potential technological breakthrough that may help to solve worldwide food shortages.

Technology constantly brings new and more efficient ways of doing things. In the home, we have already seen the introduction of garbage compacters, microwave ovens, and electronic pocket calculators. Yet to come are ultrasonic dishwashers and laundry equipment, phonovision, and a host of other developments. In industry, we have perfected new processes and techniques such as electron beam welding, ultrasonic cleaning, induction heating, computerized process controls, and electric arc furnaces. A negative aspect, however, is that all these "advances" contribute to the increased use of electric power, compounding the problem of energy shortage.

Between 1960 and 1970 industry increased its use of power by 70 percent, yet in the next decade it is estimated its use will double.[25] The accelerative tendency in man's consumption of energy is demonstrated by the fact that more than one-half of all the energy from coal consumed by man in the past 2000 years has been consumed during the last 100.[26]

The basic oxygen furnace makes steel in minutes compared to the open hearth, which takes eight or more hours, and computerized controls assure uniformity from one batch to the next. The continuous casting machine molds liquid metal into steel shapes as fast as the ladle can pour. Today's rolling mill, computer controlled, almost runs itself. There exists the near-term possibility that a completely automatic steel plant can be developed.

Technological advances in medicine have been proceeding rapidly also. With the discovery and application of cryogenics, organ transplants, plasma processing, biomedical engineering, chemotherapy, laser technology, and other scientific developments, man's longevity is being extended. Forecasts by the Rand Corporation predict an increase of 50 percent in human life span will be achieved by the year 2020. Recent studies by Smith, Kline, and French Laboratories, a large pharmaceutical company, are more optimistic and project a 50 percent increase in life span will be attained in the early 1990s.[27] With people living longer, fuller lives, a host of challenging prob-

---

[25]"Heat or Light," *Barron's*, February 22, 1971, p. 11.

[26]Alvin Toffler, *Future Shock* (New York: Random House, 1970), p. 24.

[27]Joseph P. Hrachovec, *Keeping Young and Living Longer* (Los Angeles, Ca.: Sherbourne Press, 1972), p.7.

lems and opportunities unfold that will require additional managerial decision making. Social scientist Bernice Neugarten suggests that if just five years were added to the average life span it would mean more rapid changes in our economic institutions, family institutions, systems of health services, social services, and all of the ways in which society is organized.[28]

While technology and science have brought us much that is wanted, they have also brought us much that is unwanted. There have been penalties as well as rewards. The introduction of the basic oxygen furnace has been accompanied by a decline in steel industry employment. In 1960 the industry required 462,000 production and maintenance workers to produce 99.3 million tons of ingots; in 1969, with the increase in BOF, it took only 428,000 men to produce 141.3 million tons. A major share of the credit for the gain in productivity has been attributed to the advanced technology.

In the electrical industry, while output increased during the decade, production jobs dropped by 10 percent (89,000 workers). In the soft coal industry, productivity has increased 96 percent, but employment of miners has decreased by 260,000 men. In New York City, 25,000 elevator operators have been replaced by automatic elevators.

For most firms, the goals of research and development traditionally have been new products, improvement of existing products, and reduction of costs. For many, however, R&D has become more defensive. Automobile manufacturers and petroleum refiners are now devoting much of their research efforts to eliminating pollution. Bottle and can manufacturers are seeking ways to reclaim and recycle their used containers. Chemical companies are developing replacements for enzymes and phosphates in laundry detergents that have been polluting our waters.

A long-range effect of mechanization, and of automation, is the impact on the labor force. A machine is substituted for labor, and jobs are eliminated. Offsetting this is the fact that building the new machine requires workers; operating the machine requires others; maintaining and repairing them demands new skills. A problem arises when displaced workers cannot be placed in these new jobs quickly. They remain out of work while the newly created jobs are filled slowly, giving rise to **structural unemployment.**

The worker's reaction to automation in the automobile industry, and its impact on him as a consumer, is revealed in the following statement:

> When they took the unimates on, we were building sixty an hour. When we came back to work, with the unimates, we were building a hundred cars an hour. A unimate is a welding robot. It looks just like a praying mantis. It goes from spot to spot to spot. It releases that thing and it jumps back into position, ready for the next car. They go by them about 110 an hour. They never tire, they

---

[28]Bernice L. Neugarten, "Age Groups in American Society and the Rise of the Young-Old," *Annals of Political and Social Sciences,* September 1974, pp. 187–198.

never sweat, they never complain, they never miss work. Of course, they don't buy cars. I guess General Motors doesn't understand that argument.[29]

Still another impact of automation is the elimination of occupations rendered obsolete. When a particular trade or skill is no longer needed in industry, for the displaced worker it is not a matter of looking for a job but rather of finding a new occupation which may require new training. Even if some re-training is all that is required, a worker must begin at the bottom learning a new skill for a new occupation. This is less difficult for younger workers to do than it is for older workers. The latter may lack the ability and mobility to make the adjustment.

GOVERNMENT SPENDING

Spending by federal, state, and local governments has a tremendous impact on the economic environment. Whether it is spending for defense, housing, welfare, or public works, it is concentrated spending. Government purchases, especially federal, are in huge quantities or large dollar amounts, and often represent appreciable dollar volume for industries that supply the government. For some, like the aerospace industries, the government is their only customer. No one else buys billions of dollars worth of rockets, spacecraft, lunar modules, and space shuttles. When government reduces its spending in such an area, the repercussions are immense, not only on the industry but on the local community as well. There is an observable "ripple effect."

The magnitude of government spending and its impact can be perceived in a statement made by the president of the Federal Reserve Bank of St. Louis.

> It took 186 years for the Federal budget to reach the $100 billion mark, a line we crossed in 1962, but in only nine more years we reached the $200 billion mark, and in only four more years we broke the $300 billion barrier.[30]

Total government spending as a percentage of gross national product is shown in Table 26-2. Although GNP has increased 14-fold since 1929, government spending has increased more than 35-fold.

While all forms of government spent 22.2 percent of the gross national product in 1970, it is estimated that the federal government alone spent $215 billion, or approximately 20.5 percent of the GNP. By 1975 total government spending accounted for 32 percent of our GNP. Federal spending alone

---

[29]Gary Bryner, president of Lordstown Local 1112, UAW, as quoted in Studs Terkel, *Working* (New York: Pantheon Books, 1974), p. 187.

[30]Darryl R. Francis, "Public Policy for a Free Economy," *Washington University Magazine*, Vol. 45, No. 4, Summer 1975, p. 9.

Table 26.2.   All government spending as a percentage of GNP*

Year	GNP (billions of dollars)	Government spending (billions of dollars)	Percentage of GNP
1929	103.1	8.5	8.2
1930	90.4	9.2	10.2
1940	99.7	14.1	14.1
1950	286.2	38.5	13.5
1955	399.3	75.0	18.8
1960	506.0	100.3	19.8
1965	688.1	138.4	20.1
1970	982.4	218.9	22.3
1975†	1,400.0	440.0	32.0

*From Statistical Abstract of the United States, United States Department of Commerce; Survey of Current Business, Bureau of Economic Analysis, United States Department of Commerce, Vol. 56, No. 1, January 1976.
†Estimated.

accounted for almost 22 percent of GNP and about 70 percent of all government spending. Francis estimates that if present trends continue, government spending could account for as much as 60 percent of GNP by the year 2000.[31] As the country grows, so does government spending. When the federal government spends beyond its budgeted income and operates at a deficit (deficit spending), the pressure is inflationary. Knowing this, business planners adjust their own strategies to conform to conditions that result from government spending.

SUMMARY

One of the most important facets of the total environment to which business organizations must adjust is the economic sector. It is composed of many sub-areas that are in a continuing state of flux. These contain economic forces that constantly bombard the firm and cause action and reaction. They constantly bombard each other also, so that changes in one area of the economic arena cause changes in other areas. This compounds the adjustments that commercial and industrial organizations must make.

Changes in GNP, location and extent of markets, income levels, standards of living, consumer buying habits, competition, technology, and government spending influence each other and collectively influence organizational decision making. It is a never-ending interaction and accounts, in part, for the dynamic nature of managerial activity.

---

[31]*Ibid.*

KEY CONCEPTS

Gross National Product	Competition
Net Economic Welfare	Technology
Markets	Structural Unemployment
Discretionary Income	Deficit Spending.

GLOSSARY

deficit spending   Government spending which exceeds revenues in a given fiscal period.

discretionary income   That portion of disposable income beyond what is required for the necessities of life (especially food, shelter, and clothing).

gross national product (GNP)   The total output of final goods and services at their market prices.

inflation   An economic condition in which prices rise at a more rapid rate than does productivity.

net economic welfare (NEW)   A substitute for GNP as an indicator of economic growth.

structural unemployment   A temporary type of unemployment that results when old jobs are eliminated because of new technology and displaced workers must be re-trained to fill new jobs.

technology   The technical process by which new methods and new products are discovered to improve or replace old or obsolete ones.

REVIEW QUESTIONS

1. What is the economic environment? Why would it be important to you as a manager to understand it?

2. What are some of the major sub-sectors of the economic environment?

3. Can inflation be reduced by increasing the rate of fixed capital investment? Why do you believe as you do?

4. Describe the chief kinds of markets that exist.

5. What is the difference between intra-industry, inter-industry, and extra-industry competition? Give some examples. What are these organizations competing for?

6. Give an example of a favorable result of technology. Give an example of an unfavorable result.

7. How does government spending affect business managers?
8. Why should managers be very aware of deficit spending by government?

Chapter 27

Conforming
to the Political Environment

Another important segment of the macro-environment which influences business and is influenced by it is the political environment—that complex of governmental institutions, laws, and political concepts devised to reconcile the interests of business with those of society.

What happens to business depends to a large extent on our country's foreign and domestic policies. The past, present, and future of American business are very closely linked with the past, present, and future of America itself. Government regulates public utilities, sets rail and truck rates, licenses television and radio, censors advertising, monitors securities markets, establishes import and export quotas, and enacts laws to control mergers and acquisitions, reduce pollution, protect consumers, and conserve our natural resources.

Although there are many facets to this political environment, four have been selected here to illustrate the impact of political circumstances on the manager as he guides his firm toward its objectives. They are (1) legislation and regulation, (2) philosophy of the political party in power, (3) taxation, and (4) government assistance. These segments are very much interrelated and interdependent as we shall observe.

LEGISLATION AND REGULATION

In the area of business–government relations, there has been a steady broadening of government regulation of business. Today the force of government is felt directly or indirectly in all areas of activity, from pricing decisions to product content to consumer protection. A business leader's view of the situation is expressed as follows:

> Some is proper regulation in the public interest, such as that relating to resource conservation, pollution control, and maintenance of competition. But some—price control, for example—is highly improper because it impinges on the operation of market forces. This has damaged the ability of business to per-

521

form in the public interest, and is a root cause of our most troublesome economic problems.[1]

If the business leader can anticipate changes in governmental programs and laws that may be introduced, he may be able to adapt his strategies and perform more successfully than would otherwise be the case.

Each year the federal legislative program is spelled out in the president's State of the Union message, the Budget, and the Economic Report. Included may be adjustments in social security benefits to match cost-of-living increases. This could mean increased social security contributions by all employers. Every business firm must contribute whether it is operating at a profit or not. This is a mandate from which there is no appeal.

The minimum wage paid to employees by institutions engaged in interstate commerce started at 25 cents per hour in 1938. By 1973 it had risen to $1.60 per hour; it was raised to $2 in 1974; to $2.30 in 1976, and it will probably reach or exceed $2.75 per hour in the near future. When this occurs, business will have to comply, thereby increasing its cost of operation. Without a corresponding increase in productivity or the ability to raise its prices, the marginal firm may find itself at a competitive disadvantage. In addition, the formerly successful firm may become a marginal one.

All firms must operate within the regulations established by various administrative agencies of government. Transportation companies and others involved in interstate commerce come under the rules of the Interstate Commerce Commission. In the trucking industry, for instance, regulations force many trucks to return empty after making a delivery. The National Commission on Productivity has estimated this regulation costs $250 million a year. Eliminating it could also save a quarter of a billion gallons of gasoline a year.[2] Some observers have estimated that ICC regulations have inflated truck and railroad freight rates by 20 percent or more.

Some firms are greatly influenced by regulations of the Federal Trade, Federal Power, or Federal Communications Commissions. If they are publicly held, corporations must also comply with requirements of the Securities Exchange Commission. Some regulations have in effect reduced productivity and created inefficiencies.

In the highly fragmented textile industry consisting of many comparatively tiny companies (Burlington Industries, the largest textile firm in the world with $1.8 billion in 1969 sales, held only 8 percent of the domestic market), consolidation could be a vital step toward combating the competition from low-wage mills in Asia. But for this to be achieved, the Federal Trade Commission would have to reevaluate its policy on textile firm

---

[1]Robert G. Dunlop (Chairman, Sun Oil Company), "The Quiet Revolution in American Business," *Our Sun*, Summer 1974, p. 4.

[2]Z. D. Bonner (President, Gulf Oil Company), "Untying America's Hands." Gulf Oil Publication, November 19, 1974, p. 3.

mergers. In 1968 the FTC barred horizontal mergers between firms in the textile industry where sales or assets of the merged companies exceeded $300 million and those of the acquired concern were greater than $10 million. In contrast, the Japanese government offers tax incentives to encourage its small textile companies to merge. In May of 1975 the FTC rescinded its textile mill merger policy "because industry conditions have changed."[3]

In the famous Phillips case, the Supreme Court ruled in 1954 that the Federal Power Commission had the legal responsibility to regulate field market prices for natural gas. Initially, the FPC proposed a traditional utility-type rate formula. In 1960 it switched to an area rate formula which was challenged in the courts the following year. The test case finally reached the Supreme Court, which gave its approval in 1968. This delay was important because natural gas prices were frozen between 1961 and 1968 pending the judicial outcome. The rate ceiling for new natural gas was set at 3.2 percent *below* the ceiling established for the test case area eight years earlier. Producers lost interest in exploration and drilling.

Other fuels were also affected. Since gas and oil are often found together, reduced natural gas development meant less domestic exploration and drilling for oil. Coal felt the impact also. In addition to environmental restrictions, the coal industry also suffered from the rush to convert to cheap natural gas. In April 1974, electric utilities could purchase natural gas for 44 cents per million BTU, as compared with 64 cents for coal and $1.89 for oil.[4] Regulation has made natural gas a bargain energy commodity, relative to other fuels. Recognizing that its low pricing policies have led to shortages of natural gas, the FPC is now taking steps to remedy its error. Such correction, of course, will cause new adjustments to be made through the market mechanism.

Another far-reaching effect can be seen in the FCC regulation that became mandatory January 2, 1971, barring the advertising of cigarettes on radio or television. These had accounted for nearly 15 percent of all network TV revenue. Regulation of the tobacco industry also includes the requirement that the following message must be printed on every package of cigarettes: "Warning: The Surgeon General has determined that cigarette smoking is dangerous to your health." Cigarette manufacturers have no option. They must comply.

The Equal Employment Opportunities Commission decided in 1966 that men and women must be treated equally in employee benefit plans including life insurance and illness and accident benefits. As a result, LTV Corporation extended hospitalization insurance to husbands of women workers, and

---

[3]*The Wall Street Journal,* May 13, 1975, p. 3.
[4]Z. D. Bonner, *op. cit.,* p. 6.

established a six-month sick leave policy for its male employees to match women's maternity leave benefits. A large New York bank with an established widow's benefit plan extended it to include widowers.[5]

Title VII of the Civil Rights Act of 1964 outlaws age discrimination by employers, employment agencies, and labor unions. Today a help wanted advertisement cannot indicate any preference, limitation, specification, or discrimination based on age, sex, religion, or race. Under the Age Discrimination in Employment Act of 1967, employers are specifically prohibited from favoring a younger employee over an older one, not only in hiring but also in promotions, wages, and firing, unless age can be shown to be a "bona fide job qualification," as in modeling clothes for teen-agers.

In a case dealing with racial discrimination under the Civil Rights Act, the Court ruled in 1971 that job tests including general intelligence tests and aptitude tests which screen out blacks without realistically measuring their qualifications for the job are unconstitutional. If an employment practice that operates to exclude Negroes cannot be shown to be related to job performance, it is prohibited.

Since their inception, antitrust laws have regulated the activities of business firms, prohibiting contracts, combinations, or conspiracies in restraint of trade. Later they were broadened to include ownership of the assets of another corporation engaged in commerce anywhere if the effect of such acquisition may be to lessen competition or *tend* to create a monopoly. In 1957, the Supreme Court of the United States ruled that Du Pont Company had violated the antitrust act by controlling 23 percent of the stock of General Motors Corporation. Although these two companies do not compete, the Court concluded that Du Pont supplied the largest part of General Motors' paint, chemical, and plastic requirements chiefly because of its stock interest in GM, rather than because of its competitive edge. Du Pont was forced to dispose of its GM stock and completed the divestiture in 1965. An interesting sidelight is that Du Pont had acquired the stock in 1917, 48 years earlier, when it came to the financial aid of the then almost bankrupt General Motors.

In other recent cases the Supreme Court has expanded antitrust boundaries. In 1967 it upheld Justice Department challenges of "conglomerate" mergers between companies in unrelated fields by ordering Proctor & Gamble to divest itself of Clorox Chemical Company.

Federal regulation dictates safety standards which must be observed in the automotive industry. Early in 1971 the U.S. Department of Transportation established standards for crash-worthiness of automobile bumpers on 1973 model cars. As a result, auto manufacturers are committed to install bumper systems that will withstand a five-mile-per-hour solid impact without damage to the vehicle.

---

[5]*The Wall Street Journal,* July 16, 1966.

The Clean Air Act of 1970 also affects the automobile industry. Among other things, that act requires that by the 1975 model year automobile emissions of carbon monoxide and hydrocarbons must be reduced 90 percent from 1970 levels. By 1976 emissions of oxides of nitrogen have to 90 percent below average levels of uncontrolled 1971 vehicles.[6] For the industry, that is a difficult target to reach. It will involve the development of new types of carburetors or perhaps new emission control devices. For the petroleum industry, it may mean developing more efficient gasolines. For the consumer, it will probably mean higher costs of owning and operating a car. It has been estimated that a buyer of a 1975 automobile paid $500 for federally mandated safety and emission equipment.[7]

Under a flammability standard issued by the Deparment of Commerce in 1971, after July 30, 1973 all children's sleepwear in sizes up to 6x had to be flame-resistant. For textile producers, this meant developing processes to flame-retard, and placed a strain on their facilities to meet the temporary shortages produced by the sudden demand for such fabrics. For manufacturers of robes, pajamas, nightgowns, and related items, it is unlawful to make garments of fabrics that do not meet the standard. For retailers, it is unlawful to sell such garments. For the consumer, it means higher prices for the finished garments.

One industrialist sums up business–government regulation in this way:

> It should be pointed out that rampant inflation and wide-spread shortages are not characteristic of the free market. Such dislocations are the result of Government intervention and regulatory policies which have hampered the market in its ability to adjust and function normally. While factors such as supply, demand, prices, wages, interest rates and profits are still by and large operational they have been seriously distorted by Government regulation.[8]

The same executive later takes this more moderate position:

> Doubtless there are areas where regulations and controls are necessary. Certain social goals, such as product and worker safety and air and water pollution control, can seemingly only be accomplished through regulation. Perhaps someday methods or procedures will be developed whereby these goals can be accomplished through regular market channels. Until that day, there is need for regulation in these areas. And certainly the government should pursue a firm anti-trust policy to assure that American industries remain competitive. However, our present anti-trust laws are antiques.[9]

---

[6]"Let's Have Clean Air—But Let's Not Throw Money Away," Chrysler Corporation, Research and Editorial Services, Detroit, Michigan, 1973, p. 2.

[7]Z. D. Bonner, op. cit.,p. 4

[8]Z. D. Bonner, (President, Gulf Oil Company), "How Industry Can Regain Public's Trust," The New York Times, September 1, 1974.

[9]Z. D. Bonner, "Untying America's Hands," op. cit., p. 11.

PHILOSOPHY OF THE POLITICAL PARTY IN POWER

Closely related to the influence of legislation and regulation is the impact on business of the prevailing philosophy of the political party in power. Businessmen will be influenced also by what they anticipate will be the attitude of the new administration about to take office. This holds not only at the national level, but at the state and local levels as well.

A plan for sharing federal tax revenues with states and local communities; a "full employment budget," basing government spending on revenues projected for full employment levels; a call for fairness in American life, including improvement in the health care of its citizens and a minimum income for every family—these may be part of the prevailing philosophy. How they are implemented is of considerable concern to managers.

Businessmen must ascertain what the attitude of government will be toward curbing inflation, maintaining full employment, discouraging mergers, encouraging solutions to the energy crisis. Will government apply fiscal and monetary policies to stimulate economic expansion or to discourage it? Will the result be tight credit with prime interest rates rising to 12 percent as they did in July 1974 (an all-time high), or low bank rates with money supply plentiful? Even an 8 to 9 percent prime interest rate increases inventory holding costs.

Will the administration encourage business growth by offering an investment tax credit or an accelerated rate of depreciation of business assets? A substantial increase in investment tax credits normally spurs business modernization and expansion. Will repeal of the oil depletion allowance influence decision makers? If federal taxes permit more rapid write-offs, will state taxes follow suit?

In implementing its social and economic philosophy there are countless ways that a political party in power can influence the decision-making process of business managers. When Bethlehem Steel boosted prices up to 12.5 percent on certain of its products in 1971, President Nixon condemned the action and threatened to permit additional imports of steel. U.S. Steel, therefore, boosted its prices by only 6.8 percent, and Bethlehem had to roll back its increase to that level.

The government's position on mergers can aid or hinder the operation of business firms. Steel industry leaders believe that some of its smaller firms should be merged with larger ones in order to increase efficiency in the industry. This would, of course, require a Justice Department policy that permitted such consolidations. Some steel companies may be able to merge under the **failing-company doctrine,** an antitrust provision that would permit the amalgamation of competing firms that otherwise might collapse. In recent years the industry has been revising its strategy, from merely getting along with government to turning to it for help. It seeks tighter restrictions on steel imports, relaxed antitrust attitudes on mergers, more flexible interpretations and enforcement of anti-pollution laws, and more favorable tax considerations. Professional lobbyists are often employed to achieve these ends.

To curb inflation in 1971, the Nixon administration instituted wage–price controls and appointed boards and commissions to administer them. Business was subject to penalties if it failed to follow the prescribed "voluntary guidelines."

The political philosophy of the Ford administration is expressed in a speech delivered by the president in which he stated that government should not be stampeded into writing new federal regulations on such social issues as job safety, the environment, and consumer protection.

> The question is not whether we want to do something about noise and safety but whether making changes in our regulations would make sense in terms of costs and added benefits gained.
>
> For example, is it worth as much as $30 billion a year of consumers' dollars to reduce the level of occupational noise exposure by approximately five decibels? Have airbags been proven sufficiently cost-effective for us to require their installation in all cars at between $100 and $300 for each?
>
> All too often, the federal government promulgates new rules and regulations which raise costs, and consumer prices at the same time, to achieve small or limited benefits. We must either revise proposed rules and regulations to lower their costs or we must not adopt them.[10]

President Ford also indicated there is an urgent need to overhaul or eliminate many federal business regulations, especially those governing competition in industries like railroads, trucking, airlines, utilities, and banking.[11] Many of these regulations are obsolete and impose a hidden tax on the American consumer by costing more than they provide in benefits.

The government is the largest single employer, the biggest purchaser of goods and services, and the greatest borrower of money. Government financing, undeclared wars, adverse balances in international trade payments, and deficit financing have an impact on prices, purchasing power, and the soundness of the dollar, an impact which managers cannot fail to observe. In the final analysis, actions or inactions of government agencies are a reflection of the philosophy of the political groups that staff them.

TAXATION

All sorts of taxes exist in our society. Most of them have a direct or indirect effect on how our businesses operate.

Federal income tax laws require all organizations with one or more employees to withhold a portion of their pay and, under the Federal Insur-

---

[10]Gerald R. Ford, President of the United States, in an address to the 63rd annual meeting of the U.S. Chamber of Commerce, Washington, D. C., April 28, 1975.

[11]*Ibid.*

ance Contributions Act, to deduct Social Security. For large companies this requires a staff of persons, perhaps a department, to handle withholding taxes, payroll deductions, social security collections, and the like. Without compensation, institutions act as the collecting agent for the government. It is true that costs for performing this service are deductible as a cost of doing business, but a business firm must subsidize the difference between its actual cost and its tax allowance.

Some firms, particularly those engaged in retail transactions, have to collect and forward to their state or city governments sales taxes which may have been imposed by law. Some municipalities have city earnings taxes which are also collected by business firms and other institutions from their employees.

At one time telephone companies and automobile manufacturers were compelled to charge an excise tax. This amounted to 10 percent on a telephone bill and 5 percent on the retail price of a car. Oil companies collect and forward federal, state, and city taxes on each gallon of gasoline their stations pump.

Corporations must pay an annual franchise tax to every state in which they do business. This tax is based either on the dollar amount or on the par value of authorized capital stock. In addition, they pay a corporate income tax at a rate that is higher than it is for individuals. The federal tax requires corporations to pay 48 percent on all net income in excess of $25,000. However, the Tax Reduction Act of 1975 temporarily liberalized the "surtax exemption." The first $50,000 of corporate income was taxed at 21 percent, rather than the first $25,000 at 22 percent as had been the practice.

Sometimes, after paying the federal income tax, the corporation may distribute a portion of its earnings that remain to the stockholders (that is, the owners). Dividends in excess of $100 received by a shareholder are then taxed again, as part of his *personal* income. Only corporations are subject to this **double taxation** feature. Imagine the impact on the business and investment community if the federal government were to eliminate the double taxation on dividends, either by allowing companies to deduct dividend payments from taxable income as they now do with interest, or by allowing shareholders to do so.

Tax revenues which flow to governments from business, and from governments to various segments of society, have a marked impact upon the way in which business firms operate.

GOVERNMENT AID AND ASSISTANCE

From providing hundreds of millions of dollars for the development of aircraft and sophisticated weaponry to publishing booklets like "Insurance and

Risk Management for Small Business," the government offers monumental assistance in research and advisory services.

Through its national and international agencies, it accumulates more economic information from public and confidential sources than any other organization in the world. Its forecasts of business trends, though generally on the cautious side, have usually proved more accurate than most.

Almost every subject dealing with the many phases of business activity has been investigated and researched. Much of this information is available to business managers at little or no charge. Publications are available from the U.S. Government Printing Office in Washington, D.C. Even lists of patents that have expired are available to business firms interested in a product or process whose monopoly protection has ended.

Scientific grants to industry make possible research into many areas which might not otherwise be investigated. Assistance ranging from weather reports and meteorological surveys to advice on planting seed crops is available for the asking. Many alert business managers take advantage of the wealth of information and aids available to their respective enterprises.

In times of misfortune and tragedy, when hurricanes, earthquakes, or tornadoes strike an area, the government also offers aid and assistance to sectors designated "disaster areas." The impact of all forms of aid and assistance is a sizable one.

SUMMARY

In the normal course of its operations, an organization is greatly influenced by changes that occur in the political environment which surrounds it. The impact of the political milieu on the managing process in business organization is inescapable and often dramatic.

Any time a law is passed or a decision made by a regulatory agency or government commission, business enterprise is affected. Much regulation is in the public interest, such as that dealing with resource conservation, pollution control, consumer protection, and maintenance of competition. Other regulations like price controls, import and export quotas, and the routing of airlines may stifle productivity and disrupt the normal behavior of institutions in the marketplace,

The philosophy of political parties in office or about to come into office also influences managerial decision making. Implementation of government policies bears on business operations. In many ways, government competes with industry—for example, in labor markets or capital markets.

Local, state, and federal taxes greatly influence all organizations and must be collected or paid by almost all institutions. The levying of taxes can make marginal firms from sound ones, and may sound the death knell of marginal companies. Sometimes lightening the tax burden aids profit oriented institutions, enhancing their growth or survival.

Government aid for research and pilot projects, and assistance ranging from weather reports to crop subsidies are additional influences present within the political environment.

KEY CONCEPTS

Regulatory Agencies	Failing-Company Doctrine
Influence of Legislation	Taxation and Business
Political Philosophy	Double Taxation of Corporations
Prime Rate	Government Aid

GLOSSARY

double taxation   When corporations pay a tax on net income, and again when shareholders pay an income tax on dividends received from corporate "after-tax earnings."

failing-company doctrine   A government antitrust provision that permits mergers of competing firms which otherwise might fail.

prime rate   The interest rate that banks and lending institutions charge their most credit-worthy borrowers.

REVIEW QUESTIONS

1. Name four important segments of the political environment which influence business operations.

2. How does raising the minimum wage affect the operation of a business? What do you see as its advantages? Disadvantages?

3. Do you believe that government regulation of the price of natural gas contributed to the gas shortage? Explain.

4. What is the "failing-company doctrine"?

5. Assume you are the owner of a gasoline filling station. What kinds of taxes would you have to charge and collect in the course of operating your business?

6. What kinds of government aid are available to universities? Hospitals? Steel mills? To you as a citizen?

7. Explain "double taxation" of corporations. What would you suggest to correct it? How would this affect financial planning?

Chapter 28

Reacting
to the Ethical Environment

The ethical environment deals with standards of moral conduct to which business must subscribe as it serves society.

The term *ethical* is derived from the Greek word "ethos," meaning custom or character. Hence ethics are concerned with moral values—the good or bad, right or wrong of particular practices. Since mores or societal customs change slowly, so too do ethical standards.

It is essential for managers of business enterprises to determine that their goals and motives are worthy and that their means of attaining them are ethical. Whether a firm is considered **ethical** in its actions is a *moral,* rather than legal, consideration. Many actions that are legal may not be ethical; some that are ethical are not legal. Business, however, is expected to comply not only with civil laws, which often lag behind changing mores, but with moral laws as well.

Since ethical behavior is a moral phenomenon, involving value judgments based on experience rooted in cultural values, the question may be asked, "Should all business conduct be ethical?" It is not a simple question to answer.

One must take into consideration that most businesses are small. A retail store whose annual sales do not exceed $1 million is relatively small; for a wholesaler, annual sales of less than $5 million is a small business; a factory with 100 employees is a small manufacturer. As a matter of fact, most firms are even smaller than these. The average retail store, for example, has less than $5,000 in assets, does less than $25,000 in annual sales, is individually owned, and has no paid employees. The average business in the U.S. employs fewer than seven people; approximately three-fourths of all business firms have fewer than four paid employees. A small business, particularly a marginal firm struggling for survival, may be concerned with simply staying alive. In that event, it may be more concerned with the legality than with the ethics of its actions. When it has passed the stage of fighting for economic survival, it can then "afford" to develop an ethical posture as well. Antony Jay points out the dilemma of the salesman in such a survival situation.

He must be loyal to the firm which pays him, and yet very often the man he will have to sell this new product to has become over the years a personal friend. If he has an urgent command to push this product which he knows is not right for his friend, what should he do? He is in the classic dilemma. It is no good saying that the long-term interest of his firm will not be served by selling a customer the wrong product—unless he sells it, the firm may have no future at all.[1]

Addressed to the larger, economically successful firm, the question may be stated, "Can such a company afford not to be ethical in its behavior toward customers, suppliers, employees, stockholders, the community, and the government?" The answer, obviously, is no. For the company to continue to be successful, it must adhere to ethical as well as legal standards of behavior.

It is not an easy matter to determine when actions of organizations, that is, of their executives, are ethical or unethical. It is not always a simple black or white situation. Many grey areas exist between what is or is not a conflict of interest, insider information, or deceptive advertising. Since actions that may be technically or legally correct are often ethically incorrect, as a matter of good business practice an organization should make it a policy to avoid deception and unfair representation at all stages in the process of offering products and services. How this principle can be applied is indicated in the following examples.

Usually displayed among dairy products in grocery supermarkets is a carton labeled "Half and Half." This label conveys the impression to the consumer that he is purchasing a food product containing half milk and half cream. Until recently, nowhere on the carton was the word "cream " or "milk " printed, nor were the actual contents revealed. Actually, the product does not contain 50 percent of any ingredient. Investigation in one city (St. Louis, Missouri) indicated that it is "a product consisting of a mixture of milk and cream which contains not less than 11.5 percent of milk fat." In another city (Youngstown, Ohio), cartons state "blended homogenized milk and cream, 10.5 percent butterfat." Although revealing the contents is an improvement, labeling the product "Half and Half" is obviously still misleading and probably deceptive.

For years Shell Oil Company ran its Platformate commercials on television. These depicted two cars in a mileage performance test, one containing Shell gasoline with Platformate; the other containing an equal amount of gasoline without Platformate. The one using Platformate out-performed the other. The audience gained the impression that only Shell with Platformate can give superior performance. Actually, all brands of commercial gasoline contain the chemical equivalent of Platformate. In addition, gasoline without Platformate or its equivalent is not even available to the consumer. Shell later discontinued these commercials.

---

[1]Antony Jay, Management and Machiavelli (New York: Holt, Rinehart and Winston, 1968), p. 205.

The following statement appeared in "Consumer Reports":

> My wife purchased a tin of nuts labelled "Mixed Nuts" which listed as the contents the following: Virginia peanuts, cashews, Brazil nuts, almonds and pecans. The picture on the tin depicted a rather even mixture of all of these. I was somewhat amazed to find upon opening it that it seemed to consist almost solely of peanuts. I decided then to make a count in order to determine whether or not the package was deceptive. The results were as follows: peanuts, 435; cashews, 12; Brazil nuts, 3; pecans, 2; almonds, ½.[2]

Thus the attractively lithographed can depicted mixed nuts only in a technical or legal sense. Actually, it contained 96 percent peanuts and only 4 percent of all others combined. Is this an ethical representation?

A final example of a practice that is legally correct but ethically questionable involves a well-known insurance company. It sells hospital coverage for illness or accident. Its advertisements state that a person *hospitalized* can collect up to $50,000, with payments up to $600 per month. This means that a person would have to be hospitalized almost seven years to collect the full amount. Most hospitalizations cover a period of only five to ten days. Moreover, in its first eleven years of doing business this company, with 1.6 million policy holders, had only one payment that exceeded $40,000.

To adopt an ethical posture in business, managers must subscribe to at least three principles: (1) social responsibility; (2) justice; and (3) self-regulation. These principles apply, as well, to the ethical operation of all non-business organizations.

SOCIAL RESPONSIBILITY

Major new forces have emerged in the ethical environment. Business has become a primary focus of strong pressures to preserve the environment, protect consumers, expand opportunities for the underprivileged, and improve the quality of living. The American people have shown a rising level of expectations for economic and social progress, and they look to business and government for solutions to national and international problems. A growing perception of this shared responsibility is slowly drawing business and government closer together. One international company makes this statement:

> Industry sources estimate Americans will use about twice as much paper and wood in the year 2000 as they use today. And the U.S. Forest Service predicts that our nation's commercial timberlands won't be able to keep up with the demand.
>
> One of our solutions is to help private landowners increase their yield. They own about 60 percent of America's forest lands—yet produce only 30 per-

---

[2]*Consumer Reports*, Consumer Union of U.S., Inc., 1967 brochure.

cent of the wood fiber. (Forest products companies own only 13 percent of America's forest lands—and produce 34 percent of the wood fiber.)

We do it through the Landowner Assistance Program. We'll show a private landowner how to prepare a site, plant, protect, thin, and harvest—at no charge. This way, he can get the most from his forest land—in some cases, he can actually *double* his yield. We'll even find a contractor to do the actual work. Or do the job ourselves at cost.

For this help, IP (International Paper) gets the right to buy a landowner's timber at competitive prices. We've got more than 300,000 acres in the Landowner Assistance Program now. We're aiming for 1,000,000 before 1980.

At International Paper, we believe forest products companies, private landowners and the government should work together to develop more constructive policies for managing America's forests.[3]

When he stepped down from his position as a successful chief executive officer of Sun Oil Company, Robert Dunlop observed:

I have been privileged over the past 40 years to be a part of a revolution in American business.

That revolution is compounded of vast change in virtually every aspect of business activity. Change in the way businesses are managed. In the relationships of business to people. In the external forces that impact on business operation. In the public's perception of business responsibilities. In the response of business to the shifting needs of society.[4]

Specialists from business-oriented fields warn that business is living on borrowed time if it ignores changing social needs and expectations. They insist that business can exist and prosper *only* if it integrates its needs with public expectations and social responsibility.[5]

Business activity is intertwined with the "economic problem," which Heilbroner defines as "the need to devise social institutions that will mobilize human energy for the production and distribution of goods and services."[6] In the American economy, the corporation is the primary institution undertaking the mobilization of physical, human, and technological resources for productive and distributive purposes. Society thus charges the corporation with responsibility for solving the economy problem.[7] The sur-

---

[3]"Why International Paper Is Helping to Develop a 1,000,000-acre Forest on Land It Doesn't Own," International Paper Company advertisement in *MBA*, Vol. 10, No. 7, July–August 1976, p. 3.

[4]Robert G. Dunlop (Chairman, Sun Oil Company), "The Quiet Revolution in American Business," *Our Sun*, Summer 1974, p. 2.

[5]S. Prakash Sethi, *The Unstable Ground: Corporate Social Responsibility in a Dynamic Society* (Los Angeles, Ca.: Melville Publishing Company, 1974).

[6]Robert Heilbroner, *The Making of Economic Society*, 4th ed. (Englewood Cliffs, N.J.: Prentice-Hall, 1972), p. 18

[7]For a discussion of "natural objectives" of business as society views them, the reader is referred to Chapter 1.

vival of the corporation depends on its successful fulfillment of this responsibility. Should it fail, it will go the way of the primitive clan, the Roman villa,
the feudal manor, and the medieval guild.

The development and acceptance of the idea that business leaders have
a responsibility to the community is the result partly of inceasing government regulation and partly of business leaders' gradual awareness of
changing values in American society. Having moved through eras of rugged
individualism, under a laissez-faire philosophy that saw the rise of industrial capitalists and "social Darwinism" (the survival of the industrial
fittest), the value system of American society now stresses greater protection and freedom for individuals and groups. Recognition of these new
values has become part of current managerial enterprise philosophy.

In contrast to the position taken by Charles E. Wilson, who stated, "For
years I thought what was good for our country was good for General Motors,
and vice versa,"[8] business statesmanship today accepts the positive
philosophy that what is good for society is good for business (omitting the
vice versa).

In developing an awareness of changing social and cultural values,
business leaders have learned that the philosophy of "caveat emptor"—let
the buyer beware—is no longer acceptable from an ethical point of view.
Today's consumer wants and expects two things: to be fully *informed* and to
be *heard*. Today's manager has a deep obligation to fulfill both expectations.
He must practice social statesmanship.

As part of their business philosophy and their role as managers, responsible business leaders must strive to make society a better place in which to
live and work. They are now taking the leadership in developing the cultural
and educational aspects of the community; supporting the local symphony,
opera, and arts; and contributing to scholarship funds and endowments. By
virtue of their training, education, and experience, managers are often best
qualified to head the local United Fund drives, slum clearance campaigns, or
pollution control actions. As managers, they must recognize that they have
an obligation to do so. Theirs is a responsibility of stewardship of the entire
concept of capitalism and free enterprise.

The current concept of the business manager's "social responsibility"
is that he must be a social and economic leader, concerned with problems
beyond the operation of his own enterprise. This point of view is well expressed by the chairman of a major container company:

> One of the greatest responsibilities of the corporate executive is to ensure the
> climate that makes it possible to grow in the future. . . . executives must concern

---

[8]Statement made before the Senate Armed Services Committee, as reported in the *New York
Times*, January 23, 1953. Wilson was later confirmed as Secretary of Defense under President
Eisenhower.

themselves with public affairs and with social change—equal rights, equal opportunities, hard-core unemployed, the whole bit. Today these matters are equal with the obligation of making a profit, in contrast with former times when the businessman was only interested in profit.[9]

Peter Drucker and others strongly suggest there is no conflict between profit and social responsibility. He states his position:

> To earn enough to cover the genuine costs which only the so-called "profit" can cover, is economic and social responsibility—indeed it is the specific social and economic responsibility of business. It is not the business that earns a profit adequate to its genuine costs of capital, to the risks of tomorrow and to the needs of tomorrow's worker and pensioner, that "rips off" society. It is the business that fails to do so.[10]

Many problems in our society can best be solved by business firms. Reducing unemployment is not only a government problem; business can help, through imaginative leadership. The only answer to unemployment is jobs. The business sector has most jobs under its jurisdiction. It has most of the financial resources that can be brought to bear, and most of the administrative skills available. It has the ability to wage a massive assault on many of society's woes. It also has the obligation to do so within the limits of its capabilities.

JUSTICE

Closely related to its willing acceptance of responsibility to the community is management's belief in the principles of justice, particularly social and distributive justice, founded on the Judeo-Christian ethic. **Justice** implies firm adherence to the canon "to each his due." Everyone is entitled to fair and impartial consideration. This includes the employee, supplier, consumer, stockholder, community, and government. What does justice mean to each of these groups?

- **To an employee**—fair wages, decent working conditions, equality of opportunities.
- **To a supplier**—equitable dealings, a fair price for the goods or services supplied.
- **To the consumer**—fair price and good workmanship in the finished product.
- **To the stockholder**—fair return on investment and risk.

---

[9]John McDonald, "How Social Responsibility Fits the Game of Business, *Fortune*, December 1970, p. 106.

[10]Peter F. Drucker, "The Delusion of Profits," *The Wall Street Journal*, February 5, 1975, p. 14.

- **To the community**—fair consideration to its problems, and for the use of its resources.
- **To the government**—fair evaluation for taxes, willingness to assist in times of emergency.

Any business act is unethical if the end result of that act violates the principles of social and distributive justice.

No longer can a business shut down a factory or move a warehouse to another city without regard to the social consequences. Before closing its unprofitable salt mining operations in Saltville, Virginia, and thus putting 900 of the town's residents out of work, Olin Corporation discussed the matter at length with union and civic leaders, then signed an agreement giving Saltville $600,000 in cash, its entire plant complex, 3,500 acres of land, and mineral rights to an additional 6,000 acres. These actions made it possible for the community to recover economically by offering plant sites and other inducements to new industry. Giving the plant to the town also avoided a costly demolition and salvage operation for the company.[11] The responsible action was mutually beneficial.

To prevent a community from becoming a "ghost town," to provide alternate employment in the event of plant relocation, to provide workers financial assistance in moving, to consider the impact that business decisions will have on the entire community—these are new and broader dimensions in today's business philosophy.

There is evidence that a slight shift has been taking place in American corporate philosophy about priorities in dealing with various segments of the community. In a study by Lorig, chief executives and financial officers of 300 large U.S. companies expressed the following priority of responsibilities: stockholders, employees, customers, creditors, and society.[12] In a survey by Renas and Kinard, the priority reported by corporation presidents, financial officers, chief production officers, and top marketing executives was as follows: stockholders, employees, customers, society, and creditors.[13] During the five-year interval between these studies, the three highest priorities remained unchanged, but the positions of creditors and society were interchanged. Top management apparently now considers its responsibilities to society to be greater than its responsibilities to creditors. Perhaps the shift is a reflection of favorable economic conditions and one which could reverse itself should the business cycle decline.

---

[11] *The Wall Street Journal,* December 28, 1972.

[12] A.W. Lorig, "Where Do Corporate Responsibilities Really Lie?" *Business Horizons,* Spring 1967, pp. 51–54.

[13] Stanley R. Renas and Jerry L. Kinard, "Corporate Responsibilities Revisited," *Idaho Business & Economic Journal,* Vol. 4, No. 1, February 1974, pp. 26–29.

SELF-REGULATION

Most industries have adopted ethical standards, often represented by a **code of ethics,** to encourage member firms to conduct themselves in a manner that is best for the common good.

Self-regulation stems both from management's desire to stress higher standards of ethical behavior because to do so is morally right, and from its fear that failure to do so may encourage unethical practices on the part of some to the detriment of others, with subsequent retaliation. Moreover, to the extent that unethical industry-wide practices produced a negative effect upon society, government regulation would soon follow.

Instances of self-regulation are common. In retailing furs in St. Louis, for example, dealers have mutually agreed not to show comparison prices in their newspaper advertising, nor to use misleading descriptions of furs and their colors. What formerly may have been promoted as "sable dyed coney" is now described as "dark brown rabbit." In its television code, the National Association of Broadcasters states that "advertising of beer and wine is acceptable only when presented in the best of good taste and discretion. This requires that commercials using beer and wine avoid any representation of on-camera drinking."[14]

One area in which managers can provide for self-regulation is in the formulation of corporate policy.[15] Corporate leaders can establish guidelines that require all communications, claims, and overt actions to be straightforward and accurate, and not deceptive or misleading. Product labels can carry an unconditional money-back guarantee of consumer satisfaction. Actions at all levels of management in all functional areas can be guided by high standards of good taste, contemporary values, and sensitivity to the wishes and needs of social groups.

In the conduct of business, managers deal with many questions that are of an ethical or moral character, involving societal and cultural values. It must be recognized that as society's expectations of business change, so must managerial behavior alter to accommodate these expectations. Today, society expects business leadership to conduct itself in a socially responsible way. This requires business leaders to respond by accepting ethical responsibility as part of the managerial role.

A good place for managers to start is to establish realistic sales and profit goals that can be achieved by accepted business practice so that bribery, price-fixing, allocation of markets, reciprocity, insider information, illegal campaign contributions, and other corrupt practices become unnecessary and unacceptable.

---

[14]"Action Line," *St. Louis Post-Dispatch,* September 26, 1966.

[15]For a review of the concept of corporate policy the reader is referred to Chapter 7.

How should an organization respond to an individual who deliberately and flagrantly violates its ethical code? The chairman of Pitney–Bowes, Inc. offers the following advice:

> From the pinnacle of its corporate pyramid to its base, there can be only one course of action: dismissal. Chief executive or junior sales representative, there can be no other choice. By so doing, the corporation is saying as clearly as it can that it will not tolerate wrongdoing of any kind by anyone.[16]

If a business manager, union leader, or government officer wants to be ethical, he or she must abide not only by the letter but also by the spirit of the law. This, too, is a managing principle.

SUMMARY

The ethical environment has become an increasingly important influence on business activities.

Whether a practice is ethical or not is a value judgment rooted in mores rather than civil laws. Many legal actions are unethical; many ethical actions are illegal. When survival is not an issue, business managers should conduct their operations in an ethical as well as legal manner. This often calls for calculated action since what is ethical or unethical is not always crystal clear.

To avoid grey areas, business leaders can subscribe to three principles which should become essential components of their managerial philosophy: social responsibility; social and distributive justice; and self-regulation.

The philosophies of "caveat emptor" and "social Darwinism" are no longer appropriate. Today's business leader must be concerned with problems beyond the portals of his own organization. Justice demands that all segments of society be accorded fair and impartial consideration. Any act is unethical if it violates the principles of social and distributive justice. Codes of ethics are steps in the direction of self-regulation, through which organizations and groups of organizations act in ways that are best for the common good.

KEY CONCEPTS

Ethical Conduct	Self-Regulation
Social Responsibility	Code of Ethics
Justice	

---

[16]Fred T. Allen (Chairman and President of Pitney–Bowes, Inc.), "Corporate Morality: Is the Price Too High?," an address before the Swiss–American Chamber of Commerce, Zurich, Switzerland, October 18, 1975.

GLOSSARY

code of ethics   A standard of ethical behavior adhered to by each for the good of all.

ethical behavior   Action that is morally correct regardless of its legal aspects.

justice   The principle "to each his due." Fair and impartial consideration to which all segments of the community are entitled.

REVIEW QUESTIONS

1. Define or explain what is meant by the ethical environment.
2. Based on your own experience give an example of an action that is legal but unethical. Can you provide an example of an action that is illegal but ethical?
3. Do you agree with the statement, "If it's good for General Motors it is good for the country"?
4. What are the two fundamental things that consumers want and expect from business today? Do you agree with them?
5. Suggest some ways in which business leaders can exercise social responsibility. What can union leaders do to act as social statesmen?
6. Do you agree with Peter Drucker that there is no conflict between profit and social responsibility? Explain your position.
7. Why are social and distributive justice essential to a managerial philosophy?
8. Do you believe that managers' first responsibility is to stockholders, followed by employees, customers, society, and creditors?
9. How is self-regulation beneficial to business organizations?
10. How would you determine that a business action was not ethical?

Chapter 29

Accommodating
to the Physical Environment

Nature, plus land and the many influences upon it, are the factors that constitute the physical environment to which firms must accommodate. Although it is true that business can alter the components of the physical environment in a limited way, to a far greater extent it is influenced by them. Tornados, floods, earthquakes, forest fires, freezes, droughts, and hurricanes are violent natural forces that often affect business operations in a dramatic and sometimes traumatic way.

While there are a great many components to the total physical environment, our purpose is served by dealing only with the following: (1) topography; (2) water supply; (3) fertility; (4) climate; (5) ecology; and (6) man-made improvements. The first five of these are usually included in the "natural environment," which consists of the geophysical and biological processes on the surface of the earth as they have evolved without significant influence by man. All six, however, influence decisions affecting the firm's location, accessibility to markets, transportation routes, public services, power sources, and other important areas of decision making.

TOPOGRAPHY

The physical characteristics of land, its shape and contours, whether it is hilly or flat, are of great concern to managers, especially if they are considering the location of a new plant. Topography may be an important factor in the final determination. It was so in the case of Union Electric Company of St. Louis. This company designed and engineered its Taum Sauk generating plant to fit the topography of the region. It decided to build the facility at the top of a mountainous area and to pump water uphill during the night, when there is low demand for electric power. During the day, when power demand is greater, the water descends via gravity, generating electricity as it flows. The water is recycled as part of a complete system, conserving this natural resource. Taking advantage of the topography provided the basis for making this plant economically feasible.

The influence of topography is readily observed in the home construction industry where hills, contours, and drainage influence not only location but also the design of buildings and improvements. Split-level houses are often the result of accommodation to existing topography. The magnificent Crown Center built by Hallmark in Kansas City, Missouri is an outstanding example of a structure built on a huge rock outcrop in the middle of the downtown area.

WATER SUPPLY

Availability of water is another factor which many business firms must consider. Topography was not the only consideration in locating the generating plant referred to above; a dependable supply of water was another. In this case relatively scarce water is used again and again in the system.

Steel mills, chemical plants, and paper mills are examples of firms that consume large amounts of water in the production process. In the production of soft drinks, beer, or other beverages, not only abundance but also the quality or purity of the water becomes a determining factor.

LaChoy Food Products Company, packers of Chinese foods and sauces, found its growth and expansion to meet increased demand for its products limited by the unavailability of additional water in Archbold, Ohio. The town did not have additional water to support this food processor's request. LaChoy's future depends to a large extent on its ability to find new sites with the capability of supplying the necessary water. Genesee Beer points with pride to the fact that its quality is based in large part on the purity of the mountain spring water with which it is brewed.

FERTILITY

How fertile the soil is will influence how abundant a crop will be. Closely allied to the richness of the soil is its chemical or mineral composition. For some purposes, such as developing groves of citrus fruit, alkalinity and salinity of the soil are considerations. For most agricultural production, particularly on a commercial scale, chemical properties of the soil are assessed. Campbell Soup Company selects geographic areas where fertility of the soil is favorable for raising the vegetables that go into its food products. Its processing and packing plants are located close to these regions.

There have been dramatic increases in national and global consumption of food, feedstuffs, forest products, and natural fibers. Paralleling these have been escalating demand and rising costs for energy-dependent fertilizers and crop-protecting chemicals. These have become matters for national concern. Fortunately, the products of agriculture, forestry, fisheries, wildlife, and range are renewable resources. Food, fiber (cotton, wool, silk) and timber are reproducible, says S. H. Wittwer, "because solar energy fixation through photosynthesis and biologically fixed nitrogen are free and essentially inexhaustible. You can go back to the land, the water, and the air year after year and renew them, or reproduce the process."[1]

At current levels of food and fiber production plants draw approximately 15 billion tons of carbon dioxide a year from earth's atmosphere. Man has created strategies for manipulating plants and their environment to optimize this energy conversion process. These include soil fertilization with mineral nutrients, spacing, irrigation, pest and disease control, pruning, and weeding.

CLIMATE

Related to fertility is climate. Climate includes temperature, humidity, and rainfall. It is not difficult to see how these factors influence business decisions.

Specific climate features that favor the growth of plants or animals are often obscure and difficult to detect. Temperature and stable humidity could well be prerequisites for certain types of business operations; adequate rainfall for others.

A semi-tropical climate with year 'round temperature in the 80's, and sufficient rainfall are necessary to raise oranges and grapefruits. This explains why citrus fruits are grown in Florida, California, Texas, and Arizona, and cannot be grown in New York, Ohio, or Missouri. Tobacco and cotton are produced where it is warm; cocoa and coffee where it is hot; fur where it is cold. A freeze is the greatest risk faced by an entrepreneur in raising a citrus crop in Florida or Texas.

The ability of the automotive industry to develop a system to control noxious car emissions that pollute the atmosphere, at the lowest possible cost to the consumer and within the standards established by the Environmental Protection Agency, is dependent upon several variables aside from those in the manufacturing process. They include temperature, humidity, and operating conditions. When a cold engine is first started, carbon monoxide and hydrocarbon emissions are at a peak. One oil company has estimated that an extra 160 million barrels of crude oil will be required annually to provide the kind of low-volatility gasoline needed to meet the 30-second cold-start test requirements established by the EPA.[2]

The operation of a textile plant, in which fibers are twisted into thread, requires conditions of controlled temperature and humidity lest the fibers shrink. If the plant is to be built where climate changes are frequent or

[1]S. H. Wittwer, Director, Agricultural Experiment Station, Michigan State University, "Agricultural Productivity and the Energy Crisis," *Phi Kappa Phi Journal,* Winter 1975, p. 36.

[2]"More Partnership, Less Partisanship," an address by Thomas A. Murphy, Vice Chairman General Motors Corporation, before Seventh Annual Detroit Management Conference, November 2, 1972.

drastic, it may have to be designed with air conditioning, humidity control, and other forms of artificial climate control.

Building a pipeline in the climate of Louisiana or Texas is quite different from building one through the arctic tundra at 36° below zero. Few companies have the technical capability or experience to build a pipeline in sub-zero temperatures like those of Alaska.

Obviously, climate also has a vast influence on markets. It is unlikely that major tire companies will ever carry a large stock of snow tires in Florida.

ECOLOGY

The study of maintaining a balance in nature, including harmonious relationships between people and their natural environment, constitutes **ecology.** In recent years pollution has come to be recognized as a serious threat to ecological balance. Environmental pollution takes many forms, including air, water, trash, and noise pollution, and each of these may have many facets. Air pollution may be smoke from stacks and exhausts from tailpipes; trash may include tin cans, discarded bottles, used paper, and abandoned automobiles; noise can mean jackhammers or subsonic booms; water pollution includes untreated sewage as well as mercury from chemical plants, and the destructiveness of enzymes and phosphates in laundry detergents as they enter rivers and streams.

There have been estimates that it will take $90 billion during a five-year span to deal with pollution. The federal government's concern with these problems has created the Environmental Protection Agency. Local governments have passed pollution abatement laws to which business must adhere. Industries that face major environmental cleanup problems include:

- **Mining:** To restore the landscape torn in strip-mining operations;
- **Steel:** To eliminate solid emissions and sulphur oxide, and to combat water pollution;
- **Electric utilities:** To clean up dust and fly ash, and to find ways to eliminate sulphur oxide emissions;
- **Pulp and paper:** To eliminate water pollution, and to re-plant trees and re-forest the soil;
- **Chemicals:** To eliminate odors, chemical emission, and water contamination;
- **Petroleum:** To eliminate sulphur oxide and hydrocarbon emissions, and to develop non-leaded gasoline and low-sulphur fuels;
- **Automobile:** To develop noiseless mufflers, and to re-design engines and carburetors to eliminate exhaust pollutants, including deadly

sulphur dioxide (produced by catalytic converters that were designed to eliminate the *original* pollutants).

Aluminum, cement, copper, and asphalt industries also face cleanup chores. Despite the fact that many millions of dollars will have to be spent by these companies with no compensating return likely in many instances, as in the case of steel, society demands for its own self-preservation that pollution be eliminated. Buying, installing, and operating pollution control equipment adds to the cost of doing business so that weaker or marginal companies will be unduly penalized. By whom is the ultimate cost to be borne?

Billions of dollars are involved. In 1972 industry and governments spent about $13.9 billion on air, water, and solid waste pollution control. The estimate for 1977 was $20.5 billion, including a predicted expenditure of $12.3 billion for water treatment alone.[3]

A study commissioned by the American Iron and Steel Institute found that the domestic steel industry will have to make capital expenditures averaging $5.5 billion a year from 1974 through 1983 of which about $1.4 billion will go for pollution-control equipment.[4] The study further estimates that complying with 1983 pollution control regulations will add 8 percent to 10 percent to operating costs. This translates into an increase of $25 to $30 per ton of steel.

Firms and governments have been tackling the trash and waste types of pollution with attempts at **recycling.** The City of Paris has been burning trash and garbage as a fuel for half a century. Similar plants are operating in Tokyo, Sweden, and Germany. In recent years, there has been considerable interest in the U.S. in exploiting organic heat sources, particularly from municipal solid wastes. The Union Electric Company in St. Louis has been burning a mixture of 20 percent shredded solid residential waste with 80 percent pulverized coal since 1972. The project was initiated as an Environmental Protection Agency demonstration grant and reportedly "has hardly any bugs at all."[5]

According to Edwin Owen, a specialist in corrosion of metals, it will take 500 years for an aluminum beer can tossed into the woods to decompose and return to nature; a conventional steel can will take only 100 years; a tin can will require 1,000 years.[6] Some brewers and bottlers are buying back their used cans and bottles. They are sorting, cleaning, and re-using the bottles; shredding and selling the cans to companies in the tin, aluminum, and copper recovery business.

---

[3]Terry W. Rothermal, "Pollution Control," *Financial Analyst's Handbook* (Homewood, Ill.: Dow Jones-Irwin, Inc.), Vol. 2, Chapter 23, April 1975.

[4]*The Wall Street Journal,* May 15, 1975.

[5]Bill A. Stout, "Organic Energy Resources," *Phi Kappa Phi Journal,* Winter 1975, p. 11.

[6]Boyce Rensberger, "Nature Will Recycle Cans—Eventually," *Youngstown Vindicator* (Ohio), September 24, 1972.

A corn products company has developed a use for corn cobs by grinding them up and selling the grit as an abrasive for polishing purposes. Several firms have developed huge shredders and compacters that make it possible for automobile carcasses to be reduced to small, solid cubes that can be re-smelted as scrap for steel.

Opportunities for innovation in packaging are abundant. Manufacturers can package their products in containers designed to have a use in addition to the originally intended one. Cottage cheese and dairy whip are examples of food products sold in polyethelene containers that can later be used as refrigerator containers for leftover foods. Perhaps in the not too distant future, technology will also find a way for empty cans to self-destruct without polluting the atmosphere, or for food containers to be as edible as their contents.

The U.S. uses over 300 million gallons of ethanol annually in chemicals, toiletries, and cosmetics. Ethanol is produced from ethylene, which is derived from petroleum. Researchers have discovered ways to make ethanol (ethyl alcohol) from glucose derived from cellulosic wastes. As an example, newspaper is converted to cellulose; cellulose is converted to glucose; glucose is converted to ethanol by a process of fermentation. Scientists predict that if the ethanol process becomes economic the chemical could be used as a major ingredient for gasoline and thus further reduce reliance on petroleum.[7]

Water, too, can be recycled through a process of purification and recovery brought about by an innovation known as "membrane technology."[8] Through a process of reverse osmosis salty or brackish water, even water from industrial waste and treated sewage, can be recovered, purified, and re-used. Membrane technology is said to be a low energy consumer. A yachtsman, for example, could turn sea water into drinking water by using a portable, hand-operated pump powered only by the energy of his arm muscles.[9]

ECOLIBRIUM

It must be borne in mind that while a balanced ecology is a desirable goal toward which to strive, there are costs involved which society must be prepared to pay. It may have to give up something in exchange. There is a vital need to balance our concern for ecology (the harmony of organisms and their environment) with a concern for economy (the managing of resources to maintain productiveness). This is known as **ecolibrium.**[10]

---

[7]Jeffrey A. Tannenbaum, "Energy Alchemy," *The Wall Street Journal,* February 13, 1975, p. 26.

[8]John Oldaker, "Purity Plus Recovery," *Oxy Today,* No. 6, 1975, p. 18.

[9]*Ibid.*

[10]Athelstan Spilhaus, "A City in the Sea," *Petroleum Today,* American Petroleum Institute, Washington, D.C., 1972, Vol. 13, No. 3, p. 1.

Industry's experience with waste treatment reveals that substantial amounts of energy and raw materials can be consumed in meeting water-quality regulations. One scientist calculated the amount of energy that would be required to meet the goal of zero effluent at one industrial location. To get rid of 4,000 tons of waste material would require the use of an additional 40,000 tons of natural resources.[11]

Here is an example from Du Pont's experience. Water pollution facilities at one of its chemical plants cost $8 million to install and $3.7 million per year to operate. They remove 90 to 95 percent of pollutants. Present federal laws will require that 98 percent be removed by 1983. This small difference will make no measurable improvement in the water, which already is used for swimming, boating, and fishing, yet the extra facilities will cost $6 million to install and an additional $5 million per year to operate.[12] These figures indicate that in trying to reach our social goals it is easy to take two steps backward for each step forward.

To protect workers against hearing loss from excessive noise, OSHA supports a permissible level of 90 decibels. The Environmental Protection Agency wants to reduce this to 85 decibels. Yet it has not been shown that such a reduction would provide increased protection to employees. Scientists at Du Pont and other companies indicate that any threat posed by noise can be managed through the use of ear protectors and audiometric testing.[13] In this case, the expenditure of an estimated $32 billion dollars to reduce noise levels by 5 decibels would not improve worker safety by any commensurate degree.

One way to reduce the potential global food shortage would be to produce beef of grade "good" rather than "choice." This would reduce feeding requirements of over 1,000 pounds of grain per animal and release 1 billion bushels of grain annually.[14] Society would have to be willing to change its buying habits to make this economy possible.

Much of what is purchased in a modern supermarket may be seen through the unlabeled part of a glass bottle or jar. Undoubtedly this is an excellent way to merchandise food products and household items. However, it takes only 35 percent as much energy to produce a metal or paper container, whose walls cannot be seen through, as it does to produce a glass container.[15]

---

[11]Charles B. McCoy, "Can We Avoid a Crisis in Resources?" An address before The Economic Club of Detroit, Detroit, Michigan, December 4, 1972, p. 5.

[12]Edwin A. Gee (Senior Vice President, E.I. duPont de Nemours and Company, Inc.), "Keynote Address," Professional Development Conference of the American Society of Safety Engineers, Denver, Colorado, June 23, 1975, p. 7.

[13]*Ibid*, p. 6.

[14]S.H. Wittwer, *op. cit.*, p. 38.

[15]Archie N. Solberg, "The Role of Honor Societies in Crises," *Phi Kappa Phi Journal*, Winter 1975, p. 29.

Environmental goals have had a special impact on the demand for gasoline, which accounts for almost half of every barrel of oil that goes through the average domestic refinery. Sites for new refineries have become more difficult to obtain in the face of strong opposition from environmental groups. This is especially true of the East Coast area which consumes 40 percent of all petroleum products but possesses only 12 percent of the nation's refining capacity. One state has prohibited refinery construction in its coastal zone. Three others have enacted similar legislation which effectively rules out refinery construction in coastal areas.

In 1973 the East Coast consumed an estimated 2500 million barrels of oil products, yet produced only 40 million barrels, or 1.6 percent, of the amount it used.[16] In addition, the East Coast used 4100 billion cubic feet of natural gas but produced only 328 billion, or 8 percent, of what it consumed.[17] The ecolibrium question that must be answered is this: Can people living on the Eastern seaboard continue to block the search for natural gas and crude oil that may lie offshore of their states, and the refinery construction required to process it?

MAN-MADE IMPROVEMENTS

Part of the physical environment bearing on managerial decision making has to do with man-made improvements. It includes such factors as the availability of roads and parking facilities.

The building of a giant pipeline in Alaska or Canada to transport oil through the tundra involves many ecological problems, from the disruption of wildlife to the possibility of destructive oil spills from a broken line. But a pipeline could not be built at all if highways and service roads had not already been built. The availability of roads is often an essential determinant of whether or not a project can go forward. To know that precious metals exist on top of a mountain would mean little if they could not be transported out. Real estate developments, mining, and logging operations depend on good, all-weather roads.

Parking is another important consideration, particularly in a business where the customer must come to the establishment, as in the case of a department store or shopping mall. The development of suburban shopping centers has been successful in part because of the availability of adequate parking areas for customers. Based on experience, the ratio between square feet of floor space and number of car spaces required has been estimated as

---

[16]Maine, New Hampshire, Vermont, Connecticut, Rhode Island, Massachusetts, Delaware, New Jersey, North Carolina, South Carolina, and Georgia produce no petroleum; Florida, New York, Pennsylvania, Maryland, Virginia and West Virginia do.

[17]Charles J. DiBona (Executive Vice President, American Petroleum Institute), "Energy, Jobs and Offshore Drilling," a statement presented at hearings held by the Department of the Interior on Accelerated Outer Continental Shelf Lease Sales, Trenton, New Jersey, February 12, 1975.

one parking space for each 150 square feet of selling area. To open a store with less than the correct ratio of parking to selling area would be self-defeating.

In addition to roads and streets and parking considerations, man-made improvements embrace grading, drainage, land fills, and similar modifications of land surfaces. Such factors may have far-reaching implications in man's attempt to adapt to nature's provisions or the lack of them.

The influence of various facets of the macro-environment on each other and upon strategic decisions that managers must make to accommodate to external change has been pointed out in each of the previous chapters. These dynamic interrelations can all be observed in actual practice.

SUMMARY

One doesn't often think of the physical environment as a part of the total external environment in which organizations operate. Yet it is always present and its forces, sometimes violent in nature, pose threats and challenges to success.

Part of the physical environment is the natural environment, consisting of geophysical and biological processes in nature. These include topography of the land, water supply, fertility, climate, and ecological factors. Another segment of the physical environment consists of man-made influences like parking, roads, landfills, and other modifications of the earth's surface.

To some extent man's actions produce changes in the physical environment in which his institutions operate. To a much greater extent physical forces, often unpredictable, influence the way managers of organizations must make plans to accommodate to the threats and opportunities produced by the physical environment. As is true for all forces in the macro-environment which affect the operation of business organizations, failure on the part of the manager to adapt successfully to the physical environment may spell the demise of the organization.

KEY CONCEPTS

Topography	Pollution
Water Supply	Recycling
Fertility	Ecolibrium
Climate	Man-Made Improvements
Ecology	

GLOSSARY

ecolibrium   A balance between a concern for ecology and a concern for economy.

ecology   The study of the relationships between organisms and their natural environment.

fertility   The capacity for producing, developing, or growing, especially as it applies to soils.

pollution   A condition of impurity or contamination. Frequently refers to air, water, trash, and noise pollution.

recycling   A multi-stage natural or physical process through which resources are reclaimed and re-used.

topography   The shape and contour of the land.

REVIEW QUESTIONS

1. In your own words, explain why you think the physical environment is or is not an important influence on the operation of business organizations.

2. What does the "natural environment" mean?

3. Give an example of a situation in which water supply would be an important consideration to a manager.

4. Give an example of an industry in which humidity might influence its operations.

5. Give some examples of forms that pollution takes.

6. Who is going to pay for the cost of pollution control?

7. Give some examples from your own experience of things society may have to do without in order to conserve its scarce resources.

8. Do you think a minority group of environmentalists, sincerely concerned with preserving our ecology, should destroy our "ecolibrium"? Explain.

9. Of what importance is it to know the ratio of parking spaces to store selling space in a shopping mall?

Glossary

abstraction   Expressing a quality apart from the actual object or specific situation so that details are omitted.

accountability   An appraisal or evaluation of the extent to which performance was discharged satisfactorily.

accounting system   A set of related procedures designed to provide management with continuing information covering business and financial transactions.

activating   The cluster of activities in the managing process that, through the exercise of leadership and the proper use of incentives, causes the organization to carry out its planned activities.

actuating   The process of getting things started.

ad-hocracy   A term used to describe the rise of project-oriented organization.

administration   A term used outside of business in place of management.

algorithm   A well-defined systematic mathematical procedure used to deal with a well-structured problem.

anomie   A condition of rootlessness or lack of personal attachment in which normative standards of conduct are weak or non-existent.

art   A skill in doing something that is learned by experience, study, and observation.

attitude   A mental set based on the relationship between expectations and reality.

authority   The right to discharge one's duties, to perform a task that has been assigned and accepted.

autocratic management   An authoritarian leadership style, in which authority is highly centralized in the manager. Sometimes it is called "be strong" or "be firm" management.

automation   The substitution of machines for physical and mental effort.

bisociation   Unplanned creativeness in which two unconnected ideas or concepts form a single new one.

bleeding the line   Speeding up production, with little regard for negative effects, in order to meet a production quota by the deadline.

brainstorming   A technique of problem solving through group effort of suggesting spontaneous ideas in quantity.

break-even point   That level of output at which total costs are equal to total revenues, and there is neither a profit nor a loss.

budget   A single-purpose detailed plan used to allocate resources.

business function   Any business activity designed to achieve a business objective.

business population   The total number of business firms in our economy.

centralization   Concentration of resources (plant, personnel, and equipment) or decision-making authority.

code of ethics   A standard of ethical behavior adhered to by each for the good of all.

coercive controls   Procedures, rules, and regulations that require compliance or restraint to avoid penalties for non-compliance.

collateral organization   Adjuncts to line and staff organization, including task forces and special committees that operate on a continuing basis.

collegial management   A leadership style that recognizes fellow workers as colleagues or co-equals rather than as subordinates.

committee   A group of persons, elected or appointed, who meet by intent to consider matters assigned to it.

communication   An interchange of thoughts or information between two or more persons, in which the recipient must respond.

comparison   Determining the degree of relevance between actual performance and planned performance.

composite plan   An overall plan that may utilize two or more major types of plans concurrently.

conceptual skill   The ability to recognize and understand broad relationships, to work with ideas.

control report   A control function in which oral or written information can be used for evaluating performance and deciding whether some change is necessary.

control system   The sum of all control sub-systems plus their patterns of relationships.

controlling   A major function of managing which measures and evaluates the effectiveness of the organization and takes corrective action if necessary.

corporation   A legal form of business organization owned by stockholders.

corrective action   Control steps taken to reduce significant variance between planned results and actual results.

crash program   Speeding up the time required to perform a job or complete an activity, despite the increased costs, by assigning additional personnel and capital resources in order to "buy time."

critical path   The sequence of connected events in a project which takes the longest time to complete.

current master plan   A short-range master plan that prepares six months to a year in advance.

decentralization   Dispersion of resources (plant, personnel, and equipment) or decision-making authority.

decision   Commitment to a choice from among two or more alternatives.

decision tree   A graphic tree-like presentation of a sequence of decisions to be made and the possible outcomes of each.

deductive reasoning   Logical process that draws conclusions from general premises.

deficit spending   Government spending which exceeds revenues in a given fiscal period.

demography   The study of the size, density, growth, and distribution of human populations.

depreciation   An allowance in the form of a charge against earnings for replacement of worn-out or obsolete facilities.

deterministic   A situation in which a decision maker has all the necessary facts and can decide under conditions that approach certainty.

direction   A control function concerned with interpreting plans for others and giving instructions on how they should be carried out.

directive   An order, applying to a specific situation, to initiate action toward a stated goal.

disciplinary action   A type of remedial or corrective action in which the performance or behavior of a person or group is brought into conformity with organizationally prescribed patterns of conduct.

discretionary income   That portion of disposable income beyond what is required for the necessities of life (especially food, shelter, and clothing).

discrimination training   Training an already trained worker to adapt to a new machine or piece of equipment.

dispatching   An actuating function concerned with releasing orders and authorizing the commencement of work. Sometimes associated with scheduling as a control device.

dissatisfiers   Job conditions which, when absent, tend to dissatisfy employees but do not motivate very strongly when present.

double taxation   When corporations pay a tax on net income, and again when shareholders pay an income tax on dividends received from corporate earnings "after taxes."

eclectic   Composed of the best elements drawn from many sources.

ecolibrium   A balance between a concern for ecology and a concern for economy.

ecology   The study of the relationships between organisms and their natural environment.

economic environment   That portion of the macro-environment that deals primarily with production and consumption activities of individuals and organizations and their impact on all other organizations.

economic order quantity   The optimum quantity to order because ordering costs and carrying costs are equal.

empirical   Based on observation or experience.

employee-oriented   A managerial attitude in which concern for the employee's welfare dominates; concern for output is important but secondary.

equilibrium point   A situation in which marginal costs and marginal revenues are equal and profits are greatest.

ethical behavior   Action that is morally correct regardless of its legal aspects.

exception principle   Only significant deviation between actual performance and planned performance should be brought to an executive's attention.

expectancy   The belief, expressed as a subjective probability, that a given act of an individual will lead to a particular organizational goal.

expected elapsed time   A weighted average of three time estimates (optimistic, most likely, and pessimistic) used in determining how long an activity will take to complete.

extension   A type of creativity based on refinement, development, or adaptation of an existing idea.

extrinsically significant incentives   Intangible incentives of a social nature.

failing-company doctrine   A government antitrust provision that permits mergers of competing firms which otherwise might fail.

feedback   A form of return flow of information, formal or informal.

fertility   The capacity for producing, developing, or growing, especially as it applies to soils.

float   The same as "slack" in critical path scheduling.

forecasting   An aspect of planning that deals with predicting changes in the environment in which an organization operates.

free rein management   A laissez-faire style of management that leaves all decision making in the hands of subordinates.

function   Any activity necessary to accomplish some organizational objective.

functional authority   Authority that is exercised across organizational lines rather than through the normal chain of command.

grapevine   A type of indirect, informal communication.

gross national product   The total output of final goods and services at their market price.

hedging   A strategy to protect one's self from loss by a counter balance transaction.

heuristic technique   A decision-making technique used to solve ill-structured problems by making reasonable assumptions in a search for reasonable rather than mathematically precise answers.

hierarchy   A structure of concepts or events arranged in a series in either ascending or descending order.

human relations skill   Ability to direct human activities toward organizational goals.

hygiene factors   Another term for maintenance factors in motivation theory; job conditions that support a reasonable level of satisfaction. They describe the job environment.

inbreeding   Developing and perpetuating organizational characteristics that are ingrained and deeply rooted.

incentive   An inducement to perform.

inducive controls   Programs and procedures that offer rewards for compliance.

inductive reasoning   A logical process that draws generalizations from specific facts or data.

inflation   An economic condition in which prices rise more rapidly than does productivity.

innovation   The product or end result of some type of creativity, usually extension, substitution, synthesis, or bisociation.

instrumentality   An individual's perception of the probability of organizational goals leading to the achievement of personal goals.

insufficient reason   A decision criterion that assumes equally likely probabilities of any event occurring.

internal control   A system of checks and balances to safeguard an organization's assets. It separates the performance of an act from the auditing of that performance.

interview guide   A planned format designed to standardize personnel selection interviews.

interview report   A form that summarizes the results of the selection interview and rates the job applicant on points that do not appear in the interview guide.

intrinsically significant incentives   Intangible incentives of a personal nature.

intuition   Power of attaining an insight into a problem without deliberate, rational thinking.

iterative   Characterized by being repeated.

job   The kind and amount of work to be performed by a person or piece of equipment within a given time period.

job analysis   Breaking a job down into its components to determine its content.

job classification   Grading of jobs based on similarities in job descriptions and/or job specifications.

job definition   A detailed statement consisting of a job description and a job specification.

job description   That portion of a job definition consisting of a statement of the content of a job in terms of major tasks, sequence of tasks, conditions under which they are to be performed, and the job's authority, responsibility, and accountability.

job-oriented   A managerial attitude in which concern for output and the job to be done is of primary importance; employee welfare, though important, is less so.

job specification   That portion of a job definition which states the qualifications a person should have to fill the job that has been described.

justice   The principle "to each his due." Fair and impartial consideration to which all segments of society are entitled.

lateral promotion   A transfer to a new position at the same classification level.

law of effect The psychological phenomenon, described by Thorndike, that rewarded behavior tends to be repeated and unrewarded or punished behavior tends to be eliminated.

leadership Getting people to do what the leader wants them to do because he has influenced or inspired them to believe it is what they want to do.

line organization The basic form of organization structure that results from authority relationships. Authority flows in a straight line from superior to subordinate through successive levels of management.

linear relationship A relationship in which one value varies directly with any change in another value.

long-range master plan A type of master plan that prepares five to twenty-five years ahead.

macro-environment The external environment to which organizations must adapt.

maintenance factors Job conditions that tend to support and maintain mental health of employees. Their absence causes dissatisfaction, although their presence does not motivate very strongly. Sometimes referred to as hygiene factors.

management by objectives A system in which superior and subordinate jointly establish goals and the subordinate determines the means to be utilized to achieve those objectives.

managing The process consisting of planning, organizing, activating, and controlling enterprise resources for the purpose of achieving the goals of the organization.

managing function Any managerial activity designed to achieve management objectives.

markov process Mathematical model dealing with steady state probabilities.

matrix organization An intricately linked cooperative relationship between project organization and functional organization.

maximax A decision-making criterion for maximizing greatest possible gain.

maximin A decision-making criterion for maximizing minimum possible gains.

measurement A control function that provides information about the quantity, quality, and economy of group response to managerial decisions.

mechanization The substitution of machines for physical effort.

megalopolis   A population center that includes several contiguous metropolitan areas.

method   A routine plan that is a component of a procedure.

minimax   A decision-making criterion for minimizing maximum possible loss.

monte carlo method   A method of predicting the frequency of occurrence of random variables.

morale   The willingness of members of a group to seek individual satisfactions by pursuing the purposes for which the group exists.

motivation   A person's inner drive or urge to fulfill a need.

motives   Basic inner drives of individuals based on unfulfilled needs, desires, wants, and fears.

net economic welfare   A substitute for GNP as an indicator of economic growth.

objective   An organizational goal, end, purpose, aim, destination, or reason for being toward which managers direct their efforts.

on-the-job training   A type of formal training in which proficiency is developed in the actual job situation.

operant conditioning   Modifying behavior by offering rewards or punishments as a consequence of a subject's behavior.

operations research   A type of decision-making procedure using scientific and mathematical techniques.

opportunity cost   Alternative use cost.

optimizing   Attempting to obtain what is most desirable for the enterprise as a whole.

organization   A social structure in which two or more individuals interact to achieve a mutual goal that neither could accomplish as effectively alone. The end result of the organizing process.

organizing   A major component of managing which consists of selecting and combining appropriate resources (personnel and capital) and integrating them into a structure of relationships that enables them to carry out the planned activity in a coordinated and controlled way.

overhead   Fixed or indirect costs of an operation.

partnership   An association of two or more co-owners of a business.

paternalistic management   A management style that tends to be fatherly and benevolent in its philosophy toward workers. Sometimes it is called ''be good'' management.

perception   The process of constructing meaning from sensations.

personality   That part of one's self that is exhibited to others.

PERT   Program Evaluation and Review Technique. A type of critical path scheduling used for control purposes.

philosophy   Beliefs, concepts, and attitudes held by individuals or groups in their relationship with each other and with society.

planning   A major function in the management process that consists of formulating objectives and establishing ways to reach them.

plural executive   A staff committee with full authority to enforce or implement its decisions.

poisson process   A statistical technique utilized where the population is infinite, the probability of an event occurring is constant, and its occurrence is independent of any previous occurrence.

policy   A type of plan that deals with a recurring problem for which there is no routine solution, by requiring the organization to recognize particular objectives and to work toward their fulfillment in some broadly defined way.

pollution   A condition of impurity or contamination. Frequently refers to air, water, trash, and noise pollution.

positive reinforcement   The use of positive external rewards to increase the probability or frequency of occurrence of a desired response.

power   The ability to enforce managerial authority.

primacy effect   Of two successive communications, the first tends to inhibit or block the comprehension of the second.

primacy of planning   Planning must precede performance.

prime rate   The interest rate that banks and lending institutions charge their most credit-worthy borrowers.

principle   A generalization having widespread application based on the causal relationship between an action and the perceived results of that action.

problem   An uncertainty about the best way to establish or achieve some objective.

procedure   A routine detailed plan that provides a step-by-step sequence of tasks in a specific order.

program   A single-purpose metaplan that is an aggregate of several related projects with a common objective.

project   A single-purpose detailed plan that is usually part of a broader plan called a program.

promoting from within   A system of filling job openings with present members of the organization.

proprietorship   An individually owned enterprise.

random variables   Events that occur by chance in an unpredictable manner.

rational approach   The objective definition of a problem and search for a valid, reliable solution.

recency effect   Of two successive communications, the second tends to be more effective because of the phenomenon of retention.

recycling   A multi-stage natural or physical process through which resources are reclaimed and re-used.

reflective thinking   A decision-making process that integrates past and present experience in "thinking through" a problem.

reliability   Internal consistency of any means, device, or technique that indicates it is dependable.

reporting   Transmitting information upward or laterally to advise a manager of work progress.

representation   Portraying the organization to the internal or external community.

reprimand   A negative type of disciplinary action involving formal reproof or censure.

responsibility   An obligation to discharge one's duties to the best of one's ability.

rule   A routine plan, usually in the form of specific statements from which there can be no deviation.

rumor   Grapevine information that is hearsay and usually a distortion of the true facts.

satisficing   Working toward a sufficient, though not necessarily optimum, level of satisfaction.

satisfiers   Job conditions which help build higher levels of job satisfaction and motivation but which do not cause much worker dissatisfaction when not present. They are centered within the job itself. Sometimes called motivators.

scalar principle   The downward flow of authority in which authority decreases by degrees through successively lower levels.

scheduling   A detailed planning of the time sequence of operations or tasks.

scientific method   Objective collection of data, classification of data, formulation of hypotheses, and verification of hypotheses by testing for reliability and validity.

semantics   The meaning and connotation of words.

slack (float)   In critical path scheduling, the difference between a job's earliest start time and its latest start time (or between earliest finish time and latest finish time).

social environment   That portion of the total external environment that deals with behavior patterns of people and relationships among groups in society.

sociometry   The study and measurement of feelings of members of a group toward each other.

span of authority   Sometimes called span of supervision or span of control. It refers to the number of subordinates a manager can supervise effectively.

span of management   The number of subordinates a manager can supervise effectively. This term is interchangeable with span of authority.

staffing   An organizing activity that includes placing the right persons in the right jobs by carefully selecting, training, assigning, and indoctrinating them.

standard   Either the result of a scientific search for the best way to do something (technical standard) or a norm or accepted level of attainment or performance (general standard).

states of nature   Events beyond a manager's control which could actually occur (uncontrollable variables).

statistical quality control   A sampling technique to standardize quality by using statistical methods based on the law of probability.

statistics   A branch of mathematics dealing with the process of collection, analysis, interpretation, and presentation of numerical data.

status   The rank or position of prestige one enjoys relative to others in the social order.

stochastic process   A decision-making technique that assigns probability of occurrence to states of nature and to random variables since all factors or relationships are not known or are imprecise.

stock option   The right usually given to an executive to purchase shares in the corporation at some future date at a price based on their market value at the time the option is issued.

stockouts   A merchandising term indicating that items are "out of stock" or unavailable because of inadequate inventory.

strategic management   Dealing with the problem of adapting the organization to external environmental changes.

strategic managing   Adapting to macro-environmental changes.

structural unemployment   A temporary type of unemployment that results when old jobs are eliminated because of new technology and displaced workers have to be re-trained to fill new jobs.

sub-optimizing   Setting performance in a sub-unit at less than optimum in order to achieve balanced organizational performance.

substitution   A type of creativity that results from finding a replacement for an existing product or concept.

supervision   A major activating function that insures that planned events are understood and are taking place currently.

supportive management   A management style that encourages participative activities. It is sometimes called democratic management.

synergistic   Producing a total effect greater than the sum of the component effects.

synoptic   Providing a broad view of the whole.

synthesis   A type of creativity that results from combinations or consolidations.

system   A routine metaplan comprised of several related procedures with a common objective. Also, any situation in which two or more elements interact for a common purpose.

tangible incentives   Material inducements, either monetary or nonmonetary.

task environment   That portion of the total environment which exerts an influence on goal setting and goal attainment.

teamwork   A situation in which members of a group subordinate personal ambition or achievement to the effectiveness of the group.

technology   The technical process by which new methods and new products are discovered to improve or replace old or obsolete ones.

telic   Purposive in intent, leading toward an end.

thematic apperception test   A projective type of psychological test used to measure personality traits.

theory   A coherent system of propositions advanced to explain a phenomenon.

therblig   A unit or element of motion.

three-tiered rating   A rating system in which a person is evaluated by subordinates, peers, and superiors so as to provide a composite appraisal.

tolerance   Permissible variation in an engineering or technical standard.

topography   The shape and contour of the land.

total cost   Fixed costs plus variable costs.

traits   Distinguishing qualities or characteristics.

uncertainty   Existence of doubt because of a lack of definite or complete knowledge about an outcome.

unity of command   A situation in which each subordinate is accountable to or subject to the authority of only one superior.

unity of direction   A situation that prevails when a group of activities is directed toward a central or common objective.

valence   A component of instrumentality–expectancy theory which indicates the strength or intensity of an individual's desire for a given outcome.

validity   A criterion of effectiveness, predictability, or successful achievement.

variable costs   Direct or prime costs that fluctuate upward or downward with the level of operation.

variance   Any deviation of the actual from the norm.

vestibule school   A training situation away from the normal operating area that prepares the trainee to take his place in a similar activity when his training has been completed.

working standards   Engineering standards with built-in tolerances.

Name Index

Subject Index